HISTORY IN DISPUTE

ADVISORY BOARD

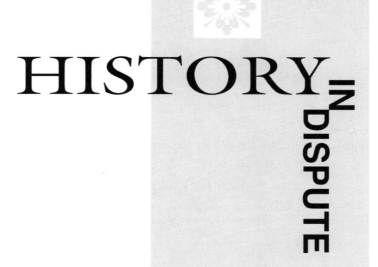

HISTORY IN DISPUTE

Volume 16

Twentieth-Century European Social and Political Movements: First Series

Edited by **Paul du Quenoy**

A MANLY, INC. BOOK

St J

ST. JAMES
PRESS

THOMSON
————*————
GALE

Detroit • New York • San Diego • San Francisco • Cleveland • New Haven, Conn. • Waterville, Maine • London • Munich

History in Dispute
Volume 16: Twentieth-Century European Social and Political Movements, First Series
Paul du Quenoy

Editorial Directors
Matthew J. Bruccoli and Richard Layman

Series Editor
Anthony J. Scotti Jr.

LIBRARY OF CONGRESS CONTROL NUMBER: 00-266495
ISBN 1-55862-479-1

Printed in the United States of America
10 9 8 7 6 5 4 3

CONTENTS

CONTENTS

CONTENTS

CONTENTS

CONTENTS

ABOUT THE SERIES

History in Dispute is an ongoing series designed to present, in an informative and lively pro-con format, different perspectives on major historical events drawn from all time periods and from all parts of the globe. The series was developed in response to requests from librarians and educators for a history-reference source that will help students hone essential critical-thinking skills while serving as a valuable research tool for class assignments.

Individual volumes in the series concentrate on specific themes, eras, or subjects intended to correspond to the way history is studied at the academic level. For example, early volumes cover such topics as the Cold War, American Social and Political Movements, and World War II. Volume subtitles make it easy for users to identify contents at a glance and facilitate searching for specific subjects in library catalogues.

Each volume of *History in Dispute* includes up to fifty entries, centered on the overall theme of that volume and chosen by an advisory board of historians for their relevance to the curriculum. Entries are arranged alphabetically by the name of the event or issue in its most common form. (Thus, in Volume 1, the issue "Was detente a success?" is presented under the chapter heading "Detente.")

Each entry begins with a brief statement of the opposing points of view on the topic, followed by a short essay summarizing the issue and outlining the controversy. At the heart of the entry, designed to engage students' interest while providing essential information, are the two or more lengthy essays, written specifically for this publication by experts in the field, each presenting one side of the dispute.

In addition to this substantial prose explication, entries also include excerpts from primary-source documents, other useful information typeset in easy-to-locate shaded boxes, detailed entry bibliographies, and photographs or illustrations appropriate to the issue.

Other features of *History in Dispute* volumes include: individual volume introductions by academic experts, tables of contents that identify both the issues and the controversies, chronologies of events, names and credentials of advisers, brief biographies of contributors, thorough volume bibliographies for more information on the topic, and a comprehensive subject index.

ACKNOWLEDGMENTS

James F. Tidd Jr., *Editorial associate.*

Philip B. Dematteis, *Production manager.*

Kathy Lawler Merlette, *Office manager.*

Ann M. Cheschi and Carol A. Cheschi, *Administrative support.*

Ann-Marie Holland, *Accounting.*

Sally R. Evans, *Copyediting supervisor.* Phyllis A. Avant, Caryl Brown, Melissa D. Hinton, Philip I. Jones, Rebecca Mayo, Nadirah Rahimah Shabazz, and Nancy E. Smith, *Copyediting staff.*

Zoe R. Cook, *Series team leader, layout and graphics.* Janet E. Hill, *Layout and graphics supervisor.* Sydney E. Hammock, *Graphics and prepress.*

Scott Nemzek and Paul Talbot, *Photography editors.*

Amber L. Coker, *Permissions editor and database manager.*

Joseph M. Bruccoli, *Digital photographic copy work.*

Donald K. Starling, *Systems manager.*

Kathleen M. Flanagan, *Typesetting supervisor.* Patricia Marie Flanagan, Mark J. McEwan, and Pamela D. Norton, *Typesetting staff.*

Walter W. Ross, *Library researcher.*

The staff of the Thomas Cooper Library, University of South Carolina, are unfailingly helpful: Tucker Taylor, *Circulation department head, Thomas Cooper Library, University of South Carolina.* John Brunswick, *Interlibrary-loan department head.* Virginia W. Weathers, *Reference department head.* Brette Barclay, Marilee Birchfield, Paul Cammarata, Gary Geer, Michael Macan, Tom Marcil, and Sharon Verba, *Reference librarians.*

PERMISSIONS

ILLUSTRATIONS

Pp. 5, 17: Photograph courtesy of the David King Collection, London, by permission of David King.

P. 10: Courtesy of the National Archives, Washington, D.C.

P. 26: Radio Times Hulton Picture Library, by permission of Getty Images.

P. 31: Photograph from Z. A. B. Zeman, *Twilight of the Habsburgs: The Collapse of the Austro-Hungarian Empire* (New York: American Heritage, 1971), p.119.

P. 47: Hulton/Hulton Deutsch Archive/Getty Images.

P. 55: Photograph from Gwyneth Hughes & Simon Welfare, *Red Empire: The Forbidden History of the U.S.S.R.* (New York: St. Martin's Press, 1990), p.25.

P. 62: © Ron Haviv/CORBIS.

P. 68: By permission of the British Library, London.

Pp. 77, 195, 295, 309: Photographs from Stefan Lorant, *Sieg Heil! Hail to Victory: An Illustrated History of Germany from Bismarck to Hitler* (New York: Bonanza Books, 1979), pp. 52, 71, 125, 160.

P. 86: By permission of Vietnam News Agency; collection of Ngo Vinh Long.

P. 93: Photograph by Novosti.

P. 101: Photograph from Vera Olivova, *The Doomed Democracy: Czechoslovakia in a Disrupted Europe, 1914–38* (London: Sidgwick & Jackson, 1972), insert #2b.

P. 110: AP/Wide World Photo.

P. 119: Photograph from Archives Documentation Française.

P. 123: AP Photo/Lehtikuva, Hans Paul (APA4904512).

P. 136: Photograph from photographe anonyme d'agence.

P. 142: Photograph by Rene Dazy.

Pp. 149, 169, 219: Library of Congress, Washington, D.C.

P. 157: Photograph by permission of Bundesbildstelle from *Europe: Dream, Adventure, Reality* (New York: Greenwood Press, 1987).

P. 172: Branger/Roger-Viollet Collection.

P. 182: Lafayette Studios/Victoria and Albert Museum, London.

P. 190: Photograph from the Christopher Ailsby Historical Archives.

P. 205: Photograph from A La Vielle Russie, Inc., New York.

P. 210: Range/Bettman/UPI.

P. 229: AP Photo/B.I. Sanders (APA5043867).

P. 241: Photograph from Marcus Cunliffe, *The Times History of Our Times* (London: Weidenfeld & Nicolson, 1971), top left p. 339.

P. 244: ©Hulton-Deutsch Collection/CORBIS.

P. 253: Ullstein Bilderdienst/ullstein bild Berlin (Photo ID#00011787).

P. 260: Photograph from Lewis Siegelbaum and Andrei Sokolov, ed., *Stalinism as a Way of Life: A Narrative in Documents* (New Haven: Yale University Press, 2000), insert #23.

P. 268: Photo: akg-images; Berlin.

P. 279: Hulton/Archive by Getty Images.

P. 283: Photograph from the Czech News Agency.

P. 300: Photograph from Documentation Française.

P. 318: Imperial War Museum, London.

TEXT

P. 116: Marc Bloch, *Strange Defeat: A Statement of Evidence Written in 1940,* translated by Gerard Hopkins (London & New York: Oxford University Press, 1949), pp. 52–53 courtesy of Oxford University Press.

P. 256: Lothar Metzger, "The Fire-bombing of Dresden: An Eye-witness Account," Time-witnesses: Memories of the Last Century (May 1999) <http://timewitnesses.org/english/~lothar.html> by permission of Lothar Metzger and Timewitnesses.

P. 275: George F. Kennan, "The Sources of Soviet Conduct," as X, *Foreign Affairs,* 25 (July 1947): 566–582 by permission of *Foreign Affairs.*

PREFACE

"The path to truth," one of my favorite undergraduate history professors liked to repeat, "lies in comparative analysis." That exercise is the greatest purpose of the *History in Dispute* series. The present work, devoted to topics in twentieth-century European history, examines many of the historical profession's most volatile debates in such a comparative framework.

As the world enters not only a new century but a new millennium, the events, debates, problems, ambiguities, controversies, catastrophes, and contradictions of the twentieth century continue to have a profound impact on humanity. When taking this fact into consideration, scholars of twentieth-century Europe cannot escape its negative implications. The century's destructive power was rarely short of enormous, and occurred on an incomprehensible scale. How can one avoid the fact that more soldiers died in World War I (1914–1918) alone than in all European conflicts over the previous eight centuries combined? Who could fail then to realize that this horror was compounded by the fact that World War II (1939–1945) claimed five times as many lives as World War I? The development of nuclear weapons in the twentieth century gave humanity the capacity to destroy itself for the first time in its history. This single innovation fundamentally changed conceptions of war, peace, and diplomacy that had endured since ancient times. Other technological advances enabled governments and political movements to inflict untold suffering. War, hatred, murder, and even genocide were perhaps not new to the human experience before 1900, but gas chambers, bureaucracies of death, missiles, civilian bombing, and manufactured famines certainly were. Rather than advancing toward further "enlightenment" or building on the rationalist traditions of past centuries, much of twentieth-century political and philosophical thought was strongly influenced by ideologies that pretended to monopolies on "scientific" truths determined by "immutable" laws. Communism and fascism enslaved much of humanity. The communists, who spent most of the century holding power in many areas, sacrificed as many as one hundred million people to their dream of creating a utopia that in the end (not to say in the beginning) utterly eluded them. Fascists touched off a war that killed fifty million individuals in the name of ultimately unattainable goals of racial purity. The realm of ideas was easily as culpable as the scientist's laboratory in ravaging the twentieth century. Since ideologies often furnished the organizing principles that put the new technologies to use, they should probably take some of the blame.

Yet, as one chapter in these volumes discusses, one can also argue that the twentieth century fostered positive developments for humanity. It may have seen unprecedented slaughter and deprivation, but it also brought equally unprecedented advances in health, travel, communications, information, and education. Before 1900 every European family, from the peasant's to the monarch's, could have realistically expected at least one of its children to die before reaching adulthood. A century of antibiotics, mass vaccination, steel-reinforced concrete, chemical insecticides, and other measures protecting public health and hygiene presented a solution to that problem forever, at least in the developed world. Even with the devastation of the century's man-made disasters, the population of the earth increased more dramatically than it ever had before. After an increase from about 1.5 billion people in 1900 to well over 6 billion in 2000, many now believe that chronic overpopulation will begin to outstrip the planet's resources in the current century. The West is beginning to have populations so healthy and well cared for that the number of people living into retirement may strain financial and social resources to the breaking point.

Twentieth-century innovations have made the world an unmistakably smaller place, a veritable "global village." Ideas began to flow with dramatically more freedom and vastly fewer inhibitions than ever before. The automobile, the airplane, the radio, the television, the satellite, the computer, and the Internet have changed communication and transportation so dramatically that modern conceptions of time, place, and distance seem to jump from the pages of science fiction. The nineteenth century may have given the world the train, the telegraph, and the steamship, but the innovations of the twentieth have made even these transformative technologies appear obsolescent. Christopher Columbus sailed to the New World in about ten weeks in 1492, while a nineteenth-century steamship could make the crossing in about ten days. The modern commercial airline passenger can do it in about six hours. Television and film allow images from anywhere in the world to be captured and shown anywhere else in the world. Satellite and computer technology has made this process instantaneous. World leaders, businessmen, relatives, friends, and strangers can talk instantly over the phone from one side of the globe to the other. Within seconds they can exchange letters, information, documents, and images over the Internet. After they have sent their transmissions, they can search for information on an unlimited number of topics, buy an ever increasing volume of goods, and read virtually every major newspaper—all without having to leave their chairs. As the critic and philosopher Marshall McLuhan has suggested, the way in which humans learn, process, and communicate information is undergoing profound evolutionary change.

Even the wars during the twentieth century had redeeming qualities in that they resulted in thoroughgoing triumphs for freedom and democracy. At the turn of the millennium, the West's philosophical dedication to those ideals holds a paramount place in the daily realities and hopes and dreams of billions throughout the world. The political scientist Francis Fukuyama has even suggested that the triumph of liberal democracy over fascism and communism in the twentieth century has resulted in the "end of history." In this popular and optimistic view, humanity has finally found its ideal form of political, social, and economic development.

The twentieth century's legacy is ambiguous for the entire world. It was at once immensely destructive and immensely progressive. To both extremes it far exceeded the tragedies and triumphs of any previous century and, indeed, of any combination of previous centuries. Europe shared in this ambiguity and underwent tremendous and tumultuous change. Its most powerful nations all lost their preeminence as the world's great powers, yet they are wealthier and more prosperous today than ever before. The continent survived war or lived in its shadow for most of the century, yet it is now following a determined path toward unprecedented economic and political unity. Its peoples were numerically and spiritually devas-tated by violent conflict and oppressive regimes, yet they are now freer and more populous than they have ever been. Intellectual life, political movements, and social structures were torn asunder by long periods of dissension, yet virtually every European state has embraced democracy and capitalism as its guiding ideals.

The studies contained in these volumes will examine many of these transformations, as well as their causes, effects, attributes, legacies, and inevitabilities. They also include chapters that reflect many of the arguments that scholars continue to make in the current historiography. Some of these address broad topics that developed over the course of the century, including issues of ideology, economics, demographics, and diplomacy. Others are specific to individual cases, involving particular nations, regimes, leaders, and events. My goal has been to include the broadest possible array of issues in a manner that reflects current trends in the historical profession. Those presented in *History in Dispute, Volume 16: Twentieth-Century European Social and Political Movements, First Series* are rather traditional, examining problems in "high" politics, diplomatic (or, as it is increasingly called, international) history, and military affairs. These fields have long been studied, but fresh arguments continue to appear while older ones are continually reexamined.

It is, of course, the contributors who should receive most of the credit for this work. Without their efforts it would not be. They vary greatly in age, background, outlook, and profession. Many are accomplished professors of considerable reputation and experience. An effort has been made to include scholarship by experts who have pursued careers outside of academia, in the belief that their professional insights will enhance the overall quality of the work and add perspectives that are not often found in the ivory tower. The reader should be aware that some contributors either elected to argue sides of issues that do not reflect their personal or professional opinions, or responded affirmatively to my request that they do so. It is my belief that the ability, willingness, and courage to express an argument that contradicts one's own view represents an exercise in skill as well as in wisdom. Indeed, my mentor Professor David Goldfrank and I have indulged in this idea by writing both sides of some chapters, in effect arguing against ourselves. The staffs at Manly, Inc., and St. James Press also deserve meritorious recognition. Coordinating the work of more than forty contributors and an editor who was in Russia much of the time was no small feat and deserves respect and admiration. Errors of editorial judgment are my own; views expressed and facts presented are those of the contributors.

—PAUL DU QUENOY,
GEORGETOWN UNIVERSITY

CHRONOLOGY

1900

Twenty-five percent of the world's population resides in Europe; six of the eight major world powers are located in this region.

29 JULY: Italian king Umberto I is assassinated by an anarchist; he is replaced on the throne by his son Victor Emmanuel III. (*See* **Monarchy**)

1901

22 JANUARY: Victoria, the queen of England, dies, and her eldest son takes the throne as Edward VII. (*See* **Monarchy**)

1902

30 JANUARY: Great Britain and Japan form an alliance in order to block Russian expansion in the Far East.

31 MAY: Great Britain and the Boer Republics sign a peace treaty ending the Boer War, which began in 1899. (*See* **Colonialism**)

1904

8 FEBRUARY: Japan breaks diplomatic relations with Russia, with whom it had been contesting control of Korea and Manchuria, and attacks the Russian fleet at Port Arthur, sparking the Russo-Japanese War.

8 APRIL: Largely in response to the growing power of Germany, Great Britain and France agree to settle outstanding disagreements, especially concerning their colonies, and establish the Entente Cordial. (*See* **Colonialism**)

1905

22 JANUARY: Russian soldiers in St. Petersburg fire upon demonstrators who are calling for shorter working hours and better labor conditions; more than 130 people are killed and hundreds injured in this incident, known as "Bloody Sunday."

5 SEPTEMBER: The Treaty of Portsmouth ends the Russo-Japanese War; Russia loses control of Port Arthur and Sakhalin Island.

1906

16 JANUARY–7 APRIL: The international Algeciras Conference is held to settle a dispute between Germany and France over French claims to a protectorate in Morocco. France succeeds in getting its claims recognized. (*See* **Colonialism** *and* **Outbreak of World War I**)

FEBRUARY: The battleship HMS *Dreadnought* is launched, resulting in the start of a naval arms race.

10 MAY–21 JULY: The Duma, the national representative body of Russia, meets for the first time; the assembly is the result of Tsar Nicholas II's October Manifesto (1905), in which he changed Russia to a constitutional monarchy. (*See* **Monarchy**)

22 NOVEMBER: Land-privatization reforms, giving peasants control of their land, are decreed by Russian prime minister Petr Stolypin.

1907

Great Britain and Russia sign the Agreement Concerning Persia, Afghanistan, and Tibet (establishing the Anglo-Russian Entente).

1908

7 OCTOBER: Bosnia-Herzegovina is annexed by the Austro-Hungarian Empire.

1911

10 AUGUST: The British Parliament limits the power of veto of the House of Lords.

18 SEPTEMBER: Stolypin is assassinated.

1912

8 OCTOBER: Bulgaria, Greece, Montenegro, and Serbia unite to fight against Turkey

when the Turks refuse to grant Macedonian autonomy. By 1913 the Turks are defeated, but internal squabbling soon leads to a second Balkan conflict.

1914

28 JUNE: Archduke Franz Ferdinand, heir to the Habsburg throne, and his wife, Sofia, are assassinated by Serbian anarchist Gabriel Princip in Sarajevo. (*See* **Outbreak of World War I**)

28 JULY: Austria declares war on Serbia.

1 AUGUST: Russia and France mobilize for war; Germany declares war on Russia; World War I begins. (*See* **Russia in World War I**)

3 AUGUST: Germany declares war on France.

4 AUGUST: Britain enters World War I against Germany. (*See* **British Entry into World War I**)

26–30 AUGUST: The Germans defeat Russian troops in northeastern Poland at the Battle of Tannenberg.

5 SEPTEMBER: Russia, Great Britain, and France sign the Treaty of London, stating that there will be no separate peace with Germany.

6–15 SEPTEMBER: The Russians suffer another defeat at the Battle of the Masurian Lakes.

1915

JANUARY: Austro-Hungarian forces launch an offensive in the Carpathian Mountains.

22 MARCH: Russian forces capture the Galician fortress of Przemysl. (*See* **Russia in World War I**)

7 MAY: The British passenger liner *Lusitania* is sunk by a German U-boat in the Irish Sea, killing 1,198 people and enraging American sentiment against the Germans.

1916

JANUARY–FEBRUARY: U.S. president Woodrow Wilson sends adviser Colonel Edward M. House to Europe to seek mediation between the conflicting sides, but they are unreceptive to the overture. (*See* **World War I Peace Settlement**)

21 FEBRUARY–JULY: A battle is fought for control of the area around the fortress at Verdun, with casualties to both sides reaching eight hundred thousand men. (*See* **Total War**)

24–29 APRIL: Irish republicans revolt against British rule in the Easter Rebellion; the rebels are defeated and put on trial.

4 JUNE: A massive Russian attack against Austro-Hungarian forces, known as the Brusilov Offensive, commences on the Eastern Front. The Germans are forced to remove troops from the Western Front to counter the threat. (*See* **Russia in World War I**)

1 JULY–19 NOVEMBER: More than one million men are killed during the Battle of the Somme in France.

21 NOVEMBER: Austro-Hungarian emperor Franz Joseph dies. (*See* **Monarchy**)

5 DECEMBER: Germany institutes the "Auxiliary Service Law," which declares that all able-bodied men between the ages of fifteen and sixty not already in the army are liable for civilian service. (*See* **Total War**)

12 DECEMBER: German chancellor Theobald von Bethmann-Hollweg proposes peace negotiations; it is turned down by the Allies.

18 DECEMBER: Wilson renews an offer to mediate a compromise between the belligerents, as Germany agrees that it will evacuate occupied territories in Western Europe but not lands held in Eastern Europe; the offer is rejected by the Allies. (*See* **World War I Peace Settlement**)

1917

King George V of England changes the royal name from Saxe-Coburg-Gotha to Windsor. (*See* **Monarchy**)

22 JANUARY: President Wilson, during a speech to the U.S. Senate, appeals to the World War I combatants to seek "peace without victory." (*See* **World War I Peace Settlement**)

31 JANUARY: Germany announces its decision to renew unrestricted submarine warfare against all shipping in British waters. (*See* **Total War**)

15 MARCH: Tsar Nicholas II abdicates the throne; he and his family are arrested on 21 March; members from the Russian Duma form a Provisional Government. (*See* **Collapse of Tsarist Russia** *and* **Monarchy**)

6 APRIL: The United States enters World War I on the side of the Allies.

1 AUGUST: Pope Benedict XV proposes a compromise peace, including Germany's withdrawal from Belgium and France; Allied withdrawal from German colonies; withdrawal of Central Powers troops from Serbia, Montenegro, and Romania; and the creation of an independent Poland. The proposal is rejected by both sides. (*See* **World War I Peace Settlement**)

3 SEPTEMBER: The United States recognizes the Czecho-Slovak National Council as the ruling government in Austria-Hungary.

7–8 NOVEMBER: Bolsheviks seize the Russian capital, Petrograd, overthrow the provisional government led by Aleksandr Kerensky, and touch off a brutal civil war that lasts until 1920. Vladimir Lenin becomes the leader of the Soviet state. (*See* **Bolshevik Revolution**)

20 DECEMBER: The Extraordinary Commission to Combat Counterrevolution, Speculation, and Sabotage (Cheka, or Soviet secret police) is established.

1918

8 JANUARY: Wilson issues the "Fourteen Points," his vision for postwar peace, to include such elements as open covenants, freedom of navigation, free trade, reduced national armaments, and a cooperative international league.

19 JANUARY: Russia's democratically elected Constituent Assembly meets and is dispersed by the Bolshevik government.

3 MARCH: Soviet Russia and the Central Powers sign the Treaty of Brest-Litovsk, ending the war on the Eastern Front. (*See* **Russia in World War I**)

SPRING: Fifteen Allied nations—including Britain, France, the United States, and Japan—send troops into Soviet Russia in an attempt to intervene in the Revolution. (*See* **Allied Intervention**)

16/17 JULY: Nicholas II, along with his wife and children, is executed.

29 OCTOBER: The National Council of Croats, Serbs, and Slovenes declares the formation of Yugoslavia.

9 NOVEMBER: The German Republic is proclaimed.

11 NOVEMBER: An armistice ending World War I goes into effect.

1919

JANUARY: A radical uprising of the German Spartacists, a communist group, is suppressed by the republican government.

5 JANUARY: The *Nationalsozialistische Deutsche Arbeiterpartei* (National Socialist German Workers' Party, or Nazi Party) is formed in Germany. (*See* **Hitler's Rise to Power**)

18 JANUARY: The Paris Peace Conference begins.

6 FEBRUARY–11 AUGUST: An assembly meets in Weimar, adopting a constitution

that forms the government that rules Germany until 1933.

4 MARCH: Czechoslovak forces shoot fifty-four Sudeten Germans protesting the Czech annexation of their land. (*See* **Eastern Europe After World War I**)

28 JUNE: The Versailles Treaty is signed, to take effect in January 1920. Germany accepts all responsibility for World War I, limitations on the size and power of its armed forces, territorial losses, and the responsibility to pay reparations eventually fixed in the amount of $33 billion. (*See* **Versailles Treaty**)

1920

16 JANUARY: The League of Nations is formally inaugurated, and the Paris Peace Conference officially ends.

1921

The *Sturmabteilung* (SA, known as Storm Troopers or Brownshirts) is formed by the Nazi Party. (*See* **Hitler's Rise to Power**)

13 DECEMBER: The United States, Great Britain, Japan, and France sign the Four-Powers Pact, establishing procedures for settling disputes in the Pacific dependencies. (*See* **Colonialism**)

1922

6 FEBRUARY: The United States, Great Britain, Japan, France, and Italy sign the Five-Power Naval Limitation Treaty, establishing limitations on the size of naval fleets and vessels. (*See* **Disarmament**)

2 APRIL: Josef Stalin becomes general secretary of the Communist Party of Soviet Russia.

31 OCTOBER: Benito Mussolini, leader of the Fascist Party, becomes prime minister of Italy.

DECEMBER: The Irish Free State is established.

30 DECEMBER: Soviet Russia formally becomes the Union of Soviet Socialist Republics (U.S.S.R.).

1923

French and Belgian troops occupy the industrial Ruhr region after Germany defaults on its World War I reparations debt.

8–9 NOVEMBER: Adolf Hitler and the Nazi Party attempt to start an insurrection against the Weimar Republic in what becomes known as the Beer Hall Putsch. Police halt a march and Hitler later serves eight months in prison, where he starts work on *Mein Kampf* (My Struggle). (*See* **Hitler's Rise to Power**)

1924

21 JANUARY: Lenin dies and Stalin, who has been accumulating power during Lenin's last years of life, gradually emerges as the new dictator. (*See* **Totalitarianism**)

16 AUGUST: The Dawes Plan reduces Germany's reparations owed to around $9 billion and provides loans to help pay them. (*See* **Versailles Treaty**)

1925

APRIL: Paul von Hindenburg is elected president of Germany.

1 DECEMBER: Germany, France, Belgium, Great Britain, and Italy agree to guarantee peace in Western Europe by signing the Locarno Treaty. (*See* **Concert of Europe**)

1926

Germany joins the League of Nations.

1928

The right-wing *Croix de feu* (Cross of Fire) is founded in France. (*See* **French Fascism**)

Stalin launches the first Five Year Plan for economic development.

20 JUNE: Croatian Peasant Party leader Stjepan Radic is mortally wounded by a rival member of parliament (he dies on 8 August), prompting King Alexander to declare a royal dictatorship the following January and to eliminate all ethnic-based political parties. Alexander establishes Yugoslavia and divides the country into administrative districts. (*See* **Eastern Europe After World War I**)

27 AUGUST: The Kellogg–Briand Pact, an attempt to outlaw war as a weapon of national policy, is signed in Paris. (*See* **Disarmament**)

1929

7 JUNE: The Young Plan reduces Germany's reparations again and extends payments for fifty-nine years. (*See* **Versailles Treaty**)

29 OCTOBER: The Stock Market in New York crashes, signaling the start of the worldwide Great Depression.

1931

1 JULY: U.S. president Herbert Hoover proposes a moratorium on German reparations.

14 APRIL: Spain becomes a Republic after Alfonso XIII is sent into exile. (*See* **Monarchy**)

11 DECEMBER: Great Britain establishes the policy of granting self-government to its colonies, in the Statute of Westminster, leading to the "British Commonwealth." The dominions effected are Australia, Canada, Ireland, New Zealand, and Newfoundland.

1932

2 FEBRUARY: Sixty-one nations send delegations to the League of Nations Disarmament Conference in Geneva, which continues into 1934. (*See* **Disarmament**)

JULY: Elections in Germany give the Nazi Party the largest representation in parliament; Hindenburg is reelected as president, but Hitler comes in second in the vote.

1933

30 JANUARY: Adolf Hitler is appointed chancellor of Germany by Hindenburg. (*See* **Hitler's Rise to Power**)

27 FEBRUARY: A fire at the Reichstag building, allegedly set by Dutch communist Marinus van der Lubbe, allows Hitler to overthrow constitutional guarantees and aggressively attack his opponents. Elections on 5 March give the Nazi Party nearly 44 percent of the popular vote.

23 MARCH: The Reichstag passes the Enabling Bill, which gives complete power to Hitler. His government begins establishing concentration camps for opponents of the regime. (*See* **Totalitarianism**)

JUNE: The World Economic Conference is held in London.

16 NOVEMBER: The Soviet Union and the United States establish diplomatic relations.

1934

6 FEBRUARY: A right-wing mob tries to storm the French Chamber of Deputies. (*See* **French Fascism**)

29–30 JUNE: Hitler orders a bloody purge of the SA, in what becomes known as the Night of the Long Knives. (*See* **Hitler's Rise to Power**)

2 AUGUST: Hitler declares himself *Führer* (leader) of the Third Reich. (*See* **Totalitarianism**)

1935

3 MAY: The Soviet Union and France sign a Treaty of Mutual Assistance. (*See* **Soviet Union as Ally**)

16 MAY: Czechoslovakia and the U.S.S.R. conclude a mutual assistance pact.

JULY: Great Britain institutes the Government of India Act, extending representative government and suffrage in India.

15 SEPTEMBER: The Nazis pass the Nuremburg Laws, which deprive German Jews of citizenship and protect the purity of "German" blood.

3 OCTOBER: Italy invades Abyssinia (Ethiopia). (*See* **Colonialism**)

1936

7 MARCH: Hitler sends troops into the Rhineland.

APRIL–MAY: The left-leaning antifascist Popular Front, led by Léon Blum, comes to power in France.

17 JULY: Following several days of political murders, conservative generals begin an uprising to overthrow the Spanish government, leading to the Spanish Civil War. The rebels (rightists) are initially blocked by a coalition of leftist groups that support the Republic. General Francisco Franco appeals to Germany and Italy for aid to overthrow the government. The Soviet Union and France support the loyalists.

AUGUST: At the Lyon Conference, France, Germany, Great Britain, and Italy agreee to halt supplies from reaching both sides in the Spanish Civil War.

29 SEPTEMBER: A provisional ruling military junta chooses Franco as commander in chief of the Nationalists, and he is then appointed the leader of Spain.

25 OCTOBER: Germany and Italy sign a treaty forming the Axis.

25 NOVEMBER: Germany and Japan sign the Anti-Comintern Pact, aimed at stopping the spread of communist (and hence Soviet) power; Italy joins the pact on 6 November 1937.

11 DECEMBER: George VI becomes king of England after the abdication of Edward VIII. (*See* **Monarchy**)

1937

26 APRIL: German aircraft under Franco's command bomb the Basque town of Guernica.

1 JUNE: Stalin begins to purge military officers in the Red Army. (*See* **Totalitarianism**)

1938

11–12 MARCH: Nazi troops are sent into Austria, and the country is annexed by Germany.

SEPTEMBER: Hitler invades the Sudetenland (in Czechoslovakia) and annexes it to Germany.

30 SEPTEMBER: British prime minister Neville Chamberlain and French premier Edouard Daladier meet with Hitler and Italian dictator Benito Mussolini in Munich; the Munich Agreement allows Czech territory to remain in German hands. (*See* **Appeasement**)

1939

28 MARCH: The Nationalists win their fight to overthrow the Republicans, and the Spanish Civil War ends.

23 AUGUST: The Soviet Union and Nazi Germany sign the Molotov-Ribbentrop agreement, a nonaggression pact.

1 SEPTEMBER: Nazi Germany attacks Poland, initiating World War II. (*See* **Total War**)

3 SEPTEMBER: France and Great Britain declare war on Germany.

18 SEPTEMBER: In accordance with a secret provision of the Molotov-Ribbentrop Agreement, the Soviets invade Poland from the east and annex territory.

30 NOVEMBER: Soviet troops invade Finland; the Winter War lasts until Finland yields in March 1940.

1940

SPRING: More than fifteen thousand Polish officers are murdered by the Soviets (they had been prisoners since September 1939).

10 MAY: The Germans launch an offensive westward, overrunning Luxembourg, the Netherlands, and Belgium. Chamberlain resigns, and Winston Churchill becomes the prime minister of England.

10 JUNE: Italy declares war on France.

17 JUNE: The Red Army invades Latvia and Estonia, and the Soviet Union later officially annexes these countries, as well as Lithuania.

22 JUNE: France signs an armistice with Germany. (*See* **Fall of France**)

27 JUNE: The Soviet Union annexes Bukovina and Bessarabia from Romania.

10 JULY: Henri-Philippe Pétain forms the Vichy government in France. (*See* **Vichy France**)

7 SEPTEMBER: The German Blitz against England begins.

27 SEPTEMBER: The Tripartite Pact (Axis) is signed by Germany, Italy, and Japan.

28 OCTOBER: Italy invades Greece.

1941

11 MARCH: Through the Lend-Lease Act the United States provides material support to Great Britain. The act also provided help to other Allies, including the Soviet Union, which received $11.3 billion. (*See* **Lend Lease and the Soviet Union**)

27 MARCH: General Dusan Simovic leads a coup that topples Dragisa Cvetkovic's government after it had signed the Anti-Comintern Pact (25 March). Hitler responds by invading Yugoslavia.

22 JUNE: Hitler launches Operation Barbarossa against the Soviet Union. At this time Germany also begins mass executions of Jews in extermination camps and in occupied territories. (*See* **Operation Barbarossa**)

14 AUGUST: The United States and Great Britain pledge to assist each other in resisting aggression, respecting sovereign rights and territories, collaborating in economic progress, and seeking world peace in the Atlantic Charter; twenty-four additional nations affirm the charter in January 1942. (*See* **World War II Alliances**)

7 DECEMBER: Japanese planes attack the American naval base at Pearl Harbor, Hawaii, which results in the United States declaring war on Japan the following day.

11 DECEMBER: Germany and Italy declare war on the United States; the United States declares war against them.

1942

1 JANUARY: The Big Three (United States, Great Britain, and Soviet Union) and twenty-three other nations conclude a pact in Washington, D.C. not to make separate armistices with the Axis. (*See* **World War II Alliances**)

MAY: Regular deportations of Jews to Nazi death camps begin.

MAY: Soviet foreign minister Vyacheslav Molotov visits London and Washington and requests that the Allies open a second front against Germany.

AUGUST: At the Moscow Conference, Stalin, Churchill, and U.S. envoy W. Averell Harriman discuss the opening of a second front in Europe.

1943

12–23 JANUARY: At the Casablanca Conference Roosevelt and Churchill insist on the unconditional surrender of Germany. (*See* **World War II Alliances**)

2 FEBRUARY: German troops at Stalingrad surrender to Soviet forces, marking a turning point in the war.

28 NOVEMBER–1 DECEMBER: Roosevelt, Stalin, and Churchill meet in Tehran, Iran, to discuss the opening of a second front in Europe and other issues.

1944

6 JUNE: The Allies invade Normandy to open a second front in Western Europe.

JULY: The Polish Committee of National Liberation (PKWN) is established to administer territories liberated by the Soviet Red Army.

21 AUGUST–7 OCTOBER: The foundations of the United Nations (UN) are established at the Dumbarton Oaks Conference.

26 AUGUST: Free French leader Charles de Gaulle enters Paris.

1945

4–11 FEBRUARY: Roosevelt, Stalin, and Churchill meet in Yalta to discuss postwar plans, and the Soviet Union is given much latitude in how to deal with occupied countries in Eastern Europe. The text of the agreements made at the conference is published as the Declaration on Liberated Europe. (*See* **Soviet-Western Cooperation after 1945** *and* **World War II Alliances**)

13–14 FEBRUARY: The German city of Dresden is firebombed by Allied bombers; the city is destroyed and between 35,000 and 135,000 people are killed.

6 MARCH: Romania forms a communist government led by Petru Groza.

12 APRIL: While vacationing in Warm Springs, Georgia, Roosevelt suffers a cerebral hemorrhage and dies; the vice president, Harry S Truman, is sworn in as president.

28 APRIL: Mussolini and his mistress are captured while trying to flee Italy and are executed.

30 APRIL: Hitler, along with his mistress and several associates, commits suicide in Berlin.

7–8 MAY: Germany surrenders to the Allies.

26 JUNE: The UN Charter is signed in San Francisco.

17 JULY–2 AUGUST: Stalin, Churchill, and Truman meet at the Potsdam Conference, agreeing to divide Germany (and Berlin) into four occupied zones, to hold war crimes trials, and to seek the unconditional surrender of Japan.

6 AUGUST: The United States drops an atomic bomb on Hiroshima, Japan; three days later it drops another nuclear device on Nagasaki. Japan surrenders on 2 September.

29 NOVEMBER: The Federal People's Republic of Yugoslavia is established, and Josip Broz Tito becomes prime minister.

1946

1 FEBRUARY: Hungary becomes a republic.

9 FEBRUARY: Stalin declares that the world is broken into "two camps" and that the Soviets cannot coexist with their former allies. (*See* **Soviet-Western Cooperation after 1945**)

5 MARCH: Winston Churchill makes a speech in Fulton, Missouri, warning the West of a Communist "Iron Curtain" descending in Eastern Europe.

9 MAY: Victor Emmanuel III of Italy officially abdicates in favor of his son Umberto, but a plebiscite establishes a republic, and both men go into exile. (*See* **Monarchy**)

8 SEPTEMBER: Bulgaria declares itself a republic and abolishes its monarchy. (*See* **Monarchy**)

2 DECEMBER: The British and American occupied zones of Germany unite, to be later joined by the French (1948); the Soviets continue to control the fourth region.

1947

19 JANUARY: The Polish Communist Party wins power in state elections.

12 MARCH: The Truman Doctrine, which establishes the U.S. policy of blocking the spread of communism and provides assistance to Greece and Turkey, is announced by President Truman. (*See* **Eclipse of Europe** *and* **United States and Western Europe**)

5 JUNE: In an address at Harvard University, U.S. secretary of state George C. Marshall advances the concept of American help to rebuild Europe, largely to counter potential expansion of communism. Over the next four years more than $13 billion is provided to sixteen European nations.

14–15 AUGUST: Great Britain grants independence to India and Pakistan. (*See* **Decolonization**)

31 AUGUST: The communists gain power in Hungary.

4 DECEMBER: Bulgaria becomes the People's Republic of Bulgaria.

1948

25 FEBRUARY: A coup d'état in Czechoslovakia replaces a coalition government with a communist regime.

17 MARCH: Britain, France, Belgium, the Netherlands, and Luxembourg sign the Brussels Pact for common defense.

6 APRIL: Finland signs a nonaggression pact with the Soviet Union. (*See* **Finland after 1945**)

24 JUNE: Stalin orders all ground traffic into and out of Berlin to be halted. The Americans respond with an airlift of supplies into the city that lasts until the end of September 1949 (the blockade is lifted 12 May 1949).

28 JUNE: Yugoslavia is expelled from the Cominform, the agency of international communism founded by the Soviets in 1947.

1949

25 JANUARY: The Soviet Union founds the Council for Mutual Economic Assistance (COMECON).

4 APRIL: The North Atlantic Treaty Organization (NATO) is formed. Members include Belgium, Canada, Denmark, France, Iceland, Italy, Luxembourg, the Netherlands, Norway, Portugal, Spain, the United Kingdom, and the United States. (*See* **United States and Western Europe**)

23 MAY: The Federal Republic of Germany (West Germany) is established; in response the Soviets form the German Democratic Republic (East Germany) in October.

29 AUGUST: The U.S.S.R. explodes its first atomic bomb.

1950

Approximately 15.3 percent of the world's population resides in Europe. (*See* **Eclipse of Europe**)

25 JUNE: The Korean War begins as North Korean troops attack the South. The United States and United Nations respond by sending troops. Belgium, France, Great Britain, Greece, Italy, Luxembourg, the Netherlands, Norway, and Sweden will supply troops during the conflict. The war rages until 1953.

1951

18 APRIL: Belgium, France, the Federal Republic of Germany, Italy, Luxembourg, and the Netherlands sign the Treaty of Paris, establishing the European Coal and Steel Community (ECSC). (*See* **Eclipse of Europe**)

1952

30 APRIL: Tito refuses to accept an offer to join NATO.

27 MAY: A European Defense Community is proposed. (*See* **Eclipse of Europe**)

2 OCTOBER: Great Britain becomes a nuclear power with the test of its first such weapon.

1953

5 MARCH: Stalin dies.

2 JUNE: Elizabeth II is crowned queen of the United Kingdom at Westminster Abbey. (*See* **Monarchy**)

18 JUNE: Rioting erupts in East Germany, and the protesters are suppressed by Soviet troops.

1954

7 MAY: French troops are defeated at Dien Bien Phu, initiating a withdrawal of France from its colonial empire in Indochina. (*See* **Decolonization**)

1955

5 MAY: The Allied occupation of West Germany officially ends.

14 MAY: The Warsaw Treaty of Friendship, Cooperation, and Mutual Assistance (commonly known as the Warsaw Pact) establishes a mutual-defense organization including the Soviet Union, Albania, Bulgaria, Czechoslovakia, East Germany, Hungary, Poland, and Romania.

1956

14 FEBRUARY: Soviet leader Nikita Khrushchev makes a "secret speech" at the Twentieth Congress of the Communist Party of the Soviet Union, denouncing Stalin's cult of personality.

26 JULY: Egyptian leader Gamal Abdel al Nasser nationalizes the Suez Canal.

21 OCTOBER: Rioting occurs in Poland.

23 OCTOBER: Hungarian students in Budapest stage a protest, gaining public support and eliciting police response.

29 OCTOBER: Israel attacks Egypt.

1 NOVEMBER: Hungary withdraws from the Warsaw Pact.

4 NOVEMBER: Soviet tanks enter Budapest and depose Nagy, who is later abducted and executed in 1958.

5–6 NOVEMBER: Anglo-French forces land in the Suez Canal zone in response to Nasser's nationalization of the canal. (*See* **Suez Crisis**)

22 DECEMBER: Responding to Soviet and American opposition, British and French troops withdraw from Egypt.

1957

25 MARCH: Belgium, France, West Germany, Italy, Luxembourg, and the Netherlands sign two treaties in Rome, one of which establishes the European Economic Community (EEC) while the other sets plans for the peaceful pursuit of atomic energy development. The EEC goes into effect on 1 January 1958. (*See* **Eclipse of Europe** *and* **United States as a European Power**)

4 OCTOBER: The Soviet Union launches the Sputnik satellite into orbit.

1958

3 FEBRUARY: Belgium, the Netherlands, and Luxembourg form the Benelux Economic Union (to come into force in 1960).

31 MAY: The Fourth Republic ends in France as de Gaulle is named prime minister; the Fifth Republic is inaugurated 5 October.

10 NOVEMBER: Khrushchev demands that unless talks are held concerning the reunification of Germany, he will deny Western access to Berlin.

21 DECEMBER: Charles de Gaulle is elected president of France. (*See* **France after 1945**)

1959

3 NOVEMBER: De Gaulle announces his intention to withdraw France from NATO. (*See* **Independent Foreign Policy**)

1960

13 FEBRUARY: France explodes its first nuclear weapon. (*See* **France after 1945**)

1961

12–13 AUGUST: East Germany begins sealing off East Berlin from West Berlin, constructing the Berlin Wall, in an attempt to stop the exodus of East Germans to the West.

1962

1 JULY: France, after a referendum, grants Algeria independence. (*See* **Decolonization**)

1963

22 JANUARY: France and Germany sign the Treaty of Elysée, a declaration of cooperation. (*See* **France after 1945**)

1964

13–14 OCTOBER: Khrushchev is removed from power and replaced by Leonid Brezhnev.

1966

7 MARCH: France pulls out of the military component of NATO. (*See* **France after 1945**)

1967

Greek leader Stephanos Stephanopoulos is overthrown in a military coup.

1968

20 AUGUST: Warsaw Pact forces invade Czechoslovakia to counter the rise of a liberal communist government.

12 SEPTEMBER: Albania withdraws from the Warsaw Pact.

1969

27 APRIL: De Gaulle resigns and Georges Pompidou becomes president in June. (*See* **France after 1945**)

1970

West German leader Willy Brandt, seeking improved relations with East Germany and the Soviet Union, formulates his O*stpolitik* (eastern policy). (*See* **Independent Foreign Policy**)

1972

22–30 MAY: The United States and Soviet Union sign the first Strategic Arms Limitations Talks (SALT) Treaty. (*See* **Disarmament**)

5 SEPTEMBER: Eleven Israeli athletes and coaches are killed during a terrorist attack at the Munich Olympic games. Five Black September (Palestinian) terrorists and a German policeman also die. (*See* **Terrorism**)

1973

1 JANUARY: Great Britain, Ireland, and Denmark join the EEC.

1974

14 AUGUST: Greece withdraws from NATO in a dispute over the handling of the Turkish invasion of Cyprus.

1975

20 NOVEMBER: Spanish dictator Franco dies; two days later Juan Carlos becomes the king of Spain. (*See* **Monarchy**)

1976

10 NOVEMBER: The Convention on the Suppression of Terrorism is adopted by the Committee of Foreign Ministers of the Council of Europe. (*See* **Terrorism**)

1978

16 MARCH: Italian former prime minister Aldo Moro is kidnapped and later murdered by members of the Red Brigades. (*See* **Terrorism**)

1979

27 AUGUST: British Lord Mountbatten, a relative of the queen, is assassinated by the Irish Republican Army (IRA), which blows up his sailboat. (*See* **Terrorism**)

24–25 DECEMBER: Soviet troops invade Afghanistan.

1980

Approximately 10.8 percent of the world's population resides in Europe.

4 MAY: Yugoslavian leader Tito dies.

14 AUGUST: Lech Walesa leads massive shipyard strikes in Poland.

1981

23 FEBRUARY: Juan Carlos blocks a coup attempt by the Spanish military. (*See* **Monarchy**)

1982

Spain joins NATO.

9 MAY–14 JUNE: Great Britain fights against and defeats Argentine forces in the Falkland Islands.

10 NOVEMBER: Brezhnev dies.

1983

1 SEPTEMBER: The Soviet Union shoots down a Korean airliner over the Sea of Japan.

30 DECEMBER: U.S. Pershing missiles are deployed in West Germany. (*See* **United States and Western Europe**)

1985

11 MARCH: Mikhail Gorbachev is selected general secretary of the Communist Party of the Soviet Union.

7 OCTOBER: Terrorist Abu Abbas hijacks the Italian ocean liner *Achille Lauro* and murders an American Jewish passenger. (*See* **Terrorism**)

19 NOVEMBER: U.S. president Ronald Reagan meets with Gorbachev in Geneva; the two leaders talk amicably for about an hour, although they disagree about Reagan's "Star Wars" policy.

27 DECEMBER: Palestinians led by Abu Nidal simultaneously attack airports in Rome and Vienna, killing twenty travelers.

1986

Spain, Portugal, and Greece join the EEC.

11–12 OCTOBER: Reagan and Gorbachev meet in Reykjavik and propose a reduction in long-range missiles.

1987

8 DECEMBER: The United States and Soviet Union sign the Intermediate Range Nuclear Forces (INF) Treaty, which provides for the removal of their nuclear missiles from Europe. (*See* **Disarmament**)

1988

14 APRIL: The Soviet Union agrees to withdraw its troops from Afghanistan.

6 DECEMBER: Gorbachev announces Soviet troop reductions for Eastern Europe.

21 DECEMBER: Libyan terrorists destroy Pan American flight 103 over Lockerbie, Scotland, killing 270 people. (*See* **Terrorism**)

1989

9 FEBRUARY: The Soviet Union withdraws its last troops from Afghanistan. (*See* **Collapse of the Soviet Union**)

20–21 FEBRUARY: Hungary establishes a new constitution that omits the leading role of the Communist Party. (*See* **Velvet Revolutions**)

4 JUNE: Representatives of the labor party Solidarity win a majority of parliamentary seats in the first free elections in Poland since before World War II.

9 NOVEMBER: East Germany opens its borders.

22 DECEMBER: Romanian leader Nicolae Ceauşescu is overthrown; he is executed on 25 December.

1990

11 MARCH: Lithuania declares its independence from the Soviet Union. (*See* **Velvet Revolutions**)

3 OCTOBER: East and West Germany reunite.

19 NOVEMBER: The Treaty on Conventional Armed Forces in Europe (CFE Treaty), limiting the number of weapons possessed by the Soviet and Western sides on the Continent, is signed.

22 DECEMBER: Walesa is sworn in as president of Poland.

26 DECEMBER: Serbian leader Slobodan Milošević becomes president of Yugoslavia.

1991

APRIL–SEPTEMBER: As the constituent republics declare their independence, the Soviet Union begins to dissolve. (*See* **Collapse of the Soviet Union**)

12 JUNE: Yeltsin is elected president of the Russian Federation.

19 JUNE: Russian troops complete their withdrawal from Hungary.

25 JUNE: Slovenia and Croatia secede from Yugoslavia. Bosnia-Herzegovina and Macedonia soon follow. (*See* **Collapse of Yugoslavia**)

19–21 AUGUST: Gorbachev is held under house arrest during a coup attempt by hard-liners.

25 DECEMBER: Gorbachev resigns as leader of the Soviet Union. Yeltsin and the presidents of Ukraine and Belarus (Belorussia) establish the Commonwealth of Independent States (CIS).

1992

Serbia invades Bosnia, instituting a program of "ethnic cleansing" and initiating the Bosnian Civil War. (*See* **Collapse of Yugoslavia**)

7 FEBRUARY: The European Union (EU) is formally established, based on the Treaty of European Union signed in Maastricht, Netherlands. By 1995 the union will include Austria, Belgium, Denmark, Finland, France, Germany, Greece, Ireland, Italy, Luxembourg, the Netherlands, Portugal, Spain, Sweden, and the United Kingdom. (*See* **Eclipse of Europe** *and* **United States as a European Power**)

1993

1 JANUARY: Czechoslovakia peacefully divides into the Czech Republic and Slovakia.

23 JULY: The British Parliament ratifies the Maastricht Treaty.

1994

DECEMBER: Yeltsin sends Russian troops into the breakaway republic of Chechnya.

1995

Austria, Sweden, and Finland join the EU.

14 DECEMBER: The Dayton Accords, an attempt to broker peace in Bosnia-Herzegovina, are signed. U.S. troops will police the peace under UN auspices. (*See* **Collapse of Yugoslavia**)

1998

Milošević begins moving military and paramilitary units into Kosovo. (*See* **Collapse of Yugoslavia**)

17 JULY: The bodies of Nicholas II and his family are interred in the Cathedral of Saints Peter and Paul in St. Petersburg; he is granted canonization on 20 August 2000 by the Russian Orthodox Church.

1999

1 JANUARY: The euro, the monetary unit and currency of the EU, is introduced. It will replace the national currencies of all EU member states except Britain, Denmark, and Sweden in 2002. (*See* **Eclipse of Europe** *and* **United States as a European Power**)

MARCH: Poland, Hungary, and the Czech Republic join NATO.

MARCH–APRIL: A U.S.-led NATO bombing campaign commences in Yugoslavia to stop "ethnic cleansing" of ethnic Albanians in Kosovo. An international peacekeeping force subsequently occupies Kosovo. (*See* **Collapse of Yugoslavia**)

31 DECEMBER: Yeltsin resigns and Prime Minister Vladimir Putin becomes acting president of Russia. Putin is elected president in March 2000.

ALLIED INTERVENTION

Was the Allied intervention in Soviet Russia that began in 1918 intended to crush communism?

Viewpoint: Yes. The Allied military presence was aimed at eradicating the Bolshevik regime.

Viewpoint: No. The Allies were concerned mainly with protecting their own wartime and postwar geopolitical and strategic interests in the region.

The Bolshevik Revolution of November 1917 set off not just a brutal civil war in Russia but also a determined international effort to aid anti-Bolshevik forces. Beginning in the spring of 1918, the Allies sent troops eventually numbering 150,000 men from fifteen nations, including Britain, France, the United States, and Japan. In most cases these forces had been withdrawn by 1920, but Japan kept troops on the mainland Far East until 1922 and on the Russian part of Sakhalin Island until 1925. This intervention cast a long shadow over Soviet Russia and its relations with much of the rest of the world.

The true motives for this intervention have been debated. One argument suggests that it was a determined effort to crush Bolshevism by aiding domestic resistance to communist rule. Future British prime minister Winston Churchill, who served as war minister during much of the intervention, spoke of "strangling the Bolshevik baby in its crib." In addition to sending troops, both Britain and France gave large amounts of material and diplomatic aid to the "Whites," the Russian anti-Bolshevik forces.

At times, however, the intentions of the interventionist powers appeared to be less ambitious, and eradicating Bolshevism seemed only incidental to the Allies' main goals. As a counterargument suggests, many of the nations involved were less worried about the Bolsheviks than they were that Germany would exploit its World War I victory over Russia by moving unopposed into the Russian heartland. According to this argument, one major reason for intervention was preventing Allied supplies that had been intended for Russian units on the Eastern Front from falling into German hands. American intervention, the argument maintains, was mainly oriented toward preventing Japanese expansion into Asian territories of Russia.

Viewpoint:
Yes. The Allied military presence was aimed at eradicating the Bolshevik regime.

Governments in general dislike admitting to failure, and so it is not surprising that the Allied intervention in the Russian Civil War has often been portrayed as anything but what it was: a failed attempt to eradicate Bolshevism while it was still weak.

Initially, the Allied decision to help the anti-Bolshevik "Whites" against the Bolshevik communist "Reds" was part of the Allies' strategy to defeat the Germans in World War I. The Reds were committed to ending the unpopular and costly war with Germany on whatever terms necessary so they could focus on consolidating Bolshevik power within Russia. As a result they accepted the punitive terms demanded by Germany in the March 1918 Treaty of Brest-Litovsk. The Allies hoped that defeating the communists in Russia would lead to the reopening of the Eastern Front, thus preventing Germany from concentrating its forces against the Allies in the West. Then, however, the Allies won World War I without reviving hostilities on the Eastern Front. As a result they found themselves in the awkward position of intervening in Russian internal affairs without their original compelling reason to do so.

The Russian community in exile argued that, as Russian governments before the communist takeover had been loyal to the Allied cause, the Allies had a moral obligation to help the Whites defeat the Reds. Furthermore, the Soviet government, at this point still committed to "global revolution," was actively spreading communist propaganda and conducting subversive activities in many Allied countries, as well as in most of the defeated ones. War weariness, however, initially led the Allies to attempt a compromise between the two sides, while Allied troops remained in place.

As early as February 1918, even before the Treaty of Brest-Litovsk, Britain supported intervention in the civil war on behalf of the Whites, and in March it landed troops in Murmansk. They were soon joined by forces from France, Italy, Japan, the United States, and ten other nations. Eventually, more than 150,000 Allied soldiers served in Russia. Reluctant to send their own soldiers into major combat, the Allies supplied impressive quantities of war matériel and financing to the White armies. Thousands of tons of supplies poured into the camps of Admiral Aleksandr Kolchak in Siberia and General Anton Denikin in southern Russia, as well as to the forces of lesser and more-infamous commanders, such as the brutal Cossack Grigorii Semenov.

The United States, under the idealistic leadership of President Woodrow Wilson, hoped for a compromise between the warring parties. Although the British were more willing to fight than their allies, they joined the Americans in calling all Russian parties to a truce and peace talks at Prinkipo, in the recently defeated Ottoman Empire (now Büyükada, Turkey). The Reds declined the truce but accepted the call for peace talks, while the Whites declined both. The failure to bring the two sides together led War Minister Winston Churchill of Britain to call for increasing aggressive action against the communists, but the Americans continued to hope for a settlement, sending Assistant Secre-

tary of State William Bullitt to Moscow in March 1919. The peace proposals he received from the communists, including amnesty for Russians who collaborated with the Allies and a pledge of a cease-fire in return for an end of Allied aid to the Whites, came at a time when the Allies were already embroiled with the seemingly more pressing matter of the Rhineland and Germany. The communist proposals proved unacceptable to the Allies and the Whites, and the accommodationist phase of Allied intervention ended, allowing Churchill's opinions to assume temporary prominence.

The scale of the war between the Russian Reds and Whites, however, was such that the Allies soon realized they would have little, if any, direct impact on the course of the Civil War unless they were prepared to intervene on a far grander scale. By the end of April 1919 the French had withdrawn their soldiers. The Allies were involved in almost no military engagements. British and American troops saw some action in November 1918 on the Northern Front, near the port of Arkhangel'sk, but this campaign was of limited significance in the outcome of the Civil War. The last British and American soldiers were withdrawn in 1920. The main Allied contributions to the White cause thereafter were supplies and money, mostly from Britain.

After the Bolshevik Revolution of November 1917 communist power was at first concentrated mostly in Moscow, Petrograd, and the heart of European Russia; communist control was weaker in other parts of the Russian Empire, especially in the south of European Russia, the countryside outside the heartland, and Siberia. In the Far East the Japanese had established good supply lines and were willing to defend their newly gained advances. Under direct pressure from the Americans they agreed to begin withdrawing from Russian territory in summer 1920, but Japanese forces remained on the Far Eastern mainland until autumn 1922 and in the northern (Russian) half of Sakhalin Island until 1925.

To a certain extent the Allies' collective amnesia about their missed opportunity to eliminate communism in its infancy was made easier by official Soviet historiography. Soviet historians tended to portray the Civil War as a domestic struggle against segments of Russian society that resisted the consolidation of Bolshevik power (internal suppression) and as military campaigns against the White armies. Although these historians acknowledged Allied intervention on the Whites' behalf, they downplayed this aspect of Soviet history. The Soviets needed to portray Bolshevik forces as strong and their victory as inevitable. To suggest that the outcome could

ALLIED INTERVENTION

CHURCHILL'S WARNING

In an 11 April 1919 speech at an Aldwych Club luncheon in London, Winston Churchill warned of "The Bolshevik Menace":

Of all the tyrannies in history the Bolshevist tyranny is the worst, the most destructive, and the most degrading. It is sheer humbug to pretend that it is not far worse than German militarism. The miseries of the Russian people under the Bolshevists far surpass anything they suffered even under the Tsar. The atrocities by Lenin and Trotsky are incomparably more hideous, on a larger scale, and more numerous than any for which the Kaiser himself is responsible. . . .

Lenin and Trotsky had no sooner seized on power than they dragged the noble Russian nation out of the path of honour and let loose on us and our Allies a whole deluge of German reinforcements, which burst on us in March and April last year [after the Russians withdrew from World War I]. Every British and French soldier killed last year was really done to death by Lenin and Trotsky, not in a fair way, but by the treacherous desertion of an ally without parallel in the history of the world. There are still [anti-Bolshevik] Russian Armies in the field, under Admiral Koltchak and General Deniken, who have never wavered in their faith and loyalty to the Allied cause, and who are fighting valiantly and by no means unsuccessfully against that foul combination of criminality and animalism which constitutes the Bolshevist *régime.* We are helping these men, within the limits which are assigned to us, to the very best of our ability. We are helping them with arms and munitions, with instructions and technical experts, who volunteered for service. It would not be right for us to send our armies raised on a compulsory basis to Russia. If Russia is to be saved it must be by Russian manhood. But all our hearts are with those men who are true to the Allied cause in their splendid struggle to restore the honour of united Russia, and to rebuild on a modern and democratic basis the freedom, prosperity, and happiness of its trustful and good-hearted people.

There is a class of misguided or degenerate people in this country and some others, who profess to take so lofty a view that they cannot see any difference between what they call rival Russian factions. . . . Their idea of a League of Nations is something which would be impartial as between Bolshevism on the one hand, and civilization on the other. We are still forced to distinguish between right and wrong, loyalty and treachery, health and disease, progress and anarchy. There is one part of the world in which these distinctions which we are bound to draw can translate itself into action. In the North of Russia the Bolshevists are continually attacking the British troops we sent there during the course of the war against Germany in order to draw off pressure from the West, and who are now cut off by the ice from the resources of their fellow countrymen. . . . We have no intentions whatever of deserting our lads and of leaving them on this icy shore to the mercy of a cruel foe. The Prime Minister has given me the fullest authority to take whatever measures the General Staff of the Army think necessary to see that our men are relieved, and brought safely through the perils with which they are confronted. . . .

Very great perils still menace us in the world. Two mighty branches of the human race, the Slavs [of Russia] and the Teutons [of Germany], are both plunged at the present time in the deepest misery. The Great Power which was our foe, and the Great Power which was our friend, are both in the pit of ruin and despair. It is extremely undesirable that they should come together. Germany is struggling against breaking down into Bolshevism. But if that were to happen it would produce a reaction which it is no exaggeration to say would reach as far as China.

The Russian Bolshevist revolution is changing in its character. It has completed the Anarchist destruction of the social order in Russia itself. The political, economic, social, and moral life of the people of Russia has for the time being been utterly smashed. Famine and terror are the order of the day. Only the military structure is growing out of the ruin. That is still weak, but it is growing steadily stronger, and it is assuming an aggressive and predatory form, which French Jacobinism assumed after the fall of Robespierre, and before the rise of Napoleon. Bolshevist armies are marching on towards food and plunder, and in their path stand only the little weak States, exhausted and shattered by the war.

If Germany succumbs either from internal weakness, or from actual invasion, to the Bolshevist pestilence, Germany no doubt will be torn to pieces, but where shall we be? Where will be that peace for which we are all longing; where will be that revival of prosperity without which our domestic contentment is impossible. . . .

. . . I say to you, keep a strong Army loyal, compact, contented, adequate for the work it has to do; make peace with the German people; resist by every means at your disposal the advances of Bolshevist tyranny in every country in the world.

Source: Robert Rhodes James, ed., Winston S. Churchill: His Complete Speeches, Volume III, 1914–1922 *(New York & London: Chelsea House/Bowker, 1974), pp. 2771–2774.*

have been otherwise would have highlighted the tenuous nature of early Bolshevik rule in Russia and thus undermined the subsequent legitimacy of the Soviet state. Furthermore, after the Civil War the Soviets desperately needed to normalize relations with the West in order to secure foreign investment in their war-torn country and promote foreign trade. Lenin and his associates believed that stabilizing the domestic economy was critical to the survival of their regime, and such stabilization was impossible without a return of healthy foreign trade and investment.

After the end of World War I in November 1918 the only reason for continued Allied intervention in Russia was the menace of international communism to global security and the Western capitalist way of life; the Allies' goal was to eradicate Bolshevism. Because of their recent heavy fatalities in World War I, however, the Allies lacked the resolve to involve their troops in a full-scale intervention. Neither the French nor the Americans had much appetite for the new adventure. The United States had entered World War I late and with reluctance, and the idealistic government of Woodrow Wilson was unwilling to countenance the loss of American lives to restore a conservative autocracy or to install what would almost certainly have been an undemocratic military government. France had paid such a high price in lives and property during the war that its only interest was extracting a suitable degree of reparation from Germany at Versailles. Moreover, many influential French socialists viewed the Soviet state with a degree of optimism that prevented them from supporting intervention on the behalf of its domestic enemies.

Britain was the Allied nation most heavily involved in the Russian Civil War, largely because Churchill viewed communism as an abomination, a threat to world peace and security. Foreseeing that the menace to Western society posed by a communist Russia was potentially greater than the upheaval inflicted by Germany, he called on the Allies to "strangle the Bolshevik baby in its crib." As British public opinion was tired of involvement in military action, however, the British contribution against the Reds ultimately consisted mostly of financial support and military matériel.

One could attempt to argue, by virtue of the Allied attempts at mediation in early 1919, that there was a genuine willingness to allow the Reds to continue to exist. Yet, the presence of Allied troops in Russian territory during these supposedly honest attempts at compromise leads to some skepticism. Furthermore, the volume of Allied material support was great, and the Whites' failure to use it in an effective, united, and well-organized effort—not an insufficiency of

Allied supplies—was largely responsible for their failure to win the Civil War. Finally, the Allies' unwillingness to consider the ideas brought back from Moscow by the Bullitt mission indicates that the main purpose of the mission, from the Allied leadership's perspective, was to give them a pretext for rejecting the Reds' proposals and thus legitimize continued action against the Reds. The chief purpose of Allied intervention in Soviet Russia was to help the Whites defeat the Reds and destroy Bolshevism.

–VASILIS VOURKOUTIOTIS,
UNIVERSITY OF OTTAWA

Viewpoint:
No. The Allies were concerned mainly with protecting their own wartime and postwar geopolitical and strategic interests in the region.

In the past the official Soviet historiography described the Allied intervention in Russia as a large-scale, well-coordinated, and ideologically motivated crusade of "international capitalism" against Soviet Russia. During the Stalin era this approach went even further. The Russian Civil War was officially renamed a "Patriotic War Against the Interventionists and the White Guards." Some Western scholars, while doubting that the Allied endeavor in Russia was well coordinated, also view anticommunist intentions as the Allies' primary motive. Some scholars, particularly left-wing critics of the intervention, have even defined it as the real beginning of the Cold War between the Soviets and the West. Surely there was a strong and persistent element of natural hostility on the part of the West toward the Bolshevik regime installed in Russia in 1917. The West took note of its radical ideology, extremist tactics, and brutality and also suspected links with the Germans during World War I. Moreover, the Bolsheviks withdrew Russia from the war and thus from the Allied camp.

Nevertheless, even those historians who share the view that intervention was intended to crush communism could not deny several paradoxes of the Allied involvement in the Russian Civil War. First, most of the Allied contingents sent to Russia were not large enough to participate in major combat. After the end of World War I the Western powers deployed only a small portion of their forces to Russia. Second, as many Western diplomatic documents reveal, the Allies, at least initially, were reluctant to fight the Bolsheviks, and the British and U.S. governments repeatedly made it clear that they did not

Czech, American, Japanese, and British soldiers and sailors in Vladivostok, Russia, circa 1918

(David King Collection)

intend to take sides in the Russian turmoil. Third, most of the Allied troops in Russia were deployed in theaters of operation far removed from the Bolshevik-controlled heartland. The Allied forces' confinement to the periphery prevented them from playing any decisive role in the clash with the Reds. Finally, in the diplomatic sphere the Allied powers did not use all the opportunities available to create an effective anti-Soviet coalition involving the states bordering Russia.

The Bolsheviks later admitted that they could not have withstood a concerted French and British attack in the end of 1918, but such an attack had not occurred. Historians have also identified three critical moments in 1919 when the Reds were in grave danger of defeat, and the Allies did not employ stronger intervention tactics, which had realistic chances for success. In the late spring and early summer of 1919 Admiral Aleksandr Kolchak's forces in Siberia made substantial gains in their march on Moscow, the new capital, before they were turned back. In the fall of that year the forces of General Anton Denikin in southern Russia moved north with some success and were stopped only about a hundred miles south of the new capital. Another army's simultaneous attack on the former capital of Petrograd (as St. Petersburg had been renamed in 1914) reached the suburbs of the city before

stalling. Each of these campaigns received tentative Allied assistance, but it was mostly confined to material supplies and some limited naval operations in the Baltic. Substantive Allied aid to any one of these White campaigns might have made the difference in the Civil War.

Many historians have pointed out that the Allied adventure in Russia was motivated by more complex considerations than just anticommunism. Until the armistice was signed on the Western Front in November 1918, the continuing war with Germany and its allies (the Central Powers) dominated the Allied approach to the Russian problem.

Having been exhausted by the uncertain and bloody standoff in the West, the British and the French particularly wanted to reestablish an Eastern Front, which had virtually disintegrated after the Bolsheviks took power in Russia and declared their intention to leave the war. The Allies were concerned that the peace in the East could allow the Germans to transfer some one million troops to the West and defeat the Allied cause. The Allies hoped that the emerging anti-Bolshevik movements in Russia—which, as a rule, strongly opposed separate peace talks between the Russians and the Germans—would carry on fighting against the Central Powers if they were successful. These considerations, rather than just anticommunism, prompted the British and

French decision of 1 December 1917 to establish contacts with the anti-Soviet forces in Russia.

After the collapse of the first round of the separate peace talks between Russia and the Central Powers in February 1918 the rapid and successful advance of the Central Powers deep inside Russia added new elements to the situation. On the one hand, the Allies began to consider how to prevent the Central Powers from making use of Russian agricultural, mineral, and industrial resources. Addressing this problem might have required Allied operations in southern Russia and the Caucasus. If, however, the Reds continued to fight the Germans, any Allied confrontation with the Bolsheviks would have been unnecessary and counterproductive for the reestablishment of the Eastern Front.

Moreover, the Allied governments, though for a brief period of time, even considered cooperating with the Reds in fighting the Germans. The United States, Britain, and France maintained unofficial contacts with the Soviets in 1917–1918 and attempted to sponsor peace talks between the two sides in the Civil War in 1919.

In the growing chaos surrounding the German advance in Russia, the Allies, particularly Britain and the United States, also became concerned that the Germans might seize the huge quantities of war supplies that they had delivered to Russia in 1916–1917. Many of these supplies were stockpiled at the ports of Murmansk and Arkhangel'sk in the north and at Vladivostok in the Far East. The perceived need to protect these supplies strengthened the Allied (particularly the British) desire to intervene in Russia.

After Soviet Russia and the Central Powers signed the Treaty of Brest-Litovsk in March 1918, the Allies had raised one more concern about the Russian situation. They feared that, when the Russians released their enemy prisoners of war, those roughly one million men might easily take over Siberia with its infrastructure, including the port of Vladivostok. In addition, the British were haunted by visions of enemy armies invading the Caspian region on their way to India. Such fears, realistic or not, contributed to the Allies' decision to intervene in Russia.

In May 1918 an armed conflict broke out between the Reds and the Czechoslovak Legion, a unit that had been formed in Russia to fight the Germans and was on its way to Vladivostok to be transported to the Western Front. The Allies, particularly the United States, decided to help the Czechs. When the well-disciplined Czechs easily took over the Trans-Siberian Railway, the Allies began to view them and the pro-Allied and anti-Bolshevik Russians as the possible nucleus of an army to reopen a new Eastern Front. Thus the interrelated imperatives of keeping the Germans occupied in the east, helping the Czechoslovak Legion, and keeping strategically important areas and resources of Russia from the enemy provided strong motives for the Allies to go into northern Russia, Transcaucasia, the Caspian region, and Siberia in March–April 1918. The Allied troop presence was increased with the arrival of French forces in Ukraine in December 1918.

Japan sent more troops to Russia (seventy-three thousand) than all the other Allies combined. Many historians agree that the Japanese intervention was much less motivated by anti-communism than by a desire to establish de facto Japanese control in Siberia and the Far East, which Tokyo considered its special "sphere of interest." Some scholars stress that sending American troops to Siberia was primarily an attempt to offset unilateral Japanese action there. Moreover, as some students of the intervention have concluded, the mission of the U.S. expeditionary forces in Siberia was a continuation of the traditional "Open Door" policy that Washington had long advocated in the Far East. The U.S. troops in Siberia were instructed to remain strictly neutral in the civil war. For that reason the White leaders in Siberia later advocated the removal of the Americans from the Russian territory.

The U.S.-Japanese rivalry in Siberia and the Allied occupation of other parts of Russian territory stimulated many complaints from the Whites as well as the Reds, both of whom charged that the Allies were pursuing their own expansionist goals and economic interests. Adherents of this view often refer to the 23 December 1917 convention in which Britain and France defined their "spheres of influence" in southern Russia. While the Allies' immediate aim was to keep the area and its resources from the Central Powers, the convention divided up the region strictly according to the economic interests of the signatories. Britain took responsibility for Caucasus and its oilfields, while France made itself responsible for Ukraine with its coal and iron mines.

At least in the immediate aftermath of World War I the Allies considered themselves bound by obligations of honor to the Russian anti-Bolshevik regimes that had emerged under the shelter of the Western military presence. Also, the Allied powers had some sense of responsibility toward the newly independent states that were proclaimed on the periphery of the former tsarist empire and were threatened by the continuing Civil War in Russia. The British Navy, for example, was instrumental in safeguarding the independence of the Baltic States, while Allied diplomatic pressure and a French military mission helped Poland survive Bolshevik attempts to conquer it.

ALLIED INTERVENTION

Some British leaders, particularly Foreign Secretary George, Lord Curzon, justified the British presence in Transcaucasia by arguing that they needed to maintain a buffer between Russia and India—the classic British imperial strategy regarding the East. A well-known historian of the Russian Revolution, Richard Pipes, has said that on the British side there was a "fear not of White defeat, but of White victory." Some private statements by the British politicians, including Prime Minister David Lloyd George, reveal that they were ready to deal with the Bolsheviks as the de facto government in the part of Russia they controlled, and that they favored dividing the country into separate states with none of sufficient size and power to threaten the general peace.

During the Paris Peace Conference of 1919 the Allies viewed the pacification of Russia as an integral part of postwar reconstruction. President Woodrow Wilson and Prime Minister George endorsed the idea, trying to bring together the belligerents in the Russian Civil War at an Allied-sponsored peace conference. This initiative, though unsuccessful, would have placed the Bolsheviks on an equal plane with the Whites in the peacemaking process.

Even the staunchest anti-Bolshevik Allied leaders—including Prime Minister Georges Clemenceau of France, Allied Supreme Commander Marshal Ferdinand Foch, and War Minister Winston Churchill of Britain—who repeatedly advocated stronger Allied intervention in 1918–1920 were not motivated solely by anticommunism. Broader geopolitical and strategic considerations were at stake, including not only the danger of aggressive Bolshevism but also the possibility of revived German militarism and Japanese imperialist ambitions—all of which could combine to create the most formidable threat the West had ever faced.

Thus, many considerations other than anticommunism motivated the Allied intervention in Russia. This fact, as well as a growing post–World War I rivalry among the Allies, precluded a large-scale, coordinated, and successful Western assault on Soviet Russia.

—PETER RAINOW,
SAN MATEO, CALIFORNIA

References

John F. N. Bradley, *Allied Intervention in Russia* (London: Weidenfeld & Nicolson, 1968).

George F. Kennan, *The Decision to Intervene,* volume 2 of his *Soviet-American Relations, 1917–1920* (Princeton: Princeton University Press, 1958).

William J. Morley, *The Japanese Thrust into Siberia, 1918* (New York: Columbia University Press, 1957).

Richard Pipes, *The Russian Revolution* (New York: Knopf, 1990).

John Silverlight, *The Victors' Dilemma: Allied Intervention in the Russian Civil War* (New York: Weybright & Talley, 1971).

Ilya Somin, *Stillborn Crusade: The Tragic Failure of Western Intervention in the Russian Civil War, 1918–1920* (New Brunswick, N.J.: Transaction, 1996).

Richard H. Ullman, *Intervention and the War,* volume 1 of his *Anglo-Soviet Relations, 1917–1921* (Princeton: Princeton University Press, 1961); *Britain and the Russian Civil War,* volume 2 of his *Anglo-Soviet Relations, 1917–1921* (Princeton: Princeton University Press, 1968).

Betty Miller Unterberger, *America's Siberian Expedition, 1918–1920: A Study of National Policy* (Durham, N.C.: Duke University Press, 1956).

ALLIED INTERVENTION

APPEASEMENT

Was the British and French policy of appeasing Nazi Germany during the 1930s based on a belief that Adolf Hitler's demands and actions were reasonable?

Viewpoint: Yes. The majority view in the British and French governments was that Adolf Hitler was a "rational actor" who would guarantee peace if his "reasonable" demands were met.

Viewpoint: No. The British and French governments had serious reservations about their military preparedness, and they followed a policy of appeasement, hoping to avoid conflict with Nazi Germany.

Faced with aggressive territorial expansion by Nazi Germany in the 1930s, Britain and France—victorious powers of World War I—responded with a series of measures designed to placate Adolf Hitler. Collectively known as *appeasement,* these concessions allowed Germany to violate treaty limitations on the size, power, and deployment of its armed forces and to use its military might to expand its borders. Arguing at first that Germany had a right to govern all German-speaking areas of Europe, Hitler annexed Austria in March 1938. The following September he invaded the German-populated areas of Czechoslovakia (the Sudetenland). Prime Minister Neville Chamberlain of Britain and Premier Edouard Daladier of France had conceded the Sudetenland to the Germans, believing that in return Hitler would make no further territorial demands in Europe. In March 1939, however, Hitler overran much of the remaining part of Czechoslovakia. A growing chorus of critics began to argue that appeasement had enabled Hitler's aggression.

A traditional explanation for why the British and French governments decided on this appeasement policy has pointed to the Allies' belief that many of the sanctions imposed on Germany by the peace settlements after World War I were too harsh. According to this theory, they considered Hitler—despite his bluster and authoritarianism—a rational politician and believed many of his demands were reasonable responses to unfair treaty sanctions. In hindsight it is easy to call such beliefs foolish, but—if this view had been correct—Hitler's development of an army comparable to that of any other European power and his desire to establish the "natural" hegemony of Germany over Central Europe might not have been causes for alarm.

A recent reinterpretation of appeasement, however, argues that it sprung from a profound sense of military weakness on the part of Britain and France. Although the politicians did not admit their fears publicly, Germany's military potential, dramatic rearmament, and impressive economic rebound from the Great Depression presented a difficult challenge to the British and French, whose economies and military preparedness were still suffering the effects of the worldwide economic crisis. Particularly in such modern categories of weaponry as aircraft and tanks, Germany appeared superior. From this perspective appeasing Hitler might have been seen as an attempt to buy time or to avoid fighting a war that the British and French believed they might lose.

Viewpoint:
Yes. The majority view in the British and French governments was that Adolf Hitler was a "rational actor" who would guarantee peace if his "reasonable" demands were met.

Many scholars have argued that, after the heavy casualties of World War I and the limits of the Great Depression on their military expenditures, the governments of Great Britain and France allowed German territorial expansion in the 1930s to go unchecked because they hoped never to go to war again. While there is some basis for this argument, the main impetus for this policy of appeasement was the strong belief on the part of successive French and British governments that Adolf Hitler behaved in a rational manner and could be convinced to limit his demands by appeals to reason.

During the Great Depression of the 1930s many people considered strong governments necessary to solve the world's economic problems. Germany was especially vulnerable to an authoritarian takeover. Its government under the Weimar Constitution, which took effect in 1919, was too weak to govern effectively, and economic dislocation was rampant at critical points in the 1920s and 1930s. Nor were Britain and France immune to the appeal of authoritarianism. Fearing the sort of takeover that had occurred in Russia in 1917, many people in France and Britain, as well as Germany, considered fascism a viable defense against communism.

Furthermore, Hitler at first behaved like a rational actor on the world stage. Having learned an important lesson from his failure to overthrow the German government by force in November 1923, he followed the law until he was strong enough to ignore it. In the years after his early release from prison in 1924, the Nazi Party fielded candidates for the Reichstag (the German legislature) with increasing success. By July 1932 the Nazis were garnering 37 percent of the national vote. Although his nomination for chancellor was the result of backroom negotiations, it was not radically out of step with parliamentary democracy. The Enabling Act of March 1933, which granted Hitler emergency dictatorial powers, was legally enacted with the support of political centrists. Even when Hitler began his program of territorial expansion, he moved carefully and slowly, calculating each move to avoid frightening Great Britain and France. He wanted a war, but on his terms, when he was ready. He wanted to prevent them from declaring war before he was prepared to fight.

Hitler's every move was carefully planned out. He did not immediately throw out the Treaty of Versailles (signed 1919) and launch the Holocaust. He started with small steps, building on the Allies' latent guilt over the harsh provisions of the treaty and on the anti-Semitism that already existed throughout Europe. By the time the world realized what was happening, it was too late. Indeed, Hitler's definitive program of outright genocide of European Jews was formulated after the war began.

After coming to power in 1933, Hitler embarked on a secret plan to remilitarize Germany and bring its armed forces to parity with the other Great Powers of Europe. The Versailles Treaty included provisions limiting the size of the German Army, restricting the navy even more severely, and forbidding it to form an air force or to deploy its troops. Other nations, however, had begun to feel that the treaty had been too harsh, not only in its military sanctions on Germany but also in its requirement that the Germans pay heavy financial reparations for war damages, especially to France and Belgium. Guilt over these demands and the world economic crisis that followed 1929 had led to lax enforcement of the reparation provisions, which were suspended in a U.S.-sponsored 1931 moratorium. As a result Hitler had no reason to believe that the Allies would attempt to enforce the rest of the treaty too vigorously, and he was right.

In 1935 Hitler's announcement of a peacetime military draft and his revelation that Germany had established a modern air force aroused little protest from the British and French governments. In the same year the British and Germans negotiated a new naval agreement that revised the Versailles Treaty provisions regarding the German surface fleet and allowed Hitler to increase its size. Hitler then set out to remilitarize the Rhineland, a German territory bordering France, from which the Treaty of Versailles had barred German troops. He offered an explanation designed not to alarm Britain and France, using as a convenient pretext the Franco-Soviet treaty of 1935. According to Hitler, this pact surrounded Germany with enemies, with no chance to defend itself until enemy troops were well into German territory. By presenting his reason in this way, he circumvented objections to violations of terms in both the Treaty of Versailles and the Locarno Pact (1925). Therefore, on 7 March 1936, the day after the Franco-Soviet treaty was ratified by the French Senate, he sent troops into the Rhineland. By calling these troops a defensive force, Hitler offered a reasonable alternative to the interpretation that he was remilitarizing the region in preparation for an attack on France. No reasonable nation could argue that

British prime minister Neville Chamberlain, French premier Edouard Daladier, German dictator Adolf Hitler, Italian dictator Benito Mussolini, and Italian foreign minister Count Galeazzo Ciano (l.-r., front) after signing the Munich Agreement in 1938

(National Archives, Washington, D.C.)

another sovereign nation did not have a right to defend itself on its own territory. No one disputed that the Rhineland was German territory and that Germany had a right to defend it. Why, the British asked, should they intervene to stop Hitler from invading "his own back garden"?

After remilitarizing the Rhineland, Hitler made no further overt moves for some time, preferring to continue his plans in secret. He was helped in this deception by the outbreak of the Spanish Civil War in July 1936, deflecting the attention of the Great Powers toward containing that conflict. Germany publicly went along with France and Great Britain in their calls for nonintervention. Privately, however, Hitler helped General Francisco Franco, using the war as a chance to test his forces and new weapons.

During this apparent respite, Hitler continued planning to control Europe. His next move was again carefully calculated to seem nonthreatening. He set his sights on uniting Austria and Germany as one country. Because of French worries about a strong Germany, the Treaty of Versailles forbade this union. Yet, there were strong arguments favoring the *Anschluss* (union). The two nations shared the same ethnic makeup, culture, and language. In 1931 Germany and Austria had attempted to enter into a customs union, but the other Great Powers, notably Great Brit-

ain and France, had blocked it. For his plan to be successful, Hitler knew that the first step toward unification could not come from Germany. He sent agents who managed to gain control of the Austrian National Socialist Party. During a political crisis over the possibility of unification in February and March 1938, the agents managed to gain control of the government. The day before a 13 March plebiscite in which the people of Austria were scheduled to vote on the union of their country with Germany, Hitler sent troops over the border "to protect the vote" from fraud. With this military "persuasion" the vote was overwhelmingly in favor of unification.

The *Anschluss* occurred almost without bloodshed. As democratic nations, Great Britain and France felt they could not argue with the results of an apparently free election that purportedly reflected the will of the Austrian people. Given the commonalties between Germany and Austria, the Great Powers decided that it seemed foolish to deny unification any longer. Finally, since the disturbances that preceded the *Anschluss* were believed to have been caused by communist agitators, unification of Austria with anti-Bolshevik Germany seemed preferable to a communist takeover of Austria. By agreeing beforehand to abide by the results of the election and by describing his troops as protectors of civil order rather than a conquering army, Hitler again convinced Britain and France of his peaceable, reasonable intentions.

After the successful unification of Austria and Germany, Hitler moved quickly to achieve his next objective: acquiring the Sudetenland. Part of Austria-Hungary before 1918, this region became part of Czechoslovakia under the Treaty of Versailles. The majority of its inhabitants were ethnic Germans. Again sending agents to cause unrest, Hitler demanded that the Sudetenland be ceded to Germany to protect its ethnic Germans from persecution by the Czechoslovak government. Realizing that the Sudetenland included the most defensible parts of his country and most of its natural resources—as well as the Škoda munitions works—President Eduard Beneš of Czechoslovakia initially refused. Hitler then appealed to the other Great Powers, stating the ostensibly sensible desire to protect his ethnic brethren in a region whose government was unwilling to do so.

Faced with this impassioned request, Britain and France examined their options. France was in a difficult position because it had a treaty of alliance with Czechoslovakia. The French and British governments reasoned, however, that the entire nation of Czechoslovakia was not threatened and decided that giving up a border region seemed a small price for continued peace in Europe. Additionally, Hitler had sworn this demand was his last territorial claim. He even stated in a speech that he did not want the whole country, proclaiming, "We don't want any Czechs!" Prime Minister Neville Chamberlain of Great Britain and Premier Edouard Daladier of France took him at his word and set out to convince the Czechs to agree.

On 22 September Chamberlain flew to Bad Godesberg, Germany, to meet with Hitler and negotiate a resolution to the ethnic German situation that seemed more agreeable to the Allies. France and Britain told Czechoslovakia that if it wanted to resist its larger, better-armed neighbor, it would fight alone. Faced with the possible loss of his entire country if he did not give up the Sudetenland, Beneš agreed. On 28 September 1938 Chamberlain and Daladier met with Hitler and Italian dictator Benito Mussolini in Munich, where they signed the Munich Agreement, giving Czech sovereign territory to Germany. The isolated Czechs gave in, and the crisis ended. Chamberlain returned home to announce that they had achieved "peace for our time."

Throughout these encounters with Germany one belief prevailed among the leaders of the Western powers. They were convinced that Hitler was a rational, logical leader who would keep his promises and behave in a sane, reasonable manner. Fueling this attitude toward Hitler was the strongly held belief that anyone, including Hitler, who had been through the horrors of World War I would be loathe to go to war again. The leaders of Britain and France persisted in treating Hitler as if he were one of them—a well-educated career politician who "knew how the game was played." They seemed to ignore that Hitler was not well educated, that he had not had the traditional preparation for a political career, and that he had held no government posts before becoming chancellor. The only game Hitler played was his own, and he cared little for the rules of civilized political life, except when he used them cynically to his own advantage. Their blindness caused Britain and France to ignore Hitler's growing power and his apparent path to complete domination of all Europe. When Hitler took the rest of Czechoslovakia and then invaded Poland in 1939, Britain and France finally realized his true intentions.

Hitler had encouraged their illusions as long as possible. Between 1933 and 1939 each step he took toward his ultimate goal was carefully calculated to assuage the fears of the only two nations strong enough to stop him. He seemed to act within the bounds of international law until it was too late to stop him without resorting to all-out war. As long as Hitler seemed to act rationally, Britain and France believed that the policy of appeasement was a reasonable response.

—MARY PARKS,
AUSTIN, TEXAS

Viewpoint:
No. The British and French governments had serious reservations about their military preparedness, and they followed a policy of appeasement, hoping to avoid conflict with Nazi Germany.

During the 1930s the Western democracies failed to respond adequately to threats presented by Germany, Italy, and Japan. The rise of Nazi Germany and Adolf Hitler's ambition to dominate Europe destabilized international relations. As Germany repeatedly violated the international treaties on which European order rested, Britain and France followed a policy of appeasement, trying to make concessions in exchange for peace. In fact, their actions encouraged Hitler and led to the outbreak of World War II.

Scholars have devoted much time to examining why the governments of Britain and France tried to avoid taking on the challenge of Nazism.

"PEACE FOR OUR TIME"

On the evening of 30 September 1938, after returning to London from the Munich Conference, where he and Premier Edouard Daladier of France had ceded the Sudetenland region of Czechoslovakia to Adolf Hitler, Prime Minister Neville Chamberlain made the following statement to the press outside his official residence at 10 Downing Street:

We, the German Fuhrer and Chancellor, and the British Prime Minister, have had a further meeting today and are agreed in recognizing that the question of Anglo-German relations is of the first importance for our two countries and for Europe.

We regard the agreement signed last night and the Anglo-German Naval Agreement as symbolic of the desire of our two peoples never to go to war with one another again.

We are resolved that the method of consultation shall be the method adopted to deal with any other questions that may concern our two countries, and we are determined to continue our efforts to remove possible sources of difference, and thus to contribute to assure the peace of Europe.

My good friends, for the second time in our history, a British Prime Minister has returned from Germany bringing peace with honor. I believe it is "peace for our time." Go home and get a nice quiet sleep.

Source: "Sources of British History," Britannia Historical Documents <http://www.britannia.com/history/docs/peacetime.html>.

Left-wing historians have described appeasement as an attempt to redirect German aggression against the Soviet Union, exploiting the Nazis' virulent anticommunism. Yet, although many conservatives in the 1930s believed that the West should drive the Soviet Union and Germany into a ruinous war in which the two great dictatorships would destroy one another, they represented only a minority view within the British and French governments and contributed little to the appeasement policy. The real reason for appeasement may be found in a series of complex and interrelated military and nonmilitary factors that led the British and French governments to have serious reservations about their abilities to face Nazi Germany militarily and to try to avoid such a conflict at all costs.

Historical studies and primary documents have both shown that, while Germany and its allies were concentrating all their efforts on a speedy military buildup, Britain and France were unready for war and were doing little to strengthen their armed forces. Their rearmament programs were seriously neglected and underfunded until just months before the outbreak of World War II in 1939. The Western powers were particularly weak in tanks, military aviation, and air defenses. In 1939 the German Luftwaffe (air force) was numerically superior to the air forces of Britain and France combined.

Great Britain had no desire to fight a major war at all. From 1937 onward its military chiefs of staff constantly warned the British government that its armed forces could not hope to defeat Germany, Italy, and Japan, even with France as an ally. As Winston Churchill, a long-time advocate of confronting Hitler, wrote in *The Second World War* (1948–1953), "we were hideously unprepared for war." This belief was responsible for British concessions to Germany. By agreeing to German demands for Czechoslovak territory at Munich in 1938, for example, the Western powers tried to gain time to regenerate their military might and prepare for the coming war. As John F. Kennedy wrote in his *Why England Slept* (1940), "I feel that Munich was inevitable on the ground of lack of armaments alone." Another motive for the appeasement policy was the great suffering caused by World War I. Historical memories of that conflict left Britain and France with the feeling that nothing could be solved by war and that almost any compromise was preferable to another conflagration.

The Allies' military reluctance was also heavily influenced by the effects of the Great Depression. Their limited resources were absorbed in the struggle to overcome continuing economic problems. In 1935–1937 Britain was producing an average of 11.8 million metric tons of steel, the most basic commodity for military production. Germany was averaging 20.4 million tons.

Preoccupied with economic recovery, the British government refused to participate in any strong counteractions when Germany withdrew from the International Disarmament Conference, which had been meeting at Geneva since 1932. Moreover, the British began to explore the possibility of meeting Hitler's demand that he be allowed to raise Germany to a position of military equality with other European nations. In 1935 the British not only acquiesced to the creation of a German air force, which the Treaty of Versailles had explicitly banned, but also negotiated a naval deal that allowed Germany to abandon Versailles restrictions on ship construction and to build a fleet 35 percent the size of the Royal Navy. The weakness of Britain's strategic position was further illustrated in 1937, when the Treasury warned the government that increasing rearmament expenditures might well cause economic disaster. The government was convinced that another war with Germany would bankrupt Britain, destroy it as a major world power, and leave the Soviet Union as the dominant power in Europe.

APPEASEMENT

French economic problems had somewhat different origins from those of the British. The Depression had arrived later in France than in Britain and had more-profound effects, including increasing social unrest and demographic stagnancy. These factors contributed to a general sense of national decline and military weakness. The French government was greatly influenced by the advice of its military leaders, who remembered the horrors of World War I and put almost mystical faith and most of the national military budget into the Maginot Line, a chain of fortifications along the Franco-German border. Obsessed with memories of World War I, the French military was convinced that the main lesson of the war was the superiority of defense over attack. Also, as a result of the reduced birthrate in France in the aftermath of World War I, the French Army was greatly understrength. Because the cost of constructing the Maginot Line reduced funding for regular army troops, any sort of military response to German expansionism would require the mobilization of French reservists. No French government was willing to undertake such an unpopular measure. As the Nazis were spending ten times as much as France on aviation alone, the French government could not afford to invest comparable sums in military preparedness. Increases in defense spending did not come until 1938, and only after France finally declared war on Germany in 1939 did France dispatch agents to the United States to buy American combat aircraft to augment the weak French air force.

International factors, many of which were also of a military nature, contributed to the appeasement policy as well. Britain was limited by the decline of its empire. Dominions such as Canada, Australia, New Zealand, South Africa, and the Irish Free State—which were given de facto independence in 1931—had provided more than a quarter of British troops in World War I, but they were unwilling to offer similar support to Britain during the Czechoslovak crisis of 1938. Moreover, the British appeasers considered it folly to plunge into a war in Central Europe when the empire and its communications were under threat from Germany's allies, Italy in the Mediterranean and Japan in the Far East—both of which had been British allies in World War I. At the same time large numbers of British and Indian troops were tied down in the costly occupation of Palestine and other territories held as mandates under the League of Nations. Much of the Royal Navy's battle fleet was antiquated and laid up for refitting. Britain's rearmament program still had far to go, and the government believed that it lacked the resources to win another war with Germany.

For these reasons the British government hoped to find agreeable solutions to satisfy German aspirations such as military equality with other major European nations, the unraveling of what the British perceived to be the least-tenable and least-sensible aspects of the Versailles settlement, and recognition of German preeminence in Central Europe. Nazi diplomacy and propaganda exploited the British desire for peace with numerous assurances that Germany wanted nothing so much as the trust and friendship of Britain.

The general Anglo-French appeasement policy was also influenced by the desire of both powers to develop friendly ties with Italy while exploiting German-Italian disagreements. In January 1935 Italian dictator Benito Mussolini persuaded the French to agree to allowing Italy a free hand in Ethiopia. In April of that year Britain, France, and Italy formed the "Stresa Front" opposing German rearmament and expansionism during a conference at the Italian lakeside resort of Stresa. When the Italian-Ethiopian War broke out in October and the League of Nations imposed sanctions on Italy, Britain and France hesitated to apply the most effective one—an embargo on oil supplies. After the Rhineland crisis of March 1936 France effectively surrendered control of French foreign policy to Britain. Despite their initial willingness to help the Loyalist side in the Spanish Civil War, which broke out that July, the French found it impossible to do so because Britain took a neutral stance, and the two nations turned a blind eye as the Germans and Italians provided aid to the forces of General Francisco Franco in that war.

Despite the creation of the German-Italian Axis in October 1936, the British and French continued trying to conciliate Italy. In January 1937 Britain and Italy signed an innocuous "gentlemen's agreement" in which each power recognized that the other had interests in the Mediterranean. In April 1938 the two nations signed a more important treaty in which England recognized Italy's conquest of Ethiopia.

Domestic problems also weakened France and Britain. The permanent domestic instability of France in the 1930s was not conducive to vigorous and consistent foreign and security policies. The French had weak and unstable governments at the time of Hitler's occupation of the Rhineland and annexation of Austria. The politicians and the public in Britain were deeply divided on international issues. The ruling Conservative Party (with rare exceptions such as Churchill) tended to minimize the German danger and took an optimistic view about the possibility of coming to peaceful terms with the Germans. Some influential groups in Britain accepted the revisionist view that Germany had

APPEASEMENT

been unfairly treated after World War I and that it would become a satisfied and peaceful power if these injustices were removed. Some British policymakers even believed that Germany was entitled to hegemony in Central and Eastern Europe. British leftists tended to support a policy of appeasement because they felt Germany had been treated unfairly in the Treaty of Versailles, and the Labor Party steadily opposed rearmament and conscription measures until the outbreak of war in 1939. Ignoring the reality, both the government and the opposition competed for ballots by exploiting the strong antiwar sentiments of a vast majority of British voters—a public that welcomed the Munich settlement of 1938 with relief and jubilation, agreeing with Prime Minister Neville Chamberlain that it meant "peace for our time." A majority of French citizens shared their sentiments.

The democracies and the dictators had mutually contradictory sets of values, which left no common ground for compromise. The conciliatory gestures of Britain and France encouraged Germany and Italy to believe that the Allies would acquiesce to future conquests just as they had in the past. Chamberlain announced the end of the appeasement policy in his 17 March 1939 speech at Birmingham, after Germany occupied the remnants of Czechoslovakia. Hitler's invasion of Poland on September 1 ended the peace.

–PETER RAINOW,
SAN MATEO, CALIFORNIA

References

Winston Churchill, *The Second World War*, 6 volumes (Boston: Houghton Mifflin, 1948–1953).

Richard Lamb, *Drift to War, 1922–1939* (London: W. H. Allen, 1989).

Gustav Schmidt, *The Politics and Economics of Appeasement: British Foreign Policy in the 1930s* (New York: St. Martin's Press, 1986).

Telford Taylor, *Munich: The Price of Peace* (Garden City, N.Y.: Doubleday, 1979).

Amos Yoder, *World Politics and Causes of War since 1914* (Lanham, Md.: University Press of America, 1986).

APPEASEMENT

BOLSHEVIK REVOLUTION

Was the 1917 Bolshevik uprising in Russia truly a popular revolution?

Viewpoint: Yes. The Bolsheviks gave voice to the concerns of the Russian masses and harnessed their discontent to bring about a successful revolution.

Viewpoint: No. The Bolsheviks had much less popular backing than they later claimed and succeeded only through terrorist tactics and the incompetence of their opponents.

World War I doomed Imperial Russia. By March 1917 its armies were suffering defeat, its internal order was collapsing, and its monarchy had fallen. The Provisional Government that assumed power failed to solve the country's many problems, and within just a few months it teetered on the verge of collapse. On 7 November 1917 revolutionary forces of the radical Bolshevik party seized power in the capital, Petrograd (formerly St. Petersburg). In the weeks and months that followed, the Bolsheviks spread and consolidated their authority over much of Russia. By late 1920 they were the undisputed masters of most of the territory of the Russian Empire.

Part of the Bolsheviks' founding ideology was the claim that their victory resulted from the genuine popularity of their ideals and the freely given support of the Russian people. According to the Bolsheviks, the great majority of Russians had made a conscious "choice" in favor of the world's first socialist government. This explanation for the triumph of communism remained an important part of Soviet ideology, and many Western scholars have found evidence of mass support for Bolshevism and legitimate popularity of its ideals.

Other scholars have argued, however, that Bolshevism was forced on a largely unwilling Russian population. These critics of the Soviet system point to the almost immediate appearance and long duration of armed resistance to the Bolsheviks as an indication that many Russians did not favor socialism. The new government's use of a secret police and concentration camps, its reliance on terror and coercion, and its suppression of civil liberties and the democratic process, they argue, demonstrate that it might not have engendered widespread popular support.

An assessment of the degree to which Russians welcomed the Bolshevik Revolution offers insights not only into what became of the Russian Empire but also into the popularity of socialism and communism throughout Europe. It also allows students of history to understand the emergence of one of the two Cold War superpowers and the final collapse of the Soviet Union in 1991.

Viewpoint:
Yes. The Bolsheviks gave voice to the concerns of the Russian masses and harnessed their discontent to bring about a successful revolution.

The Bolshevik Revolution of November 1917 was not sudden and unexpected. It resulted from the fifty-year failure of the Russian monarchy to address pressing social concerns. Even after being defeated in the Crimean War of 1853–1856, tsarist Russia did not abandon its adventurous foreign policies. Instead of building on the efforts of Alexander II (ruled 1855–1881) to reform rural society, public life, and the autocratic political system, his successors, Alexander III (ruled 1881–1894) and Nicholas II (ruled 1894–1917), preserved the basic features of the autocracy and remained deaf to the demands of an increasingly radicalized society. The ideology of "Orthodoxy, Autocracy, and Patriotism" accompanied renewed political censorship and repression in the reign of Alexander III. Nicholas II's brutal suppression of domestic unrest, his unwillingness to create a genuinely democratic parliament, and his imprudent involvement in wars against Japan (1904–1905) and the Germany-led coalition in Europe (1914–1918) were all steps by which he deprived himself of historic opportunities to prevent revolution and civil war. The never-implemented "reform from above" had to give way to a "revolution from below."

Alexander II's reforms provided an opportunity to narrow the growing gap between a socially and economically backward Russia and a rapidly modernizing Europe. The defeat of Russia in the Crimean War resulted from its insufficient domestic capital, its poorly developed infrastructure, its predominantly rural economy, and its extremely small middle class. Attempting to remedy these problems and responding to the growing acceptance of constitutional principles in Europe, Alexander devised a far-reaching reform agenda. He abolished the institution of serfdom by formally allowing peasants to leave their noble overlords and find other employment. He initiated policies of glasnost (openness) in public life and encouraged education, particularly in rural primary schools. By establishing elected local governments and an independent judiciary, he made critically important steps in reforming the autocratic political system. Had he not been killed by a terrorist bomb in 1881, the Russian Empire might have evolved into a constitutional monarchy with a state council—an advisory body—as a protoparliament. In fact, his key adviser, Count Mikhail Loris-Melikov, recommended the creation of a state council to address

the problem of domestic terrorism and provide "the government's attentive and positive response to the needs of the people." Though these reforms were incomplete, they might well have put the country on the path of economic development and liberating social initiative. Alexander II's foreign minister, Prince Aleksandr Gorchakov, also pursued a relatively moderate external agenda and emphasized that the important lesson of Russia's defeat in the Crimea was the need to concentrate on domestic issues and social reform.

Alexander III, however, interpreted Russia's external and domestic situation differently from his father. He rejected the idea of developing a state council as a protoparliament. The tsar's tutor, Konstantin Pobedonostsev, who was also procurator of the Holy Synod (the chief administrative official for religious affairs), recommended instead that Alexander emphasize the old "Orthodoxy, Autocracy, and Patriotism" and introduce new censorship and repression of dissidents. Pobedonostsev referred to the idea of a state council as a "foreign falsehood" and the first step on the dangerous road to Western-style constitutionalism. Externally, Russia continued to expand in the Far East despite the growing tensions in its relations with Japan.

In many ways Nicholas II continued Alexander III's policies of domestic repression and external overstretch. When he came to power in 1894, Russia was going through growing political instability, as well as economic and social polarization. Leading Russian intellectuals were pointing to widespread poverty, corruption, diseases, and low morale, trying to warn the tsar about the possible consequences of social discontent. In 1898 the Marxist Social Democratic and Labor Party, which later spawned the Bolshevik movement, was established and awaited chances to capitalize on the tsar's inconsistencies and unwillingness to accommodate the social needs of the population. Such opportunities soon began to present themselves.

In 1903 Nicholas dismissed a key economic reformer, Finance Minister Sergei Witte, and the following year he went to war against Japan, suffering humiliating defeats both on land and at sea in 1905. Reputedly encouraged by Interior Minister Viacheslav Plehve as "a little victorious war to stop the revolutionary tide," the Russo-Japanese War instead caused tremendous losses for the ill-prepared and poorly led Russian military and, even worse, immediate domestic unrest. In 1905 Russia went through its first revolution, which included strikes by urban workers, widespread peasant uprisings, and forcefully articulated political opposition. The revolution, which further narrowed chances of preventing the 1917 revolution, was sparked mainly by two events. The first was the tsar's brutal suppression of a peaceful

workers' demonstration on 9 January 1905 ("Bloody Sunday"). Despite the moderate demands of demonstrators (shorter working hours and better labor conditions), the local police and military authorities ordered the army to open fire. At least 130 people were killed, and hundreds more were injured. The second factor was the losses of Russian forces in the Far East, particularly the defeats on land at Mukden and at sea at the Tsushima Straits in the spring of 1905.

Nicholas II's response to the 1905 revolution was grossly inadequate, failing to address any of the population's serious concerns effectively. Politically, the tsar promised more freedoms and established the Duma, a quasi-parliament. A step in the right direction, the Duma was never able to articulate the vital needs of Russian society and, instead, became a facade in front of the old autocratic regime. The first two Dumas, elected on a restricted, yet somewhat inclusive, franchise, were dismissed by Nicholas as too reformist for their advocacy of a constitution and the redistribution of land to the peasants. The third Duma, which was elected under a more conservative election law and excluded the lower classes, somewhat satisfied the tsar and Prime Minister Petr Stolypin. The proposed land reform was unable to satisfy popular expectations, as it allowed peasants to separate from the traditional communal tenure of agricultural land, which had the effect of reducing resources for peasants who remained in the communes. A defender of the interests of nobility and landed property, Stolypin argued against tak-

ing land away from nobles without compensation, but he provided no answer as to where the mostly poor peasants, the majority of the Russian population, were supposed to raise the money to buy their own land.

Perhaps the worst failure of tsarist state policies was the involvement in World War I against Germany. Bound by previous alliance commitments to Serbia and France, Nicholas and his advisers insisted that Russia fight on the side of France and Serbia. The war became domestically unpopular. Poorly armed, Russian soldiers were being slaughtered. (In 1914 about one-third of the Russian army had no rifles.) Most felt they had no reasons to be in the war. In a primarily rural country, most soldiers were peasants hungry for land, and the idea of fighting a brutal war with Germany to honor alliance commitments had little appeal for them. While Nicholas was at war, Russians grew to hate Empress Alexandra, who was German-born and reputed to favor her native land.

The state was increasingly unable to maintain social order, and its replacement by a Provisional Government in March 1917 had little effect. The slow movement of foodstuffs, which had been critical in causing the collapse of the monarchy, fell off by 40 percent in April and May 1917. Prices, inflation, and unemployment levels were growing. The number of strikes rose, almost doubling in May. In the radicalized political spectrum the new government's support for the war found little sympathy. Only the radical Left, espe-

Vladimir Lenin addressing soldiers and civilians in Sverdlov Square, Moscow, May 1920

(David King Collection)

cially Vladimir Lenin's Bolshevik Party, argued for peace. The Mensheviks (the moderate wing of the Social Democratic Labor Party) and Socialist Revolutionaries sat in the government trying to build a compromise and close the rapidly growing gap between the upper, middle, and lower classes. Outside the government the words of Bolsheviks, who had no real voice in the political system, became louder and more convincing to workers, soldiers, and peasants. Bolsheviks opposed Russian involvement in the war, even to the point of advocating "the defeat of our own government." Although they initially had no mass support among the population, eventually—within an emerging power vacuum—they were able to draw support and seize power.

Despite their highly conspiratorial tactics, at a time of desperation and social anarchy the Bolsheviks were the only party able to offer the right slogans to the masses of peasants, soldiers, and workers. Lenin's slogan "peace to the people, land to peasants, and power to the soviets [councils]" resonated with much of Russian society. Obviously, the slogan was clever political rhetoric, and the system that the Bolsheviks eventually created was neither peaceful nor democratic—as the subsequent bloody civil war, the Red Terror unleashed by the Bolsheviks against their political opponents, the dissolution of the democratically elected Constitutional Assembly, and many other events abundantly demonstrated. Although they were not the only party who voiced mass popular feelings and aspirations—Mensheviks and Socialist Revolutionaries also had a wide appeal— the Bolsheviks were the most prepared to act during a time of growing social anarchy. Over the stormy course of 1917 this small but tightly organized group, reminiscent of a secret sect (a "party of the new type," to quote Lenin), proved to be the only one capable of taking advantage of the social unrest and state weakness.

–ANDREI P. TSYGANKOV,
SAN FRANCISCO STATE UNIVERSITY

Viewpoint:
No. The Bolsheviks had much less popular backing than they later claimed and succeeded only through terrorist tactics and the incompetence of their opponents.

"Those against the insurrection were 'everybody'—except the people. But the Bolsheviks were the people," wrote Lev Trotsky in his history of the Bolshevik Revolution of Novem-

ber 1917. Bolsheviks such as Trotsky argued— and may have believed—that their party's revolution represented the will of the Russian people. Yet, the facts—and some of Trotsky's own writings—indicate otherwise. If an empire-wide referendum on their plans had been held on 7 November 1917, the Bolsheviks would have received far less than 51 percent of the vote. In terms of sheer numbers of supporters, the Bolsheviks took second place, behind the more moderate socialist Revolutionary Party. In addition to the opposition they faced from members of the middle and upper echelons of Russian society—most of whom (quite understandably) opposed the installation of a regime that later labeled them "former persons"—the Bolsheviks lacked the support of large segments of the rest of the Russian empire's population. The difficulties they faced even in their strongholds, the results of post-November elections for a national Constituent Assembly, and the events of the subsequent civil war are further, definitive evidence against their interpretation of the Revolution.

The non-Russian parts of the empire wanted autonomy far more than they wanted a Bolshevik revolution. Poland, Finland, Ukraine, the Transcaucasian Federation (Azerbaijan, Armenia, and Georgia, which acted together), Lithuania, Latvia, Estonia, and Belorussia all declared their independence from Russia in 1917 and 1918. Communists in Finland lost a civil war there for control of the government. In Ukraine the newly established Rada (parliament) and the Ukrainian Military Congress responded to the news of the Bolshevik uprising by continuing to make their own plans to establish a constituent assembly for an independent Ukraine. Russian domination of Ukraine's soviets created resentment and helped to ensure Ukrainian support for their own nationalists against "Russian interlopers." It took an invasion and civil war for the Bolsheviks to gain control of Ukraine. Similarly, it took years for the Red Army to inaugurate their rule in the Caucasus and areas further east. The Soviets regained only partial control of Poland and reincorporated the Baltic States (Lithuania, Latvia, and Estonia) only after Nazi Germany recognized the Soviets' hegemony over them in the 1939 German-Soviet nonaggression pact.

Within Russia itself, the key to a popular majority was the peasantry. As the Bolsheviks admitted, they had little support among the peasantry compared to the Socialist Revolutionary Party. Bolshevik strength lay not in the countryside but in the cities. Yet, even in urban areas the party found only partial and conditional support. In the Petrograd garrison, Trotsky wrote, "a thousand soldiers ready to

THE BOLSHEVIK COUP

In his History of the Russian Revolution to Brest-Litovsk, *written in February 1918, during the treaty negotiations with Germany at Brest-Litovsk, Lev Trotsky offered his perspective on the Bolsheviks' successful 7 November 1917 coup against the Provisional Government headed by Aleksandr Kerensky:*

The Government was still in session in the Winter Palace, but it had already become a mere shadow of its former self. It had ceased to exist politically. In the course of November 7th the Winter Palace was gradually surrounded from all sides by our troops. At one o'clock in the afternoon, in the name of the Military Revolutionary Committee, I announced at the sitting of the Petrograd Soviet that Kerensky's Government no longer existed, and that, pending the decision of the All-Russian Congress of Soviets, the Government authority would be assumed by the Military Revolutionary Committee.

. . . The bourgeois Press had shrieked so much about the coming revolt, the march of armed soldiers in the streets, the pillage, and the inevitable rivers of blood, that it did not perceive the insurrection which, in reality, was now taking place, and accepted the negotiations between ourselves and the Military Staff at their face value. All this time, quietly, without any street fighting, without firing or bloodshed, one Government institution after another was being seized by highly disciplined detachments of soldiers, sailors, and Red Guards, in accordance with the exact telephone instructions emanating from [Vladimir Lenin in] the little room on the third floor of the Smolny Institute.

In the evening, the second All-Russian Congress of the Soviets held a preliminary meeting.

. . . [Menshevik F. I. Dan] delivered an indictment against the rebels, the usurpers, and sedition-mongers, and tried to frighten the meeting by predicting the inevitable collapse of the Insurrection, which in a day or two, he said, would be suppressed by troops from the front. His speech sounded exceedingly unconvincing and very much out of place in a hall in which the overwhelming majority of delegates were following with the greatest enthusiasm the victorious march of the Petrograd rising.

By this time the Winter Palace was surrounded, though not yet taken. From time to time shots were fired from the windows at the besiegers who were slowly and very carefully closing in upon the building. From the Peter and Paul Fortress a few shells were fired at the Palace, their distant sounds reaching the Smolny. [Menshevik Y. O.] Martoff, with impotent indignation, was speaking from the rostrum of civil war, and particularly of the siege of the Winter Palace where, among the other Ministers, there were—oh, horror of horrors!—members of the Menshevik Party. Two sailors, who had come to give news from the scenes of struggle, took the platform against him. They reminded our accusers of the [Bolsheviks'] July offensive, of the whole perfidious policy of the old Government, of the re-establishment of the death penalty for soldiers, of the arrests, of the sacking of revolutionary organizations, and vowed that they would either conquer or die. They it was who brought us the news of the first victims on our side on the Palace Square.

Every one rose as though moved by some invisible signal, and with a unanimity which is only provoked by a deep moral intensity of feeling sung a Funeral March. He who lived through this moment will never forget it. The meeting came to an abrupt end. It was impossible to sit there, calmly discussing the theoretical question as to the method of constructing the Government, with the echo reaching our ears of the fighting and firing at the walls of the Winter Palace, where, as a matter of fact, the fate of this very Government was already being decided.

The taking of the Palace, however, was a protracted business, and this caused some wavering amongst the less determined elements of the Congress. The Right wing, through its spokesmen, prophesied our early doom. All were waiting anxiously for news from the Winter Palace. After some time, [Bolshevik V. A.] Antonoff, who had been directing the operations, arrived. At once there was dead silence in the hall. The Winter Palace had been taken. Kerensky had taken flight. The other Ministers had been arrested and conveyed to the Peter and Paul Fortress. The first chapter of the November Revolution was at an end.

The Right Socialist Revolutionaries and the Mensheviks, numbering altogether about sixty persons, that is, about one-tenth of the Congress, left the meeting under protest. As they could do nothing else, they "threw the whole responsibility" for whatever might now happen on the Bolsheviks and the Left Socialist Revolutionaries. The latter were still wavering. . . . But the insurrection forced them to choose either for or against the Soviet. Not without hesitation, they were concentrating their forces on the same side of the barricade where we stood.

Source: *Lev Trotsky, "The Decisive Day," in his* History of the Russian Revolution to Brest-Litovsk *(London: Allen & Unwin, 1919), Marxist Internet Archive <http://www.marxists.org/archive/trotsky/works/1918/hrr/>.*

BOLSHEVIK REVOLUTION

fight on the side of the revolution were scattered here and there among the more passive mass." Trotsky counted industrial workers as solidly Bolshevik and most soldiers as "standing for the Bolsheviks insofar as they had a legal soviet cover." Fellow revolutionaries Grigorii Zinoviev and Lev Kamenev agreed: "In Russia the majority of the workers and a significant part of the soldiers are for us. But all the rest is questionable." With workers and soldiers behind them, the Bolsheviks won a third of the votes for members of the Petrograd Soviet (a council of workers and soldiers) in September 1917, attained a bare majority (51 percent) in a mid-September election in Moscow, and took 390 of the 650 seats filled in the November Congress of Soviets by its opening day. These numbers, impressive but far from unanimous, strongly suggest that "politically conscious" peasants and more-conservative workers and soldiers sided not with the Bolsheviks but with the establishment of soviets as an institution. In fact, the Bolsheviks did not achieve easy victories in the cities. In some areas, they resorted to a kind of gerrymandering to achieve a majority in the local soviet and take power. In Voronezh only a minority of the populace, even in the party itself, was willing to carry out the Revolution. Granted, the hesitation of some Bolsheviks may have been related to the timing rather than to the Revolution itself, but it does raise questions about their level of commitment to the party. Even more damning, however, are the results of the long-awaited elections for the Constituent Assembly, which took place in the first weeks after the Bolshevik Revolution. The Bolsheviks received 9.8 million votes of the nearly 50 million cast, just over 24 percent of the total. In contrast, their rivals, the Socialist Revolutionaries, received 15.8 million votes, or 40 percent. Even these figures probably inflate the level of support for the Bolsheviks. Much of the election campaign was carried out in an atmosphere of intimidation. Opposition candidates for the Constituent Assembly were subject to harassment by Bolshevik gangs before the elections and later by the Cheka, the Bolshevik secret-police force, established in December 1917. When the Assembly met in January 1918, its president, Socialist Revolutionary leader Viktor Chernov, attended in defiance of a government arrest warrant. Once it met, the popularly elected Assembly refused to recognize the Bolshevik government, despite the menacing presence of armed guards in the meeting hall. On that first day the delegates had begun to pass land-reform laws when the guards forced them out of the hall and shut the Assembly forever. It is inaccurate to label as "popular" a government that has to disperse a popularly elected assembly by force in order to establish its own power.

Anti-Bolshevik protests were not confined to Petrograd. The Bolsheviks had to fight a full-scale civil war to consolidate their power. Their enemies included not only the "Whites"—a diverse assortment of political opponents including aristocratic supporters of the deposed tsar—but the population at large. In the first twelve months after November 1917, approximately one million soldiers deserted the Red Army, and, as Orlando Figes has documented, armed "Green" bands of former soldiers and peasants formed in provinces across Russia to oppose both Whites and Reds. The victory of the Bolsheviks despite such opposition can be credited to their military power, their determination, their willingness to end Russian participation in World War I, the strategic advantage of their central location relative to the Whites, and the fact that many Russians did not actively oppose them. Both Reds and Whites used force to extract grain and recruits from the countryside. To the general populace the Reds were at least no worse than the Whites. In many areas Bolsheviks benefited from White plans to return seized agricultural land to its original (often noble) owners. If they could not have the Socialist Revolutionaries, at least the agrarian masses could have the party that promised "peace, land, and bread." In general, for many Russians it seemed best to hoard as much grain as possible, cooperate with the Bolsheviks when necessary, and lay low until the civil war was over. This pragmatic passivity (which Figes has pessimistically and inaccurately called the Russians' "fail[ure] to become their own political masters") aided the Bolsheviks, but it cannot be construed as popular support. Historians such as Ronald Grigor Suny may write that the Bolsheviks "rode a wave of popular discontent and enthusiasm for Soviet power." They cannot, however, show that the Bolshevik revolution was popular. Too much evidence exists to the contrary.

—CATHERINE BLAIR,
GEORGETOWN UNIVERSITY

References

Stephen F. Cohen, *Rethinking the Soviet Experience: Politics and History since 1917* (New York: Oxford University Press, 1985).

Robert V. Daniels, ed. and trans., *A Documentary History of Communism in Russia: From Lenin to Gorbachev,* third edition, revised and updated (Hanover, N.H.: University Press of New England, 1993).

Orlando Figes, *A People's Tragedy: The Russian Revolution, 1891–1924* (New York: Viking, 1997).

Geoffrey Hosking, *The First Socialist Society: A History of the Soviet Union from Within,* second edition, enlarged (Cambridge, Mass.: Harvard University Press, 1993).

Tim McDaniel, *Autocracy, Capitalism, and the Revolution in Russia* (Berkeley: University of California Press, 1988).

Richard Pipes, *The Russian Revolution* (New York: Knopf, 1990).

Alexander Rabinowitch, *The Bolsheviks Come to Power: The Revolution of 1917 in Petrograd* (New York: Norton, 1976).

Nicholas V. Riasanovsky, *A History of Russia,* sixth edition (New York: Oxford University Press, 2000).

Ronald Grigor Suny, *The Soviet Experiment: Russia, the USSR, and the Successor States* (New York: Oxford University Press, 1998).

Leon Trotsky, *The Essential Trotsky* (New York: Barnes & Noble, 1963).

Robert C. Tucker, *The Marxian Revolutionary Idea* (New York: Norton, 1969).

Bertram D. Wolfe, *Three Who Made a Revolution: A Biographical History* (New York: Dial, 1948; fourth edition, revised, 1964).

BOLSHEVIK REVOLUTION

BRITISH ENTRY INTO WORLD WAR I

Did the Germans have reason to doubt that the British would declare war in 1914?

Viewpoint: Yes. The British leadership was highly fragmented and reluctantly went to war only after it identified specific threats from Germany.

Viewpoint: No. British entry into World War I was inevitable, especially after Germany invaded Belgium, because Britain could not permit the domination of the continental Channel ports by any other nation.

As the nations of Europe moved toward war in the summer of 1914, one of the burning questions was whether Britain would enter the fray. Despite its growing closeness to France and Russia in the decade before the war, Britain had avoided firm alliance commitments to both powers. Although its relations with Germany had become strained, a series of diplomatic visits and talks suggested that these tensions might be ameliorated. Observers could only speculate what the British might do.

Britain entered World War I on 4 August 1914 after Germany failed to concede to an ultimatum and withdraw its forces from neutral Belgium, which it had invaded as part of its strategy to fight France. Just as contemporary Europeans speculated about the possibility of British involvement, historians have wondered about its probability. One argument suggests that it was unavoidable. Although London's strategic commitments appeared tenuous, its alienation from Germany was so pronounced and its relationship with its wartime allies so developed that it would go to war in any case. Allowing Germany to defeat France and Russia would be tantamount to conceding the hegemonic domination of Europe to one power, a development against which Britain had been willing to fight for centuries.

Yet, revisionists argue that the British decision to enter the war was not predetermined. Britain's talks with Germany portended a peaceful resolution of the two nations' strategic differences, one that would have mirrored earlier talks with Japan, France, and Russia. Even as London considered entering the war, several high-level officials entertained major doubts, and foreign diplomats were until the last minute guessing about Britain's course. The debate, which continues in this chapter, gives fascinating insight into how nations make the decision to go to war.

Viewpoint:
Yes. The British leadership was highly fragmented and reluctantly went to war only after it identified specific threats from Germany.

Great Britain's intervention in World War I (1914–1918) was hardly inevitable. In August 1914 Britain was not bound specifically by an alliance to defend France, nor was there an outcry to defend the 1839 treaty defining Belgium as neutral. Britain's entente with France, reached in 1904, had been organized as a colonial deal rather than as a binding encirclement of Germany, a country with which Britain had a strong cultural affinity and therefore had little reason to fear. Additionally, there were major factions within the governing Liberal Party, and within the cabinet itself, which opposed intervention. Even after its formal declaration of war, the British government still had the option to forgo an expeditionary force and rely on the Royal Navy to enforce a blockade rather than commit troops to the European continent.

The Entente Cordiale with France was not made because of a threat from Germany. Rather, Britain identified France as its primary rival in the colonial theater and as the European power that most threatened the far-flung British Empire. In particular, the French were in a position to recognize British possession of Egypt, a long-standing point of contention, and to work out spheres of influence in North Africa. The British government had vivid memories of the threat that the French could pose as a rival for overseas resources and could point to the recent Fashoda Incident (1898) as a reason to coordinate military and diplomatic action with France.

The Entente offered the additional bonus of leverage with the Russian Empire, with which France had forged diplomatic and financial ties. Britain's defensive alliance with Japan (1902) made it possible to deal with the Russians in the Pacific, as well as in their traditional area of conflict, Central Asia. Far from an encirclement of the Germans, Britain aimed to safeguard the British Empire though regularized relations with France and Russia.

Although Anglo-German diplomatic proposals had failed, it was not because of a deep or lasting enmity. The Germans were not an advantageous ally for a country whose weak points were scattered around the globe—Germany's formidable army would be of little use in India, Canada, or the Caribbean, while Britain's great navy had little to offer a Central European land power. Germany had lost the

naval race by 1912, and the rivalry spawned by naval construction had lost its potency as a real military threat. Britain's borders did not figure in German war planning—despite paranoid newspaper serials, the Germans did not plan a cross-Channel invasion and had little interest in cutting ties that had bound the two countries together for three centuries.

Since 1714 the British monarchy had been almost entirely German by blood, and the reigning dynasty had continued to marry its children into the princely houses of Germany. The aristocracy and upper middle classes had followed this pattern, and many families were part of an extended Anglo-German elite. Examples included Robert (von) Ranke Graves, a great-nephew of the German historian, and popular authors such as Australian-born Elizabeth von Arnim Russell (widow of a German count and wife of Earl Russell). In the nineteenth-century world of social Darwinism the Germans and the British felt themselves closely connected by their shared Germanic ancestry. The musical compositions of Richard Wagner, George Frideric Handel, and Johannes Brahms were played during the proms season of 1914; German students flocked to Oxford on Rhodes scholarships until 1916; and many educated Britons studied in Germany.

If the two nations could not benefit from a formal alliance, they certainly could from financial cooperation. Multinational banking families such as the Warburgs and Rothschilds aided Anglo-German business in profitable investment in Chinese railroads and Venezuelan oil. Britain had a great deal to gain from friendly cooperation with Germany in the Near East, using German influence in the crumbling Ottoman Empire and its Berlin-to-Baghdad railway project to deal more easily in areas such as Mosul and the Suez Canal zone.

Britain's experience in the Boer War (1899–1902) had been shocking, expensive, and unpleasant. The British were not a nation anxious to engage in another war—even promilitary projects such as Robert Baden-Powell's Boy Scouts had limited success in recruiting the next generation of soldiers before 1914. The British Army, to keep its place in competition with the Royal Navy, engaged in war planning with the French and, having lost them as a primary enemy, produced elaborate anti-German scenarios, but these were cautious and dwelled on the potential casualties, expense, and unpopularity of a European war. Even Belgium, whose neutrality became a cause célèbre, had little pull on British sympathy, since the army's planning also contained a violation of Belgium's borders to make their hypothetical stand on the French frontier.

Liberal noninterventionists, including Chancellor of the Exchequer David Lloyd George, pointed out that Britain had bigger priorities in pacifying Ulster, confronting women's suffrage demands, and finding funds for increased social programs than in settling European border disputes. Labour Party leaders, such as James Keir Hardie and Ramsey MacDonald, had strong ties to the German Social Democrats and engaged in internationalist talks focusing on the power of the working classes to stop any European war. Influential socialists, including members of the prominent Fabian Society, spent much of the summer of 1914 touring Germany and making favorable comparisons between the German social welfare system and the one they pushed for in Great Britain.

During the war crisis of July–August 1914, pro-French cabinet members, led by Foreign Minister Sir Edward Grey, muddled the position of Great Britain so badly that none of the other powers, nor many Britons, knew where the British government stood on intervention. Grey had to tell the House of Commons that the Entente did not require Britain to aid France, even while he warned the German and Austrian ambassadors that Britain might yet enter the conflict if no diplomatic solution could be found. Had the position been strongly stated for intervention, the Central Powers might have been warned off, but as it stood, the Germans gambled that Britain would stay out of the war. France had fallen to the Germans before, in the Franco-Prussian War (1870–1871), and the world had not come to an end. Nor had there been a one-power Europe created to threaten Britain. If Britain truly felt threatened, it had unquestionably the most powerful navy on earth and could easily use it without committing men to European fighting.

Ultimately, it was this survival of France as an independent power that formed the most convincing argument for men such as Grey, who labored through the first days of August to swing the cabinet to commit Britain to intervention and a declaration of war. If Germany won without Britain as an ally, it would be contemptuous in victory. If France lost without British help, it would be unforgiving in defeat. If France successfully defended itself without British aid, it might renounce the Entente and work against British interests. Either way, Britain's long-term interests and reputation as a great power would suffer. In one of the most tragic decisions of British history the Asquith government went to war against Germany, not because of territorial threats, national enmity, a legal commitment to France, or even a serious rivalry, but because Great Britain's reputation

was at stake in the aftermath of whatever came out of the declaration of hostilities.

In retrospect British politicians justified the hideous losses of World War I as an unavoidable commitment to an ally, as a crusade against the unspeakable "Hun," or as a response to Germany's aggression against neutral Belgium. In early August 1914 none of these explanations was true. Britain, with little at stake in a continental war, might have stood aside and let the situation resolve itself, as had the Franco-Prussian War and the wars for German and Italian unification. Instead, for the sake of "interests," namely the reputation of Britain as a European and world power, she hitched herself to the charnel wagon of World War I.

—MARGARET SANKEY,
MINNESOTA STATE
UNIVERSITY, MOORHEAD

Viewpoint:
No. British entry into World War I was inevitable, especially after Germany invaded Belgium, because Britain could not permit the domination of the continental Channel ports by any other nation.

The nineteenth-century British concept of "splendid isolation" proved to be an effective tool for British economic, military, and political security. As the twentieth century emerged, however, the prospect of maintaining this isolation, even with less splendor, appeared increasingly difficult. British involvement in the Fashoda Incident (1898), Boer War (1899–1902), and other late-nineteenth-century military and diplomatic confrontations evidenced the problems with British isolationism. As the twentieth century commenced, Britain began to explore opportunities for alliances and agreements, first and unsuccessfully with Germany, and then successfully with Japan (1902), France (1904), and finally Russia (1907). Consequently, by the conclusion of the first decade of the twentieth century any contention that Britain had maintained its isolation was invalid. Departure from this isolation emphasized the economic and strategic importance of maintaining friendly relations with their closest neighbors on the Continent. Consequently, British interests in Europe prohibited London from considering nonparticipation in a general European war; any geopolitical reordering of the Continent involved British national security and the security of the British Empire.

WHO BEGAN IT?

Below is the British government's response in 1914 to the German assertion that Russia was to blame for starting World War I:

First, it is difficult enough to tell "who began it" when the negotiations are spread over months, but it is practically impossible to do so when, as here, it is a question of hours.

The actual mobilization measures are taken in the midst of a cloud of accusations and threats, and it is impossible to separate cause from effect. Secondly, in any attempt to state the facts, the minor accusations and innuendoes must be discarded as of slight importance, except as a guide to the psychology of the moment.

The same may be said of rumours of violations of frontier. They have their value, but to put them forward, as does the German and Austrian correspondence, as the actual ground for the commencement of hostilities is to assume the impossible position that the fate of nations is subject to the reported action of a roving patrol. A marked insistence on such reports, as in the German Book, shows a poor appreciation of the value of the evidence.

Thirdly, mobilization "orders" are not mobilization. The mobilization systems of different countries are radically different; the precise nature of those systems, the lines of the railways and a hundred other points must be taken into consideration in judging mobilization measures, and any statement which ignores these factors is a mere bid for uninformed public opinion.

The hard fact that though Germany only proclaimed "Kriegsgefalzrzustand" on July 31st and mobilization on August 1st, to take effect on August 2nd, the German troops were across the Luxemburg frontier at dawn on August 2nd, will probably be judged to be historical evidence of far more value than any isolated reports received during the crisis.

As to Russian mobilization, it was fully realized in Germany that the Russian system was so complicated as to make it difficult to distinguish the localities really affected by mobilization.

Germany accuses Russia of mobilizing against Germany, not Austria, because she is reported to be mobilizing at Vilna and Warsaw, but both those towns are nearer to the Galician frontier than Prague is to the Serbian frontier, and Austria was reported to be mobilizing at Prague four days before she declared to Russia that she was only mobilizing against Serbia. The bare facts are of very slight value as evidence without a knowledge of the points already mentioned.

If the charges as to the priority of Russian mobilization are examined in the light of these considerations, it will be admitted that the evidence for those charges is remarkably slight, and that, given the admitted extreme slowness of Russian, and the extreme rapidity of German, mobilization, a fact which is frequently alluded to in the correspondence, there is no indication in favour of, and an overwhelming presumption against, the theory that the Russian measures were further advanced than the German when war was declared on August 1st.

The charge that the Czar's telegram of July 31st was misleading, and that the mobilization orders issued about the time of its dispatch destroyed the effect of sincere efforts then being made by Germany to mediate between Russia and Austria, is also unestablished.

In the first place, a glance at the Czar's telegram is sufficient to show that this charge is, to put it frankly, of the flimsiest character. His Majesty gave his "solemn word" that, while it was "technically impossible to discontinue our military preparations," the Russian troops would "undertake no provocative action" "as long as the negotiations between Austria and Serbia continue."

There was no promise not to mobilize; there was nothing but a statement which is almost word for word the same as that contained in the German Emperor's telegram to King George twenty-four hours later—the statement that, under certain circumstances, mobilization would not be converted into hostilities.

As a matter of fact, a somewhat unscrupulous use, in effect though perhaps not in intention, has been made of the Czar's telegrams to substantiate the theory of "betrayal."

Take for instance the German Chancellor's statement on July 31st (British Book, No. 108), that "the news of the active preparations on the Russo-German frontier had reached him just when the Czar had appealed to the Emperor, in the name of their old friendship, to mediate at Vienna, and when the Emperor was actually conforming to that request."

The telegram referred to must be that of July 29th (German Book, No. 21), since this is the only one which mentions "old friendship"; but this telegram, though it asks the Emperor to restrain Austria, also says in so many words that popular opinion in Russia would soon force measures which would lead to war.

Source: "British Reaction to Official Statement of the German Government: 'How Russia Betrayed Germany's Confidence,'" in Source Records of the Great War, volume 2, edited by Charles F. Horne (New York: National Alumni, 1923), FirstWorldWar.com <http://www.firstworldwar.com/source/britishreactiontogermanstatement.htm>.

BRITISH ENTRY
INTO WORLD WAR I

British crowd outside the
House of Commons as
members of Parliament
leave after the declaration
of war on Germany in
August 1914

(Radio Times Hulton Picture Library)

BRITISH ENTRY
INTO WORLD WAR I

Although the British entered World War I
(1914–1918) because of strategic concerns, some
historians contend that British participation
resulted from threats they associated with Germany: specifically, long-term Anglo-German
commercial and military competition. This argument is seductive because of the frequent antagonism that defined Anglo-German relations
during the early twentieth century. The launching of the HMS *Dreadnought* in 1906 catalyzed
this friction, resulting in a naval arms race and
increased bellicosity; of the many conflicts
between these two states this rivalry offered the
foremost prospect for war. Yet, this rivalry
started no later than 1906, fully eight years
before World War I, and it never produced a
martial conflict. Thus, while assertions that the
Anglo-German naval rivalry of the early twentieth century produced discord between these two
powers are correct, contentions that it provided
sufficient cause for either party to declare war are
erroneous.

The second important historical axiom is
the belief that the British entered the war
because of increasing German economic competition. The historic importance of international
trade to the British is well known, and in the
twentieth century the Germans threatened components of this economic staple. While concerns
over economic discord traditionally dominated
discussions of Anglo-German commercial relations during the early twentieth century,
increased commercial cooperation between Britain and Germany largely compensated for this
friction. In fact, between 1905 and 1914 Britain
and Germany enjoyed a reciprocally profitable
trade. British bankers and insurers provided
financing and protection for many, possibly
most, of the German merchant marine, and
German exports to Britain exceeded those of
both France and Russia. Further, the growing
dependence in both these countries on international commercial trade illustrated the economic
incentive to avoid war. This incentive became

more important with the resolution of established conflicts, such as the completion of the Berlin-to-Baghdad railroad, in the year preceding the war. Thus, the economic relationship between Britain and Germany during the early twentieth century should not be understood as a threat that provided a spur for the British to declare war but instead as a tool that worked against increased hostility between these two powers.

In spite of the series of Anglo-German conflicts, none of these tensions was present when the war started on 1 August 1914. Instead, the assassination of Austrian archduke Franz Ferdinand in Sarajevo precipitated the war (which the British did not officially join until three days later). Although the British and Germans had different and sometimes conflicting ambitions in the Near East, especially in the Ottoman Empire, this assassination did not have to result in conflict between Britain and Germany. In fact, in 1912–1913 these two countries cooperated in peacefully concluding the brief Balkan wars. The lack of any traditional Anglo-German conflict on 1 August, or even in the interim period before Britain declared war, permits the obvious deduction that the British decision to enter World War I was not the product of long-standing antagonism with Germany but something else.

The increasingly cordial Anglo-German relations produced one of the most noteworthy, and ultimately misguided, elements in German chancellor Theobald von Bethmann Hollweg's strategic planning. He believed that if Britain could be convinced that German military action was defensive, British neutrality in a broad European war could be assured; such efforts extended at least until February 1912. Although the Germans never received a promise of neutrality, they believed that their relations with Britain were sufficiently good that this policy was viable. If Anglo-German commercial and naval antagonisms were insufficient to bring about a war, if the relative interests of the two powers were sufficiently coordinated that they could work for peace in the Balkans only a year before the start of World War I, and if the Germans believed that the tension between themselves and the British was sufficiently minimal that the British would avoid conflict with Germany, then why did these two powers go to war in 1914?

The single most important explanation for why the British entered World War I is that they could not afford to permit the entire European continent, or even just the western half, specifically the Channel ports, to fall under the dominion of one country. French emperor Napoleon Bonaparte's Continental System, implemented just over a century before the start of World War I, reminded the British of the necessity and fragility of trade with the Continent. The Channel ports represented to the British the most important strategic locations in Europe. Should these ports fall under German dominion, not only would German dreadnoughts have greater access to the sea but Britain also could be subjected to a blockade and even invasion. The prospect of a victorious attack on France and Belgium by any third power required British intervention.

Diplomatic exchanges among Britain, Germany, Russia, and France in July 1914 indicated that if the Austro-Serbian conflict resulted in war, it would not remain localized. Moreover, it was well known that should a European war materialize, Germany would invade France at once, probably through Belgium, in order to handle one front presented by the Franco-Russian alliance. This possibility compelled British participation to protect the Channel ports. This understanding was enhanced by the assumption that should the Central Powers be victorious, the Germans would appropriate Belgian and French territories, probably including the Channel ports. If for no other reason than British concerns for their own security (especially as related to the Channel ports), the war obliged British participation.

Although British security concerns mandated their participation in the pending war, British diplomats endeavored to avoid a conflict. During July 1914 the British initiated no less than four different offers for mediation as alternatives to war. None of these appeals succeeded in convincing the Germans to pressure the Austrians to seek anything but a military solution to the Serbian problem. Instead of embracing British offers for mediation, the Germans sought British promises for neutrality in the event of a general European war.

The considerable British efforts to secure a mediated peace failed, and on 1 August 1914 World War I started with a German declaration of war against Russia. The three-day delay in Britain's joining the war has permitted many to argue British indecisiveness. Such a conclusion is not valid, and when put into historical context, the British leadership exhibits comparatively little apprehension. Most countries did not declare war on 1 August or even the next day. The Germans presented the Belgian king with an ultimatum on 2 August requiring the latter to permit German troops to cross his country. Even with this German demand to cross Belgium, neither the French nor the British declared war; finally, on 3 August, facing the reality of a German invasion and honoring their secret agreement with Russia, the French entered the war, but only after Germany declared war on them. When the German ultimatum to Belgium expired on 4 August without the Belgians relenting, the Germans invaded Belgium, providing the pretext for a British declaration of war. The British decision to wait to declare war made them the last major European participant to enter the war, but only by hours. Why has this decision produced accusations of British indecisiveness and not French indecisiveness? Any hope that the British would remain neutral in a broad European war was misguided and should have been evident from the diplomatic correspondence from July 1914. The decision to delay a declaration of war until Germany invaded Belgium illustrated an effort to bolster domestic support and was not governmental indecisiveness.

The British decision to wait until Germany invaded Belgium was entirely political. The Germans had already received notification from the British that any invasion of Serbia would result in a continental war that would necessitate British participation, but the decision to delay permitted the British to enter the war with both just cause and unity at home. Although ordinary people greeted the declaration of war with cheers, members of the government were more alarmed and consequently more somber. While most of the cabinet supported Prime Minister Herbert Henry Asquith in the declaration of war, two members resigned in protest. Though the decision was not unanimous, the British, both elite and ordinary citizens, fully supported the government's decision.

Anglo-German antagonisms during the early twentieth century represented little more than the traditional and expected struggle between states with competing interests. None of these antagonisms was sufficient for either side to declare war. Instead, good relations were important to the economic capabilities of the two countries. While antagonisms existed, they were insufficient causes for the British declaration of war. Instead, Britain could not permit the Channel ports to fall under the influence of one power and therefore could not have assumed a passive position in a broad European war.

–NILES ILLICH,
TEXAS A&M UNIVERSITY

References

J. M. Bourne, *Britain and the Great War 1914–1918* (London & New York: Arnold, 1989).

John Charmley, *Splendid Isolation?: Britain, the Balance of Power, and the Origins of the First World War* (London: Hodder & Stoughton, 1999).

Niall Ferguson, *The Pity of War* (New York: Basic Books, 1999).

Bentley B. Gilbert, *Britain, 1914–1945: The Aftermath of Power* (Wheeling, Ill.: Harlan Davidson, 1995).

Cameron Hazlehurst, *Politicians at War, July 1914 to May 1915: A Prologue to the Triumph of Lloyd George* (London: Cape, 1971).

Paul Johnson, *The Offshore Islanders* (London: Weidenfeld & Nicolson, 1972).

J. S. McDermott, "The Revolution in British Military Thinking from the Boer War to the Morocco Crisis," in *The War Plans of the Great Powers, 1880–1914,* edited by Paul Kennedy (London & Boston: Allen & Unwin, 1979), pp. 99–117.

Zara S. Steiner, *Britain and the Origins of the First World War* (London: Macmillan, 1977).

John Turner, *British Politics and the Great War: Coalition and Conflict, 1915–1918* (New Haven: Yale University Press, 1992).

Keith M. Wilson, *The Policy of the Entente: Essays on the Determinants of British Foreign Policy, 1904–1914* (Cambridge & New York: Cambridge University Press, 1985).

BRITISH ENTRY
INTO WORLD WAR I

COLLAPSE OF THE HABSBURGS

Was the Habsburg Empire doomed from the beginning of World War I?

Viewpoint: Yes. The war accelerated long-standing patterns of disintegration while creating new challenges to the unity of the empire.

Viewpoint: No. Major threats to the cohesion of the empire came only after several years of fighting, and the empire might have survived if the Allies had not sided with Slavic nationalist movements as a means of weakening Habsburg domination in Central and Eastern Europe.

By the end of World War I several European empires had disintegrated, among them the Habsburg-ruled empire of Austria-Hungary. Patched together over several centuries through marriage, inheritance, and conquest, the Habsburg domains included more than a dozen major ethnic groups and territory covering much of Central and Eastern Europe with terrain as diverse as the mountainous coast of the Adriatic and the farmlands of the Ukrainian breadbasket. The dominant German and Hungarian populations were minorities. The language of command in its small navy was Italian. By 1914 its subject peoples were clamoring with greater and greater urgency for independence or unification with their brethren in neighboring countries.

Historians have often wondered whether the House of Habsburg could have held on to its rule of Austria-Hungary if it had not become embroiled in World War I. Some scholars have argued that, even though Austria and Hungary were held together by ties as seemingly tenuous as loyalty to a dynastic monarchy and a continual reorganization and renegotiation of its political structures, it had proven over the years that these relationships were all it needed to survive. From their perspective the rough separation of the Habsburg Empire into its constituent parts after 1918 came about because the Allies supported minority nationalists who wanted independence from the empire and needed to weaken the Austrians militarily. Thus, they argue, losing the war is a sufficient explanation for the empire's collapse.

Another argument maintains, however, that no matter what loyalty the Habsburg emperors may have enjoyed in the past, their day was done by 1914. Even without the war, the growing internal tensions within the empire, Vienna's increasingly ineffective role as an international power, and the pan-European growth of ethnically based modern nationalism doomed it to destruction. World War I may have accelerated forces of political, social, and economic decay, but they would have eventually brought about the disintegration of the empire even without the war. As modern Europe faces new challenges in the Balkans and debates the future of other lands once ruled by the Habsburgs, a consideration of why their empire collapsed commands the attention of contemporary audiences.

Viewpoint:
Yes. The war accelerated long-standing patterns of disintegration while creating new challenges to the unity of the empire.

The history of the Habsburg Empire may be described as a series of compromises spanning nearly five hundred years. As the pace of change in Europe increased, the compromises that kept the Empire together became more drastic—even its name changed three times in its final decades. The carefully constructed and confusing balance of power within the empire did not survive World War I (1914–1918), but it was not the war itself or misfortune on the battlefield that dethroned the Habsburgs. Indeed, their military performed remarkably well given the circumstances. The unfortunate truth is that by 1914 the empire was doomed.

In 1909, after declining to run for a third term in office, American president Theodore Roosevelt traveled through Europe. He later described the venerable Habsburg emperor Franz Josef (ruled 1848–1916) as if he were a creature of myth. Seen from the American perspective at the turn of the twentieth century, emperors and empires were, indeed, things of myth; yet, Vienna—a city renowned for its opera, fine arts, symphonies, and ballet—was the capital of an emperor, one of the last rulers to hold supreme power over his state.

Franz Josef had been crowned in 1848, the Year of Revolution in Europe; by 1914 he must truly have seemed a relic from an earlier time. Managing the state and its tottering pillars of compromises and half-solutions was more than a full-time job. He worked sixteen-hour days at his desk, sleeping on a cot in his office surrounded by mounds of paper. Widowed when his wife was murdered by an anarchist in 1898, he was estranged from his children. Many of Franz Josef's contemporaries linked the empire to the emperor. Franz Josef seemed to be holding the empire together by force of will, and it seemed unlikely to outlast him.

The Habsburg Monarchy as it stood in 1914 dated from 1867, following defeat by Prussia at the Battle of Sadowa the previous year. Rising Hungarian nationalism and weakening German domination had forced a compromise (or *Ausgleich*), subject to renegotiation every ten years, to keep Austria and Hungary together in a single state. Franz Josef ruled as emperor in Austria and as king in Hungary. Austria and Hungary had separate parliaments, which sent delegates to a weak central legislature in Vienna. The principal minis-ters in each realm were appointed by the monarch. All major decisions required the support of the Hungarian prime minister.

The Habsburg Empire had no clear ethnic majority; Germans, Hungarians, Poles, Czechs, Slovaks, Romanians, Ruthenes, Serbs, Croats, Jews, Gypsies, Italians, and Slovenes each made up significant percentages of the population. The only official languages were German and Hungarian, just as only the Hungarians and Germans had their own parliaments. The other peoples routinely faced legal discrimination, and some of them (notably the Slovenes) faced cultural annihilation through absorption into their larger neighbors. As a result a vast percentage of the population was becoming increasingly dissatisfied with its second-class status. Furthermore, the Hungarians no longer wished to be equal partners in the "Austro-Hungarian Empire" and sought to create their own independent state. Each time they renegotiated the *Ausgleich* treaty (in 1877, 1887, 1897, 1907, and 1917), the Hungarians secured progressively greater autonomy from Vienna.

The national divisions within the empire exacerbated an increasing disparity between agricultural regions and highly industrialized mining and manufacturing areas. Each felt slighted by the central government, and neither was particularly supportive of the central authority. The problem was complicated by the fact that the rural areas were largely Slavic and the industrial areas largely German. A religious divide also existed, between the Roman Catholic Germans and Hungarians and the Eastern Orthodox Slavs (with the Uniate Poles, Ruthenes, and Ukrainians perennially in the middle).

When the empire annexed Bosnia-Herzegovina in 1908, the existing problems multiplied. Several million more Slavs, mostly Orthodox Serbs, were added to the empire by force, as were a large number of Muslims. Many historians call this last Habsburg conquest "the final straw" that broke the back of the empire. If all the Slavs—Serbs, Poles, Czechs, Croats, and others—were counted together, they outnumbered either Germans or Hungarians. The Slavs demanded an equal share in the government. Even more ominous for the Habsburgs, many of their subject peoples could look to significant populations of their brothers living in freedom in bordering states. It was only a matter of time before Serbs would demand to unite their part of the empire with Serbia, or Romanians would want to unite with Romania.

Combined with these internal pressures were significant external threats to the stability of the empire. From the independent Balkan states on the southern border of the empire came not invading armies but dangerous ideas.

**Crowd gathering at the
Austrian Reichstag in
November 1918 after the
declaration of a new
socialist republic**

(from Z. A. B. Zeman, Twilight of
the Habsburgs, *1971)*

COLLAPSE OF THE
HABSBURGS

Nationalism is the death of empires. One people cannot rule another except by force, and force was too expensive for the Habsburgs to maintain for long. The Habsburgs perceived a more-material threat from Russia to the east, the only direction in which the empire might still expand. An 1884 Austro-Hungarian Foreign Office memorandum read:

> The developments of the past twenty years pushed Austria-Hungary back from her old historic position. We have only the East. We cannot allow [a] Slav conformation of the Balkan peninsula under Russian material or moral protection [that] would cut our vital arteries.

Habsburg foreign policy, largely responsible for World War I, had its basis in this fear of Russian influence. The Habsburgs were less afraid of Russian attack than they were that Russia, an independent Slavic state, might serve as a beacon for the captive Slavs in the Habsburg Empire.

On the north the Habsburg Empire bordered a rapidly expanding Imperial Germany—to which it increasingly looked for protection in the event of a war with Russia. Believing such a war was inevitable if the empire was to survive, Austria-Hungary also made defensive pacts with Italy and Romania against Russia (and her entente partners, France and Britain). This anti-Russian coalition, however, was not enough to save the Habsburg Empire.

World War I may be seen as the inevitable explosion following a century of growing hubris and pride, based largely on the fanatical belief that mankind was constantly progressing toward a better society. The world was changing too fast, and governments had not kept up. For the Habsburgs, war was the only way to deal with tensions in the empire, which were eroding the empire from within. All the underpinnings of the regime were melting away.

Their first target was Serbia. Demonstrative of the extreme tensions in the empire, the assassination of Archduke Franz Ferdinand, the heir to the Habsburg throne, on 28 June 1914 gave Austro-Hungarian military commanders a convenient excuse to set in motion long-laid plans. Serbia had been presented with an ultimatum by Austria that was geared to lead to war; from this exchange it is clear the reply did not matter, Austria was going to start the war it thought it was prepared for. Twelve divisions (about a quarter of the army) were slated to attack Serbia. Habsburg foreign minister Count Leopold von Berchtold telegraphed Army Chief of Staff Franz Conrad von Hötzendorf on 26 July 1914, "We should like to present the declaration of war as soon as possible. . . . When do you want the declaration of war against Serbia?" Conrad replied, "Only when we have made enough progress with mobilization for operations to begin. About 12 August." Considering themselves ready and able to wage a quick, victorious war against Serbia, the Austrians declared war on Serbia on 28 July, two days after the exchange between Berchtold and Conrad, and quickly learned just how unprepared they were.

The Serbians fended off three successive Austrian attacks. Eventually, Austria was victorious in late 1915, but only after much loss of life, the involvement of their German ally, and a surprise attack on Serbia by Bulgaria. The Serbian front, however, was only part of a larger Austrian battle plan.

Austria had also planned a major war of conquest against Russia, mainly for the purpose of adding much more of Poland and Ukraine to the Habsburg Empire. Because of European defensive alliances, the Great Powers were brought into the war in August 1914, pitting Germany and Austria-Hungary against Russia, France, and Britain and soon drawing the rest of Europe into what is now known as World War I. This invasion was by far the largest military undertaking in the history of the empire. By 1917 more Habsburg troops had been killed or captured on the Russian Front than during all other military engagements of the past three centuries combined. During the same period Austria was eventually forced to defend itself against attacks by two of its prewar allies, Italy (after May 1915) and Romania (after August 1916).

The Austrian generals faced an enormous handicap. The Austro-Hungarian army was less than 50 percent Austrian or Hungarian. It was 47 percent Slav, with roughly even numbers of Czechs, Poles, Ruthenes, and "Serbo-Croats" (Vienna considered Croats and Serbs as one people). Twenty-nine percent were German-speaking and therefore called "German"; 18 percent were Hungarian, 5 percent Romanian, and a little more than 1 percent Italian. (Italian was the language of command in the small Austro-Hungarian navy.) The Austrian generals thus found themselves in the unenviable position of fighting Slavic Russia and Serbia, Romania, and Italy with an army in which more than half the men were Slavs, Romanians, or Italians.

Perhaps the second-largest problem facing the Habsburg Empire was its generals. Conrad and his staff devised many plans for deploying troops in the event of war, but trouble began when they attempted to put all of them into action. In the opening weeks of the war Austro-Hungarian units were sent first to the Russian border, then to the Serbian front, and then back to Russia. Conrad seemed unable to decide whom to attack first.

Similar problems plagued the Austrian army for the rest of the war. Every time a new front opened up, there was confusion and disorder among Austrian troops until the German army intervened, as it did against the Russians in Galicia in 1914–1916, against Serbia in 1915, and against Italy in 1915–1917. Conrad buried the government of Vienna in communiqués complaining of German "interference," but without German intervention the Habsburg Empire might have collapsed well before the autumn of 1918.

Two key elements defeated the Habsburg armies in the field: an inability to adapt and an inability to plan ahead. Following the Russian Revolution of November 1917 and Russia's withdrawal from the war the following March, more than five hundred thousand prisoners of war flooded back into the Habsburg Empire. They brought with them the contagion of communism; "peace, bread, land" was the cry of the Russian Bolsheviks, and the Habsburgs' soldiers returned home with the same demands. Beginning in the spring of 1918, the Austrians set up *Heimkehrerkordon*, (roughly, "homecomers' quarantine") and put these men in detention camps if they were believed to be dangerous.

Strategic planning, efficient supply, and internal organization are the hallmarks of a victorious army. By early 1918 the infrastructure of the patchwork Habsburg Empire was incapable of supplying units in the field—even after the Austrians and Germans appropriated nearly the entire Ukrainian and Romanian grain harvest of 1918. Men began to desert or to resort to brigandage. Between the ideological quarantine of half a million men on one front, and the desertion of hungry men on another, it is a wonder the empire made it to autumn 1918.

Another issue also undermined the cohesion of the army and the empire. By early 1917 the Allied powers, hoping to turn the Habsburg Empire's fractious multiethnic character to their advantage, had endorsed the idea of "self-determination" for its subject peoples, a principle that for all practical purposes included their national independence from Austria-Hungary. This policy was also supported by the United States, which entered the war in April 1917. President Woodrow Wilson's "Fourteen Points," a blueprint for a postwar world announced in January 1918, included a strong statement favoring self-determination. For many this announcement meant the end of the Habsburg Empire.

In October 1918 Croatian units mutinied at Fiume, Croatia, and fought with Hungarian units. At the captured Russian port of Odessa, units of Slovenian, Italian, and German troops revolted, killed their officers and demanded to return to their homes, which soon would be states independent of the empire. One official Austrian history said that by 31 October, "the

realm lay in ruins. The Army and the Fleet were broken in pieces by the revolution." The war had ended, and so had the Empire.

The collapse was quick in coming. Stalemated on multiple fronts, the Austrian General Staff had spent three years trying to patch things together. Even after the defeats of Serbia, Romania, and Russia there were always too many losses and not enough recruits to replace them. Untrained and poorly equipped troops fought a series of battles and retreated on the Balkan Front. Better units were wasted in battle after battle on the Italian border. Eventually too many competing problems proved beyond the abilities of the General Staff.

As dexterous as the Habsburgs had been in holding together their empire, some compromises—including the 1867 agreement on which the Austro-Hungarian Empire was based—are unworkable. The question is not whether the Habsburg Empire could have survived the war, but rather "how it survived so long."

–LAWRENCE A. HELM,
NASA

Viewpoint:
No. Major threats to the cohesion of the empire came only after several years of fighting, and the empire might have survived if the Allies had not sided with Slavic nationalist movements as a means of weakening Habsburg domination in Central and Eastern Europe.

In November 1918, during the closing days of World War I—with his armies beaten and his government in disarray—Emperor Karl, who had ruled the Habsburg Empire since the death of Franz Josef in November 1916, signed a message renouncing all participation in the affairs of state; thus ending the Austro-Hungarian Empire. Some observers have said that the empire would have failed even if there had been no war. They have called it a "prison house of nations" holding captive more than a dozen nationalities and have asserted that the autocratic officials in Vienna could have found no just resolution for the claims of these peoples. The record of events, however, shows that the demise of Austria-Hungary was not caused by internal weakness but rather was the result of conscious efforts by a few individuals, assisted by a favorable set of circumstances, to gain independence for their peoples at the expense of Austro-Hungarian territory. Without the work of these nationalists the empire could have survived.

Throughout the latter half of the nineteenth century subjects of the Habsburgs suggested several constructive solutions to the problems of the various nationalities. Acknowledging the historic role of the empire as a check on German and Russian imperialism, most of them envisioned converting the Habsburg Empire into a federal union, rather than breaking it up into separate nations. The best-known of these ideas, "Austro-Slavism," was put forth by the Czech historian Frantisek Palacky. He supported the monarchy and called for subject nationalities to remain "*Habsburgtreue*" (loyal to the Habsburgs). Even the Austrian socialist leaders Otto Bauer and Karl Renner favored the preservation of the multiethnic empire; as international socialists, however, they were convinced that nationality or ethnicity was a false identity that would become irrelevant.

The Austro-Hungarian Empire received its deathblow from three academics: philosophy professor Tomáš Masaryk, law professor Eduard Beneš, and astronomer Milan Štefánik. In 1914 Masaryk decided that the future of the inhabitants of Moravia, Bohemia, Slovakia, and Austrian Silesia lay in unified independence. He elicited the support of his friend Beneš, and they took their message abroad. A fugitive in the empire, Masaryk escaped to London, where for two years, while teaching at the University of London, he worked with influential people to spread the cause of Czech independence. After the overthrow of the tsar in February 1917, he went to Petrograd, where he organized newly released Czech prisoners of war into a military force, the Czechoslovak Legion, which ended up fighting the Bolsheviks in the Russian civil war while attempting to reach the Western Front.

Until early 1917 neither the British nor the French were seriously interested in dissolving the Habsburg Empire. They changed their minds only after the desperate battlefield situation on the Western Front forced them to consider steps that would promote disloyalty in the enemy camp. Earlier, the Russians had talked about a Slavic kingdom of Bohemia under a Russian prince and looked to annex the ethnic Ukrainian regions of Galicia, but their declining fortunes in the war made their achieving either goal unlikely.

After the Bolshevik Revolution of November 1917 Masaryk went to the United States to seek support from Czech and Slovakian immigrants and attempt to influence the American government. Initially, he was not successful with President Woodrow Wilson and Secretary of State Robert Lansing, but his cause captured the imaginations of the immigrant communities and the American public in general, who saw parallels between Masaryk's cause and the American struggle for independence. Masaryk was ultimately successful in creating enough grassroots pressure on the U.S. government that the United States recognized the Czecho-Slovak National Council as a de facto government.

While Masaryk was busy in Britain and the United States, Beneš was active in France. The Czecho-Slovak National Council, with Beneš in charge, came to have easy access to influential French officials, who began to view support for Czech independence as an opportunity to confound the Austrian war efforts. While Beneš dealt with the official side, his deputy, Štefánik, courted public opinion. Handsome, charming, and audacious, the Slovakian astronomer became a French citizen, joined the air corps, and shot down enough German planes to be declared an ace and become a popular hero. The Czecho-Slovak Council could influence Czechs captured from the Austro-Hungarian army to fight on the side of the Allies, and it was resolutely anti-Bolshevik, thus gaining sympathy from the French government. Only in June 1918, however, did the French formally recognize the National Council as the future government of an independent Czechoslovakia.

Romania had special status among claimants to Austro-Hungarian territory by virtue of its having declared war on Germany, not once but twice. After protracted territorial negotiations with the Allies, Romania went to war with Germany in August 1916. By December, however, German and Austrian armies had overrun Romania, and it had dropped out of the war. In November 1918, when the war was nearly over, it again declared war on Germany. Premier Georges Clemenceau of France was not eager to honor Romania's desertion with territory, but other forces were at work that eventually enabled Romania to take possession of Transylvania, Bukovina, and half of the Banat of Temesvar after the war. Paris was the favorite city of the Romanian aristocracy, vocal supporters of Romanian claims. Ion Bratianu, the Romanian prime minister, arrived in Paris after the Armistice of November 1918 to make his case for territorial concessions. He was not entirely convincing. Then, however, Queen Marie of Romania arrived on the scene. A grandchild of Queen Victoria, the lovely and vivacious monarch was the rage of "le tout Paris," using her style and dynastic connections to gain her country a role in carving up the Austro-Hungarian Empire. Both Clemenceau and Prime Minister David Lloyd George of Britain were enchanted, and Romania was given most of the territory it had been promised in 1916. Furthermore, soon after the Armistice that ended the war, Romania and Slovakia, taking advantage of a weakened Hungary, invaded

WAR PLANS

On 2 July 1914, a few days after the assassination of his nephew and heir, Archduke Franz Josef sent Kaiser Wilhelm II of Germany a letter to which he attached a document that had been drafted by the Hapsburg minister of foreign affairs a month before the murder afforded Austria-Hungary a pretext for invading Serbia. It included the following passages:

Serbia whose policy has for years been animated by hostility toward Austria Hungary, and which is completely under Russian influence, has achieved an increase of territory and of population that exceeded by much her own expectations. Turkey, whose community of interests with the Triple Alliance was progressing well, and who constituted an important counterpoise against Russia and the Balkan States, has been almost entirely pushed out of Europe, and has seen her situation as a great power gravely compromised. Territorial proximity with Montenegro and the general strengthening of the Pan-Serbian idea have brought closer the possibility of a new expansion of Serbia by means of a union with Montenegro. Lastly in the course of the crisis, the relations of Roumania with the Triple Alliance have essentially changed. . . . We see, on the other hand, that Russian and French diplomacy have carried on a unified action, in conformity with a preconcerted plan to exploit the advantages obtained and to change certain factors that were from their point of view unfavorable. . . .

The thought of freeing the Christian Balkan people from Turkish rule, in order to use them as a weapon against central Europe, has been for a long time the secret thought of Russian policy, by the traditional interest of Russia for these people. In these latter days has been developed the idea, put forward by Russia and taken up by France, of uniting the Balkan States into a Balkan alliance, in order by this means to put an end to the military superiority of the Triple Alliance. The first condition before the realization of this plan was that Turkey should be pushed back from the territory inhabited by the Christian nations of the Balkans, in order to increase the strength of these States and to render them free to expand to the west. This preliminary condition has been, on the whole, realized by the last war. On the other hand, after the end of the crisis, a division separated the Balkan States into two opposing groups of nearly equal strength: Turkey and Bulgaria on the one hand, and the two Serbian States, Greece and Roumania, on the other.

To put an end to this division in order to be able to use all the Balkan States or at least a decisive majority, to upset the balance of European power, was the latest task to which, after the end of the crisis, Russia and France applied themselves. . . .

There is no doubt of the basis upon which . . . these differences and rivalries might be reconciled and a new Balkan alliance created. What could be the actual aim of such an alliance in the present circumstances for the Balkan States? There is no longer reason to consider a common action against Turkey. It can, therefore, only be directed against Austria-Hungary and can only be accomplished on the basis of a program that should promise to all it[s] members extensions of territory by a graduated displacement of their frontiers from the east to the west, at the expense of the territorial integrity of the Monarchy. A union of Balkan States upon any other basis would be impossible to imagine, but on this basis not only is it not impossible, but it is in a fair way to be realized. One cannot question that Serbia under Russian pressure would consent to pay a considerable price in Macedonia for the entry of Bulgaria into an alliance directed against the Monarchy and looking forward to the acquisition of Bosnia and the adjacent territory. . . .

The relations of Austria-Hungary with Roumania may be at this moment characterized by the fact that the Monarchy relies entirely upon its alliance and, before as since, is ready to uphold Roumania with all its force if the *casus foedoris* shall arise, but that Roumania detaches itself one-sidedly from its obligations of alliance and shows to the Monarchy only the prospect of neutrality. Even the neutrality of Roumania is only guaranteed to the Monarchy by the personal affirmation of King Charles which naturally is of value only for the duration of his reign. . . .

Under these conditions it is impossible to consider the alliance with Roumania as of sufficient certainty and extent to serve Austria-Hungary as a pivot in her Balkan policy. . . .

To destroy, with the assistance of the Balkans, the military superiority of the two Imperial powers is the objective of Russia. . . .

For Russia has recognized that the relation of her plans in Europe and in Asia, plans which correspond with internal necessities gravely affect the important interests of Germany, and must inevitably arouse her to resistance. . . .

For these reasons those in charge of the foreign policy of Austria-Hungary are convinced that it is in the common interest of the Monarchy, as in that of Germany, to oppose energetically and in time in this phase of the Balkan crisis, the development foreseen and encouraged by Russia by a pre-concerted plan.

Source: *World War I Document Archive <http:// www.lib.byu.edu/~rdh/wwi/1914/frzwilly.html>.*

COLLAPSE OF THE HABSBURGS

it and claimed territory. As Winston Churchill remarked, "the war of the Giants is over, the war of the pygmies has begun."

The idea of a union of peoples speaking South Slavic languages had emerged in the mid nineteenth century and coalesced into a movement championed by Serbian and Croatian intellectuals. At first "Yugoslavism" did not necessarily entail independence from Austria-Hungary and unification with the small kingdom of Serbia, but in 1914 Ante Trumbic, the chief spokesman for the movement, decided that his people would fare better in an enlarged South Slavic state, and the following year he set up the Yugoslav National Committee in London. As with the Czech national organization, the Yugoslav National Committee was largely funded by immigrants in North America. By 1917 it had accumulated a powerful body of supporters, including Robert Seton-Watson, a wealthy British scholar and linguist, and London *Times* correspondent Wickham Steed. The committee's efforts, Serbia's wartime suffering, and the Allies' need to encourage more separatism within the Austro-Hungarian Empire generated greater sympathy for their goals. On 29 October 1918 the National Council of Slovenes, Croats, and Serbs declared the formation of a united kingdom, with much of its territory coming from Austria-Hungary.

Sometimes the most perceptive critic of his own policy of self-determination, President Wilson commented, "it will be a turbulent nation as they are a turbulent people." Indeed, the artificial nation of Yugoslavia, born of a coincidence of interests between minority dissidents and increasingly desperate Allied governments, experienced little stability in the interwar period, during World War II, or after its emergence from communism in the 1990s. Few of the people in the annexed territory had anything in common with the people of the Serbian kingdom. Croatia had been tied to Hungary in dynastic union since the twelfth century, while the Banat of Temesvar had been an organic part of the Hungarian kingdom since its reconquest from the Turks in 1718. The Serbian populations of these regions had largely immigrated there in the seventeenth century to live and serve under a Christian ruler while their homeland was under Ottoman occupation. Slovenia had for centuries been an integral component of the Austrian crown lands. The Adriatic coast of Austria-Hungary, including the provinces of Istria and Dalmatia, was heavily Italian, with communities dating back to the Middle Ages. The treaty that secured Italian adherence to the Allied side in the war had promised it to Rome, but when the Allied governments proved unwilling to back these promises, the new South Slavic state swallowed

most of it up. The small state of Montenegro, which had long existed as an independent nation, was also annexed, even though Montenegro had fought on the Allied side in the war. Bosnia-Herzegovina, technically part of the Ottoman Empire until its annexation by Vienna in 1908, had an ethnically mixed population of Serbs, Croats, and a plurality of Muslims. Macedonia had remained Ottoman territory until 1913 and was coveted by Serbia, Bulgaria, and Greece. Also including large populations of Germans, Hungarians, Italians, and Albanians, in addition to its five recognized nationalities, Yugoslavia was only a little less diverse than the Austro-Hungarian Empire. It is difficult to identify any long-term causes that would have brought these far-flung, ethnically distinct, religiously separate, and historically unconnected regions together in the absence of a major international upheaval and an ambitious Serbia supported by victorious wartime allies.

The Habsburg Empire was sustained by an ongoing negotiation between Vienna and the nationalities. World War I interrupted that exchange. Through the dynamics of a nation at war, criticism—which in peacetime would lead to constructive debate—became a demonstration of disloyalty. Even a thoughtless word could cause trouble. One breach developed between Vienna and the provinces and another between the government and the people. These gaps grew as the war went on, and forces favoring radical change prospered. By 1918, 60 percent of the Empire's men of breadwinning age were at the front, while Allied blockades and economic dislocation caused starvation.

To the average subject of the Habsburg Empire, who thought more about his religion, his emperor, and his neighborhood than about his nationality and its politicians, the death of the aged Emperor Franz Josef in November 1916 was a severe blow. The hallmarks of the Dual Monarchy at the turn of the century were its comfortable and predictable routine and the pomp and gaiety of the Danube culture. This pervasive way of life was personified by Franz Josef, who commanded loyalty from his diverse subjects for nearly seven decades. The public applauded his sober work habits and followed with sorrow the sad stories of the violent death of his brother Maximilian, the ill-fated Emperor of Mexico in 1863–1867; his son Rudolf, who committed suicide in a bizarre pact with his mistress in 1889; his wife Elizabeth, who was stabbed to death by an anarchist in 1898; and his nephew and heir Franz Ferdinand, whose murder set the war in motion in 1914. For most subjects Franz Josef was the only leader they had ever known, and his loss dealt a critical blow to the stability he and his dynasty had long represented.

It is often said that the army was the glue that held the Habsburg Empire together. Although the people became more restless and unruly as the war progressed, with some exceptions the army fought loyally and well until almost the end. Only a few cases of desertion occurred before 1917, and most mass desertions only came in the last days of the war, and then because many national minorities realized the war and Empire were coming to an end and wished to avoid prisoner-of-war camps. In fact, desertion was a greater problem in the French and Russian armies. The mutinies of 1917 affected more than half the units in the French army and paralyzed the French military capability along two-thirds of the Western Front. The Imperial Russian army disintegrated in a wave of mass desertions.

Franz Josef expressed the mission of the Empire in these words, which might seem self-serving if they were not precisely true: "the Monarchy is not an artificial creation but an organic body. It is a place of refuge, an asylum for those fragmented nations scattered over Central Europe who, if left to their own resources would lead a grim existence, becoming the pawns of more powerful neighbors." Within a generation of the end of his empire, nearly all his former subjects lived under the control of Nazi Germany. Less than a decade later most of them lived under a communist rule, which lasted for nearly half a century. Perhaps it was not beyond the imagination of the Habsburgs' loyal subjects that there were worse alternatives to empire.

–JOE KING,
BOCA RATON, FLORIDA

References

Oszkár Jászi, *The Dissolution of the Habsburg Monarchy* (Chicago: University of Chicago Press, 1929).

Lonnie Johnson, *Central Europe: Enemies, Neighbors, Friends* (New York: Oxford University Press, 1996).

Margaret MacMillan, *Peacemakers: The Paris Conference of 1919 and Its Attempt to End War* (London: Murray, 2001); republished as *Paris 1919: Six Months That Changed the World* (New York: Random House, 2002).

John Terraine, *White Heat: The New Warfare 1914–18* (London: Sidgwick & Jackson, 1982).

COLLAPSE OF THE SOVIET UNION

Was the collapse of the Soviet Union inevitable?

Viewpoint: Yes. The Soviet system had inherent political and economic flaws that made it unsustainable.

Viewpoint: No. The Soviet Union had the potential to remain stable; it was brought down by foreign pressures and bad leadership decisions.

When Soviet leader Mikhail Gorbachev resigned on Christmas Day 1991, the country he led had only a few more days left to survive. By New Year's Day 1992 the monolithic superpower Union of Soviet Socialist Republics (U.S.S.R.) that had dominated Eurasia for more than seventy years had been replaced by a shrunken Russia, reduced to borders that had in some cases not been seen on the map since the seventeenth century, and fourteen other nations, some of which had known independence in the distant past and others that were completely new. All of these lands shared the absence of their main governing principle for seven decades: Soviet communism.

The enormous ideological and geopolitical ramifications of the Soviet Union's collapse have left enduring questions about the inevitability of that event. Indeed, before 1991 the Soviets themselves and most Western observers believed unflinchingly that the U.S.S.R. would remain a major factor in world politics long into the future. Confident scholarly studies predicted its economic growth to the year 2000, and military planners accustomed to decades of bipolarity planned the next phase in the arms race. Indeed, few cartographers imagined that they would have to redraw their maps of Europe a dozen times between 1990 and 1995.

As some scholars maintain, the fall of Soviet communism was unavoidable. The Soviet state's dependence on terror, reliance on uncompetitive economics, and devotion to a political philosophy that brought it into conflict with most of the rest of the world ultimately doomed it to destruction. The U.S.S.R. was caught between an angry and stagnant society at home and a hostile community of nations abroad, and its eventual demise was a foregone conclusion. Others argue that the pre-1991 status quo could have continued. Had it not been for the bullish anticommunism of U.S. president Ronald Reagan's administration in the 1980s, existing challenges to Soviet social and economic problems could have become manageable. Western goodwill, financial assistance, and favorable trade relations, all advocated by proponents of détente in the 1970s, might have enabled the Soviet state to reform successfully and survive intact into the twenty-first century.

Viewpoint:
Yes. The Soviet system had inherent political and economic flaws that made it unsustainable.

When the Soviet Union expired on the last day of 1991, a variety of trends and forces arrived at their logical outcome. Seventy-four years of communist rule proved that the Union of Soviet Socialist Republics (U.S.S.R.) was doomed in every sense important to the survival of a nation. Politically and economically, the dictatorship established by the Bolshevik coup d'état (November 1917) was unsustainable over the long term and, despite its own boasting and the sober predictions of most Western observers, could never have survived into the twenty-first century.

Terror lay at the center of the Soviet system. The establishment of communist rule in Russia depended on nothing less for its survival. Within days of the Bolsheviks' seizure of power, they subjected their real and potential political opponents to intense coercion and intimidation and quickly applied terrorist methods to cow into submission the independent media, religious life, cultural sphere, and all other aspects of civil society. Measures that began as arbitrary and improvised, and that the Bolsheviks claimed would be "temporary," soon grew into a vast system of repression presided over by revolutionary leader Vladimir Lenin and his successor Josef Stalin. With a powerful and unchecked secret police, a gigantic network of concentration camps, and far-reaching government control over the lives and minds of its citizens, the Soviet Union sank into a totalitarian abyss that destroyed millions of lives.

The scope of this terror betrayed an important fact. The U.S.S.R.'s revolutionary leadership believed from its first days in power that terrorist methods were their only reliable means of control. And they were right. Despite determined attempts to evangelize communist ideology to the Soviet people, capture minds and hearts through programs of education and modernization, and inculcate a Soviet patriotism, arbitrary repression was their only real means of remaining in power. Yet, over time the iron will and malevolent sense of purpose required to maintain this system faltered. On the eve of World War II (1939–1945), even Stalin acknowledged that terror was counterproductive to effective government and announced at a 1939 Communist Party Congress that its use would be curtailed. This admission did not stop him from continuing to employ terror during and after the war, but his statement reflected a growing body of elite opinion. After Stalin's death in 1953, his successors swiftly eliminated the dangerous secret police chief, Lavrenty Beria, and renounced the use of terror. Nikita Khrushchev, who won the power struggle after Stalin's death, followed this policy and partially exposed some of the state's crimes in a February 1956 speech to the party elite. Under Khrushchev's leadership the prison camps emptied, the state's arbitrary powers were somewhat curtailed, and a new law code introduced at least the pretense, if not the actual fact, of civil rights and due legal process.

While Lenin and Stalin had the tremendous power and will to crush any actual or imagined resistance, their successors, beginning with Khrushchev, lost both and became vulnerable to dissent. The Soviet government's abandonment of mass terror allowed dissenters to grow in number. Direct criticism of the regime remained a crime, but the corresponding punishments declined in severity as well as in deterrent value. Dissident activity that would have resulted in one's disappearance and secret murder in earlier decades instead brought on official harassment, shorter prison terms, subjection to psychological quackery, and exile in the 1960s, 1970s, and 1980s. These punishments were still terrible violations of human rights and were certainly characteristic of an ugly authoritarian regime, yet their relative leniency and reactive nature ensured that the Soviet government would never be able to keep a lid on dissent. Official harassment and shorter prison sentences left dissidents to function more freely in society, and allowed them to interact with each other and with a growing numbers of foreign visitors who could relate their stories and political statements to the West. The Soviet government's use of psychology to repress dissidents who were held to be "morally sick" or "social misfits" exposed Moscow to tremendous international criticism, not only by other nations but also by the international scientific community. Exile removed dissidents from Soviet society only to deliver them to free countries where they could spread word of conditions in the U.S.S.R. and continue their activities and criticism unhindered. Technicalities of the Khrushchev law code, furthermore, gave defendants the right to trials that widely publicized the regime's treatment of dissidents. Consequently, more and more Soviet citizens were emboldened to speak out, knowing that reprisals against them would become national and international news. Indeed, as the Cold War reached its apogee, Moscow's treatment of dissidents became a major issue in its international relations, a factor linked explicitly to trade and arms-control negotiations with the West. When Soviet leader Mikhail Gorbachev increased political democracy and freedom of expression in the late 1980s, the dissident community used the concessions not, as Gorbachev had hoped, to help reform the Soviet system and rejuvenate communist ideology, but instead to attack communism per se and undermine the existence of the Soviet state. Lacking the will and desire to crack down on the emerging anticommunist consensus within his country, Gorbachev's reforms spiraled out of control. By the time some of his hard-liner opponents in the leadership attempted to remove him in an August 1991 coup, communists had lost any pretense to govern by popular mandate, exposure of their crimes had become total and unrestrained, and their seventy-year-old rule of the U.S.S.R.'s minority nationalities had all but ended. Devoid of legitimacy, and rightly seen by the majority of the Soviet people as morally bankrupt, the linchpin provided by the Communist Party disintegrated and the country collapsed.

Dissent alone did not bring about the Soviet collapse. Lenin seized power with the conviction that state ownership of the economy would lead to material abundance and social harmony. Yet, as he and his successors tried to translate theory into practice, their economic policies merely contributed to the U.S.S.R.'s decline. Criminalizing commerce, collectivizing farmland, and placing all economic decisions in government hands deprived the Soviets of the very initiative, experience, creativity, and incentive that the capitalist world employed to compete with and ultimately defeat them. In contrast to tsarist Russia's burgeoning economic development in the decades before the 1917 Revolution, Soviet economic history was a long, sad story of squandered resources, wasted talents, embarrassing shortages, and slow decline. Industrial management rested with Communist Party hacks whose only asset was their ideological orthodoxy and whose only concerns were keeping the Party's good favor and jealously guarding their privileges. The forced nationalization and collectivization of agriculture physically eliminated the country's best farmers and reduced the rest to day laborers with no compelling motivation or incentive. Private enterprise remained illegal in virtually any form, and most Soviet citizens had to rely on their own wits and vast black markets to meet even basic needs. Indeed, many of the Soviet Union's greatest economic "achievements," including its ambitious industrialization campaign in the 1930s, its impressive World War II military production, and its successful atomic energy and space flight programs, depended on the acquisition, borrowing, or theft of capitalist industrial products, technical know-how, and managerial experience.

By the 1980s these factors began to take their toll. The Soviet Union's failure to compete with capitalist skill and innovation caused its entire economy to lag far behind that of the West, and the gap only grew with time. Dramatic new developments in information technology, consumer industry, health care, transportation, infrastructure, popular culture, and other areas impacting daily life largely passed the U.S.S.R. by. Widespread environmental damage—which, in an oppressive police state, could not be checked by civic action or independent "watchdogs"—harmed public health, polluted landscapes, and jeopardized future well-being. As impoverished Soviet citizens became more and more aware of the West's superior material quality of life—a process that was itself largely a product of the information age—domestic unrest grew. Convinced that their government and its ideology had failed and deceived them, many coveted the West's prosperity and associated their ability to achieve it with fundamental political and economic change.

The Soviet government also became deeply preoccupied with the implications of the West's economic superiority. It worried about the discontent generated by the increasingly obvious economic disparity and took measures to curtail popular dissatisfaction. Propaganda campaigns tried to persuade the Soviet people that they were better off than Westerners, or promised them that despite their woes, they would live better in the future. Western radio transmissions were jammed. Western popular culture was censored and disparaged. Travel abroad, even to other communist countries, was virtually forbidden. Contact with foreigners outside official circumstances remained a risky undertaking. Yet, no matter what Moscow did, its people still craved Marlboro cigarettes, McDonald's fast food, rock music, and *Playboy* and only resented their government the more for trying to forbid them. Soviet leaders began to look like desperate old men who would do anything to keep themselves in power and the people they ruled in poverty and ignorance.

The strategic ramifications of the economic chasm were even more serious. By the 1980s a new generation of high-tech weaponry created an insurmountable gap in military technology. Several proxy conflicts, in which exported U.S. and Soviet hardware squared off on Third World battlefields, demonstrated the marked inferiority of Soviet weaponry. American advances in computer, satellite, laser, missile, and other technologies translated into huge combat advantages, and U.S. president Ronald Reagan's 1983 announcement of the Strategic Defense Initiative (SDI), a prospective space-based missile defense system, threatened to neutralize the effectiveness of the U.S.S.R.'s nuclear arsenal, its only remaining strategic asset. As Gorbachev and many other Soviet leaders realized then and admitted later, economic weakness left them with no hope of competing or even standing their ground in the arms race. Reducing Cold War tension to cut the U.S.S.R.'s crushing military budget and promote economic development became a centerpiece of Gorbachev's strategy. Yet, by pursuing this goal, Gorbachev was forced to abandon strategic positions that the U.S.S.R. had long held, in some cases for decades. In 1989–1991 Soviet troops, advisers, supplies, and subsidies were withdrawn not only from the recent Cold War battlefields in Afghanistan and southern Africa, but also from the U.S.S.R.'s oldest client regimes in Eastern Europe, North Korea, and Cuba. As the contraction of Soviet power continued, the military made no effort to defend the unity of the U.S.S.R. itself and failed to support the anti-Gorbachev hard-liners who wanted to keep it together. These momentous changes were direct consequences of the Soviet Union's inability to modernize its economy; their result was its complete collapse.

The importance of confrontation in the collapse of the Soviet Union was yet another long-term process. Although the West's most bullish anticommunism and greatest military superiority emerged in the 1980s, both were the end result of decades of justified suspicion of and resistance to Moscow. In their doctrinaire adherence to revolutionary Marxism, the Bolsheviks arrived in power determined not only to transform Russia but also to fulfill what they viewed as their historic mission to export communism to the rest of the world. Of course this strategy set them at odds with the entire international community. Contrary to later claims that the Bolsheviks were the misunderstood victims of narrow-minded and aggressive anticommunists, their messianic fervor informed all other governments that they were enemies and threatened them with subversion, war, and overthrow, all planned in Moscow. Indeed, as soon as 1919 Soviet-supported communists briefly established revolutionary governments in Germany and Hungary. Foreign communist parties were coordinated under Moscow's control through the Communist International, established in 1919, and until 1991 communists in Europe and elsewhere executed political intrigues, labor unrest, assassinations, and terrorist activities with Moscow's blessing. Just what were foreign powers supposed to think? International communism openly proclaimed its goals of destroying the diplomatic order that they had fashioned and of overturning the social and economic principles that guided their societies. It only followed that many in the West would advocate intervention against the Bolsheviks in the Russian Civil War, refuse to acknowledge the Soviet government's legitimacy, and, even if most Western governments eventually established diplomatic relations with Moscow, isolate and ostracize the Soviets in the international arena.

The rise of Adolf Hitler's Germany and the danger it posed in World War II produced a tentative cooperation between the U.S.S.R. and the West, but the end of that conflict only renewed tensions. As the Soviets attempted to expand their military presence throughout the world, installed loyal communist regimes throughout Eastern Europe, and lent assistance to emerging communist movements elsewhere, Western leaders by consensus viewed their actions as a renewal of their ambition to impose communism upon the entire world. By 1947 the United States formally committed itself to resisting Soviet expansion on a global scale, a strategy that came to be known as "containment." Two years later the United States formed the North Atlantic Treaty Organization (NATO), an anti-Soviet defensive alliance, which eventually included almost every country in Europe outside the Soviet bloc, as well as Canada and Turkey. Washington made similar anticommunist defensive arrangements with Japan, most other nations of the Pacific Rim, and its Latin American neighbors. When the U.S.S.R. attempted to project power into the emerging "third" (in other words, nonaligned) world, the United States and its allies responded to the challenge directly and with great effort. Indeed, Soviet advances and pretensions were so great that even other communist powers, including China, the most populous country, and Yugoslavia, openly broke with Moscow and looked toward favorable relations with the United States and its allies. Although the Soviets in some cases successfully sponsored the emergence of communist regimes in the Third World in the 1960s and 1970s, these successes convinced Western leaders and peoples that Moscow had to be dealt with not merely through vigilant containment but with an aggressive "rolling back" of Soviet gains. Heightened support for anticommunist resistance movements, renewed military intervention in the Third World, determined economic warfare, and engagement in a formidable arms race left the Soviets with the unenviable choice between fighting and losing or retreating and accepting quiet death. They chose the latter.

–PAUL DU QUENOY,
GEORGETOWN UNIVERSITY

COLLAPSE OF THE
SOVIET UNION

GORBACHEV RESIGNS

Below is the resignation speech given by Soviet leader Mikhail Gorbachev on 25 December 1991:

Dear fellow countrymen, compatriots. Due to the situation which has evolved as a result of the formation of the Commonwealth of Independent States, I hereby discontinue my activities at the post of President of the Union of Soviet Socialist Republics.

I am making this decision out of considerations based on principle. I have firmly stood for independence, self-rule of nations, for the sovereignty of the republics, but at the same time for preservation of the union state, the unity of the country.

Events went a different way. The policy prevailed of dismembering this country and disuniting the state, with which I cannot agree. And after the Alma-Ata meeting and the decisions taken there, my position on this matter has not changed. Besides, it is my conviction that decisions of this caliber should have been made on the basis of popular will.

However, I will do all I can to insure that the agreements that were signed there lead toward real concord in society and facilitate the exit out of this crisis and the process of reform. Shackled by Bureaucracy— Addressing you for the last time in the capacity of President of the U.S.S.R., I consider it necessary to express my evaluation of the road we have traveled since 1985, especially as there are a lot of contradictory, superficial and subjective judgments on that matter.

Fate had it that when I found myself at the head of the state, it was already clear that all was not well in the country. We had a lot of everything—land, oil and gas, other natural resources—and there was intellect and talent in abundance. Yet we lived much worse than developed countries and keep falling behind them more and more. The reason was obvious even then. This country was suffocating in the shackles of the bureaucratic-command system, doomed to serve ideology and bear the terrible burden of the arms race. It had reached the limit of

its possibilities. All attempts at partial reform—and there had been many—had suffered defeat, one after another. We could not go on living like that.

Everything had to be changed radically.

That is why not once—not once—have I regretted that I did not take advantage of the post of [Communist Party] general secretary to rule as czar for several years. I considered it irresponsible and amoral. I realized that to start reforms of such a scale in a society such as ours was a most difficult and even a risky thing. But even now, I am convinced that the democratic reform that we launched in the spring of 1985 was historically correct. Society Liberated Itself—The process of renovating this country and radical changes in the world community turned out to be far more complicated than could be expected.

However, what has been done ought to be given its due.

This society acquired freedom, liberated itself politically and spiritually, and this is the foremost achievement—which we have not yet understood completely, because we have not learned to use freedom. However, work of historic significance has been accomplished.

The totalitarian system that deprived the country of an opportunity to become successful and prosperous long ago has been eliminated. A breakthrough has been achieved on the way to democratic changes. Free elections, freedom of the press, religious freedoms, representative organs of power, a multiparty [system] became a reality. Human rights are recognized as the supreme principle.

Movement has been started toward a multi-tier economy, and the equality of all forms of ownership is being established. Within the framework of land reform, peasantry began to reemerge as a class. Farmers have appeared, billions of hectares of land are being given to urbanites and rural residents alike. Economic freedom of the producer has been legalized, and entrepreneurship, shareholding, privatization are gaining momentum. In turning the economy toward a market, it is important to remember that all this is done for the sake of the individual. At this difficult time, all should be done for his social protection, especially for senior citizens and children.

We live in a new world. The Cold War has ended, the arms race has stopped, as has the insane militarization that mutilated our economy, public psyche and morals. The threat of world war has been removed. Once again I want to stress that on my part everything was done during the transition period to preserve reliable control of the nuclear weapons.

We opened ourselves to the rest of the world, abandoned the practices of interfering in others' internal affairs and using troops outside this country, and we were reciprocated with trust, solidarity and respect. We have become one of the main foundations for the transformation of modern civilization on peaceful democratic grounds.

Opposed by Obsolete Forces—The nations and the peoples (of this country) gained real freedom of self-determination. The search for a democratic reformation of the multinational state brought us to the threshold of concluding a new union treaty. All these changes demanded immense strain. They were carried out with sharp struggle, with growing resistance from the old, the obsolete forces: the former party-state structures, the economic elite, as well as our habits, ideological superstitions, the psychology of sponging and leveling everyone out.

They stumbled on our intolerance, low level of political culture, fear of change. That is why we lost so much time. The old system collapsed before the new one had time to begin working, and the crisis in the society became even more acute. I am aware of the dissatisfaction with the present hard situation, of the sharp criticism of authorities at all levels including my personal activities.

But once again I'd like to stress: Radical changes in such a vast country, and a country with such a heritage, cannot pass painlessly without difficulties and shake-up.

The August coup brought the overall crisis to its ultimate limit. The most dangerous thing about the crisis is the collapse of statehood. And today I am worried by our people's loss of the citizenship of a great country. The consequences may turn out to be very hard for everyone.

Heirs of a Great Civilization—I think it is vitally important to preserve the democratic achievements of the last years. They have been paid for by the suffering of our whole history, our tragic experience. They must not be given up under any circumstances or any pretext, otherwise all our hopes for the better will be buried. I am telling you all this honestly and straightforwardly because this is my moral duty.

Today I'd like to express my gratitude to all citizens who supported the policy of renovating the country, got involved in the implementation of the democratic reforms. I am grateful to statesmen, public and political figures, millions of people abroad, those who understood our intentions, gave their support and met us halfway. I thank them for their sincere cooperation with us.

I am leaving my post with apprehension, but also with hope, with faith in you, your wisdom and force of spirit. We are the heirs of a great civilization, and its rebirth into a new, modern and dignified life now depends on one and all. I wish to thank with all my heart all those who have stood together with me all these years for the fair and good cause. Some mistakes could surely have been avoided. Many things could have been done better. But I am convinced that sooner or later our common efforts will bear fruit, our nations will live in a prosperous and democratic society. I wish everyone all the best.

Source: *"The Resignation of Mikhail Gorbachev, Russia,"* Freeserve <http://freeserve.i-resign.com/uk/halloffame/viewHOF_22.asp>.

COLLAPSE OF THE SOVIET UNION

Viewpoint:
No. The Soviet Union had the potential to remain stable; it was brought down by foreign pressures and bad leadership decisions.

An overwhelming consensus among historians suggests that the breakup of the Union of Soviet Socialist Republics (U.S.S.R.) in 1991 was the most significant geopolitical transformation the world witnessed since World War II (1939–1945). Yet, it is one of the most controversial developments of contemporary history. A nuclear superpower with a global presence, massive manpower and economic potential, an enormous military and vast arsenal of armaments, disappeared without firing a shot. As former U.S. secretary of state Henry Kissinger noted, "No world power had ever disintegrated so totally and so rapidly without losing a war."

Although some historians argue that the Soviet collapse occurred mainly because of the systemic flaws in the communist system, there is also a view that credits U.S.-led external pressures with undermining the Soviet Union's international posture, weakening the Soviet economy, and destabilizing the communist regime. Adherents of this approach credit the Reagan administration's stern military and economic pressure on the U.S.S.R. as well as harsh ideological attacks as key elements in forcing the Soviets into decline and subsequent collapse, a condition that would not otherwise have developed.

The Reagan administration outlined basic elements and goals of its anti-Soviet strategy in 1982–1983 based on an understanding of the growing disparity between overextended global and military ambitions of the Kremlin on the one hand and mounting Soviet internal economic and resource problems on the other. The new strategy in many ways presented a radical break with the policies of previous U.S. administrations. It emphasized the political, economic, and moral weaknesses of the Soviet system and its inevitable breakdown if the U.S.S.R. were seriously challenged. The strategy also reflected the fact that while the economic sphere was a major weakness of the Soviets, it, at the same time, was a huge advantage for America. As Caspar Weinberger, U.S. Secretary of Defense at the time, recalled, "we adopted a comprehensive strategy that included economic warfare to attack the Soviet weakness."

Negotiations with the Soviet Union would be considered only after restoring U.S. military strength with American technological and economic advantages, reversing the West's posture of the détente-era retreat, and mounting political and ideological pressure on the Communist bloc. Another innovative element was the readiness of the United States to engage the Soviets and their clients in costly military conflicts in the Third World, as well as to challenge the Soviet domination of Eastern Europe and assist anti-communist forces around the world. The primary goal of the strategy was rather simple—to force the Soviets to choose from among three options: abandoning their global ambitions, withdrawing from the confrontation with the West, or facing increasingly devastating pressures with the possibility of complete collapse. In sum, it was a strategic offensive based on the coordinated use of economic, military, technological, and diplomatic factors against the Soviets. The strategy was designed to shift the focus of the superpower struggle to the Soviet bloc and even the Soviet Union itself.

The defensive buildup was a major element in the unfolding confrontation with the Soviets. Between 1980 and 1985 U.S. military expenditures doubled and as a result exceeded those of the U.S.S.R. for the first time since the late 1960s. Of much importance were the reinforcement of the strategic arsenal and, particularly, the rapid rise of research and development programs. The aim was to invest in a new generation of expensive high-tech weapon systems that would render Soviet military equipment obsolete. This strategy presented an enormous problem for Moscow. Between 1981 and 1985 the Soviets raised their defense budget by 45 percent, but their expenditures were insufficient to match the American challenge.

In 1982 the U.S. Army adopted the AirLand Battle doctrine—which capitalized on the use of American improvements in electronics and communications equipment—aimed to surprise, outmaneuver, disorient, and defeat an enemy. The United States strengthened its military posture across the world, particularly in Western Europe, the Persian Gulf, and the Far East. Thanks to the endorsement of U.S. allies and despite the pacifist protests, the North Atlantic Treaty Organization (NATO) managed to deploy U.S. Pershing and Tomahawk intermediate-range missiles in Europe in 1983. The new American missiles, far superior to their Soviet counterparts, changed the military balance in Europe and placed a wide range of Soviet command, control, and communications targets under effective threat.

The United States also actively capitalized on the huge technological gap between the superpowers. According to U.S. Department of Defense assessments, the U.S.S.R. was ten years behind America in computers and trailed in many of the most important technologies: electro-optic sensors, robotics, stealth, and so on. In high-tech weaponry, the Soviet Union was in 1983 a generation behind the United States and its allies, according to the former Chief of the Soviet General Staff Marshal Nikolai Ogarkov. Anatoly Cherniaev, an aide to Soviet leader Mikhail Gorbachev, estimated the Soviet technological gap with the West was ten to thirty years.

Also in 1983 U.S. president Ronald Reagan announced the Strategic Defense Initiative (SDI), which was intended to protect U.S. territory from Soviet intercontinental ballistic missiles (ICBMs) by destroying them in space. The far-reaching goal of SDI was twofold. On the one hand, an effective antimissile defense would make the ICBMs—the bulk of the Soviet nuclear forces—irrelevant and powerless, decisively changing the overall strategic balance to favor the United States. On the other hand, SDI presumed the full-scale use of U.S. technological advances in the arms race with the Soviet Union. While the possibility of creating an effective antimissile shield was a matter of a great controversy at the time, SDI contributed to the U.S.S.R.'s collapse, conjuring up for an already declining Soviet economy the prospect of an enormous burden by forcing it to participate in the new round of the high-tech rivalry. In this way SDI virtually threatened to bankrupt the Soviet military- industrial complex and was, as former British prime minister Margaret Thatcher put it, "one vital factor in the ending of the Cold War."

On the geopolitical front of the U.S. offensive against the Soviet Union there were two situations of critical importance for the Soviets: the crisis in Poland (1980–1981) and the war in Afghanistan, which the Soviets began in 1979. Since 1980 Poland—the largest Soviet satellite in Eastern Europe—was an arena of open mass struggle, led by an independent trade union, Solidarity, against the ruling communist regime. In December 1981 martial law was declared and the regime, decisively supported by the Soviets, banned the opposition. As Edwin Meese III, Reagan's policy adviser from 1981 to 1985, mentioned in his memoirs, Poland was "one of the earliest test cases for the president's anti-Soviet strategy." The Central Intelligence Agency (CIA) in concert with the Vatican, and cooperating with French Intelligence, organized covert logistic, intelligence, and financial support to Solidarity (AFL-CIO efforts, as well as help from Sweden, were instrumental in this area) that ensured its survival underground. The operation was a part of a wide range of American activities aiming to undermine Soviet domination in Eastern Europe. At the same time U.S. sanctions against Poland, declared in response to the introduction of martial law, prompted the Soviets to provide the military regime in Poland with emergency financial aid of $1 billion to $2 billion per year. Polish authorities and their Soviet patrons,

however, proved unable to suppress political opposition. By 1989 the communists were forced to enter into negotiations with the opposition, which led to the election of the first noncommunist government in Eastern Europe since 1945.

Covert CIA operations played a decisive role in supporting Afghan resistance to the Soviet occupation and the pro-Soviet regime in the country. The CIA—in concert with Britain, Pakistan, Saudi Arabia, and China—provided training for the Afghan *mujahideen* (holy warriors) and gave them financial, military, and logistic support. The United States also used CIA spy satellites to make guerrilla operations more effective and help them target strategically important areas of the country. The United States sponsored the largest paramilitary operation in CIA history, with total estimated costs at $3 billion. All these measures, particularly supplies of high-tech weaponry, allowed the United States to shift the focus of the Afghan war from harassing the Soviets to turning them back. By the spring of 1984 Afghan resistance took the war into neighboring Soviet Central Asia. By 1986 the cost of the war for the Soviets reached $4 billion per year. By 1989, when Soviet troops withdrew from the country, the U.S.S.R. had lost some 13,000 men killed. The defeat in Afghanistan had far-reaching revolutionary effects, discrediting the Soviet military and undermining the stability of the communist regime.

The U.S. economic "assault" on the U.S.S.R. unfolded from several directions. The first was the U.S.-initiated efforts to reduce dramatically hard-currency earnings by limiting Soviet energy exports to the West and by manipulating oil prices. By 1983 oil and gas exports made up between 60 and 80 percent of Soviet hard-currency earnings. At the same time, the main vulnerability of the Soviet energy industry was its almost total dependence on Western technology. The Americans instituted a comprehensive global campaign to reduce Soviet access to Western technology and promoted a technological disinformation campaign designed to undermine the Soviet economy.

The main tool of the U.S. strategy to coordinate Western efforts to curtail this flow of technology was the Coordinating Committee for Mutual Export Controls (COCOM), which included the NATO countries (except Iceland) and Japan. In 1982 COCOM banned the export of critically important technologies to the U.S.S.R., including advanced computers and electronics, and limited technical and other contacts with the Soviets. The United States also pressured neutral countries—particularly Austria, Sweden, and Switzerland—to tighten control of high-tech exports to the U.S.S.R. by threatening to leave them without access to U.S.-licensed technology.

The technological shutoff had a dramatic effect on the Soviet oil and gas industry, particularly on one of the most ambitious Soviet projects—the Siberian pipeline to Western Europe. In 1982, in response to Soviet involvement in the Polish crisis and despite protests from its European allies, the United States imposed an embargo on technology for the pipeline. Historians note that this act was a real declaration of economic war on the Soviet Union, one with devastating consequences. Instead of earning $8 billion to $10 billion per year from oil exports by 1985 and $15 billion to $30 billion by 1990, as the Soviets expected, Moscow lost $15 billion to $20 billion in revenue because of the resulting delays. The Soviets tried to complete the pipeline without U.S. technology and failed, at an additional cost of $1 billion.

The third direction of the U.S. economic war dealt with one more crucial factor for Soviet hard-currency earnings—oil prices on world markets. To lower prices the United States needed cooperation from Saudi Arabia—one of the world's main oil producers. The United States intensified diplomatic contacts with the Saudis, increased military assistance, gave Saudi Arabia security guarantees, and coordinated its policies in the Persian Gulf and Afghanistan with Saudi Arabia. In return, in late 1985 the Saudis rapidly increased production, and oil prices dropped from $30 per barrel in November 1985 to $12 per barrel in May 1986, with devastating costs to the Soviet energy sector. The Soviets lost more than $10 billion a year—almost half of their previous earnings from oil exports. Thus by 1985–1986 expected technology supplies, credits, and hard currency from the West were drying up or being cut back. The Soviet economic crisis was aggravated tremendously.

On the diplomatic front, the United States successfully exploited several of Moscow's blunders—such as the deployment of SS-20 missiles targeting Western Europe (late 1970s), the occupation of Afghanistan (1979–1989), and the shooting down of a South Korean passenger plane (1983)—to unite all major centers of power in the world, including Western Europe, the oil-rich Arab countries, China, and Japan, into a de facto anti-Soviet coalition. The United States intentionally used an aggressive rhetoric, unprecedented since the early 1950s. This strategy of psychological and ideological warfare as well as aforementioned U.S. pressures fueled indecision and fear inside the Kremlin, paralyzed the will of the Soviet leadership, and forced it to concede. Additionally, U.S. propaganda efforts ("public diplomacy") actively used Western examples of prosperity and freedom to undermine the Soviet regime.

Personally, President Reagan played an important role in the anti-Soviet crusade, particularly in its psychological warfare. Reagan's assertive anticommunist declarations, motivated by his instinct and strong belief in the fatal inevitability of a Soviet crash, presented Moscow with a surprise. Reagan's self-confidence and optimism were a striking contrast to the pre-Gorbachev gerontocrats in the Kremlin, who were more concerned with their own physical survival than with reacting to the American challenge. When Reagan was asked why he failed to meet with Gorbachev's predecessors, his answer was, "they kept dying on me."

As historian Paul M. Kennedy noted, "historically, none of the overextended, multinational empires ever retreated to its own ethnic base until they had been defeated in a great power war." Theoretically speaking, the Soviet leadership, facing enormous external pressures, could have used its immense military abroad and security apparatus domestically to hold power, regardless of the cost. Yet, as Princeton historian Stephen Kotkin mentioned, the Soviets "did not even attempt to stage a cynical foreign war to rally support for the regime." Many historians credited Gorbachev and his *perestroika* (in other words, domestic Soviet developments) for the relatively peaceful collapse of the Soviet monster. For sure, many ills of the communist regime, which Gorbachev tried to reform, had a domestic nature; they were inherent in the system itself. However, the United States masterfully and decisively exploited Soviet vulnerabilities and exacerbated the U.S.S.R.'s crisis. Moreover, the United States forced the Soviets to face growing international isolation. As Eduard Shevardnadze, former Soviet foreign minister, admitted, the race for absolute parity with almost the rest of the world and the maintenance of a global military presence had brought the Soviet Union to the brink of economic catastrophe.

The U.S. anti-Soviet strategy had many forms: secret diplomacy, covert actions, an intense arms race, economic pressure, demoralizing psychological warfare, and propaganda. Moscow found itself under the enormously destructive effects of a high-tech arms race, geopolitical setbacks in crucially important areas of the world, hard-currency shortages, a Western technological embargo, and growing international isolation. Thus, one could say that Gorbachev's ill-fated

Soviet soldiers resting
during a lull in
intercommunal riots,
Dushanbe, Tajikistan,
in 1989

(Hulton Deutsch Archive)

❀ПРИМЕРОЧНЫЕ КАБИНЫ❀

COLLAPSE OF THE
SOVIET UNION

reforms were, to a large extent, late attempts to respond to external pressures.

The U.S. anti-Soviet assault was a nontraditional kind of war. It was waged on many fronts: economic, geostrategic, and ideological, as well as in an intense arms race. To their misfortune, Soviet leaders, including Gorbachev, failed to comprehend the multifaceted nature of this war and the comprehensive character of U.S. strategy, in which all elements mutually reinforced each other. In the absence of massive U.S. pressure, the Soviet Union may well have survived into the twenty-first century. Had the United States continued its 1970s policies of détente, the U.S.S.R. and its communist system may have grown stronger and more entrenched. The pundits who predicted the continued existence of the Soviet Union, however, were wrong.

-PETER RAINOW,
SAN MATEO, CALIFORNIA

References

John Lewis Gaddis, *The United States and the End of the Cold War: Implications, Reconsiderations, Provocations* (New York: Oxford University Press, 1992).

Paul M. Kennedy, *The Rise and Fall of the Great Powers: Economic Change and Military Conflict from 1500 to 2000* (New York: Random House, 1987).

Stephen Kotkin, *Armageddon Averted: The Soviet Collapse, 1970–2000* (Oxford: Oxford University Press, 2001).

David M. Kotz and Fred Weir, *Revolution from Above: The Demise of the Soviet System* (London & New York : Routledge, 1997).

Edwin Meese III, *With Reagan: The Inside Story* (Washington, D.C.: Regnery Gateway, 1992).

Don Oberdorfer, *The Turn: From the Cold War to a New Era: The United States and the Soviet Union, 1983–1990* (New York: Poseidon Press, 1991).

Peter Schweizer, *Victory: The Reagan Administration's Secret Strategy that Hastened the Collapse of the Soviet Union* (New York: Atlantic Monthly Press, 1994).

Paul A. Winters, ed., *The Collapse of the Soviet Union* (San Diego, Cal.: Greenhaven Press, 1999).

COLLAPSE OF TSARIST RUSSIA

Was the fall of the Russian monarchy in 1917 an inevitable result of the tsarist government's inability to deal with political, social, and economic change?

Viewpoint: Yes. Russia's undemocratic monarchy, its fragmented society, and its troubled economy made radical revolution inescapable.

Viewpoint: No. The defeats and failures of domestic leadership during World War I drove Russia to revolution.

By early 1917 the military defeats and social strains of World War I had created a political crisis in Imperial Russia. Over several unseasonably warm days in February and March of that year, angry crowds gathered in the capital of Petrograd (formerly and once again St. Petersburg), and the capital garrison refused to suppress the disturbances. Isolated at military headquarters near the front, Tsar Nicholas II did not realize the gravity of the situation until too late. He waited too long to return to the seat of his government and was forced to abdicate in Pskov, where his train was diverted.

Historians have often wondered if Nicholas's abdication was inevitable. The Soviets, who came to power in November 1917, and sympathetic Marxist historians have argued that it was an unavoidable step in a scientifically determined progression of history. In their view the old-regime autocracy gave way to a "bourgeois-democratic" government that in turn gave way to socialism. While most Western historians disagree with this dogmatic explanation, many nevertheless believe that Imperial Russia was doomed. That is, its highly authoritarian character, its reliance on anachronistic social structures, its inability to cope with rapid social and economic change, and its general inflexibility were bound to result in violent upheaval. Thus, they argue, the nature of the tsarist regime contained the seeds of its destruction.

Yet, an emerging school of thought on late Imperial Russia argues that, despite the persistence of authoritarian political structures, there seem to have been many promising developments in Russian social and political life, which might have allowed Imperial Russia to evolve peacefully into a modern democratic country if the pressures of World War I had not led to the revolutions of 1917. The creation of a national representative body (the Duma), which first met in 1906, the increasing activism of local governmental bodies, the growth of an independent civil society, and a vast expansion of educational institutions were a few of many developments that suggest Russia was moving toward social and economic modernization and political liberalization. In this view, if the disasters of World War I had been avoided, Russia might have followed a peaceful course to a prosperous future.

Viewpoint:
Yes. Russia's undemocratic monarchy, its fragmented society, and its troubled economy made radical revolution inescapable.

In November 1913 moderate Octobrist Party leader Aleksandr Guchkov warned that Nicholas II's government was carrying Russia "toward an inevitable and grave catastrophe." He was right about the catastrophe. Historians, however, differ on whether it was inevitable. "Optimists" point to developments such as the 1905 creation of the Duma, a quasi-parliamentary body that met for the first time in 1906, and Prime Minister Petr Stolypin's 1906 land-privatization reforms as proof that Russia was progressing politically, socially, and economically in the years before World War I. If the war had not intervened, they argue, Russia could have transformed itself into a modern constitutional monarchy. "Pessimists" maintain that the war was only the final blow to an antiquated autocracy incapable of solving Russia's many social and economic problems.

The pessimists are right. By 1913 the collapse of the autocracy had long been inevitable. Nicholas II could not solve Russia's problems and would not cede power to those who thought they could. The coming war was certain to overtax Russian resources and exacerbate popular dissatisfaction with the existing regime. Furthermore, Russians from all walks of life considered revolution not only a possibility but a probability. Their expectation that things would change was the most important factor in the revolution of February–March 1917. Once the tsar had been overthrown, personalities, socio-economic circumstances, and popular expectations led inexorably to the Bolshevik Revolution that occurred in November.

The prerevolutionary Russian government was incompetent. As historian Dominic Lieven has written, Nicholas "could not co-ordinate and manage his government effectively but was in a position to stop anyone else from attempting to do the job for him." He viewed with suspicion any proposal that threatened to infringe on the autocratic power he had inherited. Most of his advisers and top officials rose and fell based on their loyalty to him rather than their merits, while the bureaucracy they oversaw was inefficient and riddled with corruption. After Nicholas dissolved the first two popularly elected Dumas in 1906 and 1907 and rewrote the election law to ensure that a disproportionate number of Duma representatives came from "trustworthy" social groups, especially the nobil-

ity, the members of the Duma learned from their predecessors' mistakes, preferring to cooperate with mediocrity rather than put forth any significant legislation of their own. Government activity, in Guchkov's words, consisted of "a conflict of personal intrigues and aspirations, a continual attempt to settle personal accounts, and dissensions between various departments," so that "the ship of state has lost its course, and is aimlessly tossing on the waves."

Of course, these circumstances were not peculiar to Russia, nor to revolutionary situations. Many incompetent regimes throughout the ages have muddled along in spite of themselves. When they are faced with serious problems, however, they are likely to falter. Russia did have a serious problem: chronic discontent. Peasants wanted more land. Workers wanted higher wages, better working conditions, and the political right to articulate their demands. The intelligentsia and the "middle classes" wanted more say in the government. Revolutionaries from various walks of life wanted socialism to replace capitalism, or they sought the abolition of the central government. Some wanted both. These groups had tasted power during the Revolution of 1905 and smaller strikes and uprisings in later years, as well as through participation in local-government institutions (*zemstvo;* plural: *zemstva*) permitted by the tsarist government and in voluntary organizations. They wanted more participation in government.

In a 1914 memorandum to Nicholas, Interior Minister Petr Durnovo attributed such discontent to "the excessive nervousness and spirit of opposition of our society." Indeed, historian Richard Pipes has argued that "the Revolution was the result not of insufferable conditions but of irreconcilable attitudes, of a clash between those who wanted sweeping changes in government and a government whose ruler refused to change anything." It is irrelevant, however, whether Durnovo and Pipes were correct in implying that Russians were overreacting to their country's difficulties. It is irrelevant that generations of scholars have measured the extent to which Russian society was becoming open and democratic, and that statistics showing Russian economic progress under Nicholas may be more reliable than statistics indicating economic stagnation. What is relevant was the belief among Russians that their lives could be better, and that in failing to bring about that improvement, the state proved itself inadequate. The omnipresence of this belief made Russia susceptible to revolution even before its military defeats, supply problems, and economic privations during World War I. As Guchkov put it, "people of the most sharply opposed political views, of the most varied social groups, all agree with a rare, an unprec-

COLLAPSE OF TSARIST RUSSIA

edented unanimity" that Russia in 1913 was approaching catastrophe.

In fact, a revolution was inevitable precisely because everyone believed it was coming. Members of the Duma warned of it: "Never has the authority of the Imperial government sunk so low," wrote Guchkov; "Not only has the government failed to arouse sympathy or confidence; it is incapable of inspiring even fear." The media trumpeted the coming revolution. One article by a liberal politician, Vasilii Maklakov, compared Nicholas II to a "mad chauffeur," ignoring passengers who were more capable drivers and piloting the automobile of state headlong down steep roads toward catastrophe. In urban areas such as Petrograd, where the revolution eventually began, residents who could not read newspapers heard articles expressing similar sentiments read aloud or discussed in public. Even if they supported the monarchy, many people started to believe the widespread voices of doom. Thus, when spontaneous protests over bread shortages and working conditions reached a critical point in February 1917, everyone decided that it was the long-awaited, or long-feared, revolution and acted accordingly. Most soldiers of the garrison in the capital went over to the side of the revolutionaries. More workers all over Russia took to the streets. Members of Nicholas's cabinet, seeing what they thought was a revolution, resigned even before the tsar abdicated, thus confirming the perception that a revolution was occurring. Most of the tsar's generals told him that he could no longer rely on the support of the field armies to keep the monarch in power.

The Provisional Government established after this revolution likewise fell prey to a lethal combination of circumstances and perceptions. From the beginning its leaders had to share power with the newly established soviets, or "councils," of workers and soldiers; Guchkov, who had become minister of war, believed that "the provisional government exists only so long as it is permitted by the Soviet." The new government could not implement reforms quickly enough to suit its constituents, whose sympathies seemed to lie somewhere to the left of the government and whose attitude was often typified by the complaint of a Riazan peasant that "nothing has changed yet, and the revolution is already six weeks old." The Provisional Government further alienated large numbers of Russians by continuing the war with Germany and maintaining the imperialist goals of its tsarist predecessor. Furthermore, politicians' assertions that they held only provisional power forfeited them any chance they might have had to hold full power. They did not have the faith in themselves and in their politics that the socialists, and especially the Bolsheviks, displayed.

They could not hold out against socialists who might not always have believed that the revolution would come in their lifetimes but who were convinced that it was coming.

"Optimistic" historians of the Russian Revolution argue that things could have been different. If Stolypin had not been assassinated in 1911, they say, or if the war had been postponed until 1920, or if Nicholas had behaved differently in February 1917, perhaps there would have been no revolution. Stolypin was "dying" politically before the assassin's bullet hit him. It seems unlikely that Nicholas II would have been any more competent in 1920 than he was in 1917; nor does it seem probable that by 1920 he would have brought the Russian military up to par with Germany's. Even if Nicholas had proved more sensitive to public opinion in February 1917, it would have been too late. As Durnovo predicted in 1914, the war brought about social unrest and "a Weakening of the Monarchist Principle" that made revolution inevitable not only in Russia but in Germany, Austria-Hungary, and the Ottoman Empire as well. If Lenin had died in a train wreck on his way to Petrograd, Russia might have had Socialist Revolutionaries in December rather than Bolsheviks in November, but it could not have avoided socialism entirely.

The Revolution was like an avalanche. One can look at the gathering weight of stones and snow and predict an avalanche, but one cannot predict precisely when it will occur and what path it will take. Once it starts, however, it is unstoppable.

—CATHERINE BLAIR,
GEORGETOWN UNIVERSITY

Viewpoint:
No. The defeats and failures of domestic leadership during World War I drove Russia to revolution.

The reign of the last tsar of Russia, Nicholas II (ruled 1894–1917), has come under increasing scrutiny since the collapse of the Soviet Union in 1991 reawakened scholarly interest in late Imperial Russia. Before that time most of the literature dealing with the period between 1894 and 1917 sought narrowly for the reasons underlying the fall of the Romanov dynasty rather than examining Russian history of the period as a whole. Leopold Haimson's 1964–1965 article "The Problem of Social Stability in Urban Russia, 1905–1917" presented the thesis that Russian society was so afraid of

THE FIRST DUMA

When the Russian Duma met for the first time in April 1906, it presented an ambitious agenda to Tsar Nicholas II, who rejected their demands and dissolved the legislative body in July. The Duma's message to the tsar included the following points:

The country has concluded that the arbitrariness of the administrative officials who separate the Tsar from the people is the fundamental shortcoming in the national life. With a united voice the country has loudly declared that the renewal of national life is possible only on the basis of freedom, the right of independent popular action, popular participation in the legislative power, and popular control over the executive power. . . .

Together with the establishment of administrative responsibility to the legislature, it is imperative to follow the basic principle of true popular representation, so that the unity of the monarch with the people can be the sole source of legislative power. Thus all barriers between the Supreme Power and the people must be removed. Likewise no limits should be set to the legislative competence of the popular legislature in unity with the monarch. The State Duma feels obliged to declare to Your Imperial Majesty in the name of the people that the entire population can join in the creative task of renewing the national life with true inspiration and true faith in the development of national prosperity only when nothing will stand between the people and the Throne, no State Council of officials chosen only from the highest class of the people; when the levying of taxes and duties becomes the responsibility of the popular legislature alone; and when no special laws whatever will set limits to the legislative competence of the popular legislature. . . .

The State Duma . . . considers it urgently necessary to agree upon precise laws guaranteeing personal immunity, freedom of conscience, freedom of speech and the press, freedom of union and assembly, and freedom to strike. . . .

The State Duma holds firmly to the conviction that neither freedom nor order founded on right can be strong or lasting without strict observation of the principle of the equality of all citizens before the law (without exception). The State Duma will therefore work out bills for the full equalization of all citizens, and for the abolition of all restrictions and privileges accruing to anyone by reason of class, nationality, religion, or sex. . . . The State Duma considers the use of the death penalty intolerable, even by judicial sentence. . . .

Clarification of the needs of the rural population and the undertaking of legislative measures appropriate to meet them is the most immediate problem facing the State Duma. The working peasantry, the largest part of our population, are impatiently awaiting satisfaction of their acute need for land. The first Russian State Duma will not have fulfilled its duty if it does not work out a law providing land for the peasants. . . .

The State Duma also deems it necessary to work out laws which will secure equal rights for the peasant and do away with the arbitrary and tutelary authority which they have so long endured. The State Duma recognizes as equally urgent the satisfaction of the needs of the working class by legislative measures which will protect the rights of the wage laborer. . . .

The State Duma likewise considers it its duty to do all it can to raise the level of popular enlightenment; thus we should turn our attention to laws concerning universal free education.

The Duma will also give special attention to an equitable distribution of the tax burden, which today weighs disproportionately on the poorest classes of the people, and to the study of the most advisable use of the state revenues.

Fundamental reform of local administration and local self-government is no less essential a legislative task. The entire population should be enlisted for equal participation in local self-government according to the principles of universal suffrage. Remembering the burden of service which the people bear in your Majesty's army and navy, the State Duma is concerned with the strengthening of the principles of equity and justice in the armed forces.

Finally, the State Duma considers it necessary to list among our urgent problems the satisfaction of the long-pressing demands of the various nationalities. Russia is a state populated by many tribes and peoples. A true spiritual union of all these tribes and peoples can be possible only when each is enabled to live its own peculiar and separate way of life. The State Duma will thus concern itself with ways to satisfy those demands.

Your Imperial Majesty! . . . The first word which was spoken in this hall . . . was the word *amnesty*. The country awaits it; an amnesty granted to all those convicted for religious or political reasons, and for all violations of agrarian laws.

. . . Sire, the Duma awaits from you a full political amnesty, as a first guarantee of the mutual understanding and mutual agreement between the Tsar and the people.

Source: *"The Reply of the State Duma," in* Imperial Russia, 1700–1917, *volume 2 of* Readings in Russian Civilization, *edited by Thomas Riha, second edition, revised (Chicago & London: University of Chicago Press, 1969), pp. 446–449.*

revolution that it was unwilling to force social and political reforms lest they spark the conflagration. Also published in 1964, the first edition of Theodore H. von Laue's *Why Lenin? Why Stalin?* echoed Haimson's argument, concluding that there was no chance whatsoever for Russia's peaceful evolution because the rapid pace of industrialization had separated the elite from the people. This approach was largely the result of uncritical acceptance of Lev Trotsky's observation that the revolution in 1905 was only a "dress rehearsal." Much attention was paid to the dramatic growth of the labor movement after 1905, even though an increase in its size and activity should have been expected given the legalization of trade unions by the tsarist government in that year. Since the end of the Soviet Union, however, the reign of Nicholas II is no longer being judged merely by the historical fact of its ultimate demise. Recent scholarship has begun to focus on Russia's considerable achievements in the political, social, and economic realms during the two decades prior to the outbreak of World War I.

New research suggests that the surge of reform that swept through the Russian towns and countryside prior to World War I led to a clear commitment of the emerging "middle" groups to civic activity in order to effect the regeneration of Russian social and political life. Such works as Adèle Lindenmeyr's *Poverty is Not a Vice: Charity, Society, and the State in Imperial Russia* (1996) and the 1998 collection *Emerging Democracy in Late Imperial Russia* suggest that educated Russian society (*obshchestvo*) was in fact becoming increasingly active and reformist. This marked increase in social and political activism refutes the once dominant paradigm in the field that contends that *obshchestvo* was demoralized and marginalized and thus unable to play any constructive role in Russian life, especially after the so-called reaction that set after the revolution of 1905.

Other scholars have found evidence to support this more positive assessment of developments in late Imperial Russia, especially in studies of the entrepreneurial skills of the Russian business community. Also, in contrast to earlier scholarship, most recent studies of urban life in Russia during the period have concluded that living conditions in the towns and cities were rapidly improving. Historians have discovered that industrial workers not only enjoyed opportunities for advancement, but also—contrary to the findings of an earlier generation of social and labor historians—were not united in their support for destroying the Russian social and political order. To be sure, the tsarist government was still authoritarian on the eve of World War I. Nevertheless, autonomous civic groups were beginning to play a role in the transformation of Russia from a servile to a civil society.

Despite limits on the initiative of the emerging Russian "middle" groups, there is clear evidence that Russia was moving, however slowly, away from a service state with an estate-based society of orders (*sosloviia*) toward a modern polity. These groups actively sought to work with the government to resolve the social problems that inevitably arise in modernizing societies. Although the tsarist regime continued to espouse outdated ideals and to extol the virtues of autocracy, it was meanwhile pursuing a modernization process that would fundamentally alter Russian society. Indeed, the industrialization programs of Nicholas II and his predecessor, Alexander III (ruled 1881–1894), brought into existence a middle class, which in turn demanded an end to the restrictions imposed on it by the state.

This new middle class perhaps represented tsarist Russia's best hope for a modern democratic government and a thriving capitalist economy. In Moscow and several other industrial centers various philanthropic organizations, members of the municipal governments (many of whom came from the business community), and liberal industrialists committed themselves to urban and democratic reform. Some notable individuals from this class of Russians—such as Octobrist Party members Pavel Riabushinskii and Aleksandr Guchkov and Constitutional Democrats Aleksandr Konovalov and Mikhail Tereshchenko—became national leaders between 1907 and 1917. Even as the social and economic crises attendant to modernization escalated, however, the tsar clung to his outdated notions of personal rule based on the traditional estate system—despite the efforts of far-sighted ministers such as Petr Stolypin, prime minister from 1906 to 1911, who sought to integrate the peasantry into the social, economic, and political life of the nation as a necessary step toward the creation of a civil society.

If it had been fully realized, Stolypin's program could have forced Russia to evolve from its traditional political culture, where authority was based on legitimacy and precedent, to a modern political order along the lines of those in Western Europe, with legal protection of civil liberties, legal political parties, and public involvement in governance. Stolypin had convinced Nicholas to issue the *ukaz* (decree) of 6 October 1906, which restored the peasantry's right to elect its own delegates to the *zemstva* (singular: *zemstvo*)—elected institutions of local government established in most provinces of European Russia after 1864—which had been taken from them by a counterreform measure in 1890. The *ukaz* of 1906 also gave peasants the right to participate in the second, nonnoble electoral curia and congresses (usually reserved for townspeople) for provincial *zemstva* if they held private farmsteads, as increasing numbers of peasants did in the years before World War I. Further plans were drawn up, though not realized, to establish an all-class local (*volost'*, or canton) level of the *zemstvo*, and one below the *volost'* that would have transferred much local political power to the peasantry while greatly reducing that of the nobility.

Since Stolypin hoped to make the peasants into citizens with a stake in the system, these plans were designed to break down the estate system and to give the peasantry equal voting rights to the nobility. Stolypin was determined to end the system of apartheid that maintained the Old Regime's society of orders in Russia. He accomplished this goal through a series of decrees passed between 1906 and 1910, finally breaking the stultifying grip of the peasant commune, the structure set up to govern the legal, social, and economic aspects of peasant life after the emancipation of serfdom in 1863. The practice of collective responsibility for the commune's tax burden and legal obligations had already been ended, and Stolypin's granting of passports to the peasantry enabled them to move freely. More important, he wanted to give the peasants the right to own as private property their allotments of communal land, which were periodically redistributed and usually uneconomically dispersed over a wide area. Once these strips of land were consolidated into private farms, as they increasingly were in the years before 1914, the emergence of a prosperous, stable, and property-owning peasantry reached toward rural political stability.

The seizure of the *zemstva* by conservative landowners in the aftermath of the revolution of 1905 has been well chronicled. Special emphasis has been placed on the broad array of programs that were immediately slashed or shut down. The fact that conservative gentry controlled the *zemstva* after 1905 has been repeatedly cited as proof that these organs of local self-government could not serve as agents for change in the countryside and thus could not further the development of a civil society. The problem with this standard view, however, is that it looks at events before 1907 and does not take into account the historical record from 1908 to 1914 and even during the war years. After 1907 the nobility soon realized that not only would continued repression undermine the stability of the countryside and increase the peasantry's disaffection but that the nobility would ultimately become irrelevant and lose their influence in Russia unless they reinvigorated the *zemstva* and limited state authority over them. While they defeated many of Stolypin's proposals to democratize the *zemstva*, they also began to reassemble programs they had cut and to implement broad-ranging programs for educational, health, and welfare reforms that were even more impressive than those of their predecessors. The noble delegates also began a protracted, well-organized campaign—in many ways reminiscent of the struggle conducted by their liberal forbears—to allow society more autonomy and leeway in governance.

During the years 1907–1914 *zemstvo* activity increased dramatically. Budgets skyrocketed after Stolypin removed the restriction placed on the *zemstva* by the law of 12 June 1900, which limited tax increases to no more than 3 percent per annum. By 1912 the overall budget of the thirty-four *zemstvo* provinces was 220 million rubles, a sum more than triple their combined budgets in 1895. Just two years later—after nine additional provinces had been allowed to establish *zemstva*—the total budget of the forty-three *zemstvo* provinces was 347.5 million rubles. Fully three-quarters of these funds went to health, education, and welfare; only 12 percent went toward administrative overhead. Entirely new fields of endeavor, such as agronomy and adult education, were created. This process was accelerating on the eve of the war. In arguably the most important *zemstvo* field, education, *zemstvo* activists *(zemtsy)* entered into negotiations with the Ministry of Education over how best to implement plans for universal schooling, which the tsarist government planned to achieve by the 1920s. In 1913 the total *zemstvo* budget increased by 39.8 million rubles over the previous year, with more than 40 percent of the increase (16.5 million rubles) going to education. While it is true that state subsidies increased dramatically (from a mere 2 million rubles in 1907 to more than 40 million rubles in 1913), *zemstvo* contributions grew at an even faster rate, with the result that by 1914 spending on schools surpassed spending on medicine.

This expansion of *zemstvo* services in turn made necessary the hiring of tens of thousands of specialists (the so-called Third Element) such as doctors, teachers, veterinarians, agronomists, accountants, and others who saw themselves as public servants, as opposed to government officials. This group's cooperation and expertise were crucial if the state and educated society were to resolve the myriad social and economic problems brought about by modernization. One need only look at *zemstvo* schools to understand how crucial the Third Element was in prewar development. In 1879, 22,767 rural schools in the provinces of European Russia employed 24,389 teachers. Thirty-two years later 62,913 teachers filled the classrooms of a new generation of learners. As Jeffrey Brooks has indicated in his *When Russia Learned to Read: Literacy and*

Tsar Nicholas II blessing Russian troops, circa 1915

(from Gwyneth Hughes and Simon Welfare, Red Empire, *1990)*

Popular Literature, 1861–1917 (1985), of all the areas of *zemstvo* activity, primary education showed the most impressive growth between 1880 and 1914.

On the eve of World War I the political and social transformation of Russia was well under way. The political experience of state and educated society working together to succor victims of famine and disease, to hasten the acculturation of the peasantry through mass education, to facilitate the breakup of the commune, and to resettle several million peasants in the empty spaces of Siberia promoted a détente between these two important elements of the Russian polity. This cooperation of intellectuals and the state undercuts the traditional "state versus society" argument found in the writings of prerevolutionary liberal activists. Recent scholars have found, for example, that provincial governors welcomed the assistance of the *zemstva*, especially in the areas of public education and health.

Looking on from his exile abroad, Vladimir Lenin cautioned his few followers not to take Stolypin's policies lightly. Contrary to the standard view, the coming of World War I did not entirely derail this slow evolution toward a civil society. Russia's educated society responded to the crises that the conflict engendered by assuming many burdens that normally would have been the responsibility of the state in time of war. These activities included providing munitions to the army, rendering assistance to refugees and medical services to wounded soldiers, and administering vaccination programs. The increasing confidence of Russian "middle" groups and the impetus given to peasant demands for education about the Germans or how an airplane worked—demonstrating, as Scott Seregny has noted, their interest in the larger world—shows how the war acted as an accelerator of change.

Proof that some elements of a democratic, civil society were at least incipient might be found in the *zemstvo* elections in the fall of 1917, before the Bolshevik coup, and those for the Constituent Assembly in November of that same year. Some scholars have pointed to the low turnouts for the *zemstvo* elections as evidence of the intransigence and isolation of the peasantry from political life. But considering that the election was held at harvesttime and that women (who were eligible to vote for the first time) generally stayed away from the polls, the turnout of 40 to 50 percent was remarkably high. (The turnout in the American presidential election of 2000 was just under 50 percent.) The political progress of Russian society was revealed in the Constituent Assembly elections: even in the intimidating circumstances of the Bolsheviks' "temporary" dictatorship, fifty million citizens expressed their will through the ballot box and not in the street. After the demise of the Soviet Union, Russians began looking to the last years of Romanov Russia as a way to guide or legitimize Russia's current democratic experiment. One should take note of the symbolism involved in reinstituting the State Duma as the national legislature, the readoption of the traditional tricolored flag and double-headed Romanov eagle, and even the reburial and canonization of Nicholas II. Developments during the reign of the last tsar had important implications for peasant integration and the evolution of a civic identity. By minimizing or ignoring countervailing trends that do not fit into prearranged political categories, historians run the risk of accepting historical outcomes as being inevitable.

COLLAPSE OF TSARIST RUSSIA

There were alternative paths open to Russia in 1917, and those opportunities, which reflect a long-standing political reality, remain open.

–THOMAS EARL PORTER,
NORTH CAROLINA A&T STATE UNIVERSITY

References

Abraham Ascher, *P. A. Stolypin: The Search for Stability in Late Imperial Russia* (Stanford, Cal.: Stanford University Press, 2001).

Jeffrey Brooks, *When Russia Learned to Read: Literacy and Popular Literature, 1861–1917* (Princeton: Princeton University Press, 1985).

Hélène Carrère d'Encausse, *Nicholas II. The Interrupted Transition* (New York: Holmes & Meier, 2000).

Mary Schaeffer Conroy, ed., *Emerging Democracy in Late Imperial Russia: Case Studies on Local Self-Government (the Zemstvos), State Duma Elections, the Tsarist Government, and the State Council before and during World War I* (Niwot: University of Colorado Press, 1998).

James Cracraft, ed., *Major Problems in the History of Imperial Russia* (Lexington, Mass.: Heath, 1994).

Orlando Figes, *A People's Tragedy: The Russian Revolution, 1891–1924* (New York: Viking, 1997).

Paul Gregory, *Before Command: An Economic History of Russia from the Emancipation to the First Five Year Plan* (Princeton: Princeton University Press, 1994).

Leopold Haimson, "The Problem of Social Stability in Urban Russia, 1905–1917," *Slavic Review,* 23 (December 1964): 620–642; 24 (March 1965): 1–22.

Michael F. Hamm, *Kiev: A Portrait, 1800–1917* (Princeton: Princeton University Press, 1993).

Geoffrey Hosking, *The First Socialist Society: A History of the Soviet Union from Within,* second edition, enlarged (Cambridge, Mass.: Harvard University Press, 1993).

Stephen Kotkin, "1991 and the Russian Revolution: Sources, Conceptual Categories, Analytical Frameworks," *Journal of Modern History,* 70 (June 1998): 384–425.

Dominic Lieven, *Nicholas II: Twilight of the Empire* (New York: St. Martin's Press, 1994).

Adèle Lindenmeyr, *Poverty is Not a Vice: Charity, Society, and the State in Imperial Russia* (Princeton: Princeton University Press, 1996).

Nicolai N. Petro, *The Rebirth of Russian Democracy: An Interpretation of Political Culture* (Cambridge, Mass.: Harvard University Press, 1995).

Richard Pipes, *The Russian Revolution* (New York: Knopf, 1990).

Thomas Porter and Scott Seregny, "The *Zemstvo* Reconsidered," in *Russian Local Government: Power, Authority and Civic Participation,* edited by Alfred B. Evans (Lanham, Md.: Rowman & Littlefield, forthcoming).

Nicholas V. Riasanovsky, *A History of Russia,* sixth edition (New York: Oxford University Press, 2000).

Thomas Riha, ed., *Imperial Russia, 1700–1917,* volume 2 of *Readings in Russian Civilization,* second edition, revised (Chicago & London: University of Chicago Press, 1969).

Scott Seregny, "Zemstvos, Peasants, and Citizenship: The Russian Adult Education Movement and World War I," *Slavic Review,* 59, no. 2 (2000): 290–315.

Ronald Grigor Suny, *The Soviet Experiment: Russia, the USSR, and the Successor States* (New York: Oxford University Press, 1998).

Leon Trotsky, *The Essential Trotsky* (New York: Barnes & Noble, 1963).

Theodore H. von Laue, *Why Lenin? Why Stalin? A Reappraisal of the Russian Revolution, 1900–1930* (Philadelphia: Lippincott, 1964); revised and enlarged as *Why Lenin? Why Stalin? Why Gorbachev? The Rise and Fall of the Soviet System* (New York: HarperCollins, 1993).

COLLAPSE OF YUGOSLAVIA

Was the disintegration of Yugoslavia caused by the opportunism of nationalist politicians?

Viewpoint: Yes. Secessionist leaders used Western support of their nationalist goals for personal, political, and economic aggrandizement.

Viewpoint: No. The breakup of Yugoslavia into smaller states was an inevitable consequence of its multiethnic character and Tito's failure to create a unified nation.

The death of dictator Josip Broz Tito of Yugoslavia in 1980 was followed not only by the collapse of its communist government but also by the breakup of that country into separate states. Founded after World War I and known until 1929 as the Kingdom of Serbs, Croats, and Slovenes, Yugoslavia included the prewar kingdoms of Serbia and Montenegro and territory taken from the fallen Austro-Hungarian Empire. The diversity of the Yugoslav population, which included many ethnic and religious groups, stood as a potential threat to the viability of Yugoslavia throughout its history. Authoritarian governments subdued ethnic and religious tensions until Tito's death, but then conflict flared up. In 1991 four of the six constituent republics of Yugoslavia—Croatia, Slovenia, Bosnia-Herzegovina, and Macedonia—declared their independence, leaving only Serbia and Montenegro in Yugoslavia. Two of the secessionist republics, Croatia and Bosnia-Herzegovina, had substantial minority populations of Serbs, most of whom opposed independence and feared that the new states, the first populated predominantly by Roman Catholic Croats and the second by a large plurality of Bosnian Muslims and a substantial Croat minority, would not serve their interests. The result was a bloody war between Serbia and Croatia and an even bloodier civil war among the warring factions in Bosnia. News of the siege of Sarajevo, the discovery of mass graves, and other shocking events in Bosnia captured international headlines. Calls for international intervention led to the deployment of United Nations (UN) peacekeeping forces, which proved incapable of ending the conflict. In 1995 U.S. president William Clinton sponsored negotiations to conclude the Bosnian conflict. Held in Dayton, Ohio, these talks resulted in a cease-fire to be policed by American troops. After their arrival in December 1995 the situation remained tense, with occasional outbreaks of violence. By 1998 ethnic tension in Kosovo, a province of Serbia populated predominantly by ethnic Albanians, produced more international intervention, culminating in a U.S.-led NATO bombing campaign against Yugoslavia in March–April 1999 and in the subsequent occupation of Kosovo by an international peacekeeping force.

One explanation for the collapse of Yugoslavia suggests that it was inevitable because of its multiethnic and multireligious population. Proponents of this view assert that in an age of intense and resurgent nationalism, no such state could continue to exist without major challenges to its legitimacy. Thus, in the absence of a strong central authority after Tito's death, national division became unavoidable. Yet, as opponents of this view point out, Yugoslavia remained a cohesive state from its founding in 1918 until its occupation by Germany and Italy in 1941, and then from its liberation in 1945 until the early

1990s. They point out that its internal problems during these periods were not markedly different from those of many other countries, and, they argue, its collapse did not necessarily follow from its multiethnic character. Rather, the general collapse of communist authority in Eastern Europe after 1989 allowed the ethnic elite of Yugoslavia to pursue personal agendas and interests at the expense of the existing state. Many communists remade themselves into nationalists, believing that it would be better to rule a small nation-state than to remain functionaries of a larger multinational entity. Many also knew that the West, which renewed its defense of the principle of national self-determination in the postcommunist world, would likely support them if they presented their cause as one of freedom.

Viewpoint:
Yes. Secessionist leaders used Western support of their nationalist goals for personal, political, and economic aggrandizement.

Accompanied by bloodshed, human dislocation and suffering, and economic hardship, the disintegration of Yugoslavia in the 1990s has often been presented as an inevitable consequence of ethnic and religious diversity in the Socialist Federal Republic of Yugoslavia. The breakup has also been blamed on the authoritarian nature of its government and on the uneven economic development of the six republics in the Yugoslav federation. That is, Slovenia and Croatia were considered the most advanced, while Bosnia-Herzegovina, Serbia, Montenegro, and Macedonia were evaluated as economically backward.

European historical experience, however, has clearly demonstrated that uneven economic development or the multiethnic character of a specific country does not necessarily lead to disintegration. Uneven economic development in Italy (where the south is far behind the north) has not brought about any significant threats to the national unity of that country. Switzerland, with its four ethnolinguistic communities, has always been a stable federal state. The same may be said of bilingual Belgium. Protestant and Catholic communities in Germany have not experienced significant conflicts throughout the twentieth century.

Moreover, ethnic and economic diversity do not explain why the breakup of Yugoslavia was accompanied by so much bloodshed. In contrast, the division of the former socialist republic of Czechoslovakia into the independent Czech Republic and the Republic of Slovakia took place in a remarkably peaceful fashion and did not have any obvious negative impact on the socio-economic and political development of the two new republics.

A far more likely explanation for the violent breakup of Yugoslavia during the 1990s may be found in the opportunistic policies pursued by specific politicians from the various republics of

Yugoslavia and in the ineptitude with which the international community responded. Politicians who embraced nationalist separatism largely as a means to personal political and economic gain, precipitated the dissolution of the Yugoslav federation. The tragic consequences of this collapse were to a considerable extent facilitated by the imbalanced and precipitate policies of outside powers. The governments of Western Europe, the United States, and Russia often failed to reach agreement among themselves about what course to take. They promoted solutions that clearly favored a particular side, or sides, in the conflict and often exploited the conflict for gains in their own domestic politics. Nationalist leaders in the Yugoslav republics often counted on support from outside powers—and in some cases on those powers' lack of consistent policy—to mobilize followers in their quest to gain from the breakup of Yugoslavia. Such opportunism was apparent not only in pro-Western Yugoslav republics such as Slovenia and Croatia, which tried to separate from the federation immediately after the fall of the Berlin Wall in 1989, but also in the behavior of Slobodan Milošević. This Serb leader consolidated support for his government by skillfully exploiting Western backing for the separatist claims in Slovenia, Croatia, Bosnia-Herzegovina, and Kosovo to present Serbia and its people as victims in the game of international diplomacy.

At the beginning of the Yugoslav crisis in 1991 many well-established politicians in the different member republics of the Yugoslav federation found it profitable to switch from communism to nationalism. Slovenia's proclamation of independence in June 1991 did not meet with significant resistance from the Yugoslav government. The republic of Slovenia was small, ethnically homogenous, and remote from the federal capital of Belgrade. At the same time, however, Croatia seceded and was soon followed by Bosnia-Herzegovina and Macedonia. Unlike Slovenia, these republics were not ethnically homogenous and had Serb minorities. Croatia had a sizable Serb population (six hundred thousand people); approximately one-quarter of the Macedonian population was Albanian, together with a sizable Serb minority; and Bosnia-Herzegovina was a mix of Serbs, Croats, and Mus-

SPEECH BY MILOŠEVIC

On 28 June 1989 Slobodan Miloševic gave a speech at a ceremony honoring the six-hundredth anniversary of the Battle of Kosovo, in which the forces of Serbia and its Balkan allies were defeated by troops of the Ottoman Empire. In the following passages Miloševic expressed his desire to maintain the unity of Yugoslavia, with a strong and unified Serbia at its head.

The lack of unity and betrayal in Kosovo will continue to follow the Serbian people like an evil fate through the whole of its history. Even in the last war, this lack of unity and betrayal led the Serbian people and Serbia into agony, the consequences of which in the historical and moral sense exceeded fascist aggression.

Even later, when a socialist Yugoslavia was set up, in this new state the Serbian leadership remained divided, prone to compromise to the detriment of its own people. The concessions that many Serbian leaders made at the expense of their people could not be accepted historically and ethically by any nation in the world, especially because the Serbs have never in the whole of their history conquered and exploited others. Their national and historical being has been liberational throughout the whole of history and through two world wars, as it is today. They liberated themselves and when they could they also helped others to liberate themselves. The fact that in this region they are a major nation is not a Serbian sin or shame; this is an advantage which they have not used against others, but I must say that here, in this big, legendary field of Kosovo, the Serbs have not used the advantage of being great for their own benefit either.

Thanks to their leaders and politicians and their vassal mentality they felt guilty before themselves and others. This situation lasted for decades, it lasted for years and here we are now at the field of Kosovo to say that this is no longer the case.

Disunity among Serb officials made Serbia lag behind and their inferiority humiliated Serbia. Therefore, no place in Serbia is better suited for saying this than the field of Kosovo and no place in Serbia is better suited than the field of Kosovo for saying that unity in Serbia will bring prosperity to the Serbian people in Serbia and each one of its citizens, irrespective of his national or religious affiliation.

Serbia of today is united and equal to other republics and prepared to do everything to improve its financial and social position and that of all its citizens. If there is unity, cooperation, and seriousness, it will succeed in doing so. This is why the optimism that is now present in Serbia to a considerable extent regarding the future days is realistic, also because it is based on freedom, which makes it possible for all people to express their positive, creative and humane abilities aimed at furthering social and personal life.

Serbia has never had only Serbs living in it. Today, more than in the past, members of other peoples and nationalities also live in it. This is not a disadvantage for Serbia. I am truly convinced that it is its advantage. National composition of almost all countries in the world today, particularly developed ones, has also been changing in this direction. Citizens of different nationalities, religions, and races have been living together more and more frequently and more and more successfully.

Socialism in particular, being a progressive and just democratic society, should not allow people to be divided in the national and religious respect. The only differences one can and should allow in socialism are between hard working people and idlers and between honest people and dishonest people. Therefore, all people in Serbia who live from their own work, honestly, respecting other people and other nations, are in their own republic.

After all, our entire country should be set up on the basis of such principles. Yugoslavia is a multinational community and it can survive only under the conditions of full equality for all nations that live in it. . . .

Equal and harmonious relations among Yugoslav peoples are a necessary condition for the existence of Yugoslavia and for it to find its way out of the crisis and, in particular, they are a necessary condition for its economic and social prosperity. . . .

This year, the Serbian people became aware of the necessity of their mutual harmony as the indispensable condition for their present life and further development.

I am convinced that this awareness of harmony and unity will make it possible for Serbia not only to function as a state but to function as a successful state. Therefore I think that it makes sense to say this here in Kosovo, where that disunity once upon a time tragically pushed back Serbia for centuries and endangered it, and where renewed unity may advance it and may return dignity to it. Such an awareness about mutual relations constitutes an elementary necessity for Yugoslavia, too, for its fate is in the joined hands of all its peoples. . . .

Let the memory of Kosovo heroism live forever!

Long live Serbia!

Long live Yugoslavia!

Long live peace and brotherhood among peoples!

Source: *"Miloševic's Speech, Kosovo Field, June 28, 1989"* <http://emperors-clothes.com/articles/jared/milosaid.html>.

COLLAPSE OF YUGOSLAVIA

lims. The North Atlantic Treaty Organization (NATO) powers were divided in their attitudes toward the secession of these republics. President George H. W. Bush feared that recognizing the independence of the separatist republics might facilitate the breakup of the Soviet Union and invigorate smoldering separatist movements in Western Europe, such as those of the Basques and Catalans in Spain, the Scots and Irish in the United Kingdom, and the Corsicans in France. Striving to assert its leading position in the European Union (EU), Germany, however, took a different stance. The ruling Christian Democratic Union (CDU), led by Chancellor Helmut Kohl, and especially the Christian Social Union (the sister party of the CDU in Catholic Bavaria) strongly sympathized with Catholics in Croatia and Slovenia and supported those republics' claims to self-determination. Germany soon recognized them as independent nations. Other EU member-countries and most of the other countries of the world soon did so as well. Nationalist politicians in Croatia interpreted this recognition as tacit approval of Croatian policies that did not favor an equitable settlement regarding the status of the Serb minority in the Krajina region of Croatia.

The developments regarding Croatia encouraged separatist claims elsewhere in Yugoslavia. In Bosnia-Herzegovina the Bosnian Serbs sought to achieve independence from the Muslim-dominated government and set up their own republic. They also initiated "ethnic cleansing," killing or driving out of the country all but their own ethnic group. Their example was soon followed by the Croats in Bosnia and Croatia (especially against the Serbs in Krajina). Hostilities escalated, and in 1993 the United Nations sent peacekeeping forces from several countries. Lacking coordinated leadership and experience, they were generally ineffective, encouraging Croat, Muslim, and Serb separatist political leaders and military commanders to continue hostilities. The situation was only exacerbated by the futile efforts of international peace negotiators who arranged many cease-fire agreements, which were usually violated within days of their signing. The U.S.-sponsored Dayton agreements of 1995, signed under the increasing pressure of the international community, did not bring lasting stability. The agreements called for the creation of two constituent federal regions—a Bosnian-Serb republic and a Muslim-Croat federation—each enjoying self-rule but remaining a part of an internationally recognized Bosnia-Herzegovina. The Muslim-Croat federation was a fragile entity and was soon torn by internal contradictions, while the Bosnian Serbs were developing closer ties with the republic of Serbia. The West persistently placed all the blame for the hostilities on the Serbs, who increasingly saw themselves as victims of an international double standard and sought support from Russia and Greece. In addition to illuminating the considerable weaknesses of international peacekeeping missions, the Bosnian crisis also intensified long-standing rifts in the world community. Western European states, led by Germany, continued to support Croatia, which had successfully reconquered Krajina, while Russia and Greece backed the Serbs, fellow practitioners of Orthodox Christianity. In turn, Turkey and other Muslim countries vowed support for Bosnian Muslims and Kosovar Albanians.

Ethnic strife in the predominantly Albanian-populated Serb province of Kosovo flared up in 1998–1999. Separatist claims in the province began in the early 1990s, after Serbian president Milošević abrogated the province's autonomous status in 1989. In 1992 the Albanians of Kosovo responded with an ineffectual declaration of independence, which the Serbs ignored. The issue of Kosovo became internationalized in 1998–1999, after Milošević started moving military and paramilitary units into the province. These troops began a program of ethnic cleansing similar to the one that occurred during the Serbian invasion of Bosnia in 1992–1993. After Serbia refused to withdraw its forces and accept a peace agreement, NATO launched a war, primarily through air strikes in March and April 1999, and brought the Milošević regime to its knees. Russia strongly objected to the NATO campaign, which was supported on the ground by the Kosovo Liberation Army (KLA), an underground Albanian paramilitary organization founded in 1993. Before, during, and after the 1999 NATO operation the KLA is reported to have participated in retaliatory ethnic cleansing of Kosovo Serbs, who were a minority in Kosovo. Throughout the 1990s the KLA also played important regional roles in drug smuggling and in the weapons trade. The leaders of this group clearly took advantage of the West's justifiable concern for the plight of Kosovo Albanians to consolidate their control in the area. After the 1999 war the international peacekeeping forces sent to oversee Kosovo's peaceful transition to independence have proven ineffectual in stabilizing the region, largely leaving power in the hands of KLA leaders who do not seem sufficiently committed to building a stable democratic regime in Kosovo.

Thus, an examination of the events suggests that the violent breakup of Yugoslavia is less related to the multiethnic character of that federation than it is the result of opportunistic policies pursued by leaders in virtually all the constituent republics. The indecisiveness of Western leaders and their inability to handle the Balkan crises in the 1990s contributed to the success of self-serving separatist politicians while destroying the federation of Yugoslavia.

—YORK NORMAN,
GEORGETOWN UNIVERSITY

COLLAPSE OF YUGOSLAVIA

Viewpoint:
No. The breakup of Yugoslavia into smaller states was an inevitable consequence of its multiethnic character and Tito's failure to create a unified nation.

With its multiethnic makeup and its inability to build unifying, nonethnically based governing institutions, Yugoslavia was bound to collapse. A key player in the demise of Yugoslavia was Josip Broz, known as Tito, who during his nearly forty years as dictator of Yugoslavia laid the foundation for the violence of the 1990s. Five parts of Tito's legacy—his devolution of centralized power to the six constituent republics, his inability to construct an accepted nonethnically based national identity, his creation of arbitrary boundaries, his inadequate distribution of resources, and his failure to train a cadre of leaders to succeed him—created conditions that contributed greatly to the demise of Yugoslavia.

The standard Balkan state that emerged from the breakup of the Ottoman Empire and the aftermath of World War I usually had one dominant nationality. Majority populations exploited suspicions of "alien" minorities to justify seizing power and creating strong centralized governments, leaving little decision-making power to regions or minority populations. In the case of the Kingdom of Serbs, Croats, and Slovenes (founded in 1919), which became Yugoslavia after 1929, power was centralized in Belgrade, and virtually all the senior government officials were Serbs, the dominant ethnic group in the country. By contrast, Catholic Croats and Muslim Bosnians had little say in governing the country, while the Slovene and Macedonian populations—as well as the substantial Albanian, Hungarian, Montenegrin, and German minorities—had even less power. These groups had no desire to be part of a centralized Yugoslavia, wanting instead to be a part of a loosely federated state or united with countries where they would have been part of an ethnic majority.

When Tito came to power after World War II, he began changing the Yugoslav governing system by implementing political and economic self-management reforms in the constituent republics. This new system of government put real administrative power in the hands of the six republics, even allowing them to form local territorial militias. Tito also gave nationality status to the Croats and Muslims, guaranteeing Muslims equal political and administrative representation with Serbs and Croats. The 1974 Yugoslav constitution further decentralized the country by creating two new autonomous provinces of Ser-bia, Kosovo and Vojvodina, and by creating a rotating presidency to give all republics and autonomous provinces a chance to head the state.

Tito's devolution of power caused problems in the 1960s and early 1970s. During this period Yugoslav reformists, who were often the same politicians who wanted more economic and political autonomy for Croatia, Slovenia, and Bosnia-Herzegovina, started arguing along ethnic lines. Croatia became the most vocal proponent of autonomy. Although the 1974 constitution was not repealed, Tito eventually turned against the reformists and used the secret police and the army to boost Belgrade's power over the republics. The arguments along ethnic lines prevented the development of supraethnic loyalties and identities and laid the groundwork for ethnic mobilization and political fragmentation even before Tito's death.

Tito's idea of *bratstvo i jedinstvo* (Serbian for "brotherhood and unity") was inextricably tied to his decentralization of Yugoslavia. The idea behind this slogan was that the strength of Yugoslavia came from the unity of all its peoples and what they had in common—their "Yugoslavness." This unity was precarious at best; both Serbia and Croatia had designs on Bosnia-Herzegovina. Tensions among the ethnic groups had been high since World War II, during which the Bosnians, Croats, and Serbs fought each other in a civil war, and the wrangling over liberalization during the 1960s and 1970s kept them from resolving their differences. Although Tito's *bratstvo i jedinstvo* campaign prevented open ethnic conflict under communism, political loyalties and national identities remained an important part of Yugoslav society, and interethnic grievances continued. By the 1990s it was clear that pan-Yugoslavism had not taken root. Only 10 percent of those living in the territories of Yugoslavia identified themselves as Yugoslavs. Tito's attempt to create a pan-Yugoslav identity was artificial and had little meaning for the various peoples of that nation.

A key reason for the failure of pan-Yugoslavism was Tito's creation of arbitrary administrative units, which left large numbers of ethnic minorities outside the homelands of their ethnic groups. For example, large Serb populations were located in Croatia and Bosnia. In the Yugoslavian census of 1991, 62.3 percent of those living in the republics of Serbia and Montenegro were Serbs, 16.6 percent Albanians, 5 percent Montenegrins, 3.2 percent Muslims, and 1.1 percent Croats. Croatia was more homogenous with 77.9 percent Croats, but 12.2 percent of the population was Serbian and 1 percent was Muslim. Bosnia-Herzegovina was the most heterogeneous republic with no majority population:

Men with the old Yugoslav flag at a peace demonstration in April 1992

(Ron Haviv)

43.7 percent Muslim, 31.3 percent Serbian, 17.3 percent Croatian, and 7 percent Yugoslav and other nationalities.

The heterogeneous mix of the Yugoslav republics was a recipe for problems, and the federal institutions were so weak that they were unable to regulate relations among national groups. In Bosnia—where each ethnic group believed that the Yugoslav Parliament, courts, and police favored the others—minorities turned to their national groups, which later became national-religious groups, for protection. Nationalist feelings were strengthened by the perceived poor treatment of minorities in Croatia, Bosnia, and Serbia. In this environment historical myths

and political loyalties were perpetuated, making it all but impossible for even a limited pan-Yugoslav identity to last.

Economic disparities among the republics also contributed to the failure of pan-Yugoslavism and increased ethnic tensions. Because Bosnia-Herzegovina was a poor region with no port, it needed resources and food from Serbia or Croatia. As a result Serbs and Croats perceived that their wealth was being given to their neighbor. As the Yugoslav economy stagnated in the early 1980s, the Greater Serbia idea emerged, maintaining, among other things, that Serbian economic problems resulted from Tito's policy of keeping the Serbs divided and underdeveloped by giving away their resources. In their rhetoric the republic presidents turned economic differences into new ethnic or religious nationalisms, setting the stage for the collapse of Yugoslavia, with people thinking that "their" republic would help them fight other minorities to get their share of limited economic resources.

Tito's death in 1980 left Yugoslavia with no unifying figure to hold the country together and balance the Yugoslav republics' competing aspirations. While on paper a multiethnic Presidium with a rotating presidency seemed to be a good mechanism to ensure that all regions had an equal say in government, in practice it created rifts among the ethnic groups as each tried to use its turn at the presidency to further its own goals at the expense of the state. From 1980 until 1986 real power lay in the regional party organizations, which came together in the Presidium to discuss their joint concerns. Thus, the Presidium was no longer organizationally unified, and there was no leadership at the top to make the new arrangement work. Party leaders used the Presidium and rotating presidency to make their local-ethnic interests a priority, pitting the interests of one region against another. In 1986 Slobodan Milošević became chief of the Serbian Party, and in 1987 he assumed de facto control over Serbia.

Milošević used the lack of a unifying leader to help him rise to power. In 1989 he became president of Serbia and reversed Tito's unifying state ideology to create divisions among Yugoslavia's ethnic groups by highlighting their differences. For example, Milošević portrayed Bosnia as Stalinist because of its stricter local version of communism and as Islamic fundamentalist because of Bosnia's large Muslim population and its contacts with other Muslim countries. He depicted Croats as fascists, reviving the memory of World War II when Croatia (with the aid of Bosnians, who were part of a Croatian federation at the time) was a German protectorate and killed many Serbs. The Serbs also criticized Tito, a half-Croat, half-Slovene communist, for taking away power from Serbia in the 1974 constitution to distribute it more evenly among the other groups in Yugoslavia. In addition to his use of ethnic propaganda, Milošević tried to recentralize power. Ethnic tensions came to the fore.

By the early 1990s Croatian president Franjo Tudjman and Bosnian president Alija Izetbegovic were using nationalist propaganda to encourage separatism among their citizens. Izetbegovic and Tudjman portrayed Serbia as a "hegemon" that oppressed the other groups in Yugoslavia. Although religious attitudes were generally flexible in Croatia and Bosnia, and people often changed religions, Tudjman and Izet-

begovic also used religious propaganda to further their power. Few politicians were left to counter the extreme nationalist rhetoric because those who wanted a multiethnic state were driven out of the country or silenced toward the end of the communist era. The nationalities began to believe the inflammatory rhetoric, including the idea that each nationality deserved its own state.

Even with the republics' separatist aspirations, they needed to believe that they could survive as small independent states. After the fall of the Berlin Wall and the collapse of the Soviet Union the Soviet republics moved successfully toward national independence, providing a provocative example for Yugoslavia's constituent republics. Slovenia, Bosnia-Herzegovina, Croatia, and Macedonia all declared their independence in 1991, leaving a rump Yugoslavian state that included the pre–World War I kingdoms of Serbia and Montenegro, including the Kosovo and Vojvodina provinces of Serbia.

From its resurrection after World War II Yugoslavia was a troubled state. Tito recognized that for Yugoslavia to survive he would have to create a supraethnic Yugoslav identity and take other steps to stem the rise of nationalism. But local identities were so ingrained that Tito's attempts were doomed to failure, and he succeeded instead at angering minorities. With the end of the external threat of the Soviet Union and the republics' growing perception that they could survive on their own, there was no incentive for them to remain united. Nobody wanted to fight for the preservation of the state when Slovenia declared independence, precipitating the end of Yugoslavia.

–KERRY FOLEY,
WASHINGTON, D.C.

References

Bogdan Denitch, *Ethnic Nationalism: The Tragic Death of Yugoslavia*, revised edition (Minneapolis: University of Minnesota Press, 1996).

Misha Glenny, *The Balkans: Nationalism, War, and the Great Powers, 1804–1999* (New York: Viking, 2000).

Ron Haviv, *Blood and Honey: A Balkan War Journal* (New York: TV Books, 2000).

Sabrina Ramet, *Balkan Babel: The Disintegration of Yugoslavia from the Death of Tito to the Fall of Milošević*, fourth edition, enlarged (Boulder, Colo.: Westview Press, 2002).

COLONIALISM

Did European nation-states systematically plan to become colonial powers?

Viewpoint: Yes. European nation-states deliberately engaged in colonialism to dominate markets, trade routes, and sources of raw materials.

Viewpoint: No. Colonial empires were not the result of deliberate planning; they were the products of European attempts to maintain regional stability.

By the turn of the twentieth century, European nations ruled directly or indirectly over most of the world. After decades of expansion and competition few peoples in what is now called the "developing world" retained their independence. Why would the most materially prosperous nations go to such great effort and expense to create worldwide hegemonies?

The traditional explanation for this phenomenon is economic. As European societies and economies grew more complicated in the industrial age, the continent demanded a steady stream of natural resources to ensure production and a network of reliable markets to ensure consumption. Maintaining overseas territories guaranteed both. The control of strategic points such as Gibraltar, Suez, Hong Kong, and Singapore, furthermore, provided secure routes of transit for imperial commerce. It was to promote these ends that European governments and populations were willing to make vast deployments of military power and spend lavishly on colonial rule.

A counterargument maintains that regardless of the economic factors, few European colonial powers established their rule over the developing world in a planned or systematic fashion. European rule expanded more because existing interests were threatened by the instability of local political, economic, and social conditions. In a spiraling process the more European powers suppressed instability, the more they encountered it in newly adjacent territories, and the more regional responsibility they were forced to accept. Once these regions were pacified, or once the colonial powers' concerns about them disappeared, control became unnecessary and unpopular. According to this argument, European colonial rule almost always developed haphazardly and was never planned to last.

Viewpoint:
Yes. European nation-states deliberately engaged in colonialism to dominate markets, trade routes, and sources of raw materials.

In the last half of the nineteenth century, European states, along with their junior partners, Japan and the United States, constructed a system of imperial domination that came to control the entire globe economically and politically. Utilizing technological advances from the industrial revolution, Europeans, Americans, and Japanese imposed their will relatively easily on others through a variety of schemes: military occupations, unequal treaties, financial trusteeships, and spheres of influence. China, the Ottoman Empire, and other imperial states, which had previously been key rivals of Europe, succumbed to varying degrees of foreign tutelage, occupation, and loss of territory. European settlers and financiers provided human and economic capital to make the imperial schemes both profitable and enduring. Social Darwinism and other ideas of racial and cultural superiority both justified and gave historical and scientific "context" to the new system of imperial domination.

Since the appearance of the imperial order, scholars have sought to understand the factors that gave rise to this rapid expansion of European control of the non-European world between 1870 and 1945. Many agree that the period marked a heyday of European power and influence in global affairs that was shaken by World War I (1914–1918) and then vanquished by World War II (1939–1945), the Cold War, and decolonization. One of the chief explanations for this expansion is economic. Nineteenth-century capitalists required the raw materials and markets of extra-European territories in order to compete internationally and to supply their societies with essential goods. Economic rivalries were particularly fierce between capitalists of the older "status quo" powers with those of the newly industrialized powers in North America, Asia, and Central Europe. Other historians touch on the religious fervor and nationalism of the time and the popularity of many ideas such as social Darwinism, the "civilizing mission," and racial and cultural classifications and hierarchies. Another explanation highlights elite fear of class revolution and shows how those feelings convinced governments to pursue aggressive foreign policies and opportunities for their nationals to enrich themselves overseas, most often through new settlements or capital investments with interest rates higher than available at home.

By 1914 a quarter of Britain's, and a fifth of France's and Germany's, wealth was invested overseas.

Of these explanations those dealing with rival capitalists and overseas capital investments factored most prominently in the calculations of the two states whose overseas empires and influence grew the most between 1870 and 1945: Great Britain and the United States. Throughout this seventy-five-year period Britain's empire dwarfed the size of any other great power and controlled much of Africa, the Middle East, South Asia, the Indian Ocean, and the Pacific. At the same time no economic system on earth matched the dynamism and growth of global influence of the American economy. Following the Venezuelan Crisis (1895) and the Spanish-American War (1898), the United States emerged as the dominant power in the Western Hemisphere and a major player in the Pacific Ocean. Britain and the United States also controlled the crucial arteries of world trade—the Suez Canal, Panama Canal, Straits of Gibraltar, and Straits of Malacca—and global petroleum production, the most important industry and natural resource of the age. The two empires were closely linked by bonds of language, culture, and commerce and grew in tandem with each other. A comparison of their foreign policies—though Britain was an "old" great power and the United States a "new" great power—shows that the factors guiding their and their rivals' expansion were a desire to control foreign markets, trade routes, and raw materials, and the fear of the consequences if others won control of these resources.

It is important to bear in mind that the economic and political goals of both British and U.S. leaders were similar to those their predecessors had pursued and that their expansion was a change in tactics rather than outlook. For Britain those tactics were forged by the logic of Liberals who rescued the nation from economic problems in the 1820s after consecutive poor harvests and the loss of Britain's traditional overseas markets. Liberals argued that global wealth was not finite and that free trade should replace monopolies and managed trade. This new system would allow states to produce what they were most suited for and thereby increase everyone's standard of living. Liberals were driven by their religiousness, patriotism, and faith in the material and spiritual benefits of British civilization. Given an open market, they asserted that Britain—the world leader in commerce and technology—could trade profitably and maintain considerable influence over regions without physically controlling them. The keys to the system were Britain's strong navy to protect seagoing trade, a series of free-trade treaties, and the preservation of a European balance of power that would prevent the

COLONIALISM

emergence of any challenger. This subtle form of imperialism became known as the "imperium" of free trade.

The underlying logic of American economic and political policies before 1870 mirrored those of Britain. In the eyes of many nineteenth-century Americans, their nation and civilization were the most moral in history, and the survival of their republican institutions hinged on the expansion of U.S. power and influence. Leading politicians as disparate as Thomas Jefferson and Alexander Hamilton agreed on this principle and used imperial and ahistorical rhetoric to articulate their visions of U.S. foreign affairs. Both men understood that foreign policy could be an indirect tool of domestic reform, allowing the transformation or maintenance of institutions without having to make wrenching choices about the distribution of wealth or power. Domestic reform was an important issue to the United States for two reasons: first, the nation's wealth, size, and diversity grew rapidly in the nineteenth century; second, since the nation's inception it was divided into regional blocs with differing cultural outlooks, economic systems, and views of international trade. Americans argued that the international economy operated principally for their benefit and that they had the right to reconstruct it—even if that process was highly detrimental to others. They also sought to create an open international commercial order without accepting any competing presences, economic or political, in the Western Hemisphere. At the same time, many leading Americans saw dangers in entanglements beyond North America and were able to convince their fellow citizens to limit the nation's relationships with peoples and nations beyond the continent almost entirely to economic ones. This "tension" between a desire to organize the world economy and an unwillingness to commit resources to achieve that desire was in large part resolved by the power of the British navy, which indirectly guaranteed American security in the Western Hemisphere and that of U.S. merchants overseas. The American vision of an imperium of free trade certainly had a British tinge.

The events of the last four decades of the nineteenth century shook the foundations on which both Britain's and America's imperiums rested. The most important of these events were Germany's victory in the Franco-Prussian War (1870–1871), the Meiji Restoration in Japan (1868–1912), and Italian unification (ended 1870). These events signaled the emergence of three powers—Germany, Japan, and Italy—intent on altering global military and economic balances. Germany sought to project global power to match its military victories, economy, and overseas trade, which were rapidly overtak-

ing those of Great Britain. Germany also seized colonies in both Africa and Asia and, along with Britain, discussed intervening in a Latin American debt crisis—something no European nation had done since the 1820s. Japan's and Italy's policies in Asia and the Mediterranean, respectively, were important as well. Japan's defeat of China (1895) intensified the partition of China, while Italy's expansion hastened the Ottoman withdrawal from Europe and exacerbated Russian-Austrian tensions over the Balkans. The Franco-Prussian War also marked the beginning of a forty-year period of attempts by France to restore its international status through aggressive diplomacy, strategic investment of capital overseas, the forging of new alliances, and expansion, adding 3.5 million square miles to an already formidable extra-European empire.

All the great powers also followed France in raising their tariff barriers. The new restrictions were a reaction to competition and instability in the international economy and financial insolvency in much of the extra-European world, a dilemma as serious as the new global politics. Since the mid nineteenth century, Europeans had lent millions overseas, usually with high rates of interest. Though bankruptcy was not unheard of in either Europe or overseas (Austria declared bankruptcy five times, as did every nation in Latin America), the consequences of bankruptcies became far more acute after 1870. First, the long "depression" in the international economy from 1873 to 1893 and the decline in the price of commodities meant that non-European nations were far more likely to enter and remain in debt than previously. (Cotton and other commodities were often the chief exports of non-European regions.) Second, bankruptcies often took place in regions adjacent to important trade routes and generated civil unrest. Together, these events threatened global trade and peace. Britain and Russia nearly came to blows over who would dominate the Turkish Straits during the Ottoman financial crisis (1878); Britain and France nearly clashed following Britain's invasion of Egypt to resolve the Egyptian Khedive's bankruptcy (1882); and the United States threatened military action against Germany if Berlin did not withdraw its warships from the Caribbean and agree to the Hague Tribunal's arbitration of Venezuela's debt crisis (1902).

These changes threatened to limit British access to overseas markets and resources and to force Britain to pay a high price to retain the territories it already controlled. They could not have come at a worse time: Britain's trade balances were declining; British goods were losing their competitive position internationally; and Britain's economy was not as dynamic or modern as

THE AFFAIRS OF THE WORLD

In 1884 French prime minister Jules Ferry, a proponent of colonial expansion, offered some thoughts on the process:

The policy of colonial expansion is a political and economic system . . . that can be connected to three sets of ideas: economic ideas; the most far-reaching ideas of civilization; and ideas of a political and patriotic sort.

In the area of economics, I am placing before you, with the support of some statistics, the considerations that justify the policy of colonial expansion, as seen from the perspective of a need, felt more and more urgently by the industrialized population of Europe and especially the people of our rich and hardworking country of France: the need for outlets [for exports]. Is this a fantasy? Is this a concern [that can wait] for the future? Or is this not a pressing need, one may say a crying need, of our industrial population? I merely express in a general way what each one of you can see for himself in the various parts of France. Yes, what our major industries [textiles, etc.], irrevocably steered by the treaties of 1860–1 into exports, lack more and more are outlets. Why? Because next door Germany is setting up trade barriers; because across the ocean the United States of America have become protectionists, and extreme protectionists at that; because not only are these great markets . . . shrinking, becoming more and more difficult of access, but these great states are beginning to pour into our own markets products not seen there before. This is true not only for our agriculture, which has been so sorely tried . . . and for which competition is no longer limited to the circle of large European states. . . . Today, as you know, competition, the law of supply and demand, freedom of trade, the effects of speculation, all radiate in a circle that reaches to the ends of the earth. . . . That is a great complication, a great economic difficulty; . . . an extremely serious problem. It is so serious, gentlemen, so acute, that the least informed persons must already glimpse, foresee, and take precautions against the time when the great South American market that has, in a manner of speaking, belonged to us forever will be disputed and perhaps taken away from us by North American products. Nothing is more serious; there can be no graver social problem; and these matters are linked intimately to colonial policy.

Gentlemen, we must speak more loudly and more honestly! We must say openly that indeed the higher races have a right over the lower races. . . .

I repeat, that the superior races have a right because they have a duty. They have the duty to civilize the inferior races. . . . In the history of earlier centuries these duties, gentlemen, have often been misunderstood; and certainly when the Spanish soldiers and explorers introduced slavery into Central America, they did not fulfill their duty as men of a higher race. . . . But, in our time, I maintain that European nations acquit themselves with generosity, with grandeur, and with sincerity of this superior civilizing duty.

I say that French colonial policy, the policy of colonial expansion, the policy that has taken us under the Empire [the Second Empire, of Napoleon III], to Saigon, to Indochina [Vietnam], that has led us to Tunisia, to Madagascar—I say that this policy of colonial expansion was inspired by . . . the fact that a navy such as ours cannot do without safe harbors, defenses, supply centers on the high seas. . . . Are you unaware of this? Look at a map of the world.

Gentlemen, these are considerations that merit the full attention of patriots. The conditions of naval warfare have greatly changed. . . . At present, as you know, a warship, however perfect its design, cannot carry more than two weeks' supply of coal; and a vessel without coal is a wreck on the high seas, abandoned to the first occupier. Hence the need to have places of supply, shelters, ports for defense and provisioning. . . . And that is why we needed Tunisia; that is why we needed Saigon and Indochina; that is why we need Madagascar . . . and why we shall never leave them! . . . Gentlemen, in Europe such as it is today, in this competition of the many rivals we see rising up around us, some by military or naval improvements, others by the prodigious development of a constantly growing population; in a Europe, or rather in a universe thus constituted, a policy of withdrawal or abstention is simply the high road to decadence! In our time nations are great only through the activity they deploy; it is not by spreading the peaceable light of their institutions . . . that they are great, in the present day.

Spreading light without acting, without taking part in the affairs of the world, keeping out of all European alliances and seeing as a trap, an adventure, all expansion into Africa or the Orient—for a great nation to live this way, believe me, is to abdicate and, in less time than you may think, to sink from the first rank to the third and fourth.

Source: *Jules François Camille Ferry, "Speech Before the French Chamber of Deputies, March 28, 1884," in* Discours et Opinions de Jules Ferry, *edited by Paul Robiquet (Paris: Armand Colin & Cie., 1897), pp. 199–201, 210–211, 215–218; translated by Ruth Kleinman in Brooklyn College Core Four Sourcebook, Internet Modern History Sourcebook <http://www.fordham.edu/halsall/mod/1884ferry.html>.*

COLONIALISM

Burmese rebels undergoing punishment, circa 1900

(British Library, London)

Germany's or America's. Nor could Britain compensate for these deficiencies domestically, given the relatively small population and natural-resources base of the British Isles. Consequently, the British abandoned liberalism and expanded overseas.

The British started this process by formalizing control over several regions where they previously had informal influence and then acquiring other areas. That strategy, like that of the Liberals, rested on the strength of the Royal Navy and the financial strength of the city of London. It also looked to British officials to reorganize the finances of non-European peoples in order to make certain that debts were paid on time and that foreign investments were protected. Britain guaranteed free trade and protection of trade and investments within the empire, which, by 1920, included nearly a quarter of the world's population and land surface. Markets, trade routes, and important raw materials were paramount to the new imperial rubric. Their importance is shown by the enormous sums in men and material that Great Britain spent to ensure that the diamond mines of the Transvaal, oil fields of Iraq, and Suez Canal stayed in British hands. At the same time, London withdrew from areas that were not valuable to Britain financially—Central Asia, the Caribbean, North and Central Africa, and the Levant—as long as another power guaranteed

British access and stable financial conditions. The British were certainly interested in the growth of their empire, but only if it was done profitably.

For the United States the political and economic changes presented a more existential but no less threatening strategic conundrum. Unlike Britain, the United States boasted one of the most modern and fastest-growing economies in the world, with an enormous continental-sized hinterland with large markets, cities, and important natural resources. America's governing institutions and ideologies facilitated a relentless program of settlement and economic development of that hinterland, which freed the United States from a dependence on overseas trade and kept the nation free from extensive overseas commitments or powerful neighbors. Much of the nation's capital remained safely invested at home, while Britain and other nations poured millions of dollars annually into the economy. Abundant supplies of food, coal, and petroleum meant that the nation was virtually self-sufficient. An extensive rail network brought goods and services across the nation quickly.

Many of these strengths, however, were potential weaknesses after 1870. The rise of German and Japanese naval power revised fears of the vulnerability of the nation's long coastline and the possibility of having to choose between

COLONIALISM

defending the Pacific or Atlantic coasts, which were thousands of miles apart. The lack of overseas bases meant that the nation had to continue to depend on the benevolence of other powers to retain access to markets and the natural resources in Latin America, the Caribbean, and China. This point was important for two reasons. Within the new competitive international environment Americans could hardly count on Britain, as they had for decades, or on any other power to guarantee their access to the relatively close markets in the Caribbean or to the considerably farther and even more valuable markets in Asia. Americans for generations had taken it as an article of faith that their institutions depended on the growth of the nation's wealth and size. Deprived of overseas trade routes, natural resources, and markets, could the United States achieve enough growth to maintain national harmony?

The solution to this dilemma was to expand the nation's holdings overseas to include enough territories with access to trade routes, natural resources, and overseas markets to achieve the needed growth. Over the next two generations Washington increased U.S. influence by expanding the nation's navy, establishing colonies and bases in the Pacific and the Caribbean, and strategically investing assets overseas. Among the most important of these bases and colonies were the Philippines, which gave access to Asia, and Puerto Rico and the Panama Canal in the Caribbean. Completed in 1914, the Panama Canal was particularly important to the United States because it shortened by weeks the maritime trip between the Eastern and Western U.S. coasts by eliminating the need to go around South America. By 1925 the United States possessed economic power, a navy, and overseas influence second to none and was poised to become the dominant global power of the century. No longer would Washington depend on other powers to protect American interests overseas.

The decision of both Britain and the United States to abandon their old rubrics for dealing with the outside world and to expand their overseas empires illustrates the challenges that faced the great powers in the period between the Franco-Prussian War and the end of World War II. The spread of industrialization from Great Britain to continental Europe, North America, and Asia and the appearance of new states desiring to change the international balances of power after 1870 made the competition for modern power and wealth—markets, trade routes, and raw materials—fierce and unrelenting. Neither Britain and other status quo powers nor the United States and other rising powers could escape these pressures and the

logic of that period: the only way to survive internationally was to expand. Too much was at stake for any individual great power to trust that others would allow access to a given territory unless that power physically controlled it completely. That same notion held true for the local elite, whose access to European credit had led to the construction of the Suez Canal and other modern infrastructure projects as well as to enormous bankruptcies that threatened global financial and political security. Because of all these factors, it comes as no surprise that by the turn of the twentieth century just ten states dominated the entire globe.

–SEAN FOLEY,
GEORGETOWN UNIVERSITY

Viewpoint:
No. Colonial empires were not the result of deliberate planning; they were the products of European attempts to maintain regional stability.

Since the disappearance of Europe's overseas empires, historians and other scholars have advanced two explanations for the rise of modern colonialism. One view, strongly influenced by critical theorists in such disciplines as sociology and comparative literature, has argued that Europeans needed colonies to satisfy a racist desire to rule over an inferior "other," and to use that rule as a source of the national pride that they needed to solve domestic political dilemmas. A more traditional and deterministic view posits that European nation-states acquired colonies for purely economic reasons. Seizing control of resources in the underdeveloped world enabled them to compete more effectively with each other, while captive markets provided guaranteed outlets for the products of their growing industrial economies.

Yet, both of these interpretations ignore a fundamental and important detail in the history of colonial expansion. Colonial empires were almost never the result of deliberate planning. More often they were the haphazard and undesired products of the European pursuit of regional stability. Although this quest included the need for stable markets, secure trade routes, and local government favorable to commerce, it also mandated broad strategic imperatives and almost never had domination as its goal.

Several cases of European colonial expansion prove this point. Britain's control of India, which began in the mid eighteenth century, is an excellent example, for it was incremental and never reached the point where India was totally under Britain's authority. Britain's early commercial interest in the subcontinent only became a political game when the collapse of the hegemonic Moghul Empire devolved authority to local princes, chieftains, and other strongmen. Preserving trading rights, battling rival French interests, and securing other advantages in practice meant lending support to individuals or coalitions of indigenous rulers who in turn upheld British interests. So haphazard was the British presence that the management of Indian affairs long lay with the commercial East India Company rather than the main government in London. Even after a league of Indian rulers rebelled against the British presence in 1857, Britain—then at the height of its global power—still relied largely on other indigenous forces to defeat the uprising and still resisted establishing direct British rule over the entire subcontinent. Direct authority was only imposed in the absence of stability. Indeed, when Queen Victoria was formally crowned Empress of India in 1876, she reigned not as the direct sovereign of all India but rather as the patroness of vassal Indian princes. These rulers retained their rights throughout the rest of the British presence and only lost them to the independent Indian state founded after Britain's withdrawal in 1947. The regions under direct British rule were subjected to what the British themselves long realized would be a temporary interval. Rather than establishing an indefinite military occupation of India, their main purpose was to prepare the subcontinent (and their other colonies) for eventual self-government on the basis of the rule of law and political legitimacy. The Government of India Act (1935) established local government for the British-ruled areas in anticipation of eventual independence. At every step in Britain's two-hundred-year involvement in India its control was tentative, improvised, and self-consciously finite; its main goal was not to keep the land and its people in permanent thrall to racist European exploiters but to achieve stability in a region of strategic and economic importance.

France's involvement in Algeria was another case of a European state having to act against its will to take possession of an overseas territory. With little prior interest in North Africa the French only began to move in when the local rulers' continuing piracy posed an unacceptable threat to the security of France's expanding commercial and strategic interests in the Levant. Although the American naval commander Stephen Decatur had temporarily put a stop to the Barbary Pirates with his 1815 expedition, they soon resumed their operations. France's invasion in 1830 was a direct response to the rising threat. The contradiction, however, was that as much as France wanted to tame the local rulers, the resis-

tance of indigenous Berber tribes required a deeper penetration into North Africa than it had planned and mandated a long-term occupation. France's ultimate solution was to pacify Algeria by turning it partly into a settlement colony, where hundreds of thousands of Europeans ultimately dwelled. The presence of these settlers made France's eventual withdrawal much more difficult, but the original purpose of their presence in North Africa had much more to do with securing the region's stability than with ensuring the permanent subjugation of the indigenous people or exploiting commercial resources that were (at least at that time) of negligible value.

Inertia also accelerated the Russian Empire's expansion into Central Asia in the latter half of the nineteenth century. Long faced with a porous eastern frontier, Russian rulers relied on military expeditions and conquests to combat raids, disruptions in communication, and other threats to stability. In earlier eras this policy had led to the conquest of the Khanates of Kazan (1552), Astrakhan (1556), and the Crimea (1783)—Muslim states that bordered Russia to the east and south—and to the absorption of the Ukrainian steppe and the Caucasus region in the eighteenth and early nineteenth centuries. By the mid nineteenth century, Russia's growing trade with China, Persia, and other lands in the east brought its travelers and traders more frequently into contact with the Muslim tribes and states of Central Asia. Britain's growing involvement in India, as incidental and haphazard as it may have been, was another threat on the horizon. Frictions that portended wider instability prompted the Russians—rarely the central government in St. Petersburg but rather local military authorities on the frontier—to march out into the steppes and solve whatever problem confronted them.

Like the French in Algeria, the Russians were confronted with a dilemma. Every time they moved forward to enforce stability on the border, they merely found more instability awaiting them. By 1864 the Russian Foreign Ministry could only endorse the impromptu actions of the frontier commanders and recommend that they take all opportunities presented to enforce stability. Within twenty years Russian armies had brought the frontiers of the empire fully across the heartland of Asia, to the western borders of China and to the borders of Afghanistan. Most of this land was desert that the Russians did not (before the discovery of oil) necessarily want to have, but the desire to secure their frontier and trade routes led them into a long-term military presence that only ended (and then only partially) with the collapse of the Soviet Union in 1991.

These three cases were not the only instances of colonial expansion, but they figure among the most notable, occurred in vastly different parts of the world, and had concerns about instability at their root. The British in India, French in Algeria, and Russians in Central Asia all had as their main goals securing the stability of borders, protecting trade routes, defending strategic positions, and cutting out the competition of other European powers. In the long run, all of these powers became more involved in the colonized regions than they would have liked, and all eventually left when their concerns about stability had become, if not satisfied, then at least anachronistic.

This essay is by no means intended to excuse colonialism or ignore the crimes and suffering to which it led, but it is nevertheless worth noting that all three of the regions under discussion witnessed the return of great instability almost immediately after the withdrawal of the colonial power. India was partitioned into a larger Hindu state and the smaller Muslim state of Pakistan, a process that included a violent population transfer that cost millions of lives, frequent conflict over disputed areas, and a nuclear arms race. After winning independence from France in 1962, Algeria was consumed by a bloody civil war that resulted in military dictatorship and continuing challenges from Islamic fundamentalism. After Soviet withdrawal Central Asia suffered from the establishment of oppressive dictatorships in most of the new states established there, a bloody civil war in Tajikistan, and, ironically, the continued presence of Russian troops to attempt to keep order. Additionally, the Soviet Union's extension of power into Afghanistan after 1979 destabilized that country, which continued to fight a civil war after Soviet troops pulled out in 1989, came under the control of the Islamic fundamentalist Taliban by 1996, and became the main base of operations for the al-Qaida terrorist organization that has carried out several terrorist attacks against American targets—including the devastating attacks on the World Trade Center and the Pentagon in September 2001. In another irony of imperialism the U.S. military response in the Middle East, which deposed the Taliban in Afghanistan in late 2001 and attacked Saddam Hussein's Iraq in March 2003, has frequently been described as another great power attempt to secure its interests by seeking to enforce stability over a faraway place.

-PAUL DU QUENOY,
GEORGETOWN UNIVERSITY

References

John Braeman, "Power and Diplomacy: The 1920s Reappraised," *Review of Politics,* 44 (July 1982): 342–369.

Niall Ferguson, *Empire: The Rise and Demise of the British World Order and the Lessons for Global Power* (New York: Basic Books, 2003).

Michael H. Hunt, *Ideology and U.S. Foreign Policy* (New Haven: Yale University Press, 1987).

Ivan Musicant, *Empire by Default: The Spanish-American War and the Dawn of the American Century* (New York: Holt, 1998).

Roger Owen, *The Middle East in the World Economy, 1800–1914* (London & New York: Methuen, 1981).

David Painter, "Research Note: Explaining U.S. Relations with the Third World," *Diplomatic History,* 19 (Summer 1993): 526–529.

R. R. Palmer and Joel Colton, *History of the Modern World,* sixth edition (New York: Knopf, 1984).

COLONIALISM

CONCERT OF EUROPE

Was the nineteenth-century Concert of Europe an effective model for twentieth-century diplomacy?

Viewpoint: Yes. The international system established at the Congress of Vienna was a model of reasonable foreign relations and managed international peace for twentieth-century politicians.

Viewpoint: No. The Concert of Europe depended purely on interests that coincided in certain sets of circumstances and frequently became irreconcilable; twentieth-century aspirations to imitate it were inappropriate and futile.

When a coalition of European powers defeated French emperor Napoleon Bonaparte in 1814, they put an end to twenty-two years of almost constant war, a conflict that had permanently altered the political landscape of the continent and left its future stability in question. Napoleon's brief return from exile in 1815, though ultimately unsuccessful, highlighted this instability. In these circumstances the powers of Europe assembled at an international conference, the Congress of Vienna (1814–1815), to settle outstanding diplomatic questions peacefully. In the years that followed, the major European powers—Austria, Prussia, Russia, and Britain—formed an alliance, which France was later allowed to join, to keep the general European peace. Most continental powers also entered into the Holy Alliance, an international agreement to conduct diplomatic relations in accordance with Christian principles. On several occasions representatives of the powers met at international conferences to discuss and agree upon the resolution of new challenges to European stability. This system of cooperation in international affairs became known as the Concert of Europe.

In the troubled twentieth century many statesmen looked back to the Concert of Europe as a healthy alternative to conflict, one that was to be emulated. This chapter seeks to assess whether the nineteenth-century diplomatic model was valid for twentieth-century politics. As one argument presented here suggests, Europe's shared values, reasonable compromises, and cooperative solutions during the earlier century were splendid alternatives to naked aggression, global conflict, and, potentially, nuclear war. Even if the Concert of Europe did not always work perfectly and occasionally broke down, the successes and good intentions of those who directed it were a lesson for twentieth-century leaders. Yet, as opponents of this view argue, the nineteenth century contained too many failures and conflicts to qualify it as a time of successfully managed peace. When interests of the major powers collided in a way serious enough to cause war—as it did before the Crimean War (1853–1856), the Wars of German Unification (1864–1871), and World War I (1914–1918)—conflict became unavoidable. Other conflicts they also argue, were solved not by tame negotiations but by raw calculations of power and national interest.

Viewpoint:
Yes. The international system established at the Congress of Vienna was a model of reasonable foreign relations and managed international peace for twentieth-century politicians.

A twentieth century that too often experienced the force of international relations as a zero-sum game conducted in a state of anarchy may be pardoned for regarding with nostalgia the "simpler place and time" represented by the Concert of Europe. The Concert, however, was more than a last-ditch manifestation of statist politics and aristocratic societies. The notion of a European order based on flexible negotiation of wedge issues among interested parties remains as valid—and as elusive—in the twenty-first century as it proved in the twentieth.

The concept behind the Concert of Europe involved developing a general alliance among the great powers that would be focused on neither aggression and territorial gain nor defense against external threats in the classic balance-of-power model. Instead, the Concert of Europe was intended to facilitate the preservation of peace through mutual restraint. Its roots were Austrian and arguably extended back to some general ideas presented by Holy Roman Emperor Leopold II (reigned 1790–1792) relative to the Polish Question. The idea is more generally, and accurately, connected to Austrian foreign secretary Prince Clemens von Metternich, who at the Congress of Vienna (1814–1815) repeatedly stressed the desirability of regular consultation among the powers to maintain peace and increase prosperity.

The underlying principle of the Concert idea was the postulate that no great power would take action in Europe, even in a matter it described as engaging its vital interests, without preliminary consultation with its counterparts. The underlying strength of the Concert idea was its recognition that peace was a positive concept, something requiring action to sustain. Eighteenth-century diplomatic deism, the notion of a self-regulating polity expressed in the phrase *balance of power,* was a dangerous mirage. In these contexts the Concert of Europe asserted the primacy of the great powers—Britain, France, Russia, Austria, and Prussia—while recognizing the independence and rights of the lesser states. It accepted as well the special position of the two "wing" or "fringe" powers—Russia in Asia and Britain in the non-European world in general—each of which had interests and responsibilities inconvenient to include in a continental context.

The Concert of Europe allowed them relative freedom of action, while simultaneously exercising a "watching brief" to ensure responsible behavior.

Metternich's original notion of periodic direct meetings collapsed within a decade—largely because face-to-face contact among the powers tended to exacerbate tensions rather than resolve them. The pattern of exchanging notes persisted, however, and was facilitated by the development of transportation and communications technology that sped the processes of multiple exchanges of information. Concert diplomacy still required time, but delay in taking action on foreign-policy questions was generally considered an acceptable trade-off in return for support—or at least tacit consent—from the other major states.

Central to the Concert's functioning was that no lesser state took a significant diplomatic initiative without the support and patronage of a great power. That pattern was facilitated because after 1815 the high levels of armament maintained by the great powers meant that no lesser state by itself could hope to do more than fight a delaying action against one of them. Time was correspondingly less important as a force multiplier. The same was true for the counterrevolutionary operations that were the other pillar of Concert activity. The years since 1789 had taught Europe's governments enough about urban crowd control and rural search-and-hang missions.

During the first half of the nineteenth century, Concert diplomacy worked well enough in maintaining order and sustaining communication—as long as its activity was restricted to Europe. In Spain, Italy, and Germany the Concert proved an effective force for international peace and domestic stability for twenty years after the fall of French emperor Napoleon Bonaparte (1814). Once the Powers interacted systematically outside of that charmed circle—specifically in the Balkans and Middle East—ground rules grew strained. Russia's refusal to cooperate with the Western powers over the Ottoman question in the 1830s led to an Anglo-Russian entente at the expense of Britain's relations with France. That led in turn to a series of French initiatives in the German question that strained the Concert almost to the breaking point and indeed by some accounts reduced it to a fiction on which states agreed until agreement became inconvenient. The Crimean War (1853–1856) marked the end of Concert diplomacy in its pristine form as the Western powers—France, Britain, and their allies—went to war to counter what they regarded as unacceptable Russian initiatives in an Ottoman Empire that they had marked for their own exploitation.

Critics of the Concert, then and now, suggest it could have been no more than a temporary institution under any circumstances. In the absence of any integrating external threat the clashing self-interests of powers essentially equal in strength would in any case have stretched the post-Vienna concord to the breaking point even without the Ottoman temptations and imbroglios. Yet, in the years prior to World War I (1914–1918) Concert diplomacy made a second appearance on the European stage, this time as the central element in an effort to integrate the Balkans into a network of alliances and multinational agreements that, for all its inconsistencies, had kept Europe's peace since its introduction by German chancellor Otto von Bismarck in the 1870s. The effort failed, in good part because neither of its principal advocates, Germany and Britain, had the diplomatic finesse to sell the idea to Europe's chanceries or the military power to command attention when they warned of the risks of the Near East—and by extension the Ottoman Empire—becoming the tail that wagged the European dog.

The notion of a Concert of Europe retained a significant half-life in the twentieth century. It reemerged in the Locarno Pact (1925), the terms of which provided for systematic negotiations among the nations of Western Europe while recognizing the great powers' need for flexibility. If the Warsaw Pact, the military alliance of the Soviet Union and the other communist nations of Eastern Europe, was substituted for European revolution during the Cold War, the North Atlantic Treaty Organization (NATO) owed much of its structure and behavior to Metternich's original concept. The comparison might be extended in order to argue that the turn-of-the-century strains on NATO reflect the same "out of area" issues that plagued the original Concert. European Union (EU) efforts to establish a military counterpoint/counterweight to what one French foreign minister called America's "hyperpower" have so far met the same fate, and for roughly the same reason, as the efforts to revive the Concert before World War I: the absence of a sufficiently strong, convincing rallying point relative to the perceived threat. Concert diplomacy is likely to remain an option in any international system built around several states of roughly equal strength. In turn, the flexibility that gives Concert systems their initial viability is the most likely reason for their eventual failure, as participants seek to maximize their interests individually.

—DENNIS SHOWALTER,
COLORADO COLLEGE

Viewpoint:
No. The Concert of Europe depended purely on interests that coincided in certain sets of circumstances and frequently became irreconcilable; twentieth-century aspirations to imitate it were inappropriate and futile.

The Concert of Europe, the regular meeting of the great European powers after the downfall of French emperor Napoleon Bonaparte (1814) until the outbreak of World War I (1914–1918), has frequently been perceived as a model for guiding diplomatic relations during the twentieth century. The leaders of the United States and Western Europe often uncritically saw the actions of Britain, Prussia, Austria, Russia, and France to maintain Europe's balance of power, territorial integrity, and monarchies as historical precedents for their own attempts to balance the international order. These attempts, such as the League of Nations, the Yalta (February 1945) and Potsdam (July–August 1945) conferences, and various Western European international bodies, largely resulted in political and socio-economic instability. Like Austrian foreign secretary Prince Clemens von Metternich, British politician Viscount Castlereagh, and German chancellor Otto von Bismarck, twentieth-century statesmen often sought to reinstate the old European club of states without taking into account the rapid developments of the modern age. Yet, political leaders of the twentieth century also ignored the consequences of rapid technological development, total war, ethnic and racial hatred, industrialization, demographic growth, and popular alienation from existing regimes. These misunderstandings undoubtedly contributed to the totalitarian movements and destruction and massive loss of life that have plagued Europe.

The League of Nations had many similarities to the Concert of Europe. Like the Concert of Europe, the League of Nations was founded in the immediate aftermath of a war that threatened to overturn the political order. Just as Article Six of the Vienna Settlement called for the Concert of Europe to maintain order in the postwar years so, too, Article Thirteen of the Versailles Treaty (1919) authorized the League of Nations to prevent a world war from ever recurring. Although the League of Nations included far more than just five European powers and was a formal international institution, France and Britain, the victorious powers of the

IMPORTANT ARRANGEMENTS

In 1815 German writer and journalist Frederick von Gentz made the following observations on divisions among the participants at the Congress of Vienna:

The Emperor of Russia has come to Vienna, in the first place to be admired (which is always the principal thing in his thoughts), and next to direct personally the important arrangements which should fix the boundaries and future position of the many states who claim their share of the immense spoil which is placed at the disposal of the Allies, by their success against the common enemy. The three principal objects of the Emperor Alexander were: 1st, to take possession for ever of the whole, or almost the whole, of the Duchy of Warsaw, with the exception of some small portions, which he would give to the two neighbouring powers; 2nd, to prevent Austria from profiting too much by the advantages of her new position; 3rd, to enrich Prussia as much as possible, not only to compensate her for her ancient Polish provinces, which he had carried away from her by surprise, and which he retained because it pleased him to do so, but also to make her a useful and powerful ally, the only one on whom he could rely in the future. Such were the *real* objects he had in view; the *ostensible* object was to mingle in all the affairs of Europe, and to pass as the arbiter of their destinies.

On arriving at Vienna the Emperor was already more or less embroiled with Austria, England, and France. His displeasure with Austria was chiefly on account of the many and deep grievances which he had, or pretended to have, against Prince Metternich. The first and true origin of these grievances dated from the opposition of that minister to the Emperor's proposal to become himself the commander-in-chief of the allied armies. His resentment, which was restrained during the first period of the war, and even hidden under an appearance of great friendliness, broke out for the first time in the month of December, 1813, on the occasion of the Allies entering Switzerland, a plan which all good generals had approved, but which the Emperor opposed, because, in one of his philanthropic moods, he had given his word to some Vaudois apostles of liberty that the neutrality of Switzerland should be respected. Since that moment there has been no return of harmony. Angry and bitter discussions took place almost every day during the last part of the campaign, and by the time the Allies reached Paris they preserved, with difficulty, the outward appearance of a friendliness which had no longer any foundation. The Emperor accustomed himself to look on M. de Metternich only as a permanent obstacle to his designs, as a man occupied without intermission in opposing and thwarting him; at last, as a sworn enemy. The calmness and serenity which M. de Metternich always opposed to these prejudices, instead of softening the Emperor, appeared only to embitter him the more; private feelings, above all a strong jealousy of M. de Metternich's success, both in politics and society, increased this irritation. At last it reached the point of an implacable hatred, and during his stay in Vienna, his daily explosions of rage and frenzy afforded an inexhaustible fund of curiosity and amusement to frivolous minds at the court, whilst sensible men deplored them as a great calamity. This hatred is the key to most of the events of the Congress; if it has done infinite harm to the affairs, and essentially spoilt the most important interests of Europe, we have at least the poor consolation that it has not turned to the personal advantage of the Emperor. His perpetual tirades against Prince Metternich, the details into which he entered with twenty women of society, to indoctrinate them with the crimes of this minister and designs for overthrowing him, as badly conceived as foolishly carried out, and only succeeding in adding to his credit—all this has given the Emperor Alexander an irreparable blow in public opinion; and it is perhaps one of the most useful effects of this Congress, and one of the greatest benefits it has given to Europe, to have cooled the general admiration with which some of this sovereign's brilliant qualities had inspired almost all his contemporaries. The true worth of his character is now seen, and if men have ceased to admire, they have also entirely ceased to fear him.

His relations with England (a Power which he had always cordially detested, and which he only cultivated either from interest or fear) have been sensibly disturbed since his visit to London. Lord Castlereagh was particularly disagreeable to him; he called him cold and pedantic, and there were moments in Vienna when he would have treated him as he did M. de Metternich, if extreme fear of openly compromising himself with the British Government (the only one before whom he trembled) had not forced him to dissimulate. Neither was the Emperor inclined to friendly relations with France. He had not pardoned the King for having adopted a system of government contrary to the advice which he had wished to give him; he was furious against Prince Talleyrand, who, at the time of the Allies entering Paris, had appeared to recognise no law but the will of the Russian Emperor, and who, four weeks afterwards, had found the means of rendering himself independent. In the first months of his stay in Vienna there were some violent scenes between the Emperor and M. de Talleyrand; subsequently Talleyrand understood how to impress the Emperor by his cleverness, his repartees, and his *savoir-faire;* but the secret aversion remained the same. The King of Bavaria, although his brother-in-law, was odious to him on account of his close relations with Austria, and because he believed Marshal de Wrede to be one of the blind instruments of Prince Metternich. The King of Denmark was equally insupportable to him, because he had had the courage to reproach him for his wrongs and evil conduct. The King of Prussia, therefore, was the Russian Emperor's only friend, a prince whose personal attachment was secured by his gratitude, his weakness, his infatuation, and by his distrust of everyone else, whose cabinet, foreseeing the general opposition to its schemes for self-aggrandisement, had allied itself with Russia, and made the first principle of her policy a blind submission to the will of that Power.

Source: *Prince Richard Metternich, ed.,* Memoirs of Prince Metternich, 1773–1815, *volume 2, translated by Mrs. Alexander Napier (New York: Howard Fertig, 1970), pp. 554–556.*

war, hoped to control the assembly, while the United States never joined.

In fact, the main problem of the Paris Peace Settlement (1919) was that it followed the Paris agreements of 1815 too closely. Similar to Metternich's attempts to reduce French territory to the borders of 1792 and allow the Prussian and Habsburg Empires to take back territories they had lost, French premier Georges Clemenceau, British prime minister David Lloyd George, and U.S. president Woodrow Wilson tried to restore the balance of power that existed before the 1870s, when Germany's military victories, unification, industrialization, and demographic boom propelled it beyond its rivals. The victors of World War I sought to accomplish this task by stripping Germany of much of its territory and breaking the Habsburg Empire into various successor states. Also, reparations and the occupation of the industrial heartland devastated the German economy. Finally, Wilson and Clemenceau devised a cordon sanitaire of newly established Eastern European nations—namely Poland, Czechoslovakia, Yugoslavia, and Romania—to contain Germany, Austria, Hungary, and Bulgaria, which sought to revise the peace settlements.

Unlike Metternich's arrangement, whose border settlements were left largely intact for approximately fifty years, the measures of Clemenceau, Lloyd George, and Wilson were an almost immediate failure. France, Britain, and the United States were unwilling to enforce the harsh terms of Versailles, as demonstrated by German leader Adolf Hitler's remilitarization of the Rhineland, annexation of Austria, and diplomatic triumph over Czechoslovakia. The allies would have been better off to acknowledge Germany as the predominant power of continental Europe in the beginning rather than bolster the Nazis by stripping significant chunks of territory and then catering to German demands. France and Britain, the world powers of the eighteenth and nineteenth centuries, were no longer capable of redrawing the map of Europe.

The allies had also attempted the nearly impossible task of imposing liberal democratic regimes upon the losing powers. The first step in this process was the provisions in the peace settlements that formally ended the German, Habsburg, and Ottoman Empires in favor of new nation-states. President Wilson in particular called for the new successor states to be based on the principle of national self-determination, believing that democratic forms of government should naturally take root. Indeed, he refused to negotiate with a German government that was dominated by the military or supporters of the monarchy. His efforts, like those of Metternich before him, underestimated the determination of the defeated populations to resist the imposed form of government. Just as the French Revolutions of 1830 and 1848 aimed at restoring the republic, many Germans also sought to reinstate a strong, nationalist regime. The allies' failure to stop antidemocratic movements throughout the continent was obvious throughout the interwar period. The Molotov-Ribbentrop Pact (1939), which precipitated the outbreak of World War II (1939–1945), revealed that totalitarianism, not democracy, was the only form of government that could be exported.

The wartime conferences of the "big three" allies—the United States, the Soviet Union, and Britain—from 1942 to 1945 were the second instance in the twentieth century where the U.S. government attempted to emulate the Concert of Europe. President Franklin D. Roosevelt believed in a common mission with Russian leader Josef Stalin and British prime minister Winston Churchill to end the German threat and establish antifascist regimes throughout Europe. The allies indeed ensured that Germany would never again dominate the continent. Britain, the United States, and the Soviet Union never came to a true consensus about Stalin's demand for "Soviet-friendly people's democracies" in the countries adjacent to the Soviet Union. Although American support for democracy seemed compatible with this demand, the Red Army installed Communist regimes throughout Eastern Europe by 1948.

Attempting to reestablish a European-dominated balance of power was also a futile task. Western Europe was so devastated by the conflict that American dollars could only partially succeed in rebuilding it. Despite the Marshall Plan (1947)—the massive influx of U.S. cash into Western Europe—France, Britain, the Netherlands, and Belgium were all forced to give up their colonial possessions throughout Africa and Asia. The United Nations (UN), founded immediately after the war by American demand, reflected the new reality. Even though Roosevelt envisioned that the institution would promote worldwide consensus, the veto power of the Soviet Union almost always stopped the UN from responding to major crises. The UN failed to approve any significant American initiative until the fall of the Soviet Union (1991), except for UN intervention in Korea (1950–1953), and that vote was taken during a Soviet boycott of the institution. The real balance of power was maintained by the mutually assured nuclear destruction of the Western democratic capitalist governments and their dependents and non-Western Communist-inspired regimes

in the event of war. The American and Soviet nuclear powers saw Europe merely as a battle-field for global power politics.

The fall of the Eastern European Commu-nist regimes in 1989 and the subsequent breakup of the Soviet Union were opportuni-ties for the Western powers to reestablish a common consensus among European nations for democracy and capitalism. Perhaps the most ambitious project was the absorption of East Germany into the Federal Republic of Germany in October 1990. Former East Germany's tran-sition into the Western European economy was harsh and swift. Consequently, most East Ger-mans had to accept that reunification did not lessen the economic gap between themselves and their Western counterparts. Meanwhile, the European Union (EU) has planned to expand its membership by accepting countries such as Hungary, Poland, and the Czech Republic. With the help of the International Monetary Fund (IMF), World Bank, and other Western-dominated financial institutions, other previ-ously excluded Eastern European nations have also prepared themselves to join the EU.

Although the Eastern European governments were initially in favor of cutting public expendi-tures in order to qualify for Western loans and integration, the population soon grew weary. Reformed communist parties have recently won elections in most Eastern European states on the promise of slowing down the pace of reforms. Similarly, the former Communist Party of Democratic Socialism (PDS) has become a leading party in the former East Germany, presenting a constant challenge to reintegration in the West.

These ongoing integrative efforts once again have overestimated the ability of Western Europe to impose a common political and eco-nomic consensus on the continent. The failure of the EU to prevent the outbreak of war in the former Yugoslavia revealed the inability of this organization to deal with internal European affairs. While the American-led forces finally intervened in the Bosnian and Kosovo con-flicts, this intervention was done at the price of injuring Russian pride. Russian president Boris Yeltsin signaled that his country would no longer tolerate further interference in what its elite considered its traditional sphere of influ-

Delegates at the Locarno Conference, in which the leading states of Europe agreed to maintain their existing boundaries, October 1925

(from Stefan Lorant, Sieg Heil! Hail to Victory: An Illustrated History of Germany from Bismarck to Hitler, *1979)*

CONCERT OF EUROPE

ence. Continued Russian campaigns against Chechnya also augured the end of any common geopolitical consensus.

The inescapable conclusion is that Western Europeans and Americans never established a common political and ideological consensus at the end of the twentieth century's three great conflicts. Many leaders looked back to the Concert of Europe, thinking that they too had the ability to redraw the frontiers of Europe to fit this vision and their own nation's strategic interests. The reality was that Britain and France, the two surviving members of the old Concert of Europe, would never effectively dominate continental affairs like they did in the previous century. America, an outside power, was only partially successful in filling the gap. Hitler's Germany, the Soviet Union, and an Eastern Europe disenchanted with the West have always stood in opposition to democratic capitalism as a common form of governance. This hostility is unlikely to go away.

–YORK NORMAN,
GEORGETOWN UNIVERSITY

References

Richard Langhorne, *The Collapse of the Concert of Europe: International Politics, 1890–1914* (New York: St. Martin's Press, 1981).

Richard Rosecrance, "A New Concert of Powers," *Foreign Affairs,* 71 (Spring 1992): 64–82.

Georges-Henri Soutou, "Was there a European Order in the Twentieth Century?: From the Concert of Europe to the End of the Cold War," *Contemporary European History,* 9 (2000): 329–353.

DECOLONIZATION

Did European colonial powers give up their empires after World War II because they were too weak to maintain them?

Viewpoint: Yes. European nations gave up their colonies as a result of military weakness and international pressure.

Viewpoint: No. Europeans gave up their colonies because their leaders determined that such possessions were no longer necessary or profitable.

The impact of two world wars permanently damaged the ability of European powers to retain their colonial empires. Particularly after 1945, the main colonial powers Britain and France, and also Belgium, the Netherlands, and Portugal, relinquished control of their possessions in the emerging Third World. By the turn of the twenty-first century, colonialism had become anachronistic and was confined to only a few remote corners of the world.

This chapter examines why European powers so readily divested themselves of wealthy and prestigious colonies. One argument traces the decision to military factors. As the European colonial powers found themselves weakened economically and threatened militarily, few of them had the resources, stamina, and will to fight the independence movements growing in their empires. In some cases, particularly France's debacle in Indochina, they suffered absolute military defeats at the hands of indigenous forces. In others, including France's involvement in Algeria, Portugal's drawn-out struggles with independence movements in its colonies, and the Soviet Union's long battle in Afghanistan, mounting costs led to the realization that the occupying power could not win without unacceptable sacrifice. Much of the time these and other colonial powers recognized in advance that they could not sustain a war to preserve their positions.

In counterpoint the other argument suggests that European colonialists were craftier in their rationales. One major reason for decolonization, the author argues, was that long-term European presence had created a legacy of secure markets, mature infrastructures, and a reliable elite that ensured that the regions would remain stable trading partners and trustworthy members of the community of nations. In other words, the colonial empires had done their job by integrating previously turbulent regions into the international system. When the colonial powers left their possessions, they were fulfilling a process that was and had always been conceived of as limited in ambition and finite in duration. As concerns about the Third World play a greater role in the new millennium, understanding its emergence is of considerable importance.

Viewpoint:
Yes. European nations gave up their colonies as a result of military weakness and international pressure.

Military weakness and international pressure were crucial factors in hastening the decline of European imperialism. Facing dwindling resources and new challengers in the developing world, retreat from colonial possessions was the only viable option for European powers, particularly after World War II (1939–1945).

Although most of the colonial world became free after 1945, there were nevertheless several earlier developments underscoring the military and diplomatic necessity of decolonization. Even by 1900 continuing trends of relative decline and rising trends of heavy domestic spending indicated that the two foremost European colonial powers, Britain and France, were losing their competitive edges and would soon have to face serious challenges from rising powers such as the United States, Germany, Japan, and, to a lesser extent, Russia and Italy. Indeed, France's defeat by Germany in 1870–1871 proved that it was moving into a position of inferiority vis-à-vis its fellow great powers. For the moment, however, the two main European colonial centers perceived alternate means of preserving their empires. Britain pursued delicate relations with the United States through most of the nineteenth century and continued to do so into the twentieth. By conceding the Western Hemisphere as a de facto American zone of influence and accommodating a growing U.S. presence in the Pacific, it avoided potentially costly confrontations. Although Britain's relationship with France long remained contentious, in 1904 the two nations negotiated a comprehensive settlement of their competing claims in the colonial world and, while not explicitly becoming allies, entered into a de facto strategic partnership. Two years earlier Britain had entered into a defensive alliance with Japan to avoid conflict in the Far East, and in 1907 it settled outstanding colonial disputes with Russia. As a leading revisionist account has suggested, Britain's purpose in pursuing these agreements was to eliminate as much as possible the threat of a destructive war. France's purpose in negotiating with Britain and in maintaining a long-term defensive alliance with Russia (in place after 1892) was to make certain that it would not have to fight Germany alone in the future.

Such diplomacy masked growing economic weakness, which, as the British and French elite realized, would translate into military weakness.

The costs of World War I (1914–1918) were instrumental in proving that the two nations' relative positions were indeed on the decline. Germany came close to proving that it had the economic and corresponding military potential to defeat Britain, France, and Russia in combination. Only German domestic turmoil and timely U.S. intervention prevented that catastrophe. Nevertheless, the consequences of the war for the victors and their ability to control their empires were almost immediately apparent. Within only a few years of the peace settlement Britain was actively withdrawing from many of its imperial commitments. After fighting an inconclusive guerrilla struggle with Irish nationalists, it conceded Ireland's status as a "free state" in 1922, a development that soon allowed most of the island to move toward full independence and the formal proclamation of a republic from Great Britain. That Parliament had been debating Irish Home Rule for decades and had already tentatively approved it in 1914 (the outbreak of war prevented its implementation) was a powerful admission of Britain's inability and unwillingness to defend its centuries-old occupation by force of arms. Such weakness had also been evidenced by Britain's willingness to grant autonomy to South Africa—which had been forged by conquest in the Boer War (1899–1902) but could no longer command its declining military resources—as a quasi-independent dominion in 1910. In 1922 Britain also ended its forty-year-old protectorate over Egypt, even if it retained political influence, base rights, and a major stake in the Suez Canal Company. Within ten years it followed a similar course in Iraq. The Statute of Westminster (1931) provided for the formal transition of Britain's former settlement colonies—Canada, Australia, New Zealand, and South Africa, as well as the Irish Free State—into new entities that enjoyed de facto independence and only nominal ties to the British Crown. This retraction of British influence continued through the 1930s, as London abandoned its more formal regime of protectorates and mandates in the Middle East in favor of informal networks of advisers and diplomats. The decision to give up India—which only reached fulfillment in 1947—was largely already made in 1935, when Parliament passed a bill creating native local government in preparation for eventual independence.

Had the British suddenly become humanitarians who rejected the evils of colonization? If that were true, they certainly kept enough colonies to make them look like hypocrites. Did they believe that they had accomplished their original tasks of bringing stability to strategically important regions and promoting their economic interests? For a variety of reasons this conclusion was unlikely. Some of the territories let go in the interwar period were recent acquisitions of limited economic value, particularly the Middle Eastern protectorates, which had not yet built up their oil industries. Egypt had the Suez Canal, but the British held on to their control of the waterway. The more developed territories that left imperial control—Ireland, Canada, Australia, and New Zealand—actually used their new domestic powers at the expense of British economic interests. All of them dramatically raised import tariffs on British goods, partly to foster domestic industry and partly to reduce potential political influence deriving from British economic penetration. The Irish Free State immediately adopted radical and punitive land-reform policies that were designed to break British and Protestant domination of agriculture and land-ownership.

A better explanation was that the British leadership, and to a lesser extent the French as well, realized that keeping up costly commitments in contentious environments was more than their military and economic resources could bear. Each country had lost several hundred thousand men in World War I, and the rest of the population was war weary. When Britain looked at possible acquisitions in the Caucasus, the Middle East, and Central Asia immediately after the war and considered a policy of intervention in the Russian Civil War (1918–1920), its military leaders came to the conclusion that their country had neither the will nor the resources to play such roles. Rising unrest in Ireland, Egypt, and India—all of which eventuated Britain's withdrawal—indicated that limited military resources would be needed for problems within the existing empire.

The expense of modern warfare had been impressive as well, even if it was not quite as devastating as it would be in the next world war. Neither Britain nor France ever repaid its World War I loans to the United States. France maintained that it could not recover domestically without the enforcement of reparations payments on Germany. Both Britain and France suffered economically in the 1920s. France's failure to secure German reparations or stimulate economic growth led to a major currency crisis in 1926 that caused the devaluation of the franc to 20 percent of its prewar value. Britain chafed under the expense of war pensions and suffered a series of strikes and other economic dislocations. Afflicted by the Great Depression, Britain took its currency off the gold standard and devalued the pound in 1931. France devalued the franc once again in 1936. Clearly neither country had the economic, and therefore the military, wherewithal to compete alone on the world stage. One of the main motivations behind the policy of appeasement toward Nazi Germany was that neither Britain nor France believed it could stand up to German military power on its own, or even in combination with the other. German leader Adolf Hitler's victorious six-week campaign against France in 1940 and Britain's desperate struggle alone over the next year proved their weakness.

Although the involvement of the United States and the Soviet Union secured Germany's defeat, World War II reduced Britain's and France's economic and military power even further. From a military standpoint they faced huge difficulties in reestablishing authority over their empires. Britain withdrew from potentially dangerous situations in India (1947) and Palestine (1948) largely because it did not wish to shoulder the costs of remaining. Its "bush wars" against rebel movements in Kenya, Malaya, and other colonies were costly and unpopular and had to compete with the resources demanded by Britain's vast postwar welfare state. Both Kenya and Malaya were independent within just a few years of the postwar colonial conflicts. Most of Britain's colonies in Africa became independent from 1956 to 1962, and few did so in a stable or prosperous fashion. Britain's already reduced presence in the Middle East began to vanish at the same time and was completed following the 1967 decision of Prime Minister Harold Wilson's government to withdraw from points "East of Suez." Only small colonial possessions such as Hong Kong (returned to China in 1997), Gibraltar (rejected a joint-sovereignty arrangement with Spain in a 2002 referendum), and the Falkland Islands (sparsely inhabited territories retaken from Argentina with U.S. assistance in 1982) remained of its once mighty empire.

France, which had been psychologically shattered by the defeat of 1940, was more tenacious, but its military effort to regain control of Indochina, which had been occupied by Japan during the war, ended in absolute military defeat at the hands of the Vietnamese rebels at Dien Bien Phu (1954). Indeed, France's efforts were so challenging for the country's depleted resources that it had to plead for U.S. financial assistance to fund the war (which was granted) and for U.S. air strikes to break the siege at Dien Bien Phu (which were not). The defeat caused the weak government of France to let go of most of its remaining colonies by the end of the decade.

The remaining trouble spot of the French Empire, Algeria, presented considerable military challenges. Although French forces won the "Battle of Algiers," a rising of Arab nationalists, when it flared in 1957, a bitter guerilla war continued. France's failure to capitalize on its initial tactical victory led to a major political crisis in May 1958 that portended military resistance to the democratic order and resulted in its replacement by a brief, but de facto, dictatorship under

STATUTE OF WESTMINSTER (1931)

Whereas the delegates to His Majesty's Governments in the United Kingdom, the Dominion of Canada, the Commonwealth of Australia, the Dominion of New Zealand, the Union of South Africa, the Irish Free State and Newfoundland, at Imperial Conferences holden at Westminster in the years of our Lord nineteen hundred and twenty-six and nineteen hundred and thirty did concur in making the declarations and resolutions set forth in the Reports of the said Conference: And whereas it is meet and proper to set out by way of preamble to this Act that, inasmuch as the Crown is the symbol to the free association of the members of the British Commonwealth of Nations, and as they are united by a common allegiance to the Crown, it would be in accord with the established constitutional position of all the members of the Commonwealth in relation to one another that any alteration in the law touching the Succession to the Throne or the Royal Style and Titles shall hereafter require the assent as well of the Parliaments of all the Dominions as of the Parliament of the United Kingdom: And whereas it is in accord with the established constitutional position that no law hereafter made by the Parliament of the United Kingdom shall extend to any of the said Dominions as part of the law of that Dominion otherwise than at the request and with the consent of that Dominion. And whereas it is necessary for the ratifying, confirming and establishing of certain of the said declarations and resolutions of the said Conferences that a law be made and enacted in due form by authority of the Parliament of the United Kingdom: And whereas the Dominion of Canada, the Commonwealth of Australia, the Dominion of New Zealand, the Union of South Africa, the Irish Free State and Newfoundland have severally requested and consented to the submission of a measure to the Parliament of the United Kingdom for making such provision with regard to the matters aforesaid as is hereafter in this Act contained: Now, therefore, be it enacted by the King's Most Excellent Majesty by and with the advice and consent of the Lords Spiritual and Temporal, and Commons, in this present Parliament assembled, and by the authority of the same, as follows:

Section 1 [Meaning of "Dominion" in this Act] In this Act the expression "Dominion" means any of the following Dominions, that is to say, the Dominion of Canada, the Commonwealth of Australia, the Dominion of New Zealand, the Union of South Africa, the Irish Free State and Newfoundland.

Section 2 [Validity of laws made by Parliament of a Dominion] (1) The Colonial Laws Validity Act, 1865, shall not apply to any law made after the commencement of this Act by the Parliament of a Dominion. (2) No law and no provision of any law made after the commencement of this Act by the Parliament of a Dominion shall be void or inoperative on the ground that it is repugnant to the law of England, or to the provisions of any existing or future Act of Parliament of the United Kingdom, or to any order, rule, or regulation made under any such Act, and the powers of the Parliament of a Dominion shall include the power to repeal or amend any such Act, order, rule or regulation in so far as the same is part of the law of the Dominion.

Section 3 [Power of Parliament of Dominion to legislate extra-territorially] It is hereby declared and enacted that the Parliament of a Dominion has full power to make laws having extra-territorial operation.

Section 4 [Parliament of United Kingdom not to legislate for Dominion except by its consent] No Act of Parliament of the United Kingdom passed after the commencement of this Act shall extend or be deemed to extend, to a Dominion as part of the law of that Dominion, unless it is expressly declared in that Act that that Dominion has requested, and consented to, the enactment thereof.

Section 5 [Powers of Dominion Parliaments in relation to merchant shipping] Without prejudice to the generality of the foregoing provisions of this Act, sections seven hundred and thirty-five and seven hundred and thirty-six of the Merchant Shipping Act, 1894, shall be construed as though reference therein to the Legislature of a British possession did not include reference to the Parliament of a Dominion.

Section 6 [Powers of Dominion Parliaments in relation to Courts of Admiralty] Without prejudice to a generality of the foregoing provisions of this Act, section four of the Colonial Courts of Admiralty Act, 1890 (which requires certain laws to be reserved for the signification of His Majesty's pleasure or to contain a suspending clause), and so much of section seven of that Act as requires the approval of His Majesty in Council to any rules of Court for regulating the practice and procedure of a Colonial Court of Admiralty, shall cease to have effect in any Dominion as from the commencement of this Act.

Section 7 [Saving for British North America Acts and applications of the Act to Canada] (1) Nothing in this Act shall be deemed to apply to the repeal, amendment or alteration of the British North America Acts, 1867 to 1930, or any order, rule or regulation made thereunder. (2) The provisions of section two of this Act shall extend to laws made by any of the Provinces of Canada and to the powers of the legislatures of such Provinces. (3) The powers conferred by this Act upon the Parliament of Canada or upon the legislatures of the Provinces shall be restricted to the enactment of laws in the relation to matters within the competence of the Parliament of Canada or of any of the legislatures of the Provinces respectively.

Section 8 [Saving for Constitution Acts of Australia and New Zealand] Nothing in this Act shall be deemed to confer any power to repeal or alter the Constitution or the Constitution Act of the Commonwealth of Australia or the Constitution Act of the Dominion of New Zealand otherwise than in accordance with the law existing before the commencement of this Act.

Section 9 [Saving with respect to States of Australia] (1) Nothing in this Act shall be deemed to authorize the Parliament of the Commonwealth of Australia to make laws on any matter within the authority of the States of Australia, not being a matter within the authority of the Parliament or Government of the Commonwealth of Australia. (2) Nothing in this Act shall be deemed to require the concurrence of the Parliament or Govern-ment of the Commonwealth of Australia, in any law made by the Parliament of the United Kingdom with respect to any matter within the authority of the States of Australia, not being a matter within the authority of the Parliament or Government of the Commonwealth of Australia, in any case where it would have been in accordance with the constitutional practice existing before the commencement of this Act that the Parliament of the United Kingdom should make that law without such concurrence. (3) In the application of this Act to the Commonwealth of Australia the request and consent referred to in section four shall mean the request and consent of the Parliament and Government of the Commonwealth.

Section 10 [Certain sections of Act not to apply to Australia, New Zealand or Newfoundland unless adopted] (1) None of the following sections of this Act, that is to say, sections two, three, four, five and six, shall extend to a Dominion to which this section applies as part of the law of that Dominion unless that section is adopted by the Parliament of the Dominion, and any Act of that Parliament adopting any section of this Act may provide that the adoption shall have effect either from the commencement of this Act or from such later date as is specified in the adopting Act. (2) The Parliament of any such Dominion as aforesaid may at any time revoke the adoption of any section referred to in subsection (1) of this section. (3) The Dominions to which this section applies are the Commonwealth of Australia, the Dominion of New Zealand and Newfoundland.

Section 11 [Meaning of "Colony" in future Acts] Notwithstanding anything in the Interpretation Act, 1889, the expression "Colony" shall not, in any Act of the Parliament of the United Kingdom passed after the commencement of this Act, include a Dominion or any Province or State forming a part of a Dominion.

Section 12 [Short title] This Act may be cited as the Statute of Westminster, 1931.

Source: "Statute of Westminster 1931," Internet Modern History Sourcebook <http://www.fordham. edu/halsall/mod/1936westminster.html>.

DECOLONIZATION

General Charles de Gaulle. By September 1959 France's new democratic government, which de Gaulle led and had been instrumental in installing, came to terms with the realization that its long-term presence in Algeria was a losing proposition. Growing international pressure was beginning to harm France's foreign relations, and domestic support for an expensive and brutal war was declining. Terrorist attacks by Algerian nationalists worsened the situation. Facing these pressures and knowing that his country could no longer afford to fight for a French Algeria, by 1961 all de Gaulle could do was throw up his hands and announce a referendum on independence. It was approved the following year.

Lesser European powers also faced military challenges that they could not support. Denmark, which had been conquered by the Germans in just twelve hours in April 1940, failed to recover Iceland, which was occupied by the Allies and became independent in 1944. Dutch attempts to regain the East Indies, occupied by Japan during the war, failed militarily and ended with the creation of an independent Indonesia in 1949. The Dutch subsequently declined to fight to retain Western New Guinea, which they abandoned in 1962. Belgium's long attempt to maintain its position in the Congo dragged on in a bitter guerilla struggle until it withdrew in 1960. Portugal managed to hold on to its African possessions longer than any other power, but the growing strain of its battles with proindependence forces led in large part to the country's revolutionary takeover by the military in 1974 and to unilateral withdrawal from its colonies the following year.

The Suez Crisis (1956) added another military dimension to decolonization: the concern that fighting for colonial possessions might touch off a major war between the West and the Soviet Union. Egypt's nationalization of the largely Anglo-French-owned Suez Canal Company that year elicited a British and French military response. In cooperation with Israel, Anglo-French forces quickly seized the canal and attacked Egyptian military installations. Within days, however, Soviet premier Nikolai Bulganin relayed a veiled threat from his government that suggested Moscow might resort to nuclear attacks if the occupying forces were not withdrawn. Surely this stance was a reckless blunder for which Soviet premier Nikita Khrushchev later paid, but the larger message was that from a military standpoint decolonization was no longer about weakened colonial powers dealing with rebellious subject peoples. It was now about superpower strategic interests as well. The U.S.S.R.'s nearly simultaneous invasion of Hungary indicated that it meant business and suggested that it might not have been bluffing. Since

Washington not only failed to support London and Paris against Moscow's threats but actually voted with Moscow against them in the United Nations (UN) Security Council, they had no choice but to back down and acknowledge that their independence of action as great powers was hamstrung by broader geopolitical questions.

The end of arguably the last colonial empire, the Soviet Union, also had much to do with military weakness. As its economy ossified and its military became less competitive with that of the combined West, the U.S.S.R. came to realize that it could never fight to hold on to its neighboring satellite nations or, eventually, even its own territory. In another major defeat for a "colonial" power Moscow fought a long, bloody, and inconclusive war against Muslim rebels in Afghanistan after invading that country in 1979. Although it could win in direct combat and maintain control of military bases and cities, its losses through attrition were so high that one observer has identified the campaign as a major factor in the general collapse of the Soviet military. By February 1989 the last Soviet troops withdrew and Afghanistan's unpopular communist government was left to its speedy demise.

Increased general weakness and the resources consumed by Afghanistan further compromised Moscow's ability to maintain its influence in Eastern Europe. With one hundred thousand combat troops tied down in Asia it declined to intervene in Poland's domestic crisis of 1980–1981, an event that set the stage for the "velvet revolutions" (1989). The collapse of the Soviet position throughout Eastern Europe that year and the dissolution of the Soviet state itself (1991) largely resulted from the governing elite's realization that its military was not strong enough to support a confrontational policy with rebellious peoples. The ruthless use of military power, furthermore, was expected to trigger negative reactions from an already hostile West at a time when the Soviet economy and society desperately needed favorable relations in trade, finance, and other categories. Just as the British and French hegemons of the previous generation wanted to rid themselves of destructively high military budgets, unpopular commitments abroad, and actual and potential cases of drawn-out guerilla fighting that they probably would not be able to win, so too did the Soviets acquiesce to the collapse of their empire out a sense of military weakness.

While France's defeat at Dien Bien Phu was perhaps a singular example of decolonization caused by a battlefield military defeat, there are compelling reasons to regard decolonization as the product of military causes. Especially after World War II the costs of military involvement were simply higher than the battered colonial powers could afford. Postwar European societies lacked the resources to fight what were increasingly drawn-out, painful wars of attrition. France found this truth out in Indochina, and with all its power and wealth the United States did not do much better there. Many former colonies became independent in peaceful transitions—even if postindependence developments were seldom free from conflict—but the transitions were peaceful precisely because the colonial powers involved knew that they could not pay bills to win or bear the costs of losing. In many important respects this was an admission of relative decline that the colonial powers could no longer mask.

As the Cold War superimposed its agenda over developments in the Third World, moreover, it became increasingly clear that holding on to colonial possessions might now also involve risking direct confrontation with Moscow. Neither Britain nor France could have won that battle, and it is doubtful that the U.S. would have fought it for them. In the final denouement of decolonization the need for a peaceful transition to a new world order precluded the use of military power to keep many of the structures of colonization in place. The U.S.S.R.'s implosion was as deeply rooted in military weakness as its possible explosion would have been.

—PAUL DU QUENOY,
GEORGETOWN UNIVERSITY

Viewpoint:
No. Europeans gave up their colonies because their leaders determined that such possessions were no longer necessary or profitable.

Among the most important events of the postwar world was the breakup of informal and formal colonial regimes across Asia, Africa, and the Middle East. In the space of a few decades dozens of nation-states—some of minuscule size and scant natural resources—replaced the large empires of European states (and their junior partners, such as Japan), some of which had existed since the fifteenth century. Though the Cold War would profoundly shape the course of these events and of politics in Europe, decolonization outlived the fall of the Berlin Wall (1989) and remains, at the start of the twenty-first century, paramount to the lives of peoples living in regions as diverse as the Caribbean, the Middle East, Central Asia, and Southeast Asia. European leaders abandoned their colonies following

World War II (1939–1945), yet had more control over the process than is traditionally maintained; decolonization was part of a longer-range historical process that preceded the Cold War by decades.

Traditionally, scholars have argued that Europeans withdrew from their colonies because of economic and political weakness after 1945. This weakness reflected the enormous costs of reconstruction after World War II, the military and political success of nationalist movements throughout the Third World, and Western Europe's dependence on financial and military support from the United States to meet the costs of reconstruction and to counterbalance the Soviet Union. The connection to the United States was significant because American interests were often parallel but not identical to those of Europe; key pillars of U.S. foreign policy—free trade and anticolonialism—were antithetical to the very existence of European empires. The Suez Crisis (1956), in which the United States and the Soviet Union, ordinarily bitter international competitors, cooperated to compel France and Britain to withdraw from Egypt, revealed clearly the dangers of this dependence and the degree to which Europe was a "junior partner" to the United States. That crisis, along with France's defeat at Dien Bien Phu (1954) in Indochina, are often portrayed as key turning points in the twentieth century signifying the rise of American power in global affairs and the start of a process that would, by the end of the 1960s, lead to the liberation of all but a handful of European overseas possessions.

There is little question that this explanation neatly links several international crises in the 1950s with the process of decolonization, but it has four important drawbacks and actually distorts the factors that led to decolonization. To begin with, the theory misrepresents the historical framework in which decolonization actually occurred. While much of the extra-European world won independence in the late 1950s and early 1960s, the process of decolonization and the factors that shaped it existed decades before the Cold War. Equally important, Washington's influence over London and Paris in the 1950s and 1960s was not absolute, and there were socio-economic changes within postwar European societies that created pressures that were as strong for European withdrawal as American ideology and economic power. At the same time, many of the other external factors that compelled Britain and France to withdraw from their overseas commitments permitted other states in Europe to maintain their empires well into the postwar period.

Centered on Europe, a global system of imperial domination controlled much of the

Regiment of Vietminh soldiers parading through the streets of Hanoi in October 1954

(Vietnam News Agency; collection of Ngo Vinh Long)

non-European world through colonial rule or informal governance maintained by military occupation, unequal treaties, or spheres of influence. These regions were expected to support their occupations, not impinge greatly on the treasuries of Great Power governments, and to succumb to the precise use of modern weapons. German imperialist Carl Peters perhaps best summed up this formula when he noted: "The purpose of colonization is, unscrupulously and with deliberation, to enrich our own people at the expense of other weaker peoples." Europeans imposed the new system to manage two key problems of the international system: the intensification of Great Power rivalries within and without Europe, and the perceived failure of governments from Latin America to the Middle East to East Asia to maintain political and economic conditions suitable for foreign direct investment and global trade.

The desire to protect global commerce and the financial structures of overseas colonies is the most important consideration because it reflected the objectives of that European state with the most extensive extra-European empire: Great Britain. British leaders had long striven to create and protect a global system of free-trade capitalism. The entire system functioned "like a multinational company." Britain withdrew from countries and turned them into "associated concerns" when "reliable economic links and national organizations emerged—while it extended into others in need of development." The other post-1870 nation-state "multinationals" (France, Russia, Germany, Japan, Portugal, Italy, Belgium, Spain, and the United States) were rivals and, more importantly, partners, who shared the burdens and dividends of the international economy.

Central to this process was the United States. In the 1870s London started a century-long process of ceding to Washington the costs and responsibilities of playing the principal "guardian," or organizer, of nation-state "multinationals." By 1940 Britain had ceded control of the Caribbean, much of the Atlantic, and the Western Pacific; within a decade Britain eventually conceded the Western Mediterranean and the Indian Ocean. Even in areas where British power appeared to be predominant, such as the Arab Middle East during the interwar period, London's authority owed a great deal to U.S. financial power. This position became even more apparent following World War I (1914–1918), when the center of the global economy shifted from Britain to the United States. Britain's Dominions (Canada, New Zealand, South Africa, and Australia) facilitated this process. They, like the United States, were partners for Britain's international economy and secured independence when London's international influence was at its twentieth-century zenith, shortly before World War I. Boasting mature socio-economic institutions and secure financial and cultural links to Britain, the Dominions showed that Europeans could withdraw from overseas and not worry that their influence or global business conditions would be diminished.

The success of the withdrawal from the Dominions was of crucial importance because it coincided with the rise of social justice movements in Europe and in Europe's colonies stressing universal norms of human rights, exemplified by the legalization of trade unions and the creation of the International Red Cross. The mass mobilizations of Europeans during World War I, the creation of the Soviet Union, and U.S. president Woodrow Wilson's Fourteen Points legitimized the ideas and dreams of nationalists in Asia and Africa, trade unionists in Europe, and progressive reformers everywhere. Though the major European colonial powers emerged in 1918 as victors with unrivaled power and much larger empires, they had to balance the needs of rising social classes at home and abroad with the needs of empires. Furthermore, Europeans had to balance their commitments with the bitter ideological rivalry between the United States and the Soviet Union. Because of the two states' military potential, that rivalry became ever more important internationally in the 1950s, as both states extended ever greater help to proxies abroad. Thus, the factors that traditionally explain decolonization existed decades before the great European colonial military defeats at Suez and Dien Bien Phu.

This insight leads to a critical question: why did the chief European colonial powers choose to withdraw from their colonies at mid century instead of sooner? First, they no longer needed to occupy colonies to maintain global political-economic stability or retain influence overseas. Second, the costs of occupying colonies became prohibitive. These two changes reflected the new global institutions of the postwar era: the World Bank, the International Monetary Fund (IMF), the United Nations (UN), the General Agreements on Tariffs and Trade (GATT), North Atlantic Treaty Organization (NATO), and other regional security-political organizations. The burdens formerly shouldered by British and other "multinational" states for global stability were spread to all states of the world directly or indirectly through these new global organizations.

Europeans could now, in the language of modern business, outsource the responsibility for extra-European problems if the costs of remaining in a particular colony were perceived as high. In the Middle East, Central Africa, and South Asia, Europeans rapidly withdrew their

DECOLONIZATION

colonial administrators and military forces and left the UN and the two superpowers to sort out any remaining problems, such as conflicting claims over Palestine or Kashmir. The withdrawal of Europe's political accountability, in turn, eliminated any responsibility to raise the health, education, and labor standards of extra-European nations to those of Europe. That task too would be outsourced. Indigenous rulers, international agencies, and the superpowers would assume the mantle of developing extra-European nations and both pay and manage the indigenous workforces formerly administered by Europeans. Equally importantly, the new indigenous leaders could be won over as true friends or clients through arms deals, financial development schemes, and other forms of foreign aid. The logic of this approach was borne out by a report written by British prime minister Harold Macmillan's government in 1957, which evaluated the profitability of every colony in the British Empire. The results were predictable: the report concluded that Britain's trade and finances would improve as it withdrew from its remaining colonies.

Conversely, when Europeans chose to stay in a territory, they were generally successful. The Dutch reoccupied Indonesia shortly after liberation from Germany. Britain crushed resistance movements in Kenya, Malaysia, and South Arabia. France, despite its loss at Dien Bien Phu, won the Battle of Algiers (1956–1957) against nationalist rebels in North Africa, and along with the British easily defeated the Egyptian forces at Suez. What is more, the worst military and political disasters for European colonialism were rarely complete losses: U.S. power meant that the retreating Europeans could usually expect politically congenial successor regimes and favorable business conditions. This situation allowed Britain, only twelve years after the Suez Canal crisis, to withdraw from the oil fields whose access it had gone to war to protect in 1956.

Nor did large-scale European decolonization signify the end of European military, cultural, or economic influence. More than a decade into the postwar period Britain and France still maintained important overseas bases in former colonies as well as the right to fly over their airspace and to use their soil as bases for military operations. Despite pressure on their currencies and domestic pressures to invest in social-welfare programs, the British and the French invested large sums overseas. The British Council, the Commonwealth, *Francophonie,* and postwar migration to Europe from Africa and Asia intensified the long-standing linkages between Europe and its former colonized nations. Europeans also provided financial, professional, and technical services and arms to their former colonies and were often a preferred alternative for nations not wishing to choose between the two superpowers for development programs.

The same factors that compelled most European powers to contract their empires also reinforced those of Portugal and the Soviet Union. Portugal's strategic assets in Africa, Europe, and Asia meant that it could expect unconditional U.S. support for the maintenance of its empire as a bulwark against Soviet expansion in Africa and as a staging ground to repel a Soviet invasion of Europe. Similarly, the U.S.S.R. maintained control in Eastern Europe and parts of Asia, which Russia had controlled since the eighteenth and nineteenth centuries. The seemingly "inevitable" forces of decolonization had little relevance to the peoples of the Baltic States, Ukraine, the Caucasus, and Central Asia until the early 1990s, nearly four decades after decolonization occurred in Asia and Africa.

As scholar Gordon Martel cautions in "Decolonization After Suez: Retreat or Rationalization" (2000), it is easy to be misled as to the importance of the rapid changes in political borders, withdrawal of colonial governing officials and structures, and rise of indigenous governments and leaders. Rather than the start of a new era of European defeat and weakness, postwar decolonization was simply another stage in a long process by which European states reorganized their resources to make their presence better felt on the world stage. In the nineteenth century that process entailed occupying and administering large parts of the extra-European world. By 1950 global institutions, the superpowers, indigenous elite, and new partner states permitted Europeans to withdraw without a substantial loss of global prestige. Through investing in new economies and economic institutions, Europe boomed economically in the postwar period, while its governments still played an important role in international affairs. Forty years after decolonization, Europe possesses economic and political influence internationally nearly equal to that of the United States and greater than that of the Soviet Union or any of its successor states. Europe is also wealthier than it was before decolonization and carries on more overseas trade than it did during the height of the continent's colonial age.

—SEAN FOLEY,
GEORGETOWN UNIVERSITY

References

Glen Balfour-Paul, *The End of Empire in the Middle East: Britain's Relinquishment of Power in Her Last Three Arab Dependencies* (Cambridge & New York: Cambridge University Press, 1991).

D. George Boyce, *Decolonization and the British Empire* (New York: St. Martin's Press, 1999).

John Darwin, *Britain and Decolonisation: The Retreat from Empire in the Post-war World* (New York: St. Martin's Press, 1988).

Kent Fedorowich and Martin Thomas, eds., *Diplomacy and Colonial Retreat* (London & Portland, Ore.: Frank Cass, 2001).

Marc Ferro, *Colonization: A Global History,* translated by K. D. Prithipaul (Quebec: World Heritage Press, 1997).

Lawrence James, *Imperial Rearguard: Wars of Empire, 1919–85* (London & Washington, D.C.: Brassey's Defense Publishers, 1988; Elmsford, N.Y.: Pergamon Press, 1988).

James, *The Rise and Fall of the British Empire* (London: Little, Brown, 1994).

Paul M. Kennedy, *The Rise and Fall of the Great Powers: Economic Change and Military Conflict from 1500 to 2000* (New York: Random House, 1987).

Dominic Lieven, *Empire: The Russian Empire and its Rivals* (London: Murray, 2000).

Wm. Roger Louis and Ronald Robinson, "Imperialism of Decolonization," *Journal of Imperial and Commonwealth History,* 22 (1994), pp. 462–511.

Gordon Martel, "Decolonization After Suez: Retreat or Rationalization," *Australian Journal of Politics and History,* 46 (September 2000), pp. 403–417.

William E. Odom, *The Collapse of the Soviet Military* (New Haven: Yale University Press, 1998).

William Stivers, "International Politics and Iraqi Oil, 1918–1928: A Study in Anglo-American Diplomacy," *Business History Review,* 55 (Winter 1981): 517–540.

DECOLONIZATION

DISARMAMENT

Were the twentieth-century attempts at disarmament in Europe effective?

Viewpoint: Yes. Disarmament negotiations in the 1920s and 1990s helped to reduce international tensions and to limit dangerous arms races.

Viewpoint: No. Disarmament negotiations usually produced only tactical truces that were transient and ineffective solutions to problems of great-power politics.

The twentieth century was humanity's bloodiest era, but the carnage was nevertheless punctuated occasionally by international attempts to reduce the size and power of military arsenals, usually in the hope that such agreements would alleviate international tension and limit the destructiveness of war. Whether the issues concerned land forces, warships, or nuclear missiles, negotiators and diplomats made determined efforts over the course of the century to promote disarmament among nations.

Were their efforts successful? Disarmament has appealed to many people, including some historians, as an ideal way to end dangerous arms races, ease general international tension, and promote greater communication and understanding between adversaries who would otherwise plot war. In the view of these individuals, disarmament talks during the twentieth century enjoyed significant successes; even in the cases where they failed, the good intentions that lay behind them and limited results they achieved were better than nothing.

Other historians argue that disarmament's effectiveness in the twentieth century did not supersede its many failures. Even when friendly nations reached disarmament agreements, political, strategic, and military developments made them irrelevant or led to situations in which they became unsustainable. Several agreements proved simply unenforceable as they depended on mutual trust and good faith, often between bitter adversaries who had little patience. Other agreements resulted less from legitimate peaceful intentions than from governments trying to avoid expensive arms races. Still others caused nations to look for ways—either covertly or overtly—to circumvent the treaties they signed.

Viewpoint:
Yes. Disarmament negotiations in the 1920s and 1990s helped to reduce international tensions and to limit dangerous arms races.

The twentieth century was Europe's bloodiest. Many civil wars, several attempts at genocide, brutal totalitarian regimes, and two world wars plagued Europe. Why this civilized region should have descended into such savagery has been one of history's greatest debates. Europe's troubles clearly began with World War I (1914–1918). One of the most common explanations for "the Great War" has been that a prewar arms race created paranoia among states locked in a long, drawn-out competition. This condition created a hair-trigger situation that finally erupted into a general war. Once the troops were mobilized, heavily armed states took over, and Europe found itself locked in a senseless and seemingly endless slaughter. If Europe's problems were rooted in this kind of mindless military system, then it should hardly be surprising that it became increasingly believed that it was a good idea to prevent arms races. Thus, the diplomacy of the century accordingly was marked by several efforts at disarmament. Though not every case was completely successful, it can nevertheless be argued that such efforts were both wise and fruitful and that they helped greatly to defuse international tensions.

At the Paris Peace Conference (1919) at the end of World War I the victors demonstrated their commitment to the principle of disarmament by tying Germany to a future of multilateral disarmament. Article 8 of the League of Nations Covenant specifically called for international disarmament talks. The interwar years were marked by popular pacifist movements that went beyond the traditional religious-based movements, such as the Quakers, to include veterans' groups and other more widely based citizens' groups: disarmament soon became a central pillar of Europe's left-wing and socialist parties. In 1920 the League of Nations set the machinery of disarmament talks into motion. The next year the first multilateral disarmament conference met in Washington and successfully negotiated naval reductions and a freeze upon naval installations and fortifications in the Pacific Ocean region. Even the distinctly realist historian E. H. Carr grudgingly referred to the Washington naval conference as "an outstanding success." From 1927 to 1929 negotiations under League of Nations auspices aimed to duplicate such successes for other weapons, and by 1930 the League of Nations Preparatory Commission called for a general Disarmament Conference to be held in Geneva beginning in 1932. Sixty-one nations sent delegations to the Conference, but in 1934 the effort fizzled out in the wake of the Nazi ascension to power the previous year and the ensuing German withdrawal from the Conference.

The 1930s were notoriously unsuccessful for those who sought disarmament, but the question arises whether the process as well as the goal was beneficial or detrimental to European stability. That a general conflict broke out in 1939 seemed at first glance to discredit everything that happened in the years leading up to the war. British prime minister Winston Churchill, for example, argued in his memoirs of World War II (1939–1945) that the conflict was an "unnecessary war." Churchill, in a bout of postwar self-justification, believed that if Britain had not chosen appeasement—a policy that he believed was based upon craven pacifism and pursuit of disarmament—the war would never have happened. This argument has circulated widely and has colored the entire Cold War. It bears, however, only passing resemblance to the historical reality. Churchill certainly was not the staunch opponent of disarmament in principle that his reputation makes him out to have been. As secretary of state for war and air in 1919, Churchill helped promote Britain's much-maligned Ten Years Rule, whereby Britain concluded that no general war threatened Britain for the next ten years, and that therefore it ought to make no serious armament expenditures. The Ten Years Rule was abandoned in 1932.

Britain certainly was not disarmed in 1939. The abandonment of the Ten Years Rule resulted in a focused rearmament effort that coincided roughly with that undertaken by Germany. When German leader Adolf Hitler's invasion of Poland triggered a British ultimatum, he threw a characteristic tantrum and blamed his foreign minister, Joachim von Ribbentrop, for having misled him about London's intentions. Hitler believed that he was launching a colonial war to subjugate the subhuman Poles. He judged that the British and French would not fight, not on the basis of intelligence reports on the levels of British and French armament but instead upon his insistence that he could read anyone with his special powers as a master politician. Indeed, Hitler singularly ignored any professional advice from the military or its intelligence for his entire career. Had he listened to them in August 1939, he would have learned that German arms lagged behind those of his Western adversaries in many important categories. Hitler had arbitrarily decided that he would be ready for a war with the West in 1942. When the West did not oblige him in this timetable and instead gave him a war three years early, he began his four-and-a-half-year-long improvisation that ultimately caused the utter destruction of his country. This tragedy had nothing to do with disarmament. Once a lunatic was given the reins in Germany, the West promptly abandoned its goal of disarmament and was able to stop him, albeit at a terrific cost. Disarmament in the interwar years was never given a chance. The real problem lay in the peace treaty and the way it was negotiated, not in disarmament.

The other great era of European disarmament occurred during the Cold War. The wisdom of disarmament was even clearer in this case, despite some of the rhetoric of the time. Despite its desirability, Cold War disarmament was only attempted sporadically. Like the arms race that preceded World War I, the Cold War arms race was driven by logic external to the antagonists' security needs. In this case a great incentive grew from the Western "military industrial complex." The profitability and economic stimulus of weapons purchases became apparent by the 1950s, as the European economy bounced back with the help of increased weapons expenditures triggered by the Korean War (1950–1953). One of the great ironies is that the most memorable words ever uttered by President Dwight D. Eisenhower, a career soldier, would be an admonition against allowing the military-industrial complex to dictate American policy, for it was on his watch that the Cold War began its astonishingly dangerous shift from a reliance upon conventional weapons to a dependence upon atomic weapons. By the 1970s thousands of nuclear weapons were holding the world hostage. One must wonder whether any conceivable economic, social, or political gain was worth the potential cost of launching such a war. When the Soviet Union finally collapsed (1991), advocates of further arms expenditures argued that this implosion was caused by the Soviets' inability to keep up with the West in the development of arms. However, subsequent studies seemed to indicate that in fact the Soviets were withering away all on their own. Some scholars now claim that had the United States not blundered into a costly war in Vietnam (ended 1975), the Soviet leadership would have given up hope of keeping up with the West by 1970. Such prosaic material goods as plastics and medical equipment proved to be beyond their ability to produce. It was obvious that in the competition between East and West the Soviets were losing badly. Soviet leader Mikhail Gorbachev's attempts at reconciling Soviet reality with the potential of the West immediately exposed this gap, and the regime collapsed fairly peacefully. The arms race, though expensive for Moscow, was only one of the many things that brought down the Soviet regime. Even such a "Cold Warrior" as U.S. president Ronald Reagan saw the fallacies and dangers inherent in an unbridled arms race and at a sum-

mit with the Soviets in Reykjavik stunned the world (and his staff) by proposing a complete abandonment of nuclear weapons. In the absence of any good purpose for an arms race the wisdom of disarmament is even more apparent. Had the West pursued arms control and disarmament with more conviction during the Cold War, the world would have been far safer and precious resources could have been dedicated to more productive ends.

–PHIL GILTNER,
ALBANY ACADEMY

Viewpoint:
No. Disarmament negotiations usually produced only tactical truces that were transient and ineffective solutions to problems of great-power politics.

Twentieth-century disarmament talks usually failed in practice and often became mere tools in nations' extensive arsenals of diplomacy. Although some disarmament treaties became anachronistic, most failed because one or more parties violated their terms or attempted to enforce them in untenable or unrealistic ways.

The first truly modern disarmament negotiations, initiated by the Russian Empire in 1898 and conducted in The Hague the following year, were begun for no other purpose than to allay Russia's fears that foreign militaries would outpace its conventional weapons capability. Innovations in a wide range of weapons, especially sophisticated mechanized artillery, virtually guaranteed that Russia's general underdevelopment and particular deficiencies in precision manufacturing would hinder its battlefield performance. Rather than waste huge sums on research and development in what would probably have been a futile attempt to counter their expected enemy, Germany, the Russians advanced the cheaper and shrewder diplomatic solution of an international disarmament conference. If Russia could not beat its prospective opponents on the field or firing range, it could use pacifist diplomacy to try to persuade them to abandon weapons more lethal than those that it could produce.

Little came of these talks. Most nations saw through Russia's rather obvious attempt to overcome its deficiencies by convincing everyone else to disarm, and no agreement was signed. Japan used its superior guns to blast Russian troops and bases in the Far East in 1904–1905. During World War I (1914–1918) superior German artillery blasted Russian troops all over Eastern

Europe. Nascent arms-control talks designed to reduce a growing naval arms race between Britain and Germany, held periodically in the years before World War I, failed to achieve any success. Britain's navy was its major defense and principal link to its empire; Germany believed it needed major seapower to compete with Britain and to advance its position in the world. Reducing their fleets was impossible for either power given their national goals and strategic imperatives, and both went to war in 1914 with huge fleets.

Germany's overall defeat in World War I led to renewed international support for disarmament. Many believed that the arms race before 1914 had both led to the war itself and facilitated its unprecedented carnage. Avoiding those two outcomes in the future, they posited, depended on broad multilateral disarmament. The provisions of the November 1918 armistice that ended the fighting and the Versailles Treaty (1919) that brought formal peace began this process by forcing Germany to disarm unilaterally.

Its army was reduced to one hundred thousand men (20 percent of its prewar total), and it was banned from having tanks, aircraft, a general staff, and a substantial navy. The victorious Allies' ideal was that these limitations would be equaled by their own voluntary disarmament, a goal expressly stated in both the documents of the Paris Peace Conference (1919) and the Covenant of the new League of Nations, an international body established after the war to govern world politics peacefully. This prospect, however, faced major limitations. France, which feared another war with Germany and failed to secure British and American pledges to come to its assistance, maintained high levels of defensive military spending. Britain and the United States reduced their peacetime military strengths, but this effort was not much of a sacrifice since neither power traditionally maintained a large, expensive land force in any case. Britain, moreover, circumvented its home forces' disarmament by keeping large colonial armies, which played an

Mobile missile launcher at a military parade in Moscow, 1965

(Novosti)

DISARMAMENT

important role in World War II (1939–1945), and the paramilitary "Black and Tan" auxiliaries deployed in Ireland.

Even Germany's enforced disarmament became untenable over time. Almost immediately after the peace Germany began to violate the terms of the Versailles Treaty by maintaining a large paramilitary auxiliary militia (*Freikorps,* or "free corps") composed of former soldiers, disguising its banned army general staff as an innocuous "troop office," training tank and aircraft crews in the Soviet Union, and contracting forbidden submarine construction to Dutch and Finnish shipyards. The victorious Allies had no mechanism to prevent or even monitor these developments apart from a weak and ineffectual disarmament commission. The disarmament provisions of Versailles did have the immediate tactical advantage of ending the war while Germany's troops still stood on foreign soil (in other words, without a long, costly campaign to occupy the whole country) and ensuring that it could not take up an offensive initiative for the immediate future. Expecting Germany to remain permanently disarmed, however, was a pipe dream, and believing that the rest of the world would freely reduce its arsenals was unrealistic.

Since Germany was a defeated nation at the Allies' mercy, one should rightly wonder whether an undefeated rival could be more controllable or more honest in its approach to disarmament. Indeed, the interwar period offered two such examples. At the Washington Naval Conference (1921–1922) multilateral disarmament negotiations to reduce great-power naval forces, the object of a major prewar Anglo-German arms race, resulted in an accord. The agreement allowed the United States and Britain to maintain naval parity, while France and Japan were permitted forces equal to 60 percent of the strength of either the United States or Britain, and Italy was granted a navy equal to 35 percent of the U.S. or British figure. Even though all of these countries were World War I allies and approached the talks with general goodwill, their agreement proved unsustainable. The United States and Britain reduced their naval power not by dismantling or otherwise destroying their large fleets but by putting many of their older ships into "mothballs" and other types of storage. They may not have been deployed and ready to fight, but only a few days of preparation could return them to active service. In World War II both powers relied to an important degree on World War I–era ships to guard coasts, protect convoys at sea, and hunt submarines and other enemy vessels. Japan, which came under the control of a militarist government in the late 1920s and embarked on an aggressive expansionist course in the 1930s, simply ignored the agreement and built a

navy and other military forces that were capable of challenging both the United States and Britain when it attacked their possessions in the Pacific in December 1941. In 1935 Britain weakened naval disarmament further by concluding a bilateral agreement with Germany, which, despite the Versailles Treaty's limitations on German naval power, allowed the Germans to build their navy up to 35 percent of Britain's.

The Anglo-German naval agreement was only a symptom of the larger problem of German rearmament, however. The democratic government that came to power in Germany after World War I had almost immediately covertly violated the disarmament provisions of the peace,–but by the early 1930s it became more openly contemptuous of them. When the League of Nations sponsored an international disarmament conference, which began meeting in Geneva in 1932, German leaders argued that the West's spotty disarmament record invalidated the peace settlement's provisions for their own disarmament, which was ostensibly to be only one component within a broad multilateral framework. They argued, therefore, that Germany was entitled to rearm. France, still facing diplomatic isolation and remaining fearful of another war with Germany, repeated its refusal to disarm at the conference. After Adolf Hitler was appointed German chancellor in January 1933, he withdrew his country's delegation from both the Geneva Conference, which flagged on to no effect until 1937, and from the League of Nations, which proved increasingly powerless to stop international conflict. In 1935 Hitler's government acknowledged its possession of a three-hundred-plane air force and announced the reintroduction of conscription to build a five-hundred-thousand-man army, in addition to concluding its naval agreement with Britain, which it planned to violate in the future in any case. All of these developments were blatant violations of the Versailles Treaty, yet Germany suffered no consequences. The United States, which never ratified the treaty, was uninterested in enforcing its provisions. The British and French were too weak to intervene and, preferring appeasement, even hesitated to increase their own military spending to counter Germany's.

Hitler's growing arsenal enabled him to make a major but ultimately unsuccessful bid for European hegemony in World War II. His defeat and the subsequent Cold War between the two "superpowers," the United States and the Soviet Union, eventuated more disarmament failures. The atomic bomb, which the United States first detonated and used in war in 1945 and which the Union of Soviet Socialist Republics (U.S.S.R.) acquired in 1949, added the most lethal weapon yet known to military affairs. A growing arms race in nuclear technology created widespread fear of nuclear annihilation and led to renewed calls for arms control and disarmament talks.

Achieving the mutual willingness to engage in such negotiations remained difficult. The Soviets, motivated by the belief that they were constantly threatened and determined to expand their influence as much as possible, wanted to build a nuclear arsenal to equal and surpass those of the United States and its British and French allies, who also developed nuclear weapons. Soviet leader Nikita Khrushchev declared his intention to have nuclear missiles roll off conveyor belts "like sausages," threatened to use them during the Suez Crisis (1956), and stationed them in Cuba in 1962, provoking major crises and near war. Looking into the abyss of potential nuclear conflict, however, scared Khrushchev enough to sign a 1963 treaty with the Western nuclear powers to place limited bans on nuclear weapons testing; consider an international agreement to prevent the proliferation of nuclear weapons to other nations; agree to the installation of an emergency "hot line" between the White House and the Kremlin; and make a deal to reduce enriched uranium production.

Although proponents of disarmament lauded these efforts and expected them to lead to a general reduction or even elimination of Cold War tensions, their hopes were quickly dashed. In October 1964 Khrushchev's hard-liner opponents removed him from power, claiming that he, among other mistakes and deficiencies, had weakened the Soviet Union's international position through arms-control talks and undermined its allies' security and confidence in Soviet leadership. The latter included China, which, despite Khrushchev's movement toward a nonproliferation agreement, detonated its first atomic bomb just two days after he was ousted and developed a hydrogen bomb less than three years later. For the next twenty years Khrushchev's successors refused to negotiate nuclear or conventional disarmament or discuss nonproliferation. The Strategic Arms Limitation Talks (SALT) of the 1970s placed ceilings on the U.S. and U.S.S.R.'s arsenals of nuclear warheads, giving the Soviets a slight numerical advantage, but did not lead to their substantial reduction or elimination. Apart from the obvious technical difficulties that each power faced in verifying the other's compliance, the first round of these talks, known as SALT I, was effectively circumvented by technological breakthroughs—the fast U.S. Pershing cruise missile and an updated guidance system for the Soviet intermediate-range SS-20 missile—that shortened the delivery time for each side's nuclear warheads and thereby increased their effectiveness without adding more missiles to the existing arsenals. The second

round, SALT II, resulted in a 1979 agreement to reduce the warhead ceiling further but amounted to little in practice because President Jimmy Carter withdrew it from the U.S. Senate's consideration in response to Soviet aggression in the Third World and swelling Congressional opposition. It has remained unratified and never came into force. A related agreement to the talks, the Anti-Ballistic Missile (ABM) Treaty (1972), prevented both the United States and the U.S.S.R. from developing land-based defensive weapons systems that could intercept and destroy each other's nuclear missiles. The Soviets insisted on this agreement because they, like their tsarist predecessors before World War I, realized that they lacked the know-how to compete with the West in the requisite technological arena. Regardless of the treaty's rationale, however, both sides violated it. The United States did so in spirit after 1983, when President Ronald Reagan announced the Strategic Defense Initiative (SDI), a planned orbital antimissile defense system, and in a letter in 2002, when President George W. Bush's administration formally renounced it. In the mid 1980s the Soviets broke it by developing a coordinated, U.S.S.R.-wide radar grid, a preliminary development to an ABM system, which the treaty prohibited.

The waning of the Cold War in the late 1980s led to another round of disarmament and arms-control talks, but few of these had lasting effectiveness or importance. The Intermediate Range Nuclear Forces (INF) Treaty (1987) provided for the removal of Pershings and SS-20s from Europe, eliminating the tactical innovations that had undermined SALT I. But even as both sides appeared to sign away their nuclear advantages, both stood ready to deploy a whole new generation of submarine-based missiles that could be launched with almost no warning and in conditions of near invulnerability.

Agreements made in connection with the reunification of Germany in 1990 limited the size and power of the united German army and excluded North Atlantic Treaty Organization (NATO) activity from the territory of the former East Germany. The comprehensive Conventional Forces in Europe (CFE) Treaty, signed in November of that year, placed "permanent" limits on the size and deployment of NATO and Soviet conventional forces in what remained a divided Europe. The Strategic Arms Reduction Treaty (START), signed in January 1991, called for the U.S. and Soviet nuclear arsenals to be cut by about one-third.

These agreements soon became irrelevant. The collapse of the Soviet Union in December 1991 raised serious questions about their validity and the validity of the SALT I and ABM treaties. After all, one of their signatory powers

NUCLEAR DISARMAMENT

On 1 May 2000 the five major nuclear powers—the United States, Russia, China, the United Kingdom, and France—issued a statement announcing their support of steps toward nuclear disarmament:

1. The delegations of China, France, Russia, the United Kingdom and the United States, on the occasion of the sixth Review Conference of the Treaty on the Non-Proliferation of Nuclear Weapons (NPT), formally reiterate the strong and continuing support of our countries for this Treaty, the cornerstone of the international nuclear non-proliferation regime and the essential foundation for nuclear disarmament. We remain unequivocally committed to fulfilling all of our obligations under the Treaty.

2. We welcomed the decision on indefinite extension of the Treaty adopted in 1995 by its member States. We reaffirm our commitment to strengthening the review process of the Treaty and to the principles and objectives for nuclear non-proliferation and disarmament. We reaffirm our commitment to the resolution on the Middle East adopted in 1995. The principles established by those documents will make a continuing contribution to the review process, the Treaty remaining its fundamental guide.

3. The progress of NPT universality has been confirmed after the 1995 conference. We welcome the accession to the Treaty by Chile, Vanuatu, the United Arab Emirates, Comoros, Andorra, Angola, Djibouti, Oman and Brazil. Today, there are 187 member States. We reiterate the need for universal adherence to the NPT and call upon States that have not yet done so to accede to the Treaty at an early date. The nuclear explosions carried out by India and Pakistan in May 1998 were a cause of deep international concern. We continue to call upon both countries to undertake the measures set out in UNSCR 1172. Notwithstanding their nuclear tests, India and Pakistan do not have the status of nuclear-weapon States in accordance with the NPT.

4. We stress that compliance with the NPT by all member States is essential to further the comprehensive goals of the Treaty.

5. We reiterate our unequivocal commitment to the ultimate goals of a complete elimination of nuclear weapons and a treaty on general and complete disarmament under strict and effective international control.

6. A program of action was set out by the 1995 Review and Extension Conference as important in the full realization and effective Implementation of Article VI. In pursuit of that program, there have been highly significant multilateral, bilateral and unilateral developments since 1995.

7. The CTBT was opened for signature in New York on 24 September 1996. The five nuclear-weapon States all signed it that very day. Today, 155 States have signed it and 55 of them, including 28 whose ratification is necessary for its entry into force, have deposited their instruments of ratification with the Secretary General of the United Nations, including France and the United Kingdom in a joint ceremony on 6 April 1998. The recent ratification of the CTBT by the Russian Federation is welcome. The Preparatory Commission for the CTBT Organization has been set up in Vienna and is putting into place the international monitoring system of the Treaty. Important progress has been made so far in the setting up of the verification system. We remain committed to ensuring that, at entry into force of the CTBT, the verification regime will be capable of meeting the verification requirements of this Treaty. The first conference of States having ratified the Treaty to consider the issue of its entry into force took place in Vienna in October 1999. No efforts should be spared to make sure that the CTBT is a universal and internationally and effectively verifiable treaty and to secure its early entry into force. There should be no doubt as to the commitment of our five countries to that effect.

8. As one logical multilateral step in the full realization and effective implementation of Article VI, we reaffirm the necessity of a non-discriminatory, universally applicable and internationally and effectively verifiable convention banning the production of fissile material for nuclear weapons or other nuclear explosive devices negotiated in accordance with the 1995 statement of the Special Coordinator of the Conference on Disarmament and the mandate contained therein. We urge the Conference on Disarmament to agree on a program of work as soon as possible, which includes the immediate commencement and early conclusion of negotiations on such a treaty.

9. The contribution of the five nuclear-weapon States to systematic and progressive efforts to reduce nuclear weapons globally has been and will be highlighted by each of us nationally.

10. Emphasizing the essential importance of cooperation, demonstrating and advancing mutual trust among ourselves, and promoting greater international security and stability, we declare that none of our nuclear weapons are targeted at any State.

11. Ratification of START II by the Russian Federation is an important step in the efforts to reduce strategic offensive weapons and is welcome. Completion of ratification of START II by the United States remains a priority. We look forward to the conclusion of START III as soon as possible while preserving and strengthening the ABM Treaty as a cornerstone of strategic stability and as a basis for further reductions of strategic offensive weapons, in accordance with its provisions.

12. We are committed to placing as soon as practicable fissile materials designated by each of us as no longer required for defense purposes under IAEA (International Atomic Energy Agency) or other relevant international verification. We have launched a number of significant initiatives to provide for the safe and effective management and disposition of such materials.

13. We welcome the creation of two new nuclear-weapon free zones since 1995 as a significant contribution to the enhancement of regional and international peace and security: South-East Asia and Africa. The five nuclear-weapon States have signed and, in most cases, ratified all the relevant protocols to the treaties of Tlatelolco, Rarotonga and Pelindaba; internal processes are underway to secure the few lacking ratifications. The consultations with States parties to the treaty of Bangkok have recently been accelerated, paving the way for our adherence to the additional protocol. We are looking forward to the successful and early conclusions of those consultations. We encourage the States in Central Asia to pursue successfully their efforts to create a nuclear-weapon free zone in their region. We support and respect the nuclear-weapon free status of Mongolia.

14. We note that the actions of the nuclear-weapon States since 1995 on the relevant additional protocols to Nuclear Weapon Free Zone treaties have increased the number of non-nuclear-weapon States eligible for legally binding Negative Security Assurances to over 100. We reaffirm our commitment to United Nations Security Council resolution 984 adopted in April 1995 on security assurances for NPT non-nuclear-weapon States. According to operative paragraph 10 of resolution 984, the issues addressed in that resolution remain of continuing concern to the Security Council. We are ready to exchange views relating to the positive security assurances referred to in the resolution.

15. We consider the international safeguards system of the International Atomic Energy Agency as one of the essential pillars of the non-proliferation regime. This system acts as a guarantee for stability and the preservation of world peace. We call on all States parties, which are required by Article III of the Treaty and have not yet done so, to sign and bring into force comprehensive safeguards agreements without delay.

16. The development and the implementation of the strengthened safeguards system of the IAEA through new agreements is a significant achievement. We praise the remarkable work carried out by the IAEA in this field and hope that the strengthened system soon spreads across all regions of the world. Here again, universality is the challenge we face. To date, Additional Protocols have been signed by more than 50 non-nuclear-weapon States; nine of them have entered into force. We urge all non-nuclear-weapon States that have not yet done so to sign without delay the additional protocol with a view to its early implementation.

17. As regards States not members of the NPT, one of them has recently signed an Additional Protocol with the IAEA. We encourage the three others to negotiate an Additional Protocol with the IAEA.

18. All the five nuclear-weapon States signed an Additional Protocol with the IAEA and shall seek to ratify their agreements as soon as possible.

19. We support the promotion of transparency in nuclear related export controls within the framework of dialogue and cooperation among all interested States parties to the treaty and we welcome the initiatives taken in order to carry out this objective.

20. We reaffirm the inalienable right of all the parties to the Treaty to develop research, production, and use of nuclear energy for peaceful purposes without discrimination and in accordance with the relevant provisions of the Treaty and the relevant principles on safeguards. Pursuant to our obligation under Article IV, we have provided our support for the technical cooperation programs administered by the IAEA, which has enabled many nations to make progress in the application of nuclear technologies in important fields such as agriculture, hydrology, medicine and environment.

21. We stress the importance of international cooperation in order to maintain the highest practicable levels of nuclear safety. In this regard, we welcome the entry into force and the first review meeting of the convention on nuclear safety as well as the opening for signature of the joint convention on the safety of spent fuel management and on the safety of radioactive waste management. We call on all States which have not yet done so to sign and ratify those two conventions.

22. We are determined to take a forward-looking approach to nuclear non-proliferation and nuclear disarmament. The NPT provides an indispensable framework for future efforts against nuclear proliferation and towards nuclear disarmament. We fully acknowledge our particular responsibility and key role in ensuring continued progress in the implementation of the NPT.

23. The five nuclear-weapon States hope similarly genuine commitment to the pursuit of nuclear non-proliferation and disarmament as a contribution to enhanced peace and security will be shown by all States members of the NPT and States outside the NPT. We will continue to work together and with the non-nuclear weapon States for the success of the review process.

Source: U.S. Department of State, Office of International Information Programs, "Five Nuclear Powers Express Strong Support for NPT," *Federation of American Scientists* <http://fas.org/nuke/control/npt/news/000501-npt-usia1.htm>.

DISARMAMENT

had ceased to exist, and critics wondered whether its successor states or other signatories were bound by the terms of the agreements. The accession of Poland, Hungary, and the Czech Republic to NATO in 1999, furthermore, allowed for deployments of American and other NATO forces to those countries and rendered meaningless the earlier restrictions on NATO activity in the former East Germany. Even without that development, no disarmament treaty stopped the deployment of U.S. troops to war-torn Bosnia-Herzegovina (December 1995), the U.S.-led NATO military operation against Yugoslavia (March–April 1999), or the mainly NATO occupation of the contentious Kosovo province that followed. Expected future NATO expansion will make the 1990 disarmament agreements even less relevant and enforceable, and future deployments of military power to other conflict situations in Europe may trump them as well. A second Strategic Arms Reduction Treaty (START II) was signed by the United States and Russia in January 1993 and called for the reduction of their respective nuclear arsenals by two-thirds of pre-START figures, but this treaty, not projected to come into full effect until late 2007, still left both countries with the right to maintain more than three thousand nuclear warheads—more than enough to devastate the planet—and did not solve the inherent problems in verifying the reductions. Its greater significance was in facilitating Russia's transition from a superpower to a regional power and reducing the chance that its poorly guarded and maintained nuclear arsenal would be pilfered or cause accidental harm.

International disarmament initiatives have also failed to curb another major threat to world peace, the proliferation of nuclear weapons and other weapons of mass destruction (WMD). Since China's unhindered development of the atomic bomb, several other countries have acquired nuclear weapons technology. Israel did so in the 1960s and nearly resorted to using it against Egypt and Syria when those countries launched a surprise attack in October 1973. Both India and Pakistan, bitter enemies with long-standing and seemingly intractable territorial disputes, successfully tested nuclear weapons in 1998, after pursuing a long and unchecked arms race. North Korea, an oppressive dictatorship and sworn enemy of the United States and its Asian allies, announced its successful testing of an atomic bomb in 2002, eight years after it pledged to end its nuclear weapons program in a

disarmament agreement with Washington, yet another such accord that one obviously cannot describe as a success.

Successful nonproliferation efforts have normally resulted from another power's preemptive actions, which have not usually involved disarmament talks or enjoyed broad international sanction. In 1981 Israel bombed an Iraqi nuclear power plant that was probably designed for military purposes. Unilateral U.S. diplomatic and economic pressure played the major role in persuading Argentina, Brazil, and South Africa to abandon nascent nuclear weapons programs. Ukraine and Kazakhstan, after achieving independence in 1991, agreed to surrender leftover Soviet nuclear weapons on their territory to Russia. When United Nations weapons inspectors proved ineffective in monitoring development facilities for nuclear and other WMD in Saddam Hussein's Iraq in 1991–2003, a U.S.-led coalition attacked the country and deposed its regime to preempt its acquisition of such weapons. The future of North Korea's nuclear capability and Iran's shady nuclear weapons program remains unclear at this writing, but if history is any guide, disarmament talks are unlikely to lead to a lasting and meaningful solution.

–PAUL DU QUENOY,
GEORGETOWN UNIVERSITY

References

Richard Dean Burns, ed., *Encyclopedia of Arms Control and Disarmament,* 3 volumes (New York: Scribners, 1993).

Attar Chand, *Nuclear Disarmament and Foreign Policy* (New Delhi: Akashdeep Publishing, 1992).

Carolyn J. Kitching, *Britain and the Geneva Disarmament Conference: A Study in International History* (New York: Palgrave Macmillan, 2003).

Serge Sur, ed., *Disarmament and Limitation of Armaments: Unilateral Measures and Policies* (New York: United Nations, 1992).

Fred Tanner, ed., *From Versailles to Baghdad: Post-war Armament Control of Defeated States* (New York: United Nations, 1992).

Philip Towle, *Enforced Disarmament: From the Napoleonic Campaigns to the Gulf War* (Oxford: Clarendon Press, 1997; New York: Oxford University Press, 1997).

DISARMAMENT

EASTERN EUROPE AFTER WORLD WAR I

Were the new states created in Eastern Europe after World War I viable political entities?

Viewpoint: Yes. Despite some difficulties, the new states of Eastern Europe were adept at solving domestic problems and resolving international disputes.

Viewpoint: No. The new states of Eastern Europe were inherently unstable and lacked both legitimacy and long-term viability.

Perhaps the greatest political and geographic consequence of World War I (1914–1918) was the disappearance of four empires: German, Austro-Hungarian, Russian, and Ottoman. In their absence new states arose, ostensibly nation-states dominated by ethnic groups that had either been long repressed by imperial rule or long separated from smaller existing states. Nowhere was this situation more true than in Eastern Europe. Austria and Hungary emerged in truncated form as separate entities for the first time since 1526. Poland reemerged from the lands of the German, Austro-Hungarian, and Russian empires for the first time since 1795. The crown lands of Bohemia and Moravia, under direct Habsburg rule since 1620, emerged in the new state of Czechoslovakia, which also included the peoples of Slovakia and Ruthenia, neither of which had known self-government since the remote past. The small state of Serbia, the fate of which had started the war, became the senior partner in the multiethnic Kingdom of Serbs, Croats, and Slovenes, the future Yugoslavia. Romania's seizure of Transylvania from Hungary and Bessarabia and Northern Bukovina from the Russian Empire vastly enlarged its territorial base.

Challenges appeared in the wake of these tremendous changes, however. As one essay argues, the new states were plagued by questions of legitimacy and, ultimately, viability. Over the course of the interwar period they experienced political violence and extremism, divisive ethnic tension, major economic dislocation, and serious international weakness. Even without World War II (1939–1945), the violent confrontation that accompanied the dissolution of Yugoslavia in the 1990s and the "velvet divorce" that divided Czechoslovakia in 1993 would still have happened.

Yet, the opposing essay suggests that the question of state viability in Eastern Europe should be taken in a larger context. All of the problems experienced by the region's states in the interwar period affected almost every other country in Europe. While some of these states fell under authoritarian governments, it was merely a fate they shared with Germany, Italy, Spain, Portugal, and Greece—all non–Eastern European states. While some experienced economic problems, these troubles were a general consequence of both the war and the Great Depression. Czechoslovakia, moreover, sustained a modern democratic government with a fairly well-balanced treatment of its ethnic minorities. As contemporary Eastern Europe seeks deeper integration into the West and as the recent conflicts in Yugoslavia reach resolution, the question of the region's stability after the emergence of its nation-states is one of urgency.

Viewpoint:
Yes. Despite some difficulties, the new states of Eastern Europe were adept at solving domestic problems and resolving international disputes.

Scholars who have analyzed the breakup of Yugoslavia and Czechoslovakia at the end of the twentieth century have most often pointed to problems that plagued both states since their creation in 1918. Many people have interpreted the ultimate failure of Yugoslavia and Czechoslovakia as the inevitable outcome of U.S. president Woodrow Wilson's failed experiment for national self-determination, since these two unions of peoples were not based on the dominance of a single ethnic group or an earlier historical nation. Still, the history of both states between the world wars was largely one of domestic and foreign policy success. Both states took initial steps to ensure their own survival. Only unchecked German military aggression halted these plans.

Yugoslavia's unification of the South Slavic peoples of the former Habsburg lands with the Serbian state was legal and voluntary. The National Council of Slovenes, Croats, and Serbs (formed after Emperor Charles in October 1918 called for the federalization of the empire) voted almost unanimously for joining with Serbia, crowning the Serbian Alexander Karadjordjevic as king of the new country, and accepting the results of a constituent assembly to determine the exact makeup of the country and its institutions. Only Stjepan Radic, leader of the Croatian Peasant Party, protested this decision.

A consensus among the various Yugoslavian parties developed over time. Admittedly, there were problems in gaining a broad popular mandate after the first elections for the constituent assembly in November 1920. The Yugoslav Communist Party, which advocated socialist revolution along Soviet lines, was forbidden to take its nineteen seats in the Parliament. Radic and the Croatian Peasant Party also won eighteen seats but refused to participate once it became known that Nikola Pašic's Serbian Radical Party would form a coalition with the Serbian Democratic Party. Despite the Serbian domination of nearly all coalition governments until 1929, non-Serb parties also lent their support to the Yugoslav central government. Anton Korosec, leader of the Slovenian People's Party and a former prime minister, won the right for Slovenes to establish a separate educational system for the first time. Bosnian Muslims likewise supported the Serbs' efforts to centralize the Yugoslav state and received autonomous religious, cultural, and educational rights in

return. Even Radic eventually participated in a ruling coalition in 1925 as the minister of education, thereby recognizing Yugoslavia's legitimacy in governing Croatia. Vlatko Macek, Radic's successor, joined a unity government as a vice premier of Yugoslavia as late as 1939, when Yugoslavia increasingly felt the pressure of Nazi Germany and Fascist Italy.

King Alexander took the necessary steps to restore order after a Montenegrin member of Parliament mortally wounded Radic on 20 June 1928. Proclaiming a royal dictatorship in January 1929, Alexander eliminated all ethnic-based political parties, effectively establishing an antinationalist technocratic government to run the country's affairs until tensions between the Serbs and Croats died down. Alexander also redrew the internal boundaries of Yugoslavia into nine districts called *banovinas*. None of the *banovinas* had any historical basis; they were simply named after rivers that ran through them. The strength of these reforms can be seen in the fact that they survived after Alexander was assassinated by radical Croats and Macedonians in Marseilles in October 1934.

Dragisa Cvetkovic, the dominant political figure in Yugoslavia after Alexander's death, was able to maintain the non-ethnic-based system for four more years. In August 1939 Cvetkovic was able to regain the support of Macek and the Croatian Peasant Party by forming a separate Croatian *banovina*, which had a large degree of autonomy in administrative, cultural, and educational affairs. Macek also agreed to support the Yugoslav government.

Finally, Yugoslavia maintained a progressive foreign policy. Pašic, who had long been the prime minister of Serbia, had enjoyed good relations with the French since World War I (1914–1918). Throughout the interwar years France incorporated Yugoslavia into its cordon sanitaire, a system of alliances with Yugoslavia, Czechoslovakia, Romania, and Poland that aimed at preventing revisionist states such as Germany, Hungary, and Bulgaria from reemerging as threats to the international order. Yugoslavia also established ties with the Soviet Union in April 1941, even though the Communist Party was still prohibited.

After years of German leader Adolf Hitler's heavy-handed approach toward the region, Yugoslavia's military and Serbian public opinion would not stand for its government becoming a German satellite. A coup d'état led by General Dusan Simovic on 27 March 1941 toppled Cvetkovic's government after it had signed the German-sponsored Anti-Comintern Pact on 25 March. Hitler's troops invaded the country within days. Four years of war cost Yugoslavia enormously. Nearly 20 percent of its population died during World War II. Yugoslavia's resistance, however,

was so effective that it almost single-handedly succeeded in liberating the country from Nazi rule by the end of the war.

Czechoslovakia, like Yugoslavia, at first had been largely supported by its Slavic majority. Linguistic considerations aside, most Slovaks favored unifying with the Czech people, given the alternative of staying within Hungary. A group of key Slovakian intellectuals and political leaders signed an agreement in June 1918 with their Czech counterparts in Pittsburgh, Pennsylvania, that proclaimed the formation of a joint republic at the end of the war. Naturally, the Slovaks encountered some difficulties once the country was established. Cultural barriers compounded communication problems between Czechs and Slovaks: the Czechs were formerly attached to the Austrian crown lands, and Slovakia was a part of the Hungarian Kingdom. In addition, the civil service in Slovakia had been almost entirely dominated by the Magyars and had to be replaced almost entirely by Czechs, as the Slovaks had no trained officials themselves. The Slovaks also had difficulties adjusting to the free-market policies of the Czechs, which contrasted sharply with the protectionist measures that the Hungarians had implemented earlier. Nevertheless, the Slovaks began the long process of economic and social integration. One must also note that Slovak political parties remained faithful to the republic's constitution until just before the German invasion in March 1939.

Similarly, Ruthenians, the ethnic Ukrainian population of eastern Czechoslovakia, preferred Czechoslovakia to both the Soviet Union and Poland. In November 1918 a committee of Ruthenian representatives in Scranton, Pennsylvania, proclaimed its loyalty to Czechoslovakia. Though Ruthenian society was much less developed than the Czechs, they did not protest their position in the republic.

Only the Sudeten Germans were incorporated into Czechoslovakia against their will. Having been considered by the Allies as enemy nationals, this population was excluded from the right to national self-determination that President Wilson had proclaimed. The Sudetenland was thereby awarded to the Czechs in order to make the new state's borders defensible. The cost, however, was that some three million citizens—20 percent of Czechoslovakia's population—refused to acknowledge the government's existence.

Nevertheless, the integration of the Slovaks and Germans into Czechoslovakia progressed during the 1920s. The Czech economy flourished, bolstered by its new markets in Slovakia and Ruthenia, and the strong industrial base of the Czech lands. Many of the republic's citizens gained new opportunities to make a living. Sudeten Germans in particular became aware of these prospects and began to accept the system. In 1925 nearly a third of them voted for political parties that acknowledged the republic by taking their seats in Parliament. The stock market crash in New York on 29 October 1929 and Hitler's rise to power in January 1933 halted this trend, however. Increasingly, the Germans looked toward unification with Nazi Germany as a more favorable alternative to remaining in Czechoslovakia.

Tomas Masaryk, first president of Czechoslovakia (seated, fourth from left), and other Czech officials at the signing of the Pittsburg Declaration, a document that promised European Slovaks self-government in a postwar state, at Turciansky Svaty Martin, May 1918

(from Vera Olivova, The Doomed Democracy: Czechoslovakia in a Disrupted Europe, 1914–38, *1972)*

EASTERN EUROPE AFTER WORLD WAR I

Politically, Czechoslovakia was the only Eastern European democracy to survive throughout the interwar years. Unlike most Eastern European heads of state, the president of Czechoslovakia never annulled the Parliament or constitution. A working alliance of five mainstream Czech parties ruled through majority coalitions in a democratically elected parliament until the German invasion.

The eventual breakup of the country was largely caused by diplomatic circumstances outside of the republic's control. France, Britain, and the Soviet Union guaranteed the republic's borders until British prime minister Neville Chamberlain and the French agreed to Germany's annexation of the Sudetenland in September 1938. The British and French also failed to resist when Hitler invaded and destroyed the remaining Czechoslovakian state on 15 March 1939. Hitler created a puppet Slovak state and turned the Czech lands into the German-ruled Protectorate of Bohemia and Moravia.

In the final analysis, the governments of both Czechoslovakia and Yugoslavia scored impressive successes during the interwar period. While there were problems in integrating all their ethnic groups in the beginning, over time even the once-hostile Germans in Czechoslovakia and the Croats in Yugoslavia came to understand the benefits of remaining within the new polities. The Czechoslovak economy and political democracy set the highest standards of success for all of Eastern Europe. Both governments developed intimate ties with Western Europe. They also did not incite open conflict with their neighbors. Unfortunately, Czechoslovakia and Yugoslavia were among the first victims of Hitler's aggressive plans to expand German rule to the east. Unfortunately, the West was in large part responsible for the destruction of both of these states during the first years of World War II: their willingness to allow totalitarian powers to dominate the region was a trend that would continue for generations.

—YORK NORMAN,
GEORGETOWN UNIVERSITY

Viewpoint:
No. The new states of Eastern Europe were inherently unstable and lacked both legitimacy and long-term viability.

War has a tendency to create business for cartographers. After World War I (1914–1918) the map of Europe was redrawn significantly. The new states that sprouted in Central and Eastern Europe supposedly epitomized the principle of self-determination much touted by U.S. president Woodrow Wilson. The euphoria regarding these newly created states was perhaps misplaced, however. Future British prime minister Winston Churchill best summed up the situation by stating, "there is not one of the peoples . . . to whom gaining their independence had not brought the torture which ancient poets and theologians had reserved for the damned." The successor states to the Austro-Hungarian and Ottoman empires were confronted with weakness and instability internally, regionally, and internationally. These states were ill equipped for survival. As time would show, most did not survive.

The foundation upon which these states were built was the principle of self-determination. Unfortunately, as the historian Raymond Sontag pointed out, though self-determination seemed a noble and practical concept, it was contrary to the essential security of Europe. These small, frail states would be incapable of serving their purpose, as envisioned by France and Britain, to stand as a buffer against the Soviet Union and to balance the potential might of Germany.

Quite a chasm between ideals and reality existed. A double standard applying the principle of self-determination sowed bitter seeds of resentment that would eventually flower into friction among states and among groups within states. The new Austrian Republic, for example, desired union with Germany. As this pairing would create a German population greater than that which existed prior to World War I, the Paris Peace Settlement of 1919 denied Austria's right to unify with Germany. Much the same attitude was taken toward the three million Sudeten Germans who found themselves denied union with Germany, as such an act would deprive the newly created Czechoslovakia of mountainous territory essential to defense and historically integrated into the kingdom of Bohemia, and toward another million Germans who suddenly found themselves living in Poland. It would seem that any attempt of certain peoples, such as the Austrians or the Germans, to move toward realizing their aspirations of self-determination met with disapproval and, in certain incidents, with violence. On 4 March 1919 Czechoslovak forces, which had marched into the Sudetenland in December 1918, shot fifty-four demonstrating Sudeten Germans. Large ethnic Hungarian minorities in Czechoslovakia, Yugoslavia, and Romania likewise had no right to determine their futures. The principle of self-determination was to be granted only to particular peoples as far as the constructors of the Paris Peace Settlement were concerned.

The skeletons of these successor states were fragile. Unlike multiethnic Switzerland, these countries were unable to instill in their populations a sentiment of political nationality. The dissolution of the Ottoman and Austro-Hungarian empires did not create neat, convenient nation-states with homogenous populations containing an equal share of natural resources, a functioning infrastructure, and a balanced economy. These successor states comprised territories of varying cultural, political, and economic levels and experiences. Within Yugoslavia the legacies of the Austro-Hungarian Empire had to be reconciled with those of the Ottoman Empire. In Poland a new national system had to be built by integrating the legacies of three empires: German, Austro-Hungarian, and Russian.

Just a cursory examination of the ethnic makeup of these states illustrates the complexity confronting them. Austria was reduced to a land-locked state of 6.5 million, 2 million of whom resided in Vienna. Czechoslovakia's population of 15 million included 3 million Germans, 700,000 Hungarians, nearly 500,000 Ruthenians, and approximately 2 million Slovaks. Poland contained 1 million Germans and close to 2 million Belorussians and Ukrainians. Romania ruled over 2 million Hungarians. In addition to Serbs, Croats, and Slovenes, Yugoslavia consisted of half a million Hungarians, as well as Romanians, Germans, Italians, Roma, and Albanians. Any government would be hard-pressed to hear such a multitude of voices. To achieve agreement among so many varying peoples would be quite an accomplishment. Not only was the variety of ethnic groups an issue, but also many of these minorities resented their status in the new states. German and Hungarian minorities were particularly reluctant to concede that they were now in a position to be controlled by those they had so recently dominated. Slovaks and Ruthenians complained early on that Czechoslovakia was controlled from Prague and that their concerns had little bearing on the issues at hand. Tension and disagreement between ethnic groups would be visible in the political arena of the state.

A form of political myopia blinded Eastern Europe. Obviously, new states required new governments. Attempting to create new governments that would satisfy all of the constituents within their borders proved to be a Herculean task. In order for parliamentary democracy to succeed and prosper, majority interest and coalitions were required. States, such as Romania, Yugoslavia, and Poland, diverse in social makeup, territory, and political tradition, were hard-pressed to agree, given conflicting agendas. The political simplicity of a two-party system within a homogenous state was not possible. Given the

CORFU DECLARATION

In July 1917 Nikola Pašic, prime minister of Serbia, and Ante Trumbic, president of the Yugoslav Committee, issued an agreement known as the Corfu Declaration, providing for the establishment of Yugoslavia:

The representatives of the Serbs, Croats and Slovenes declare anew and most categorically that our people constitute but one nation, and that it is one in blood, one by the spoken and written language, by the continuity and unity of the territory in which it lives, and finally in virtue of the common and vital interests of its national existence and the general development of its moral and material life. The idea of its national unity has never suffered extinction, although all the intellectual forces of its enemy were directed against its unification, its liberty, and its national existence. Divided between several States, our nation is in Austria-Hungary alone split up into eleven provincial administrations coming under thirteen legislative bodies. The feeling of national unity, together with the spirit of liberty and independence, have supported it in the never-ending struggles of centuries against the Turks in the East and against the Magyars in the West.

. . . .All nations which love liberty and independence have allied themselves together for their common defence, to save civilization and liberty at the cost of every sacrifice, to establish a new international order based upon justice and upon the right of every nation to dispose of itself and so organize its independent life; finally to establish a durable peace consecrated to the progress and development of humanity and to secure the world against a catastrophe. . . .

To noble France, who has proclaimed the liberty of nations, and to England, the hearth of liberty, the Great American Republic and the new, free, and democratic Russia have joined themselves in proclaiming as their principal war aim the triumph of liberty and democracy and as basis of the new international order the right of free self-determination for every nation. . . .

Source: *Corum Research Group, "Material for Reflection on ex-Yugoslavia, Albania, etc: The International Minority Protection Guarantees and Pathways to Bring Them to Fruition: Towards Regaining Stability and Dignity in The Cradle of Europe" <http://www.solami.com/93-29.html>.*

increasing encirclement by hostile states along the borders and the internal political strife that became so debilitating in Yugoslavia, King Alexander was forced to dissolve parliament and declared a royal dictatorship in January 1929. Poland was also consumed by political turmoil from within. An extremist assassinated the president in 1922, and the new nation had fourteen governments between independence in 1918 and a military coup in 1926.

Many of the new states could not even agree on a basic system of government. More than one state was confronted with the dilemma of centralism versus federalism. Both Czechoslovakia and Yugoslavia adopted a centralized system of government, much to the dismay of their minority populations. Hungary was immediately torn by political strife that resulted in a communist government in 1919 and, after its suppression, in a de facto military dictatorship that posed as a regency for the deposed Habsburg dynasty until 1945. Differing views regarding the political structure of the new states resulted only in division, with each party firmly entrenched in its convictions and refusing to compromise. Finally, prior to World War II (1939–1945), Czechoslovakia offered autonomy to Slovakia, while Yugoslavia offered independence to Croatia. Ironically, both Slovakia and Croatia remained in their respective centralist states only to declare later their independence through their alliance with Nazi Germany against their former countrymen during the war.

If the successor states were bedeviled by internal problems, their regional standings were equally diseased. Divvying the spoils of the fallen empires was troublesome. Competing and conflicting claims abounded, resulting in numerous irredentist disputes. States were claiming more than was legitimate based on the principle of self-determination. Just as the complex makeup of the populations within each state was daunting, so were the many claims and disagreements within the region. Poland and Lithuania could not agree regarding Wilno (Vilnius, Vilna); Lithuania claimed historic rights, whereas Poland claimed ethnic and demographic rights. Poland and Czechoslovakia argued over Teschen (Těšin, Cieszyn), Poland claiming on the basis of ethnicity, Czechoslovakia on economics. Romania and Yugoslavia had competing claims over the Banat of Temesvàr. Italy and Yugoslavia fought over the port of Rijeka (Fiume) and the eastern coastline of the Adriatic. Hungary, reduced to a pale shade of its former self and unable to come to terms with its newfound powerless status and decreased territory, laid claims against almost all of the new states: against Czechoslovakia concerning Slovakia and Ruthenia, against Romania regarding Transylvania, and against Yugoslavia with respect to Vojvodina and Croatia.

Diplomatic cooperation among the new states was random and inconsistent and lacked long-term vision. In the 1920s Yugoslavia, Romania, Poland, and Czechoslovakia entered into a network of bilateral alliances with France, the "Little Entente," fearing Hungarian revisionism. Such efforts were worthless, not only because Hungary was a secondary threat but also because their ostracism of Hungary increased

regional discord. French hopes that these states would form a powerful and cohesive counterweight to Germany were misguided. Greece, Turkey, Romania, and Yugoslavia created the Balkan Entente, which reflected the same shortsightedness and futility as the Little Entente, for it, too, failed to address real threats from Italy, Germany, or the Soviet Union and only managed to isolate Bulgaria.

In addition to the political strife, the newly emerging states were fraught with internal socioeconomic crises. The Austro-Hungarian Empire, complex and inefficient at the best of times, dismembered was chaotic and conflicted. The main industrial sectors were now separated by new borders from necessary sources of raw materials and from their natural markets. Inadequate but formerly integrated Imperial transportation systems were now severed, adding to economic woes. Most states, devastated by world war and saddled with debt, were immediately faced with the necessity of dealing with peasant issues and land reform in their largely agarian societies. The underdeveloped industrial base was recognized as a hindrance to balanced growth. Unfortunately, adopted solutions frequently exacerbated conditions. The land reforms proved ineffective, and every country's knee-jerk reaction to its newfound independent economic status was to attempt to protect itself by imposing tariffs. This increased costs, lowered productivity, and hindered overall trade. All of these issues were relevant, and even more damaging in a regional context.

The new states were also neglected and threatened internationally. The Allies were relatively passive in many respects toward Eastern Europe. Despite many declarations to the contrary, Western Europe and the United States failed to nurture the development of these new states, either unconcerned with or doubting their viability. In 1925 the United Kingdom was willing in the Locarno Treaties to guarantee Germany's western frontier but not its eastern borders. France's Little Entente alliances were weak and ineffectual. Its defensive strategy in the 1930s and its willingness to follow Britain's lead in abandoning Czechoslovakia to German leader Adolf Hitler in 1938 made its other guarantees in the region worthless.

Other Great Powers, such as Germany and Italy, were drooling over the tender morsels of the successor states, harboring irredentist appetites. Through the interwar period, Germany looked to regain the territory it had lost to Poland. Hitler successfully sought union with Austria, the acquisition of the ethnic German-populated Sudetenland from Czechoslovakia, and the recovery of Memel from Lithuania. His desire to recover territory from Poland led to his invasion of September 1939 and the beginning of World War II. The Soviet Union wanted to recover ethnically East Slavic territory from Poland, seize strategically important territory from Finland, reincorporate the Baltic States, and retrieve territory from Romania. All of this was done, mostly with Hitler's connivance, in 1939–1940. As early as September 1919 an Italian nationalist gang seized Fiume from Yugoslavia, and Italian dictator Benito Mussolini agitated for the acquisition of ethnic Italian territory until Hitler allowed him to take it in 1941.

Economically speaking, the Allies were as unsupportive of Eastern Europe as they were politically. France traded little with its Eastern allies as it was more concerned with protecting its own agriculture from Eastern European surpluses. The West withdrew all of its capital credits to Eastern Europe following the crash of the American stock market in 1929. In the 1930s, however, Germany used its growing economic clout to expand its commercial interests in the region. These economic ties eventually facilitated German political domination.

The new states of Eastern Europe were plagued with discontent and dissension among the various ethnic minorities. They also faced myriad other challenges, including the creation of a new system of government, a bureaucracy, and a legal system; and the organization of disjointed economies and markets. Not only were the East Europeans forced to create new states, but, like the rest of Europe, they also had to restructure and develop, rising from the ashes left behind by World War I. If such internal discord and severe conditions were not sufficient obstacles to overcome, the states found themselves suffocated in regional dissonance, resulting from territorial disputes, unresolved irredentist desires, historical tension, and an utter lack of cooperation. In the international arena the great powers neglected if not undermined their protégés. Economically and politically, they protected their own interests, leaving the weak, fledgling states on their own, exposed and vulnerable to the more hostile intentions of Germany, the Soviet Union, and Italy.

Soviet foreign minister Molotov referred to Poland as "this ugly offspring of the Versailles Treaty." Perhaps it would be better stated that the offspring of the Versailles Treaty were not so much ugly as they were ill equipped for survival. In less than a generation after the Paris Peace, all of the successor states would be devoured by Germany or the Soviet Union, incapable of fending off these predators to maintain their integrity and independence. After World War II, for the majority of the second half of the twentieth century, most of the states created by the Paris Peace, lib-

erated from the Ottoman or Austro-Hungarian Empires by the principle of self-determination, would fall into the realm of the Soviet Empire, under the shadow of the Red Army. It would not be until the fall of the Berlin Wall in 1989 that these same countries would be given a second chance at independent statehood. Their odds for success were greater given that the regional and international situations were more stable and supportive to ensure viability and legitimacy. Despite such favorable conditions, some states, such as Czechoslovakia and Yugoslavia, were still unable to endure and dissolved, creating new borders and new entities. Hopefully, all of these countries have learned from the tumultuous past as they have been making efforts to address internal friction and regional issues through legal measures, economic reform, and cooperation, just as the Great Powers have been encouraging and nurturing politically and ecconomically. Given all of these new circumstances, this new generation of Eastern European states may finally be able to stand on its own feet.

–JELENA BUDJEVAC,
WASHINGTON, D.C.

References

Ivan T. Berend, *Decades of Crisis: Central and Eastern Europe before World War II* (Berkeley: University of California Press, 1998).

C. E. Black and E. C. Helmreich, *Twentieth Century Europe: A History* (New York: Knopf, 1950).

R. J. Crampton, *Eastern Europe in the Twentieth Century–and After,* second edition (London & New York: Routledge, 1997).

Barbara Jelavich, *History of the Balkans* (Cambridge & New York: Cambridge University Press, 1983).

Robin Okey, *Eastern Europe 1740–1985: Feudalism to Communism* (Minneapolis: University of Minnesota Press, 1986).

Joseph Rothschild, *East Central Europe between the Two World Wars* (Seattle: University of Washington Press, 1974).

Hugh Seton-Watson, *Eastern Europe between the Wars, 1918–1941,* third edition (New York: Harper & Row, 1967).

Raymond J. Sontag, *A Broken World, 1919–1939* (New York: Harper & Row, 1971).

ECLIPSE OF EUROPE

Was the eclipse of Europe as the arbiter of world affairs in the twentieth century inevitable?

Viewpoint: Yes. Twentieth-century shifts in demographics, military strengths, economic growth, and the global balance of power assured a diminished role for Europe in world affairs.

Viewpoint: No. Though the two world wars weakened Europe's position in world affairs, it reasserted itself as a political force by the end of the century.

The twentieth century marked the decline of Europe's position as the major arbiter of global affairs. As new centers of power and wealth emerged, Europe's colonial empires collapsed, its resources dwindled, and its ambitions faltered. By 2000 its global strategic positions, political influence, and economic power had shriveled to a pale shadow of what they had been in 1900.

Some scholars argue that the eclipse of Europe was inescapable. Even without the destruction and demoralization of two world wars, Europe would still have been challenged by rising world powers, especially the United States, Japan, and China—the first two of which began their ascent independently of any European developments before the turn of the twentieth century. Changing political, economic, and demographic realities militated strongly against Europe's perpetual preeminence.

Other historians maintain that Europe's decline was not at all foreordained. Avoiding the catastrophes of the world wars would have spared tens of millions of lost and ruined lives, saved vast treasuries, preserved tremendous economic potential, emasculated destructive political extremism, and kept alive an optimistic view of Europe's position in the world. Even if other powers were emerging, a peaceful and prosperous Europe could well have sustained its dominance over the long term—a fact supported by its continuing, if diminished, importance in the twenty-first century.

Viewpoint:
Yes. Twentieth-century shifts in demographics, military strengths, economic growth, and the global balance of power assured a diminished role for Europe in world affairs.

Prominent British historian Geoffrey Barraclough has defined a decline in Europe's global predominance and a shift of emphasis away from Europe as two of the most obvious characteristics of twentieth-century history. The date when European supremacy was succeeded by the age of global civilization is still a matter of discussion among historians and thinkers. Some historians have picked out 1917, when both the United States and Bolshevik Russia, with their programs of peace settlement and radical social transformation, respectively, challenged the old European and world order. Some authors, such as well-known Indian statesman and scholar Kavalam Pannikar, have seen the late 1940s as the end of the European age, when the independence of India (1947) and the victorious Communist revolution in China (1949) signaled the resurgence of Asia and the gathering revolt against the West.

Many historians credit the two world wars as the causes of Europe's decline, for the conflicts whittled away the resources of the European powers and, during the Cold War, led to their eclipse as the arbiters of world affairs in favor of the United States and the Soviet Union. Nevertheless, there are views that follow English historian Arnold Toynbee's note that European as well as Western civilization as a whole could not retain its global military and economic supremacy indefinitely. As famous French thinker Raymond Aron wrote, "even in the absence of the two world wars, Europe would not have avoided decline, although it would not have been so rapid nor so dramatic." There are several important dimensions that illustrate why Europe's favored position and influence in the world would not outlast the twentieth century.

At the dawn of the twentieth century a major shift in the world's population was beginning to take place, and the demographic balance was turning against Europe. The phenomenal population growth in European countries during the nineteenth century produced some 40 million emigrants, mainly to the Americas and Australia. There was also a steady decline in the birthrate in industrialized Europe caused by economic and social upheaval, higher standards of living, and the spread of contraception. At the same time major advances in hygiene and medicine—as well as the introduction of improved techniques of agriculture, irrigation, land reclamation, and food storage facilities—offset the effects of sporadic famine and led to the population explosion, particularly in Asia. Europe's proportion of the total world's population dramatically declined—from 25 percent in 1900 to 15.3 percent in 1950 to 10.8 percent in 1980. By 2000 Europe's proportion of the world's population had risen slightly to 12 percent, while Asia's reached 60.7 percent. This demographic revolution led to the formation of new centers of population, production, and power far away from Europe.

As for the military dimension, the armies and navies of the early twentieth century gave Europeans unquestionable military superiority and the power to impose their wills. In 1900, of eight major military powers, six were in Europe; the European share of the world's military power was 92 percent on land and 83 percent at sea. Yet, in the 1990s Europe had just 28 percent of the world's military manpower, 34 percent of the world's naval strength, and only 32 percent of the world's airpower.

At the beginning of the twentieth century Japan and the United States emerged as non-European centers of military and political power. The Japanese, invigorated by the Meiji Restoration (1868), successfully developed the country's industry, reformed its army, and modernized its political structure. In 1904–1905 Japan defeated Russia, showing that Asians could master Western technology and weaponry well enough to stand up to Europeans in war. In 1918–1922 Japan participated in the post–World War I peace settlement and entered the League of Nations as one of five great powers. In the early 1930s the Japanese launched a new wave of imperial conquests in Asia, trying to expel European influence and pretending to restore "Asia to the Asians"—to establish in fact a new economic and political order there, centered on Japan. These projects ended with the Japanese defeat in 1945.

As for the United States, in 1898 it fought and won a war against Spain, one of the oldest European empires. The growth of American naval power, symbolized in the voyage of the "Great White Fleet" around the globe (1907–1909), supported the transformation of the United States into a power with extensive overseas interests, discouraging further European involvement in the Western Hemisphere. At the beginning of the twentieth century the United States used its rapid and large-scale industrialization as an entrée into the club of great powers. American productivity in manufacturing was twice the average European level by the eve of World War I (1914–1918), while the United States had moved far ahead of Europe in engineering and motor transport, and the introduction of scientific farming methods turned America into a major supplier of foodstuffs.

After 1900 Britain and France gave the United States a free hand throughout the Caribbean. By 1914 America strengthened its global strategic position by securing complete control over the Panama Canal. Moreover, the United States came to see itself as an arbiter between Europe and Asia. In 1905 the United States hosted the Russo-Japanese peace conference and then participated in the Algeciras Conference (1906) to discuss concerns among the European powers, mainly France and Germany, over the control of Morocco. American might had radically influenced the outcome of World War I, while the eventual decision to enter the war in 1917 was backed by the growing belief that the United States was destined to transform the old balance of power and produce a new global order based on open diplomacy, open trade, and liberal values. In this new role the United States debuted at the Paris Peace Conference (1919), while Washington hosted an international conference in 1921–1922, which set a new balance of global naval power. In the 1920s the United States replaced Britain as a leading trader and banker,

EUROPEAN UNION

An Effective and Coherent Foreign Policy: Introduction

1. Despite the fact that it is the world's largest trading entity, the European Union is not as effective as it should be in using its diplomatic influence and its economic capacity in relations with third countries and in promoting peace, stability and prosperity in the world. One of the Conference's top priorities must be to make the external policies of the Union more coherent, effective and visible.

2. The proposed Treaty changes set out in Section III are designed to address this challenge and to ensure that the political and economic aspects of the Union's external policy are consistent, coherent and mutually reinforcing. The main elements of the approach set out in this Section are as follows:

3. More effective policy structures would be introduced under the *common foreign and security policy* and continuity would be improved in a number of ways. There would be improved support structures to assist the Presidency. There would be better preparation of decisions and more focused policy implementation. Overall consistency would be strengthened by closer involvement of the Commission. Decision-making procedures would be significantly improved.

4. In its *external economic relations*, the Community would be able to act more effectively in multilateral international organizations, notably in the World Trade Organization, to defend the interests of its Member States, its industry and workers in today's highly competitive international trading environment.

5. The Union's objectives in *security and defence* matters and the means by which the Union can pursue these objectives would be adapted to address the new challenges facing the Union.

6. The Union would be endowed with *legal personality* enabling it to negotiate and enter into international agreements with other countries or international organizations where this is required to achieve foreign policy objectives.

---

preserving its position as the largest industrial producer at the same time. Latin America, once dominated by the European powers, established closer economic and diplomatic ties with the United States. The entire world economy began to orientate itself away from Europe and toward America. The economic crisis of 1929–1933, signaled by the crash of the New York Stock Exchange, clearly proved the core role of the American center of economic and financial power in global developments.

The dramatic shift in the global balance of power in the 1940s and the Cold War further developed trends already in the making. The United States and Soviet Union became dominant players on the world stage when a divided Europe found itself militarily dependent on the superpowers. The United States maintained its military presence in Western Europe and provided its allies with security guarantees through the North Atlantic Treaty Organization (NATO) and a network of military bases and bilateral defense agreements. The Cold War also stressed a dramatic transformation of Europe's military significance: from the central role in global military balance to a "central front" in a potential American-Soviet nuclear showdown. As part of its Cold War strategy, in the 1940s and the 1950s the United States successfully persuaded European nations to accept worldwide trade liberalization (the General Agreement on Tariffs and Trade, or GATT, of 1947), helped to rebuild Europe, and promoted economic and social reforms in occupied Germany and Japan. Since the 1960s the United States has taken the lead in almost all areas of modern technology.

As far as atomic weaponry was concerned, Britain and France managed to become nuclear powers, and West Germany offered signals of its potential to do so. Nevertheless, post-Cold War strategic realities kept Europe as only one of several pivotal military players and confined it to its alignment with the United States. The slow proliferation of weapons of mass destruction (WMD)

ECLIPSE OF EUROPE

has led to the contemporary reality that of eight real and presumed nuclear powers only three (Britain, France, and Russia) are European, while five (the United States, China, Israel, India, and Pakistan) are not. Other potential candidates for membership in the "nuclear club"–including such countries as Iran, North Korea, Brazil, and South Africa–have come exclusively from outside Europe. Recent conflicts and wars–including the Persian Gulf War (1990–1991), Bosnian Civil War (1992–1995), Chechen conflict (since 1994), Kosovo War (1999), U.S.-led campaign in Afghanistan (2001), and Iraq War (2003)–have demonstrated that the Europeans and others are lagging far behind America in high-tech conventional weaponry, communications, logistics, and power projection capabilities.

In the ideological sphere Europe's international role was challenged by dynamic and violent developments in Asia. In the 1950s and 1960s there were attempts to undermine the role of the European (Moscow-dominated) center of the world communist movement by China. In Albania, the Far East, and parts of Africa and Latin America local communists followed China rather than the U.S.S.R. The revival of radical Islam since the late 1970s has seriously damaged Europe's cultural and political influence in the Arab world and endangered its energy supplies. At the same time the infiltration of radical Islam into European societies, where millions of Muslim immigrants live, and the expansion of Islamic extremist and terrorist activities throughout the continent have made it extremely vulnerable to this new challenge.

As for Europe's global economic position, in 1900 the old continent dominated the world economy. Britain, Germany, and France commanded some 60 percent of the world market for manufactured goods. Three of the world's four major investors were European (the other was the United States), and Europe's proportion of all major foreign investments was a whopping 93 percent. By 1992 Europe's share of the world's gross product had fallen to 36.7 percent. While five of the ten current major economies are still European, the two largest–the United States and Japan–are not, and the proportion of Europe's economic potential as a portion of the Big Ten's total potential is some 29 percent.

Much of this lead fell to Asia. Beginning in the 1950s and 1960s, Japan was a major player in the transformation of the Pacific Rim into the hub of world trade. China joined in this process when its communist leadership began to champion market economics in the 1980s. Additionally, since the 1970s the "four dragons" (South Korea, Hong Kong, Singapore, and Taiwan), using cheap labor and borrowed capital, ensured rapid export-led economic growth, particularly in

textile and light consumer goods. By 1976 they produced some 60 percent of the world's manufacturing exports. Partly stimulated by these developments, other regional economies, including Malaysia, Thailand, and Indonesia, began to develop. All the necessary factors of rapid export-oriented economic growth were in place there, too: a cheap and flexible workforce, low labor unrest, and the ability of governments (in contrast to Europe) to spend less on welfare and infrastructure and more on education and export subsidy. In the 1980s the Pacific Rim states began to invest their surpluses in the West, including Europe and the United States.

Economic development and transformation of material life depend on the progress of science and technology. In the twentieth century Europe began to lose its earlier unquestionable domination in this field. The recent information revolution highlights Europe's lack of competitive technology producers, such as Microsoft or Dell. Of the fifty biggest information technology companies in the late 1990s, thirty-six were American, nine were Japanese, and only four were European. Additionally, the current and prospective trend toward political and economic globalization–as well as the internationalization of crime, corruption, and terrorism–has helped to erode the power of the nation-state, which has remained the basic component of European political organization.

To Europe's political and economic decline must be added the loss of its former cultural supremacy in favor of large-scale Americanization of world culture. Since the 1920s the aggressive modernity of American life–jazz, cars, and cinema–conquered the imagination of the Europeans. New York and Los Angeles increasingly began to function as cultural centers alongside Paris, London, Berlin, and Vienna. American film studios provided much of the world's movie output. Popular music was America's most noticeable export–from Frank Sinatra in the 1940s to Madonna in the 1980s. Cultural factors were also instrumental in the growth of East Asia as the major center of economic power, because of its emphases on group loyalty, respect for hierarchy, and educational achievement.

The major European powers entered the twentieth century with what they saw as their almost complete control over the world's territory, resources, markets, and outlets for capital investments. Yet, Europe was in the process of generating social and political forces that transformed this empire. The imposition of European hegemony over much of the globe carried the seeds of its own destruction. Social and political modernization in Western Europe, promotion of parliamentary rule, civil rights, and the ideas of self-determination filtered beyond Europe to encourage political protest in the colonies. The

American and Soviet soldiers meeting on a bridge over the Elbe River at Torgau, Germany, April 1945

(Associated Press)

European empires faced growing opposition led by an educated elite who sought a role in local administration, self-rule, or even complete independence. By 1931 England had to concede full freedom of action to its "white" dominions, even in foreign policy, recognizing them as de facto independent states.

In Asia and Africa the growing anticolonial reaction was visible even on the eve of the century. Italy failed to subjugate Abyssinia (present-day Ethiopia, 1896), while the British managed to annex the Boer republics in southern Africa (1899–1902) only by concentrating tremendous resources to bloody fighting. The anti-Western Boxer Rebellion in China (1899–1901), though suppressed with a great deal of violence, signaled the awakening of a sleeping giant and stimulated Europe-wide panic about the coming "Yellow Peril."

While the European empires achieved their zenith with partition of the Ottoman Empire's Arab provinces (early 1920s) and Italy's conquest of Abyssinia (1935), anti-European forces in the Middle East, India, China, Southeast Asia, and North Africa began to confront European domination. Nationalist regimes established in Chile, Argentina, and Brazil in the 1920s and 1930s

attempted to revive native culture and values and rejected the influence of Europe. Anti-European movements in Asia and Africa, as well as growing criticism of colonialism and pressure from the United States and the Soviet Union, were important factors in the dissolution of European empires by the 1960s and 1970s.

The two world wars did much to weaken Europe's world role, but they were rather reflections of eclipse than the causes of it. The Allied powers depended heavily on the resources of Europe's colonial possessions in their war efforts. Political writers such as Hans Delbruck, Rudolph Kjellén, Paul Rohrbach, and Friedrich Naumann demonstrated their awareness that the position of Europe was changing and that its pre-1914 world domination would be inevitably lost unless something were done to restore it. That is why some historians point out that Berlin's policy of transforming Central Europe into a German-dominated continental empire, able to compete on equal terms with other world powers (Russia, the United States, and the British Empire), was, in fact, the last attempt to save Europe's world role.

One should also acknowledge that during the Cold War extra-European developments had more potential than any development in Europe to spark off a third world war. Both superpowers often considered other regions strategically more important than Europe. The system of balance of power, European in its origin and dependent for its continuation upon Europe's preeminence, gave way to a system of global polarities and the establishment of continent-wide power blocs. It was not accidental that when a chief architect of American foreign policy in the 1970s, Secretary of State Henry Kissinger, a long-time student of the European balance of power, employed a balance-of-power approach to widen the room for maneuver for the United States in world affairs, he saw two "triangles": a military-political one (the United States/NATO, U.S.S.R., and China) and an economic one (North America, Western Europe, and Japan).

For sure, the steady progress of integration did much for the restoration of Europe's importance in world affairs, particularly in trade and finance. Nevertheless, no matter how European nations conducted themselves, the rise of non-European powers could not have been avoided, and Europe, as Raymon Aron put it, had "to resign itself to a position less at odds with the size of its territory and population."

-PETER RAINOW,
SAN MATEO, CALIFORNIA

Viewpoint:
No. Though the two world wars weakened Europe's position in world affairs, it reasserted itself as a political force by the end of the century.

On 1 January 1900 no one would have disputed Europe's domination of the world. Europe led the world by any cultural, economic, political, and intellectual measure. Its colonies spanned the globe: in Africa only Ethiopia and Liberia remained independent countries. In its capital cities the heads of Europe carved up the map of the world. When the Japanese chose to imitate the world's best practices, they selected as their role models the German army, British navy, and French municipal government. European literature, music, and culture were all aped around the world, such that a family in India—in English dress and drinking French wine—might plan to attend a Mozart opera in Bombay. German universities, and their invention of the seminar, had become the model for higher education around the world. It was clear to all that the Europeans were the pinnacle of human development.

By mid century such a claim would be utterly unrealistic. Certainly, from 1945 to 1989, one could argue that Europe seemed increasingly irrelevant. By 1950 Europe's predominance seemed to be irretrievably lost. Countless cities in Germany, Poland, Britain, the Balkans, Eastern Europe, and the Soviet Union lay in ruins. Fifteen million people had been killed in the four years of World War I (1914–1918), and at least a further forty-five million were killed during World War II (1939–1945), including at least six million Jews. The same Europe that had been able to dictate to the world found itself as one of the world's greatest aid recipients. In 1945 Europe was in no position to claim the right to rule the world, but even after recovering the continent it would never regain the predominance it once held. Already in the 1940s colonies were being shed. During the Suez Crisis (1956) the United States and the Soviet Union abruptly showed Britain and France that they were no longer able to act unilaterally. By 1970 almost all European colonies had been let go. To observers the Falklands War (1982), in which Britain fought Argentina over an inconsequential archipelago in the South Atlantic, had a markedly anachronistic and futile feel about it.

Europe's weakened position in the years of the Cold War may well have been avoidable, but it is far from certain that it was inevitable. Certainly, World War I was a homegrown catastrophe, but it is arguable that blame for World War II could be laid on the troubled relationship Europe held with the United States. Had there been more genuine and fruitful cooperation between Washington and the capitals of Europe, it is conceivable that a more just and durable peace could have been built in the years after World War I. Similarly, it is possible to argue that U.S. president Woodrow Wilson's lofty pronouncements that promised unrealizable gifts of self-determination and peaceful cooperation created pent-up frustrations that burst forth once Wall Street's excesses and American selfishness created a worldwide depression. Such an argument, perhaps, leaves Europeans with far too little control over their own fate to be satisfying.

Although some observers periodically pronounce Europe's position as being as relevant as that of Imperial Rome, the case might well be made that not only are claims of Europe's inevitable eclipse unrealistic but that the conclusion that it has been eclipsed may well be premature. Admittedly, the United States and Asia are often held to be the leaders of the future, with a sclerotic Europe struggling to keep up with the dynamic societies across the Atlantic and in Asia. Europe no longer dictates to the world: no longer can a group of European foreign ministers simply carve up the map of Africa. Yet, one must wonder whether Europe is actually "finished." Europe seems to be about so much more than enforcing old colonial privileges.

The United States may be the most powerful country in terms of economic size and military force, but it seems to be in the process of learning that its military and commercial predominance may be much more limited than it thinks. Persistent pockets of poverty and a disaffected electorate whose majority does not even bother to vote mark the American economic and political landscape. Japan, once the other putative giant of the modern world, has been economically and politically paralyzed for more than a decade.

In fact, Europe may be reasserting its predominance over the world. The collapse of communism, beginning in 1989, seems to have opened the door to an era of European prosperity and growth. European ideas of freedom, democracy, and open markets are spreading across the world, aided mightily by the American example. Europe is certainly ahead of the world in terms of social justice and economic well-being for all citizens. European integration also seems to be moving ahead at a steady pace, demonstrating for all the world the power of supranational cooperation and coordination. After the economic doldrums of the 1970s and 1980s the European economy seems to be doing well and by some measures leads both the United States and Japan. In fact, American predominance in the economic sphere is overstated. Taken as a whole, Europe is more populous and produces more than the United States, Japan, Canada, or the nations of the former Soviet Union. That fact certainly does not sound like evidence of an eclipse. Nor does Europe seem to be nearly as bellicose or as resented as it once was. In fact, Europe seems to be becoming the ideal world citizen: peaceful, prosperous, and a paragon of social justice and participatory democracy.

Certainly, Europe once seemed to be able to dictate to the world, if one thinks of the imperious behavior of colonial rulers, but that domination was mostly chimerical. British domination of India, for example, was more an alliance of local Indian notables working with the British. Once Britain's suitability for partnership was drawn into question by the moral challenges posed by Mohandas Gandhi or the tragedy of World War II, the Raj fizzled out. So, too, was European domination over China more apparent than real. The Manchu dynasty collapsed under its own weight, not by dint of Europe's incursions. Internal rebellions and defeat at Japanese hands in 1895 did far more damage to China than extraterritoriality. Europe merely was standing by at the time that the Manchus collapsed. Africa arguably could be listed as having been dominated by Europe, but this domination ran mostly from 1875 to 1930, or at most three generations. Moreover, this domination was only limited to urban centers, as the Euro-peans sought to develop the political and economic infrastructure of the continent. Since the European withdrawal from Africa, European economic penetration has continued on fairly much as before. No one has since dominated the politics of that continent in the way the Europeans did for a brief time.

The question that arises, then, is if Europe has been eclipsed, then by whom? The Americans have only limited influence in those areas where Europe once held sway. China and India rule themselves. In fact, this pattern can be seen worldwide, as areas previously under the sway of Europe have taken on their own political direction. In fact, it might be more accurate to say that Europe has not been eclipsed by anyone. Rather, the huge advantage that Europe had over others in 1900 has dissipated. The greatest component of Europe's advantage was its technological advantage over Africa, Asia, and East Asia, making possible the easy conquest and management of empires. It should be considered, however, that its domination continues in other forms. Political discourse continues to be dominated by terminology and ideas invented by the Europeans (not to mention their languages). Though the United States certainly has the most dominant military and cultural influences, the values that these two factors cast around the world are not nearly as powerful as the ideas of social justice, democracy, and freedom, which were products of the European Enlightenment and which dominate the political atmosphere of Europe. Europe's power is in ideas, as the cradle of the Western civilization that is conquering the world. No doubt there are people around the world who desire to build societies with an equitable distribution of wealth, social welfare systems that work, pervasive public transportation networks, peaceful urban centers, affordable housing, and the ecologically minded consumption of energy. In many ways the European model may well be a better one for sustainable world development than the market-driven free-for-all that so often characterizes American life.

–PHIL GILTNER,
ALBANY ACADEMY

References

Raymond Aron, *In Defense of Decadent Europe,* translated by Stephen Cox (South Bend, Ind.: Regnery/Gateway, 1977).

Geoffrey Barraclough, *An Introduction to Contemporary History* (London: Watts, 1964).

Hajo Holborn, *The Political Collapse of Europe* (New York: Knopf, 1951).

Arnold Toynbee, *The World and the West* (New York: Oxford University Press, 1953).

FALL OF FRANCE

Were military factors the sole reason for the German defeat of France in 1940?

Viewpoint: Yes. France fell because of Germany's technological and strategic superiority.

Viewpoint: No. France was defeated because it suffered from psychological demoralization, political dissension, and moral decadence.

France reluctantly went to war with Germany after German leader Adolf Hitler invaded Poland in September 1939. Long fearful of a new conflict with its eastern neighbor and committed to a defensive strategy, France did little to prevent the successful conclusion of Germany's campaign in the East. The months that followed were defined by an odd lull in military operations, a "phony war," or as the French called it, the *drôle de guerre*.

That period of quiet ended explosively when the Germans launched a major offensive in the West on 10 May 1940. After overrunning Luxembourg, the Netherlands, and Belgium, the Germans' full attention turned to breaking France. Although the French and their British allies had forced their German opponents into a four-year stalemate during World War I (1914–1918), they were far less fortunate the second time around. Within just six weeks of the German attack the French government recognized its exhaustion in the field and asked for an armistice.

The astonishing defeat of a major European power in so short a time engendered a debate that continues today. Retrospective views of France's collapse, tainted by the failures and shortcomings of French government and society during the rest of the war, have focused largely on the country's long-term problems. Could a nation afflicted by restless political division, an arguably defeatist popular culture, serious social discord, and general malaise have mounted any effective resistance? French historian, officer, and later resistance fighter Marc Bloch advanced this view almost immediately after the collapse in his memoir, *Strange Defeat: A Statement of Evidence Written in 1940* (1949). As Bloch's reminiscences and one of the arguments presented in this chapter demonstrate, France's defeat was the inevitable result of preexisting national decadence.

The counterargument suggests, however, that no matter what the "mood" of France may have been before 1940, it was so outclassed militarily that its fight was hopeless. Germany's effective adaptation of new offensive battle tactics, particularly blitzkrieg (lightning war) and its emphasis on fast-moving armored columns, coordinated air attacks, and decisive frontline victories, gave its forces an insuperable advantage. France's emphasis on maintaining fixed positions and deploying its forces in reaction to enemy movements damned it far more than the nebulous influence of "decadence," which, arguably, affected every other European country before World War II (1939–1945), including Germany.

Viewpoint:
Yes. France fell because of Germany's technological and strategic superiority.

The life of France's Third Republic could be bookmarked between military defeats by Germany. The Franco-Prussian War (1870–1871) caused the collapse of the Second Empire and the rise of a new republican government. France again fought its German neighbor in World War I (1914–1918), but this time it emerged as one of the victors. Yet, twenty-two years later the French capitulated quickly to the German blitzkrieg (lightning war). German troops won after just six weeks, causing the fall of the Third Republic and the installation of a government in Vichy that collaborated with the Nazis. French citizens have had to contend with the consequences of this defeat ever since.

France's fall in 1940 confounded many observers and historians. With all due respect to the other victims of the German blitzkrieg, France should have been able to resist longer. Denmark, Norway, Belgium, the Netherlands, and Luxembourg were too small and too weak to resist the Nazi onslaught. Though their resistance was heroic, there was only so much these countries could do against the German war machine. Poland's options were also limited. Although Poland was larger than the other victims, its military was not as advanced as the German one, and it suffered from the added disadvantage of being located between Germany and the Soviet Union. Any hope that the Poles had in 1939 evaporated quickly after the Soviet invasion.

The French should have better resisted the German blitzkrieg. They had a stronger military than Germany's other victims, extensive defensive preparations, and the advantage of facing only one real enemy. As in World War I, the French had British support, including a British Expeditionary Force (BEF) in France. The French also knew that the Germans would be coming. After the Germans vanquished the Poles, the *Sitzkrieg* (phony war) began in fall 1939 and lasted through spring 1940.

There had to be reasons for this "Strange Defeat," ones that would explain how a proud country fell so rapidly. Was it the fault of decadence in French society, of the Popular Front and political dissension? There is some credibility in the doubts about France's will to fight another war. World War I was horrific; its western campaign was fought almost entirely on French soil, and nearly a generation of young men died to save the country from the Germans.

No country would want to repeat this experience.

Yet, World War I had been nearly equally as horrific for the Germans and British; citizens in these countries were not thrilled about a new war. In 1938 the German general staff was prepared to remove Hitler from power if he had been granted the war he wished for with Czechoslovakia. Germany's military leadership feared that their forces were not ready for war. Western appeasement and Hitler's popularity enabled him to continue his aggression. Many Germans, following the defeat of Poland, would have been content to end the war then and avoid attacking the West or the Soviet Union. They, too, had little desire for a long, bloody fight. The objective in blitzkrieg was a quick campaign that would avoid the risks of a long struggle in the trenches. Blitzkrieg was almost successful against the two European powers that resisted the German onslaught. The Battle of Britain (1940–1941) nearly brought the British to their knees; had the Germans concentrated on English air bases instead of shifting their attack to the cities, the outcome might have been different. Operation Barbarossa (1941) initially swept over large amounts of Russian territory, reaching the suburbs of Moscow in December, before finally being repulsed. It is possible that a concentrated German thrust instead of an attack on a wide front would have caused a Russian collapse. Though the German blitzkrieg was indeed stopped just short of its goal, the German army endangered the survival of the Soviet Union well into 1942. Evidence shows that the Germans almost defeated the two major European powers, who would later combine with the United States to defeat Nazi Germany. Germany came close to winning this war; a few adaptations in strategy might have resulted in their victory.

This simple comparison between France, Britain, and the Soviet Union shows that the traditional psychological explanations for France's rapid defeat are insufficient. No one wanted a repeat of World War I, not even the German leadership. Arguing that France lost because of its moral decadence or political dissension gives the German blitzkrieg less credit than it deserves. The British had their share of political dissension and moral decadence in the years between the world wars. Political turmoil, economic devastation, and moral "progressivism" also plagued Germany in the 1920s and early 1930s. The Soviet Union experienced considerable political turmoil in the wake of the 1917 Revolution; among the victims of Soviet leader Josef Stalin's purges in the late 1930s were many in the Russian officer corps. Therefore, any argument contending that France lost so quickly because of demoralization, dissension, and decadence wrongly presents France as exceptional among those countries that experienced similar unrest.

Robert J. Young, author of *In Command of France: French Foreign Policy and Military Planning, 1933–1940* (1978), was among the earlier scholars to address the concept of a "Strange Defeat." His objective was to separate France's military defeat in 1940 from the events that followed. France planned for a war of attrition against the Germans, one that the Germans could not sustain. Richard Overy, in *Why the Allies Won* (1995), has shown that it was not a foregone conclusion that the Germans would fall to their more resource-rich opponents, but in the end the side with the greater resources won the war. Along with its military plans, French diplomacy was active in the 1930s. France knew that another war with Germany was inevitable and that it could not fight the Germans alone. It devoted considerable energy to creating an alliance system. The results were mixed. France's "Little Entente" with states in Eastern Europe was ineffective, as was its separate alliance with Czechoslovakia; in fact, the French betrayed their Czechoslovakian allies by acquiescing to Hitler's dissolution of their country in 1938. No agreement with Russia or Italy was made. Despite their later defeat, the French had tried hard to protect their nation against Nazi aggression.

Part of France's defensive strategy lay in the development of frontier fortifications, including the construction of the famous Maginot Line. Young argues that these fortifications were quite formidable and could have forced the Germans into a war of attrition. In addition, the government of French premier Léon Blum recognized the need for some modernization of the military's weaponry; it accelerated economic planning for war and tried to refurbish the national arsenals. Although restraints were maintained on the air force, emphasis was placed on antitank and anti-aircraft weaponry, plus an ability to counterattack after a German assault. Rearmament continued through the latter part of the 1930s, making the gap between France and Germany not as wide as has been perceived. Every French parliamentary government of the 1930s took this idea of a defensive war seriously and did its best to prepare, including the left-leaning governments of the Popular Front, which were later seriously criticized for weakening the nation. Yet, they appear to have done no worse than anyone else.

Few French planners believed the Germans would be bold and lucky enough to make it through the Ardennes Forest. The Germans, however, transferred the main thrust of their attack from Belgium to the Ardennes, where French defenses were thin. The Allies and Germans committed a nearly equal number of divisions to this battle. The only area in which the Germans had numerical superiority was in aircraft, especially since the British kept the bulk of their air force at home. The German blitzkrieg won the battle, dividing the Allied forces and causing the British to evacuate. France's defensive struggle would have been more effective for a war of attrition; against bolder and more aggressive German tactics, the French crumbled quickly.

French morale must have been a factor in the rapid collapse of their nation to the German onslaught. Defeat ushered in the Vichy regime, which was too willing to collaborate with the Nazis. It is understandable that many would seek answers for this defeat and blame the nation's morale, its politicians, and the decadence of the earlier years. There is a simpler explanation—the French lost because of superior German tactics. The German blitzkrieg defeated Poland, Denmark, Norway, the Netherlands, Luxembourg, Belgium, Yugoslavia, and Greece. It almost defeated the British and Soviets. Although it is possible that all of these nations were consumed with rot and moral decay in the 1930s, it is more likely that they were contending with a formidable German foe.

–DAVID MARSHALL,
UNIVERSITY OF CALIFORNIA, RIVERSIDE

Viewpoint:
No. France was defeated because it suffered from psychological demoralization, political dissension, and moral decadence.

Historians have now pondered France's fall for more than six decades, producing interpretations that include increasingly rehabilitative, if not apologetic, accounts of key leaders and vital institutions. In this sense scholar Robert J. Young has emphasized the "ambivalence," not, he insists, the cowardice or incompetence, with which French leaders faced the challenges of the interwar period. Likewise, Martin S. Alexander recasts the reputation of General Maurice Gamelin (France's army chief of staff, 1935–1940) as an imperturbable and perceptive strategist whose insight was thwarted by the complacency of his political superiors and a somewhat uncooperative British ally.

Elisabeth du Réau, author of a 1993 biography of premier Edouard Daladier, gives Gamelin less-flattering attention. Whereas the often-vilified Daladier is portrayed as a tirelessly reso-

SHORT ON OUR LEFT FLANK

Marc Bloch, a participant in the feeble defense of France against the German onslaught in 1940, made the following comments about the Maginot Line, a system of defensive fortifications built to protect the French eastern border:

Let us, if we like, condemn the strategic blunders which compelled our troops in the Nord Department either to abandon to the enemy, or to jettison on the Flanders beaches, the equipment of three motorized divisions, several regiments of mobile artillery, and all the tanks belonging to one of our armies. This material would have come in mighty handy on the battlefields of the Somme or the Aisne, for never had the nation in arms been better 'found'. But I am not for the moment concerned with that. I want, rather, to consider the preparations that were made before war broke out. If we were short of tanks, aeroplanes, and tractors, it was mainly because we had put our not inexhaustible supplies of money and labour into *concrete.* But even so, we had not been wise enough to erect enough of it on our northern frontier, which is just as much open to attack as our eastern. And why? Because we had been taught to put our whole trust in the Maginot Line—constructed at vast expense and with much blowing of trumpets—only to see it turned, and even pierced, on the Rhine for the simple reason that it had been allowed to stop short on our left flank (but about that astonishing incident of the crossing of the Rhine I know only what the newspapers told us, which was precisely nothing at all) because, at the last moment, a hurried decision was taken to construct a number of concrete block-houses in the Department of the Nord, which, since they were designed with only a frontal field of fire, were taken from behind, with the result that our men had to expend all their efforts on digging a magnificent anti-tank ditch covering Cambrai and Saint-Quentin—which the Germans overran one fine day by the simple expedient of advancing against it *from* those two places; because the doctrine then current among our military theorists laid it down that we had reached one of those moments in the history of strategy when the power of defensive armour to resist is greater than the power of gun-fire to pierce—in other words, when the fortified position is practically impregnable—though, unfortunately, the High Command lacked the courage, when the decisive moment came, to remain loyal to a theory which would, at least, have condemned the Belgian adventure even before it had started; because many of our military pundits were profoundly suspicious of armoured units, judging them too heavy to be moved easily (and their rate of progress as shown in official statistics was, it is true, very slow, but only because it was assumed that they must move by night—for security reasons— whereas, as things turned out, the war of speed was conducted almost uniformly by day); because those attending the Cavalry courses at the Staff College had had it drilled into them that, though tanks might be tolerably useful in defence, their value for attack was nil; because of technical experts—or those who passed for such—were of the opinion that bombardment by artillery was far superior to bombing from the air, oblivious of the fact that ammunition for guns has to be brought up over great distances, while the rate at which aeroplanes can be replenished is limited only by the speed of their flight; because, to sum up, our leaders, blind to the many contradictions inherent in their attitude, were mainly concerned to renew in 1940 the conditions of the war they had waged in 1914–1918.

Source: Marc Bloch, Strange Defeat: A Statement of Evidence Written in 1940, *translated by Gerard Hopkins (London & New York: Oxford University Press, 1949), pp. 52–53.*

FALL OF FRANCE

lute leader who regrettably fell from power to Paul Reynaud just weeks before the German blitzkrieg (lightning war), Gamelin is represented as a less inspiring figure who stayed close to Paris—rather than the front—in part caused by his need for frequent medical treatments for syphilis. Finally, William D. Irvine insists that "it was not decadence that led to 1940; it is 1940 that has led us to view the late Third Republic as decadent," a strange reversal of cause and effect if ever there was one.

These "revisionist" interpretations, now a sort of historiographical orthodoxy, consign the French defeat in 1940 to the dustbin of historical accidents yet have now found themselves challenged by the "counterrevisionism" of historians who insist that France's interwar societal problems, aggravated by the mistakes of its political and military leaders, indeed helped determine the outcome of the battle. Michael Carley and Nicole Jordan's interpretations of French officialdom's shortcomings appear alongside the opposing arguments of the above-named historians in a volume edited by Joel Blatt, *The French Defeat of 1940: Reassessments* (1998).

Since the 1970s an increasing pool of declassified archival evidence has pointed to a fuller, more complicated picture of France's predicament on the eve of its showdown with the Third Reich. Virtually all historians in this debate pay homage to Jean-Louis Crémieux-Brilhac, author of the two-volume *Les Français de l'an 40* (The Frenchmen of 1940, 1990). Crémieux-Brilhac insists that "the events of 1939–40 are inseparable from their prehistory" but warns against the simplistic assumption that the Third Republic was inexorably doomed by its own decadence.

The 1940 defeat was not an historical accident unconnected to the crisis-ridden 1930s, for the present body of evidence only buttresses the seminal thesis of the venerable historian, reserve captain, and Resistance martyr Marc Bloch. For Bloch the dizzying rapidity of France's collapse and the replacement of the democratic Third Republic with Marshal Pétain's authoritarian Vichy regime cannot be explained by military factors alone. In summer 1940, in the immediate aftermath of the Nazi victory, Bloch wrote *Strange Defeat: A Statement of Evidence Written in 1940*. (It was initially published in 1946, two years after the author's death in front of a German firing squad.)

Writing on behalf of a generation with a "bad conscience," Bloch argues that neither the French military establishment nor its weapons and its plans can be analyzed in sterile detachment from French politics, culture, and society. Instead, the generals "worked with the tools put into their hands by the nation at large." And by "tools" Bloch means both military hardware and sociopsychological conditions, indeed the "totality of the social *fact*," [emphasis Bloch's] as cumulative reasons for France's strange defeat.

In the face of the Nazi menace the French experienced psychological demoralization, political dissension, and self-perceived moral decadence, all of which lay beneath the surface of France's terrible defeat. Revisionist scholars, however, employ the image of an irredeemably decadent France as a "straw man." Against overwhelming evidence, especially the defeat itself, these revisionist historians have reconstructed healthy institutions, a unified people, and wise (or at least well-intentioned) leaders—until the very hour of France's fall. However, could a defeat of this magnitude be a mere accident of history? Should one expect this kind of disaster to have no tangible antecedents?

Notwithstanding the assertions of Young, Irvine, and others, no major historian has ever really argued for the ironclad determinism of a full-blown "decadence" thesis. Even

Jean-Baptiste Duroselle's tome *La Décadence: Politique étrangère de la France, 1932–1939* (Decadence: The Foreign Policy of France, 1932–1939, 1979) eschews moralizing and pathos in favor of structural analysis. Duroselle sees in the crisis of the 1930s a "stupefying" inability of the French people and their elected officials to contemplate much-needed reforms of their fragmented and stalemated parliamentary system. The "structural instability of executive power" in France found itself dangerously aggravated by internecine economic quarrels. In agreement with Duroselle, in *La France des années 30* (France in the 1930s, 1988) Serge Berstein laments the domestic squabbles that relegated foreign and military policies to the realm of "inanity." This diagnosis of France's interwar ills hardly amounts to determinism masquerading as history. Instead, as Bloch already argued in 1940, one cannot make sense of the fall of France without taking into account all that came beforehand.

Thus, the historian encounters the persistent, stultifying memory of the 1914–1918 slaughter, the social construction of a "Maginot mentality" epitomized in France's Great Wall of the same name, the lingering stagnation of the Depression, the rise and fall of myriad governments, street riots and political polarization that culminated in the Popular Front, problems in production and procurement that retarded rearmament, and a foreign policy of abdication and abasement. Only on 3 September 1939, as the Nazi war machine enjoyed its third day of devouring Poland, did Daladier's government hesitantly decide to declare war, which remained a "phony" war until German leader Adolf Hitler chose the ideal moment to strike in the West eight months later. Of course, by that point France had yet another government. This larger context demands our attention.

France hardly won World War I—it merely survived it. The traumatic memory of the Great War was underlined by the death of 1.4 million men. The next generation heard its lessons from influential pacifist movements, a message that eventually became the policy of "peace at any price." No group voiced a more fervent and respected pacifism than those who had themselves survived the trenches. Antoine Prost's *In the Wake of War: les anciens combattants and French Society* (1992) illuminated the sentiments and demonstrated the influence of the millions of staunchly antiwar veterans after 1918. More than 1 million veterans were disabled, including War Minister André Maginot, who gave his name to France's vast system of fortifications on the German border.

Himself a former officer, Daladier would meet the former corporal Hitler at Munich in

1938, where the French premier sacrificed the territorial integrity of Czechoslovakia to avoid the unthinkable: another war. Given his abandonment of one of France's key allies, Daladier feared the wrath of angry mobs upon his return; instead, he received the rapturous applause of hundreds of thousands of grateful Parisians. In *La France et Munich: étude d'un processus décisionnel en matière de relations internationales* (France and Munich: A Study of Decision Making in International Affairs, 1992) Yvon Lacaze marvels at "how blind and naïve French leaders were in the face of a phenomenon unknown to them: totalitarian ideology." The same might be understandably said of the French people as a whole, as innumerable problems within the French democracy allowed precious little time to study other political phenomena.

In the years before World War II, French democracy experienced endemic dissension, polarization, and instability. Between June 1932 and March 1940 France had sixteen governments with an average lifespan of five months and two days. It is telling that France was between governments, in other words it lacked one, both on 7 March 1936, when Hitler remilitarized the Rhineland in violation of the Versailles (1919) and Locarno (1925) Treaties, and when the German march into Austria began on 11 March 1938. But who was paying attention? Earlier in the decade, on 6 February 1934, angry right-wing mobs had tried to storm the Chamber of Deputies, disgusted with the ineffectiveness and alleged corruption of the politicians; 15 people were killed and 1,500 were injured. The April–May 1936 elections brought the left-leaning antifascist Popular Front to power but split France between left and right, the center giving way to extremes. Rightist circles made no secret of their antipathy to France's first socialist and Jewish premier, Léon Blum. The Popular Front's reforms included a reduced, forty-hour workweek but contradictorily pushed to increase armaments production. Blum's government expired after a little more than a year in office and satisfied no one.

The Permanent Committee for National Defense met on 15 March 1938 to discuss possible responses to German-Italian intervention in the Spanish Civil War (1936–1939) and Hitler's expansionist designs in Central Europe. As the Foreign Ministry's top career official put it at the end of the inconclusive meeting, French foreign policy could only be a matter "of reaction, not initiative." According to Carley, French leaders, by failing to enter into a true military alliance with the Soviet Union, failed their own people and the rest of Europe. Fear and loathing of communism excluded Soviet leader Josef Stalin from Great Power diplomacy in 1938 and threw the "Red Tsar" into Hitler's arms in 1939. Factors other than ideological bias against the Soviet Union also came into play. Jordan emphasizes the extreme reluctance of France's leaders to face another war on French soil. Instead, they opted for a "cut-price war on the peripheries," a strategy that simultaneously hinged on alliances and predisposed France to dishonor those alliances. Meanwhile, the drift of Italy into the German camp further unbalanced France as it wagered all on its shaky alliance with the British.

Many French voices from the 1930s described their polity and its social context, if not as rotten to the core, at least as symptomatic of a nation in decline. Eugen Weber's *The Hollow Years: France in the 1930s* (1994) evokes this atmosphere: "France was not an underdeveloped country, but a developed one in a state of decay." Demographic stasis, lamented since the late 1800s, increasingly impinged on the French nation's self-concept between the world wars. To make a bad matter worse, during the Great War 1.75 million fewer babies were conceived than in the last four years of peace. The demographic trough meant, among other things, that fewer potential soldiers came of age during the second half of the 1930s. In these years deaths came to outnumber births. Meanwhile, Germany's population, already a third larger than France's, was growing daily. Had it not been for immigrants, France's population would have been in numerical decline, but the presence of these immigrants was represented as still another sign of national decadence.

While the idea of national decadence long preceded the 1940 disaster, it arguably helped bring about a self-fulfilling prophecy in the defeat and the National Revolution at Vichy that followed. In *Ni Droit Ni Gauche* (1983; translated as *Neither Right Nor Left: Fascist Ideology in France,* translated by David Maisel, 1986) Zeev Sternhell gathers France's few fascists together with many other "nonconformists." He paints a picture of antidemocratic discontent across the political spectrum based on a shared disgust of liberalism's mediocrity and bourgeois materialism. Animated by antipathies to both capitalism and communism, the disaffection of many intellectuals fed on a "sense of decadence, of decrepitude" and the conviction that only sweeping revolutionary changes could bring about "the salvation of the nation's soul." Sternhell does not credit a mood of decadence among intellectuals with helping facilitate the Wehrmacht's (German armed forces) May 1940 breakthrough, but this self-perceived decadence "no doubt helps to explain why, in the critical moments of 1940, French democracy found many fewer zealous defenders than one might have expected."

Adolf Hitler and other German leaders at the French surrender ceremony, Compiègne, June 1940

(Archives Documentation Française)

Did the above elements of psychological, political, and moral crisis affect the development of French foreign policy and national defense and thereby contribute to the fall of France? How could they not? Only after the *Anschluss* (political union of Austria with Germany, 1938), the Munich Agreement (1938), and the signing of the Nazi-Soviet Pact (1939) did France and Great Britain finally, belatedly, gather the tenuous fortitude to stand up to Hitler when he invaded Poland. In the interim so much had changed. Williamson Murray offers the damning verdict in the title of his *The Change in the European Balance of Power, 1938–1939: The Path to Ruin* (1984). Now, and in stark contrast to 1914, France and its British partner could only threaten a confident, expanded German Reich with a one-front war, and one waged passively, from behind the Maginot Line and a maritime blockade. That stance did nothing for the Poles, or eventually the French themselves.

France's defensive posture in 1939–1940 only worsened the balance of power. Ernest R. May's *Strange Victory: Hitler's Conquest of France* (2000) depicts Germany's triumph as a victory won on such a narrow margin of military superiority that within its pages the reader might at times even forget the ultimate outcome of the contest. Yet, even May argues that France stood a significantly better chance of surviving a clash of arms with Nazi Germany in the late 1930s than when the actual campaign happened in 1940. According to May, the Nazi advantage hardly existed in September 1939, "when Germany lacked many of the soldiers and much of the equipment it would have by spring 1940." As for September 1938 "Germany had almost no divisions as well trained or well outfitted as those of Czechoslovakia, let alone France."

Time had undoubtedly worked in Hitler's favor, thanks to the abstention of a somewhat insulated England and the abdication of an all-too-vulnerable France. Beginning in the late 1950s John Cairns helped pioneer a reevaluation of the fall of France. In his more recent contribution to the Blatt book he observes that French policy deliberations in the Russo-Finnish Winter War (1939–1940) reveal French confusion about whether the Allies were really at war with Nazi Germany or with the Soviet Union. This confusion soured Franco-British relations and inaugurated a "terminal period of rancour" within the Third Republic. Cairns concludes that the French government then "ran from misfortune to misfortune to final disaster three months later."

Religious philosopher and social activist Simone Weil, like Bloch, did not survive World War II. She died an exile in England in 1943, stricken with tuberculosis, her young body weakened from limiting herself to the starvation rations of her compatriots back home. And like Bloch, Weil posed the question of what had brought about France's fall, in hopes of creating a better, more stable, and humane country after the hoped-for liberation. Her answer understandably assumed a more metaphorical, if not spiritual, tone than Bloch's, but the message remains the same: "The sudden collapse of France in June 1940, which surprised everyone

FALL OF FRANCE

all over the world, simply showed to what extent the country was uprooted. A tree whose roots are almost entirely eaten away falls at the first blow." Then again, Weil had been a militant pacifist well into 1939, preferring even "German hegemony" to another war. In 1940 she, like the rest of France, got both.

–RICHARD CRANE,
GREENSBORO COLLEGE

References

Martin S. Alexander, *The Republic in Danger: General Maurice Gamelin and the Politics of French Defence, 1933–1940* (Cambridge & New York: Cambridge University Press, 1992).

Serge Berstein, *La France des années 30* (Paris: Colin, 1988).

Joel Blatt, ed., *The French Defeat of 1940: Reassessments* (Providence, R.I.: Berghahn Books, 1998).

Marc Bloch, *Strange Defeat: A Statement of Evidence Written in 1940,* translated by Gerard Hopkins (London & New York: Oxford University Press, 1949).

Jean-Louis Crémieux-Brilhac, *Les Français de l'an 40,* 2 volumes (Paris: Gallimard, 1990).

Jean-Baptiste Duroselle, *La Décadence: Politique étrangère de la France, 1932–1939* (Paris: Imprimerie Nationale, 1979).

William D. Irvine, *French Conservatism in Crisis: The Republican Federation of France in the 1930s* (Baton Rouge: Louisiana State University Press, 1979).

Yvon Lacaze, *La France et Munich: étude d'un processus décisionnel en matière de relations internationales* (Berne & New York: Lang, 1992).

Maurice Larkin, *France since the Popular Front: Government and People, 1936–1996,* second edition (Oxford & New York: Clarendon Press, 1997).

Ernest R. May, *Strange Victory: Hitler's Conquest of France* (New York: Hill & Wang, 2000).

Williamson Murray, *The Change in the European Balance of Power, 1938–1939: The Path to Ruin* (Princeton: Princeton University Press, 1984).

Richard Overy, *Why the Allies Won* (London: Random House, 1995).

Antoine Prost, *In the Wake of War: les anciens combattants and French Society,* translated by Helen McPhail (Providence, R.I.: Berg, 1992).

Elisabeth du Réau, *Edouard Daladier, 1884–1970* (Paris: Fayard, 1993).

Zeev Sternhell, *Neither Right Nor Left: Fascist Ideology in France,* translated by David Maisel (Berkeley: University of California Press, 1986).

Eugen Weber, *The Hollow Years: France in the 1930s* (New York: Norton, 1994).

Simone Weil, *The Need for Roots: Prelude to a Declaration of Duties towards Mankind,* translated by Arthur Wills (New York: Routledge, 2002).

Robert J. Young, *In Command of France: French Foreign Policy and Military Planning, 1933–1940* (Cambridge, Mass.: Harvard University Press, 1978).

FINLAND AFTER 1945

Was the post–World War II status of Finland indicative of the Soviet Union's ideal goals for Eastern Europe?

Viewpoint: Yes. "Finlandization," whereby a neighboring state was allowed to maintain its independence but did not pursue policies detrimental to Soviet security, was the Soviet goal for Eastern European countries, but security threats from the West caused the Soviets to impose strict control on Eastern European satellites.

Viewpoint: No. Finland was a special case. It was allowed to remain neutral because of its efficient army and the lack of a border with Germany, which the Soviets viewed as a possible future aggressor.

Finland emerged from World War II (1939–1945) and entered the Cold War in an anomalous position. Unlike Germany's other wartime allies in Eastern Europe and unlike other states on the Soviet Union's western frontier, Finland was allowed to maintain a democratic government and market economy. In return it maintained a scrupulous neutrality in Cold War politics and pledged to resist any diplomacy that would threaten Soviet interests. Scholars of the Cold War have looked at this curiosity and asked whether it could have been broadly applicable in Eastern Europe, where the Soviets and their local acolytes imposed rigid and monolithic communist regimes after World War II. Could "Finlandization" have been the Soviets' preferred way of dealing with their neighbors?

Some scholars have answered in the affirmative, arguing that the imposition of communism on Eastern Europe was neither planned nor immediate. Instead, they suggest that it only became an option after the United States and its Western European allies pursued diplomatic, economic, and military measures that posed potential threats to Soviet security. Strong-arm tactics to promote communism in Eastern Europe were the last resort of a Soviet Union that did not initially want to commit to the long-term occupation and policing of the region. Finland's status, which may have represented Moscow's ideal vision for its neighbors, was a holdover from the alternative course.

Others suggest that Finland's situation was always a piece of the postwar puzzle that simply did not fit. As the Soviets took steps to "communize" Eastern Europe, they saw little reason to do so in Finland. Traditional invasions of the Russian heartland, Moscow's main worry, came across Poland and other East European lands, not from the sparsely populated and geographically isolated Scandinavian permafrost. No compelling strategic necessity made strict political control of Finland necessary, so none was undertaken. Communizing Finland, moreover, may have had other consequences—including, perhaps, Western resistance or a strengthened American position in the Baltic—that could have had much more serious consequences for Soviet security than an independent Finland.

**Viewpoint:
Yes. "Finlandization," whereby a neighboring state was allowed to maintain its independence but did not pursue policies detrimental to Soviet security, was the Soviet goal for Eastern European countries, but security threats from the West caused the Soviets to impose strict control on Eastern European satellites.**

The term *Finlandization* originated in the relations that came to exist between the Soviet Union and Finland after World War II (1939–1945), in which the Finnish government enjoyed independence but did not pursue policies prejudicial to the security of the Union of Soviet Socialist Republics (U.S.S.R.). Finland was tied to the Soviets by a 1948 treaty that limited Finnish foreign-policy initiatives and obliged Finland to defend its border if Germany or any other state sought to attack the Soviet Union through Finnish territory. In a broad political sense Finlandization meant the restriction of a small state's sovereignty by the security requirements of a larger and stronger neighbor. The prospect of Finlandizing other close neighbors of the Soviet Union was frequently the subject of international speculation, particularly when it came to Eastern Europe in the aftermath of World War II.

The war left the Soviets as the unquestionable masters of Eastern Europe. At the same time, however, for the first three years after the war Moscow did little to impose monolithic communist regimes in the region. Many Western historians interpreted this interlude as a cynical and calculated approach by the Soviets and their local allies, aimed at the subversion of regional democracies step-by-step. Hungarian communist leader Mátyás Rákosi called this approach "salami tactics"—taking off one slice at a time. From the late 1960s the New Left school of revisionist historiography in America argued that while the Soviets were initially prepared to tolerate noncommunist regimes in Eastern Europe on some conditions, the Cold War forced Moscow to terminate this experiment with limited democracy because of concerns about U.S. pressure and Washington's policy, which those historians saw as efforts to impose American hegemony over the world.

At the same time, some experts on Eastern Europe, who do not share the revisionist interpretation of the motives of Soviet Eastern European policy, noted that while the phase of limited democracy in Eastern Europe proved to be short-lived, it does not mean, as Zbigniew K. Brzezinski put it in *The Soviet Bloc: Unity and Conflict* (1960), that this phase "had to last the three years it did rather than one, five, or ten." Conversely, it is possible to imagine a degree of Soviet control in Eastern Europe that would have resembled postwar relations between the Soviet Union and Finland if the historical circumstances had been different. Moreover, one could presume that the Finlandization of Eastern Europe was for the Soviets the optimal goal for all of their neighbors.

As far as international factors are concerned, during the war the "Big Three" (the United States, United Kingdom, and Soviet Union) tended to settle immediate occupation problems on the basis of traditional spheres-of-influence agreements. The rapid advance of the Red Army toward Germany gave the Soviets the advantage of predominant military force on the ground and secured Allied recognition of Soviet interests in Eastern Europe. At the Yalta Conference (February 1945) the Big Three decided that Eastern Europe was to be democratic and "friendly" to the Soviet Union. Although in later years Yalta became a symbol of betrayal for many of the region's peoples, in 1945 it was almost inevitable that the Soviet Union would come to dominate Eastern Europe. Moreover, the Allies, hoping for postwar cooperation with the Soviet Union, were obliged to recognize legitimate Soviet security concerns in Eastern Europe, which had constituted a principal route of foreign invasions of Russia throughout history. Control over the area was of critical importance for the Soviets but of only marginal interest (with an exception for Poland, because of political reasons) for the West, particularly for the United States. The relative weakness of Britain (which had some political and strategic interests in the Balkans) vis-à-vis the United States and the Soviet Union gave Soviet leader Josef Stalin additional room to maneuver in Eastern Europe. Partnership with the West and desired economic aid from the United States, as well as the establishment of Russian influence in the region, required political and ideological flexibility in Eastern Europe on the part of the Soviets. That is why Moscow agreed to sign the Yalta Declaration on Liberated Europe (1945), which called for the earliest possible free elections and establishment of democratic governments.

Besides the dynamics of interallied relations, there were other international factors working for a modus vivendi between the U.S.S.R. and the Eastern European countries. When in 1944 armistice terms were established for former Axis allies (Romania, Bulgaria, and Hungary, as well as Finland), the Soviets, as the only Allied force in the region, were granted a

position of almost exclusive influence in political and military matters. Subsequently, these nations' entrance into the Soviet orbit was the only real way to defend their national interests during the postwar peace settlement.

As for Czechoslovakia, Poland, and Yugoslavia, the situation was more complicated. In Czechoslovakia Soviet influence was established without much resistance, since the government-in-exile and President Eduard Benes de facto accepted entrance into the Soviet sphere of influence, as the Soviet-Czech treaty of 1943 had indicated. Moreover, Prague intended to play the role of a bridge builder between East and West, while retaining internal autonomy and even some foreign-policy initiatives, so long as they posed no threat to Soviet security. In contrast, Polish and Yugoslav exile governments in London were determined to resist any Soviet interference in their countries. That reason is why Moscow strongly promoted the local communists, who by 1945 were in physical control of both countries. At the same time, under Western pressure the Soviets tactically agreed with the coalition government formula for Poland (inclusion of the "London Poles" into the Communist-dominated Warsaw government).

There were other factors in play that pushed the Eastern Europeans, almost irrespective of their political or ideological orientation, into the Soviet orbit. The triumphant Red Army liberated countries of the region, which led to widespread sympathy toward the Soviet Union. This feeling sharply contrasted with recollections of the "betrayal" of Eastern European countries, particularly Czechoslovakia and Poland, by the Western powers in 1938–1939. There were also old fears and hatred of Germany, and the Soviets were perceived as natural guarantors against possible future German aggression. In addition, an historically hostile Germany gave impetus to the sentiments of Slavic solidarity in Bulgaria, Czechoslovakia, Yugoslavia, and, to some extent, Poland and moved these countries closer to Russia, the supposed historic protector of the Slavs. It was not accidental that well before the emergence of the Warsaw Pact (1955) the Eastern European alignment led by the Soviet Union came to be known in the United Nations (UN) as the "Slavic Bloc." The Soviets, for their part, strongly supported the reunification of Yugoslavia, the restoration of Czechoslovakia, and Poland's acquisition of eastern Germany up to the Oder-Neisse line.

Finnish president Urho Kekkonen (left) and Soviet leader Leonid Brezhnev shake hands after signing an economic treaty in Moscow, May 1977

(AP Photo/Lehtikuva, Hans Paul)

FINLAND AFTER 1945

In 1945–1946 Moscow crowned the Finlandization of Eastern Europe with a series of bilateral political, military, and economic agreements that guaranteed Soviet interests and influence in the region and signified the virtual subjection of these countries to the Soviet Union. As a result, in 1947 the Eastern European countries, following Finland's example, refused to participate in the U.S.-sponsored European Recovery Program (Marshall Plan). Czechoslovakia, which initially accepted an invitation to participate, suddenly and categorically withdrew from the program under Soviet pressure.

As for domestic factors militating toward the Finlandization of Eastern Europe, of much importance was the reality of the weakness of communism in the region, except in Yugoslavia and Albania. For this reason, in 1945–1946 Moscow, as well as Soviet occupation authorities in most cases, had to deal with well-established noncommunist political forces on condition of their loyalty to the Soviets. Some countries even preserved their monarchies: Bulgaria and Hungary (nominally) until 1946 and Romania until 1947. At the same time, the Soviets sponsored the formation of united fronts (National Front in Czechoslovakia; Fatherland Front in Bulgaria; National Democratic Front in Romania; Government Bloc, then People's or National Independence Front in Hungary; and Democratic Bloc in Poland), usually a coalition of left-wing elements (communists, socialists, agrarians, and miscellaneous democrats). In some cases, particularly in Czechoslovakia and Hungary, the first parliamentary elections were fair. The new coalition governments pursued reformist policies, which were generally welcomed by both local populations and by the Allies: democratization, purges of fascists and collaborators, social reforms, and the realization of a new foreign policy that was sympathetic to the Soviet Union and the West. At the same time the communists, despite being a minority, gained control over military forces, ministries of the interior, and security institutions.

The noncommunist democratic parties in most countries of Eastern Europe enjoyed some margins of liberty. However, there were exceptions, such as in Yugoslavia and Albania, where grassroots communists had the local situation firmly in hand from the beginning. In Poland, where the communists were too weak to share real power with anyone else, they kept a monopoly on power despite their formal coalition (until 1947) with representatives of the former government-in-exile. In 1946 and 1947, when coalitions in the Eastern European countries were restructured under growing pressure from the communists in their favor (Bulgaria and Romania reached this phase as early as 1945), noncommunist parties and politicians still preserved some role in governments and in political life.

Meanwhile, by 1948 the interplay of international and domestic factors put an end to any hope for Finlandization in Eastern Europe. On the one hand, the unfolding Cold War could no longer be ignored. West Berlin was under Soviet blockade, while Yugoslavia had broken with the Kremlin. In these circumstances Moscow desperately needed not merely a buffer of friendly states on its western border but a reliable, submissive, and monolithic camp of satellites. On the other hand, local communists as well as their Soviet patrons were exerting more and more aggressive pressure on their domestic opponents. Additionally, a long-term Finlandization of Eastern Europe would have required a degree of sophistication and tolerance that was alien to Stalin's character and to the characters of his closest associates. This tolerance was also quite out of accord with the whole history of previous Russian relations with its Eastern European neighbors. As early as April 1945 in Moscow, Stalin told Yugoslav Communist leader Josip Broz Tito that "whoever occupies a territory also imposes on it his own social system." By 1948 Eastern Europe was dominated by new Soviet-modeled and communist-led regimes.

Yet, despite its short-lived character, the Eastern European semidemocratic interlude of 1944–1948 had lasting effects. However latently, Eastern European societies preserved some elements of democratic political culture, traditions of pluralism and political dialogue, independent civil and religious institutions, and even legal noncommunist parties, which formally existed in the German Democratic Republic, Bulgaria, Czechoslovakia, and Poland. All these elements of civil society were highly instrumental during the so-called velvet revolutions of 1989–1990 and ensured their peaceful character. After the collapse of communism in Eastern Europe the Soviets tried to revitalize the idea of Finlandization of the region, but it was already too late, as local governments preferred integration into Western Europe. Even Finland, in a 1992 treaty with post-Soviet Russia, formally abolished its "special" relations with Moscow.

The enormous burden of maintaining their satellites in Eastern Europe—instead of having there friendly, but semi-independent, self-sufficient, and stable governments—made some Soviet leaders sorry for the lost chance of Finlandization. While observing growing unrest in East Germany, which culminated in the uprising of 1953, Lavrenty Beria, head of the Soviet secret police and a prominent leader after Stalin's death, suggested letting East Germany go in exchange for the neutral status of a united Germany.

For the Soviet Union, Finlandization was the optimal goal for the status of its neighbors. No example could better serve as a symbol of the tragic results of this missed opportunity by the Soviets than a conversation on 29 October 1956 between Soviet leader Nikita Khrushchev and Charles Bohlen, American ambassador to Moscow. When Bohlen mentioned that the Soviet Union might be better off if it had relations with Eastern European countries of the kind it had with Finland, Khrushchev, on the verge of launching a bloody and expensive invasion of insurgent Hungary to reinstall a communist regime there, agreed.

—PETER RAINOW,
SAN MATEO, CALIFORNIA

Viewpoint:
No. Finland was a special case. It was allowed to remain neutral because of its efficient army and the lack of a border with Germany, which the Soviets viewed as a possible future aggressor.

During World War II (1939–1945) collaboration between the United States and the Soviet Union gave rise to hopes that this cooperation would continue into the postwar period and ensure the preservation of peace. U.S. president Franklin D. Roosevelt, with his rhetorical devotion to self-determination as a war aim for the Allies, hoped governments in Eastern Europe would be democratically elected, yet friendly to the Soviet Union. In this way the legitimate security concerns of the Soviet Union would be met at the same time that the Eastern Europeans would enjoy rights to self-determination sanctioned by the Atlantic Charter (1941) and the Declaration on Liberated Europe (1945). Despite Roosevelt's hopes, and the efforts of such notable Eastern European statesmen as Czech leader Eduard Beneš to achieve such a state of affairs, Finland ultimately was the only European nation that combined friendship with the Soviets together with freely elected governments.

Soviet leader Josef Stalin famously told his Yugoslav comrades during World War II that "This war is not as in the past; whoever occupies a territory also imposes on it his own social system as far as his army can reach. Everyone imposes his own system as far as his army can reach. It cannot be otherwise." Recent work by historian Eduard Mark argues that Stalin simultaneously sought to maintain cordial relations with the United States and Britain while expanding communism as far west as possible. Yet, these impulses appeared not to motivate Stalin's policy toward Finland. Because the Finns were able to combine domestic autonomy within a framework of friendly relations, and foreign policy and defense coordination with the Soviets, Cold War–era commentators spoke and wrote often of Finlandization. This term, however, usually carried some pejorative connotation. Rather than seeing Finlandization as the means by which a small nation made necessary accommodation to the needs of an overweening superpower to preserve its autonomy and independence, many viewed it as a term of denigration suggesting that the Finns had been "neutralized" by sacrificing genuine independence in return for nominal observance of some of the forms of self-government. The success with which the Finns were able to preserve their national autonomy and independence during a period when similarly situated nations were reduced to communist-dominated satellites, however, suggests that the experience of Finland between 1945 and 1991 was a rather noteworthy success.

The success of this model in Finland, and its failure elsewhere in Eastern Europe, leads to the logical question of why Finland alone emerged in this fashion: was Finlandization in Eastern Europe disrupted by a variety of factors, including Western hostility, or was the success of the Finnish model the result of factors unique to Finland? Finland indeed was a special case. While some factors may have been present for Finlandization to have been implemented in other Eastern European states, only Finland had the requisite aggregation of conditions. Four major factors were crucial: Finnish governments were genuinely popular; Finnish society was more egalitarian than other Eastern European nations, and, moreover, conservative elements were committed to good relations with the Union of Soviet Socialist Republics (U.S.S.R); Finnish military performance in the Winter War (1939–1940) and the Continuation War (1941–1944) suggested that the Finns would fight hard and effectively in defense of their independence should any aggressor try to use Finland as an invasion route to the Soviet Union; and Finland shared no border with Germany, which Soviet officials considered the likely future aggressor.

Although there were ample grounds for Finnish-Soviet hostility, dating to the Finnish War of Independence (1917–1919) and continuing through 1939 to 1944, the Finns were fortunate to have in place a statesman of Juho Kusti Paasikivi's perceptivity. A conservative banker who was seventy-four years old when he became prime minister, Paasikivi had been a critic of the 1918 treaty in which the Finns gained significant territory from the Russians at a time when the fledgling Soviet government was weak. Paasikivi understood that this diminution of Russian power was temporary, and he worried that the future would bring Russian efforts to adjust the boundary by retaking territory from Finland. His willingness to accommodate Soviet interests was known as the "Paasikivi Line"; this development in foreign policy was vitally important to ensuring Finnish independence.

Paasikivi was an experienced statesman with a long history of favoring friendly relations with the Soviets; he could not be dismissed as a young opportunist seeking closer ties with Moscow to further his own ambitions. His attempt to ensure Finnish independence, and the support this policy received from the Finnish people, could not have gone unnoticed in Moscow. When Paasikivi retired, his policy was continued by his successor, Urho Kekkonen. At the same time the legacy of twentieth-century Finnish-Russian relations made clear that the Finns would forcefully resist efforts to impose a government on them. The Soviets could recognize Finnish independence and have Finns fighting with them against any eastbound aggressor, or they could attempt to conquer the Finns and bring upon themselves a costly, bloody war and an even more difficult occupation.

Unlike many other European nations with aristocratic traditions that were innately hostile to communists and even socialists, Finnish society was largely egalitarian. Even as conservative a figure as Marshall Carl Gustav Mannerheim, who led the Whites to victory in the Finnish civil war and had ties to right-wing extremists, recognized the need for friendly relations with the Soviets. Although having only attained formal independence in December 1917, the Finns had a history of democratic and egalitarian traditions dating back to when Finland had been conquered by Sweden in the twelfth and thirteenth centuries. After taking control of Finland in 1809, the Russian tsars respected Finnish autonomy; the Finns had a constitutional regime, an elected Diet, and a separate army. The Finns reciprocated with loyalty to St. Petersburg. Only when the Russians abandoned their policy of respect for Finnish autonomy in the late nineteenth century did they court trouble for themselves. Tsar Nicholas I had reportedly told his ministers, "Leave the Finns alone. It is the only part of my realm which has never given us any trouble." During the Cold War years the Soviets would return to this legacy of good Russo-Finnish relations.

Not only did the Finns have a history of friendly relations with the Russians while the Russians respected the Finnish prerogatives in self-government, but the Finns had also shown little interest in supporting communist governments on their own. This antipathy was made clear in the experience of communist Otto Kuusinen in 1939, who utterly failed to command popular support when Stalin attempted to install him as the head of a communist government to replace the Helsinki regime and facilitate Finland's inclusion in the Soviet Union. Unlike other East European countries where anti-Nazi efforts had given communists a prestige that Stalin hoped would translate into widespread popular support, the Soviet dictator could have no such illusions about the Finns. The Finns, in some respects, had an almost ideal view of the left for a society wishing to avoid Soviet interference: they lacked the visceral hostility to the left that would alarm Moscow, but they clearly would have resisted outside efforts to force a communist dictatorship upon them.

The failure of the Kuusinen effort was part of the Finns' vivid demonstration of their commitment to their own independence. While other nations with stronger militaries, older traditions, and substantial support from allies crumbled in the face of the Axis onslaught, the Finns mounted stout resistance against the Soviet invasion in the winter of 1939–1940, while receiving nothing more than rhetorical support from other nations. Although the Soviets ultimately prevailed, as they would again when the Finns fought as cobelligerents with Germany in 1941–1944, the Finnish military performance made clear to the Soviets that any effort to subjugate the Finns would be bloody and costly. This realization was particularly true at a time when the Soviets were suffering from horrific wartime devastation and sought to rebuild their strength for the future showdown Stalin expected with a resurgent, revanchist Germany. An extended, costly adventure to subdue a people who could be expected to fight hard for their independence would have been a pointless exercise for the Soviets. This situation was particularly true since the Soviets could reasonably expect that the Finns would fight any aggressor that sought to attack the Soviet Union through Finland. In fact, grueling warfare between 1939 and 1944 presumably had a chastening effect on both Finns and Soviets: after years of bloodshed and destruction both sides had a vested interest in emphasizing peace and in their relations.

A final consideration that cannot be underestimated in considering the success of the Finns in maintaining their independence is the role of geography. Stalin feared another German assault within twenty-five years, and therefore invasion routes from Central Europe would be of particular concern to him. The Finns were bordered in the west by the Gulf of Bothnia, with the much less imposing Swedes beyond that, so the Soviets

DECLARATION OF LIBERATED EUROPE

During the Yalta Conference in February 1945, the Allies published the following statement on the treatment of liberated countries in Europe:

The following declaration has been approved:

The Premier of the Union of Soviet Socialist Republics, the Prime Minister of the United Kingdom and the President of the United States of America have consulted with each other in the common interests of the people of their countries and those of liberated Europe. They jointly declare their mutual agreement to concert during the temporary period of instability in liberated Europe the policies of their three Governments in assisting the peoples liberated from the domination of Nazi Germany and the peoples of the former Axis satellite states of Europe to solve by democratic means their pressing political and economic problems.

The establishment of order in Europe and the rebuilding of national economic life must be achieved by processes which will enable the liberated peoples to destroy the last vestiges of nazism and fascism and to create democratic institutions of their own choice. This is a principle of the Atlantic Charter—the right of all people to choose the form of government under which they will live—the restoration of sovereign rights and self-government to those peoples who have been forcibly deprived to them by the aggressor nations.

To foster the conditions in which the liberated people may exercise these rights, the three governments will jointly assist the people in any European liberated state or former Axis state in Europe where, in their judgment conditions require,

(a) to establish conditions of internal peace;

(b) to carry out emergency relief measures for the relief of distressed peoples;

(c) to form interim governmental authorities broadly representative of all democratic elements in the population and pledged to the earliest possible establishment through free elections of Governments responsive to the will of the people; and

(d) to facilitate where necessary the holding of such elections.

The three Governments will consult the other United Nations and provisional authorities or other Governments in Europe when matters of direct interest to them are under consideration.

When, in the opinion of the three Governments, conditions in any European liberated state or former Axis satellite in Europe make such action necessary, they will immediately consult together on the measure necessary to discharge the joint responsibilities set forth in this declaration.

By this declaration we reaffirm our faith in the principles of the Atlantic Charter, our pledge in the Declaration by the United Nations and our determination to build in cooperation with other peace-loving nations world order, under law, dedicated to peace, security, freedom and general well-being of all mankind.

In issuing this declaration, the three powers express the hope that the Provisional Government of the French Republic may be associated with them in the procedure suggested.

Source: *"Declaration of Liberated Europe," The Avalon Project, Yale University <http://www.yale.edu/lawweb/avalon/wwii/yalta.htm>*

---

were less concerned with Finland than they were with, for example, Poland or Hungary. The chief Soviet military interest in Finland was the removal of German forces. After the Finnish-Soviet armistice of 1944 the Soviets left most of this work to the Finns. By contrast, nations such as Poland, Hungary, Romania, and Czechoslovakia were along the route to be traveled by the Red Army as it slogged toward Berlin. Accordingly, citizens in these countries witnessed firsthand the nature of the Red Army as it "liberated" them, which rarely built up goodwill.

The Red Army, expected to become a tool to enhance the prestige and popularity of communism, generally made enemies for Moscow; then it was used to subjugate the same people it had freed from Nazi subjugation. In being spared these experiences, the Finns escaped the brutality that might have greatly complicated efforts to maintain popular support for Soviet-friendly governments in Helsinki.

As the Cold War progressed, there were additional benefits of not having Finland serve as another Soviet satellite: Finland could make available to the Soviets and their satellites goods that might not be available through direct East-West trade. Furthermore, the existence of an independent Finland could be used to demonstrate an otherwise nonexistent Soviet "tolerance" of regimes of different ideological persuasions. These factors, combined with skillful Finnish diplomacy, permitted continuation of a solution that did not develop in other Eastern European nations because of a range of factors that were distinctive to Finland.

–JOHN A. SOARES JR.,
CINCINNATI, OHIO

References

Zbigniew K. Brzezinski, *The Soviet Bloc: Unity and Conflict* (Cambridge, Mass.: Harvard University Press, 1960).

Jussi M. Hanhimäki, *Containing Coexistence: America, Russia and the "Finnish Solution"* (Kent, Ohio: Kent State University Press, 1997).

Max Jakobson, *Finland: Myth and Reality* (Helsinki: Otava Publishing Company, 1987).

Eduard Mark, *Revolution by Degrees: Stalin's National-Front Strategy for Europe, 1941–1947,* Cold War International History Project, Working Paper No. 31 (Washington, D.C.: Woodrow Wilson International Center for Scholars, 2001).

Tuomo Polvinen, *Between East and West: Finland in International Politics, 1944–1947,* edited and translated by D. G. Kirby and Peter Herring (Minneapolis: University of Minnesota Press, 1986).

Joseph Rothschild, *Return to Diversity: A Political History of East Central Europe since World War II* (New York: Oxford University Press, 1989).

T. Michael Ruddy, ed., *Charting an Independent Course: Finland's Place in the Cold War and in U.S. Foreign Policy* (Claremont, Cal.: Regina Books, 1998).

William R. Trotter, *A Frozen Hell: The Russo-Finnish Winter War of 1939–1940* (Chapel Hill, N.C.: Algonquin Books of Chapel Hill, 1991).

FINLAND AFTER 1945

FRANCE AFTER 1945

Did France become a stable polity during the second half of the twentieth century?

Viewpoint: Yes. Despite the failure of the Third and Fourth Republics in the twentieth century, France has achieved a highly resilient political system that commands the respect of the people.

Viewpoint: No. The French government is still dogged by discontent, radicalism, and challenges to its political legitimacy.

French president Charles de Gaulle famously bewailed his task of governing with the rhetorical quip, "How can one govern a country with 246 kinds of cheese?" As his exasperation suggests, France faced many problems and crises over the course of the twentieth century. Still haunted by demons going back to the Revolution of 1789, France entered the century with divisive social and political conflicts and then went on to suffer tremendous losses in World War I (1914–1918), more political and social troubles in the interwar era, disastrous defeat at the hands of Nazi Germany in 1940, the definitive loss of its colonial empire, and continuing periods of unrest. This chapter investigates the extent to which France adapted and sustained itself over time. Has it achieved long-elusive social and political stability at the beginning of the twenty-first century, or does it still remain troubled by the traumas of its past? Is it, as one British journalist has recently suggested, "on the brink"?

From one perspective, France has gone a long way toward solving its problems. Despite its past instability, its republican institutions and democratic traditions are firmly entrenched in the Fifth Republic, the constitutional order founded in 1958. An integral member of the European Union (EU) and the global community at large, France is a model of stable government and a proud representative of the developed West.

Yet, other observers have seen faults that undermine this picture of stability. The fact that France had to try four other republican orders before arriving at its present Fifth Republic is itself an indictment of sorts. The failure of the Fourth Republic, the constitutional order that functioned between 1946 and 1958, suggested a continuing pattern of social and political divisiveness and a failure to reach national consensus. Subsequent narrowly avoided clashes between the military and civilian government portended more divisions in the future. Finally, the continuing dilemmas of the Fifth Republic, which, its critics believe, include undemocratic practices in government and society, widespread corruption at the highest levels of power, potentially dangerous flaws in the constitutional structure, and a political culture of alienation, leave the country lacking in stability.

Viewpoint:
Yes. Despite the failure of the Third and Fourth Republics in the twentieth century, France has achieved a highly resilient political system that commands the respect of the people.

The twentieth century proved to be a crucial test for France's political stability, both in terms of regime durability and social cohesion. The traditional saying "when France sneezes, Europe catches a cold" reflected accurately the susceptibility of the French political system to upheavals and the disruptive influence that such developments could exercise upon the whole of the European continent in the eighteenth and, especially, nineteenth centuries. Starting with the storming of the Bastille on 14 July 1789, France witnessed a wave of revolutionary situations that shook the foundations of the old order in Europe and gave political expression to various currents of political and social modernity: from the sanscullotes of the 1790s to the Napoleonic upheaval, from the 1830 liberal insurrection against the authoritarian structures of the restoration to the Revolution of 1848 and the declaration of the Second Republic, from the repudiation of democratic rule by Napoleon III in the early 1850s to the collapse of his regime in 1870, France came to epitomize the revolutionary spirit of a new era—and Paris was its indisputable heart.

The twentieth century started with rather inauspicious omens. After the overthrow of Napoleon III's regime the Third Republic was founded in the hope that a new framework of political pluralism and constitutional rule would heal the wounds of internal division and promote an enduring sense of stability. The depth of the fractures, however, dating back to the 1789 Revolution and intensified through the political conflicts of the nineteenth century, remained visible and subverted the cohesion of the new political arrangement. Historians have eloquently spoken of a genuine French civil war that continued to rage after 1870 and was not resolved until more than seven decades later, on the ruins of the Nazi "New Order" and the "ghost" of the Vichy regime. Liberals versus conservatives, proponents of secularization versus adherents to traditional Catholic values, guardians of the revolutionary tradition of Jacobinism versus nostalgic devotees to the cause of monarchical restoration—all continued to engage in bitter confrontations on every level of political, social, and cultural life.

Assessing the stability of a political system is a problematic task. There are no clear normative standards that may produce benchmarks for an accurate assessment. Is stability coterminous with government solidity, institutional permanence, and constitutional respect? Is it simply the antithesis of revolution? Does it relate solely to "high politics," or should it include a wider definition of *consensus* that involves ethical values, culture, social mobilization, and so on? Then again, basing verdicts on the nature of a country's political and social life over a long period may sacrifice accuracy for cliché. For example, one cannot judge the stability of Germany in the last century only on what happened either before or after 1945. These significant caveats render a discussion of France's stability inherently problematic and presuppose a clear definition of what stability can mean in a pluralistic, democratic, and modern sociopolitical environment.

France experienced many cataclysmic events in the twentieth century: three republics (two of which came to an abrupt and painful end, in 1940 and 1958); several governments; a rich conflict between Left and Right; an authoritarian regime (1940–1944); colonial crises that brought the country to the verge of a civil war in the 1950s and 1960s; constant constitutional reshaping; and social restlessness that reached a climax in 1968. A bitter struggle among conservative, liberal, and social democratic forces for the soul of the Third Republic during the 1920s and 1930s produced constant political alternation in power and an acute ideological polarization. One may detect terminal instability in the confrontational milieu of the 1914–1940 period in France; another may point both to the constitutional endurance of the Third Republic and the successful defense of its liberal institutions in the face of both the fascist/authoritarian challenge and socialist agitation. Unlike Italy, Germany, Spain, Portugal, Poland, and an array of other European countries, France deflected the totalitarian challenge and remained decidedly pluralistic until the time of the Nazi attack in the summer of 1940.

Why then did the Third Republic collapse so unceremoniously without even putting up effective resistance? It is true that internal forces, appalled by the left-wing experiments of the 1930s, welcomed the spectacular volte-face of 1940—not so much the Nazi invasion but the formation of an authoritarian regime under World War I (1914–1918) hero Henri-Philippe Pétain that heralded the return to traditional values. The relatively limited extent of French resistance is perhaps the most tangible evidence of the chronic lack of widespread consensus with regard to the direction of the Third Republic, but it cannot be disputed that the period of Vichy rule proved crucially formative for the postwar rejection of authoritarian alternatives to liberal parliamentary pluralism.

When General Charles de Gaulle entered Paris in August 1944 and addressed the enthusiastic crowd from the balcony of the town hall, he seemed to herald an era of national regeneration after a long period of instability and suffering for the people of France. The Fourth Republic was founded on the ruins of the war, on the painful memories of repression, and on an anxious anticipation of the type of stability that had so dramatically and catastrophically eluded its predecessor. Polarization, however, accentuated after the exceptional circumstances of the Vichy period, thwarted this expectation. The new constitution (1946) displeased de Gaulle with its combination of strong legislative and weak executive powers—the inversion of the general's expectation. With the symbolic figurehead of noncommunist resistance refusing to participate in the new political framework, perhaps the only singular force for promoting an authoritative sense of unity in the republic had been eliminated. The subsequent political wrangling between the deeply fragmented constituencies of both Left and Right produced short-lived governments (twenty-five in twelve years), political stalemate, and an atmosphere of public disillusionment that deprived the Fourth Republic of any meaningful sense of political legitimacy. In these circumstances the Algerian situation that plunged the country into crisis in 1958 was simply a catalyst, exposing the chronic deficiencies of postwar democratic restoration.

Herein lies the most fundamental transition in recent history—not simply from the disgraced Fourth to the Fifth Republic but also from disaffection with the political system to the manufacture of a pluralistic consensus. General de Gaulle returned to politics, this time determined to get his own way, by persuasion or blackmail. He called for a clean constitutional start, in other words the refounding of France's political system, on the basis of a strong, effective executive and a more flexible legislative process, all for the benefit of effectual government. He offered to resolve the Algeria crisis, but only if he felt that the new arrangements had empowered him to the extent that he could make some painful sacrifices. The new constitution was drafted under considerable pressure and was overwhelmingly approved by a plebiscite. In spite of objections to the centralization of power in the hands of the executive, the cross-party constitutional committee consented to this fundamental constitutional overturning of the Fourth Republic's principles. De Gaulle became the unelected president, bestowed with emergency powers that were deemed necessary in order to restore internal peace and resolve the colonial crisis.

The new republic differed from its precursor in much more than its constitutional makeup. The return of de Gaulle as "savior" pointed to the increased cohesive power of the former Resistance leader for a wide section of the French population (excluding, of course, the socialist/communist Left). The high level of support for both the 1958 constitution and its revision in 1961 strengthened his hand and conferred upon him a level of legitimacy that no other democratic French leader could possibly claim until then. Gaullism came to represent the spirit of democratic continuity; a tradition of strong, effective government; a vision of a rejuvenated France; as well as a categorical rejection of the Vichy. It might have been real anathema to the moderate and radical Left, whose leaders continued to pay lip service to the flaws of the Fifth Republic and what its indisputable figurehead had come to represent, but it proved to be the cornerstone of relatively stable consensus about the republic and France's position in the world.

Of course, Gaullism was a product of specific circumstances; it inevitably aged as new sociopolitical forces and conditions emerged in the 1950s and 1960s. Interestingly, however, Gaullism (as legacy and ideology) outlived even de Gaulle himself. The wave of popular discontent that swept the country in the late 1960s, culminating in the student-worker demonstrations (1968), demanded that the political system be attuned to the new social conditions that had rendered Gaullism obsolete. In one respect at least the demonstrators were successful: de Gaulle resigned in 1969 and enabled Georges Pompidou to bear the responsibility of guarding an uncertain heritage. By the beginning of the 1970s, however, despite its significant electoral strength and political leverage, Gaullism could not claim any longer to represent a form of consensus, not even for the republican Right. The 1974 election of Valéry Giscard d'Estaing on the platform of a liberal and essentially anti-Gaullist agenda signified the death of a myth that had sustained the Fifth Republic during its critical infancy and transition.

If political stability is understood only in the strict sense of government endurance and political constancy, then the Fifth Republic cannot possibly claim an encouraging record. Twenty-two cabinets in forty-three years compares unfavorably with all other European countries except the notoriously unstable Italian Republic and to a degree mirrors the high turnover in governments that France experienced under the Third and Fourth Republics. In the 1978 elections the French political system

A GREAT HOPE

On 4 September 1958 Premier Charles de Gaulle, who had been recalled from self-imposed retirement to take over the French government, defended his ideas for the new constitution:

It was at a time when it had to reform or be shattered that our people first had recourse to the Republic. Until then, down the centuries, the *ancien régime* had achieved the unity and maintained the integrity of France. But, while a great tidal wave was forming in the depths, it showed itself incapable of adapting to a new world. It was then—in the midst of national turmoil and of foreign war—that the Republic appeared. It was the sovereignty of the people, the call of liberty, the hope of justice. That is what it was to remain through all the restless vicissitudes of its history. Today, as much as ever, that is what we want it to remain.

Of course, the Republic has assumed various forms during the successive periods when it has held sway. In 1792, we saw it—revolutionary and warlike—overthrow thrones and privileges only to succumb, eight years later, in the midst of abuses and disturbances that it had not been able to master. In 1848, we saw it rise above the barricades, set its face against anarchy, prove itself socially minded within and fraternal without, but soon fade away once more through its failure to reconcile order with the enthusiasm for renewal. On September 4, 1870, the day after Sedan, we saw it offer its services to the country to redeem the disaster.

In fact, the Republic succeeded in putting France back on her feet again, reconstituting her armies, recreating a vast empire, renewing firm alliances, framing good social laws and developing an educational system. So well did it do all this that, during the first World War, it had the glory of ensuring our safety and our victory. On November 11, when the people gather and the flags are dipped in commemoration, the tribute that the nation pays to those who have served it well is paid also to the Republic.

Nevertheless, the regime contained functional defects which might have seemed tolerable in a more or less stable era, but which were no longer compatible with the social transformations, the economic changes and the external perils that preceded the second World War. Had not this situation been remedied, the terrible events of 1940 would have swept everything away. But when, on June 18, the struggle for the liberation of France began, it was immediately proclaimed that the Republic to be rebuilt would be a new Republic. The whole Resistance Movement constantly affirmed this.

We know, we know only too well what became of these hopes. . . . By reason of inconsistency and instability and—whatever may have been the intentions and, often, the ability of the men in office—the regime found itself deprived of authority in internal affairs and assurance in external affairs, without which it could not act. It was inevitable that the paralysis of the State should bring on a grave national crisis and that, immediately, the Republic should be threatened with collapse.

The necessary steps were taken to prevent the irreparable at the very moment that it was about to occur. The disruption of the State was, by a narrow margin, prevented. They managed to save the last chance of the Republic. It was by legal means that I and my Government assumed the unusual mandate of drafting a new Constitution and of submitting it to the decision of the people.

We have done this on the basis of the principles laid down at the time of our investiture. We have done this with the collaboration of the Consultative Committee instituted by law. We have done this, taking into account the solemn opinion of the Council of State. We have done this after very frank and very thorough discussion with our own Councils of Ministers. These Councils were formed of men as diversified as possible as to origin and inclination, but resolutely united. We have done this without meanwhile doing violence to any right of the people or any public liberty. The nation, which alone is the judge, will approve or reject our work. But it is in good conscience that we propose this Constitution to them.

Henceforth what is primordial for the public powers is their effectiveness and their continuity. We are living at a time when titanic forces are engaged in transforming the world. Lest we become a people out of date and scorned, we must evolve rapidly in the scientific, economic and social spheres. Moreover, the taste for progress and the passion for technical achievements that are becoming evident among the French, and especially among our young people, are equal to this imperative need. These are all facts that dominate our national existence and that, consequently, must order our institutions.

The necessity of renovating agriculture and industry; of procuring—for our rejuvenated population—the means of livelihood, of work, of education, of housing; and of associating workers in the functioning of enterprises: the necessity to do all this compels us to be dynamic and expeditious in public affairs.

The duty of restoring peace in Algeria, next of developing it, and finally of settling the question of its status and its place in our great whole, impels us to arduous and prolonged efforts. The prospects offered us by the resources of the Sahara are magnificent indeed, but complex. The relations between Metropolitan France and the Overseas Territories require profound adjustment. The world is crossed by currents that threaten the very future of the human race and prompt France to protect herself while playing the role of moderation, peace and fraternity dictated by her mission. In short, the French nation will flourish again or will perish according to whether the State does or does not have enough strength, constancy and prestige to lead her along the path she must follow.

Therefore, it is for the people we are, for the century and the world in which we live, that the proposed Constitution was drafted. The country effectively governed by those to whom it gives the mandate and to whom it grants the confidence that makes for lawfulness. A national arbiter—far removed from political bickering—elected by the citizens who hold a public mandate, charged with the task of ensuring the normal functioning of the institutions, possessing the right to resort to the judgment of the sovereign people, accountable, in the case of extreme danger, for the independence, the honor and integrity of France and for the safety of the Republic. A Government made to govern, which is granted the necessary time and opportunity, which does not turn to anything other than its task and which thereby deserves the country's support. A Parliament intended to represent the political will of the nation, to enact laws and to control the executive, without venturing to overstep its role. A Government and Parliament that work together but remain separate as to their responsibilities, with no member of one being at the same time a member of the other. Such is the balanced structure that power must assume. The rest will depend upon men.

A Social and Economic Council, appointed outside politics by the business, professional and labor organizations of France and the Overseas Territories, that gives advice to Parliament and to the Government. A Constitutional Committee, free of any attachment, empowered to judge whether the laws that have been passed are constitutional and whether the various elections have been properly held. A judicial authority assured of its independence which remains the guardian of individual liberty. Thus will the competence, the dignity, the impartiality of the State be better guaranteed.

A Community formed between the French nation and those of the Overseas Territories that so desire, within which each Territory will become a State that governs itself, while foreign policy, defense, the currency, economic and financial policies, use of raw materials, the control of justice, higher education, long-distance communications will constitute a common domain over which the organs of the Community—the President, Executive Council, Senate and Court of Arbitration—will have jurisdiction. Thus, this vast organization will renovate the human complex grouped around France. This will be effected by virtue of the free determination of all. In fact, every Territory will have an opportunity, through its vote in the referendum, either to accept France's proposal or to refuse it and, by so doing, to break every tie with her. Once a member of the Community, it can in the future, after coming to an agreement with the common organs, assume its own destiny independently of the others.

Finally, during the four months following the referendum, the Government will be responsible for the country's affairs and, in particular, will establish the system of elections. In this way, through a mandate from the people, the necessary measures may be taken for the setting up of the new institutions.

Here, women and men of France, is what inspires and what makes up the Constitution which, on September 28, will be submitted to your vote. With all my heart, in the name of France, I ask you to answer "Yes."

If you do not vote thus, we shall return, that very day, to the bad old ways with which you are familiar. But if you do, the result will be to make the Republic strong and effective, provided that those in positions of responsibility know, hereafter, the meaning of determination. But there will also be, in this positive display of the national will, the proof that our country is regaining its unity and, by the same token, its opportunity for grandeur. The world, which understands full well what importance our decision will have for it, will draw the inevitable conclusion. Perhaps it is already drawing the conclusion.

A great hope will arise over France. I think it has already arisen.

Source: "Address by Premier Charles de Gaulle outlining the draft Constitution on September 4, 1958," Charles-De-Gaulle.org <http:// charles-de-gaulle.org/article.php3?id_article=523>.

reached a stage of perfect but bewildering "quadruple bipolarity," with two left- and two right-wing parties, each receiving about one-fifth of the popular vote. Fragmentation and unstable alliance-building established the French party system as the most unpredictable and volatile in Western European politics. The election of socialist François Mitterrand as the first left-wing president of the Republic (1981), after twenty-three years of center- right monopoly, seemed to strengthen the impression that old certainties had irrevocably collapsed. Mitterrand, an erstwhile critic of both the 1958 constitution and de Gaulle's presidential style, declared soon after he took over at the Elysée Palace that the new role suited him perfectly. Undoubtedly the strongest and most charismatic president after de Gaulle, he ensured that the transition from conservative/liberal to social-democratic politics did not tamper with the institutional framework of the republic. Unlike in the history of the previous political systems in France, both the electorate and the politicians could now reject a particular model of political management without questioning their commitment to the overall framework of the political system itself. This change represented a leap toward the production of a viable and stable consensus.

This improvement does not mean that the Fifth Republic ceased to experience problems, deadlocks, and unforeseen complications. Three times since 1986 a situation arose whereby the president of the Republic and the prime minister came from different political parties. Although this development constituted a perfectly possible scenario under the 1958 constitution (the seven-year term of the president did not coincide with the five-year intervals in legislative elections), the election of a right-wing parliament in 1986 amounted to an idiosyncratic political "cohabitation." Fears, however, that this complication would bring the political system to its knees did not materialize—neither in 1986–1988 nor in the subsequent two occurrences of the same situation in 1993–1995 and 1997–2002. The major players of the Republic adapted their strategies and conduct to the new realities. The constitution and political praxis of the Republic itself proved supremely adjustable, even in the face of adversity. Change was in some cases instigated from within (for example, the 2000 referendum that approved the harmonization of the terms of the president and the prime minister and thus limited the prospect of a future "cohabitation") and was seamlessly carried out. Essentially, the last two decades constitute a testimony to the institutional resilience and stability of the country's political class and society.

In April–May 2002 France's latest presidential elections took place, in the customary two-round system. The results of the first Sunday caused a veritable tremor: with nearly 17 percent of the vote National Front leader Jean-Marie Le Pen came in second and was thus allowed to enter into a direct race against incumbent president Jacques Chirac in the second round. Many, both inside and outside France, pronounced the death of the Fifth Republic and the start of a painfully uncertain future for the country's democratic-pluralistic traditions. One week later, with more than 82 percent of the popular vote, the reelection of Chirac offered the most categorical answer to those momentarily questioning the viability of the current Republic. In his victory speech Chirac saluted the "solidarity and openness" of the French, but he also acknowledged the voters' call "to ensure the republic lives on, the nation rallies around, to make sure politics change." Faced with this and other monumental tests in its forty-five-year history but successfully ensuring the endurance of its principles, institutions, and consensus, the Fifth Republic has emerged not only as the most resilient political arrangement in the history of modern France but also as one that can effectively guarantee the progress and welfare of its people while enjoying its fundamental moral support. This constitutes the epitome of any notion of "stability."

—ARISTOTLE A. KALLIS,
UNIVERSITY OF BRISTOL

Viewpoint:
No. The French government is still dogged by discontent, radicalism, and challenges to its political legitimacy.

France turned up on the winning side of World War II (1939–1945), but its postwar history has been far from a picture of lasting stability. Over the decades since 1945 France has faced major challenges to its constitutional order; dangerous portents of military involvement in domestic political life; a chronic sense of popular alienation from government, business, and administrative elites; unsettling scandals that have threatened to undermine the foundation of its democracy; and structural problems that could potentially cause major crises.

The France that emerged from liberation in 1944 was a traumatized place. It had spent four years under a crushing German occupation that had coincided with the repressive rule of the authoritarian domestic government established at Vichy four years earlier. Parts of the country still lay under German occupation, and partisans of the Vichy government continued on in exile at Sigmaringen Castle in Germany. The suddenness of the collapse of the Third Republic in 1940 made difficult the return of prewar institutions and political structures. Authority after the liberation rested nominally in the hands of General Charles de Gaulle, a self-appointed leader with no expressed democratic mandate, but he shared this authority uneasily with various strands of the domestic Resistance movement (including a large communist force), with British and American military forces operating within France, and with last-minute crossovers from Vichy.

Establishing a national consensus on how to govern postwar France was difficult. Political realities forced de Gaulle to include members of the Communist Party, which had been banned and dissolved by the Third Republic in its last months and was slavishly loyal to the government of the Soviet Union, in his Provisional Government. Justice and law enforcement remained arbitrary and ad hoc for a considerable length of time after Paris was liberated. In 1944–1945 as many as ten thousand Frenchmen were summarily executed by kangaroo courts for alleged crimes under the occupation. Thousands more were subjected to other punishments and ostracism that they may or may not have deserved. The new government itself embraced national *épuration* (purification) as an instrument of domestic policy. About one hundred thousand people were brought to trial on charges that were often hazy or ambiguous, and that process just as often dredged up unpleasant facts and memories that arguably hindered national reconciliation more than it helped it. Despite the scope of these investigations, the French nation was almost instantly imbued with a collective amnesia, what historian Henry Rousso has called the "Vichy Syndrome," aimed at suppressing ugly truths and other facts of the recent past. Many of these truths resurfaced later with explosive and traumatic force.

The realm of high politics was not much blessed with stability, either. The Provisional Government labored for two years before it could come up with a constitutional program amenable to the newly elected Constituent Assembly, which was heavily weighted toward the Left. To many, the constitutional program presented in May 1946 seemed simply to restore a legislature that would hold most of the power, with only a nominal executive. In other words, it would have virtually created a new Third Republic, with many of the same flaws that had undermined its stability. Although the program was defeated, a second referendum in October 1946 approved a slightly modified version by a small plurality: 36 percent in favor to 32 percent against, with 32 percent abstaining. Since de

Gaulle had led the forces of liberation during the war and presided over the Provisional Government, he took the electorate's rejection of a strong executive authority, which he led and aspired to lead in the future, as a personal affront and left the national stage. In other words, the only national figure who could command near universal confidence and respect went into premature retirement to assuage his wounded personal feelings. In de Gaulle's absence the new constitutional order indeed took on many features of the failed Third Republic. Twenty-five separate parliamentary governments took office in the Fourth Republic's twelve-year existence (there had been ninety governments in the Third Republic's seventy years, 1870–1940), and coherent policies were rare.

Worse still, the popularity of the communist wartime resistance translated into strong electoral support for the postwar Communist Party, which polled as much as 26.6 percent of the vote in the October 1945 elections to the Constituent Assembly that had come up with the Fourth Republic constitution. Although the party followed Soviet leader Josef Stalin's initial instructions to cooperate with the predominantly noncommunist postwar government, it became sharply confrontational as soon as the Cold War became a new international reality. As a result, France's moderate leaders were compelled to exclude the communists from government in May 1947. Although this step was prudent, it alienated a large percentage of the electorate and led directly to violent confrontations during strikes orchestrated by communist-controlled trade unions later that year. While the communists became isolated and lost support, they nevertheless remained a potent force in French politics, not infrequently winning 10 to 15 percent of the vote in parliamentary elections. As recently as 1997 the Socialist Party had to rely on communist support to maintain a workable parliamentary majority. In the French presidential elections of 2002 the official Communist Party candidate and three dissenting communists together received nearly as many votes as the second-place candidate, right-wing extremist Jean-Marie Le Pen. The presence of committed communists among French intellectuals, university professors, and cultural figures remained, and to a degree remains, rather pronounced. The moderated rhetoric of the French Communist Party notwithstanding, the extreme Left commanded far more support in France than in any other Western nation during the Cold War and continues to command palpable support there more than a decade after the collapse of the Soviet Union.

Even without the chronic presence of left-wing extremism, France struggled to find a

Charles de Gaulle being carried by supporters at an anticommunist rally outside of Paris in May 1948

(photographe anonyme d'agence)

stable political system. The Fourth Republic quickly became mired in corruption and failed to inspire confidence. Although economic recovery proceeded apace after the late 1940s, France's declining international position had direct consequences for domestic political stability. The country's inability to reprise its former international position was psychologically jarring, but the Fourth Republic had to sustain further defeats through much of its tortured existence. After a prolonged struggle to regain possession of Indochina, French forces there were defeated by the indigenous Vietnamese armies at Dien Bien Phu (1954). Paris had no choice but to withdraw the following year. In 1956 France's cooperation with Britain and Israel in an attempt to recover the nationalized Suez Canal from Egypt was foiled by strong diplomatic pressure from the United States and the Soviet Union. As if these additional shocks did not create enough disappointment and confusion, France's relatively successful handling of the revolt in Algeria, which flared into a full-scale confrontation in 1957, seemed meaningless when the ineffectual government could find no consensus on how to pursue its advantage. In a particularly alarming development the following year, elements of the military in Algeria took control through a "Committee of Public Safety" (a facetious reference to the revolutionary body

that came to control France in the 1790s). A detachment of paratroopers sent from Algiers seized control of Corsica, portending civil war. The resulting cabinet crisis of 1958 led to the Fourth Republic's demise and the recall of General de Gaulle.

An important and frequently overlooked feature of de Gaulle's return is that it explicitly suspended democracy. A parliamentary vote gave him sweeping executive powers to draft a new constitution and rule until it came into effect. Fortunately for France, de Gaulle favored a democratic government and worked to build a stronger republic, but the National Assembly's vote to give him executive powers was far from unanimous (329 to 224, with most of the Socialists, including future president François Mitterrand, voting against). It was also uncomfortably similar to the vote that had given similar powers to the decidedly undemocratic Marshal Henri-Philippe Pétain in 1940, powers that he used to establish the Vichy regime. Nevertheless, the new constitutional order that de Gaulle ushered in provided for a powerful executive, which the general was expected to lead, and a bicameral legislature that retained strong powers.

The new Fifth Republic has endured, but de Gaulle's creation was far from perfect. The situation in Algeria presented it with an immediate challenge. Although de Gaulle initially used his personal influence to ward off the potential military challenge and courted popularity by favoring Algeria's status as an integral part of metropolitan France, the situation remained problematic. Unlike Indochina and other possessions from which France was prepared to withdraw, a million Europeans lived in Algeria, and they were fully integrated into the cultural and political life of the French mainland. The military's victory over the Algiers uprising in 1957 had established a position from which it was difficult to withdraw. Yet, the realist de Gaulle had to admit that France's long-term presence in Algeria was a losing proposition. International pressure militated in favor of France's withdrawal, domestic support for the war became increasingly tenuous as it took on the characteristics of a guerrilla struggle, and maintaining a permanent military presence threatened to become prohibitively expensive. Despite these facts, many Frenchmen strongly resented de Gaulle's eventual decision to permit a democratic referendum on Algerian independence—a measure that the Algerians were certain to win. Rather than support this unpopular step, elements of the French military seriously tested the Republic's stability by conspiring against it. In addition to several attempts on de Gaulle's life in the early 1960s, disloyal elements of the French military formed the *Organisation de l'Armée Secrète* (Secret Army Organization, OAS), which launched an attempted coup d'état in April 1961. Although the coup failed and its potential ramifications are largely understated, it represented a serious challenge to civilian rule. In a tense stand-off the coup plotters planned an attack on Paris, while de Gaulle garrisoned the capital with loyal troops and barricades. Only a series of mistakes, a lack of nerve, and some prudent deals defused the situation. De Gaulle also helped defuse the crisis with the effective employment of his constitutional power to rule by emergency decree (an undemocratic means thus ironically played an important role in saving a democratic regime), but France nevertheless came within a hair's breadth of becoming the only Western nation to lose its democratic government since World War II (1939–1945). From that important perspective it is difficult to argue that postwar France was the picture of stability, even as long as seventeen years after its liberation from the Germans.

De Gaulle's handling of the denouement of the Algeria Crisis was not accompanied by efforts to solve a host of additional problems that France has faced. Even as rebellious army officers and units were brought under control, the country continued to suffer from two major problems: first, a growing sense of alienation in the mainstream population; and second, serious shortcomings in the constitutional organization of the Fifth Republic.

In many ways the alienation that many Frenchmen have felt from their government and leaders was a product of France's centralized monarchy and its even more centralized revolutionary government. Yet, postwar France continued to suffer from stifling bureaucracy, powerful Paris-based central government, and a hierarchical social structure. Although the republican and revolutionary heritage was shrouded in the rhetoric and symbolism of liberty, equality, and brotherhood, the French continued to have many reasons not to feel free, equal, or fraternal. Perhaps the most important problem was Paris's role as a strong central authority. Local government was remarkably weak in France, with departmental prefects appointed by the state. Until recently the central government also appointed municipal mayors. Paris was free to elect its own mayor only in 1977 (the first since a revolutionary government controlled the city in 1871), while Lionel Jospin's government extended that right to other municipalities only in the late 1990s.

In addition to the sense that the people have uncommonly limited control over local issues, the nature of the national legislative government also inspires less confidence. The mainstream political parties are widely perceived as little more than groupings of self-serving civil servants, and indeed, a sizeable percentage of the deputies in the National Assembly actually are on leave from jobs in the civil administration. Many other prominent political figures have uncomfortably strong connections to private business, which has raised widespread and chronic suspicions that they serve business interests ahead of the interests of voters, parties, and the nation.

The structure of France's governing class does little to dispel these specters or lead a dispassionate observer to another conclusion. Leading figures in French political, business, and cultural life are overwhelmingly graduates of the country's *grandes écoles* (great schools), which train only the most select and talented youths. As sociologist Pierre Bourdieu observed to great resonance among his countrymen, these talented youths tend overwhelmingly to come from the upper-class families of the previous generation of *grandes écoles* graduates. Although the ideal is that the "best and brightest" are given the inside track on national leadership, the results have engendered many disappointments. At a time when the educational philosophies of most other Western countries stress the desirability of egalitarian institutions and prize diversity defined by regional provenance, ethnic background, or disadvantaged status, France's system is by definition hierarchical and exclusionary. One of its main institutions for training politicians, the *Ecole Nationale d'Administration* (National Administration School), was founded after World War II to train a closed elite. Its educational philosophy was modeled on philosopher Emmanuel Mounier's ideas of a hierarchical community and patterned after Vichy's cadres school at Uriage, which was established to train a new national administrative corps along lines similar to those advanced in Benito Mussolini's Italy. One could argue philosophically that the "best" students have a natural right to form a nation's governing class, and it may appear logical and just that they enjoy the greatest opportunities. Yet, the hard fact remains that many "average" Frenchmen feel that they are governed by an openly elitist system that controls not only the government but also business, the media, the arts, and the academy.

A disenfranchised population experiencing, or even just perceiving, serious limitations on its social mobility is seldom a good ingredient in national stability. Indeed, historians of the French Revolution (1789) have argued that this same problem was one of that upheaval's main causes. Perhaps the best explanation for France's frequent strikes, street demonstrations, riots, and other disruptions of public order is that its organized laborers, farmers, students, professionals, and special-interest groups have no other means of making their voices heard or having their grievances satisfied than by going off the job, stopping essential services, marching in the streets, or attacking McDonald's restaurants. Many nations experience such problems to a degree, but these disruptions occur with greater frequency and effect in France than in any other Western country. Civic disturbances in 1968–1969 precipitated de Gaulle's resignation and second departure from public life. Recent strike activity has involved such essential personnel as doctors, firemen, and transport workers, all of whom can deprive the entire nation of their services if their unions decide to make it happen. Even prostitutes launched a street demonstration in the fall of 2002, believing that doing so was the only way to defend their oldest of professions against new government restrictions. If members of these groups had other avenues of influence in a more open political system, then perhaps their protest actions would not be so serious or cause such major disruption.

Another practical dilemma associated with government by the "best and brightest" is that many guardians of the public trust have become embroiled in scandals so numerous and damaging that they have led many observers, French as well as foreign, to suggest that emphasizing superior academic ability might not be the wisest means of distributing authority. Certainly there are many competent and trustworthy company directors, political figures, and civil servants in France, but the 1980s and 1990s saw scandals among these high-profile groups that were virtually unparalleled elsewhere in the West. The last decade has been particularly damning. In 1993 former Social-ist prime minister Pierre Bérégovoy committed suicide after his party suffered a catastrophic loss in that year's parliamentary elections. A year later President Mitterrand was forced to admit publicly that he had received a decoration for meritorious service from the Vichy government when he was a young civil servant. Later in the decade veteran civil servant and politician Maurice Papon—who had served as a prefect, mayor, National Assembly deputy, and finally as the national budget minister—was convicted of crimes against humanity for having authorized the deportation of 1,600 Jews to Auschwitz when he was a Vichy official. He was sentenced to ten years in prison. Former prime minister Laurent Fabius and officials of his government were tried for criminal negligence in the accidental infection of more than 1,200 hemophiliacs with HIV, the virus that causes AIDS, during his term in office in the 1980s. Although Fabius was acquitted, many questions were raised about his reliability as a guardian of the public trust. In the next scandal former foreign minister Roland Dumas and his mistress were convicted of having accepted huge bribes from an oil company that wanted to buy the minister's influence and the mistress's influence over the minister. Dumas was sentenced to prison, but, to popular disgust, his conviction was quashed on appeal and he went free. Most recently, the world was astonished to hear that as many as 15,000 Frenchmen, mostly elderly, died during a heat wave in the summer of 2003. An official investigation found that appalling deficiencies in the state-run health care system caused most of these deaths. The health minister resigned. These were only the biggest and most publicized scandals among many others.

Other countries certainly have lived down major political and business scandals in recent years, but their widespread nature in France has involved a much greater than average number of high officials whose Western counterparts have not been implicated in such serious matters. Popular disgust with the prevailing political order is there to see. Political extremists command a disturbingly large share of the electorate's sympathies. The level of support for the Communist Party and other extreme left-wing political groups has been noted, but the extreme Right has been consistently much stronger in France than in any other Western nation. In the 1980s the xenophobic National Front, which has positioned itself as an antiestablishment party and has roots in discontentment going back to the 1950s, had a parliamentary presence roughly on par with the communists and enjoyed some noted successes in elections to municipal councils and the European Parliament. In 2002 its controversial leader, Jean-Marie Le Pen, placed second in the first round of the national presidential election, displacing moderate socialist candidate and incumbent prime minister Jospin. Although the center-right incumbent president

Jacques Chirac easily defeated Le Pen in the second round, Le Pen's initial share of the vote, combined with the votes for the extreme Left, demonstrated that about one out of every three French voters supported an extreme candidate who campaigned on his or her opposition to the philosophical foundations of the Republic.

Some structural features of the Fifth Republic have also called its long-range stability into question. De Gaulle's use of emergency powers during the Algiers coup (1961) has not been repeated, but the Presidency still retains the right to use them. Although they helped de Gaulle check the military threat, the two most notable democratic governments that have shared such powers in modern times were Weimar Germany, which sank into the Nazi dictatorship, and post-Soviet Russia, which has experienced many problems with its fledgling democracy. The past utility of these powers notwithstanding, they offer a real potential for misuse and for the subversion of democracy. More recently, a French judge ruled that President Chirac was immune from investigation, prosecution, or even questioning in a financial scandal involving his political party, establishing a precedent that has essentially put him and future Fifth Republic presidents above the law while in office. No Western nation shares this approach to its executive.

Another unfortunate feature of France's constitutional system is that in a particular set of circumstances the president and legislative leadership, both of which have substantial powers that are vaguely defined and not explicitly separated as they are in the U.S. Constitution or the British parliamentary system, can come from different political parties. The Fifth Republic constitution empowers the president to appoint the prime minister but also requires his appointee to be approved by a majority of the legislature. If a rival party or coalition of parties should win a majority of National Assembly seats in the course of his term (parliamentary elections must be held at least once every five years but are often held at more frequent and less predictable intervals), the president is in effect constrained to appoint, and then govern with, a member of the opposing party. Although this situation did not occur until 1986–1988, when Chirac formed a right-wing government during the Mitterrand presidency, it has always been a theoretical possibility, and it occurred again in 1993–1995 and 1997–2002. Although these "cohabitations," as they are called, did not result in major crises, they nevertheless made national government more uneasy and tentative than it has long tended to be elsewhere in the West. During the most recent cohabitation major policy differences surfaced between the president and the prime minister. The possibility of a future crisis should not be discounted. The French electorate's 2000 plebiscite vote in favor of reducing the presidential term from seven years to five (to make them more consistent with the legislative election intervals) was intended to curtail the problems of cohabitation, but many observers still wonder whether this and other problems would not best be solved by a Sixth Republic.

–PAUL DU QUENOY,
GEORGETOWN UNIVERSITY

References

Maurice Agulhon, *The French Republic, 1879–1992,* translated by Antonia Nevill (Oxford & Cambridge, Mass.: Blackwell, 1995).

John Ardagh, *France in the New Century: Portrait of a Changing Society,* revised edition (London & New York: Penguin, 2000).

Philippe Bernard and Henri Dubief, *The Decline of the Third Republic, 1914–1938,* translated by Anthony Forster (Cambridge & New York: Cambridge University Press, 1985; Paris: Maison des sciences de l'homme, 1985).

Jonathan Fenby, *France on the Brink* (New York: Arcade, 1999).

Roderick Kedward and Roger Austin, eds., *Vichy France and the Resistance: Culture & Ideology* (London: Croom Helm, 1985; Totowa, N.J.: Barnes & Noble, 1985).

Andrew Knapp and Vincent Wright, *Government and Politics of France,* fourth edition (London & New York: Routledge, 2001).

Maurice Larkin, *France since the Popular Front: Government and People, 1936–1996,* second edition (Oxford & New York: Clarendon Press, 1997).

James F. McMillan, *Twentieth-Century France: Politics and Society 1898–1991* (London & New York: Arnold, 1992).

Robert O. Paxton, *Vichy France: Old Guard and New Order, 1940–1944* (New York: Knopf, 1972).

Jean-Pierre Rioux, *The Fourth Republic, 1944–1958,* translated by Godfrey Rogers (Cambridge & New York: Cambridge University Press, 1987).

Henry Rousso, *The Vichy Syndrome: History and Memory in France since 1944,* translated by Arthur Goldhammer (Cambridge, Mass.: Harvard University Press, 1991).

Anne Stevens, *The Government and Politics of France* (New York: St. Martin's Press, 1992; London: Macmillan, 1992).

Gordon Wright, *France in Modern Times: From the Enlightenment to the Present,* fifth edition (New York: Norton, 1995).

FRANCE AFTER 1945

FRENCH FASCISM

Was fascism an important factor in French politics before World War II?

Viewpoint: Yes. Several influential militant right-wing groups in France during the 1920s and 1930s fit a general definition of fascism.

Viewpoint: No. Although a series of significant antidemocratic groups existed in France, the country never had a substantial fascist movement.

Taking advantage of demoralized societies, depressed economies, and fears of rising communism, extremists of the European Right had some success in advocating a new ideology after World War I (1914–1918). *Fascism* (derived from *fasces*, an ancient Roman symbol of power) advocated the power of the state over the individual and promised to remake divided societies into united "national communities." Under the leadership of Benito Mussolini, a fascist government arose in Italy in 1922, and, under Adolf Hitler in Germany, the fascist Nazi Party came to power in 1933.

Fascist movements were founded in other European nations, but historians dispute their significance, particularly in the case of France. Historians who believe that there was truly an "international fascism" look to the proliferation of extreme right-wing movements in interwar France in asserting that the country experienced an important fascist episode. Mass movements, political violence, and ideological statements closely resembled the Italian and German fascist movements and played an unavoidable role in French politics and society. Yet, other historians doubt that France was seriously plagued by fascism. "True" French fascists, defined by a strict definition of the political philosophy, appeared to be rather small in number and marginal in politics. Other groups might be more aptly described as "extreme Right." In other words, while they were opposed to democracy and communism, their beliefs were more reflective of the conservative and reactionary traditions that had been a part of French public life since the Revolution of 1789. Similarities with fascists of Italy and Germany were either sparing or superficial.

Viewpoint:
Yes. Several influential militant right-wing groups in France during the 1920s and 1930s fit a general definition of fascism.

Like many other European nations, France developed a large and significant fascist movement in the interwar era. By the eve of World War II (1939–1945), fascist senti- ment pervaded a significant segment of the nation. Skeptics of French fascism often argue that its failure to develop into a united movement, such as the National Socialist German Workers' Party (Nazis) or the Italian Fascist Party, doomed it to political insignificance and prevented it from playing a major role in French politics. This argument, however, ignores the existence of several French political formations that influenced interwar political life and were professedly and self-consciously fascist, or at least fit a general definition of fascism.

As was the case elsewhere in Europe, France became fertile ground for political radicalization after World War I (1914–1918). Although France lacked the recent authoritarian tradition that contributed to fascism's rise in Germany, Italy, and some of the nations of Eastern Europe, social and economic problems associated with the war bedeviled it. Even if France had emerged victorious in 1918, the occupation of much of its territory during the war, its loss of over a million men on the battlefield, serious postwar economic difficulties, and rising social tension made the victory a hollow one. In December 1920 part of the country's socialist movement branched off to form a communist party, which shared the ideals of Russia's Bolshevik Revolution (1917) and quickly aligned itself with the Soviet-led Communist International. Sensing a threat from the extreme left and continuing to suffer from economic and social problems, many Frenchmen embraced a new, right-wing radicalism. As early as 1925, a year after a leftist government came to power in France and only six years after Italian fascist leader Benito Mussolini used the word *fascism* for the first time, Georges Valois formed the *Faisceau* (from the Latin *fasces*, an ancient Roman symbol of power that Mussolini had adapted and the root word of "fascism"), an organization that directly mimicked Mussolini's movement and proudly called itself "fascist." Valois's group espoused authoritarian government, the primacy of the state over the individual, the remaking of society into a "national community," and a virulently anticommunist and antidemocratic ideology. All of these goals and values were shared by the Italian Fascist Party, which had come to power under Mussolini's leadership in October 1922, and by the National Socialist German Workers' (Nazi) Party, which became the largest political party in Germany by 1932 and, under the leadership of Adolf Hitler, came to power the following year. The symbolism of Valois's movement paralleled that of Mussolini and Hitler's, including a revered leadership, uniforms, parades, and other militaristic trappings. There were differences between the *Faisceau* and German and Italian fascism, just as there were differences between the German and Italian fascists themselves, but Valois's movement had far more in common with them than not. Although it was not a lasting force in French politics, it nevertheless assembled some 25,000 members for a rally in Rheims in 1926.

Only two years after the founding of the *Faisceau,* right-wing war veterans founded another political organization, the *Croix de feu* (Cross of Fire). Although its membership was originally restricted to veterans who had received the prestigious *Croix de guerre* (War Cross) decoration in World War I, it was soon opened not only to all veterans but to their families as well. Coming under the leadership of Colonel François de la Rocque in 1931, the *Croix de feu* also espoused an authoritarian and antidemocratic ideology. De la Rocque never developed the leadership skills and populist flair of Hitler or Mussolini, but he railed against the French Republic, advocated its replacement by an authoritarian order, and expanded his movement to the point where it had 1.5 million to 2 million members by the mid 1930s—no small feat in a country of about 40 million. Like Valois's group and the German and Italian fascists, the *Croix de feu*'s public demonstrations involved uniforms, banners, parades, and other manifestations of military prowess. Since the organization also included veterans' families, it, like both the Italian Fascist and German Nazi Parties, organized sporting events, leisure time, social clubs, and other such activities that made its members part of a "society within a society"—the potential nucleus of the "new society" advocated by bona fide fascists. The left-wing Popular Front government elected in 1936 found the *Croix de feu* so dangerous that it dissolved the organization, which nevertheless soon reemerged as an ostensible political party, the *Parti social français* (French Social Party).

Yet another group defined by its commonalities with German and Italian fascism emerged after the expulsion of Jacques Doriot, a leading communist politician, from the ranks of the French Communist Party in 1934. Skillfully using his former communist authority, connections, and media outlet, Doriot developed a mass political organization, the *Parti populaire français* (French Popular Party), which joined its rivals in denouncing the Republic, the political left, the troubled society, and the other usual targets and called for a new national community structured along authoritarian lines. In addition to these fascist attributes, Doriot's party openly advocated collaboration with Nazi Germany and fascist Italy before World War II and did so out of a professed admiration and affinity for the ideologies of those regimes. Unsatisfied with Marshal Henri-Philippe Pétain's nonfascist authoritarian government, established in Vichy after France's defeat by Germany in 1940, Doriot went to work directly for the Nazis by helping to organize the SS Charlemagne Division, a unit of French volunteers to fight on the German side against the Soviet Union that ultimately numbered 25,000 men.

These three groups were not the only fascist groups in France—there were dozens of smaller groups, as well as other right-wing groups, such

Meeting of French fascists in 1936

(Rene Dazy)

as the reactionary monarchist *Action française* (French Action) and the vaguely Bonapartist *Jeunesses patriotes* (Patriotic Youths), that cannot easily be described as fascist. But their mass memberships, public sympathy for Nazi Germany and fascist Italy, opposition to the Republic, advocacy of an authoritarian government and a "regenerated" society, and militaristic affectations make it difficult to argue that France was devoid of fascism or fascist influence. Many of these groups, furthermore, acted out to advance their ideas and attack their opponents. In February 1934 a riot in Paris, which involved several right-wing political formations, included thousands of demonstrators and caused the collapse of a democratically formed parliamentary government. Although the Republic did not collapse and another parliamentary government came to power, the threat to French democracy was clear. Two years later, in February 1936, thugs associated with a fascist-leaning youth group attempted to assassinate Léon Blum, the leader of France's Socialist Party. Blum recovered and went on to become the country's first socialist prime minister shortly thereafter, but the attack proved that the extremists were sufficiently motivated to resort to murder to accom-

plish their political objectives. As Blum's subsequent dissolution of de la Rocque's *Croix de feu* and other groups made clear, fascism was a present issue in interwar France and had a serious impact on its political life.

Apart from the troubled political atmosphere of the 1920s and 1930s, fascism also made a notable penetration into the French intellectual arena and attracted some of the best minds in France. Publicists Pierre Drieu La Rochelle and Bertrand de Jouvenel were strongly drawn to Doriot's French Popular Party and played significant roles in developing its ideology. Journalist Robert Brasillach, who had attended the elite Ecole Normale Supérieure, edited the rabidly anti-Semitic and collaborationist newspaper *Je suis partout* (I am everywhere). Another publicist and member of the French parliament, Marcel Déat, led a small political party that extolled German and Italian fascism. In 1939 he used his prominence to question bitterly his country's commitment to defend Poland against German aggression. The popular right-wing novelists Henri de Montherlant and Louis-Ferdinand Céline published widely read antiwar works and expounded profascist views. These public intellectuals and others like them reached mass audiences, some of whom came to share their views when France went to war in 1939 and after it was defeated the following year.

Most of the leading fascist politicians did not survive the war. Valois rejected fascism, embraced socialism, and died in a German concentration camp. Although de la Rocque did not renounce his authoritarian ideology, he was placed in German "protective confinement" and died shortly after his liberation. Doriot was killed when American fighter planes strafed his car in Germany in February 1945. In a backhanded recognition of fascism's importance, postwar retribution against fascist-leaning public intellectuals, most of whom survived the war, was swift and severe. Déat took holy orders in an Italian monastery to escape a death sentence. Céline fled to Denmark to escape prison and official condemnation as a "national disgrace." Drieu La Rochelle committed suicide before he could be brought to trial. Charles Maurras, the leading ideologist of the right-wing (if not explicitly fascist) *Action française,* was sentenced to life in prison. Brasillach was executed after France's postwar leader, Charles de Gaulle, rejected a plea for mercy on his behalf, declaiming that intellectuals were to be held responsible for the actions that their work propagated. Since that work in many cases propagated or complemented fascism, the ideology remains a part of France's past that cannot be ignored.

–PAUL DU QUENOY,
GEORGETOWN UNIVERSITY

Viewpoint:
No. Although a series of significant antidemocratic groups existed in France, the country never had a substantial fascist movement.

Analysis of the role of fascism in France during the interwar period is complicated by three factors. The first is the shadow of Vichy—the authoritarian government that ruled France between its defeat in 1940 and its liberation in 1944—that paradoxically seems to be growing longer with the passage of time. Associating anyone or anything, however indirectly, with Vichy's legacy is an excellent way of diminishing his or its contemporary legitimacy. A second problem is posed by the existence in France of a political Right whose roots, albeit tangled, can be traced less to the rejection of modernity than to antagonism toward the French Revolution of 1789—the two are not the same thing, however frequently they have been conflated. The third

factor is a persistent French intellectual pattern best described as "marxism with a small m," or perhaps a synergy of Marxism and Jacobinism. It is a comprehensive leftward orientation, hostile in principle to the existing orders of things and expressing that hostility in a personalized antagonism to political and intellectual opponents. In that context "fascism" runs easily off the tongue and the pen as an all-purpose term of denunciation and abuse, difficult to answer because of its vagueness. Thus, in *Neither Right Nor Left: Fascist Ideology in France* (1986), Zeev Sternhell proposes to study the "penetration" of France by "fascist" ideas, and the "Fascization" of "certain schools of thought" whose major common denominator seems to be Sternhell's distaste for them.

In any case, the intellectual result is an image of France in the interwar years as increasingly submerged beneath a creeping miasma of pitiless attacks not only on the flaws of the Third Republic but against the principles of liberal democracy and the materialism and individualism accompanying it. In its developed form French fascism is depicted as accepting even French defeat as a necessary preliminary to establishing the organic, communitarian order summarized in Vichy's slogan "Fatherland, Family, Work." Recent scholarly exposure of the "myth of the Resistance," and the accompanying demonstration that Vichy's principles, initially at least, were by no means unpopular, also contribute to a search for fascism's roots in Republican France as a means of explaining the internal corruption of the 1940s.

Closer examination reveals a much less apocalyptic situation. The interwar French Right was an efflorescently complex structure of groups and movements that drew support from prewar liberals and moderates as well as various extremists. What these men and women had in common was a growing sense of frustration at what seemed the fundamental ungovernability of France—a situation that was dissipating the promises of the victory of 1918 and retarding the economic and social developments that would fulfill the aspirations unleashed by the Great War. The issue for the Right was less what a particular government did in any particular situation than what seemed its reluctance to do anything at all that could not be immediately cancelled by the next government in succession.

Fascism at its core is a movement of opposition. It stands against liberalism as too entropic and against conservatism as too rigid. It dismisses socialism as restrictive and capitalism as institutionalized greed. In place of what it criticizes, fascism offers not programs but attitudes, and its most popular attitude is one of heroic, violent resistance to a domestic order that repre-

BOTH PRACTICE AND THOUGHT

In "The Doctrine of Fascism" Italian dictator Benito Mussolini supplies his fundamental ideas about the political philosophy that gained adherents in many European countries, including France:

Like every sound political conception, Fascism is both practice and thought; action in which a doctrine is immanent, and doctrine which, arising out of a given system of historical forces, remains embedded in them and works there from within. Hence it has a form correlative to the contingencies of place and time, but it has also a content of thought which raises it to a formula of truth in the higher level of the history of thought. In the world one does not act spiritually as a human will dominating other wills without a conception of the transient and particular reality under which it is necessary to act, and of the permanent and universal reality in which the first has its being and its life. In order to know men it is necessary to know man; and in order to know man it is necessary to know reality and its laws. There is no concept of the State which is not fundamentally a concept of life: philosophy or intuition, a system of ideas which develops logically or is gathered up into a vision or into a faith, but which is always, at least virtually, an organic conception of the world.

Thus Fascism could not be understood in many of its practical manifestations as a party organization, as a system of education, as a discipline, if it were not always looked at in the light of its whole way of conceiving life, a spiritualized way. The world seen through Fascism is not this material world which appears on the surface, in which man is an individual separated from all others and standing by himself, and in which he is governed by a natural law that makes him instinctively live a life of selfish and momentary pleasure. The man of Fascism is an individual who is nation and fatherland, which is a moral law, binding together individuals and the generations into a tradition and a mission, suppressing the instinct for a life enclosed within the brief round of pleasure in order to restore within duty a higher life free from the limits of time and space: a life in which the individual, through the denial of himself, through the sacrifice of his own private interests, through death itself, realizes that completely spiritual existence in which his value as a man lies.

Therefore it is a spiritualized conception, itself the result of the general reaction of modern times against the flabby materialistic positivism of the nineteenth century. Anti-positivistic, but positive: not sceptical, nor agnostic, nor pessimistic, nor passively optimistic, as are, in general, the doctrines (all negative) that put the centre of life outside man, who with his free will can and must create his own world. Fascism desires an active man, one engaged in activity with all his energies: it desires a man virilely conscious of the difficulties that exist in action and ready to face them. It conceives of life as a struggle, considering that it beho[o]ves man to conquer for himself that life truly worthy of him, creating first of all in himself the instrument (physical, moral, intellectual) in order to construct it. Thus for the single individual, thus for the nation, thus for humanity. Hence the high value of culture in all its forms (art, religion, science), and the enormous importance of education. Hence also the essential value of work, with which man conquers nature and creates the human world (economic, political, moral, intellectual).

This positive conception of life is clearly an ethical conception. It covers the whole of reality, not merely the human activity which controls it. No action can be divorced from moral judgement; there is nothing in the world which can be deprived of the value which belongs to everything in its relation to moral ends. Life, therefore, as conceived by the Fascist, is serious, austere, religious: the whole of it is poised in a world supported by the moral and responsible forces of the spirit. The Fascist disdains the "comfortable" life.

Fascism is a religious conception in which man is seen in his immanent relationship with a superior law and with an objective Will that transcends the particular individual and raises him to conscious membership of a spiritual society. Whoever has seen in the religious politics of the Fascist regime nothing but mere opportunism has not understood that Fascism besides being a system of government is also, and above all, a system of thought.

Fascism is an historical conception, in which man is what he is only in so far as he works with the spiritual process in which he finds himself, in the family or social group, in the nation and in the history in which all nations collaborate. From this follows the great value of tradition, in memories, in language, in customs, in the standards of social life. Outside history man is nothing. Consequently Fascism is opposed to all the individualistic abstractions of a materialistic nature like those of the eighteenth century; and it is opposed to all Jacobin Utopias and innovations. It does not consider that "happiness" is possible upon earth, as it appeared to be in the desire of the economic literature of the eighteenth century, and hence it rejects all teleological theories according to which mankind would reach a definitive stabilized condition at a certain period in history. This implies putting oneself outside history and life, which is a continual change and coming to be. Politically, Fascism wishes to be a realistic doctrine; practically, it aspires to solve only the problems which arise historically of themselves and that of themselves find or suggest their own solution. To act among men, as to act in the natural world, it is necessary to enter into the process of reality and to master the already operating forces.

Against individualism, the Fascist conception is for the State; and it is for the individual in so far as he coincides with the State, which is the conscience and universal will of man in his historical existence. It is opposed to classical Liberalism, which arose from the necessity of reacting against absolutism, and which brought its historical purpose to an end when the State was transformed into the conscience and will of the people. Liberalism denied the State in the interests of the particular individual; Fascism reaffirms the State as the true reality of the individual. And if liberty is to be the attribute of the real man, and not of that abstract puppet envisaged by individualistic Liberalism, Fascism is for liberty. And for the only liberty which can be a real thing, the liberty of the State and of the individual within the State. Therefore, for the Fascist, everything is in the State, and nothing human or spiritual exists, much less has value, outside the State. In this sense Fascism is totalitarian, and the Fascist State, the synthesis and unity of all values, interprets, develops and gives strength to the whole life of the people.

Outside the State there can be neither individuals nor groups (political parties, associations, syndicates, classes). Therefore Fascism is opposed to Socialism, which confines the movement of history within the class struggle and ignores the unity of classes established in one economic and moral reality in the State; and analogously it is opposed to class syndicalism. Fascism recognizes the real exigencies for which the socialist and syndicalist movement arose, but while recognizing them wishes to bring them under the control of the State and give them purpose within the corporative system of interests reconciled within the unity of the State.

Individuals form classes according to the similarity of their interests, they form syndicates according to differentiated economic activities within these interests; but they form first, and above all, the State, which is not to be thought of numerically as the sum-total of individuals forming the majority of a nation. And consequently Fascism is opposed to Democracy, which equates the nation to the majority, lowering it to the level of that majority; nevertheless it is the purest form of democracy if the nation is conceived, as it should be, qualitatively and not quantitatively, as the most powerful idea (most powerful because most moral, most coherent, most true) which acts within the nation as the conscience and the will of a few, even of One, which ideal tends to become active within the conscience and the will of all—that is to say, of all those who rightly constitute a nation by reason of nature, history or race, and have set out upon the same line of development and spiritual formation as one conscience and one sole will. Not a race, nor a geographically determined region, but a community historically perpetuating itself, a multitude unified by a single idea, which is the will to existence and to power: consciousness of itself, personality.

This higher personality is truly the nation in so far as it is the State. It is not the nation that generates the State, as according to the old naturalistic concept which served as the basis of the political theories of the national States of the nineteenth century. Rather the nation is created by the State, which gives to the people, conscious [of] its own moral unity, a will and therefore an effective existence. The right of a nation to independence derives not from a literary and ideal consciousness of its own being, still less from a more or less unconscious and inert acceptance of a de facto situation, but from an active consciousness, from a political will in action and ready to demonstrate its own rights: that is to say from a state already coming into being. The State, in fact, as the universal ethical will, is the creator of right.

The nation as the State is an ethical reality which exists and lives in so far as it develops. To arrest its development is to kill it. Therefore the State is not only the authority which governs and gives the form of laws and the value of spiritual life to the wills of individuals, but it is also a power that makes its will felt abroad, making it known and respected, in other words, demonstrating the fact of its universality in all the necessary directions of its development. It is consequently organization and expansion, at least virtually. Thus it can be likened to the human will which knows no limits to its development and realizes itself in testing its own limitlessness.

The Fascist State, the highest and most powerful form of personality, is a force, but a spiritual force, which takes over all the forms of the moral and intellectual life of man. It cannot therefore confine itself simply to the functions of order and supervision as Liberalism desired. It is not simply a mechanism which limits the sphere of the supposed liberties of the individual. It is the form, the inner standard and the discipline of the whole person; it saturates the will as well as the intelligence. Its principle, the central inspiration of the human personality living in the civil community, pierces into the depths and makes its home in the heart of the man of action as well as of the thinker, of the artist as well as of the scientist: it is the soul of the soul.

Fascism, in short, is not only the giver of laws and the founder of institutions, but the educator and promoter of spiritual life. It wants to remake, not the forms of human life, but its content, man, character, faith. And to this end it requires discipline and authority that can enter into the spirits of men and there govern unopposed. Its sign, therefore, is the Lictors' rods, the symbol of unity, of strength and justice.

Source: Benito Mussolini, *"The Doctrine of Fascism"* *<http://cosmo.slique.net/~vikrum/mirrored/texts/ mussolini/fascism/>.*

sents all the repressive, life-denying elements fascism denounces. To that degree fascism is fraudulent. It has never survived against a government willing to use deadly force systematically or a society willing to support that policy. Fascism can be correspondingly powerful, however, when facing societies and governments that have lost confidence in their legitimacy. In that situation, fascism can draw support from all points on a decaying political spectrum and run its bluffs alike in parliament and in the street.

Those circumstances never developed in France. Fascist organizations emerged in the late 1920s, in common with the rest of Europe. They grew in strength and influence. Yet, they never succeeded in competing with the established order either in the streets or at the ballot boxes. The fundamental reason for their failure was France's status as a satiated power. The Great War had left no territories to return, no minorities to redeem. Any national honor lost in 1870 had been recovered with interest as the victorious regiments marched into a Rhineland that would remain under French occupation for fifteen years according to the Versailles Treaty (1919), which reestablished France as the primary power of Europe.

Nor had the Great War left a domestic legacy of distrust and malaise. French morale, military and civilian, had endured to the end of the conflict. At the same time, the war experience had left little sympathy for the trappings of the paramilitary forces characteristic of fascism. Exaggerated pseudodiscipline and cadenced marching had little resonance among veterans whose wartime experience had put little emphasis on "smartness" in either the British or German sense of the word. As for racism, the wartime contributions of the Senegalese and North African *tirailleurs* (sharpshooters) had been too obvious, and their peacetime importance to France's military position too apparent, to provide fertile soil for xenophobia. Nor were the eastern Europeans, primarily Poles, who came in to work the restored mines of the northeast regarded as taking jobs from good Frenchmen. If anything, the foreigners were accepted, if not always enthusiastically welcomed, as replacements for the dead of 1914–1918.

Nor did France face the kind of economic crises that elsewhere brought men and women into the streets. The gridlocked governments that were such a source of irritation when times were good served also as a safeguard against going too far in any economic direction. The special interest groups that benefited from government support and government inaction in the 1920s gave France a balanced and diversified economy with a local and regional focus that limited—at least relatively—the Great Depression's impact and facilitated stabilization if not always recovery.

Not least of French fascism's problems was its failure to produce leaders with any more than small-scale appeal. Mainstream parties of left and right alike offered greater opportunities to ambitious men who believed they could inspire crowds. In the Third Republic, the rewards of being on the inside were surer.

In the final analysis, however, French fascism was deterred by the French Republic's unwavering commitment to use force against domestic threats from any quarter. In 1934–1935, politics seemed on the way to moving into the streets. Ad hoc nationalist leagues, bringing together hotheads of every right-wing persuasion, staged demonstrations and riots. In the background stood the *Croix de feu* (Cross of Fire), strongest of the patriotic organizations, and its enigmatic leader Colonel François de la Rocque. On the other side of the line, socialists and communists, otherwise the bitterest of enemies, made common cause against what to them seemed a fascist coup in the making. Strikes and riots proliferated, but after the Paris riots of February 1934 that left seventeen dead and hundreds injured, the government and its police showed backbone. Not only that, they showed every sign of continuing to do so. The French Right at least took heed. Able enough to make trouble, it was collectively unwilling to take the risk of crossing the line into the protorevolutionary world of fascism in the face of government rifles.

–DENNIS SHOWALTER,
COLORADO COLLEGE

References

Alice Kaplan, *The Collaborator: The Trial & Execution of Robert Brasillach* (Chicago: University of Chicago Press, 2000).

Robert Soucy, *French Fascism: The First Wave, 1924–1933* (New Haven: Yale University Press, 1986).

Soucy, *French Fascism: The Second Wave, 1933–1939* (New Haven: Yale University Press, 1995).

Zeev Sternhell, *Neither Right Nor Left: Fascist Ideology in France,* translated by David Maisel (Berkeley: University of California Press, 1986).

Eugen Weber, *Action Française* (Stanford, Cal.: Stanford University Press, 1962).

Weber, *The Hollow Years: France in the 1930s* (New York: Norton, 1994).

FRENCH FASCISM

HITLER'S RISE TO POWER

Did Adolf Hitler rise to power in Germany through a legal, democratic process?

Viewpoint: Yes. Hitler's expert management of politics enabled him to obtain power through strictly democratic means.

Viewpoint: No. Hitler rose to power by scheming with influential antidemocratic political figures and grossly violating the democratic German constitution and legal system.

On 30 January 1933 Adolf Hitler was named chancellor of Germany. Under his rule the Nazi Party achieved unprecedented levels of control over German politics and society. Hitler's Germany launched World War II (1939–1945), the most destructive conflict in human history. It carried out a horrific program of genocide and ethnic cleansing. Its institutions dominated the lives and minds of its citizens with unrestrained terror. This chapter addresses a major debate in the history of his regime: was it a legal creation? Did Hitler achieve power through a legitimate, democratic process, or was his power based on force and coercion?

An argument presented by many historians in the West, and repeated here, is that Hitler's rise to power was a perfectly legal process, one that he and the other Nazi leaders consciously intended to follow after the defeat of their "Beer Hall putsch," an attempted coup d'état, in November 1923. By winning millions of votes in national elections, using the free media to spread his message, and securing some initial legislative support for his extreme measures, Hitler pursued his path to power with complete legality.

Such an argument seems to imply that the ingredients for Nazi tyranny were present within German society. If Hitler could come to power legally, what does that say about Germany's power elite, democratic system, and ordinary voters? To refute this notion, another body of scholarship, most prominently developed by Karl Dietrich Bracher in *The German Dictatorship: The Origins, Structures, and Effects of National Socialism* (1970) and represented in this chapter, argues that the Nazis' ability to achieve and to hold on to power depended on grossly undemocratic means. Hitler's intrigues with an undemocratic elite, use of coercion to silence political opponents, and systematic violations of Germany's democratic constitution enabled him to establish his dictatorship and lead the country on the road to war.

Viewpoint:
Yes. Hitler's expert management of politics enabled him to obtain power through strictly democratic means.

People often confuse dastardly and unscrupulous with illegal. The steps by which Adolf Hitler ascended to and solidified his grip on power in Nazi Germany were undoubtedly the first two but unfortunately not the latter. In attempting to ascertain the legality of Hitler's rise to power, one must begin with an overview of the facts and events. However, in order to determine whether one should agree with historian Karl Dietrich Bracher in calling Hitler's emergence a *legal revolution,* or whether it deserves the appellation *pseudo-legal,* one must also look to the wider issues of justice and accountability.

Hitler was virtually unknown to the wider German public as a political leader as late as 1928; until that time, despite his momentary flash of fame for the "Beer Hall putsch" (November 1923), he was simply the head of a rabble-rousing group of often alcohol-soaked nationalists who commonly defined their virulent nationalism in "anti" terms: anti-Jewish, anticommunist, antihomosexual, antidemocratic, and so on. Hitler realized after his failed coup that if he wished to enter the Reichstag as anything other than a tourist, he and his fellow Nazis would have to "hold our noses" and do so through democratic means. This realization is not to say that his brown-shirted *Sturmabteilung* (SA, Storm Troopers) thugs put away their clubs and foreswore violence, but rather that they determined to direct it toward supporting their candidates in future elections.

In resorting to street violence during political campaigns, the Nazis were not unique; extremists at both ends of the political spectrum had paramilitary groups whose primary responsibility was to intimidate voters and beat up opposition groups. Hitler's fortunes began to change dramatically to his advantage in 1928, thanks to the first serious attempt by another (mainstream) right-wing leader, Alfred Hugenberg, to manipulate him.

The German government had managed to renegotiate the terms of Germany's World War I (1914–1918) reparations through the American-sponsored Dawes (1924) and Young Plans (1929). Some right-wing parties in Germany felt that the plan, in not repudiating the war-guilt clause of the Versailles Treaty (1919), merely compounded and perpetuated the humiliation of Germany. Hugenberg, a wealthy owner of many press and mass-media outlets, turned his full attention to attempting to have the Young Plan rejected in a plebiscite. To this end, he approached Hitler to do much of the grunt work. What Hugenberg did not realize was that although

his side would lose the fight against the Young Plan, putting his media empire and funds at the disposal of Hitler gave that brilliant speaker an undreamed-of opportunity to reach millions of Germans. In the political climate following the onset of the Great Depression in October 1929, voters remembered the nationalist who promised to lead them out of humiliation and back into great-power prosperity. In the five-year period leading to Hitler's appointment as Chancellor in January 1933, the Nazi Party saw its share of the national vote increase from 2.6 percent in 1928 to 37 percent in the elections of July 1932, making it the single largest party in the Reichstag. When Hitler ran for president in the 1932 elections, he finished second behind the incumbent, the aged and conservative World War I hero Paul von Hindenburg.

Under the terms of the Weimar Constitution the president was expected to call upon a political leader to be chancellor and to form a government (by coalition, if necessary) that would rule with the confidence of the deputies in the Reichstag. There was no obligation on the part of the president to choose the leader of the largest party in Parliament to be chancellor, or even to participate in government. The Social Democratic Party, despite its large showing throughout the Weimar Republic years, was almost voiceless in matters of authority, as Hindenburg would brook no participation from them in political affairs. However, the president was a snob as well as a conservative and was almost equally loath to include the impudent and vulgar Nazis, led by the upstart Austrian and former corporal Hitler. When Hitler asked for the chancellorship in 1932, Hindenburg indignantly told him to get out of his office.

Another feature of the Weimar Constitution, Article 48, gave the president the authority to rule by decree in an emergency, with the sole provision being that parliamentary elections would need to be held within four months of the failure of the president's chosen chancellor to acquire the support of the Reichstag. However, the president could simply keep holding elections every few months as long as he wished, and thus almost permanently ignore the will of the people and rule by legal dictatorship within the parameters of the Constitution. This scenario is more or less what had happened since July 1930, when a series of chancellors (Heinrich Brüning, Kurt von Schleicher, and Franz von Papen twice) ruled Germany relying almost exclusively on Article 48. The president could place turbulent regions of the country under the authority of commissars. By the summer of 1932 this step had been taken in Prussia, the core state of the German Empire, which accounted for two-thirds of the country's territory and population. Ger-

„Nimmer 1 wird das Reich zerstöret — wenn ihr einig seid und treu"

Nationalsozialisten

many was a legal presidential dictatorship well before Hitler was appointed chancellor.

That Hitler was chosen at all was a sign of Hindenburg's fatigue with the mess his other appointees were making of the situation, with the increasingly unbearable political turbulence caused by the Great Depression, and with political deals among the parties of the political right. Hitler had originally been offered the post of vice chancellor in one of Papen's governments but turned it down, betting that eventually the pressure would become so great that Hinden-

burg would appoint him to the top post; in this gamble, as in so many other political and military decisions in later years, Hitler's political instincts proved depressingly accurate: in January 1933, Hindenburg asked him to take office. The slightly more moderate right-wing parties believed that by greatly outnumbering the Nazis in the cabinet, they would be able to control Hitler and manipulate the populist into carrying out their will, and indeed, the Nazis only received two cabinet appointments in addition to the chancellorship. Hitler promptly tried to increase his command of the situation by dissolving Parliament and calling for fresh elections.

While the origins of the Reichstag Fire (27 February 1933), coming on the eve of the elections, may never be truly known, they are somewhat irrelevant for the discussion of whether Hitler rose to power legally. The presence of a probably insane, or at least slow-witted, Dutch communist in the vicinity of the burning building gave Hitler the opportunity to approach the increasingly unpredictable Hindenburg with tales of an imminent communist upheaval. The field marshal rose to the bait and, using his constitutional authority, signed an emergency decree that allowed for the temporary suspension of civil liberties. As the elections were only days away, a temporary suspension of rights was all that the Nazis needed, and under the guidance of Hermann Göring, the new government's commissar for Prussia, communists were beaten, rounded up, and harassed at the polls. Even with these brutish tactics, however, the Nazis were unable to command an overall majority in the Reichstag. They won 43.9 percent of the vote and were thus still dependent on others for the ability to pass laws.

This minor legislative hindrance was overcome soon thereafter with the passage of the Enabling Act (1933), a measure that gave the chancellor the right to pass laws for a period of four years without the consent of Parliament. For the Reichstag to acquiesce in this exercise of self-castration, however, a two-thirds majority vote was required. Even with the consent of the other right-wing parties Hitler's numbers fell short. The growing emergency situation—which the Nazis in many cases deliberately escalated—however, persuaded a sufficient number of moderates, particularly members of the Catholic Center Party, to add their votes and approve the bill.

What prevents insane parliamentary majorities from getting out of hand is usually a system of checks and balances. It is the prerogative of any parliament to pass laws as it sees fit. It is up to the courts, or the executive, to veto or strike down laws. In Germany in 1933 no one acted against the laws passed by the Parliament, neither the courts nor the president. In the strictest sense none of the legislative measures taken by Hitler's government was unconstitutional. Subsequent laws designed to weed out perceived subversives (communists, socialists, Jews, and so on) from the civil service ensured a compliant judiciary and civil service over the long term, while the death of Hindenburg in August 1934 afforded Hitler the opportunity to have his tame Reichstag vote to combine the offices of chancellor and president. The only other body that one might have expected to stand up for honor and justice was the army, but it, too, showed a compliant ability to be bought off: the murder of the leadership of his SA was a calculated move by Hitler to make his movement appear less radical and to win over the support of the army. The military pledged to support Hitler, going so far as to replace the normal oath of obedience with a pledge of personal loyalty to the Führer. Until the end of the Nazi regime the Weimar Constitution was never formally abrogated or suspended: it remained the source from which Hitler drew his legal authority to lead the German people. The emergency measures through which Hitler ruled were simply renewed and remained in effect until 1945.

Unsavory and brutish though it was, Hitler's rise and consolidation of power in Germany was a legal process. The checks and balances that might have declared them otherwise were never used. One final measure of how these moves were viewed within the context of their times can be ascertained by the actions of foreign governments. When dictators come to power, it is the prerogative of each state to decide whether to recognize the change in power as legitimate. Not only did the Vatican sign a formal treaty with the Nazi government after its accession to power, but no other state broke off diplomatic relations or indicated in any other way that they viewed Hitler as an illegal chancellor (and, later, Führer). Although it was a revolution of sorts, Hitler's rise to power was legal. To explain why such a manipulation of the laws could occur in the first place, one must look to the weaknesses of the Weimar Constitution itself, as well as the weaknesses of the other sources of power and authority in Germany.

–VASILIS VOURKOUTIOTIS,
UNIVERSITY OF OTTAWA

Viewpoint:
No. Hitler rose to power by scheming with influential antidemocratic political figures and grossly violating the democratic German constitution and legal system.

Many scholars and politicians have argued that Adolf Hitler rose to power through legal, democratic means. According to this argument, Hitler achieved power by establishing the Nazi Party as a political force that respected the Weimar Constitution. His party would eventually become the largest in Germany after the elections of July 1932, a victory that would eventually culminate in his appointment to the chancellorship by President Paul von Hindenburg in January 1933. However, these facts do not reveal the inherently antidemocratic and anticonstitutional nature of Hitler's rise to power. Hitler was always willing to use any means at his disposal to achieve power throughout his political career, from his first political activities after Germany's surrender to the victorious powers of World War I (1914–1918), to his attempted "Beer Hall putsch" (November 1923) in Munich, to his appointment and actions as chancellor of Germany in the first two years of his twelve-year rule. Flagrant acts of terror, crime, and conspiracy with the antidemocratic elite were absolutely central to these events.

Hitler's antidemocratic tendencies can even be seen in his initial political involvement in the chaotic days after the armistice of 11 November 1918. The naval revolt at Kiel shortly before the armistice and attempted communist revolutions in Berlin and Munich early the next year prompted Hitler to join the nationalist struggle to suppress the leftist threat. Participating as a member of the rightist *Freikorps* (Free Corps, private paramilitary groups), Hitler was one of many war veterans who believed that the Kaiser and the German war effort had been betrayed by the "Jewish-dominated" Communists and Social Democrats. According to this conspiracy theory, German Social Democratic leader Friedrich Ebert undermined the Reich's destiny to assert itself as the world's leading great power by usurping the Kaiser and emasculated Germany's military might by agreeing to the harsh terms of the Versailles Treaty (1919). Thus, Hitler viewed the establishment of the democratic Weimar Constitution as an act by racially degenerate traitors.

Hitler, working as a low-level intelligence agent for the German army, would take over the nascent Nazi Party within a year in the right-wing hotbed of Munich. Although many of his commanders shared similar antidemocratic sentiments, Hitler soon exceeded his original orders. Hitler acknowledged the strength of the Communists to mobilize the masses against the republic and also wished to tap into worker discontent, but he wanted to change the workers' antidemocratic ideology from class conflict and international proletarian solidarity to a national and racial struggle against the "Versailles criminals." He also enlisted his old *Freikorps* comrades to act as musclemen for the group. They were to vote with their fists and not the ballot.

Indeed, Hitler's first attempt to seize power was a coup attempt with leading antidemocratic figures. After arranging a meeting with Gustav von Kahr, self-appointed head of Bavaria who himself had taken over the former democratic provincial government by means of a military ultimatum, and General Otto von Lossow, German army commander of Bavaria who conspired with Kahr against the Social Democratic authorities in Berlin, Hitler hoped to force them at gunpoint to try to take over the central government. Hitler dreamed of duplicating Italian leader Benito Mussolini's "March on Rome" (1922)

with his own "March on Berlin." He had even gained the active support of General Erich Ludendorff, a World War I hero who avoided condemnation for the defeat by spreading the idea that Germany had been "stabbed in the back" by the Social Democrats and Communists.

Although Hitler's first attempt to seize power failed miserably, his subsequent "legal" struggle against Weimar democracy was merely tactical. Jailed for his crime, Hitler was simply not in a position to make another attempt at armed revolt. He then perfected his ability as a demagogue by using his court trial and his newly written autobiography, *Mein Kampf* (My Struggle, 1925–1927), to spread the gospel of a martyred nationalist. Hitler would not hesitate to encourage his street thugs to fight their Communist rivals upon his release in December 1924. Yet, his true success was to develop his own cult of personality as a man of action who would take the wartime struggle from the trenches to the streets.

By 1930 the political climate had changed. The appointment of Chancellor Heinrich Brüning by President Paul von Hindenburg in March without a parliamentary majority was a watershed in Germany's interwar history. From then on, election results mattered less than the relationship potential candidates had with Hindenburg. This first important movement toward an authoritarian system coincided with a new socio-economic crisis. The collapse of the American stock market (October 1929) some four months earlier resulted in a world economic crisis and a German unemployment rate of 20 percent. The conditions could not have been better for a Nazi success at the polls.

Nevertheless, the extralegal actions that Hitler's *Sturmabteilung* (SA, Storm Troopers) took on the streets and the backroom political deals that Hitler cut with the antidemocratic military elite who surrounded Hindenburg outweighed the party's success in garnering more than 37 percent of the vote in the July 1932 elections. The Nazi Party would never have received as many votes as they did without using terror to silence their opponents and to persuade "good Germans" that Nazi violence was carried out in the name of law and order. The authorities began to allow the brownshirts to act with impunity when they were confronted with the equally offensive Communist youth gangs, which were also becoming popular. Vigilantism was now allowed if it were carried out in the name of anti-communism. Political opponents were silenced, and the Nazis raised new recruits and voters.

Moreover, new rounds of political intrigue offered Hitler unforeseen opportunities. Chancellor Brüning soon fell out of favor with Hindenburg, and the general wished to replace him with an old favorite, Franz von Papen. The man

PROGRAM OF THE NAZI PARTY

The Program of the German Workers' Party is a program for our time. The leadership rejects the establishment of new aims after those set out in the Program have been achieved, for the sole purpose of making it possible for the Party to continue to exist as the result of the artificially stimulated dissatisfaction of the masses.

1. We demand the uniting of all Germans within one Greater Germany, on the basis of the right to self-determination of nations.

2. We demand equal rights for the German people (*Volk*) with respect to other nations, and the annulment of the peace treaty of Versailles and St. Germain.

3. We demand land and soil (Colonies) to feed our People and settle our excess population.

4. Only Nationals (*Volksgenossen*) can be Citizens of the State. Only persons of German blood can be Nationals, regardless of religious affiliation. No Jew can therefore be a German National.

5. Any person who is not a Citizen will be able to live in Germany only as a guest and must be subject to legislation for Aliens.

6. Only a Citizen is entitled to decide the leadership and laws of the State. We therefore demand that only Citizens may hold public office, regardless of whether it is a national, state or local office.

We oppose the corrupting parliamentary custom of making party considerations, and not character and ability, the criterion for appointments to official positions.

7. We demand that the State make it its duty to provide opportunities of employment first of all for its own Citizens. If it is not possible to maintain the entire population of the State, then foreign nationals (non-Citizens) are to be expelled from the Reich.

8. Any further immigration of non-Germans is to be prevented. We demand that all non-Germans who entered Germany after August 2, 1914, be forced to leave the Reich without delay.

9. All German Citizens must have equal rights and duties.

10. It must be the first duty of every Citizen to carry out intellectual or physical work. Individual activity must not be harmful to the public interest and must be pursued within the framework of the community and for the general good.

We therefore demand:

11. The abolition of all income obtained without labor or effort.

Breaking the Servitude of Interest.

12. In view of the tremendous sacrifices in property and blood demanded of the nation by every war, personal gain from the war must be termed a crime against the nation. We therefore demand the total confiscation of all war profits.

13. We demand the nationalization of all enterprises (already) converted into corporations (trusts).

14. We demand profit-sharing in large enterprises.

15. We demand the large-scale development of old-age pension schemes.

16. We demand the creation and maintenance of a sound middle class; the immediate communalization of the large department stores, which are to be leased at low rates to small tradesmen. We demand the most careful consideration for the owners of small businesses in orders placed by national, state, or community authorities.

17. We demand land reform in accordance with our national needs and a law for expropriation without compensation of land for public purposes. Abolition of ground rent and prevention of all speculation in land.

18. We demand ruthless battle against those who harm the common good by their activities. Persons committing base crimes against the People, usurers, profiteers, etc., are to be punished by death without regard to religion or race.

19. We demand the replacement of Roman Law, which serves a materialistic World Order, by German Law.

20. In order to make higher education—and thereby entry into leading positions—available to every able and industrious German, the State must provide a thorough restructuring of our entire public educational system. The courses of study at all educational institutions are to be adjusted to meet the requirements of practical life. Understanding of the concept of the State must be achieved through the schools (teaching of civics) at the earliest age at which it can be grasped. We demand the education at the public expense of specially gifted children of poor parents, without regard to the latters' position or occupation.

21. The State must raise the level of national health by means of mother-and-child care, the banning of juvenile labor, achievements of physical fitness through legislation for compulsory gymnastics and sports, and maximum support for all organizations providing physical training for young people.

22. We demand the abolition of hireling troops and the creation of a national army.

23. We demand laws to fight against *deliberate* political lies and their dissemination by the press. In order to make it possible to create a German press, we demand:

a) all editors and editorial employees of newspapers appearing in the German language must be German by race;

b) non-German newspapers require express permission from the State for their publication. They may not be printed in the German language;

c) any financial participation in a German newspaper or influence on such a paper is to be forbidden by law to non-Germans and the penalty for any breach of this law will be the closing of the newspaper in question, as well as the immediate expulsion from the Reich of the non-Germans involved.

Newspapers which violate the public interest are to be banned. We demand laws against trends in art and literature which have a destructive effect on our national life, and the suppression of performances that offend against the above requirements.

24. We demand freedom for all religious denominations, provided that they do not endanger the existence of the State or offend the concepts of decency and morality of the Germanic race.

The Party as such stands for positive Christianity, without associating itself with any particular denomination. It fights against the Jewish-materialistic spirit *within* and *around* us, and is convinced that a permanent revival of our nation can be achieved only from *within,* on the basis of:

Public Interest before Private Interest.

25. To carry out all the above we demand: the creation of a strong central authority in the Reich. Unquestioned authority by the political central Parliament over the entire Reich and over its organizations in general. The establishment of trade and professional organizations to enforce the Reich basic laws in the individual states.

The Party leadership promises to take an uncompromising stand, at the cost of their own lives if need be, on the enforcement of the above points.

Munich, February 24, 1920.

Source: "The Program of the National-Socialist (Nazi) German Workers Party," Yad Vashem: The Holocaust Martyrs' and Heroes' Remembrance Authority <http://www.yad-vashem.org.il/about_holocaust/documents/part1/doc1.html>.

who engineered his appointment (and also his later dismissal) was General Kurt von Schleicher. Schleicher's primary motive was to build popularity for another minority government by enlisting Hitler's support. Schleicher, like Hindenburg, did not offer the chancellorship to Hitler on the grounds that he was not a member of the army officer corps. Hitler declined the subordinate post of vice chancellor. Such prejudices, and not another election, proved to be the last great obstacle to Hitler's quest for power. However, Hitler quickly maneuvered by instigating Papen's removal with Schleicher. He then worked with Papen and Hindenburg to unseat Schleicher. Thereafter, Hitler conned Hindenburg and Papen into assigning him to the chancellorship with the promise that Papen would control the cabinet. Hitler quickly revealed the political naiveté of these conservative circles by exploiting the Reichstag Fire (27 February 1933), which convinced the nation that communist agitation was reaching new heights, to persuade the Reichstag to pass the Enabling Act in March 1933, which guaranteed him temporary emergency powers. Using his new authority, Hitler bypassed the nominal authority of the non-Nazi members of his cabinet and established a police state, complete with a political police, concentration camps, and a thorough suppression of civil liberties. In sharp contravention of the constitutional order of the Weimar Republic, the chancellor's emergency powers simply remained in effect until the end of the Nazi regime in 1945.

Hitler was determined to seize power by any means necessary. Certainly, he could not have succeeded without a significant level of popular support, as expressed in Weimar Germany's democratic electoral processes. His growing popularity during the economic crisis that followed 1929 proved that he could use legal means to advance his cause. Still, he never relied on these means alone. He did not hesitate to use armed rebellion against the Weimar authorities when he believed it might have worked, and he never flinched at using armed street gangs of his supporters to coerce and intimidate political opponents if the opportunity presented itself. The decision to use legal or extralegal methods simply depended on the time, place, and occasion. In addition, Hitler showed a distinct reluctance to act within normal parliamentary rules. Although his party enjoyed electoral successes, never once did it enter a real coalition with the other parties in the Reichstag. Its delegates frequently used tactics of obstruction, and Hitler's appointment as chancellor was the product of a series of backroom deals made by uniformly antidemocratic individuals rather than a free parliamentary vote. The only party with which the Nazis cooperated on a tactical level was the Communist Party, their great rival that shared their goal of destroying the republic. The Nazis owed their existence to the struggle to eradicate Bolshevism and international socialism, yet both movements shared an equal disdain for democracy and its institutions. Both movements also employed terror to coerce and intimidate their opponents. Not surprisingly, they both thrived after 1930, when the republic was at its greatest peril, by feeding off political and economic instability.

Finally, one needs to highlight the fact that Hitler depended on intrigues with Germany's antirepublican elite as much as he did on political demagoguery. Hitler would have never succeeded without their acquiescence, as seen in both Ludendorf's support in the Beer Hall putsch and Field Marshal Hindenburg and General Schleicher's help in his last steps to power. Army officers, officials, media barons, aristocrats, industrialists, and other traditionally conservative groups disdained a democratic civilian government that had ended World War I in what many believed to have been a dishonorable way and undermined traditional political and social values. They were unaware, however, of the monster they helped to create in their desperation. Hitler's conspiratorial skills and demagogical genius were beyond their comprehension.

–YORK NORMAN,
GEORGETOWN UNIVERSITY

References

Karl Dietrich Bracher, *The German Dictatorship: The Origins, Structures, and Effects of National Socialism,* translated by Jean Steinberg (New York: Praeger, 1970).

Alan Bullock, *Hitler: A Study in Tyranny* (New York: Harper, 1952).

Joachim C. Fest, *Hitler,* translated by Richard and Clara Winston (New York: Harcourt Brace Jovanovich, 1974).

Warren B. Morris Jr., *The Weimar Republic and Nazi Germany* (Chicago: Nelson-Hall, 1982).

Panikos Panayi, ed., *Weimar and Nazi Germany: Continuities and Discontinuities* (Harlow, U.K. & New York: Longman, 2001).

Robert Payne, *The Life and Death of Adolf Hitler* (New York: Praeger, 1973).

William L. Shirer, *The Rise and Fall of the Third Reich: A History of Nazi Germany* (New York: Simon & Schuster, 1960).

INDEPENDENT FOREIGN POLICY

Did the attempts of Western European leaders at rapprochement with the Soviet Union during the Cold War serve their best interests?

Viewpoint: Yes. The leaders of France and Germany correctly viewed the superpower confrontation between the United States and the Soviet Union as an opportunity for their nations to reemerge as independent powers in world affairs.

Viewpoint: No. Western European nations ultimately failed to establish a middle position in the Cold War and harmed their true interests and alliance relationships in the process.

By the mid 1960s the two largest and most powerful states of Western Europe, France and Germany, were beginning to move toward independent positions in global politics. Dissatisfied with playing a secondary role to the United States, both Paris and Bonn looked toward the promotion of distinct national interests by building new relationships with the Soviet Union. French president Charles de Gaulle initiated an official policy of "détente, entente, and cooperation" with Moscow and distanced his country from its alliance with the United States. West Germany began to explore independent relations with Eastern Europe in 1967 and by 1969 had initiated *Ostpolitik* (Eastern Policy), a full program of rapprochement with the Union of Soviet Socialist Republics (U.S.S.R.). A series of treaties established peaceful diplomatic relationships, new commercial ties, and West Germany's formal recognition of the Cold War status quo in Europe.

These changes in European politics were and remain controversial. To some historians they were important steps in securing the peaceful conclusion of the Cold War. Others believe they prolonged it. One argument contends that Western Europe's movement toward a middle position in the Cold War helped build the European Economic Community and European Union (EU), steps in the development of the continental integration that assures its stability. To other observers rapprochement with the U.S.S.R. only created greater tensions in the West, sacrificing unity for the pursuit of limited national goals. As France, Germany, and the integrated Europe that they helped create look toward an independent role in world affairs in the twenty-first century, the benefits and disadvantages of the Cold War origins of this process are worthy of consideration.

Viewpoint:
Yes. The leaders of France and Germany correctly viewed the superpower confrontation between the United States and the Soviet Union as an opportunity for their nations to reemerge as independent powers in world affairs.

The development of the French policy of détente reflected French president Charles de Gaulle's personal style, concern for the independence and restoration of France's great-power status, and desire to weaken the American preponderance in Europe. De Gaulle once said, "nothing could be worse for Europe than the American hegemony, which extinguished Europe and prevented the Europeans from being themselves." He tried to restrict and diminish U.S. influence in many ways. De Gaulle used every opportunity to emancipate France from the bonds that the Atlantic alliance had placed on its freedom of action. Step by step de Gaulle withdrew French forces from the North Atlantic Treaty Organization (NATO) command, and in 1966 he ended all French participation in NATO military activities.

Challenging American supremacy, the French vigorously denounced the improvement of the U.S.-Soviet relations in the wake of the Cuban Missile Crisis (1962) as a "new Yalta," referring to the February 1945 conference that in many ways established the structure of post–World War II Europe, claiming that the Americans were willing to pay the price of the de facto consolidation of Europe's partition. To achieve reunification of the continent, in the mid 1960s de Gaulle decided to outmaneuver the Americans by proclaiming his own policy of "détente, entente, and cooperation" with the communist East. De Gaulle's hope was that if Moscow perceived Western Europe, led by France, as an independent power rather than an American client, the Soviets, given their mounting problems with China, might loosen their control over Eastern Europe. This shift would dismantle the predominance of each superpower in "its half" of Europe, reunite the continent step by step, end the Cold War, and allow Europeans to play a greater role in international affairs.

De Gaulle's ambitions for European leadership led to closer ties between West Germany and the United States. Perceiving the Washington-Bonn axis as one of the main obstacles to his plans, de Gaulle wanted West Germany to separate itself to some extent from the United States and follow France's lead in rapprochement with

the Soviets. The goal of de Gaulle's approach was threefold. First, the idea was to combine the resources of the Federal Republic of Germany (FRG) with France's as a basis for a renewed claim for the leading position in Europe. The French president said at the time: "together Germany and France would unearth the treasure of a policy that would overcome the division of Europe." Second, Paris tried to use Franco-German ties, based on the Treaty of Elysée (1963), as an arrangement presaging a kind of loose defensive alliance separate from NATO that de Gaulle wanted to achieve for Europe as a whole. Third, de Gaulle was determined to prevent West Germany from filling the vacuum between the superpowers as they disengaged from Europe. If West Germany were to try to play a major role in a new Europe, de Gaulle believed that the United States and the Soviet Union would use such a development as a pretext for reimposing their control over the continent.

While appealing to the East to end the Cold War, the French did not recognize East Germany, encouraging Bonn's hopes for reunification of the country as a part of the drive against the postwar status quo. At the same time, Paris insisted that Germany must accept the Oder-Neisse line as its eastern border, for continuing doubts on this issue gave the Soviet Union an excuse to maintain its presence in Eastern Europe and delay continental unification. Yet, despite all French efforts to break the Washington-Bonn axis, West Germany—the front line of the West-East confrontation—was not inclined to turn its back on powerful America because of its security concerns and larger goal of achieving national reunification. Although de Gaulle's pan-European ambitions overestimated France's potential, his policy of détente led to significant improvement of Franco-Soviet relations and strengthened France's autonomy within the Western alliance, in Europe, and in the world.

De Gaulle's concept of détente was not lost on some West German leaders, who came to believe that the FRG might possess bargaining chips (the unresolved problems of Germany's eastern borders, the unique value of the divided Germany in the East-West strategic balance, and the powerful economy of the FRG) that Paris lacked in its European policy. Willy Brandt, who became West Germany's chancellor in 1969, recalled in his memoirs that de Gaulle's détente "paved the way for our subsequent *Ostpolitik*" (Eastern Policy).

The development of the German question until the mid 1960s demonstrated that the Cold War and West Germany's sole reliance on the Atlantic alliance produced a stalemate on the issue of reunification. A new generation of German leaders sought to approach the unification

INDEPENDENT FOREIGN POLICY

French president François Mitterand (left) and German chancellor Helmut Kohl at a battlefield ceremony, Verdun, 1984

(from Hendrik Brugmans, ed., Europe, 1987)

issue by dealing with the communist East. This turn to the East, while approved by the United States, did not require a primary reliance on America. Difficulties in U.S.-West German relations contributed to Bonn's desire to act independently. Preoccupied with the Vietnam War (ended 1975), the Johnson administration decided to withdraw troops from Germany and send them to the Far East. This act inflicted some damage on U.S.-German security relations, for Bonn believed that Washington's commitment to its defense was flagging. In the 1970s the Nixon administration's strategy of rapprochement with the communist bloc created additional fears in Bonn about U.S.-Soviet agreement on Europe at Germany's expense.

Ostpolitik–the improvement of relations with the Soviet Union and normalization of relations with East Germany and other East European countries–was the first great German diplomatic effort after World War II. In a series of treaties with the U.S.S.R. (1970), Poland (1970), Czechoslovakia (1973), and the German

Democratic Republic (1973), Bonn improved relations with the Soviet Union, accepted Germany's postwar borders with Poland and Czechoslovakia, and recognized the East German state. The objective of *Ostpolitik* was to use economic power and political dialogue as levers to increase German influence in Eastern Europe, induce the region to come closer to the West, and pave a way toward the gradual reunification of Germany. Paradoxically enough, according to the *Ostpolitik* conception, recognition of the political status quo in Europe was to be a short-term preface to dissolving it. As the collapse of communism in Eastern Europe in 1989 demonstrated, this scheme worked to some extent.

The initiative and independence exhibited by Brandt's policy represented a novel development in European politics. It also had a wider international impact. West Germany's recognition of the GDR made the admission of both German states to the United Nations possible in 1973. While the expansion of trade with Eastern Europe contributed to Germany's status as

INDEPENDENT FOREIGN POLICY

Europe's most powerful economy, political dialogue and diplomatic relations with the communist countries prevented West Germany from being outflanked diplomatically by the United States, which at the time also pursued its own policy of détente with the Soviet Union.

The Nixon administration had some reservations about Brandt's *Ostpolitik*. Above all the United States feared for the unity of the West, believing that Brandt, a Social Democrat, had no emotional attachment to the Atlantic alliance. Henry Kissinger, President Richard M. Nixon's national security adviser and later his secretary of state, repeatedly stressed that while he had no doubts about the "basic Western orientation" of German political leaders, he believed that *Ostpolitik* had "worrisome aspects." Kissinger was particularly concerned that Germany might try to act as a mediator between West and East, impairing America's leadership in Western Europe and the U.S. posture in dealing with the communist East. It should be noted, however, that Brandt was absolutely loyal to the Western alliance and understood that without an American presence in Europe his *Ostpolitik* would never succeed. Nevertheless, the West German chancellor also assumed that sooner rather than later the U.S. presence in Europe would be reduced or perhaps ended and that the FRG should establish an independent and influential role.

There were obvious similarities as well as clear differences between French détente and German *Ostpolitik*. More ambitious, though less effective in its practical results, the French approach sought to make international cooperation conditional upon its serving French national goals. De Gaulle perceived détente as a step toward the development of a fully restored, powerful, and French-led Europe. His aim was to overcome the Cold War status quo, which would prolong superpower control over Europe. *Ostpolitik* concentrated on more practical results (normalization of relations, treaties, trade) and demonstrated more devotion to Europe's transatlantic relations, particularly to the U.S.-European security link. At the same time the final vision of *Ostpolitik* was the realization of the German national goal—reunification—and the creation of a united Europe prepared by gradual rapprochement and made inevitable and acceptable to both the Soviets and the Americans.

The French and Germans, although by divergent means and in different ways, tried to prevent the United States from acting in European affairs (in the French case even in international affairs) without European consent. This effort promoted the emancipation of Western Europe from the United States and increased Western Europe's attractiveness for the eastern part of the continent. The loosening of super-power control over Europe was to be filled by a pan-European system. This new Europe was to speak with one powerful voice and required increasing coordination of French and German policies. While it was primarily addressed to Eastern Europe, French détente and German *Ostpolitik* paved a way for close Franco-German cooperation in European affairs and contributed to the development of European unification. Both developments have been good for the peace and stability of Europe and the world.

—PETER RAINOW,
SAN MATEO, CALIFORNIA

Viewpoint:
No. Western European nations ultimately failed to establish a middle position in the Cold War and harmed their true interests and alliance relationships in the process.

The European position during the Cold War was hardly enviable. Surrounded by the unprecedented ruin of World War II (1939–1945), Europeans were suddenly caught in the middle of another, potentially even greater, catastrophe not of their own making, one that would most probably be fought on their own territory and that would most likely have resulted in even greater destruction. Making matters worse, Europe's fate was not being decided in Europe but rather in Moscow and Washington, whose record on attentive listening to European concerns was far from Europe's liking. Once the Cold War thawed in the early 1960s, it seemed possible for Europe to try to explore a middle path between Moscow and Washington. To many Europeans the American approach to the Russians was either too simplistic or too dangerous, or both. America's answer to the challenges posed by the Soviet Union too often seemed to end up in confrontation or quagmire. In Europe one often saw Washington as being the protagonist in the Berlin Wall Crisis (1961) or the Cuban Missile Crisis (1962). The unfolding of a war in Vietnam (ended 1975) only helped to undermine European confidence in America's willingness to live peacefully with the Soviets. With such a seemingly unproductive record, it should not be surprising that German chancellor Willy Brandt's *Ostpolitik* (Eastern Policy) and French president Charles de Gaulle's offer to Moscow of "détente, entente, and cooperation" arose as alternative models. Each claimed to offer a rational, sustainable middle position toward the Soviets that was less dangerous and more productive.

TREATY OF ELYSÉE

On 22 January 1963 France and Germany issued a joint declaration of cooperation that included a statement on foreign policy and defense:

Convinced that the reconciliation of the German people and the French people, ending a centuries-old rivalry, constitutes an historic event which profoundly transforms the relations between the two peoples,

Aware of the solidarity uniting the two peoples, as much from the point of view of their security as from the point of view of their economic and cultural development,

Noting in particular that youth has recognised this solidarity and is called upon to play a decisive role in the consolidation of Franco-German friendship,

Recognising that a reinforcing of cooperation between the two countries constitutes an indispensable stage on the way to a united Europe, which is the aim of the two peoples:

Have given their agreement to the organisation and principles of cooperation between the two States such as they are set out in the Treaty signed this day. . . .

Foreign Affairs

1. The two Governments will consult before any decision on all important questions of foreign policy and, in the first place, on questions of common interest, with a view to reaching as far as possible an analogous position. This consultation will bear among others on the following subjects:

   •Problems relating to the European Communities and to European political cooperation;
   •East-West relations both on the political and the economic planes;
   •Matters dealt with within the North Atlantic Treaty Organisation and the various international organisations in which the two Governments are interested, notably the Council of Europe, the Western European Union, the Organisation for Economic Cooperation and Development, the United Nations and its specialised institutions.

2. The collaboration already established in the field of information will be continued and developed between the interested services in Paris and Bonn and between missions in third countries.

3. With regard to aid to developing countries, the two Governments will systematically compare their programmes with a view to

maintaining close coordination. They will study the possibility of undertaking joint projects. Several ministerial departments being competent for these questions, on the French side as on the German side, it will be for the two Foreign Ministers to determine together the practical bases of this collaboration.

4. The two Governments will study jointly the means of reinforcing their cooperation in other important sectors of economic policy, such as agricultural and forestry policy, energy, the problems of communications and transport and industrial development, within the framework of the Common Market, as well as the policy of export credits.

Defence

I. The aims pursued in this field will be the following:

1. In the field of strategy and tactics, the competent authorities of the two countries will endeavour to bring their doctrines closer together with a view to reaching common conceptions. Franco-German institutes of operational research will be set up.

2. Exchanges of personnel between the armies will be increased. They will concern in particular instructors and students of the general staff colleges. They can include the temporary detachment of entire units. In order to facilitate these exchanges, an effort will be made by both sides with a view to the practical teaching of the languages of the trainees.

3. With regard to armaments, the two Governments will endeavour to organise work in common from the stage of drawing up appropriate armaments plans and of the preparation of plans for financing them.

To this end, mixed commissions will study current researches on these plans in the two countries and will present proposals to the ministries who will examine them at their quarterly meetings and will give the necessary directives for application.

II. The governments will institute a study of the conditions in which Franco-German collaboration can be established in the field of defence.

Source: "The Treaty of Elysée . . . The Real Heart of Europe," Sovereignty <http://www.sovereignty.org.uk/siteinfo/newsround/elysee.html>.

INDEPENDENT FOREIGN POLICY

Yet, no matter how high-minded the attempts at carving out a third path might have been, they were fundamentally flawed. These approaches really can be defended only by ignoring a key element of East-West relations. Surely, Washington's policies irritated and frightened Europe, and they often might have appeared to have been oversimplified, but they were flawed more in their execution than in their intention. Even at its most vitriolic, the American stance toward the Soviets allowed for coexistence: the "bomb Moscow" extremists in the United States might well have been abhorrent to Europeans, but their influence in Washington was always negligible. What the "middle path" lobby overlooked was the fact that the United States and Europe had much more in common than either of them had with the Soviets. The European approach to the question of the Soviet Union was critically flawed, just as the appeasers' policy had been in the 1930s: these "middle position" Europeans assumed that in working with the Union of Soviet Socialist Republics (U.S.S.R.), they were dealing with a power essentially similar to them. The Soviet Union and its occupied neighbors were fundamentally different from the West and were uninterested in peaceful coexistence.

This observation can be seen briefly by examining what made the Soviets "tick." When the Soviet Union collapsed in the 1990s, one of the most profound surprises came from one of the most mundane of discoveries. Former Soviet factories and business enterprises soon became the object of Western entrepreneurial visions. Westerners believed that all that was needed was some Western know-how and the problems of Soviet economics would quickly be solved. Yet, it was not long before the profound character of the problem was revealed. As enterprises were scrutinized for their potential under Western direction, it became increasingly obvious that they had been managed since the Bolshevik Revolution (1917) as worker-directed enterprises. True, there was a level of repression that seemed contrary to the idea of a worker's paradise, but it was also discovered that to a great extent many of the inefficiencies arose out of a deliberate intent to consider worker's perspectives on questions of the business. In short, the West was shocked to discover that the communists actually seemed to believe in what they said. During the Cold War the West never believed anything of the sort; it had convinced itself that all Soviet discussion of Marxism was simply window dressing. This conclusion was not just made by hawks who saw the Soviets as an implacable enemy and inveterate liars, but also by doves who rejected—out of hand—right-wing warnings of Soviet dreams of world domination: any attribution of ideological considerations of the Kremlin was heavily discounted as right-wing hyperbole. So too was the genuine nature of Marxism, discounted by those such as Brandt and de Gaulle, who held that discussions with the Soviets were essentially the same as those with the Swedes or the Japanese. They did not—indeed could not—consider that internal Soviet decision making was as likely to be colored by considerations of Marxist dialectic as by *raison d'état*.

Indeed, the collapse of the Soviet Union reflected the central importance of Marxism-Leninism to the Soviet leadership. The only justification for the regime was its ideological basis: once the inadequacy of that justification was acknowledged, the regime completely collapsed.

Europe's failure to take the ideological aspect of the Soviet Union seriously meant that the possibility of a middle position toward the Soviets was, in negotiating terms, a "non-starter." The potential for a European-Soviet axis that was sufficiently different in character from any that might emerge between the United States and the Soviet Union or the wider West and the Soviet Union was close to zero. Long-term relationships between states have been based upon some kind of mutual interest in their maintenance. The North Atlantic Treaty Organization (NATO), for example, has lasted—even after the end of the Soviet threat—because it represents the defense of Western liberal democratic market societies. Common interests can even bring adversaries together into a tense but durable dialogue. The balance of terror between NATO and the Warsaw Pact sustained their relationship. Relationships that are based upon fleeting fears or opportunities rarely last because there is no interest to maintain them over the vicissitudes of time. The only durable relationship that could emerge between the West and the Soviet Union would have to be based upon a recognition that peaceful coexistence was desirable. The Soviets only entered such agreements under the duress placed upon them by a West whose economic and military power was vastly greater than their own. A divided West under the leadership of Bonn or Paris (or London, for that matter) did not have the weight to command Soviet respect. Such an arrangement could only offer Moscow a divided and weakened West, which certainly made Brandt's or de Gaulle's proposals attractive to Moscow but not especially beneficial to Europe or the United States.

Some facts are unavoidable. As Frederick the Great observed in the eighteenth century, diplomacy without arms is like music without instruments. As blunt as it may sound, it was the united strength of NATO that made the rocky NATO-Warsaw Pact relationship endure.

Moreover, although the largest numbers of ground troops in NATO were European, it was the American backbone of the alliance that made it formidable. Although in the 1960s no one in

INDEPENDENT FOREIGN POLICY

the West knew that the Warsaw Pact was as inept as it was revealed to be after the Soviet collapse, the relative strength of the two alliances was better known in Moscow. If NATO could have been weakened by a decrease in the American commitment to Europe, then Moscow would have gained substantially. Had the Europeans' pursuit of a middle position reached the point of alienating Washington, then there could have been serious repercussions. If the Americans decided to lower their commitment to Europe's defense, and there certainly were enough isolationists in America to make the case politically appealing, no doubt the security of Europe would have been seriously undermined. The level of European defense commitments in the 1960s and 1970s was already so high that it seems improbable that Europeans could have made up for any American withdrawal. Certainly, this conclusion is the old "Cold Warrior" argument against the establishment of a middle position, but that does not make it any less true.

This somewhat simple point might well have been obscured by attempts to explain away American frictions with the Soviet Union by European and other observers. Much European criticism of the American stance toward Moscow held the somewhat contradictory claims that either unsophisticated Americans did not understand the complexities of Marxism-Leninism or that they were making more of the differences between themselves and the Communists. The Americans, it seemed, did not understand that the Soviet Union was just another state, albeit one with an adversary ideology, and they feared it too much. Yet, sorting through the rubble of the Soviet Union, it appears that the Americans somehow understood the difference between the West and the East quite well. The difference between East and West was so profound that there was no room for a separate relationship between parts of the West and the Soviets. Any middle position under European leadership would have only divided NATO. Of course, NATO, as an alliance principally of liberal democracies, had assets that accrued to the preservation of a unified Western front that served as a model for the subjects of the Eastern Bloc. That model certainly had its value in the ideological side of the Cold War, but as seen from the Kremlin, it was the military strength of the alliance that truly mattered.

–PHIL GILTNER,
ALBANY ACADEMY

References

Willy Brandt, *My Life in Politics* (London & New York: Hamilton, 1992).

Edward E. Kolodziej, *French International Policy under de Gaulle and Pompidou: The Politics of Grandeur* (Ithaca, N.Y.: Cornell University Press, 1974).

John Newhouse, *De Gaulle and the Anglo-Saxons* (London: Deutsch, 1970; New York: Viking, 1970).

Roger Tilford, ed., *The Ostpolitik and Political Change in Germany* (Farnborough, U.K.: Saxon House, 1975; Lexington, Mass.: Lexington Books, 1975).

Philip Windsor, *Germany and the Management of Détente* (London: Chatto & Windus, 1971; New York: Praeger, 1971).

INDEPENDENT FOREIGN POLICY

LEND-LEASE AND THE SOVIET UNION

Was the American Lend-Lease aid to the Soviet Union essential to defeating Germany?

Viewpoint: Yes. American Lend-Lease aid was decisive because it provided the Soviet Union with $11 billion worth of logistical support, weaponry, and raw materials for war industries.

Viewpoint: No. American war materials sent to the Soviet Union were often too limited in quantity and quality to make a difference in the war effort.

Although the United States remained reluctant to enter World War II (1939–1945) until after the Japanese bombing of Pearl Harbor on 7 December 1941, President Franklin D. Roosevelt nevertheless showed strong sympathy for the Allied side in the early phases of the conflict. In March 1941 he secured Congress's approval for the Lend-Lease Act, a program that allowed the United Kingdom to borrow and lease American weapons, supplies, and resources to fight its desperate battle with Nazi Germany. In April aid was extended to China, and after German leader Adolf Hitler invaded the Soviet Union in June of that year, Roosevelt offered Moscow the same arrangement. Formalized in protocols signed in late September, Lend-Lease assistance to the Union of Soviet Socialist Republics (U.S.S.R.) amounted to about $11 billion by the end of the war. (Eventually more than forty nations received Lend-Lease aid, amounting to approximately $49 billion.)

How important was Lend-Lease to the Soviet war effort? A revisionist view has downplayed its importance, maintaining that American aid to the U.S.S.R. was a proverbial drop in the bucket compared to the Soviet Union's enormous sacrifices and huge wartime industrial output. According to this view, U.S. aid to the U.S.S.R. deserves little credit for the final victory.

The more traditional view insists, however, that, despite impressive Soviet production figures, American resources were essential in making them possible. On the battlefield U.S. technology made a vital contribution to Soviet mobility and communications, while shipments of tanks and planes played a notable, if not dominant, role in combat operations. Even if Lend-Lease was more important in logistical areas, its role in the outcome of the war was undeniable.

Viewpoint:
Yes. American Lend-Lease aid was decisive because it provided the Soviet Union with $11 billion worth of logistical support, weaponry, and raw materials for war industries.

The American Lend-Lease program made a crucial contribution to the Soviet Union's victory over Nazi Germany in World War II (1939–1945). Although Cold War antagonism later made the Soviet government reluctant to acknowledge its importance, the United States's delivery of $11.3 billion in military hardware, raw materials, food, and supplies kept the Red Army fighting and Soviet factories running. Without it the victorious Soviet march to Berlin would either have taken much longer or never have succeeded at all.

Those who question the significance of Lend-Lease usually argue, correctly, that the Red Army achieved much on its own without Western aid. No foreign troops fought alongside the Soviets on the Eastern Front, and the Union of Soviet Socialist Republics (U.S.S.R.) suffered approximately 25 million deaths in the war with the Germans. Much of the Red Army's military hardware was of original Soviet manufacture, and many of the leading weapons in its arsenal, including the T-34 tank and the Tiupolev and Illiushin aircraft models, were of original Soviet design. While no one can dispute these facts, it is important to realize that in modern warfare victory demands far more. Especially in the circumstances of "total war" that dominated and defined World War II, victory depended on logistical support for armies of millions, mass mobility for forces arrayed over thousands of square miles, and huge quantities of raw materials for vast war industries. It was in these three categories that American aid to the U.S.S.R. made all the difference.

In terms of logistics the Red Army quite simply depended on American farms and factories for its needs. Soviet agriculture had been problematic since the Revolution of 1917 and was even more troubled by the collectivization of farmland and related government policies in the late 1920s and early 1930s. On the eve of World War II the Soviet Union's agricultural sector still produced less than that of the Russian Empire in 1913. To make this handicap worse, Germany's early successes in the months after its invasion in June 1941 deprived the U.S.S.R. of much of its best farmland. Ukraine, containing some of the world's richest earth and producing much of the Soviet Union's

wheat, potatoes, and livestock, remained under continuous German occupation from the late summer of 1941 until the end of 1943, as did other important farmlands in the Baltic States and the western half of European Russia. In the winter of 1941–1942 starvation and malnutrition were serious national problems in the U.S.S.R.

Ultimately, American food deliveries alleviated the situation. Between late 1941 and the end of the war some 3.8 million tons of foodstuffs arrived from the United States in shipments that included not just staples such as wheat and flour but also such richer items as meat, eggs, sausage, and sugar. A quick calculation demonstrates that the amount of food delivered under the auspices of American Lend-Lease was enough to supply a half a pound of sustenance to 12 million soldiers every day for three and a half years. If, as nineteenth-century French emperor Napoleon Bonaparte said, an army fights on its stomach, then this American generosity was no small contribution to the Soviet war effort. While the Red Army's food supply was assured, American farms also fed workers in the Soviet armaments industry, starving inhabitants of the besieged city of Leningrad, and even prisoners in the gulag (the vast network of Soviet slave-labor camps), in addition to millions of others.

Having lost most of their textile industry to German occupation, the Soviets also received huge amounts of finished cloth, uniforms, and combat boots from the United States. Many a Red Army soldier woke up in an American canvas tent to go into battle in an American-manufactured uniform and one of the 15 million pairs of American boots supplied under Lend-Lease. Once again, not all of these supplies were for army consumption. When U.S. vice president Henry Wallace visited the Far Eastern Soviet city of Magadan, the administrative center of the vast Kolyma slave-labor camp, in May 1944, he noticed "free laborers" (actually prisoners whose real status was cleverly concealed) wearing American boots on their way to the mines.

The Red Army's mass mobility also depended heavily on Lend-Lease. A major deficiency in the Soviets' military operations early in the war was their inability to move large numbers of troops and equipment as fast as the Germans could. Leading proponents of military mechanization had been eliminated for political reasons in the purge of the Red Army's officer corps in 1937–1938, and their ideas were not implemented. The underdeveloped railroad network did not help—much of it quickly came under German control in any case—and the relative lack of trucks and other

LEND-LEASE ACT

An Act

Further to promote the defense of the United States, and for other purposes.

Be it enacted by the Senate and House of Representatives of the United States of America in Congress assembled, That this Act may be cited as "An Act to Promote the Defense of the United States".

SEC. 2. As used in this Act—

(a) The term "defense article" means—

(1) Any weapon, munition, aircraft, vessel, or boat;

(2) Any machinery, facility, tool, material, or supply necessary for the manufacture, production, processing, repair, servicing, or operation of any article described in this subsection;

(3) Any component material or part of or equipment for any article described in this subsection;

(4) Any agricultural, industrial or other commodity or article for defense.

Such term "defense article" includes any article described in this subsection: Manufactured or procured pursuant to section 3, or to which the United States or any foreign government has or hereafter acquires title, possession, or control.

(b) The term "defense information" means any plan, specification, design, prototype, or information pertaining to any defense article.

SEC. 3. (a) Notwithstanding the provisions of any other law, the President may, from time to time, when he deems it in the interest of national defense, authorize the Secretary Of War, the Secretary of the Navy, or the head of any other department or agency of the Government—

(1) To manufacture in arsenals, factories, and shipyards under their jurisdiction, or otherwise procure, to the extent to which funds are made available therefor, or contracts are authorized from time to time by the Congress, or both, any defense article for the government of any country whose defense the President deems vital to the defense of the United States.

(2) To sell, transfer title to, exchange, lease, lend, or otherwise dispose of, to any such government any defense article, but no defense article not manufactured or procured under paragraph (1) shall in any way be disposed of under this paragraph, except after consultation with the Chief of Staff of the Army or the Chief of Naval Operations of the Navy, or

both. The value of defense articles disposed of in any way under authority of this paragraph, and procured from funds heretofore appropriated, shall not exceed $1,300,000,000. The value of such defense articles shall be determined by the head of the department or agency concerned or such other department, agency or officer as shall be designated in the manner provided in the rules and regulations issued hereunder. Defense articles procured from funds hereafter appropriated to any department or agency of the Government, other than from funds authorized to be appropriated under this Act, shall not be disposed of in any way under authority of this paragraph except to the extent hereafter authorized by the Congress in the Acts appropriating such funds or otherwise.

(3) To test, inspect, prove, repair, outfit, recondition, or otherwise to place in good working order, to the extent to which funds are made available therefor, or contracts are authorized from time to time by the Congress, or both, any defense article for any such government, or to procure any or all such services by private contract.

(4) To communicate to any such government any defense information pertaining to any defense article furnished to such government under paragraph (2) of this subsection.

(5) To release for export any defense article disposed of in any way under this subsection to any such government.

(b) The terms and conditions upon which any such foreign government receives any aid authorized under subsection (a) shall be those which the President deems satisfactory, and the benefit to the United States may be payment or repayment in kind or property, or any other direct or indirect benefit which the President deems satisfactory.

(c) After June 30, 1943, or after the passage of a concurrent resolution by the two Houses before June 30, 1943, which declares that the powers conferred by or pursuant to subsection (a) are no longer necessary to promote the defense of the United States, neither the President nor the head of any department or agency shall exercise any of the powers conferred by or pursuant to subsection (a) except that until July 1, 1946, any of such powers may be exercised to the extent necessary to carry out a contract or agreement with such a foreign government made before July 1,1943, or before the passage of such concurrent resolution, whichever is the earlier.

(d) Nothing in this Act shall be construed to authorize or to permit the authorization of convoying vessels by naval vessels of the United States.

(e) Nothing in this Act shall be construed to authorize or to permit the authorization of the entry of any American vessel into a combat area in violation of section 3 of the Neutrality Act of 1939.

SEC. 4. All contracts or agreements made for the disposition of any defense article or defense information pursuant to section 3 shall contain a clause by which the foreign government undertakes that it will not, without the consent of the President, transfer title to or possession of such defense article or defense information by gift, sale, or otherwise, or permit its use by anyone not an officer, employee, or agent of such foreign government.

SEC. 5. (a) The Secretary of War, the Secretary of the Navy, or the head of any other department or agency of the Government involved shall when any such defense article or defense information is exported, immediately inform the department or agency designated by the President to administer section 6 of the Act of July 2, 1940 (54 Stat. 714) of the quantities, character, value, terms of disposition and destination of the article and information so exported.

(b) The President from time to time, but not less frequently than once every ninety days, shall transmit to the Congress a report of operations under this Act except such information as he deems incompatible with the public interest to disclose. Reports provided for under this subsection shall be transmitted to the Secretary of the Senate or the Clerk of the House of Representatives, as the case may be, if the Senate or the House of Representatives, as the case may be, is not in session.

SEC. 6. (a) There is hereby authorized to be appropriated from time to time, out of any money in the Treasury not otherwise appropriated, such amounts as may be necessary to carry out the provisions and accomplish the purposes of this Act.

(b) All money and all property which is converted into money received under section 3 from any government shall, with the approval of the Director of the Budget, revert to the respective appropriation or appropriations out of which funds were expended with respect to the defense article or defense infor-

mation for which such consideration is received, and shall be available for expenditure for the purpose for which such expended funds were appropriated by law, during the fiscal year in which such funds are received and the ensuing fiscal year; but in no event shall any funds so received be available for expenditure after June 30, 1946.

SEC. 7. The Secretary of War, the Secretary of the Navy, and the head of the department or agency shall in all contracts or agreements for the disposition of any defense article or defense information fully protect the rights of all citizens of the United States who have patent rights in and to any such article or information which is hereby authorized to be disposed of and the payments collected for royalties on such patents shall be paid to the owners and holders of such patents.

SEC. 8. The Secretaries of War and of the Navy are hereby authorized to purchase or otherwise acquire arms, ammunition, and implements of war produced within the jurisdiction of any country to which section 3 is applicable, whenever the President deems such purchase or acquisition to be necessary in the interests of the defense of the United States.

SEC. 9. The President may, from time to time, promulgate such rules and regulations as may be necessary and proper to carry out any of the provisions of this Act; and he may exercise any power or authority conferred on him by this Act through such department, agency, or officer as he shall direct.

SEC. 10. Nothing in this Act shall be construed to change existing law relating to the use of the land and naval forces of the United States, except insofar as such use relates to the manufacture, procurement, and repair of defense articles, the communication of information and other noncombatant purposes enumerated in this Act.

SEC. 11. If any provision of this Act or the application of such provision to any circumstance shall be held invalid, the validity of the remainder of the Act and the applicability of such provision to other circumstances shall not be affected thereby.

Approved, March 11, 1941.

Source: "Public Laws," in United States Statutes at Large Containing the Laws and Concurrent Resolutions Enacted During the First Session of the Seventy-Seventh Congress of the United States of America, 1941-1942, and Treaties, International Agreements Other than Treaties, and Proclamations, volume 55 (Washington, D.C.: Government Printing Office, 1942), pp. 31–33.

motor vehicles limited what the Soviets could do on the battlefield. Indeed, in 1941 they still relied heavily on horse-drawn carts, infantry marches, wireless radio, and personal messengers—technologies that failed to keep pace with modern mechanized warfare and resulted in many casualties. Outpacing their confused and disorganized opponents, the Germans took more than 3 million prisoners in great battles of encirclement between June and October 1941 and killed or wounded another 2 million Soviet soldiers between June and December. Mimicking the German *blitzkrieg* (lightning war) technique—which depended not only on tank breakthroughs and aerial attacks but also, and vitally, on the quick and coordinated movement of mobile infantry and support troops—was impossible until American Lend-Lease provided the Soviet Union with more than 350,000 heavy trucks, 78,000 jeeps, 13,000 railway cars, and 423,000 field telephones. To make the vehicles run, the United States supplied more than 2 million tons of oil to supplement the Soviet fuel industry, which was weakened by its poor infrastructure and by the destruction of some of the oil facilities in the North Caucasus in the summer of 1942.

Rolling on American wheels, propelled by American fuel, and talking on American receivers, vast Soviet armies were able to surround the German forces at Stalingrad in November 1942, turn back a renewed German offensive at Kursk in July 1943, and, using the Germans' own *blitzkrieg* tactics, pursue the retreating enemy out of the U.S.S.R., across Eastern Europe, and all the way to Berlin by April 1945. Without this maneuverability the Red Army stood much less chance of facing down the Germans and would have had to walk most of the way from the gates of Moscow to the heart of Germany. Like food and boots, however, American motor transport shipped under Lend-Lease also found its way into nonmilitary operations. When the Soviet government ordered the removal of the Chechens, Crimean Tatars, and other indigenous peoples from their homelands in 1944, they were moved out in American-built Studebaker trucks. Mobility, a key factor in modern warfare, and apparently in modern governance, came to the Soviets from Detroit.

As impressive as Soviet war production was, much of it too depended on Lend-Lease shipments of American raw materials. At a time when much of the U.S.S.R.'s railroad network, rolling stock, and mining facilities were under German control, nearly 2.5 million tons of American steel and 250,000 tons of American aluminum arrived at Soviet plants to be turned into tanks and planes. Although not all of the steel went into tank production, the amount delivered to the U.S.S.R. was enough to manufacture 70,000 T-34 tanks, assuming each one weighed thirty-five tons. Deliveries of rubber, plastic, engine parts, machine tools, and other components were also enormous. The Soviet government later claimed that it produced more than 30,000 tanks and 40,000 planes in 1943–1945, but it never disclosed how many could have been produced without American steel and aluminum.

Outside of these vital logistical categories, American deliveries of finished weaponry were substantial in volume and tactical importance. While most of the Red Army's tanks were of domestic manufacture (albeit with American steel much of the time), about 12,000 American tanks, self-propelled guns, and similar combat vehicles were shipped to the U.S.S.R. during the war—a figure equal to 40 percent of Moscow's claimed domestic tank production in 1943–1945. Further, the Soviets received more than 11,000 American combat aircraft, a number that accounted for about one out of every five planes in the Red Air Force by 1945. In elite fighter squadrons, long-range bomber commands, strategic air defense units, and naval air formations the contingent of American aircraft was even higher, sometimes composing as much as 60 or 70 percent of a unit's total strength. The record for the most enemy aircraft shot down by an American fighter plane still belongs to Soviet ace G. A. Rechkalov, who destroyed fifty German planes in his P-39. Soviet armed forces also received 131,000 Thompson submachine guns, 8,200 anti-aircraft guns, 300,000 tons of explosives, 22 torpedo boats, 28 frigates, and 105 submarines from the United States.

American Lend-Lease aid to the Soviet Union was a decisive factor in winning World War II. The total monetary value of this aid was itself 13 percent higher than the total U.S. defense budget in 1950. The successful Soviet offensives, which began with the Stalingrad campaign in late 1942, depended on concentrated armor and air power, mass mobility, and millions of well-fed and -clothed soldiers. None of these assets could have materialized without the huge quantities of aluminum and steel, trucks and fuel, food and boots, and tanks and planes that came directly from the American heartland to the Russian steppe. Nor can one honestly ignore—as the Red Army Museum in Moscow continues to do six decades later—the vital use of American resources and industry by the Soviets in their desperate battle with the Germans.

—PAUL DU QUENOY,
GEORGETOWN UNIVERSITY

LEND-LEASE AND
THE SOVIET UNION

Viewpoint:
No. American war materials sent to the Soviet Union were often too limited in quantity and quality to make a difference in the war effort.

Under the Lend-Lease Act of 11 March 1941 President Franklin D. Roosevelt was granted the authority to "sell, transfer title to, exchange, lease, lend or otherwise dispose of" material to any country whose defense was deemed vital for the United States's own security. The President could decide how this loan would be repaid, either in concessions or in kind, if at all. A fortnight later Congress approved an initial appropriation of $7 billion in aid to Britain. Over the course of the war, aid in the form of munitions, raw materials, food supplies, finished goods, and industrial equipment, amounting to roughly $49 billion, or 15 percent of the total American wartime expenditure, flowed from the United States to more than forty countries. The first and foremost recipient was the British Empire ($30 billion), followed by the Soviet Union ($11 billion), France ($3 billion), and China ($1 billion). Lend-Lease was primarily, though not exclusively, intended for the European theater and the struggle against Nazi Germany. The United States famously became "the Arsenal of Democracy."

During the war, and even more so afterward, American aid to the Soviet Union was the most controversial aspect of Lend-Lease, even though it amounted to only about 22 percent of total Lend-Lease expenditure. The Soviet Union had played an indisputably predominant role in holding down, destroying, and physically driving out the bulk of enemy forces from occupied Europe—a contribution that could only begin to be measured in the number of dead (upwards of 20 million soldiers and civilians) and material damage inflicted on the Soviet Union. How far the success of the Soviet war effort, and ultimate victory over Nazi Germany, was attributable to American aid became a contentious issue with profound political ramifications. As with all aspects of the wartime Grand Alliance, postwar discussion of Lend-Lease aid to the Soviet Union was subsumed into a wider ideologically driven Cold War analysis, and behind all the scholarly window dressing it could ultimately be reduced to a simple, and somewhat invidious, argument: who did more to defeat Nazi Germany, the Soviet Union or the United States?

Predictably, Soviet scholarship and official histories, if they mentioned American aid at all, sought to minimize the contribution that Lend-Lease made to the Soviet war effort.

Acknowledgment of American aid was grudging and perfunctory. One official history of the war published in the Soviet Union in the 1980s claimed that Lend-Lease was "in no way meaningful and could have [had] no decisive influence on the course of the Great Patriotic War." The Soviet critique of Lend-Lease rested on three propositions: that Lend-Lease aid was insignificant relative to overall domestic production; that the equipment delivered was often of poor quality; and that shipments were invariably delayed, even canceled, and fell far short of Soviet requirements. Americans, for their part, especially in the 1950s and 1960s, overplayed the significance of Lend-Lease. Wild claims were made that Lend-Lease, and therefore the United States, had saved the Soviet Union from defeat at the hands of the Nazis. Less ambitious, though equally sweeping, claims were made concerning Lend-Lease's contribution to Soviet offensive capabilities—that without American aid Soviet forces would have become bogged down in a debilitating war of attrition halfway across Russia. Ideology played a part in these interpretations, both sides out to prove the inherent superiority of one political and economic model (liberal democratic vs. Marxist-Leninist) over the other.

The contention here, however, is whether American Lend-Lease was "essential" to winning the war; in other words, whether it was an absolutely necessary factor, an indispensable component of victory. Or put differently: without Lend-Lease World War II could not have been won by the Allies.

At first sight, statistics on Lend-Lease to the Soviet Union are impressive. From $11.3 billion (17 million tons) of Lend-Lease aid, the Soviet Union was supplied with 11,000 combat aircraft, 12,000 tanks and self-propelled guns, 78,000 jeeps, 32,000 motorcycles, 350,000 heavy trucks, 1,966 locomotives, 15 million pairs of boots, 250,000 tons of Spam, 300,000 tons of fat, 65,000 tons of beef, 700,000 tons of sugar, 400,000 tons of copper and bronze, and 250,000 tons of aluminum. Aid, therefore, was not only in the form of military material; food, for example, accounted for a quarter, by weight, of total deliveries to the Soviet Union.

These totals by themselves, however, tell only part of the story. As a proportion of domestic production Lend-Lease imports were reasonably low. Soviet historians invariably stood by the figure of 4 percent, though it is more likely to have been somewhere in the region of 7 to 10 percent. Even when expressed as a percentage of industrial production, however, such statistics on Lend-Lease remain misleading. Totals expressed in dollars or in tonnage do not give an idea of the real value of Lend-Lease aid to the Soviet war effort. Certain items, such as aluminum, were scarce and highly sought after. With some commodities—for example, motor vehicles and telephone wire—Lend-Lease aid made up a far higher proportion of total output than for others, such as steel. Certain raw materials and machinery helped expand domestic production, and elsewhere Lend-Lease aid helped overcome supply "bottlenecks" or fill gaps in Soviet production. Food and petroleum made up the bulk of aid well into 1943. Their contribution cannot be measured in battlefield strengths. Nor do crude statistics express the qualitative value of Lend-Lease aid, especially technologically. On the other hand, it is doubtful whether certain deliveries had any wartime value at all, the most famous example being that of a Ford tire plant, transported in its entirety to the Soviet Union, which did not produce a single tire during the war. An element of misuse and waste also has to be factored in, especially during the most critical phase of the shipping crisis in 1942–1943. Moreover, it is probable that certain items, especially during the latter stages of the war, were superfluous to Soviet needs. Long after the Soviets had achieved overwhelming air superiority over the *Luftwaffe* (German air force), aircraft continued to be delivered in large quantities.

In determining how "essential" Lend-Lease was to victory, it is the timing of deliveries in relation to the course of events on the Eastern Front that is the most important consideration. There were three key developments on the Eastern Front that shaped the course of the conflict: the successful defense of Moscow between October and December 1941, as a result of which the initial German onslaught was temporarily halted and the Soviet Union survived to fight on into another campaigning season; the battle for Stalingrad between August 1942 and February 1943, seen as the turning point in the war, which again halted a phenomenal German advance and resulted in the complete destruction of a German army and the Soviets taking the offensive; and the unsuccessful German Kursk-Orel offensive of July–August 1943, after which Germany never regained the initiative.

Few, if any, historians would claim that American Lend-Lease played anything but a minor role in saving the Soviet Union from the brink of defeat in the winter of 1941. Lend-Lease deliveries to the Soviet Union in 1941 were minimal. Of the 150 aircraft, 180 armored vehicles, and 8,300 motor vehicles sent by the Americans to the Soviet Union in 1941, only 20 percent had in fact arrived by the end of the year. Being too little and too late to have had any appreciable impact on the outcome of that winter's campaigning, this aid was largely symbolic. As recent post-Soviet studies have shown, deliveries at the

end of 1941 represented less than 0.5 percent of what the Soviets had requested. Although deliveries increased in 1942, they were still far too limited for it to be said with any certainty that they had anything more than a modest share in ensuring Soviet military successes and the general improvement in the Red Army's performance. American production was unable to keep up with Soviet orders as it was, and America's own rearmament program did little to help this situation. The United States did not have adequate ammunition stocks of its own until December 1942. Nor could shipping capacity keep up with production, a situation that was not helped by the large losses in the merchant fleet to U-boats in the Battle of the Atlantic. Claims that even limited Lend-Lease supplies gave the Soviet Union "the edge" in the Stalingrad counteroffensive are unverifiable; to say that they helped, on the other hand, is to state the obvious, given that at this stage in the war any aid helped, however small.

Not until mid 1943 did substantial amounts of Lend-Lease aid flow into the Soviet Union, reaching a peak (in terms of its dollar value) in November 1943 and remaining at high levels thereafter. The bulk of Lend-Lease aid, therefore, came after the Germans had lost the initiative on the Eastern Front and after the Soviet counterattack had begun in earnest. That is not to say that deliveries received from late 1943 onward were insignificant either quantitatively or qualitatively, or that they did not have a discernible impact on the course of the war as it moved toward its final stages. There is compelling evidence that Lend-Lease was vital in increasing the mobility of the Red Army at a time when, tactically, mobility was crucial during the campaigns of 1944 and 1945. Around 410,000 trucks and vehicles were delivered under Lend-Lease. Some 140,000 of these vehicles were imported in 1944 alone—nearly five times the number in 1942. Of the total number of motor vehicles at the Red Army's disposal at the end of the war, 33 percent had been delivered under Lend-Lease. Lend-Lease, it has been claimed, put the Red Army "on wheels." In this respect Lend-Lease in the latter part of the war can be said to have helped augment the Soviets' offensive capability, and it is conceivable that Lend-Lease deliveries were vital in bringing the war to an early conclusion. As Anastas Mikoyan, a wartime member of the Politburo and the State Committee of Defence, later admitted: "Without Lend-Lease we would certainly have had another year-and-a-half of fighting." Soviet leader Josef Stalin himself said as much at the Potsdam Conference (1945). Yet, it is one thing to say that Lend-Lease brought closer the day of victory and quite another to suppose that without it this victory would have been impossible or that the Soviets would have

been ineffective offensively and reduced to a war of attrition. No doubt one can speculate on the effect that eighteen more months would have had on the development of "miracle weapons" or even on the Nazis' atomic program, and therefore on the outcome of the war.

The only remotely convincing argument in support of Lend-Lease being "essential" to winning the war lies not in the impact that American aid had on the battlefield itself, but rather on a diplomatic level, in the effect it had on the functioning of the Soviet-American wartime alliance. During 1942 and 1943 the Soviets repeatedly requested that the Anglo-Americans open up a "Second Front"; in other words, that they carry out a large-scale invasion of mainland Western Europe. The delay in establishing this Second Front was the source of much mistrust on the part of the Soviet Union and aroused suspicions that the Western Allies were banking on the combatants on the Eastern Front bleeding each other dry. Roosevelt, conscious of this belief as well as of the possibility that the Soviet Union might conclude a separate peace with Germany as Soviet Russia had in 1918, saw in Lend-Lease a firm and tangible commitment to the Soviet Union, a gesture of goodwill and solidarity. It was, as George C. Herring in *Aid to Russia, 1941–1946: Strategy, Diplomacy, and the Origins of the Cold War* (1973) has pointed out, the "principal means of holding together the uneasy alliance until the common threat could be removed." Lend-Lease to the Soviet Union, together with strategic bombing, therefore became a surrogate for a direct, full-scale commitment of American forces earlier to the European theater.

As a symbol of Allied cooperation, however, Lend-Lease was in the long run no substitute for an actual commitment of manpower and a willingness to sacrifice lives rather than just dollars to the common cause of defeating Germany. Without Lend-Lease to the Soviet Union, however, the United States would have been com-

Workers assembling Dodge WC53 Carryall trucks like those that were shipped to the Soviet Union as part of Lend-Lease aid, circa 1943

(Library of Congress, Washington, D.C.)

LEND-LEASE AND THE SOVIET UNION

pelled, in the interests of the anti-Hitler alliance, to commit itself to an invasion of Europe at a far earlier date, at a far greater risk, and with a considerably greater loss of American lives. The path to victory, at least for the United States, would certainly have been different. The outcome of the war, however, would have remained the same.

–MATTHEW FRANK,
OXFORD UNIVERSITY

References

George C. Herring, *Aid to Russia, 1941–1946: Strategy, Diplomacy, and the Origins of the Cold War* (New York: Columbia University Press, 1973).

Roger Munting, "Lend-Lease and the Soviet War Effort," *Journal of Contemporary History,* 19 (1984): 495–510.

Hubert P. van Tuyll, *Feeding the Bear: American Aid to the Soviet Union, 1941–1945* (Westport, Conn.: Greenwood Press, 1989).

United States, President, *Report to Congress on Lend-Lease Operations,* 43 volumes (Washington, D.C.: Government Printing Office, 1941–1960).

V. F. Vorsin, "Motor Vehicle Transport Deliveries through Lend-Lease," *Journal of Slavic Military Studies,* 10 (1997): 153–175.

MODERNIZATION

Did World War I initiate radical change in the nature and functions of the European state?

Viewpoint: Yes. The demands of World War I led to permanent, massive state involvement in national economies and societies.

Viewpoint: No. The modernization of European political systems was well under way by 1914; the war just accelerated an ongoing process.

It is difficult to underestimate the transformative effects of World War I (1914–1918) on modern Europe. The intense destruction and massive consumption of resources seemed to touch every aspect of life, especially in the political arena. This chapter investigates the extent to which the war enhanced the powers of the modern bureaucratic state. Some historians feel that the state emerged all-powerful, exercising extensive control over the national economy, providing comprehensively for the welfare of its people, mobilizing labor and resources for its own purposes, and taking other measures necessary for creating and maintaining a huge military machine. The demands of the greatest war in human history up to that time left governments and societies with little other choice if they were to emerge victorious, or even simply to survive.

Many observers, however, trace the rise of the powerful bureaucratic state to nineteenth-century and early-twentieth-century roots. "Statist" policies and ideologies that embraced economic interventionism, social welfare networks, conscript armies, and centralized administrations were at work enhancing government power before 1914. Such factors as industrialization, urbanization, and technological advancement were the prime movers in the rise of powerful states.

Viewpoint:
Yes. The demands of World War I led to permanent, massive state involvement in national economies and societies.

The term *total war* was first uttered in connection with World War I (1914–1918). The war effort, with millions of heavily equipped soldiers composing huge armies, was simply unprecedented. Since 1918 there has been only one occasion where this kind of war mobilization has occurred. World War II (1939–1945) may well have eclipsed the first war in terms of its massive destructiveness and attacks on civilian populations, but this difference was one of degree, not kind. No other war has been accompanied by the same degree of political and economic effort. The question is not whether states did all they could to win a war before 1914. Certainly, they did. For example, the level of violence that accompanied the Thirty Years' War (1618–1648), with massive civilian losses and rapacious armies living off their enemies' land, could stand as an example of a form of total war. Even the conflicts of the eighteenth century were supported by the full efforts of the state. Frederick

German soldiers observing French peasants with their bread rations, circa 1915

(Roger Viollet)

II of Prussia's efforts in the Seven Years' War (1756–1763) certainly displayed an all-out effort. A more famous example would certainly be the French Revolutionary Wars, with the 1793 *levée en masse*, state direction of production, and an exhortation to citizens to "stimulate the courage of the warriors and preach the unity of the Republic and the hatred of kings." The American Civil War (1861–1865) pushed both sides to employ a broad mobilization of resources, especially in the Confederacy, which was forced to draw ever more deeply from its resource base until there was practically nothing left. Yet, these wars differed from World War I in the sense that Europeans saw the first encounter between fully industrialized nations in a full-scale mobilization. This situation was most apparent between the countries engaged on the Western Front. Heavily industrialized Germany, Britain, and France deployed huge armies in efforts that required unprecedented state involvement in the affairs of the people. As the war effort became increasingly more intense, the state found itself engaged not only in fielding armies, which was a significant enough effort, but also in monitoring and directing the consciousness of its people. Public morale and public opinion became the subjects of government policy. The newly arrived industrial state made the intensity of this effort far greater than before.

On a material level the mobilization required significant effort. World War I began with the widespread belief that it would end quickly. This belief also extended to the military, which had not planned to supply its armies beyond a few months. During the first year or so both sides scrambled to adapt to their realizations that the war was not ending, as the plan had said it would. In these circumstances no other entity—except the state—existed to meet the needs of the war. Whether the agent of centralized mobilization would be distinctly civilian, as in the case of the British Ministry of Munitions, or more clearly military, as the German *Kriegsamt* (War Office), the result was the same: there arose a newly powerful and broadly empowered state agent to direct the war effort. Until the end of 1915 the belligerents scrambled to adapt to increase the output of war matériel by simply increasing the capacity of existing arrangements. However, this policy changed. In fact, 1916 marked a watershed as the distinctly different political, economic, and military character of the war sank in for all observers. The Somme and Verdun had been incredibly bloody impasses, costing hundreds of thousands of men for no noticeable gain. The only option, it seemed, was to get more out of the home front, and the entire resources of the country would have to be thrown into the effort.

The war placed tremendous demands on the belligerents. The size of the armies alone was remarkable and had been far greater than had

MODERNIZATION

been originally expected. In 1917, 505 Allied divisions faced 369 divisions of the Central Powers (at the time a division was between 10,000 and 15,000 men). Britain had expected to field an army of 100,000, but some 5.5 million eventually served. France sent two-thirds of its male population of military age (eighteen to forty), totaling some 8 million men. Each man's equipment needs were considerable: an infantryman commonly carried eighty pounds on his back. Wagons, trucks, trains, and ships carried considerably more, as the home country struggled to meet his needs for food, clothing, ammunition, and medical care. The production of weapons and, in particular, artillery shells required significant amounts of raw materials and energy. Weapons production was remarkable. Britain, for example, started the war with a mere 1,330 machine guns, but by the end of the war had produced more than 5 million rifles, almost 250,000 machine guns, 25,000 artillery pieces, almost 3,000 tanks, and nearly 5,500 aircraft. This production also required transportation and the development and maintenance of a transportation infrastructure. This effort was hugely expensive: France's 1918 budget was thirty-six times its prewar size.

All this output wound up being centrally directed, and state bureaucracies grew to meet the need. The British Ministry of Munitions, for example, began the war in 1914 as the War Contracts Office with about 20 clerks. By the end of the war in 1918 the Ministry of Munitions employed 65,000 clerks overseeing the work of 3 million employees across the nation. Shipping, agriculture, and energy all came under government supervision. The most remarkable state intervention could be found in Germany, where the military leadership had dominated the political direction of the war effort almost from the outset. A central Office of War Materials was established in 1914, in close coordination with Germany's larger industrial concerns and under the leadership of industrialist Walther Rathenau, who became Germany's foreign minister after the war. In early fall 1916 Paul von Hindenburg and Erich Ludendorff were made supreme commanders for the war effort, and the Hindenburg Program for total mobilization was launched. A War Office was established under General Wilhelm Groener, whose sweeping powers resulted in a threefold increase in production within a year. More symbolic of the level of state intervention in the affairs of society, however, was the German government's Auxiliary Service Law of 5 December 1916, which declared that all able-bodied men between fifteen and sixty not already in the army would be liable for civilian service in support of the war effort. One ought not to think that such extreme measures were limited to Germany: Britain's Defense of the Realm Act (1914) already allowed for the War Office or Admiralty to seize factories as war necessity warranted. Later acts also controlled prices and profits.

Given the ambiguity of the war's origins, it should not be surprising that governments paid attention to promoting their own views of the justice of the war cause. Propaganda until late 1916 promoted the image of enemy venality or the justness of the home nation's cause. Propaganda tended to be ad hoc, or representative of a form of "self-mobilization" by agencies such as the press or the churches. Of course, the state censored the news and controlled the release of information that might have "promoted defeatism," but the efforts of the state were less coordinated than they became in the beginning of 1917. With the intensification of the war effort the state's involvement in propaganda became more coordinated and was directed inward. The governments of Britain and France both created semiofficial "pressure groups" to coordinate public opinion. As far as the public was concerned, the link between these groups, the French *Union des Grandes Associations contre la Propagande Ennemie* (Union of Great Associations against Enemy Propaganda, UGACPE) and the British National War Aims Committee, and the government was always murky, but in fact, these were directed from the most central government agencies. The UGACPE, for example, was monitored by a representative of French premier Georges Clemenceau and an officer from the French Maison de la Presse (Press Office).

Bodies such as the German War Office or the French UGACPE were wartime exigencies, and their persistence beyond the war years was hardly expected. Yet, it ought to be remembered that certain techniques and practices did not go unlearned and unrepeated. If Britain could suddenly support a bureaucracy of 60,000 clerks, it was not unnatural to address the problems of the postwar world with a similar tool. The state learned how to grow in the war, how to direct its efforts, and how to sustain itself. New methods of management and taxation were devised during the war and would be applied to problems of the peace. The popular support for the war effort, best exemplified by the politicking of British prime minister David Lloyd George, became the norm for politics in France and Britain. The war had increased the stake of all citizens in public affairs and thus became a tremendously democratizing experience. In the years following the war the state increasingly was called upon to promote its view of events. Moreover, in the disrupted postwar world the state became more involved in the material aspects of peoples' lives, as the well-being of veterans, war widows, and

THE GERMAN IDEA

U.S. ambassador to Germany James W. Gerard recounts in his memoirs German government involvement in business during World War I:

Not long after the commencement of the war the Germans placed a prohibitive tariff upon the import of certain articles of luxury such as perfumes; their object, of course, being to keep the German people from sending money out of the country and wasting their money in useless expenditures. At the same time a great institution was formed called the Central Einkauf Gesellschaft. This body, formed under government auspices of men appointed from civil life, is somewhat similar to one of our national defence boards. Every import of raw material into Germany falls into the hands of this central buying company, and if a German desires to buy any raw material for use in his factory he must buy it through this central board.

I have talked with members of this board and they all unite in the belief that this system will be continued after the war.

For instance, if a man in Germany wishes to buy an automobile or a pearl necklace or a case of perfumery, he will be told, "You can buy this if you can buy it in Germany. But if you have to send to America for the automobile, if you have to send to Paris for the pearls or the perfumery, you cannot buy them." In this way the gold supply of Germany will be husbanded and the people will either be prevented from making comparatively useless expenditures or compelled to spend money to benefit home industry.

On the other hand, when a man desires to buy some raw material, for example, copper, cotton, leather, wheat or something of that kind, he will not be allowed to buy abroad on his own hook. The Central Einkauf Gesellschaft will see that all those desiring to buy cotton or copper put in their orders on or before a certain date. When the orders are all in, the quantities called for will be added up by this central board; and then one man, representing the board, will be in a position to go to America to purchase the four million bales of cotton or two hundred million pounds of copper.

The German idea is that this one board will be able to force the sellers abroad to compete against each other in their eagerness to sell. The one German buyer will know about the lowest price at which the sellers can sell their product. By the buyer's standing out alone with this great order the Germans believe that the sellers, one by one, will fall into his hands and sell their product at a price below that which they could obtain if the individual sellers of America were meeting the individual buyers of Germany in the open market.

When the total amount of the commodity ordered has been purchased, it will be divided up among the German buyers who put in their orders with the central company, each order being charged with its proportionate share of the expenses of the commission and, possibly, an additional sum for the benefit of the treasury of the Empire. . . .

The government handling of exchange during the war was another example of the use of the centralised power of the Government for the benefit of the whole nation.

In the first year of the war, when I desired money to spend in Germany, I drew a check on my bank in New York in triplicate and sent a clerk with it to the different banks in Berlin, to obtain bids in marks, selling it then, naturally, to the highest bidder. But soon the Government stepped in. The Imperial Bank was to fix a daily rate of exchange, and banks and individuals were forbidden to buy or sell at a different rate. That this fixed rate was a false one, fixed to the advantage of Germany, I proved at the time when the German official rate was 5.52 marks for a dollar, by sending my American checks to Holland, buying Holland money with them and German money with the Holland money, in this manner obtaining 5.74 marks for each dollar. And just before leaving Germany I sold a lot of American gold to a German bank at the rate of 6.42 marks per dollar, although on that day the official rate was 5.52 and although the buyer of the gold, because the export of gold was forbidden, would have to lose interest on the money paid me or on the gold purchased, until the end of the war. . . .

A few days before I left Germany I had a conversation with a manufacturer of munitions who employs about eighteen thousand people in his factories, which, before the war, manufactured articles other than munitions. I asked him how the government treated the manufacturers of munitions, and he said that they were allowed to make good profits, although they had to pay out a great proportion of these profits in the form of taxes on their excess or war profits; that the government desired to encourage manufacturers to turn their factories into factories for the manufacture of all articles in the war and required by the nation in sustaining war; and that the manufacturers would do this provided that it were only a question as to how much of their profits they would be allowed to keep, but that if the Government had attempted to fix prices so low that there would have been a doubt as to whether the manufacturer could make a profit or not, the production of articles required for war would never have reached the high mark that it had in Germany.

As a matter of fact, about the only tax imposed in Germany since the outbreak of the war has been the tax upon cost or war profits. It has been the policy of Germany to pay for the war by great loans raised by popular subscription, after authorisation by the Reichstag. I calculate that the amounts thus raised, together with the floating indebtedness, amount to date to about eighty billions of marks.

Source: *James W. Gerard,* My Four Years in Germany *(New York: Doran, 1917); World War I Document Archive, Brigham Young University <http://www.lib.byu.edu/~rdh/wwi/memoir/Gerard/4yrs5.htm>.*

war orphans became the object of government operations. The techniques that the state had learned during the war persisted for generations, and the modern state was born under the strain of the war.

–PHIL GILTNER,
ALBANY ACADEMY

Viewpoint:
No. The modernization of European political systems was well under way by 1914; the war just accelerated an ongoing process.

On the surface World War I (1914–1918) caused radical change throughout Europe. As a total war it required enormous amounts of resources from all its European participants. The effects were significant. The Russian Empire fell in 1917, ushering in the world's first communist regime. Empires also fell in Germany, Austria, and Turkey, all of which were followed by some sort of republican experiment. Women gained the vote in Britain, the United States, and Germany. The war brought together citizens from all over France, including peasants from regions that had been relatively isolated only a few decades before. In 1889 Germany's Social Democratic Party was still suffering from Chancellor Otto von Bismarck's persecution. In 1919 the Social Democrats headed Germany's first experiment with a republic. Obviously, the situation in 1918 had changed considerably after four years of catastrophic war.

The question is whether this change would have happened without the demands of World War I. The fallen empires were part of the older European system; what replaced them was allegedly more modern. In the late nineteenth century the Ottoman Empire was in serious danger, and by 1914 Turkey had already lost most of its European possessions. There is no guarantee that the monarchy would not have fallen without a war; it just might not have fallen in 1920. The same argument applies to the other three empires. The Austro-Hungarian Empire was experiencing considerable stress in 1914; an aggressive foreign policy was its solution to considerable domestic turmoil. In 1867 the Habsburgs had found a solution to demands of their Hungarian minority; the Dual Monarchy satisfied the Hungarians while maintaining imperial control over their territory. Could the Austrians have satisfied all the other minority groups in their empire, or would the whole structure have eventually collapsed even without a war? The

defeat of the Russians in the Russo-Japanese War (1904–1905) and the 1905 Revolution indicated that the empire was undergoing stress. The German political system was also experiencing difficulty in 1914. The Social Democratic Party, which had experienced serious discrimination from Germany's more conservative circles, had won a plurality of delegates in the 1912 German Reichstag elections. Social Democracy, the political force of the future, seriously worried German conservatives, guardians of the old order. World War I has also been seen as their solution to this domestic problem.

V. R. Berghahn, in *Germany and the Approach of War in 1914* (1973), portrays a fragile prewar German leadership struggling to resist an inevitable modernization of the country's political and economic systems. The Reich's political structure was antimodern; it favored the agrarian elite at the expense of growing industrial interests. The Germans had universal male suffrage. Nevertheless, power rested in the hands of the few, especially the Kaiser. Berghahn details a German elite in constant fear of a growing parliamentary democracy and argues that Germany's aggressive foreign policy, which included its pursuit of colonies and its attempt to build a navy comparable to Britain's, was intended to distract the public from internal concerns. These attempts were ineffective, thus necessitating an even bolder gamble by the German elite to prevent the nation from developing into a genuine parliamentary democracy. Their solution was World War I, which was initially successful in distracting the people. Modernist elements, including most German Social Democrats, rallied to the Kaiser, at least temporarily solidifying the fragile German state. However, the aggressive policies and gambles of the German leadership failed in the end. World War I ended the Hohenzollern monarchy, ushering in the parliamentary democracy that had been feared for so long.

Gordon A. Craig, in *Germany, 1866–1945* (1978), argues that one of the reasons the Weimar Republic failed was that it did not carry out a thorough purging of the German military and bureaucracy. Peter Gay, in *Weimar Culture: The Outsider as Insider* (1968), essentially argues the same point. Because of this failure, two important institutions were staffed by civil servants who were often hostile to the new republic. The army and civil service, including the German judiciary, remained dominated by individuals committed to the imperial traditions of the Reich. They often favored right-wing elements, which were dedicated to destroying the new government. This situation resulted from what Gay, Craig, and other historians, such as Hans-Ulrich Wehler, have portrayed as Germany's incomplete

MODERNIZATION

revolution in 1919. The SPD had indeed assumed power after the fall of the Hohenzollerns. However, they were faced with the threat of an even more serious leftist revolution, which could have at least resulted in more bloodshed had the Independent Socialists or German Communists gained power. To stabilize the situation, new president Friedrich Ebert made a deal with Germany's conservative elements. The leftist forces were stopped, and stability eventually returned to Germany.

Gay also argues that Weimar Germany lacked the Anglo-Saxon traditions of representative democracy and an established system of dissent. Weimar was governed instead by *Vernunftrepublikaner* (republicans by necessity), genuinely notable men and intellectuals who hated Nazism and anything similar to it but who were not passionate defenders of democracy. These notables were influenced by an undemocratic German tradition of politics and the constant quest for wholeness in a vibrant national culture. German intellectuals were used to refraining from political criticism in return for extreme intellectual freedom. At a time when Germany needed rational politics, it was influenced and governed by so-called lovers of poetry who were more inspired by Faust than parliamentary traditions. Weimar appeared sparkling and brilliant on the surface, but this illusion only covered the serious decay within.

This discussion of Weimar is relevant because it addresses the question of what changed in the German political system as a result of World War I. Most of the political parties that governed after the war already existed. There was a parliament and universal male suffrage. Women achieved more rights as a result of World War I, including the vote; however, there is no guarantee that they would not have received the suffrage anyway. The political system opened more in 1919, with local and regional elections being far more democratic. However, earlier restrictions had been unable to prevent the growth of the German Social Democratic Party nor hinder the steady gains it made in the Reichstag. It is highly possible that had there been no World War I, these gains would have continued, eventually forcing the German leadership to compromise with the most popular political party in the country.

The evidence has shown that the forces of the Old Regime persisted into the Weimar Republic. Although the vote of a worker may now have equaled that of an aristocrat, the latter and his sympathizers staffed the military and the judiciary. Therefore, there were limitations on what the state would do for its citizens. Nevertheless, the Left dissented during the Weimar period. German communists often protested on the same streets as the Nazis. The communists and their followers were not dedicated to preserving the new republic, nor did they wish for a return to the older regime. However, their vision did not prevail in 1933. The forces of the old order, the ones who had not been purged from the bureaucracy in 1919, never adjusted to the Weimar Republic. These men were ready and willing to support Adolf Hitler's rise to power.

Germany provides a good example of continuity and change through World War I. Unlike the other prominent empires on the European continent, Germany did not collapse in 1919. Its top leadership was replaced, while the main state apparatus remained relatively intact. Modernism was indeed developing in the German political system; someone observing the state in 1925 would have seen improvement from 1875. Nevertheless, these changes had been developing before the war and were only accelerated by defeat in 1919. It is highly probable that the imperial system in Germany would not have survived anyway, just as the Austrian system would have eventually collapsed from all its strains. The same applies to the Ottoman Empire and probably even to Russia.

It might be better to ask if World War II radically changed the nature of the European state and its functions. In Britain, for example, the newly elected Labour government created an extensive welfare state after 1945, which influenced all English governments until the rise of Prime Minister Margaret Thatcher. After 1945 most of Eastern Europe came under the domination of the Soviet Union. The peoples in these countries had to live under Soviet-style communist regimes. The Germans also received a new government: the Russians installed a communist regime in the eastern section, while the western zones received a parliamentary democracy. Although the eastern regime collapsed with the fall of communism, the western democracy has succeeded. Germany has developed into a modern democracy, something that resulted far more from the radical changes of World War II than World War I.

–DAVID MARSHALL,
UNIVERSITY OF CALIFORNIA, RIVERSIDE

References

V. R. Berghahn, *Germany and the Approach of War in 1914* (London: Macmillan, 1973; New York: St. Martin's Press, 1973).

Gordon A. Craig, *Germany, 1866–1945* (Oxford: Clarendon Press, 1978; New York: Oxford University Press, 1978).

Peter Gay, *Weimar Culture: The Outsider as Insider* (New York: Harper & Row, 1968).

MONARCHY

Did the monarchy play a significant role in twentieth-century European governments?

Viewpoint: Yes. Monarchies had, and continue to have, important symbolic value for European nations and have been stabilizing and cohesive influences in turbulent times.

Viewpoint: No. Monarchy is an outdated and arbitrary institution that is inappropriate and unnecessary for the government of modern states and societies.

At the close of the twentieth century ten European nations still maintained a monarchical form of government, in which a king, queen, prince, or duke reigned as the head of state. In a century torn by war and revolution, however, many of their fellow sovereigns fell from power. Has the institution of monarchy retained any value in these circumstances?

One side of the argument delivers an unqualified "yes." Nations that lost their monarchies tended to fall quickly into chasms of social and political instability that were usually breached by extremist dictatorships. The people of the remaining or restored monarchies prize their rulers for the political stability, charitable services, and national symbolism they provide. The relatively small price of royal courts, private monarchical fortunes, and other perquisites absorbs only a tiny fraction of national budgets and can provoke only symbolic opposition.

Opponents of monarchy argue, on the other hand, that since modern monarchs have little power, they are superfluous in every sense. In an age of mass media their foibles and scandals can be exposed, causing national embarrassment and undermining confidence in government. In an age of democracy the hereditary principle that guides monarchical succession appears arbitrary, outmoded, and inappropriate as a means of selecting a national head of state. Monarchy still costs taxpayers money that could be returned to them or be better spent.

Viewpoint:
Yes. Monarchies had, and continue to have, important symbolic value for European nations and have been stabilizing and cohesive influences in turbulent times.

Monarchy has played an underappreciated role in twentieth-century Europe. Although many monarchs were deprived of their thrones, when they remained, they often served as beacons of stability and powerful symbols of unity and peace. When they disappeared, their countries often later regretted it.

Great Britain's twentieth-century experience was perhaps the greatest argument in favor of monarchy as a stabilizing factor. Among Europe's great powers—Britain, France, Germany, Italy, Austria-Hungary, and

Russia—it alone had a monarchy that reigned to the year 2000 and beyond. Unlike all of the other powers, Britain remained free from major domestic strife and political instability. After the end of its monarchy in 1917, Russia fell swiftly into a brutal communist dictatorship that lasted most of the rest of the century. The abolition of Austria-Hungary's monarchy in 1918 led to that state's dissolution and disappearance as a great power. Its constituent components emerged as weak states, most of which came under authoritarian rule in the interwar era and under communist domination after 1945. The collapse of the German monarchy, also in 1918, led to its replacement by an unstable republic that was subverted by Nazism less than fifteen years after its founding. Italy's monarchy endured until it was abolished in a 1946 referendum but was succeeded by decades of parliamentary governments that on average lasted less than a year. After France first abolished its monarchy in 1792, the constitutional order of the country collapsed eleven times in the next 166 years. On three occasions (1804–1814, 1815, and 1852–1870) France tried to regain stability through the creation of a surrogate monarchy led by the Bonaparte family. In 1814–1815 and 1815–1830 it sought stability by reviving the overthrown Bourbon dynasty, and in 1830–1848 it looked to another surrogate monarchy in a branch of the Bourbons. Britain all the while successfully avoided political violence, curtailed major civil strife, and carried out a series of meaningful democratic reforms.

What role did the British monarchy play in sidestepping instability? Much evidence suggests that it was an essential institution in that regard. After having lost much of its political power in the eighteenth and nineteenth centuries—no British monarch has vetoed a parliamentary bill since 1707—the British monarchy went through the twentieth century largely as a symbolic institution. Its symbolism guaranteed its important role. Britons of all backgrounds could identify themselves as a people by referring to the monarch who reigned over them and who, as the head of state, was duty bound to guarantee the execution of parliamentary laws that elected legislators had passed. As the head of the Anglican Church the British monarch also played a role in confirming the religious identity of a majority of his or her subjects. The positioning of the monarch, beginning especially in the reign of Queen Victoria (1837–1901), as an objective figure who stood above partisan politics both separated the monarch from political controversy and made him or her the constitutional guarantor of Parliament's decisions. Although this arrangement deprived the monarch of independent political power, it nevertheless made the institution of monarchy a pillar of Britain's developing democracy and implanted the notion that it was the ultimate guardian of the people's liberties. Britain's experiences in the world wars reinforced this ideal. Members of the Royal Family served on active duty in the military in both conflicts, taking many of the same risks as ordinary people. In 1917 King George V changed the name of his dynasty from the German Saxe-Coburg-Gotha (the family name of Queen Victoria's husband, Prince Albert) to the English Windsor (after Windsor Castle) to show solidarity with his people. He and his male relatives also showed their British nationalism by renouncing their German titles and honors. During World War II (1939–1945) King George VI insisted that the Royal Family remain in residence in London to share the same risks as his subjects, even after German planes bombed Buckingham Palace. The Windsors subjected themselves to the same rationing as the rest of the nation, and the heiress to the throne, Princess Elizabeth, drove an ambulance in the auxiliary medical service. The strong spirit of public outreach that has characterized the monarchy during her reign as Elizabeth II (1952–) has included a vast array of charitable endeavors, social leadership, and arts patronage that make Britons justifiably proud. Although they were eventually divorced from their royal husbands, Diana, Princess of Wales, and Sarah, Duchess of York, touched the nation and the world with their personal charities and their generous support for the voiceless and the suffering. Princess Diana's sudden death in a car accident in 1997 elicited a huge public display of sorrow and sympathy. The deaths of Elizabeth II's mother, Queen Elizabeth the Queen Mother, and sister, Princess Margaret, in 2002 provoked similar outpourings of sympathy from a country that had felt consoled, supported, and cared for by their lives of public service. One million people lined the streets of London as the Queen Mother was laid to rest. Elizabeth II's fiftieth anniversary as queen, celebrated that summer, drew much positive attention. No matter what critics might think of the monarchy's importance, it has been so influential that all of the major political parties have consistently supported it as Britain's proper form of government. Even after the scandalous conduct of certain members of the Royal Family in the 1990s, when three of Queen Elizabeth's four children divorced amid accusations of adultery and when several family members were accused of financial and other improprieties, 70 percent of Britons favor retention of the monarchy.

Britain's experience has been shared by Europe's other monarchies. The preservation of monarchy in Belgium, the Netherlands, Luxembourg, Denmark, Norway, Sweden, Monaco, and Liechtenstein also accompanied long periods of political stability that allowed for reform and evolution without violence. Indeed, these

MONARCHY

EDWARD VIII

Edward VIII ascended the British throne in January 1936 upon the death of his father, George V. Less than one year later, he decided to abdicate the throne in order to marry Wallis Warfield Simpson, an American divorcée. His decision caused a storm of controversy in the United Kingdom, and Edward VIII remains the only British monarch ever to resign voluntarily (he was replaced by his younger brother, George VI). The following is his abdication speech, broadcast via radio to a worldwide audience on 11 December 1936:

At long last I am able to say a few words of my own. I have never wanted to withhold anything, but until now it has not been constitutionally possible for me to speak.

A few hours ago I discharged my last duty as King and Emperor, and now that I have been succeeded by my brother, the Duke of York, my first words must be to declare my allegiance to him. This I do with all my heart.

You all know the reasons which have impelled me to renounce the throne. But I want you to understand that in making up my mind I did not forget the country or the empire, which, as Prince of Wales and lately as King, I have for twenty-five years tried to serve.

But you must believe me when I tell you that I have found it impossible to carry the heavy burden of responsibility and to discharge my duties as King as I would wish to do without the help and support of the woman I love.

And I want you to know that the decision I have made has been mine and mine alone. This was a thing I had to judge entirely for myself. The other person most nearly concerned has tried up to the last to persuade me to take a different course.

I have made this, the most serious decision of my life, only upon the single thought of what would, in the end, be best for all.

This decision has been made less difficult to me by the sure knowledge that my brother, with his long training in the public affairs of this country and with his fine qualities, will be able to take my place forthwith without interruption or injury to the life and progress of the empire. And he has one matchless blessing, enjoyed by so many of you, and not bestowed on me—a happy home with his wife and children.

During these hard days I have been comforted by her majesty my mother and by my family. The ministers of the crown, and in particular, Mr. Baldwin, the Prime Minister, have always treated me with full consideration. There has never been any constitutional difference between me and them, and between me and Parliament. Bred in the constitutional tradition by my father, I should never have allowed any such issue to arise.

Ever since I was Prince of Wales, and later on when I occupied the throne, I have been treated with the greatest kindness by all classes of the people wherever I have lived or journeyed throughout the empire. For that I am very grateful.

I now quit altogether public affairs and I lay down my burden. It may be some time before I return to my native land, but I shall always follow the fortunes of the British race and empire with profound interest, and if at any time in the future I can be found of service to his majesty in a private station, I shall not fail.

And now, we all have a new King. I wish him and you, his people, happiness and prosperity with all my heart. God bless you all! God save the King!

Source: *"Edward VIII Abdicates the Throne," The History Place: Great Speeches Collection <http://www.historyplace.com/speeches/edward.htm>.*

countries, while retaining constitutional monarchies, also developed some of the most progressive, permissive, and peaceful societies in the world. Neither Sweden's generous welfare state nor the Netherlands' famously tolerant social attitudes have been contradicted or held back by national monarchs who are seen as symbols that sanction the people's will and represent national unity. The need for such symbolism has become more acute in contemporary Europe, as many nations are apprehensive about the loss of national identities and institutions in the process of European integration and attach a renewed importance to their monarchies and other distinctly national traditions. Populations that are becoming increasingly diverse through non-European immigration and through the reassertion of regional minority identities, such as those of the Scots and the Catalons, also demand more comprehensive national symbols. Regardless of the rationale, many of the current European monarchs are simply popular. Queen Beatrix of

MONARCHY

the Netherlands enjoys the approval of 80 percent of her subjects. Sweden's King Carl XVI Gustaf rates 85 percent popularity. Queen Magrethe II of Denmark tops the list with a 90 percent approval rating. Democratic opinion in these cases firmly endorses monarchy.

The value of symbolic constitutional monarchs as sources of political and social unity has not been lost on the world. After the death of Spanish dictator Francisco Franco in 1975, Spain's successful transition to a modern democracy was in many ways assured by the restoration of its monarchy (overthrown in 1931). The absence of the monarchy was accompanied by the political polarization and civil strife that led to the civil war of 1936–1939 and then to Franco's long dictatorship. Returning the House of Bourbon to the throne in the person of King Juan Carlos restored a pillar of political stability and national unity. Under his benevolent leadership Spain rapidly developed into a modern democratic polity. The new king ushered in a democratic constitution in 1978 and personally intervened to stop a right-wing military coup launched by pro-Franco officers in 1981. In the following year Spain was admitted to the North Atlantic Treaty Organization (NATO), which had by then established democratic government and civilian control of the military as prerequisites for membership. In 1986 Spain was admitted to the European Economic Community, placing it on the road to membership in a democratic, united Europe. At the present writing 80 percent of Spaniards believe their king is essential for national stability.

The potential benefits suggested by the Spanish example have not been forgotten by other former monarchies. Crown Prince Alexander of Yugoslavia, King Michael of Romania, and King Simeon II of Bulgaria have all returned to their countries, where they enjoy great personal popularity and have recovered much of their families' property (including royal palaces) since the collapse of communism in the region in 1989–1990. Although these countries have not held referenda on restoring their monarchies, a substantial percentage of their peoples believe it would be a meaningful step in promoting stability and national reconciliation after decades of Soviet domination and communist dictatorship. Exiled Prince Leka of Albania lost a 1997 referendum on the restoration of his country's monarchy, but it should be remembered that his father, King Zog, had not been a legitimate monarch with an established tradition behind him but was a ruthless military dictator who had simply named himself king. Nevertheless, nearly one-third of those who voted supported the restoration of the Albanian monarchy. Bulgaria's former King Simeon II has not publicly declared his

ambition to return to the throne, but after the restoration of his citizenship he formed a political party that in June 2001 swept half the seats in the national legislature. Since then he has served as the country's prime minister and is associated with modernization and a commitment to Bulgaria's inclusion in the democratic West. The popularity of monarchy in Russia remains controversial, but interest in the Romanov dynasty increased dramatically after the collapse of the Soviet Union in 1991. This interest culminated in July 1998 with the solemn reburial of Tsar Nicholas II and his family alongside his predecessors in the Cathedral of Saints Peter and Paul in Saint Petersburg, and in Nicholas II's subsequent canonization by the Russian Orthodox Church. Recent problems in the Middle East have led many observers to wonder whether Afghanistan would be better off if its former king, Zahir Shah, were restored, for his overthrow in 1973 was followed by communist dictatorship, massive Soviet intervention, brutal civil war, and the rule of the Islamic fundamentalist Taliban, which supported international terrorism and was overthrown by American military operations in 2001. Afghan history over the last thirty years has made the constitutional monarchy of Zahir look not bad at all.

Critics of monarchy have argued that maintaining royal families is a financial burden that far outweighs the value of their symbolism or public service. At present, however, this statement is inaccurate. Most reigning monarchs live off the income of their personal and family properties, fortunes, and investments, with only relatively small allowances from the state, usually ones that are budgeted alongside the salaries and benefits paid to professional civil servants. Queen Elizabeth II and those of her family members who carry out public duties are enumerated directly on Britain's civil list. In 1993 the Queen voluntarily agreed to pay taxes on all of her income. Many luxuries formerly kept up at the public expense, including the royal yacht and the Queen's personal train, have been given up. Repairs to Windsor Castle, one of the royal family's main residences, were largely paid for by the Queen's personal funds after a 1992 fire. The Royal Family's private art collection is considered to be state property and is not factored into annual calculations of the Queen's net worth, which, it should be noted, ranked behind that of more than one hundred of her subjects in 2002. Although the British Royal Family remains among the most generously supported monarchies in Europe, the developments of the last decade have made it more similar to the Continent's less well-supported royal families, which receive such a small amount of income and support from national treasuries that they are known as "bicycle monarchies." In a financial sense contemporary European monarchs are now in many ways indistinguishable from other individuals of great family wealth who derive additional income from public-service careers. In no case does such support make up more than a fraction of a percent of the national budget. The stability, identity, national pride, and public service which monarchs supply to their lands might well be worth that small price.

—PAUL DU QUENOY,
GEORGETOWN UNIVERSITY

Viewpoint:
No. Monarchy is an outdated and arbitrary institution that is inappropriate and unnecessary for the government of modern states and societies.

In the early days of the American War of Independence (1775–1783) English-born Thomas Paine provided the classic argument against monarchy in *Common Sense* (1776). To Paine monarchy was a hoax perpetrated upon the people to preserve the power and privileges of the descendants of some "principal ruffian of some restless gang," who came to power because he was the most capable "plunderer" or "usurper" of his age. Moreover, there was little to guarantee that the quality of a hereditary ruling class would be consistent:

> England, since the [Norman] conquest, hath known some few good monarchs, but groaned beneath a much larger number of bad ones, yet no man in his senses can say that their claim under William the Conqueror is a very honorable one. A French bastard landing with an armed banditti, and establishing himself king of England against the consent of the natives, is in plain terms a very paltry rascally original. It certainly hath no divinity in it.

Little has changed since then in royalty's suitability to have any power or privileges in a democratic society. Today ten sovereign European nations have ruling royal families: Belgium, Britain, Denmark, Liechtenstein, Luxembourg, Monaco, the Netherlands, Norway, Spain, and Sweden. Although none of these countries is ruled by families with the same kind of power that George III exercised in Paine's time, one still wonders why hereditary government should persist in a democratic era. These expensive, embarrassing, and undemocratic institutions do little to help their countries. Their time to go came long ago.

Some argue that these royal houses have helped to provide national identity and leadership for their countries in times of distress. For example, during World War II (1939–1945) the sovereigns of Norway, Denmark, the Netherlands, and Belgium all served as symbolic rallying points during foreign occupation, whether from abroad or at home. The Danes, for example, proudly refer to Christian X's daily horseback tours of Copenhagen, and still spread the myth that Christian refused to allow the Germans to require Danish Jews to wear the Star of David by proclaiming that he would be the first to don one. However, such symbolism did little to alleviate the conditions of foreign occupation. Indeed, the behavior and statements of the royals often triggered Nazi repression. Elsewhere in Europe the picture was worse. The cases in Southern and Eastern Europe under Nazi and fascist domination speak less well of the concept of monarchs as leaders and national symbols, as local monarchs gladly collaborated with the most notorious gangster regimes of the twentieth century. There is little in monarchy as such that guarantees that monarchs will do the right thing for their country in times of difficulty.

Even in much less troubling times Europe's royalty has not been especially useful as national symbols. The travails of the British royal family are well known. Three of Queen Elizabeth II's four children are divorced. The British press constantly reported the various scandals surrounding them and other members of her family. Other royals on the Continent have also drawn criticism, so much that leading newspapers of Norway and Sweden have gone so far as to call for the end of their monarchies. Nor is this phenomenon recent. Victoria went into seclusion out of despair after the death of her beloved husband, Prince-Consort Albert: getting her to attend to her duties created a small crisis in the government. Edward VIII's abdication in 1936 resulted from serious political and social scandal. It seems utterly unclear now why he was forced to choose between marrying a divorcée and commoner and being king, but such is the arbitrary nature of royalty.

Part of the problem lies in determining whether royalty has any actual power in Europe's constitutional monarchies. The defenders of royalty maintain that they have no real power and yet contradict themselves by contending that the royals ought not to have their symbolic powers curtailed. In fact, the monarchs of Europe occasionally do affect the political fortunes of their countries. Continental monarchs, presiding over proportionally representative parliamentary governments, are much more active in the formation of governments than the British sovereign, but all European monarchs have less power than

German kaiser Wilhelm II (left) posing with his cousin future British king George V (third from right) and queen Mary (in the middle between the two monarchs); the two boys in sailor suits are the future Edward VIII (left) and George VI (right), circa 1903

(Victoria and Albert Museum, London)

they had in the past. All have the right to be consulted by their parliaments and prime ministers. In the event of a hung parliament the monarch can select a prime minister. Monarchs also can dissolve parliaments and can reject legislation. In the British system the monarch exercises even more power, acting as head of state for several otherwise apparently sovereign countries. For example, for Canadian prime minister Brian Mulroney to expand the number of seats in the Canadian Senate in 1990, Elizabeth had to approve an amendment to the Canadian constitution. Elizabeth is also said to have exercised a benign influence over the fate of Rhodesia at the Lusaka conference (1979), an event that led to Zimbabwe's emergence as a nation with majority black rule the following year. King Juan Carlos

of Spain intervened to reverse a coup attempt by the Spanish military in 1981. Monarchs can exercise the opposite influence, however. Victor Emmanuel III of Italy acquiesced to Benito Mussolini's undemocratic appointment as premier in 1922 and did nothing to stop the subsequent construction of his dictatorship. The Italian people remembered that acquiescence when they deposed the monarchy in a referendum in 1946.

The problem with monarchy is exactly as Paine put it in *Common Sense*. With a hereditary monarch there is simply no guarantee that the quality of a ruler will be beneficial to the country. The same family that produced the intelligent, enlightened, and competent Frederick II of Prussia (reigned 1740–1786) also produced the bumbling, bellicose, and incompetent William II (reigned 1888–1918) who launched his country into World War I (1914–1918) and thereby brought about the end of his dynasty and the abolition of the monarchical principle throughout the German lands. Even Frederick, "the first servant of the state," the paragon of royal service to a country, does not necessarily stand out as the best of all leaders nor one who deserved the perks and privileges of royal power. He had, and rather freely exercised, the power of life and death over his subjects. He also launched several wars that served only to increase the power of his hereditary domains, and his duplicity in foreign affairs achieved the impossible by allying Austria and France against him. Similarly, the competent Louis XIV of France (reigned 1643–1715), unfettered by political opposition, drove his country into financial ruin and left his heirs with a political regime that was utterly unable to adapt to change. The result was the bloody French Revolution.

Even if the political powers of contemporary monarchs are limited in comparison to the past, they are still a drain on the public purse. Figures surrounding the House of Windsor are most readily available, but it should be remembered that the upkeep of the royal families of Europe still falls upon the shoulders of taxpayers. The queen of England is probably the wealthiest woman in the world. Her critics have pinned her wealth at a range that varies widely from the tens of millions to the billions, but there has been no public statement of her actual wealth, though her spokesmen dismiss the figure of £100 million (about $160 million) as being "wildly exaggerated." Media outlets report that she inherited some $70 million from her mother without paying the same 40 percent estate tax other wealthy Britons must pay. Her income derives from her hereditary wealth, and she is also paid some $11 million per year for her services to Britain. She has agreed to pay taxes voluntarily on her income only since 1993. British taxpayers provide more than £1.3 million ($2 million) per year for the upkeep of her family, including her husband, her children, and her cousins of royal blood. The government spends another £35 million ($55 million) per year for her servants, travel, housing, and other expenses:

much of this expenditure is not taxable, yet she benefits from it. Why the queen cannot cover her own expenses is a topic that is not brought up publicly, nor is the value of what the queen provides for all this public money.

Of course, the House of Windsor's wealth is far greater than that of other European royal houses. Yet, it is still symptomatic of an old, derelict system of land ownership and privilege. Much of the wealth of Britain's royalty and aristocracy is still derived from medieval rents on land. The Duke of Westminster, for example, is said to earn some $6.8 billion per year, mostly from leases on his land, a great deal of which lies in London.

With so much public money going to the upkeep of these millionaires, the lives of royalty in Europe are reduced to desperate or half-hearted efforts to appear somehow less than useless. The royals work on charitable projects or spend their time at symbolic ceremonies. The royals of Europe seem to be leading a rather uninteresting existence in a gilded cage: it hardly seems in keeping with the West's belief in the dignity of human life to have these people on display.

In short, European life is not about empty symbolism, nor should it be about unfair privilege. The royals, however, are living symbols of those two things. In this democratic age there is no place for royals.

−PHIL GILTNER,
ALBANY ACADEMY

References

Kenneth Harris, *The Queen: Royalty and Reality* (New York: St. Martin's Press, 1995).

Aisha Labi, "Their Modern Majesties," *Time Europe,* 159 (3 June 2002): 22.

W. M. Spellman, *Monarchies 1000–2000* (London: Reaktion, 2001).

Anthony Taylor, *"Down with the Crown": British Anti-monarchism and Debates about Royalty since 1790* (London: Reaktion, 1999).

OPERATION BARBAROSSA

Was Adolf Hitler's decision to invade the Soviet Union irrational?

Viewpoint: Yes. Blinded by his ideologically driven pursuit of a pure National Socialist empire and his fear of a Soviet attack, Adolf Hitler overestimated Germany's resources and miscalculated the strength and resolve of the Soviets.

Viewpoint: No. Adolf Hitler and his generals had valid reasons to expect a successful invasion of the Soviet Union: the Soviet army was poorly trained and equipped, and Germany needed to solidify its control over Eastern Europe.

Nazi Germany's surprise attack on the Soviet Union on 22 June 1941 was the greatest military operation in human history. More than 3 million men and 3,000 tanks invaded along a 2,000-mile front, from the White Sea to the Black Sea. The conflict that resulted lasted four bloody years, cost more than twenty-five million Soviet lives, and ended only with the Red Army's occupation of Berlin in 1945.

Many historians have ranked Adolf Hitler with Charles XII of Sweden and Napoleon Bonaparte of France as a foolish would-be conqueror of the vast Russian heartland. All failed, and Hitler's expectation that he could defeat his enormous eastern neighbor was equally hubristic and unrealistic. Germany's resources could plainly never compete with those of the Soviet Union.

Other scholars believe that Hitler's decision to attack was not altogether unsound. Soviet leader Josef Stalin had just slaughtered much of his own officer corps—including many of his top military commanders—in bloody political purges, and the Red Army was undertrained and poorly equipped. Stalin's initial reaction to the German attack suggested that he experienced a nervous breakdown, and his armies in the field suffered massive losses in the opening phases of the campaign. Only German tactical mistakes and the help of Soviet allies—neither factor being connected to the Soviet Union per se—ultimately stopped Hitler.

Viewpoint:
Yes. Blinded by his ideologically driven pursuit of a pure National Socialist empire and his fear of a Soviet attack, Adolf Hitler overestimated Germany's resources and miscalculated the strength and resolve of the Soviets.

On the day that Germany unleashed Operation Barbarossa against the Soviet Union (22 June 1941), German leader Adolf Hitler dispatched a letter to his major Axis ally, Italian dictator Benito Mussolini. In it he stated that this decision to destroy Bolshevism had set him "spiritually free," putting an end to the seemingly unholy alliance between the two regimes since August 1939. This moment was the showdown that Hitler had envisioned since the 1920s—a war between worldviews and the ultimate step in Germany's pursuit of *Lebensraum* (living space) in the east. Although the idea of an attack on the Soviet Union had been deferred in the aftermath of the signing of the Nazi-Soviet Non-Aggression Pact (1939), strategic preparations for Operation Barbarossa were authorized by Hitler personally as early as November 1940. In his early guidelines to the *Wehrmacht* (German armed forces) leadership he stated categorically that this war would be one of "annihilation" against an idea, a regime, and a people. By early spring 1941 the plan for the attack had crystallized, envisaging a colossal military assault on a 2,000-mile front, with human and material resources provided by the wide network of Nazi allies and satellite states in Europe (Italy, Hungary, Romania, and Bulgaria).

In recent years revisionist German historiography has attempted to present the decision to attack the Soviet Union as a primarily defensive campaign. According to this interpretation, the *Oberkommando der Wehrmacht* (German High Command, OKW) had received repeated warnings about Soviet military preparations for an imminent attack on Nazi Germany. Available evidence suggests that mounting problems in diplomatic relations between the two uneasy partners over control of the Baltic States and the Balkans had created an atmosphere of mistrust and increasing mutual irritation. Many conservative German diplomats and military officials realized that the purchase of Soviet friendship in August 1939 came at an immense price, especially in terms of territorial concessions. In the summer of 1940 Soviet leader Josef Stalin ordered the occupation of the whole of Lithuania, in contravention to the military protocol of the Molotov-Ribbentrop pact. Furthermore, the traditional Soviet territorial claim over the Romanian province of Bessarabia and the growing aspiration of Soviet foreign policy to become a strong player in the Balkans were not particularly welcomed in Berlin, given the importance of the region in terms of oil supplies. The deterioration in German-Soviet relations was evident in the second half of 1940—an impression that had led Stalin to order a reassessment of his armed forces' strategic plan in preparation for the eventuality of having to face a hostile Nazi Germany. Soviet foreign minister Vyacheslav Molotov's visit to Berlin in the first days of November 1940 and his largely unsuccessful talks with the Nazi leadership did nothing to assuage the fears and suspicions on either side. It was therefore to be expected that the *Wehrmacht* would plan in advance for the eventuality of a war between the two countries and that it would seize the initiative to launch a preemptive strike against the potential aggressor.

However, the theory that Hitler and the OKW were effectively forced into a defensive war against an increasingly hostile Soviet Union is contradicted by an array of parallel developments and decisions during the year before the launching of Operation Barbarossa. The most important discrepancy originates from the timing of events. Supporters of the "preventive war" thesis have stressed that prior to Molotov's visit to Berlin the OKW plans had not assumed a definitive character and that the Nazi leadership had viewed bilateral talks as a further opportunity to reassess German foreign policy. In other words, it has been argued that the erosion of the German-Soviet relationship was potentially reversible and the restoration of a climate of amicable cooperation was still possible, at least from the viewpoint of Nazi intentions. Therefore, the outright failure of the talks with Molotov constituted the final straw in a long chain of events. The Soviet reply to the German proposal for membership in the Tripartite Pact (Germany-Italy-Japan) listed several conditions that were unacceptable to the German side: complete withdrawal of German troops from Finland, access to the Dardanelles Straits, and recognition of the Soviet Union's wide strategic interest in Bulgaria. Such a reply allegedly angered the Nazi leadership and provided the definitive piece of evidence that Stalin did not wish to heal and reinvigorate his relations with Berlin. This argument, however, is not corroborated by the actual sequence of events in the autumn of 1940. It is now known that Hitler had actually issued the first general directive for the operation in the east before Molotov even set foot in Berlin. In this document the Führer stated that preparations for an attack on the Soviet Union should commence irrespective of the results of the visit. Barely a month later (5

December) Hitler spoke to a group of *Wehrmacht* generals about his decision to launch a military campaign against the Soviet Union as early as it was logistically possible. Then, finally, the issuing of Directive No. 21 on 18 December 1940 confirmed formally that Operation Barbarossa and the defeat of Bolshevism had taken official priority in Nazi foreign policy.

Further indications exist that the "preventive war" interpretation has been a misguided (if not misguiding) revisionist enterprise. If the Nazi leadership had been seriously alarmed at the alleged military preparations on the other side of Germany's eastern border and considered the Soviet Union as a threat to the Reich's security, then it would have been logical to expect that Hitler's strategic reasoning would have reflected this concern, be that as a genuine anxiety or in the form of an alibi. Yet, there was no hint of such an alarm in the Führer's speeches to Nazi and military officials in the last months of 1940. In all probability this stance reflected an accurate reading of the military situation, on the basis of the intelligence information available to the Nazi leadership, that stated the purely defensive and partial nature of the Soviet military mobilization.

Another and perhaps more crucial factor underpinning Hitler's nonchalant attitude existed—his personal ideological convictions. The 1939 pact was a largely unhappy marriage of convenience that did not signal a change in his disdainful attitude to the communist regime in the Soviet Union. For racial and ideological reasons, Hitler had always been inclined toward a serious underestimation of the Soviet Union's potential in military and political terms. The recent widespread purges in the Red Army had stimulated this belief further, creating the impression that the Soviet Union's military capacity was no match for Germany's strength in this field. The overall planning for Operation Barbarossa, and especially its overconfident assumptions that the campaign would have achieved the "annihilation of the enemy" within months, resonate a complacency that can only partly be attributed to a rational reading of the military situation. Once again, ideological presuppositions blurred the vision of the Nazi leadership and pushed Germany into the path of a confrontation on multiple fronts that even Hitler had originally ruled out as imprudent.

So why did the Nazi leadership endorse such a hazardous plan in the absence of a real or perceived military threat from the east? Obviously, the final showdown with National Socialism's ideological archenemy in the east and the acquisition of living space for the "talented" and "young" *Volksgemeinschaft* (German national community) had constituted constant themes in Hitler's worldview ever since the early 1920s. The 1939 pact with the Soviet Union had infuriated high-ranking members of the *Nationalsozialistische Deutsche Arbeiterpartei* (NSDAP, or Nazi Party), including the party's ideologue of virulent anti-Semitism, Alfred Rosenberg. Now, the prospect of an "all-out" military confrontation with Bolshevism offered the chance of reversing what for many Nazi members appeared a puzzling and unacceptable revision of National Socialism's spirit. The pivotal question here concerns the timing of the decision to launch such a colossal campaign. If Hitler had not been forced to embark on a preemptive strike in response to alleged Soviet aggressive plans, then the authorization of Barbarossa at a time when the Axis was involved in fighting on multiple fronts appears incomprehensible. The Molotov-Ribbentrop pact had been justified on purely strategic grounds as a last-ditch attempt to avoid a two-front war. By the autumn of 1940 Nazi Germany had failed to resolve the campaign in the west, had been forced to intervene in North Africa to rescue the Italian blunder in Libya, and faced the prospect of a third military entanglement in the Balkans to salvage Mussolini's ill-fated campaign against Greece. Therefore, the prospect of upsetting the balance of the Eastern Front and turning a still formidable power such as the Soviet Union from an uneasy ally to an enemy did not make any strategic sense whatever.

If one believes Hitler's strategic rationale behind the decision to authorize Barbarossa, then the impending war against the Soviet Union was primarily conceived as a parallel strategy to bring a settlement to the war against Britain. Contrary to the initial impression that the morale of the British home front would collapse under the weight of strategic bombing, the extensive air campaign of the *Luftwaffe* (German air force) in the summer of 1940 had failed to force the Churchill cabinet to the negotiating table. At the same time, planning for the invasion of the British Isles (Operation Sea Lion) was undermined by logistical problems (weather, inability to claim total air superiority) and Hitler's halfhearted commitment to the idea. By September 1940 the official "postponement" (in fact, cancellation) of Sea Lion had convinced Hitler that the war against Britain could only be won through the weakening of the government and public morale. Thus, he started referring to the Soviet Union as the only factor that explained the reluctance of the United Kingdom to acknowledge defeat in the war. So long as Stalin remained outside the war, Hitler argued, and the United States continued to exploit their position of neutrality in order to support Britain, then British prime minister Winston Churchill would nurture hopes that the situation was reversible. Thus, the attack on the Soviet Union

THE GOVERNMENT CALLS UPON YOU

On 22 June 1941 Russian foreign minister Vyacheslav Molotov reacted to the surprise German attack on his country:

Citizens of the Soviet Union: The Soviet Government and its head, Comrade Stalin, have authorized me to make the following statement:

Today at 4 o'clock a.m., without any claims having been presented to the Soviet Union, without a declaration of war, German troops attacked our country, attacked our borders at many points and bombed from their airplanes our cities; Zhitomir, Kiev, Sevastopol, Kaunas and some others, killing and wounding over two hundred persons.

There were also enemy air raids and artillery shelling from Rumanian and Finnish territory.

This unheard of attack upon our country is perfidy unparalleled in the history of civilized nations. The attack on our country was perpetrated despite the fact that a treaty of non-aggression had been signed between the U.S.S.R. and Germany and that the Soviet Government most faithfully abided by all provisions of this treaty.

The attack upon our country was perpetrated despite the fact that during the entire period of operation of this treaty, the German Government could not find grounds for a single complaint against the U.S.S.R. as regards observance of this treaty.

Entire responsibility for this predatory attack upon the Soviet Union falls fully and completely upon the German Fascist rulers.

At 5:30 a.m.—that is, after the attack had already been perpetrated, Von der Schulenburg, the German Ambassador in Moscow, on behalf of his government made the statement to me as People's Commissar of Foreign Affairs to the effect that the German Government had decided to launch war against the U.S.S.R. in connection with the concentration of Red Army units near the eastern German frontier.

In reply to this I stated on behalf of the Soviet Government that, until the very last moment, the German Government had not presented any claims to the Soviet Government, that Germany attacked the U.S.S.R. despite the peaceable position of the Soviet Union, and that for this reason Fascist Germany is the aggressor.

On instruction of the government of the Soviet Union I also stated that at no point had our troops or our air force committed a violation of the frontier and therefore the statement made this morning by the Rumanian radio to the effect that Soviet aircraft allegedly had fired on Rumanian airdromes is a sheer lie and provocation.

Likewise a lie and provocation is the whole declaration made today by Hitler, who is trying belatedly to concoct accusations charging the Soviet Union with failure to observe the Soviet-German pact.

Now that the attack on the Soviet Union has already been committed, the Soviet Government has ordered our troops to repulse the predatory assault and to drive German troops from the territory of our country.

This war has been forced upon us, not by the German people, not by German workers, peasants and intellectuals, whose sufferings we well understand, but by the clique of blood-thirsty Fascist rulers of Germany who have enslaved Frenchmen, Czechs, Poles, Serbians, Norway, Belgium, Denmark, Holland, Greece and other nations.

The government of the Soviet Union expresses its unshakable confidence that our valiant army and navy and brave falcons of the Soviet Air Force will acquit themselves with honor in performing their duty to the fatherland and to the Soviet people, and will inflict a crushing blow upon the aggressor.

This is not the first time that our people have had to deal with an attack of an arrogant foe. At the time of Napoleon's invasion of Russia our people's reply was war for the fatherland, and Napoleon suffered defeat and met his doom.

It will be the same with Hitler, who in his arrogance has proclaimed a new crusade against our country. The Red Army and our whole people will again wage victorious war for the fatherland, for our country, for honor, for liberty.

The government of the Soviet Union expresses the firm conviction that the whole population of our country, all workers, peasants and intellectuals, men and women, will conscientiously perform their duties and do their work. Our entire people must now stand solid and united as never before.

Each one of us must demand of himself and of others discipline, organization and self-denial worthy of real Soviet patriots, in order to provide for all the needs of the Red Army, Navy and Air Force, to insure victory over the enemy.

The government calls upon you, citizens of the Soviet Union, to rally still more closely around our glorious Bolshevist party, around our Soviet Government, around our great leader and comrade, Stalin. Ours is a righteous cause. The enemy shall be defeated. Victory will be ours.

Source: "Molotov: Reaction to German Invasion of 1941," Modern History SourceBook <http://www.fordham.edu/halsall/mod/1941molotov.html>.

OPERATION BARBAROSSA

was both a primary and a secondary strategy: primary in the sense of the confrontation between two ideologies and secondary as a device to end the war in the West.

However plausible this argument might appear in strategic terms, the decision to launch Barbarossa and the rationale behind the planning for the war in the east were severely flawed. Hitler's references to a war of "annihilation" against the Soviet Union indicated that he perceived this campaign as the culmination of his regime's foreign policy. However, the promiscuity of Nazi foreign policy objectives seriously weakened German capacity to wage a successful war in the east. From November 1940 to June 1941 the Nazi leadership entertained the idea of a "parallel war" in the Mediterranean against Britain, prepared for the occupation of Gibraltar (Operation Felix, which was canceled), planned and executed the operation in the Balkans (Operation Marita, April–May 1941), and increased its involvement in North Africa. By June it had become clear that Barbarossa would have had to take place with a limited time horizon because of the severe Russian winter and under far-from-optimal military circumstances. That Hitler chose to ignore such warning signs and proceeded with the campaign, still believing that the war would be concluded by the end of 1941, reflects a mixture of arrogance and flagrant underestimation of his enemy in the east that, in hindsight, proved suicidal. Even a mildly rational assessment with regard to Germany's capabilities in 1941 would have at least postponed the plan: war production had not yet reached optimal levels, both in ammunition and in basic raw materials; Nazi forces were widely dispersed and could not be fully mobilized for the war against the Soviet Union; Britain was resisting the German onslaught, both in Europe and North Africa; and the forces mobilized by Germany's allies (primarily Italy and Romania) were not as capable as the infinitely more committed, trained, and equipped *Wehrmacht* units. Thus, although on 21 June 1941 the German figures appeared staggering, the *blitzkrieg* (lightning war) strategy formidable, and the Soviets unprepared, the fatal flaws of the campaign were only temporarily camouflaged.

In spite of initial impressive advances, as early as August 1941 Hitler admitted to his inner circle that the operation had started two months too late. He still clung to the hope that further successes would force the collapse of Stalin's regime, but as the speed of the troops' advance slowed down dramatically, because of worsening weather conditions, lack of fuel, supply problems, and difficulties in coordinating such a massive campaign, no timely provisions were made for the prospect of extending the campaign into

1942. The absence of winter clothing for the troops and the nonsensically belated retreat of the Axis forces to defensible positions for the winter cost time, valuable resources, and, above all, many human lives.

By the end of 1941 the Soviets had displayed a startling capacity for persevering and mobilizing fresh resources, in spite of the initial terrifying rate of losses. Yet, the tendency of the Nazi leadership to underestimate the enemy's morale and military potential continued unabated in 1942. Hitler maintained his resolute (yet totally erroneous) conviction that the enemy was close to collapse, that it was running out of resources, and that it had been rendered incapable of mounting a serious challenge to the Axis forces. This illusion remained unchallenged even late in 1942, in spite of the highly successful Soviet counteroffensives in late 1941 and early 1942. Having dismissed the last independent-minded generals and assumed full control of all aspects of the operation, the Führer committed significant mistakes. Throughout the campaign he kept changing his mind about the priorities of the operation and caused chaos in the German High Command with his often contradictory directives. He failed to appreciate the danger of encirclement in Stalingrad in the autumn of 1942 and refused to contemplate the notion of timely, preventive retreat. As a result his responsibility for the dramatic failure of Operation Barbarossa—and, subsequently, the whole military effort of the Third Reich—was total in gambling the lives of millions of soldiers, in ravaging Eastern Europe, and in sacrificing the future of his own country.

—ARISTOTLE A. KALLIS,
UNIVERSITY OF BRISTOL

**Viewpoint:
No. Adolf Hitler and his generals had valid reasons to expect a successful invasion of the Soviet Union: the Soviet army was poorly trained and equipped, and Germany needed to solidify its control over Eastern Europe.**

German leader Adolf Hitler's decision to invade the Soviet Union was one of the most consequential decisions of World War II (1939–1945). Many historians refer to it as an obvious strategic blunder. Hitler himself ranked his order to invade the Soviet Union as one of "the most difficult decisions" he had to make. He had always said that Germany must avoid a two-front war—a situation that had proved to be fatal for Germany during World War I (1914–1918)—at all cost. Soviet leader Josef Stalin was also convinced that a German attack on the Soviet Union was unbelievable. He said once: "Germany is busy up to her ears with the war in the West and I am certain that Hitler will not risk creating a second front by attacking the Soviet Union. Hitler is not such an idiot and understands that the Soviet Union is not Poland, not France, not even England."

Hitler's decision to engage in a two-front war had many drawbacks: the unfortunate experience of previous Western invasions of Russia with the insuperable spaces of the country; the military weakness of German allies; and the risk of squandering German forces in a manner that could put the course of the war under question. As a result many historians view Hitler's decision as a fatal act of desperation rather than a rational strategic calculation. As Hitler's biographer Joachim C. Fest wrote, "it was the last and most serious example of his suicidal impulse to double his stake once the game was going against him." Yet, surprisingly enough, experienced German generals did not oppose Hitler's decision. Several important factors and developments, mainly connected with the German-Soviet military balance as well as trends connected with the overall course of the war, influenced Hitler's decision to invade the Union of Soviet Socialist Republics (U.S.S.R.).

By the summer of 1941 the Third Reich was at its military high point, controlling the resources of almost all of continental Europe. The rapid success of *blitzkrieg* (lightning war) in Western Europe profoundly demonstrated the value of mechanized forces. In 1941 Germany reorganized its panzer divisions so that two-thirds of the armored strength of each division would consist of medium tanks, and as a result the number of the armored divisions rose from ten to twenty-one. This reorganization enhanced the capability of the *Wehrmacht* (German armed forces) to wage maneuverable warfare, particularly its ability to strike deeply inside Soviet territory. For the invasion of the U.S.S.R., Germany assembled the largest force ever deployed for a single military operation: 3,150,000 men (plus 530,000 men provided by Italy, Hungary, Romania, and Finland), 3,332 tanks, 7,184 pieces of artillery, and 2,770 aircraft.

Against the Axis forces the Soviets had 2 million troops with 24,000 tanks, 8,000 aircraft, and 5,900 artillery pieces. Although the balance of forces on the ground actually implied Soviet superiority, there were many factors that weakened Soviet military posture and put the U.S.S.R. on the brink of complete catastrophe in 1941. The Soviet military machine had clearly demonstrated a huge gulf between paper strength and reality. Only 30 percent of Soviet troops had automatic weapons; about 70 percent of the aircraft and 91 percent of the tanks were obsolete; and just 22 percent of Soviet tanks were in any sort of running order. There were also significant organizational and technological problems of reequipping the Red Army with modern weaponry. The widespread shortage of motor transport highlighted the Soviet Union's military and logistical backwardness. Difficulties existed in command structure and the coordination of services. Moreover, the rapidly growing armed forces lacked adequate training. As the Bulgarian ambassador in Moscow at the time reported, "the Soviet army was no more than a joke."

The German assault on 22 June 1941 also caught the Red Army in the midst of far-reaching redeployment to protect the newly expanded borders in western Ukraine, western Belorussia, and the Baltic States, territory gained by Stalin's deal to partition Poland with Hitler in 1939. The Great Purges of 1937–1938, which almost completely annihilated the prewar Soviet High Command and significantly damaged the whole Soviet officer corps, had a lasting impact on the Red Army, creating an atmosphere of total insecurity and limiting initiative of the commanders. Many historians also mention the deficiencies of Soviet strategic thought and military planning, which underestimated the speed and power of German *blitzkrieg*.

One more important factor contributed decisively to Soviet military unpreparedness and damaged the Soviet ability to resist a surprise attack: Stalin's inexplicable self-delusion about German motives and actions. Stalin refused until the last moment to believe that Hitler would attack him and even continued to harbor this idea a few hours after the German armed forces had broken into the Soviet Union. This delusion happened despite intelligence reports and credible espionage that suggested the dramatic opposite. For nearly two weeks after the attack, Stalin disappeared from public view, apparently suffering from some kind of nervous breakdown, before reasserting his leadership.

Some strategic concerns also developed in the course of the war that influenced Hitler's decision to take on the U.S.S.R. Paradoxically, while trying to avoid a two-front war, Hitler attacked the U.S.S.R. in order to persuade the British to surrender or to sue for peace. The determination of Britain to continue to fight only made sense as long as it could hope that American aid would take effect and that the British military might gain support on the Continent, including, if necessary, from the Soviet Union. As Hitler said to a group of his top generals on 31 July 1940, the British had two hopes

A column of German troops in the Soviet Union during the initial stages of Operation Barbarossa in June 1941

(Christopher Ailsby Historical Archives)

left: America and the Soviet Union. Hitler's war efforts also required the natural resources of the U.S.S.R. and the solidification of German hegemony in Eastern Europe.

In addition, Hitler was obsessed with the fear that Stalin might attack Germany. There were political disagreements between Germany and the U.S.S.R. in the Baltic, Finland, and the Balkans, and the Germans displayed concern about a military buildup in the Soviet Union. Some German and Austrian historians have argued that Stalin was preparing to launch a war of aggression in Central Europe in order to spread communism and that Hitler's invasion of the Soviet Union was nothing more than a necessary preemptive strike. This thesis found support in the writings of Viktor Suvorov, a Soviet defector who maintained that Stalin had planned to invade Germany on 6 July 1941. While some current Russian historians claim to have confirmed Suvorov's conclusions from their own research, most important studies of the Soviet war efforts by Western and Soviet scholars dismiss these revisionist views, arguing that the Soviet Union was not ready for war in 1941 and that Stalin had no intention of launching one. Nevertheless, the fact that the main Soviet forces were deployed in or moving into forward positions along the U.S.S.R.'s new frontiers gave the Germans both the perception that an attack was on the way and that their best chance of defeating Soviet forces was in a surprise attack.

To escape getting drawn into a protracted slogging match, the German High Command designed the operation as a short and speedy campaign to be completed before the outset of winter. Soviet forces were to be dislocated by savage armored thrusts and by the continued appli-

cation of firepower—ground-to-ground and air-to-ground—at critical points along the front, which were to deny a breathing space for Soviet forces to assemble reserves in their vast rear areas. The Germans also aimed to disrupt and overwhelm the Soviet command system. Hitler's deceptive strategy on the eve of the invasion was of much importance as well. It made the desired impression, while the Soviets behaved rather passively, hoping to appease Germany, trying to avoid conflict, and showing little sign of defensive preparations.

The disposition of the Red Army and Stalin's ignoring of all warnings only facilitated the initial German strategy and ensured its success. Attacking without warning, the Germans neutralized the Soviet air force, cut off large parts of the Red Army, and penetrated quickly and deeply into the Soviet Union, which was expected to collapse under the hammer blows of the German attack. Military strategy and politics were interdependent in the operation. The Germans sought to capitalize on and exploit the widespread unpopularity of the Bolshevik regime, particularly in the areas seized by Stalin in 1939.

Early German operations enjoyed much success and went some way toward fulfilling the aims of the Barbarossa Directive. The bulk of the Soviet forward units had been smashed—particularly the air force, which lost 3,800 aircraft, mostly on the ground on the first day of the war. Germany's initial success was the result of surprise, superior training at all levels, and better strategic and tactical planning. It was also indebted to the intelligent way in which the Germans capitalized on the advantages of their power and resources. Yet, even in the midterm perspective the Germans, although they refused to admit it, failed to wipe out completely the Soviets as a fighting force. The Soviet Union had substantial manpower reserves even after its massive initial losses. Its air force remained powerful despite calamitous losses, thanks to a large aircraft industry. Most important, the Soviets could concentrate their military resources on one fighting front (this fact made the Soviet Union exceptional among the major belligerents). The Soviets rebuilt their power even as they paid with huge losses for past strategic miscalculations. As for Hitler, he had fallen into the trap he had sworn to avoid—a war on two fronts.

—PETER RAINOW,
SAN MATEO, CALIFORNIA

References

Alan Clark, *Barbarossa: The Russian-German Conflict, 1941–1945* (New York: Morrow, 1965).

Joachim C. Fest, *Hitler,* translated by Richard and Clara Winston (New York: Harcourt Brace Jovanovich, 1974).

Bryan I. Fugate, *Operation Barbarossa: Strategy and Tactics on the Eastern Front, 1941* (Novato, Cal.: Presidio Press, 1984).

John Keegan, *Barbarossa: Invasion of Russia, 1941* (New York: Ballantine, 1971).

Robert J. Kershaw, *War without Garlands: Operation Barbarossa, 1941/1942* (Shepperton: Ian Allan, 2000).

H. W. Koch, "Hitler's 'Programme' and the Genesis of Operation 'Barbarossa'," in *Aspects of the Third Reich,* edited by Koch (London: Macmillan, 1985; New York: St. Martin's Press, 1985).

Michael Parrish, ed., *Battle for Moscow: The 1942 Soviet General Staff Study* (Washington, D.C.: Pergamon-Brassey's, 1989).

Geoffrey Roberts, *The Soviet Union and the Origins of the Second World War: Russo-German Relations and the Road to War, 1933–1941* (New York: St. Martin's Press, 1995).

Bernd Wegner, ed., *From Peace to War: Germany, Soviet Russia and the World, 1939–1941* (Providence, R.I.: Berghahn Books, 1997).

Alexander Werth, *Russia at War, 1941–1945* (New York: Dutton, 1964).

Barton Whaley, *Codeword BARBAROSSA* (Cambridge, Mass.: MIT Press, 1973).

Joseph L. Wieczynski, ed., *Operation Barbarossa: The German Attack on the Soviet Union, June 22, 1941* (Salt Lake City: Schlacks, 1993).

OUTBREAK OF WORLD WAR I

Did Germany cause World War I?

Viewpoint: Yes. World War I arose from a multilateral attempt to restrain the burgeoning power and expansionist tendencies of Germany.

Viewpoint: No. World War I was caused by clashing strategic interests, interlocking alliance structures, and widespread desires to stabilize turbulent domestic politics.

The assassination of Archduke Franz Ferdinand, heir to the throne of the Austro-Hungarian Empire, in Sarajevo on 28 June 1914 set in motion a monthlong diplomatic crisis that ended with all of Europe's major powers going to war. What were the long-term trends and conditions that resulted in the unprecedented conflagration of World War I (1914–1918)? The traditional view long held that Germany, principal combatant of the "Central Powers" (Germany, Austria-Hungary, the Ottoman Empire, and Bulgaria), was primarily responsible for initiating the war. Its pursuit of world power, the challenges posed by its ambitious naval development, and its alienation of other powers by seeking a European hegemony led the "Entente" or "Allied" nations (initially Britain, France, and Russia) to collude against it diplomatically and then challenge it militarily.

Revisionist historians have suggested, however, that Germany should not bear the full burden of responsibility for World War I and that the blame it was forced to accept in the peace settlement of 1919 was just another example of the winners writing history. All European governments, in this view, had compelling reasons to enter the conflict. The Sarajevo crisis forced them to choose between honoring their long-standing alliance commitments and standing aside, an option that would soil their national honor and lead to their future diplomatic isolation. War also offered the attractive prospect of national unity to the elite, who feared the domestic dissension that accompanied rapid social and political change. Most of Europe looked to war in 1914 as the best means of preserving their status quo, and that belief guided their decisions.

Viewpoint:
Yes. World War I arose from a multilateral attempt to restrain the burgeoning power and expansionist tendencies of Germany.

The deepest causes of World War I (1914–1918) were embedded in changes in the European balance of power after the emergence of a united and powerful Germany in the heart of Europe. With Wilhelm II's ascension to the imperial throne in 1888, the rapid development of Germany as a great power seemed to require an aggressive policy of unrestricted colonial and naval expansion. In embarking upon this policy, the ruling elite of Germany disregarded concerns that it elicited from other European powers. In striking contrast to the moderate foreign-policy course conducted by Chancellor Otto von Bismarck until his dismissal in 1890 (aimed at developing a prosperous and powerful Germany through active alliance diplomacy in Europe and moderate colonial programs), the new government encouraged an assertive foreign policy of global scale—*Weltpolitik* (world policy).

The rapid expansion of the German economy after 1871 was extraordinary and caused growing concerns among the major industrialized powers. In 1872 the coal output of Germany was 33 million metric tons; in 1912 it was 175 million tons. Between 1870 and 1914 Germany's output of iron increased about sixteen times, and the country became the second leading iron producer in the world—after the United States. From 1890 to 1910 Germany's output of steel increased seven times as fast as that of Britain, and by 1914 Germany's total production of steel was twice that of Britain. There was a significant growth of Germany's foreign trade as well. Between 1870 and 1914 it increased from $1 billion to $5 billion. Expanding German industries required larger markets, and tremendous population growth (from 41 million in 1870 to 65 million in 1910) demanded raw materials and food supplies. As the existing German colonial empire was inadequate to this end, and as new colonies were difficult to acquire by peaceful means, Germany turned to active commercial and economic penetration of other countries.

Beginning in the 1890s the Germans economically infiltrated the declining Ottoman Empire, and through trade agreements and concessions, particularly the construction of the Berlin-Baghdad railway, they succeeded in establishing a huge economic presence. This economic success antagonized other great powers—Britain, France, and Russia—which had economic and political interests in the Middle East. Germany also had plans for wider expansion to the east as well as a hegemonic German-dominated economic and political association in Central Europe.

After 1898 Germany also began the construction of a high-seas navy. "Our future," said the Kaiser, "lies on the water." Because of its colonial expansion Germany already had extensive overseas possessions and maritime trade to protect, but the naval buildup was performed in a manner to alarm and antagonize other powers, especially Britain, whose predominance was directly threatened. Moreover, arrogant Germany rebuffed or ignored British attempts during 1898–1901 to appease it, and the British, in alarm, increased their navy-building programs. By the beginning of the twentieth century the great Anglo-German naval race had begun. There was also a colonial rivalry between Germany and Britain, particularly in Africa.

The rise of Germany's ambitions and its new influential and assertive world role aroused concerns and suspicions of other Great Powers. In 1894 France and Russia drew closer together and entered into an alliance to counter Germany. By 1902 concerns about Germany also influenced Britain to abandon finally its "splendid isolation" policy toward European affairs and to seek some kind of an agreement with France, despite colonial rivalry between the two powers. Edward VII, the new king of England and a Francophile, did much to promote the Anglo-French rapprochement, or Entente Cordiale, as it came to be called after its signing in 1904.

The Anglo-French Entente resolved the conflicting colonial claims of both powers and brought about a real diplomatic revolution. While at first without military obligations or cooperation, it counterbalanced Germany's growing influence in Europe and its advance in the Middle East. While the agreement caused France and Britain to resist German hegemonic schemes more decisively, it also widened the rift between Italy on the one hand and Germany and Austria-Hungary on the other hand and forced Rome to reconsider its alliance with those two powers. The Franco-Italian secret agreement of 1902 marked de facto Italian neutrality if France were to be involved in a defensive war.

The common fear of an expansionist Germany also moved Great Britain and Russia closer together. German penetration in the Middle East particularly influenced Russia and Britain to end their long-standing rivalry in Asia. Checked by Japan in the Far East, Russia welcomed Britain's help in arranging a settlement with its Oriental protagonist (a British ally) and favored reconciliation with Britain. The Anglo-Russian Entente was based on the bilateral convention concluded in August 1907. The agreement sought to prevent the growth of German influence in the Middle East and envisaged the division of Central Asia into British and Russian spheres of influence.

Thus, by 1907 Great Britain, France, and Russia had settled their rivalries and created a loosely constructed coalition capable of challenging German power. The determination of the Entente to contain Germany was revealed during a series of international crises—the First Moroccan Crisis (1905–1906), the Bosnian Crisis (1908), the Agadir Crisis (1911), and the Balkan Wars (1912–1913). These crises, particularly the Moroccan Crisis, stimulated the development of military cooperation within the Anglo-French Entente; French, British, and Belgian militaries made arrangements for disposition of their forces in the event of a war with Germany. In 1912–1914 several steps were taken to transform the Entente into an effective anti-German military alliance. Great Britain transferred most of its naval power to the North Sea in order to balance there the growing German navy. Conversely, France, by special agreement, stationed most of its navy in the Mediterranean.

Some steps were also taken to bring France and Russia into a closer understanding regarding the Balkans. The growing rivalry there between Austria, backed by Germany, and Russia, which counted on support from its Entente partners, created many obstacles for German expansion in the Ottoman Empire and in the Middle East as a whole. France and Russia also concluded a naval convention, and their general staffs conferred annually to perfect military plans for a joint offensive against Germany in case of war, while Britain and Russia were looking to a naval agreement as well. Fearing the rise of the German influence on Turkish military (German general Otto Liman von Sanders was invited to reorganize the Ottoman army in 1913), the Russians were working hard on plans to seize the strategic Turkish Straits and strengthen their support for Serbia vis-à-vis Austria in the Balkans.

Germany, for its part, had come to believe that it and its "faithful ally"—as Wilhelm II called it—Austria-Hungary, were menaced on all sides by a deliberate policy of encirclement. This strategic situation forced Germany to support Austro-Hungarian ambitions in the Balkans almost unconditionally. The kaiser also came to the conclusion that "Russia and France are working full steam for an early war against" Germany. At the same time in Britain, France, and Russia the feeling that the nations were moving toward an unavoidable war grew from day to day. Multilateral attempts to restrain burgeoning German power and expansionist tendencies had dramatically increased mutual fears and suspicions, and automatically and rapidly transformed the Austro-Serbian conflict into World War I.

—PETER RAINOW,
SAN MATEO, CALIFORNIA

Viewpoint:
No. World War I was caused by clashing strategic interests, interlocking alliance structures, and widespread desires to stabilize turbulent domestic politics.

World War I (1914–1918) began because the elite in Serbia, Austria-Hungary, Germany, and Russia considered war, or the risk of war, an acceptable policy option. To explain the outbreak of World War I, one must examine both the environmental as well as the immediate factors that attributed to those decisions to go to war. Historians have traditionally dismissed the events surrounding July 1914 as trivial and have concentrated on the role of Germany. This approach underplays the significance of developments in Serbia, Austria-Hungary, and Russia in the months leading up to July 1914. Although the war itself quickly developed into one of Germany (and the ineffectual Austria-Hungary) against the rest of Europe, one must take care not to displace these conditions as primary among the causes of the conflict. A deeper analysis reveals that interlocking alliance structures, widespread desires to stabilize turbulent domestic politics through foreign adventures, and the clashing strategic interests of all parties led to the outbreak of World War I.

Much has been written of the inflexible nature of the alliance structures in place prior to World War I. The Triple Entente and Triple Alliance had crystallized by the end of the Bosnian Crisis (1908). France, Britain, and Russia (along with its client, Serbia) formed the Triple Entente. From 1912 France and Russia worked to strengthen their position vis-à-vis German power and Austrian ambition in the Balkans. In 1912 and 1913 Raymond Poincaré, first as French premier and later as president, demonstrated the import of France's relationship with St. Petersburg. To ensure immediate Russian pressure on Germany's eastern front in case of war, France went so far as to invest in Russian railway construction. Paris also entreated London to coordinate its naval arrangements with Russia, which it began doing in early 1914. Meanwhile, Russo-Serbian relations continued to bear fruit. Russia actively encouraged and supported the formation of the Balkan League and maintained ties to Premier Nikola Pašic's regime in Belgrade. Such developments served to increase Germany's anxiety about its relative position in Europe and the world as well as to antagonize Austria in its bids to dominate the Balkans.

The leaders of the Triple Alliance (Germany, Austria-Hungary, and Italy) were also active during this period. At the end of 1912 they agreed to renew the Alliance for another five years and reinstituted coordination of military and naval planning. The Alliance, however, showed cracks. Austria-Hungary and Italy vied for position in the Balkans and the potential division of Turkish Asia Minor. Moreover, Austria-Hungary was uncertain of Germany's reaction to a potential conflict. Even as the Triple Alliance seemed a strong basis for foreign policy formulation, one had to contend with the possibility of its sudden demise and an utter lack of alternatives. In this light both alliances moved in opposite directions. The Triple Alliance, underpinned by a

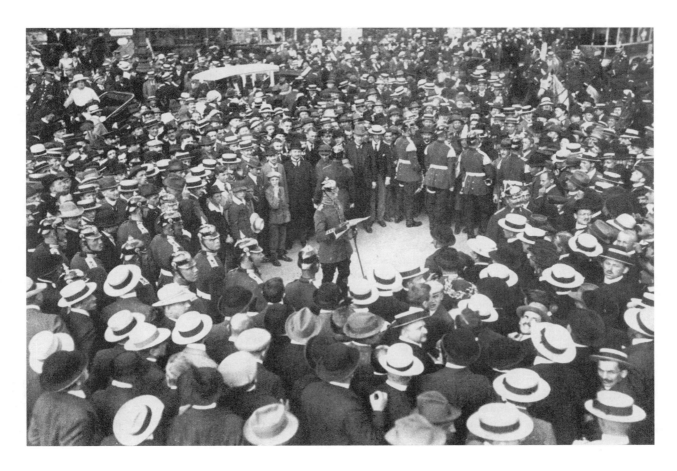

treaty, became fraught with insecurity and angst while its members sought ways to satisfy their foreign ambitions. The Triple Entente, loosely formulated to provide defensive security while its members pursued their ambitions beyond the theater of Europe, was in a period of solidification and deepening cooperation. The static nature of these two alliance structures, moreover, added to the frailty of the system by denying flexible solutions to allow states to recast their lots in a different configuration.

Russia and Austria-Hungary were central players in the events of July 1914. The role of turbulent domestic politics in the formulation of these declining monarchies' foreign policies should not go overlooked. For Vienna, questions of *Innenpolitik* (home policy) and *Aussenpolitik* (foreign policy) were intrinsically intertwined. In Romania nationalism was stirring and beginning to gather force, undermining the government's support for the Triple Alliance. Indications that King Carol might withdraw from his adherence to the Triple Alliance had twofold implications for Austria-Hungary. For one, Romania's departure would present Vienna with a potent strategic problem. Perhaps more significant, however, was the potential unrest generated by the 3 million Romanians living in Transylvania under Magyar rule. For Russia, the line between domestic and foreign policy was far clearer; nevertheless, both the Romanovs

and the Habsburgs believed that success in foreign theaters translated to domestic support, peace, and, thus, power at home. As historian Samuel R. Williamson Jr. has noted, "the decay in effectiveness of the political structures of the Habsburg, Hohenzollern, and Romanov regimes is noted as a final long-term cause of the war." The experience of the Balkan Wars (1912–1913) strengthened this resolve on both sides.

Rivalry and tension between Austria-Hungary and Russia heightened, though not without some détente, in the period prior to 1914. Russia did much to exacerbate the situation during this period. Vienna sent Ottokar Czernin as minister to Bucharest in late 1913 to try to retain Romania's support for the Triple Alliance. Then, while the tsar and tsarina were on a visit to Romania, Russian foreign minister Sergei Sazonov defiantly crossed into Transylvania in a show of support for the Romanians living in Austria-Hungary. This event served to convince Austrian policy makers that Russia was determined to undermine Austro-Hungarian efforts everywhere.

Despite these and other manifestations of tensions among the powers of Central Europe, it was hardly clear that a conflict resembling World War I lay on the horizon. First of all, there were periods of détente and concession. Although the "Eastern Question" had become a significant one for all foreign ministries, the Great Powers cooperated to manage the situation somewhat.

German officer reading the declaration of war, Berlin, 31 July 1914

(from Stefan Lorant, Sieg Heil! Hail to Victory: An Illustrated History of Germany from Bismarck to Hitler, *1979)*

OUTBREAK OF WORLD WAR I

There were no indications that these events would lead to a major conflagration. Indeed, in the period just prior to 1914 all war ministries seemed to subscribe to the "short war illusion." The doctrine that only offensive warfare contained the possibility of success was pervasive. Little evidence exists that any war planners provided for the possibility of military stalemate and what would happen if success did not come quickly. Meanwhile, military leaders continued to warn their regimes of the dangers of falling behind in the ongoing arms race.

Core strategic interests and military concerns had a tremendous impact in shaping Austro-Hungarian decision making in June and July 1914. Habsburg commanders faced an impossible situation. Their southern front faced a confident and battle-seasoned Serbia aware of its Russian support. Elements within the Serbian regime, moreover, openly sought to undermine Austrian control of Bosnia by violent means, if necessary. The possible defection of Romania from the Triple Alliance exposed the empire to an unbearable threat: Russian assault. Reports in Berlin indicated that the Russians had shortened their mobilization timetables by several weeks. To Berlin, this move raised the importance of a Habsburg assault on Russia in case of war. Vienna and the chief of the Austro-Hungarian general staff, General Franz Conrad von Hötzendorf, in particular, asked that Germany provide a greater presence on the eastern front so that Vienna could commit itself to Serbia. This question of coordination remained unanswered prior to July's events.

To the Habsburg general staff and policy makers, Serbia must have been perceived as the greatest immediate threat. Southern Slav unity propaganda aside, Serbia and elements within the empire exuded renewed confidence with the successes of the second Balkan War (1913). Moreover, reports of connections between the Serbian regime and organizations such as the Black Hand in Bosnia underscored the need to resolve the Serbian threat. Since the Eastern Question ensured that the Balkans would remain the Habsburgs' primary theater for foreign adventures, the significance of Serbia in foreign policy and military formulation cannot be underestimated. The stage had been set for the decisions of June and July 1914.

The events that unfolded on this stage reveal not only an acceptance of the risk of some kind of war by all parties but also the absence of any comprehension of the character that war would take. Though efforts were made to confine the scope of the crisis, misperception and miscalculation of the impacts of certain decisions eventually led to all-out warfare as the only ready option available. It is important to note that this analysis applies to Germany as well. Though Germany was anxious to assert its position in the world, it does not follow that Berlin drove the escalation of the crisis to world war.

The assassination of Archduke Franz Ferdinand and his wife Sophie on 28 June 1914 shocked Vienna and the world. Though their presence in Sarajevo was arguably part of a wider game of provocation being played out between Serbia and Austria-Hungary, it is unlikely any one expected them to be in grave personal danger. Upon news of their deaths, Austrian foreign minister Count Leopold von Berchtold quickly formulated a policy of retribution against Serbia and convinced Emperor Franz Josef of its merits. The emperor's complicity with this policy stemmed partly from "evidence" of connections between the Black Hand and some members of the Serbian government. At this point Vienna entreated Berlin to support action against Belgrade, not the other way around.

Berlin acquiesced. Kaiser Wilhelm II and Chancellor Theobald von Bethmann Hollweg proved receptive to the Habsburg mission sent to secure assurances of German support of the Austrian plan to undertake major military action against Serbia. By 6 July Vienna had received a pledge of German support and thus, it was hoped, a deterrent against possible Russian intervention. Austria-Hungary was unlikely to have gone to war without German support, though some kind of action would have likely ensued. Thus, one must ask: why did the German leadership lend its support to Austro-Hungarian retaliatory action against Serbia? There is a myriad of possible reasons: alliance obligations, Berlin's pursuit of a more assertive German foreign policy, personal feelings of sympathy for the death of an archduke of an allied country, and so on. Furthermore, there was the understanding that Serbia presented a major obstacle to German military planning by diverting Habsburg interests toward the south.

Although Germany must have known that Austrian action against Serbia would antagonize Russia, it did not unilaterally seek to escalate the conflict. German leaders saw war as a real possibility (as they had throughout the years immediately prior to 1914), but they did not push for it to happen at this point (nor did they actively seek to prevent it). The Habsburg ministers kept Berlin completely in the dark about the features of their retaliatory action against Serbia. That Berlin did not demand at least to be notified of Vienna's plans constituted the oft-mentioned carte blanche for Austrian military action in the Balkans. However, there was no clear reason to believe this conflict would differ fundamentally from the two Balkan Wars that preceded it.

THE ANGLO-RUSSIAN ENTENTE

Signed in August 1907, the Anglo-Russian Entente was an attempt to prevent the growth of German influence in the Middle East as well as to divide Central Asia into British and Russian spheres of influence:

AGREEMENT CONCERNING PERSIA

The Governments of Great Britain and Russia having mutually engaged to respect the integrity and independence of Persia, and sincerely desiring the preservation of order throughout that country and its peaceful development, as well as the permanent establishment of equal advantages for the trade and industry of all other nations;

Considering that each of them has, for geographical and economic reasons, a special interest in the maintenance of peace and order in certain Provinces of Persia adjoining, or in the neighborhood of, the Russian frontier on the one hand, and the frontiers of Afghanistan and Baluchistan on the other hand; and being desirous of avoiding all cause of conflict between their respective interests in the above-mentioned Provinces of Persia;

Have agreed on the following terms:—

I.

Great Britain engages not to seek for herself, and not to support in favour of British subjects, or in favour of the subjects of third Powers, any Concessions of a political or commercial nature—such as Concessions for railways, banks, telegraphs, roads, transport, insurance, etc.—beyond a line starting from Kasr-i-Shirin, passing through Isfahan, Yezd, Kakhk, and ending at a point on the Persian frontier at the intersection of the Russian and Afghan frontiers, and not to oppose, directly or indirectly, demands for similar Concessions in this region which are supported by the Russian Government. It is understood that the above-mentioned places are included in the region in which Great Britain engages not to seek the Concessions referred to.

II.

Russia, on her part, engages not to seek for herself and not to support, in favour of Russian subjects, or in favour of the subjects of third Powers, any Concessions of a political or commercial nature—such as Concessions for railways, banks, telegraphs, roads, transport, insurance, etc.—beyond a line going from the Afghan frontier by way of Gazik, Birjand, Kerman, and ending at Bunder Abbas, and not to oppose, directly or indirectly, demands for similar Concessions in this region which are supported by the British Government. It is understood that the above-mentioned places are included in the region in which Russia engages not to seek the Concessions referred to.

III.

Russia, on her part, engages not to oppose, without previous arrangement with Great Britain, the grant of any Concessions whatever to British subjects in the regions of Persia situated between the lines mentioned in Articles I and II.

Great Britain undertakes a similar engagement as regards the grant of Concessions to Russian subjects in the same regions of Persia.

All Concessions existing at present in the regions indicated in Articles I and II are maintained.

IV.

It is understood that the revenues of all the Persian customs, with the exception of those of Farsistan and of the Persian Gulf, revenues guaranteeing the amortization and the interest of the loans concluded by the Government of the Shah with the "Banque d'Escompte et des Prits de Perse" up to the date of the signature of the present Arrangement, shall be devoted to the same purpose as in the past.

It is equally understood that the revenues of the Persian customs of Farsistan and of the Persian Gulf, as well as those of the fisheries on the Persian shore of the Caspian Sea and those of the Posts and telegraphs, shall be devoted, as in the past, to the service of the loans concluded by the Government of the Shah with the Imperial Bank of Persia up to the date of the signature of the present Arrangement.

V.

In the event of irregularities occurring in the amortization or payment of interest of the Persian loans concluded with the "Banque d'escompte et des Prits de Perse" and with the Imperial Bank of Persia up to the date of the signature of the present Agreement, and in the event of the necessity arising for Russia to establish control over the sources of revenue guaranteeing the regular service of the loans concluded with the first-named bank, and situated in the region mentioned in Article II of the present Agreement, or for Great Britain to establish control over the sources of revenue guaranteeing the regular service of the loans concluded with the second-named bank, and situated in the region mentioned in Article I of the present Agreement, the British and Russian Governments undertake to enter beforehand into a friendly exchange of ideas with a view to determine, in agreement with each other, the measures of control in question and to avoid all interference which would not be in conformity with the principles governing the present Agreement.

Source: "1907 The Anglo-Russian Entente," World War I Document Archive, Brigham Young University <http://www.lib.byu.edu/~rdh/wwi/1914m/anglruss.html>.

OUTBREAK OF WORLD WAR I

Russia, meanwhile, continued its policy of antagonizing Austria and Germany and directly contributed to the escalation of the crisis. With fresh guarantees of French support in case of war and open displays of French sympathy for the Serbs, Russia seemed to actively pursue conflict. Even though Vienna had received word of Berlin's backing against Serbia on 6 July, the ultimatum was not presented to Belgrade until 23 July—more than two weeks later. The Austrians rejected Belgrade's answer as insufficient and ordered a partial mobilization for 28 July. Senior Russian ministers had met in St. Petersburg on 24 and 25 July and decided to initiate a partial mobilization. Thus, even before St. Petersburg was aware of the Serbian reply or the Austrian response, it began preparing for war. This turn of events served to accelerate the crisis, reducing available options and the time necessary to consider them.

Although Austrian intentions were clear in the text of the ultimatum and provided sufficient reason to believe that a conflict was inevitable, mobilization of Russian forces was not the only policy option available. Conflict may have been unavoidable between Austria-Hungary and Serbia, but not with Russia. Russian responses to the July crisis (with French backing) betray the same belligerent and provocative characteristics as the German-backed Habsburg policy toward Serbia. Indeed, Russia's general mobilization in the last days of July constituted the end of any chance at containment of the crisis. Russian involvement obliged the Germans to enter the war and enact their standing strategy in case of military confrontation with Russia: the Schlieffen-Moltke Plan. Violation of Belgian neutrality obliged Great Britain to enter the fray.

Vienna desired, sought, and pursued war with Serbia. It hoped that German support would act as a deterrent to direct Russian involvement. Germany failed to recognize the implications of its decision to back the Austrian retaliatory action against Serbia blindly and remained aloof and uninformed as to the details of that action. France made a similar miscalculation to that of Germany by making clear its support to Russia to oppose any action against Serbia. The Russian response exuded confidence and belligerence and served to escalate the conflict beyond a localized conflict to one of pan-European proportions.

Nevertheless, none of the protagonists of July 1914 either foresaw or sought out a conflict on the scale of World War I. Rather, developments in both alliances, the premium that domestic turmoil placed on success abroad, and clashing strategic interests set the stage for total war. The "short war illusion" persisted up to the outbreak of actual fighting and facilitated a rather casual approach to the possibility of conflict. Indeed, each of the agents clearly considered war an acceptable policy option. However, the evidence does not support the idea that Germany alone sought and instigated the conflict. Although it undeniably played an essential role, Germany mirrored France in its reckless support for the policies of a belligerent power, giving insufficient consideration to the ramifications of that support. These miscalculations manifested in grave consequences for the whole of Europe and beyond.

–SCOTT VARHO,
ARLINGTON, VIRGINIA

References

L. L. Farrar Jr., *The Short War Illusion: German Policy, Strategy & Domestic Affairs, August–December 1914* (Santa Barbara, Cal.: ABC-Clio, 1973).

Niall Ferguson, *The Pity of War* (New York: Basic Books, 1999).

Catherine Karolyi, "The Outbreak of World War I," *New Hungarian Quarterly,* 5 (Autumn 1964): 62–97.

Laurence Lafore, *The Long Fuse: An Interpretation of the Origins of World War I* (Philadelphia: Lippincott, 1965).

Joachim Remak, *The Origins of World War I, 1871–1914* (New York: Holt, Rinehart & Winston, 1967).

Jerome Thale, "World War I and the Perception of War," *Southern Humanities Review,* 16 (Summer 1982): 185–210.

Samuel R. Williamson Jr., "The Origins of World War I," *Journal of Interdisciplinary History,* 18 (1988): 795–818.

OUTBREAK OF
WORLD WAR I

RUSSIA IN WORLD WAR I

Was Imperial Russia doomed to defeat in World War I?

Viewpoint: Yes. Russia could not cope with the demands of modern warfare or the military might of Germany.

Viewpoint: No. Russia was much more resilient than has commonly been recognized and fought until its domestic political situation collapsed.

Russia was one of the greatest losers of World War I (1914–1918). Its armies were defeated on the battlefield; much of its territory was occupied by enemies; both its reigning Romanov dynasty and the vaguely democratic government that replaced it were toppled by domestic political turmoil; authority fell into the hands of extremists, who presided over one of the most repressive regimes in history; and the price of peace was a massive loss of territory, population, and resources. Was Imperial Russia doomed to such terrible catastrophe?

Some scholars believe that it was. Despite the Russian Empire's economic and social advances in the decades before 1914, it remained underdeveloped and militarily weak in comparison with its main adversary, Germany. With superior technology and training, German armies not only inflicted huge defeats on the Russians but also simultaneously waged an aggressive campaign in Western Europe. Russia, facing major consequences from its low military and civilian morale, overtaxed infrastructure, and exhausted resources, could never have mounted effective resistance and should rightly be considered one of the conflict's most vulnerable powers.

Yet, others believe that in military terms Russia was not that far out of step with its adversaries. Despite its ultimate defeat in the war, it launched successful campaigns against Austria-Hungary and the Ottoman Empire, Germany's main allies, and held off some German attacks in the earlier stages of the war. Its supply problems were no more severe than those of the other combatants, all of which struggled to coordinate industry and orient it toward war production. Like its allies and competitors, moreover, Russia was capable of finding solutions. In terms of casualties, the Russians, who had the largest population and mobilized more men than any other power, did not suffer more on the battlefield, either in absolute or relative terms. The argument follows that it was not an inherent inferiority that imperiled Russia's ability to fight and remain competitive but rather the domestic political and social crises that had begun brewing before the war.

Viewpoint:
Yes. Russia could not cope with the demands of modern warfare or the military might of Germany.

When Imperial Russia went to war in 1914, it was certain to lose. In almost every major category it lagged far behind its principal adversary, Germany, and for many reasons it was incapable of competing in a modern war. Ultimately, Russia's inability to fight in World War I (1914–1918) deprived its political leadership of legitimacy and precipitated the collapse of its expanding prewar economy and burgeoning civil society.

That Russia could not stand up to a modern European opponent should have come as no great surprise. No Russian army had won a major battle against a European power since the victories over Napoleon Bonaparte in 1812–1814. Although Russia won its wars against the Ottoman Empire (1828–1829 and 1877–1878) and against the native peoples of Central Asia and the Caucasus throughout the nineteenth century, European powers could effectively scale back its victories by threatening military intervention. When Russia engaged modern industrial powers in direct combat, as it did when it battled the Ottomans' European allies in the Crimean War (1853–1856) and Japan (1904–1905), it suffered crushing defeats.

The defeat in the Crimean War directly spurred a long period of reform intended to modernize Russia and increase its military and economic competitiveness. Particularly in the years after 1890, under the leadership of its finance minister, Sergei Witte, the empire experienced rapid industrial growth, expanding international trade, and major improvements in infrastructure. Yet, the results of this long-term strategy were insufficient to help Russia in 1914, when its economy still ranked a distant fifth among the world's great powers. Since modern military prowess depended more than ever before on economic power and raw industrial strength, the numbers already doomed Russia on the battlefield.

This point was not lost on European strategic planners as they looked toward future conflict. Indeed, the Russian government's sponsorship of modernization and industrial growth in the decades before 1914 derived from its realization that it would remain hopelessly uncompetitive without them. Russia's unsuccessful war with Japan, which helped touch off a domestic political revolt, reinforced that perception. In addition to partial political modernization, in which Tsar Nicholas II conceded some power to an elected legislature and abridged the authoritarian strictures of his government, the Russian elite redoubled their efforts to modernize the economy and society, at least partly in preparation for a general European war. Petr Stolypin, who served as premier from 1906 to 1911, famously declared, "Give me twenty years of peace, and you will not recognize Russia!" He meant that avoiding war for the foreseeable future would give him time to expand Russia's industrial sector, increase literacy and primary education, and modernize the military and civilian infrastructure to the point where the empire could compete with its potential adversaries.

France, Russia's ally, also realized its need for development. Concerned about its own ability to defend against a German attack, France did all it could to promote Russia's modernization. Beginning in the 1890s, French loans provided much of the capital for Russia's public and private development in industry and infrastructure. After the Russo-Japanese War demonstrated Russia's military and economic weakness, the French made their annual loans increasingly conditional on projects of military significance, including railroads connecting the rest of the country to the German borderlands.

Russia's adversaries were also aware of the importance of its development. Otto von Bismarck, the German chancellor until 1890, closed his country's financial markets to Russian borrowers because he realized that investment would only make Russia stronger. This move was a factor in driving Russia to form its alliance with France in 1892. As a result German military planners, confronted with a potential two-front conflict, began to believe that every mile of new Russian railroad track would reduce their battlefield advantage. Concluding that it would be better to fight the war sooner rather than later, they eventually estimated that a failure to attack Russia before 1916 would jeopardize their ability to win a war on two fronts. The sense that Russia's continuing economic development was closing a window of opportunity convinced many in the German leadership to advocate conflict in 1914.

The Russians, their allies, and their enemies all were right. Further development, Stolypin's "twenty years," was essential for Russia's military competitiveness. But it never happened. Stolypin had only five years in power before his assassination; his less effective successor had just three before his dismissal in 1914. Within a few weeks of Germany's declaration of war, this shortfall became painfully clear. Russia's initial and unexpected penetration into East Prussia in August 1914 ended in a costly rout at Tannenberg at the end of the month, and German reinforcements halted the Russian march into the Austro-Hungarian province of Galicia in September. After inconclusive winter positioning, the Germans and Austrians checked a renewed Russian advance in Galicia in March 1915. A German attack in the spring and summer of that year forced the Russians out of their Polish territories, depriving the empire of a significant amount of its industrial base and railroad infrastructure. The Russians regained some ground in Galicia in a counteroffensive in the summer of 1916, but as soon as German reinforcements arrived, the attack ground to a halt.

Deficiencies in tactics and technology went a long way toward explaining these reverses. Many senior Russian commanders in 1914 were still enamored of dated tactics. The commander of the Northwestern Front, which included Russian forces deployed against Germany, insisted on concentrating men, artillery, and supplies in strategic fortresses, an idea that rendered them useless for ground operations and, as the mobile Germans could easily bypass and reduce these fortresses, superfluous in the war at large. Military modernizers had been consistently sidelined in the prewar years by a largely corrupt and geriatric high command that mistrusted them. The war minister, General Vladimir Sukhomlinov, proudly declared in 1913 that he had not read a military manual in twenty-five years. Emerging military technologies—including tanks, machine guns, aircraft, and telephone communications—were explored on a relatively small scale by the Russian military. While tanks and aircraft were of only marginal use elsewhere, the machine gun was one of the war's most decisive weapons. The telephone became essential for coordinating ground operations on the Western Front, but the Russians almost never used it, even at military headquarters after Tsar Nicholas II relocated there after assuming personal command of the army in August 1915. The cavalry, which all the other European powers had relegated mainly to ceremonial and supply roles, remained an essential component of the Russian military, even though horses could do little against German machine guns and artillery, and despite the challenges of moving horses and fodder around on already overtaxed railroads. One recent study of Russian military policy before World War I makes the point clearly with its title: *Bayonets before Bullets: The Imperial Russian Army, 1861–1914* (1992).

Behind the lines Russia's war effort was for the most part a bleak endeavor. No combatant power expected World War I to last as long as it did, and all experienced military and civilian shortages of various kinds, but in Russia they were especially acute. The army was so dramatically undersupplied that as many as one-third of its soldiers went into battle unarmed and supplied only with the unpromising instructions to pick up weapons from fallen comrades to con-

tinue the attack. German and Ottoman control of strategic waterways placed major limitations on Russia's ability to import foreign military matériel. Even supplies that could get through to the northern ports of Murmansk and Arkhangelsk, or to Vladivostok on the Pacific, had to wait for months on the faraway docks before they could be moved across Siberia or the Russian north to the front. French loans, on which Russia had been so dependent before 1914, disappeared as France found itself in the fight of its life and had to borrow heavily from the United States and Britain for its own needs. American finance, which became essential for Britain as well as France, was not made available to Russia. Although domestic industry partly succeeded in making up for shortfalls in weapons production, one expert has calculated that by April 1915 Russian artillery units could fire only two shells per day. When Nicholas II took personal command of the army in August 1915, his near permanent absence from the capital, Petrograd, hindered the coordination of government ministries and left increasing amounts of authority in the hands of Empress Alexandra and her favorites, most of whom were dubious nonentities of limited competence.

Exhausted and strained beyond endurance, by winter 1916–1917 the Russian infrastructure could neither supply the front adequately nor transport a sufficient amount of food to urban centers. When the supply of bread in Petrograd began to run low in February 1917, several days of demonstrations and rioting caused the tsarist government to lose control of the city. The troops in its garrison defected to the demonstrators. In early March, Nicholas II, warned that the army would longer support him, abdicated in favor of a provisional government formed by members of the legislature to which he had delegated limited powers, a group that uneasily shared authority with a spontaneously assembled body of workers' and soldiers' deputies, the Petrograd Soviet (council). Like their tsarist predecessors, however, these authorities were also incapable of fighting the war to a successful conclusion. Crisis followed crisis through 1917, and the authority of the new government ebbed. By November of that year the radical Bolshevik Party—promising bread, land, and freedom—seized control of the capital in a coup d'état. As the new government swiftly became a brutal dictatorship, one of its first acts was to sign an armistice with Germany, followed by the harsh peace treaty of Brest-Litovsk in March 1918. Both the communist dictatorship and the punitive peace were the sad fate of a nation doomed to defeat in World War I.

–PAUL DU QUENOY,
GEORGETOWN UNIVERSITY

FIGHTING THE RUSSIANS

Austrian officer Octavian Taslauanu recounts in his memoirs an engagement with Russian forces in the Carpathian Mountains on 20 November 1914:

I had just put on my shirts again—I always wore two or three—when I heard a shout from all sides: "The Russians are on us!"

Private Torna came to our shelter to announce: "Sir, the Russians are breaking through our line on the top!"

I did not yet believe it, but, at any cost, I asked my friend Fothi to conduct the company to the trenches. Meanwhile I hastily put on my boots, took my rifle, and rejoined the company as it was emerging from the wood.

There I stopped. I could hardly believe my eyes. What was it I saw? Along the whole front, the Russians and our men were in contact, staring at, threatening (with bayonets fixed), shouting at, and, in places, blazing away at each other.

Among the junipers, near to the trench we had dug three days back, the Russians and our men were scrambling together, fighting and kicking, around a supply of bread intended for the 12th Company. This struggle of starving animals for food only lasted a few seconds. They all got up, each man having at least a fragment of bread, which he devoured voraciously.

With a rapid glance I counted the Russians. They were not more numerous than ourselves, and I saw them drag our men away one by one by pulling at the corners of their blankets—for our shepherds had turned their blankets into overcoats.

One or two of them, a little more knowing than the rest, unfastened these coverings and, with a shake of the shoulders, left them in the hands of the Russians. The latter, well content with their prize, went their way laughing, while our men came back to us. I thought to myself that, after all, it could not be much worse in Siberia than it was here.

Some of the Russians now tried to surround us. One raw young recruit came quite close up to us and raised his rifle at me. I held mine to the ready in response. It was a thrilling moment. I don't know what it was, but something in my look prevented him from firing, and I too refrained.

He took to his heels and fled. But the shock had been too much for me, and, like a savage, I yelled in a fury: "Disarm them!"

I threw myself on to the group nearest to us, and Fothi and I together wrenched the rifles out of the hands of the two Russian soldiers. They all surrendered forthwith like lambs. We took sixty of them. All our men wished to escort the prisoners.

I selected three as a guard, the third to walk behind and carry the Russian's rifle. I was obliged to have recourse to threats before I could induce them to enter the trench, and I then marched them off in file to the Commander-in-Chief.

And this is how bread, holy bread, reconciles men, not only in the form of Communion before the holy altar, but even on the field of battle. The peasants, who, in their own homes, whether in Russia or elsewhere, sweat blood in order to insure the ripening of the golden ear of corn which is to feed their masters, once they are on the battlefield forget the behests of these masters who have sent them forth to murder their fellows, and they make peace over a scrap of bread.

The bread which they have produced and harvested makes them brothers. After this scene not a single shot disturbed the forest, and those who had been able to preserve a whole loaf, quickly shared it brotherly fashion with the prisoners, the latter offering them tobacco in exchange. All this, of course, took place in front of our bivouacs in the heart of the forest.

I sent Fothi to the Major to ask for reinforcements, as I was expecting a second attack. The prisoners told me that the Russians had come about four hundred strong.

I did not have long to wait. An hour later, on the edge of the wood, a party of Russians appeared. They were standing with their rifles at the slope, beckoning to us to approach. One of our men left his party and came to tell us that the Russians wished to surrender, but that we ought to surround them.

It was no doubt a fresh ruse. A quarter of an hour before I had sent out a patrol of two men—a Rumanian and a Saxon—and they had not returned. The Rumanian had surrendered and the Saxon had been killed.

My reinforcements arrived, sixty men of the 10th Company, under Second Lieutenant Szollosy, the man who was always the best hand at cursing and belabouring our Rumanians. I sent his sergeant-major, a brutal and thoroughly repellent Saxon, together with twenty men, to the right to surround the Russians.

I certainly doomed them to death. I reckoned that if the Russians wished to surrender they would not wait for us to surround them first. They would lay down their arms and give themselves up. On the other hand, if they did fire on our men, all who had gone out to the corner of the forest would fall victims. But calculations are all very fine; on the field of battle they are apt to be misleading.

Surrender was the last thing in the world that the Russians against whom our men were advancing with fixed bayonets had in mind.

I went over the top, clambering over the body of a man whose brains were sticking out of his head, and signed to them to surrender—they were at most 200 yards away.

But they still continued to call to us without attempting to move. I thereupon gave the command, "Fire!" and held my own rifle at the ready. At this point my calculations broke down. My Rumanians refused to fire, and, what was more, prevented me from firing either. One of them put his hand on my rifle and said "Don't fire, sir; if we fire, they will fire too. And why should Rumanians kill Rumanians?" (He was thinking of the Bessarabians.)

I accordingly refrained, but, beside myself with rage, tried to rejoin my right wing, where incredible things were happening.

The schoolmaster Catavei and Cizmas barred my way, exclaiming: "Stop, don't go and get yourself shot, too!"

Our men were advancing towards the Russians, and, with their arms at the slope, were shaking hands with them; and the fraternizing business started again.

"Surrender, and we will surrender, too. We're quite ready."

Our men were bringing in Russians, and vice versa. It was a touching sight.

I saw one of my Rumanians, towards Saliste, kiss a Russian and bring him back. Their arms were round each other's necks as though they were brothers. They were old friends, who had been shepherd boys together in Bessarabia.

We took ninety Russians as prisoners in this way; whilst they took thirty of our men.

But this was not the last of the adventures of that wonderful day.

I was afraid of a third attack. A Moldavian from Bessarabia, noticing what a handful we were, said to me: "If we had known there were so few of you we should have gone for you with sticks."

I again applied to the Major for reinforcements and a machine gun. As it happened, he had just called up a company of the 96th Infantry Regiment; they arrived almost immediately—125 men, under Lieutenant Petras—and went to lengthen our right wing.

As for me, the Major sent me to a bank on the left, to direct two machine guns where to fire in order to cut off the retreat of those Russians who had remained in the wood. I had hardly advanced a hundred yards before I heard a shout of "Hurrah!" in my sector.

I called out to the Major to find out what it meant, and went on. In a hollow I found a field officer—unfortunately, I have forgotten his name—who sent a lieutenant to accompany me to the machine guns.

But it was a Russian machine gun that welcomed us as soon as we reached the trenches. The bullets whizzed by, thick and fast. One grazed my leg, another came within a hand's-breadth of my head.

The Russians employ detachments of snipers, who creep into advanced positions and pick off officers only. Major Paternos had the fingers of his left hand shot off in his observation post. They are wonderful shots. I showed my respect for them by not leaving the trench until nightfall, when I returned to my sector.

Lieutenant Petras had attacked the Russians in the wood. That was the meaning of the cheers I had heard, of which the most patent result was the reduction of the relieving company of the 96ths to twenty-five men. Those who had entered the wood never returned, and had certainly fallen a prey to the Russians.

Once again I had escaped the dangers of that fateful day, which the Commander-in-Chief assured us, in a special Army Order, would be inscribed on the page of history.

Our scrap with the Russians may have been extremely comic, but at least we had held our positions—and that alone was a victory. We had been allotted the task of keeping the crest, from which, if they had been able to seize it, the Russians would have threatened our line in the rear and on the flank; and we had fulfilled it.

Source: *Octavian Taslauanu, "Memoirs & Diaries: An Austrian Officer's Memoir of the Battle of the Carpathian Passes," in* Source Records of the Great War, *volume 3, edited by Charles F. Horne (Indianapolis: American Legion, 1930); First World War.Com <http://www.firstworldwar.com/diaries/carpathianmemoir.htm>*

RUSSIA IN WORLD WAR I

**Viewpoint:
No. Russia was much more
resilient than has commonly been
recognized and fought until its
domestic political situation
collapsed.**

It is always difficult when examining the past to separate the end result from what was actually happening as the events were occurring. One prime example of this situation is World War I (1914–1918) and Russia's role in it. Russia had military plans and capabilities that matched those of the other Great Powers. What led to its defeat was a combination of the course of the war and its effect on the internal situation of the empire. While it is often hard to separate the domestic and foreign aspects of war in the twentieth century, Russia was defeated mainly by pressures within the Russian Empire. This defeat was not preordained. Rather, the new type of war unleashed on Europe was one where all of society was mustered in order to succeed. Russia fell because it was not able to hold up under all of these pressures.

Russia had adequate military plans for the war that everyone in Europe believed was imminent. By the fall of 1913 Russia had completed work on Mobilization Order #20, a comprehensive set of war plans that called for rapid advances into both German and Austro-Hungarian territory, supplemented by a network of strategic fortresses. Because of the lack of time to implement it (moving divisions to their new locations, logistical problems, and so on) before the outbreak of hostilities on 1 August 1914, however, Russia was forced to implement Mobilization Order #19, which had been completed and accepted by the monarchy on 1 May 1912 and was intended to focus on one enemy at a time. Nevertheless, both of these Mobilization Orders were the full equivalent of either the Joffre Plan (Plan XVII) in France or the Schlieffen Plan in Germany. All four plans envisioned quick offensive maneuvers intended to knock out enemy forces in a few weeks. In many ways the Russian and French military plans were more current than the German plans. Field Marshall Joseph Joffre became the French chief of staff in 1911 and drew up his plans shortly thereafter. This preparation occurred at the same time the Russian General Staff was writing Mobilization Order #19. The German plan was written and revised by the chief of the German general staff, Count Alfred von Schlieffen, between his appointment in 1891 and retirement in 1906, and it was subsequently modified and substantially weakened by his timid succes-

sor, Count Helmuth von Moltke. At the start of the war Germany was operating with a weakened plan originally conceived more than two decades before the conflict broke out, while the Russians and the French were organizing under two- or three-year-old military plans.

Mobilization Order #19 was important in understanding Russian military strategy—both offensive and defensive. One of the most important aspects of this plan was that it actually consisted of two separate plans: one to fight Austria-Hungary (Plan A) and another to fight Germany (Plan G). Plan A focused on a strong offense against Austria-Hungary across the Carpathian Mountains, while troops stationed along the East Prussian border would focus on holding the border. Plan G was operationally the opposite of Plan A: the troops along the Austria-Hungary border would hold the line against attack, while the bulk of the Russian forces attacked Germany. In the end, even though the more ambitious Mobilization Order #20 could not be implemented, having these dual strategies within the military planning proved beneficial to Russia because there was no joint strategy and planning between the Central Powers.

When Russia made the decision to mobilize on 31 July 1914, its leaders focused initially on Plan G and marched into East Prussia. They quickly suffered two major defeats at the hands of Germans: the Battle of Tannenberg (26–30 August) and the Battle of the Masurian Lakes (6–15 September). By December the Germans had captured the industrial city of Lodz in Russian Poland. The front was not just a story of defeat after defeat for the Russians, however. During the winter months Russian forces in Poland successfully defended Warsaw against German attacks and held a stable front. Bringing Plan A into operation, the Russians successfully captured Lemberg (Lvov), the capital of the Austro-Hungarian province of Galicia, in September. When Austro-Hungarian forces launched an offensive in the Carpathians in January 1915, they were defeated by weather and a Russian counteroffensive. In March 1915 the Russians captured the Galician fortress of Przemysl, taking 120,000 Austrian prisoners. The Russians bested the Austro-Hungarian forces throughout the entire war, and Germany constantly had to divert troops from other fronts to aid its beleaguered allies. After the fall of Przemysl the Austrian general staff worried that the Russians had imminent plans to march into Hungary. In the spring of 1916 the Russians launched another huge offensive under General Aleksei Brusilov against Austria and made important gains. Given these successes, it was entirely possible that Russia could have beaten Austria-Hungary if it were not also fighting the

RUSSIA IN WORLD WAR I

Germans. Indeed, part of the diplomatic rationale for Berlin's involvement in World War I was that it knew that Austria—its oldest and only reliable ally—could not stand up to the Russians and their Serbian clients alone. At the same time, Russia was also successful in fighting the Ottomans in the Caucasus, capturing a series of Turkish fortresses. Since Russia had not lost to the Turks in any military engagement since the eighteenth century, it is likely that it would have defeated them, too, had Germany not been in the war. Although Russian Poland fell to the Germans over the summer of 1915, Russia's other successes should not be discounted.

The Russians were defeated by the Germans, but many of the reasons for this result were not because of poor battlefield performance. Most had to do with the economic situation within Russia. There are many accounts of how backward economic development inside the Russian Empire limited its military strength. First, there was a short supply of money. Russia had a weak domestic tax base; its revenue-yielding foreign trade dried up because the Germans and Turks controlled the Baltic and Black Sea egresses used by Russian shipping; and its traditional foreign-capital markets in France were taken over by the desperate French war effort. The war caused the highest inflation experienced by any combatant power, while real wages declined faster than anywhere else. Second, the transportation system within Russia was minimal in comparison to that of Germany and the other major powers. The Russian Empire was much larger than any of the Central Powers and had a much lower population density, but its railway development was smaller in absolute as well as relative terms when compared to its adversaries. Third, Russia faced a chronic shortage of guns and other military equipment. Rampant corruption in the War Ministry prevented an effective allocation of resources before the war. Russia's smaller industrial base was uncompetitive with Germany's, but Russia was nevertheless able to stockpile a relatively impressive supply of arms by 1916, relying on assistance from the Western allies and dramatically increased domestic production.

Despite these limitations, Russia was still able to mobilize more than 12 million soldiers over the course of the war. Only Germany, which mobilized 11 million soldiers, was able to come close to matching its actual numbers of soldiers in the field. The casualty figures were even more telling. Russia lost about 1.8 million dead, compared to more than 2 million for Germany, 1.1 million for Austria-Hungary, and more than 325,000 for the Ottoman Empire. While one must remember that the Central Powers also had to fight Russia's allies in other theaters, it is important to note that Russia lost only half as many men as they did in the field. In proportional terms 11.5 percent of Russia's mobilized troops were killed. This figure was by no means insignificant, but for Austria-Hungary it was 12.2 percent, for Germany it was 15.4 percent, and for the Ottoman Empire it was an enormous 26.8 percent. Russia lost a huge number of men to enemy captivity—3.5 million between 1914 and 1917—but the Germans, Austrians, and Turks together also had more than 3 million men taken prisoner over the course of the war. Russia's high rate of capitulation, moreover, had much to do with the apathy that its undersupplied soldiers felt about defending a country devastated by domestic political dissension, a situation that likewise came to cause mass surrenders of German, Austrian, and Turkish troops in the last year of the war.

Russia's utility in the field was recognized by its allies. The Treaty of London, signed on 5 September 1914 by Russia, Great Britain, and France, stated that there would be no separate peace. In war aims talks held in the first months of the war, Western diplomats gave Russia substantial territorial concessions—including the strategically important and long-contentious Turkish Straits—in the hope that these prospective gains would keep Russia in the war. Even after the collapse of the Russian monarchy in February 1917, Allied missions continued to urge the Provisional Government that succeeded it to remain in the war.

Aside from the domestic limitations listed above, Russia was in a difficult political situation as it fought the war. Russia was fighting for two separate goals at the same time: to maintain its Great Power status and to maintain the monarchy. German diplomatic pressure had already forced Russia to back down from protecting its Serbian client twice during the Balkan Wars (1912–1913), and Russia had been forced to swallow Austria-Hungary's enhanced position after its annexation of Bosnia-Herzegovina in 1908. If Russia could not stand up to other powers, then it would lose its position in world politics. It was also felt that if Russia lost the war, the monarchy would be forced to take the blame and would fall. Russia experienced the same initial enthusiasm for the war that every other European country went through. Where there had previously been dissent and even strikes, there was near unanimous support for the war and the monarchy, even among dissident socialists. Widespread strikes only started to return in mid to late 1915, following military defeats. Even so, there were only about 100,000 individuals who went on strike at that time. By the end of 1916, as the situation got worse, there were massive strikes all over the country, but these increasingly had to do with short supplies of food. In Petrograd (the renamed St. Petersburg) more than 250,000 individuals participated in strikes at the end of 1916. The war effort had put a strain on Russia's economy and society. It was a new type of war that, because of the large number of troops as well as military goods necessary to fight it, meant that all of society, not just the soldiers on the front lines, had to participate in the war effort. Military supplies had precedence over civilian goods and food. Military defeats created refugees, led to the loss of agricultural land, reduced the production of civilian goods (even as the supply of military goods was increasing), and seriously impacted the country's transportation network. These factors fed the discontent of workers and citizens of the Russian Empire. By February 1917 there was only a few days' supply of bread left in the capital. Peaceful demonstrations against the war, aided by warm weather, grew. The ineffective government failed to counter them until it was too late, and within just a few days the tsarist regime had vanished. The Provisional Government that followed was determined to keep the country in the war, but the same problems on the home front weakened its tenuous position just as they had weakened the tsarist regime.

Russia was able to hold its own in the field in World War I, not only until the domestic political order collapsed but also for several months thereafter. Even after the monarchy fell, the Provisional Government was able to launch an attack into Galicia in July 1917, an offensive that was not tactically unsound. However, this attack also failed in the end because the domestic situation did not permit the government to focus fully on the war effort. There was a larger war brewing within Russia. Domestic problems within the Russian Empire were the key to its defeat in World War I. However, neither victory nor defeat was preordained in this new type of war that involved all of society, not just the political and military elite. No one was prepared for it, and only the last parties standing could win. Russia was just one of the first to fall.

–BRANDON C. SCHNEIDER,
GEORGETOWN UNIVERSITY

References

Niall Ferguson, *The Pity of War* (New York: Basic Books, 1999).

Orlando Figes, *A People's Tragedy: The Russian Revolution, 1891–1924* (New York: Viking, 1997).

Bruce W. Menning, *Bayonets before Bullets: The Imperial Russian Army, 1861–1914* (Bloomington: Indiana University Press, 1992).

Richard Pipes, *The Russian Revolution* (New York: Knopf, 1990).

Norman Stone, *The Eastern Front: 1914–1917* (London: Hodder & Stoughton, 1975; New York: Scribners, 1975).

RUSSIA IN WORLD WAR I

SECOND THIRTY YEARS' WAR

Can the period 1914–1945 be compared usefully to the Thirty Years' War?

Viewpoint: Yes. In both the period 1914–1945 and the Thirty Years' War European powers attempted to thwart the hegemonic designs of a Germanic state.

Viewpoint: No. The two world wars had different causes and results than the Thirty Years' War, and comparisons between them are misleading.

Historians, looking for long-term continuities in European history, have wondered whether it is apt to categorize the period from 1914 to 1945—a time that included World War I (1914–1918), World War II (1939–1945), and a troubled interwar era—as a repetition of an earlier period of European conflict, the Thirty Years' War (1618–1648). The seventeenth-century struggle, which involved a series of attempts by Austrian Habsburg emperors to gain definitive control of Central Europe, is seen by some scholars as a Germanic power bid for a European hegemony, only to be defeated by a coalition of opponents. These academics argue that Germany's aggressive role in World War I and World War II, and its neighbors' successful resistance to it, repeated this pattern in the twentieth century.

Another view maintains that the more one studies the two conflicts, the more different they truly appear to be. Habsburg ambitions were largely limited to consolidating control over the German lands; twentieth-century German ambitions were to create a hegemony over all Europe, and in certain cases beyond. The twentieth-century conflicts were separated by a long period of peace that had no seventeenth-century counterpart. Finally, modern Germany had three different regimes in power from 1914 to 1945, each with different structures, goals, and ideologies. Habsburg rule and ambition remained steady and consistent for all of the Thirty Years' War. These and other differences suggest that the conflicts have only superficial similarities.

Viewpoint:
Yes. In both the period 1914–1945 and the Thirty Years' War European powers attempted to thwart the hegemonic designs of a Germanic state.

The treaties concluded in 1919 that ostensibly ended World War I (1914–1918) were the product of exhaustion and anxiety. The exhaustion was a function of four years'

worth of improvised mobilization for mass war, the dimensions and endurance of which no reasonable authority had predicted. All the combatants except the United States had been stretched to their limits to keep pace. Russia, Austria-Hungary, and finally Germany had imploded one after the other. France and Britain were at the end of their resources. Even marginal players, such as Japan, saw limitations to their ambitions. Secondary states from Belgium to New Zealand had been trampled under conquerors' boots or exsanguinated by the casualties of remote fighting fronts. Colonial empires had been destabilized by the unending demands for manpower and material—and by prima facie evidence that European civilization might well have been the oxymoron eventually suggested by Indian nationalist Mahatma Gandhi.

The fear in 1919 is usually described as a bourgeois/capitalist response to the emergence of an avenging proletariat guided by the emerging Soviet Union. In fact, the Bolshevik bogey was a convenient focus for a spectrum of anxieties that involved issues of gender, generation, identity, and stress reaction—to name only a few. In the aftermath of the struggle in the trenches the main goal of the war's losers, its winners, and everyone in between was to restore at least a facade of stability behind which individuals and communities could begin reconstructing their lives.

Altogether this environment was unpromising ground for a stable, comprehensive settlement of the issues that created the war and those created by it. Four particular factors, each reflecting and shaping the politics of specific Great Powers, nurtured continuity with a later, larger conflict. First was the German Question. Germany prior to 1914 had been in the anomalous position of being not quite strong enough to support its European and global pretensions. The Great War had diminished Germany's absolute capacity for war making—but left it relatively stronger in the context of an east-central Europe reorganized into a clutch of medium-sized states whose own pretensions far exceeded their capacities, and a Russia excluded from the councils of Europe that was even more dangerous than Germany.

The consequences of this situation were further exacerbated by a postwar climate of victimization, encouraged by successive governments of the Weimar Republic, that fostered a revanchist/revisionist mentality extending deeply into the postwar German Left. That mindset, it should be emphasized, involved more posturing than substance. Apart from the practical fact that the Versailles Treaty (1919) left Germany disarmed to a point where even self-defense was a dubious effort, ordinary citizens were by no means anxious to don uniforms and pick up guns in an effort to overturn the new order. It was rather that Germany's voice and weight, even when Minister of Foreign Affairs Gustav Stresemann was orchestrating policies of fulfillment and conciliation in the 1920s, were too often thrown behind the forces of entropy. When, beginning in 1933, Adolf Hitler challenged the Germans by transforming beer-hall rhetoric into public policy, they followed him to eventual ruin rather than

admit to themselves their nationalism had been only braggadocio.

Second, France contributed to the temporary nature of the Versailles settlement from the opposite end of the spectrum. After 1918 France recovered its long-lost status as the Continent's primary power—but found the position unsustainable with its own material and moral resources. Expedients such as stationing increasing numbers of troops from their empire in the *metropole* to compensate for the low birth rates of the war's "hollow years" failed to bridge the gap. French national policy during the interwar period instead developed around the aphorism that a general European war, while in no way desirable, should be fought on someone else's soil and involve spilling as little French blood as possible. The Maginot Line was part of a strategy whose projected complement was a forward defense in Belgium—with, let it be understood, full cooperation of the latter, to be gained by diplomacy. The other half of the strategy involved creating a network of alliances in Eastern Europe, for the purpose of deterring, distracting, and containing the Germans. The time thus bought would be used for the total mobilization of France's resources, with the eventual aim of a decisive offensive into the Reich.

France was so committed to the concept of a total war that it lacked what would later be called a "graduated deterrence capacity." As a result French policy moved toward a "bullying influence" pattern: the use of negative inducements to compel assent. In the final analysis French threats and warnings—however accurate as 1939 approached—proved no more effective when applied to allies and potential allies than to Hitler's Reich. When the alternative was a secondary role in another total war, the temptation to hope for a miracle proved overwhelming.

Third, the consequences of France's propensity for buying more time with its diplomatic efforts than its military force were exacerbated by Britain's reaction to a continental commitment initially assumed more by default than from a sense of self-interest. Prior to 1914 Britain's plans for general war involved replicating the Napoleonic experience: developing the island kingdom as the Triple Entente's arsenal and warehouse, emphasizing sea power to weaken the Central Powers, and committing no more forces in Europe than necessary to maintain its credibility with France and Russia. Even the New Armies raised in 1914–1915 were projected as a makeweight, to be introduced into battle

German soldiers viewing the Eiffel Tower following the French surrender in 1940

(Range/Bettman/UPI)

only when both sides had worn each other down.

The reality symbolized and epitomized by the network of park-like military cemeteries constructed in France and Belgium in the 1920s left successive British governments committed to nothing deeper than avoiding a similar experience. Even supporters of European involvement saw airpower and mechanization as substitutes for the bodies of a new generation of Britain's young men. An empty treasury and an overextended imperium further encouraged intellectual and emotional rewriting of the history of the Great War in terms of a moral equivalence in turn legitimating Britain's withdrawal to a moral high ground that left a blank space in the ranks of states consequently committed to maintaining the peace of Versailles.

The fourth factor in the way Europe addressed its wartime issues in a postwar context was the behavior of the emerging world powers. For ideological and geopolitical reasons Soviet dictator Josef Stalin yearned for leadership in Europe. Outside of the "useful idiots" of the political and intellectual Left, the grim tyranny of the Union of Soviet Socialist Republics (U.S.S.R.) was so prima facie off-putting that, if it were indeed "the future, and it works," in the words of American socialist Lincoln Steffens, then better by far to tinker with the present and buy time before the darkness fell. The United States, on the other hand, nursed the burned fingers of its brief wartime involvement by withdrawing into economic and diplomatic isolation. The notion that entry into the war had been a fundamental mistake was part of the American myth even before 1929 as the Great Depression plunged the country into a self-preoccupation that arguably endured through most of World War II (1939–1945).

Added up, the behavior of the major players in the Euro-Atlantic system of the interwar years created a power vacuum whose dynamics could be changed almost at will by the behavior of any single participant. With no country of significance willing to accept the Versailles order as a primary element of its own interest, the point is not that it disintegrated but rather that it lasted as long as it did. That fact at least testifies to the West's deep reluctance to go to war again—which in turn proved vital both directly and indirectly to Hitler's diplomatic and military successes from 1934 to 1942. For these reasons both conflicts are correctly linked and in many ways represented a second Thirty Years' War centered around a struggle to thwart Germanic hegemony in Europe.

—DENNIS SHOWALTER,
COLORADO COLLEGE

Viewpoint:
No. The two world wars had different causes and results than the Thirty Years' War, and comparisons between them are misleading.

To describe the period 1914–1945 as a "second Thirty Years' War" (1618–1648) is a simplification that no comparative study of the two eras of conflict can support. Like any analogy, however, there is a grain of truth to it. Both the seventeenth-century conflict and the two world wars of the twentieth century were largely fought to restrain the hegemonic aspirations of a Germanic state. In the first case the Holy Roman Empire, a feudal conglomerate ruled by the Austrian Habsburgs, sought political as well as religious predominance in Central Europe. The second case involved two distinct regimes that despite their differences pursued ambitious war aims designed to ensure Germany's preeminence in Europe.

The comparisons largely end there. Perhaps the most obvious implication of stressing the similarity of the two conflicts is that historians should consider World War I (1914–1918) and World War II (1939–1945) to be nothing more than the same conflict separated by a twenty-year truce. Indeed, future British prime minister Winston Churchill, distinguished French marshal Ferdinand Foch, and many other participants perceived these events in this manner as they were happening. Such historians as A. J. P. Taylor and Sir Michael Howard have reached a similar conclusion in their studies.

There are several problems with this approach, however. First, it rests on the assumption that in the twentieth century the Germans, perhaps because of their "national character" or the "special path" of their history, were consistently predisposed toward using force to seize a European or world hegemony. No one can deny that this goal was true for German leader Adolf Hitler, and as scholar Fritz Fischer has argued, it is not an implausible approach to the study of Imperial Germany's motivations in World War I. Yet, there are many reasons to question whether such ambitions were a constant over the entire thirty-one-year period. Despite the unpopularity of the Versailles Treaty (1919), elite opinion in interwar Germany generally favored the nation's rehabilitation as a pacific European power and sought future revision of the treaty, either through longtime Foreign Minister Gustav Stresemann's "fulfillment" policy of accepting new international realities peacefully or a variant thereof. Conciliatory steps such as paying a revised war reparations bill on schedule, participating in international organizations, engaging in economic cooperation with the victorious allies, signing the Locarno Pact (1925) to guarantee the West European territorial status quo, and generally (albeit not always) following the military provisions of Versailles were intended to convince the victors of World War I that Germany could be trusted as a partner in upholding European security and thus could redeem itself as a respectable great power. In other words, for fifteen years of the supposed "second Thirty Years' War," the Germanic power was actively seeking a respectable role in a European order based on reconciliation and cooperation. Even if the Weimar Republic failed to manage its domestic challenges and was subverted by Nazism, the hard fact remains that for nearly half the period 1914–1945 Germany was neither engaging in nor planning to engage in a military démarche to achieve hegemonic domination.

There was no comparison to this situation during the Thirty Years' War. This series of conflicts may have proceeded in what historians call "phases," but each phase only resulted from the exhaustion of successive Habsburg enemies. The conflicts were not broken up by Habsburg defeats, lasting attempts at peacetime international reconciliation, and relapses into aggression. Indeed, Holy Roman Emperor Ferdinand II actually used the pauses that resulted from his military victories to consolidate greater authority over Germany, first by revoking the long-established political and confessional rights of Protestant rulers through confiscation and other forms of "restitution" and later by trading his acknowledgment of individual rulers' authority over religious matters in their domains for political loyalty. Even if French marshal Foch wanted to think of the 1919 peace settlement as a twenty-year truce in a single conflict—which, given the ostentatiously peaceful diplomacy of the 1920s, was not necessarily accurate—there was no comparable period in 1618–1648 that could have matched this description. The desperate rebels of the Kingdom of Bohemia, ill-fated Danish armies, effective but ultimately retiring Swedes, and finally French troops and subsidies may have taken their turns, but the challenge to a Central European Habsburg hegemony lasted consistently and virtually without interruption for thirty years. Indeed, since the French and Spanish remained at war with Vienna for a further eleven years after the Peace of Westphalia ended the intra-German conflict in 1648, restraining Habsburg hegemony might be described as an even longer and more determined process.

It is significant that there were consistent challenges to the Habsburgs, for resisting their attempts to establish hegemony over Germany was a consistent imperative for their enemies. The prospect of decisive Habsburg victories presented their Protestant subjects with the chance of long-term rule by a "heretical" and "devilish" Catholic superpower that they expected to rule through the Inquisition and Spanish troops. Habsburg victories would restrain the autonomy of the Protestant princes of the Holy Roman Empire and thwart their moves toward independence. Habsburg domination also would present Denmark and Sweden with the loss of their strategic and commercial positions in Central Europe, without which they were meaningless as powers. Moreover, it would reduce France to a satellite power. A failure to resist the aspirant Germanic power was impossible in these circumstances.

At certain times in 1914–1945, however, many leaders of the "antihegemonic" powers believed that they could reach some kind of accommodation with the Germans. The West reciprocated Stresemann's fulfillment policy in meaningful ways. Germany entered the League of Nations in 1926, its reparations debt was twice reduced and restructured (in 1924 and 1929), some aspects of its territorial dissatisfaction were vaguely promised future redress, and the Versailles armaments limitations became negotiable over time. Even after Adolf Hitler came to power in Germany in 1933, the core of Britain's policy of appeasement lay in the belief that Hitler—despite his belligerent rhetoric, less-than-affable political manifesto, and increasingly harsh treatment of Jews and political opponents—was at bottom a "reasonable fellow" who would gratefully reciprocate Western concessions with peaceful diplomacy and a cooperative foreign policy. Of course, the British were tragically wrong about Hitler, but it is significant that for most of the time outside of war, even during the Nazi period, they believed that Germany's aspirations within Europe were manageable. Right down to British prime minister Neville Chamberlain's "peace in our time" speech, after the Munich Crisis (September 1938), many British leaders even indicated that at least some of these aspirations were natural and acceptable.

The French were less willing to see the Germans as a nonthreat in the interwar period, but they were still unwilling to go to war on their own to confront Berlin. Indeed, France's failure to secure unilateral alliance commitments from Britain or the United States indicated how decisively the leaders of those countries believed that they would not have to go to war with Germany again. Even when there was substantial evidence of a rising German threat (for example, the remilitarization of the Rhineland in March 1936), France failed to form any serious coalition-style response to restrain it. Naturally, this policy meant that in relative terms France was not as strong as it had been in 1618–1648, but therein lies another crucial distinction. In the earlier period France could take the lead to build coalitions, subsidize the anti-Habsburg German and Scandinavian powers, and become directly involved in the conflict without having to rely on help from across the English Channel or the Atlantic Ocean. In the 1920s and 1930s the essential British and American allies from World War I were unwilling to back any French activity to check Germany. The "Little Entente" alliances that France made with Poland, Yugoslavia, Romania, and Czechoslovakia in the 1920s and the defense pact it concluded with the Soviet Union in 1935 were either ineffectual or burdensome or both.

During twentieth-century wartime, furthermore, France, like Denmark and Sweden, could scarcely defend itself from German expansion. In the seventeenth century the French could involve themselves in a major Central European conflict and remain reasonably secure in their ability to defend their own territory, from the Habsburgs and from other enemies as well. King Charles I of England's unsuccessful descents on La Rochelle and the nearby islands in the 1620s were disasters that led directly to the English constitutional crisis and created the conditions for his country's civil war. Spanish mercenaries crossed the Rhine into France in the 1640s but met with disastrous results. Infringements on French soil were in any case peripheral to what was happening in Germany. In the twentieth century this security was a luxury that belonged to a past era. British intervention in 1914 was decisive in stopping the German advance toward Paris. The expanded presence of British forces, the introduction of forces from the British overseas dominions, and the arrival of several hundred thousand American combat troops in 1918 were all necessary for France's survival and essential for victory in World War I. In World War II organized French resistance to the Germans crumbled in scarcely six weeks, even with British help, while national liberation depended on Anglo-American efforts. On the other side of the lines, leading Nazis could talk about France as though it were the next Switzerland (in other words, a marginal, powerless state in a German-ruled Europe) in a way that no Holy Roman Emperor could ever have imagined. France was unable to reprise its seventeenth-century role in the twentieth.

Whether France's de facto elimination as an effective counterweight to German power resulted from decadence, demographics, or diplomacy is not important here. Its diminished strategic role in Europe fundamentally altered the constellation of anti-German resistance. France had been the financial reservoir, armory, and protector of last resort in 1618–1648, but by the twentieth century the ability as well as the responsibility for restraining Germany shifted to the "Big Three"—Britain, the United States, and the Russian Empire/Soviet Union.

Yet, even if there was a coalition that challenged German hegemony in the twentieth century, the geographic dispersion and divergent worldviews of the powers that took up the roles formerly played by France, Denmark, Sweden, and the minor Protestant states dramatically altered the terms and conditions of resistance and intervention. For at least some period during 1914–1945 all three wartime centers of anti-German resistance saw no reason to confront and restrain Germany. Neither Germany's actual nor potential power was sufficient to provoke an isolationist United States, an isolated Soviet Union, or an accommodationist Britain to engage in constant vigilance, even—in the case of the United States and the Soviet Union— during time of war. For a substantial period none of these nations felt any specific strategic threat from, for instance, the remilitarization of the Rhineland, the fate of Memel (the Lithuanian district returned to Germany in 1939), or the existence of a German air force. In the Soviet case, on two occasions it made more immediate sense for them to reach a bilateral agreement with Germany, as they did in the separate World War I peace of March 1918 and in the Nazi-Soviet nonaggression pact of August 1939. Divided public and elite opinion kept the United States out of both world wars until it was directly attacked—after having issued repeated warnings in 1917 (World War I) and until it received an explicit declaration of war from Germany in 1941 (World War II). In the seventeenth century the consistent threat that the Protestant states and France saw in a consolidated Habsburg-led Holy Roman Empire made the prospect of a Germanic hegemony a much more immediate cause for concern and led them into the fray without the need for direct provocation.

The centrality of German lands in the Thirty Years' War also sharply distinguished that conflict from the period of the world wars. While the latter wars were in every sense pan-European, and even global, the seventeenth-century conflict was confined almost exclusively to what later became Germany or the Austrian Empire and to powers that had a direct interest in German affairs. France's determination to preserve a fragmented Holy Roman Empire was a matter thoroughly concerned with Germany. Spain operated from dynastic loyalty to its rulers' Austrian Habsburg cousins, but then only hesitantly and with a view toward establishing control over land communications with its rebellious Dutch provinces. Sweden and Denmark had territorial, religious, and commercial interests in Germany that dictated their stance as champions of the Protestant cause.

For these reasons it is more apt to describe the Thirty Years' War as a German civil war or a failed war of German unification. The Habsburgs responded first to a threat to their control of the Bohemian crown lands (which because of the nature of their political history and social composition counted as German rather than Czech) and thus the integrity of their familial holdings in Central Europe. Protestant resistance, led by outside powers (Denmark and Sweden) and supported by one (France) that also had strategic interests in German lands and affairs, allowed the Habsburgs to seek greater control over their nominal imperial subjects. Whether, and to what extent, they could have succeeded are open questions. Their aims, however, were mainly limited to securing the stricter obedience of their German subjects. Military activity was concentrated heavily within the German lands. Of the major battles, only the French victory at Rocroi (1643) occurred outside German territory, and it was fought against a Spanish army that had crossed the border from campaigning within Germany. Several non-German powers and armies may have fought, but their victories and defeats were virtually all at places with names such as Breitenfeld (1631), Lützen (1632), and Nördlingen (1634).

This point of divergence between 1618–1648 and 1914–1945 is perhaps the strongest refutation of the notion that the two periods of conflict were similar enough to bear the same name. If the historian should properly see the Thirty Years' War as an intra-German conflict, how could it be favorably compared to World War I and World War II? In an age of increasing European integration it has become fashionable to argue that the world wars were more events of a long "European Civil War," in which "adolescent" national rivalries worked themselves out and resulted in the settlement of what progressively seems to be a common European future. It is most accurate to argue that the period 1914–1945 was no second Thirty Years' War simply because the full and effective unification of Germany had occurred by 1914. If World War I and World War II were fought in response to growing German hegemonic aspirations over Europe, it is entirely correct to argue that the conflicts of 1618–1648 were fought to prevent a Germanic state from acquiring the power, resources, and unity necessary to make such a bid vis-à-vis the rest of the Continent—a challenge it could only have made if Germany had been consolidated as a more cohesive state. The logical step from contemplating a more complete hegemony within Germany to indulging in real bids for hegemonic power over Europe, and indeed the world, may appear small in a cursory study of European diplomatic history, but few of those who died in either world war would probably agree.

One should also compare outcomes. If two events are said to have been similar enough to share the same name, should they not have ended in a like manner? Of course, these two eras did not, and this fact reflects the broader differences in the nature of each conflict. The Peace of Westphalia (1648) effectively prevented the Habsburgs from achieving the further consolidation of imperial authority over Germany. German lands remained politically fragmented between the Habsburg crown lands and more than three hundred lesser states, which exercised greater amounts of autonomy and de facto independence. This condition of the peace created an entrée for Brandenburg-Prussia, which developed into a major European power in its own right and in just over two centuries seized the mantle of German leadership from Vienna. Westphalia also gave Denmark and Sweden expanded territorial and commercial rights within Germany and ensured their viability at least as major regional powers for another century or so. The recognition of Dutch and Swiss independence further decreased the Empire's potential power and resources. The net effect of the peace, then, was to restore most of the status quo and alter the rest of it in ways that permanently weakened the Habsburgs in favor of the lesser German states, the Protestant powers, and the French, who automatically benefited from a divided Germany and received some strategic territory.

In essence, there was nothing about the 1918 or 1945 Allied victories that was intended to restore a modified status quo. In both cases the Allies were determined to crush the German state (and, in World War I, the Austro-Hungarian Empire, which had grown diplomatically, economically, and militarily dependent on it) to the point where it could never again function as a potentially hegemonic power. That Germany could nevertheless recover after 1919 and present a second challenge twenty years later reveals only how poorly the Allies dealt with its aggressive potential in the aftermath of World War I. Despite the ultimate shortcomings of the Treaty of Versailles, the Allies entertained major plans to partition and partially occupy German territory, cripple the German economy with huge reparations payments, and permanently limit the size and offensive power of the German armed forces. Their lack of vigilance and decisiveness in 1914–1945 indicated once again how differently they perceived twentieth-century Germany from

DAWN OF THE GERMAN RULE

On 22 August 1939 German leader Adolf Hitler told army officers his thoughts on upcoming expansion and his belief that he would achieve it in a war some scholars have seen as a continuation of the efforts of the Germans in World War I:

Our strength lies in our quickness and in our brutality; Genghis Khan has sent millions of women and children into death knowingly and with a light heart. History sees in him only the great founder of States. As to what the weak Western European civilization asserts about me, that is of no account. I have given the command and I shall shoot everyone who utters one word of criticism, for the goal to be obtained in the war is not that of reaching certain lines but of physically demolishing the opponent. And so for the present only in the East I have put my death-head formations in place with the command relentlessly and without compassion to send into death many women and children of Polish origin and language. Only thus we can gain the living space *[lebensraum]* that we need. Who after all is today speaking about the destruction of the Armenians?

Colonel-General von Brauchitsch has promised me to bring the war against Poland to a close within a few weeks. Had he reported to me that he needs two years or even only one year, I should not have given the command to march and should have allied myself temporarily with England instead of Russia for we cannot conduct a long war. To be sure a new situation has arisen. I experienced those poor worms Daladier and Chamberlain in Munich. They will be too cowardly to attack. They won't go beyond a blockade. Against that we have our autarchy and the Russian raw materials.

Poland will be depopulated and settled with Germans. My pact with the Poles was merely conceived of as a gaining of time. As for the rest, gentlemen, the fate of Russia will be exactly the same as I am now going through with in the case of Poland. After Stalin's death—he is a very sick man—we will break the Soviet Union. Then there will begin the dawn of the German rule of the earth.

The little States cannot scare me. After Kemal's [i.e. Ataturk] death Turkey is governed by cretins and half idiots. Carol of Roumania is through and through the corrupt slave of his sexual instincts. The King of Belgium and the Nordic kings are soft jumping jacks who are dependent upon the good digestions of their over-eating and tired peoples.

We shall have to take into the bargain the defection of Japan. I gave Japan a full year's time. The Emperor is a counterpart to the last Czar—weak, cowardly, undecided. May he become a victim of the revolution. My going together with Japan never was popular. We shall continue to create disturbances in the Far East and in Arabia. Let us think as "gentlemen" and let us see in these peoples at best lacquered half maniacs who are anxious to experience the whip.

The opportunity is as favourable as never before. I have but one worry, namely that Chamberlain or some other such pig of a fellow *(Saukerl)* will come at the last moment with proposals or with ratting *(Umfall)*. He will fly down the stairs, even if I shall personally have to trample on his belly in the eyes of the photographers.

No, it is too late for this. The attack upon and the destruction of Poland begins Saturday early. I shall let a few companies in Polish uniform attack in Upper Silesia or in the Protectorate. Whether the world believes it is quite indifferent *(scheissegal)*. The world believes only in success.

For you, gentlemen, fame and honour are beginning as they have not since centuries. Be hard, be without mercy, act more quickly and brutally than the others. The citizens of Western Europe must tremble with horror. That is the most human way of conducting a war. For it scares the others off.

The new method of conducting war corresponds to the new drawing of the frontiers. A war extending from Reval, Lublin, Kaschau to the mouth of the Danube. The rest will be given to the Russians. Ribbentrop has orders to make every offer and to accept every demand. In the West I reserve to myself the right to determine the strategically best line. Here one will be able to work with Protectorate regions, such as Holland, Belgium and French Lorraine.

And now, on to the enemy, in Warsaw we will celebrate our reunion.

Source: *"Adolf Hitler: The Obersalzberg Speech," in* Documents on British Foreign Policy, 1919–1939, *edited by E. L. Woodward and Rohan Riftlep, third series, volume 7 (London: HMSO, 1954), pp. 258–260.*

the way the anti-Habsburg powers perceived the seventeenth-century Holy Roman Empire.

The second German challenge was met by a much firmer response. Demanding the country's unconditional surrender, the Allies utterly destroyed the Nazi regime, placed the entire country under long-term military occupation, removed a substantial amount of territory in the east, liquidated the predominant state of Prussia, and oversaw the development of a peace settlement that kept what remained of Germany divided for more than forty years. Plans to divide the country into several smaller states or create a united but neutralized and "pastoralized" state were not explored, but the extreme measures that were taken succeeded in incapacitating Germany's offensive potential. The essential difference was that in the twentieth-century conflicts, the powers that resisted German hegemonic aspirations were obliged to find a lasting solution. They failed once, but succeeded the second time. In the seventeenth century, however, the Germanic power that had to be resisted was only strong enough to pursue a Central European hegemony. Its success could potentially have led to aspirations to a European hegemony, as indeed happened after Germany was unified in 1871, but in the Thirty Years' War the antihegemonic powers had the desire, interest, and resources only to prevent its consolidation of German power.

The periods 1618–1648 and 1914–1945 are for several reasons far too different to be called by the same name. First, governments, ideas, aspirations, and strategies were on all sides too fluid over time to be defined by any consistency. Germany may have been in a position to launch a gambit for European hegemony twice in the twentieth century, but to say that it did so for precisely the same reasons and in precisely the same circumstances belies too many facts. Second, the lack of cohesion in the events of 1914–1945 was caused largely by the failure of the resisting powers to pursue a consistent policy toward Germany. While they were committed to restraining or destroying Germany when it presented them with direct challenges, the long period of peace in between was characterized by hesitation, aloofness, concessions, appeasement, and ineffectual multilateralism. For two of the "Big Three" anti-German powers, several of these attitudes were also sometimes present during actual wartime. Part of the reason for this situation originated with the dramatic fluctuations in German foreign policy: for almost fifteen years the German government expressly renounced striving for hegemonic power through military force. For a substantial amount of time in both wars it refrained from making direct challenges to one of its major opponents and abided by separate deals that served the immediate interests of another. In 1618–1648, however, the Austrian Habsburgs remained consistent in their desire to establish hegemony over their imperial possessions. Their array of enemies was equally determined to prevent them from doing so and to weaken their ability to try again in the future. For this reason it is quite plausible to refer to the four separate wars, or "phases," of the era as one integrated conflict. Third, the Thirty Years' War was almost solely about Germany. Virtually all the fighting, diplomacy, and strategic thought that went into the conflict had to do with the future status of the German lands in relation to the authority of the Holy Roman Empire and its Habsburg rulers. In the two world wars an already consolidated German state (with an ancillary Germanic state tethered to it in World War I and subsumed within it during World War II) made vast efforts to secure hegemonic domination over the whole of Europe. Whether one chooses to describe these conflicts as a "European Civil War" is irrelevant; they were about Europe and Germany's place in the Continent, not about Germany and one Germanic power's place in a potential nation-state. Fourth, the results of the two conflict periods were radically different. The Peace of Westphalia checked Austrian Habsburg ambitions within Germany, but the Austrian Empire remained a major power in different incarnations for the next 270 years. Its eventual challenger, Prussia, grew increasingly powerful and eventually created a united Germany on its own terms. The post-1945 settlement, however, completely eliminated Germany's capacity to function as a major power and replaced its role with enhanced positions for the United States, the Soviet Union, and more recently a united Europe. As convenient as it may be to compare the two periods' relatively similar time frames and destructive capacities, it is wholly simplistic to call 1914–1945 a second Thirty Years' War.

—PAUL DU QUENOY,
GEORGETOWN UNIVERSITY

References

Michael Howard, *War in European History* (London & New York: Oxford University Press, 1976).

Paul M. Kennedy, *The Rise and Fall of the Great Powers: Economic Change and Military Conflict from 1500 to 2000* (New York: Random House, 1987).

Richard A. Preston, Alex Roland, and Sydney F. Wise, *Men in Arms: A History of Warfare and Its Interrelationships with Western Society*, fifth edition (Fort Worth, Tex.: Holt, Rinehart & Winston, 1991).

A. J. P. Taylor, *The Second World War* (London: Athlone Press, 1974).

SOVIET UNION AS AN ALLY

Would the Soviet Union have been a reliable partner in a collective-security alliance with Western Europe against Nazi Germany during the interwar years?

Viewpoint: Yes. A Western European alliance with the Soviet Union during the interwar years would have been helpful in deterring German aggression.

Viewpoint: No. Despite its bluster, the Soviet Union was neither ideologically willing nor militarily able to become an Eastern counterweight to Hitler's Germany.

Although they had defeated Germany in World War I (1914–1918), the nations of Western Europe, particularly Britain and France, feared its potential resurgence and looked for a collective means of resisting it in the 1920s and 1930s. Over the course of these two decades this endeavor included bilateral security alliances with Eastern European nations, faith in international organizations such as the League of Nations to keep the peace, multinational antiwar agreements, lobbying for a formal security commitment from the United States, and the official appeasement of German demands to revise the World War I peace settlement. Yet, all these efforts failed. Germany was not deterred from its aggressive course, and its invasion of Poland in September 1939 drew Britain and France into conflict for the second time in twenty-one years.

Some scholars argue that interwar attempts to create a collective security alliance ignored one promising avenue: alliance with the Soviet Union. Indeed, Imperial Russia had been France's principal ally before World War I, and during that conflict its efforts had tied down enough German troops and resources to give the Western allies a fighting chance. Even though a bloody revolution and civil war had transformed tsarist Russia into a communist dictatorship, its potential as an ally in deterring German aggression was great. Communism and fascism were already strident ideological enemies; Soviet leader Josef Stalin's crash program of industrialization was making Russia into a major military power; and Moscow's focus on domestic development caused it to play down its antagonism to creditors, traders, and other business partners in the capitalist West. Cooperation with the Union of Soviet Socialist Republics (U.S.S.R.) against Nazi Germany was, in the view of these scholars, a viable option for Britain and France. Only irrational anticommunism led their elite to resist exploring it.

Yet, critics of this argument maintain that the Soviet government would have been neither competent nor reliable as a collective security partner. The U.S.S.R.'s revolutionary ideology made its own immediate interests paramount and rendered its diplomacy fickle and mercenary. Stalin's reorganization of the Soviet economy actually weakened its potential to battle the Germans, and his brutal purges of the 1930s, especially of the Red Army's experienced officer corps, left it totally unprepared for war. Ultimately, when it suited him, Stalin worked to improve relations with Nazi Germany and signed a nonaggression pact with it just days before the outbreak of World War II (1939–1945). What would have happened had the British and French made a more serious attempt to woo Stalin, and would it have succeeded?

Viewpoint:
Yes. A Western European alliance with the Soviet Union during the interwar years would have been helpful in deterring German aggression.

The rise of aggressive ambitions of militaristic Japan, fascist Italy, and Nazi Germany, which denied the rule of international law and sought to overturn the post–World War I (1914–1918) settlement, radically transformed the whole pattern of international relations in the 1930s. Worried by this challenge, particularly by the mounting threat from Japan in the east and from the resurgent Germany in the west, the Union of Soviet Socialist Republics (U.S.S.R.) gradually abandoned its previous semi-isolationist policy and opposition to the Versailles settlement (1919) and sought to create counterbalances of power against the new threats to its security. At the same time the specter of a new war drew the U.S.S.R. and the Western democracies, which Moscow had previously regarded as its main enemies, closer in the face of common danger.

Although the shift toward reconciliation with the West was a real breakthrough in Soviet foreign policy, some important elements of this new course were detectable even in the late 1920s, when the Soviets, anticipating troublesome international developments, signed the Kellogg–Briand Pact (1928), which denounced war as an instrument of foreign policy, signaling their willingness to adopt international norms and patterns of behavior accepted in the Western world. Moreover, the Soviet Union constructed similar arrangements applicable more practically to its immediate neighbors. In 1929 the U.S.S.R., Poland, Lithuania, Latvia, Estonia, Romania, Turkey, and Persia signed a protocol that affirmed the Kellogg–Briand Pact. In the 1930s the new reconciliatory trend in Soviet foreign policy came into full bloom. In 1931–1932 the Soviets signed a series of nonaggression pacts with Afghanistan, Turkey, Lithuania, Finland, Latvia, Estonia, Poland, France, and Italy. At the World Economic Conference in London in 1933 the Soviet delegation proposed a multilateral convention defining aggression. The convention was signed by the U.S.S.R., Finland, Lithuania, Latvia, Estonia, Poland, Czechoslovakia, Yugoslavia, Romania, Turkey, Persia, and Afghanistan.

The new course of Soviet foreign policy, which could be summed up by the term *collective security*, was aimed at developing formal international arrangements whereby protection against aggression would be maintained by the strength and actions of an international community and peace-loving allied countries. The spirit of this new Soviet policy was fundamentally pragmatic and accommodative. While lowering revolutionary rhetoric, it had a sort of commonsense and business-like approach and favored establishing close ties with the democracies of Europe, the United States, international bodies such as the League of Nations, and, generally, all forces that strove to maintain a system of collective security against the forces of aggression and fascism.

A personal factor was of significant importance in this new Soviet policy. Maksim Litvinov, people's commissar for foreign affairs (foreign minister) from 1930 to 1939, declared that peace is "indivisible," and he became a convincing spokesman for Soviet cooperation with the West. While the concept of collective security did not transform Litvinov's internal Marxist-Leninist beliefs, he was ideally equipped to present Moscow's foreign policy in a new, attractive guise, for he was an old Bolshevik with an English wife and strong personal ties with the West. Since Litvinov was a Jew, few could doubt that he was strongly anti-Nazi. Harry Hopkins, an aide to U.S. president Franklin D. Roosevelt during World War II (1939–1945), remarked that Litvinov "had a Western kind of mind."

While playing a major role in the formulation and realization of Soviet foreign policy, Litvinov, contrary to some Western assumptions, never made policy. He merely executed the strategic decisions adopted by Soviet leader Josef Stalin and the Politburo. The decision to cooperate with the West was based on a cold-blooded calculation of Soviet national interests rather than on sympathy toward Western democracies or pacifist intentions. As Stalin put it at the Seventeenth Congress of the Soviet Communist Party (1934), "we were not in the past oriented towards Germany, and we are not now oriented towards Poland and France. Our orientation, past and present, is exclusively towards the USSR."

The rationale underpinning the Soviet approach to collective security, which made the new course stable and firm, was based on an understanding of the growing internal and external insecurities of the state. Internally, the Soviets experienced enormous and destabilizing costs of their large-scale socio-economic transformation (collectivization and industrialization)

WONDER HOW LONG THE HONEYMOON WILL LAST?

American political cartoonist Clifford Berryman's depiction of the Nazi-Soviet Pact of 1939

(Library of Congress, Washington, D.C.)

and desperately needed economic cooperation with the West. Externally, the rise of Germany in Europe and Japan in the Far East posed, for the first time in Russia's history, a two-front security threat of the first magnitude. This combination of external threats and potential internal instability made the search for collective security and new cooperation with the West an urgent imperative for Moscow. The Soviet Union, with its growing economic potential and formidable armed forces, emerged as a leading advocate and a determined promoter of collective security in Europe and beyond.

The League of Nations, an international organization created in 1919 to preserve peace and ensure cooperation between states, was the primary international institution supporting collective security. Moscow, marking a fundamental shift in Soviet foreign policy, abandoned its long-term hostility toward the League. Japanese and German withdrawal from the League in

1933 presented an opportunity to the Soviet Union to gain international respectability. In September 1934 the U.S.S.R. joined the League of Nations, hoping to meet the growing threat of aggression and to organize an effective system of international security.

The ability of the League of Nations to resist aggression was tested in 1935 when Italy invaded Ethiopia. The Soviets called upon the League to punish the aggressor, but the Western powers, which hoped to exploit German-Italian disagreements at that time, hesitated to apply the most effective sanctions—an embargo on oil supplies to Italy. Diminution of the League's prestige and authority as a result of its failure to deal effectively with this aggression, as well as the lack of progress at the International Disarmament Conference, which had been meeting in Geneva since 1932, strengthened the Russian search for new alliances and bilateral security cooperation as another road toward collective security. The

SOVIET UNION AS AN ALLY

Soviets were quick to understand this reality and redirected their foreign policy.

Moscow revitalized its ties with France, while the latter in its turn tried to erect a European alliance system, including the Soviet Union, to contain Germany. The rapprochement between the Soviet Union and the Western democracies proceeded promisingly with the negotiations of British foreign secretary Anthony Eden and French prime minister Pierre Laval in Moscow, in March and May 1935, respectively. On 3 May 1935 the U.S.S.R. and France signed a Treaty of Mutual Assistance, in which they pledged to come to one another's assistance in the event of unprovoked aggression. Nevertheless, there was not much trust between the Soviets and their Western partners. When on 16 May 1935 Czechoslovakia (a French ally) and the U.S.S.R. concluded a similar mutual assistance pact, both parties agreed that the Soviet Union would come to aid Czechoslovakia only if France acted similarly in fulfillment of its responsibility within the Franco-Czechoslovak treaty. Later this escape clause played a tragic role in the collapse of Czechoslovakia. Even earlier, on 16 November 1933, the Soviet Union and the United States established diplomatic relations. The Soviet-American rapprochement was another integral part of Russia's collective security policy.

The Soviet turn toward partnership with the Western democracies also required a shift in policy of the Communist International (Comintern)—the Moscow-based and Soviet-dominated international association of the world's communist parties. The Seventh Congress of the Comintern that met in Moscow in July 1935 called for the establishment of a united front (Popular Front) with moderate socialists, liberals, and other political forces that favored resistance to fascism and aggression. This step was a radical departure from Comintern's earlier opposition to "reformist and bourgeois" parties. Popular Front governments came to power in France and Spain in 1936. On one hand, the introduction of the Popular Front strategy demonstrated Moscow's long-term commitment to cooperation with democracies. On the other hand, by promoting broad antifascist coalitions, it widened political support inside Western Europe for Soviet collective security initiatives.

The policy of collective security in its multilateral (the League of Nations) and bilateral forms was put to the test by growing Nazi aggression and instability in Europe. In March of 1936 Germany remilitarized the Rhineland in violation of the Locarno Treaty (1925). The League of Nations and Western powers failed to either act with conviction or intervene militarily. The Spanish Civil War (1936–1939), in which Germany and Italy decisively intervened, acceler-

ated the disintegration of the collective security in Europe. The Soviets, initially maintaining an official policy of noninterference, acted cautiously. Seeing that Paris and London's neutral stand in fact did nothing about German and Italian actions in Spain, however, the Soviet Union began limited intervention in Spain to help the loyalists. These developments undermined the Franco-Soviet alliance and caused growing Soviet disillusionment about collective security.

In March 1938, immediately after the *Anschluss* (union) of Germany and Austria and despite Western passivity, Litvinov declared the Soviet Union's readiness to begin discussions with other powers about practical measures to punish the aggressors. Again, Britain and France, hoping to appease German leader Adolf Hitler, failed to respond to the Soviet initiative.

Throughout the Czechoslovak (Sudeten) Crisis (1938) the Soviet government repeatedly affirmed its willingness to support all decisions and recommendations of the League of Nations to combat aggression and preserve peace, irrespective of whether these decisions coincided with the Soviet immediate national interests. The Soviets declared their readiness to come to the aid of Czechoslovakia, provided France did likewise. But France and Britain ignored the Soviet Union and tried to come to peaceful terms with Hitler at Czechoslovakia's expense. Despite the fact that the French refusal to help Czechoslovakia against Germany had formally freed the U.S.S.R. from the obligation to render aid to Prague, the Soviets were ready to provide military support to the Czechs if their government wished it. The Czechoslovak government, however, opted to concede to the German-British-French ultimatum adopted in Munich about the settlement of the crisis, and ceded the Sudetenland to Germany.

The question of whether the Soviet Union was really ready to provide Czechoslovakia with effective military support remains a matter of controversy. On one hand, many Western observers pointed out that the Red Army, particularly in the aftermath of the Great Purge (1930s), was in no condition to operate against a powerful foe beyond the Soviet borders, while neither Poland nor Romania (the U.S.S.R.'s immediate neighbors) was prepared to accept Soviet troops on their way to Czechoslovakia. On the other hand, many critics of official British and French policy at the time, such as Winston Churchill and Joseph Paul-Boncour, insisted that unique opportunities to stop the Nazis were lost when the Soviet offers of cooperation were rebuffed. Moreover, in 1938, before Munich, most German generals expected that a simultaneous war with Britain, France, the Soviet Union, and

Czechoslovakia would be a disaster. For sure, Soviet military aid to Czechoslovakia would have been indirect but still a potent strategic factor in the situation. Thus, during the Sudeten Crisis the Soviet Union proved to be the only country that kept faith with its international obligations in relations with Czechoslovakia and collective security in Europe.

Moscow drew the worst possible conclusions from Munich. The Soviets found out that the shortsighted Western democracies ignored the Soviet offer to help them and accepted Czechoslovakia's dismemberment by Germany. With the evident failure of the collective security policy to halt German aggression, Stalin removed Litvinov from the Foreign Ministry and ended the pro-Western policy identified with him. The Soviets again changed their foreign policy course and became amenable to approaches from Berlin. This shift culminated in the Soviet-Nazi Pact of August 1939. When Britain and France went to war against Germany the following month, the Soviet Union was already a virtual ally of the latter.

During the 1930s the Soviet Union was a determined champion of collective security and a reliable partner for a possible alliance against Nazi Germany. Western Europe's resistance to forming a firm alliance with the Soviet Union was indeed an irresponsible and ill-considered rejection of a viable strategic option. It should be noted also that many misunderstandings rooted in the past, continued suspicions and antagonisms, and mutual ideological hostility precluded politically necessary adjustments between the U.S.S.R. and the Western democracies and undermined long-term and stable security cooperation between Moscow and the West. The failure of collective security was to bring tragedy to the Soviet Union and to all Europe.

—PETER RAINOW,
SAN MATEO, CALIFORNIA

Viewpoint:
No. Despite its bluster, the Soviet Union was neither ideologically willing nor militarily able to become an Eastern counterweight to Hitler's Germany.

The question of Soviet willingness to engage in collective security arrangements is important to scholars looking to make sense both of World War II (1939–1945) and the origins of the Cold War. If the Soviets were willing and able to engage in a revival of the World War

I (1914–1918) Triple Entente (Britain, France, and Russia) focused on countering resurgent Germany, then the Western democracies failed to avail themselves of a genuine opportunity to halt German leader Adolf Hitler's aggression earlier and at much lower cost than they did. Arguably even more important, the Western democracies' failure to enter a collective security arrangement might justify Soviet leader Josef Stalin's depredations against his Eastern European neighbors between 1939 and 1941, and the later activities of the Red Army and secret police in "liberating" Eastern Europe. After all, the suggestion of Western hostility inherent in the democracies' refusal even to consider a security arrangement in their best interests because it also would protect the Soviets suggests hostility that made bold unilateral action by Stalin understandable.

A careful consideration of the historical record in the 1930s and beyond makes clear that while the Soviets made some gestures toward collective security, reasons of ideology compelled them to make these overtures in hopes of emboldening the British and French to launch a war with Germany. The Soviets expected such a war to have the same revolutionary consequences for Western Europe that World War I had for Imperial Russia. While reasons of national self-interest eventually might have drawn Stalin into a war in Central Europe, he was not serious about collective security with capitalist nations. The Soviet dictator made this stance clear with his performance during the Czechoslovak Crisis that culminated with the Munich Conference in 1938. Perhaps more important, any Soviet military assistance in the 1930s would have been of questionable value given the state of its armed services at that time. The democracies would not have been allying themselves with the relentless, battle-proven Red Army of the later years of World War II. Rather, any assistance would have been provided by the utterly inept Soviet military whose abundant limitations were on display against the Finns during the Winter War (1939–1940).

Soviet foreign minister Maksim Litvinov made several suggestions for possible combinations against the growing threat of Nazi Germany during the 1930s, but there is good reason to doubt Soviet willingness actually to engage in any meaningful efforts against the Nazis. While any German collapse likely would have brought the Soviets into a war to ensure that they got their share of the spoils, R. C. Raack, in *Stalin's Drive to the West, 1938–1945: The Origins of the Cold War* (1995), makes a strong case that Soviet overtures to the West were designed chiefly to encourage the West to attack Nazi Germany. Not anticipating the rapidity with which the French collapsed in the face of the German onslaught,

KELLOGG–BRIAND PACT (1928)

The President of the German Reich, the President of the United States of America, His Majesty the King of the Belgians, the President of the French Republic, His Majesty the King of Great Britain, Ireland and the British Dominions beyond the seas, Emperor of India, His Majesty the King of Italy, His Majesty the Emperor of Japan, the President of the Republic of Poland, the President of the Czechoslovak Republic.

Deeply sensible of their solemn duty to promote the welfare of mankind;

Persuaded that the time has come when a frank renunciation of war as an instrument of national policy should be made to the end that the peaceful and friendly relations now existing between their peoples may be perpetuated;

Convinced that all changes in their relations with one another should be sought only by pacific means and be the result of a peaceful and orderly process, and that any signatory Power which shall hereafter seek to promote its national interests by resort to war should be denied the benefits furnished by this treaty;

Hopeful that, encouraged by their example, all the other nations of the world will join in this humane endeavor and by adhering to the present treaty as soon as it comes into force bring their peoples within the scope of its beneficent provisions, thus uniting the civilized nations of the world in a common renunciation of war as an instrument of their national policy;

Have decided to conclude a treaty and for that purpose have appointed as their respective plenipotentiaries:

The President of the German Reich: Dr. Gustav Stresemann, Minister for Foreign Affairs;

The President of the United States of America: The Honorable Frank B. Kellogg, Secretary of State;

His Majesty the King of the Belgians: Mr. Paul Hymans, Minister for Foreign Affairs, Minister of State;

The President of the French Republic: Mr. Aristide Briand, Minister for Foreign Affairs;

His Majesty the King of Great Britain, Ireland and the British Dominions beyond the seas, Emperor of India:

For Great Britain and Northern Ireland and all parts of the British Empire which are not separate members of the League of Nations:

The Right Honourable Lord Cushendun, Chancellor of the Duchy of Lancaster, Acting Secretary of State for Foreign Affairs;

For the Dominion of Canada: The Right Honourable William Lyon Mackenzie King, Prime Minister and Minister for External Affairs;

For the Commonwealth of Australia: The Honourable Alexander John McLachlan, Member of the Executive Federal Council;

For the Dominion of New Zealand: The Honourable Sir Christopher James Parr, High Commissioner for New Zealand in Great Britain;

For the Union of South Africa: The Honourable Jacobus Stephanus Smit, High Commissioner for the Union of South Africa in Great Britain;

For the Irish Free State: Mr. William Thomas Cosgrave, President of the Executive Council;

For India: The Right Honourable Lord Cushendun, Chancellor of the Duchy of Lancaster, Acting Secretary of State for Foreign Affairs;

His Majesty the King of Italy: Count Gaetano Manzoini, His Ambassador Extraordinary and Plenipotentiary at Paris;

His Majesty the Emperor of Japan: Count Uchida, Privy Councillor;

The President of the Republic of Poland: Mr. A. Zaleski, Minister for Foreign Affairs;

The President of the Czechoslovak Republic: Dr. Eduard Benes, Minister for Foreign Affairs;

who, having communicated to one another their full powers found in good and due form have agreed upon the following articles:

ARTICLE I

The high contracting parties solemnly declare in the names of their respective peoples that they condemn recourse to war for the solution of international controversies, and renounce it as an instrument of national policy in their relations with one another.

ARTICLE II

The high contracting parties agree that the settlement or solution of all disputes or conflicts of whatever nature or of whatever origin they may be, which may arise among them, shall never be sought except by pacific means.

ARTICLE III

The present treaty shall be ratified by the high contracting parties named in the preamble in accordance with their respective constitutional requirements, and shall take effect as between them as soon as all their several instruments of ratification shall have been deposited at Washington.

This treaty shall, when it has come into effect as prescribed in the preceding paragraph, remain open as long as may be necessary for adherence by all the other Powers of the world. Every instrument evidencing the adherence of a Power shall be deposited at Washington and the treaty shall immediately upon such deposit become effective as between the Power thus adhering and the other Powers parties hereto.

It shall be the duty of the Government of the United States to furnish each government named in the preamble and every government subsequently adhering to this treaty with a certified copy of the treaty and of every instrument of ratification or adherence. It shall also be the duty of the Government of the United States telegraphically to notify such governments immediately upon the deposit with it of each instrument of ratification or adherence.

In faith whereof the respective Plenipotentiaries have signed this Treaty in the French and English languages both texts having equal force, and hereunto affix their seals.

Done at Paris the twenty-seventh day of August in the year one thousand nine hundred and twenty-eight.

Source: *"Treaty Providing for the Renunciation of War as an Instrument of National Policy," World War I Document Archive, Brigham Young University <http://www.lib.byu.edu/~rdh/wwi/1918p/ kellogg-briand.html>.*

SOVIET UNION AS AN ALLY

Stalin expected that France, Britain, and Germany would bog down into another costly bloodletting such as occurred on the Western Front during World War I. Stalin believed the cost and destructiveness of this war would cause the collapse of social structures in those nations. After they had bloodied themselves sufficiently, ravaged their armies, and caused unrest among their populations, the nations would have been ripe for the fresh Red Army to assist revolutionary forces in seizing power. To facilitate this revolutionary process, and not to encourage a resurrection of the World War I Triple Entente, the Soviet made efforts toward collective security agreements.

Another issue facing the West would have been the cost of reaching an agreement with Stalin. Put simply, Hitler was willing to concede Soviet domination over parts of Eastern Europe, with a cynical disregard for the people of those nations. Given Hitler's disdain for Slavs, Jews, and other Eastern Europeans, he could hardly have been troubled over the fate of the people he was abandoning to Stalin's tender mercies. This "sacrifice" was a cost Hitler could pay easily to ensure that the Soviets did not interfere with his conquest of Poland. In contrast, it is hard to see how Stalin and the Western democracies could have reached a similar agreement in peacetime. The leaders of Western democracies could hardly have been so casually cynical about the disposal of populations, and Stalin demanded precisely such accommodations in his limited talks with Britain and France in 1939.

Those unconvinced about Stalin's brutality in making territorial demands need only consider his performance with his newfound American and British allies after the German attack on the Soviet Union, which commenced in June 1941. Even when his regime's survival was in peril, Stalin continued to demand that his new democratic allies recognize the territorial plunder he had obtained from his agreement with Hitler. It is unlikely that Western nations, at least before World War II, would have been willing to give Stalin any such blandishments. It was true that in the final analysis the Western democracies did virtually nothing to prevent Stalin from taking much of what he wanted in Eastern Europe after the war anyway. Wartime cooperation broke down less over Stalin's disdain for the principles of the Atlantic Charter (1941) and the Declaration on Liberated Europe (1945) than over his refusal to permit even a fig leaf of democratic procedure to conceal his naked brutality. The West was willing to deal with Stalin on his terms, however, only after the astonishingly rapid collapse of the Western European democracies in the spring of 1940 demonstrated the necessity of Soviet participation in the anti-Nazi coalition. Moreover, in the wake of the German attack it was possible for those in the West to read events backward and see Stalin's efforts between 1939 and 1941 as part of a shrewd strategy to prepare for the coming war. Western qualms about Soviet acquisitiveness by the end of World War II were assuaged by the perception that four years of grinding warfare against the Nazis in the East had both purified the Soviets of some of their more unseemly qualities and earned for Moscow the right to take additional territory to assure its security needs.

Additional evidence of Stalin's unsuitability for participation in a collective security arrangement lay in his control of Poland and his attempt to establish a Soviet-style government over Finland. These events also suggested strong ideological incompatibility with Western ideas of self-determination and the territorial and administrative integrity of small nations. Stalin was unwilling to permit even a rump Poland to retain some vestiges of independence. During the Winter War (1939–1940) Stalin presaged his postwar schemes for dominance in Eastern Europe by organizing a Finnish People's Democratic Government that was to be established in the first Finnish town that Red forces captured. The Soviets planned to install this government in Helsinki as soon as they overran the Finns. Again, such naked designs on domination of neighboring territory would have been difficult for Western democracies to accept.

While Stalin's desire to impose a Communist government on Finland would have posed problems for Western democracies looking to make a diplomatic deal with him, he had greater limitations as an ally that were on display during his conflict with the Finns. Arguably, even more problematic was the disarray into which Stalin had plunged his military through his purge of leaders and his own inept leadership. The purge was a public display of Communist cynicism and brutality that could not help but raise doubt about Stalin in the West. The damage done to the Soviet military, combined with ineptitude, was amply displayed during the Winter War. The Soviets, with 171 million people, struggled for months to defeat 3.5 million Finns. Stalin's military leaders underestimated the fighting capacity of the Finns, misjudged the difficulty of maneuvering a mechanized army through subarctic wilderness lacking finished roads, and appeared completely to misunderstand what was involved in winter fighting. While there was much in the Finnish performance that complicated the Red Army's efforts, the Finnish leadership understood their difficulties in trying to face down the Soviets. During Soviet efforts to arrange the surrender of Finnish territory before they launched their attack, Finnish marshal Carl Gustav Mannerheim was imploring his government to reach some settlement because his army was not prepared or supplied for war against the Soviets.

If Soviet ineptitude in the Winter War was not enough to raise doubts about Soviet value to a collective security arrangement with the West, their performance during the Czechoslovak Crisis (1938) demonstrated Stalin's lack of interest in taking meaningful steps in concert with Western powers. The Soviets were bound by an alliance with the Czechs that took effect when the French acted in accordance with their defensive treaty with the Czechs. Yet, during the crisis that culminated with the agreement at Munich to surrender the Sudetenland to the Nazis, the Soviets made no effort to prod the French or Czechs into action. Had Stalin been seriously committed to collective security, he had the perfect opportunity to do so in a crisis situation in which the French were committed to act, and the Czechs were confronted by an adversary that could be fought on fairly favorable terms given the rugged terrain of the Sudeten Mountains. The logical time and place to try collective security was at hand, yet the Soviets did not take advantage of it.

Raack argues that the reason the Soviets made no move toward collective security at a time when it could have paid dividends was because of Stalin's determination to see the British, French, and Germans embroiled in war. Had Stalin taken steps to signal the U.S.S.R.'s willingness to enter the fight, this move might have conjured up German visions of another two-front war against France and Russia. Given Germany's experience twenty years earlier, Raack argues, this situation might have induced restraint in Hitler that was the opposite of what Stalin wished to see. In other words, the Soviets were more interested in seeing the rest of Europe consumed by war than they were in taking meaningful steps that might have restrained Hitler and prevented war.

A final argument against Soviet willingness to address collective security was their performance in the summer of 1939. By this time the Western nations saw clearly the true magnitude of the threat posed by Hitler, and their diplomats were looking for common ground with the Soviets from which to build an anti-Nazi security apparatus. Negotiations between the Soviets and Western diplomats dragged on that summer, inconclusively. Meanwhile, German foreign minister Joachim von Ribbentrop appeared in Moscow and was able to negotiate an agreement with Soviet foreign minister Vyacheslav Molotov in a single day. This pact was not attributable to particular skill on the part of von Ribbentrop, nor of Molotov. Rather, it was a logical result of Stalin's greater comfort level in working with another totalitarian dictator and his determination to facilitate the general European war from which he hoped to profit.

It is true that Western leaders were slow to understand and respond to the truly revolutionary threat Hitler posed to European civilization. Yet, when they were ready to coordinate defense efforts with the Soviets, at a time when Stalin supposedly was already concerned about possible eventual German aggression, Stalin did not respond like a man serious about addressing the threat or preventing war. It was neither the hostility of capitalists nor the obtuse diplomacy of the West that prevented agreement with the Soviet Union. Rather, it was Stalin's revolutionary agenda and confidence that it would be promoted by another general European war that prevented such agreement. The Western democracies ought not to have felt guilty over the slowness to act, only their foolishness in failing to see the duplicity of the Soviet dictator who in a couple of years would be their cobelligerent in the effort against the Nazis.

–JOHN A. SOARES JR.,
CINCINNATI, OHIO

References

Michael Jabara Carley, *1939: The Alliance That Never Was and the Coming of World War II* (Chicago: Dee, 1999).

John Lewis Gaddis, *We Now Know: Rethinking Cold War History* (Oxford: Clarendon Press, 1997).

R. H. Haigh, D. S. Morris, and A. R. Peters, *Soviet Foreign Policy, the League of Nations, and Europe, 1917–1939* (Aldershot, U.K.: Gower, 1986; Totowa, N.J.: Barnes & Noble, 1986).

Jonathan Haslam, *The Soviet Union and the Struggle for Collective Security in Europe, 1933–1939* (New York: St. Martin's Press, 1984).

R. C. Raack, *Stalin's Drive to the West, 1938–1945: The Origins of the Cold War* (Stanford, Cal.: Stanford University Press, 1995).

William R. Trotter, *A Frozen Hell: The Russo-Finnish Winter War of 1939–1940* (Chapel Hill, N.C.: Algonquin Books of Chapel Hill, 1991).

SOVIET-WESTERN COOPERATION AFTER 1945

After World War II did the Soviet Union honor its wartime pledge to Western Allies to allow democratically installed governments within its Eastern European spheres of influence?

Viewpoint: Yes. The Soviet Union generally honored its pledges to the Western Allies in order to preserve the partnership that had existed during the war, and it installed communist regimes in Eastern Europe only after the West appeared hostile.

Viewpoint: No. The Soviets always intended to "Bolshevize" Eastern Europe in order to satisfy their security requirements, and they did so without regard for their wartime agreements with the West.

As the tide of World War II (1939–1945) turned in favor of the Allies, their primary shared concerns were preparing for the peace settlement and reshaping the postwar world. One of the main points of contention involved the future of Eastern Europe. Occupied by or allied to Nazi Germany during the war, the future of the region seemed inevitably linked to the battlefield fortunes of the Soviet Union. The United States and Great Britain, however, resisted conceding the region to postwar Soviet domination. To do so offended their philosophical commitment to liberty and democracy and made a mockery of their determination to avoid carving the world up into spheres of influence. In a series of "Big Three" (American, British, and Soviet) conferences held in Teheran (November 1943), Yalta (February 1945), and Potsdam (July–August 1945) the Western Allies extracted promises from the Soviet government not to impose communist systems on the liberated nations of Eastern Europe. Moscow retained the right to promote "friendly" governments there, but those governments were to be installed and elected by "democratic" means.

Even before the war ended, controversy broke out over what exactly "friendly" and "democratic" would mean. As a result, the question of whether the Soviets kept their wartime promises in postwar Eastern Europe became highly debatable. One school of thought argues that Moscow was largely faithful to its agreements. Despite the ambiguities in the conference talks, democratic elections were held throughout Eastern Europe after the war, noncommunist governments came to power alongside the presence of the Red Army, and subsequent communist regimes only came to power after the West hardened its attitudes toward the Soviet Union.

Another perspective posits that the Soviets were master deceivers. Although they may have gestured toward the fulfillment of wartime agreements, their presence in Eastern Europe guaranteed that communism would have an unnaturally large presence in the region, that the non- or anticommunist elite would disappear or be cowed into submission, and that institutions of a truly democratic government and society would be stifled. Further evidence suggests that the Soviets were actively preparing to carry out this policy before and even during their negotiations with the Western Allies. "Bolshevizing" the region, in other words, was always Moscow's intention. The ambiguities in the wartime agreements were purposely formulated to deceive the West and give the Soviets the time and opportunity they needed to control Eastern Europe.

Viewpoint:
Yes. The Soviet Union generally honored its pledges to the Western Allies in order to preserve the partnership that had existed during the war, and it installed communist regimes in Eastern Europe only after the West appeared hostile.

Though generations of journalists, politicians, and historians have tried to prove otherwise, Josef Stalin and the Soviet leadership generally honored their pledges to the Western Allies to preserve the strategic partnership in Eastern Europe. Stalin only resorted to more-aggressive measures in response to Western moves that appeared to him hostile and provocative.

Recent scholarship on postwar Soviet relations with the United States and Great Britain has demonstrated that the Soviet leadership hoped and expected that relations would continue on a similar course to those during wartime. Despite and, perhaps, also because of America's atomic monopoly, the Soviet Union wished to pursue favorable relations with its wartime allies. Soviet policy makers, such as Deputy Foreign Minister Maksim Litvinov and Ambassador to the United States Andrei Gromyko, saw cooperation with the West as essential to ensuring peace in Europe. A stable relationship with the United States and Great Britain would enable the Soviet Union to begin recovery from the war and prevent such future destruction. The Soviets were especially interested in American economic and technical assistance. Soviet foreign policy was motivated by state interests, not by ideology. Continued cooperation was in Stalin's best interests.

In the final years of the war and in its immediate aftermath, Stalin and his advisers focused primarily on the threat from Germany. Their greatest fear was not American atomic power or British aggression, but a resurgent Germany. The Soviet leadership hoped to avoid confrontation with the West and focus on its own security. This orientation has led historian Carolyn Kennedy-Pipe to argue that the Soviets were not opposed to the introduction of U.S. troops to Germany because it allayed their fears of future German aggression. Even if one does not agree with her interpretation, it is clear that the Soviets were not following a policy of confrontation with the West.

Political scientist William Taubman notes that the Soviet Union pursued détente with the West throughout its history. For example, he cites Soviet leader Vladimir Lenin's desire for détente in the 1920s and Stalin's drive for collective security with the West in the 1930s. Stalin

hoped for such a state of relations in the postwar years. Indeed, Taubman even asserts that Stalin shifted away from a policy of entente, or active engagement, with the West to détente in response to American actions.

In order to achieve his policy goals, Stalin adhered to the agreements that he had reached with the United States and Great Britain at the conferences held in Teheran (November 1943), Yalta (February 1945), and Potsdam (July–August 1945). Critics of Stalin charged that he repeatedly broke his commitments to his wartime allies, most egregiously on the question of Poland. They contend that Stalin had promised a "democratic and independent" Poland, a stark contrast in their eyes to the makeup of the postwar government. This complaint is most often the result of a misunderstanding of the Yalta agreement, caused by the deliberate effort by U.S. president Franklin D. Roosevelt and others to deceive the American people about the true content of the accord. Therefore, Western observers frequently interpreted the accords differently than the "Big Three" (Roosevelt, Stalin, and British prime minister Winston Churchill) had. Observers such as U.S. ambassador to the Soviet Union W. Averell Harriman and others repeatedly chastised Stalin for the supposed betrayal. Yet, Roosevelt, and certainly Stalin, recognized that the Polish government would not conform to Western democratic standards. Roosevelt did not regard Stalin as having gone against his word, a fact made clear in his telegram communication with Churchill and Stalin in the weeks and days before his death on 12 April 1945. Churchill and Roosevelt each recognized Stalin's intense concern about the future security of the Soviet Union and the extent to which he saw a friendly Poland as essential to that security. Roosevelt and Churchill focused on the domestic political implications of Stalin's actions in Poland. Their understanding of Soviet security needs was not advertised in the American debate about the future of Europe, leading to much confusion and finger-pointing in the subsequent decades.

Stalin, however, had been clear about his postwar aims throughout his wartime negotiations with his allies—the establishment of friendly regimes in countries that bordered the Soviet Union. He repeatedly stressed the historic threat of Germany to the Soviet Union and argued that the only way to prevent a resurgent Germany from invading the Soviet Union again was to create a buffer zone of security. Stalin was not breaking any agreements with the Allies when he took steps to ensure that the creation of this zone would become a reality.

The Soviets felt Western pressure on their southern flank as well. After the war, Stalin wanted to secure an oil concession from Iran, such as those granted to the other Allies. The United States and Great Britain, however, joined forces to convince Stalin to withdraw from Iran without the concession. Many observers have pointed to the Iran crisis (1945–1946) as one of the early signals of Soviet expansionism. Yet, Stalin only remained in Iran in an effort to gain a concession that would mark parity with his Western allies. It is worth noting that when Greek communists were engaged in a civil war for control of their country, Stalin complied with his agreement and did not aid them in their struggle. This restraint was exercised in spite of growing Soviet fears about Western attempts to infiltrate Eastern Europe.

Soviet policy toward Eastern Europe did not become aggressive until Stalin felt he was being provoked by the West. The most notable example of this change was the American offer of Marshall Plan aid to Europe and the Soviet Union in June 1947, and the Soviet bloc's subsequent rejection of that aid. Over the years, scholars have argued about the reasons for this refusal and have often attributed it to Soviet hostility toward the West. Recent scholarship, however, has demonstrated that the Marshall Plan was perceived by the Soviet Union as hostile and invasive. Indeed, American policy makers never desired Soviet acceptance of their offer; it was extended primarily for purposes of appearance. It was regarded by the Soviet Union as a hostile effort to infiltrate the Soviet sphere of influence in Eastern Europe with American capitalism. Such aid would have mandated economic transparency, something that the Soviet Union did not wish to allow in its new sphere, much less in its own domestic economy. Although some observers have argued that Stalin rejected Marshall Plan aid because he believed that the United States economy would soon collapse, as it had after World War I (1914–1918) during the Great Depression, historical research points to Stalin's fear of American economic power and its influence on Eastern Europe. Many scholars agree that the Soviet rejection of the Marshall Plan was a turning point for the worse in the relationship between the United States and the Soviet Union. Yet, it was the Soviets who modified their behavior in response to a threat from the West.

In his memoirs Gromyko writes that Stalin genuinely liked Roosevelt. He suggests, as do others, that Roosevelt's death was also a turning point in the Soviet relationship with the British and the Americans because Harry S Truman, the new American president, was not cognizant of the real terms of the wartime agreements among the Big Three. Because of this lack of knowledge, and the extent to which he was influenced by more-experienced hard-line offi-

cials, Truman increasingly adopted a confrontational attitude toward Stalin. Initially, this attitude was manifested in a fractious meeting with Soviet foreign minister Vyacheslav Molotov, in which he flatly accused the Soviets of not carrying out the terms of their agreements. As his presidency progressed, this attitude could be seen most clearly in the proclamation of the Truman Doctrine (March 1947) of resisting communist expansion, the formulation of the Marshall Plan (June 1947), and eventually the creation of the North Atlantic Treaty Organization (NATO, 1949), an organization that could only be seen as anti-Soviet. These policies were interpreted by the Kremlin as signaling a new, confrontational, and expansionist foreign policy by the Americans. The perception of a shift led the Soviets to modify their foreign policy as well. Analyzing the origins of the Cold War has sparked a wide range of historical inquiry with many observers studying the shift in American policy in 1946–1974. This shift, however, was not caused by any general Soviet efforts to renege on the agreements with their wartime allies as Soviet actions were only taken in response to Western provocation.

–SARAH SNYDER,
GEORGETOWN UNIVERSITY

Viewpoint:
No. The Soviets always intended to "Bolshevize" Eastern Europe in order to satisfy their security requirements, and they did so without regard for their wartime agreements with the West.

The brutality and human costs of Soviet expansion into Eastern Europe were appalling and must not be forgotten, but exclusive emphasis on these factors obscures the complex circumstances that guided the occupation policy. European security issues, Allied strategic concerns, Soviet economic interests, and the internal situation of East European states greatly contributed to the successful establishment of the Soviet bloc. World War II (1939–1945) was the primary cause of these seismic international shifts and crucial domestic changes. To maintain that Moscow "tricked" its allies is to state the obvious and to presume mistakenly the innocence of the Western capitals. Did Moscow intend to "Bolshevize" as many of its western neighbors as possible after the tide of the war turned? Of course it did. Did it send intentionally confusing messages to the allies? Yes. The "socialist revolution" in

Eastern Europe effectively constructed a buffer zone for what Soviet leader Josef Stalin foresaw as an inevitable clash of East and West.

When did plans for "Bolshevization" first appear? Is there a document to which the policy can be traced? Was westward expansion a natural consequence of the October coup of 1917? The Bolsheviks split on the issue of exporting the Revolution in the 1920s, with Lev Trotsky as the main proponent of internationalism and Stalin the supporter of internal development. After Stalin's victory over his opponents within the Bolshevik Party, the Soviet Union was put steadily on the rails of industrialization, which required peace and a defensive foreign policy. Stalin even began a purge in the armed forces in the late 1930s, which he could hardly have thought timely on the eve of expansion. Throughout the 1920s and 1930s the Kremlin was preoccupied with ideological battles and internal Party affairs, but the Nazi invasion of the Soviet Union on 22 June 1941 allowed the Revolution to be exported. World War II dramatically changed the situation in Eastern Europe, producing effects similar to those of a revolution, and allowed the Soviet army to occupy territories it had liberated

from the Nazis. This occupation not only facilitated Bolshevization but made it inevitable.

If Bolshevization had roots, they were ideological. In the 1930s the Communist International (Comintern) became Stalin's foreign-policy tool that launched ideological colonization long before the first gunshots of World War II were fired and promises made to the Allies. The case of Poland is particularly demonstrative. The Moscow-directed purge of the Polish Communist Party eliminated almost the entire leadership by 1937–1938. Survivors continued to serve the Soviet Union as employees of the Comintern or of the international branch of the *Narodny Kommisariat Vnutrennikh Del* (People's Commissariat for Internal Affairs or NKVD, Soviet secret police), which organized a training center for Polish recruits in September 1940 near Smolensk, not far from the forest at Katyn, where more than four thousand Polish officers had been executed by the NKVD a few months earlier following their capture in the Nazi-Soviet partition of Poland in 1939. Those soldiers shared the fate of more than ten thousand other Polish officers and nearly fifteen thousand "socially dangerous" civilians, while as many as

Hungarian communists and Freedom Party members fighting at a Freedom Party meeting in Szeged, Hungary, June 1947

(AP Photo/B.I.Sanders)

SOVIET-WESTERN COOPERATION AFTER 1945

five hundred thousand Poles were arrested and deported to remote regions of the Soviet Union in 1939–1941. By the end of 1940 the NKVD center had two hundred recruits—Poles, Ukrainians, and Belorussians—all former residents of the eastern areas of the Polish Republic.

After the battle of Stalingrad, which ended with a crushing German defeat in February 1943, it became clear that Europe would be divided into Soviet and capitalist camps and that Poland was an important square on this chessboard. The NKVD began secret operations there in 1942 while the country was still occupied by the German army. Moscow set up additional special schools and political organizations for Polish Communists inside the Soviet Union to make sure that they saw the postwar situation the way the Kremlin did. Polish partisans and soldiers were taught to fight and to "think correctly." Some of these men were parachuted into Polish territory to establish communications with partisan groups, and others marched in later with the Red Army. One of these men was Jakob Berman, who had spent the war in the Soviet Union as a leading member of the Union of Polish Patriots and the Central Bureau of Polish Communists. In a 1980 interview he said:

> The world *has* changed can't you see that? There aren't any sovereign states any more, only semi-sovereign ones. The degree of dependence can be lesser or greater, but it's always there. And thinking that we'll sit down in our little corner and smile a little at each in turn is stupidity; it shows ignorance of geography and of elementary political principles. Poland can only be either pro-Soviet or pro-American; there's no other possibility. There isn't [shouting]! Poland can't be uprooted from the Soviet Bloc. How? Uproot it and then where would you put it? On the moon? Poland lies on the road between the Soviet Union and Western Europe, and its position is clear: either/or. There are no half-shades, because Poland can't float in the air.

Indeed, Poland could not float in the air, and circumstances placed it squarely into the Soviet sphere of influence. The question of Polish borders was discussed at the Teheran Conference (November 1943) and settled by British prime minister Winston Churchill and Stalin during the last session. Eastern Polish territories taken under the Nazi-Soviet Pact of 1939 (which had partitioned Poland between German leader Adolf Hitler and Stalin) remained part of the Soviet Union, while Poland annexed eastern parts of Germany. The Soviets used one of Poland's historical weaknesses, its geography, to make it dependent on Moscow. The country was shifted to the west and the new border along the Oder-Neisse line made an alliance with the Soviet Union "indispensable" for the country's security. Geographically, Poland was given to Stalin even before the war with Nazi Germany came to an end. The Polish compromise does not sound so surprising given that the principal aim of the conference was to coordinate the struggle against Nazi Germany.

The structure of the Polish government, a point of bitter controversy, came up fifteen months later at the Yalta Conference (February 1945). Stalin insisted that the West recognize the Polish Committee of National Liberation (PKWN, established in July 1944 to administer territories liberated by the Red Army) and ignore the London-based anticommunist government in exile. The American and British sides insisted that the interim government include Stanislaw Mikolajczyk, leader of the Polish Peasant Party, and other moderate Poles from abroad. Soviet foreign minister Vyacheslav Molotov introduced a plan that called for the inclusion of several democratic leaders from Polish émigré circles and promised democratic elections as soon as possible. An American draft called for a fully representative government. Three days of negotiations ensued, and on 9 February the issue was settled. The formula called for a provisional government "more broadly based than was possible before the recent liberation of western Poland," a meeting in Moscow between the members of the Lublin government and democratic Polish leaders, and free and unfettered elections.

Again, Polish independence was not the primary concern at the conference. The Americans obtained Moscow's pledge to open a second front against the Japanese three months after Germany surrendered. Stalin also accepted a voting formula that made the United Nations (UN) functional, an achievement for which U.S. President Franklin D. Roosevelt eagerly fought, and acquiesced to Churchill's goal of rebuilding France as a European great power. Many in the West also hoped that giving Stalin what he wanted in Eastern Europe would leave him better disposed toward international cooperation after the war. Poland was but a bargaining chip in this game. At the time a war over it between the Allies was a distinct possibility, and none of the parties, except perhaps the United States (but least of all Poland itself), could afford another conflict. Yalta effectively left Poland in the Soviet sphere of influence in exchange for other American and British strategic gains. U.S. President Harry S Truman recorded his instructions to an aide dispatched to meet Stalin in late May 1945:

> That Poland, Rumania, Bulgaria, Czechoslovakia, Austria, Yugoslavia, Latvia, Lithuania, Estonia et al. made no difference to U.S. interests only in so far as World Peace is concerned. That Poland ought to have a "free election," at

least as free as Hague, Tom Pendergast, Joe Martin, or Taft would allow in their respective bailiwicks. That Uncle Joe should make some sort of jesture [sic] whether he means it or not to keep it before our public that he intends to keep his word. Any smart political boss will do that.

The war wreaked havoc with Polish politics, and, in addition to geography, Stalin took full advantage of two more historical Polish weaknesses: internal political instability and military weakness. Hatred of Nazi Germany shared by all Poles united the country in the struggle against the common enemy, but the resistance movement was severely factionalized. Two governments (one in exile in London, the other directed by Moscow) claimed legitimacy. Political parties formerly opposed to the prewar dictatorship vied for power. The Polish People's Army (PAL) was a guerrilla force established in April 1943 by various leftist noncommunist groups. The National Armed Forces (NSZ) was formed in 1942 as the military wing of the extreme nationalist National Radical Camp (ONR). The Home Army (AK) was the London-controlled underground body established in 1942. The Peasant Battalions (BCh) were a guerrilla force established by the Peasant Party (SL). In November 1944 right-wing elements within the AK created the National Military Union (NZW), an underground partisan body, to undertake an armed struggle against the communists. Poland experienced two wars simultaneously: a war for independence and a civil war. The military units grew out of political factionalism, and the Soviets played one actor against another, just as the tsarist courts had done for two and a half centuries.

There is ample documentation of the carefully planned Soviet penetration of Polish politics. First emphasized were political reconciliation and consolidation. In its support for the Polish Workers' Party (PPR) between 1944 and 1947, Moscow stressed a moderate approach to other parties, fearing that openly radical measures would alienate badly needed support for the Polish communists. In essence, the Soviet policy followed the idea of creating a greater national symbol as a rallying point for Poland. Moscow found it easy to use the struggle against Nazi Germany. This plan was accompanied by playing up the myth of the communists' leading role in that struggle. Officially organized violence was kept to a minimum, and consolidation was based on an all-inclusive goal of a liberated Poland. Soviet strategy changed as the leftist regime became stronger and more Stalinist and openly turned on its initial supporters through direct political persecution.

Without sufficient presence behind the descending Iron Curtain, the Western powers could not affect the region's fate. Moscow lost no time in getting back to the Imperial Russian tradition of eliminating resistance inside the country in preparation for a protectorate. The Soviet Union was a step ahead of the West—the presence of the Red Army was crucial in establishing the Communist regime. Parallel to consolidation, a Polish military force was created under the aegis of the Red Army as NKVD and Soviet military intelligence officers worked closely with Polish units. Marshal Konstantin Rokossovskii, a prominent Soviet military commander of Polish ancestry, took up pro forma Polish citizenship to become the country's defense minister. To control the country in the Soviet interest meant to Bolshevize the political and military elite.

The Soviet task was made more urgent and at the same time easier by several crucial domestic factors. First, the economic situation played into Moscow's hands. The Nazi occupation stimulated raw materials production. Coal extraction increased by 50 percent between 1939 and 1944. Oil fields increased production by 60 percent. The production of natural gas doubled. Could an economy such as this one be allowed to fall into "enemy" hands? Could it not be used to bolster Soviet security instead? Moscow wasted no time in ordering the dismantling and transportation to Soviet territories of Polish factories. The territory that Moscow had annexed under the terms of the Nazi-Soviet Pact of 1939 and retained after 1945 included most of Poland's oil reserves. Poland's foreign trade was heavily biased in favor of the Soviet Union through a series of bilateral treaties.

Second, German wartime occupation policies centralized the Polish economy and largely eliminated its prewar leaders, owners, and proprietors. Millions of Polish civilians were enslaved by German big business and by enterprises managed directly by the SS or the German state. The adaptation of the Polish economy to command management, the removal of the existing elite, and the devastation of the war made it much easier to nationalize significant sectors of the economy after the war. Before the Soviet Union even established its domination in Poland, the economy was already severed from Western markets, centralized, and increasingly government-managed.

Third, immense population losses and demographic changes led to the homogenization of Polish society. Nazi and Soviet occupation policies radically reduced the upper classes, most of which fled or were killed. Ethnic Germans and Jews made up the bulk of the prewar urban bourgeois population. Virtually all Jews were killed in the Holocaust, while most Germans either fled or were expelled after the war. This fate was the same for ethnic German populations

LIVE AND PROSPER

Soviet leader Josef Stalin gave the following speech upon the signing of a treaty between the Soviet Union and Poland in April 1945:

Mr. President, Mr. Prime Minister, Gentlemen!

I think that the Treaty of Friendship, Mutual Assistance and Post-War Collaboration between the Soviet Union and Poland, which we have just signed, is of great historic importance. The importance of this Treaty lies, first of all, in that it marks the radical turn in the relations between the Soviet Union and Poland towards alliance and friendship that was brought about in the course of the present struggle for liberation against Germany, and which is now formally sealed in this Treaty. The relations between our countries during the past five centuries, as is known, were replete with elements of mutual estrangement, unfriendliness and often with open military conflicts. These relations weakened both our countries and strengthened German imperialism.

The importance of the present Treaty lies in that it puts an end to these old relations between our countries, nails them in their coffin, and creates real basis for substituting relations of alliance and friendship between the Soviet Union and Poland for the old unfriendly relations. During the last twenty-five to thirty years, *i.e.*, during the last two world wars, the Germans succeeded in utilizing the territory of Poland as a corridor for invasion in the East, and as a jumping off ground for an attack on the Soviet Union. This could happen because there were then no relations of friendship and alliance between our countries. The former rulers of Poland did not wish to have allied relations with the Soviet Union. They preferred a policy of playing between Germany and the Soviet Union. Of course, they lost. . . . Poland was occupied and her independence was annulled; as a result of this fatal policy the German troops were given the opportunity to reach the gates of Moscow.

The importance of the present Treaty lies in that it does away with the old fatal policy of playing between Germany and the Soviet Union and substitutes for it a policy of alliance and friendship between Poland and her Eastern neighbor.

Such is the historic importance of the Treaty between Poland and the Soviet Union

for Friendship, Mutual Assistance and Post-War Collaboration, which we have just signed. It is not surprising, therefore, that the peoples of our countries have been impatiently looking forward to the signing of this Treaty. They feel that this Treaty is a guarantee of the independence of new democratic Poland, a guarantee of her might and her prosperity.

But this is not all. The present Treaty is also of great international importance. While there was no alliance between our countries, Germany was able to take advantage of the absence of a united front between us; she could play off Poland against the Soviet Union and vice versa, and thereby fight them one by one. The situation radically changed after the alliance between our countries was established. Now it is no longer possible to play off our countries against each other. Our countries now have a united front, from the Baltic to the Carpathians, against the common enemy, against German imperialism. It can now confidently be said that German aggression is hemmed in in the East. There can be no doubt that if this barrier in the East is supplemented by a barrier in the West, that is, by an alliance between our countries and our Allies in the West, it may be boldly asserted that German aggression will be curbed, and it will not be easy for it to run riot.

It is not surprising, therefore, that the freedom-loving nations, and primarily the Slavonic nations, have been impatiently looking forward to the conclusion of this Treaty, for they realize that this Treaty signifies the consolidation of the united front of the United Nations against the common enemy in Europe.

Hence, I have no doubt that our Western allies will welcome this Treaty.

May free, independent and democratic Poland live and prosper!

May her Eastern neighbor—our Soviet Union—live and prosper!

Long live the alliance and friendship between our countries!

Source: *J. V. Stalin, "Speech Delivered at the Signing of the Treaty of Friendship, Mutual Assistance And Post-war Collaboration Between The Soviet Union And The Polish Republic, April 21, 1945," in* On the Great Patriotic War of the Soviet Union *(Moscow: Foreign Languages Publishing House, 1946), pp. 186–188.*

SOVIET-WESTERN
COOPERATION AFTER 1945

that had lived in the historically German territory east of the Oder-Neisse line that Poland annexed in 1945. Ethnic Ukrainians or Belorussians lived largely in the territories retained by Moscow after the war, but more than 1 million Poles were forcibly relocated from those lands to the new Polish state. Before the war, national minorities constituted almost one-third of Poland's population. After the war the country became 97 percent ethnically Polish. This homogenization made it easier for the communist regime to take credit for satisfying nationalist aspirations by providing upward mobility for the ethnic majority. In the early stages of Bolshevization the PPR repeatedly appealed to the population as a distinctly Polish Communist Party, not as a Soviet agent, and Moscow fully supported this approach. Ultimately, of course, these nationalistic aspirations created tensions within the Soviet bloc, but for the moment it helped the communists consolidate control.

Finally, the social consequences of the waves of mass violence experienced during the occupation had a profound effect on how brutalized, displaced, and frightened communities interpreted the concepts of commonwealth, collective good, and group interests. A homogenized and psychologically shocked society was more susceptible to strong government, a policy of nationalizing major industries, and the promise of a planned and predictable future. The Communist Party offered youth and women the hope of social advancement, success, and power, which allowed a Bolshevik message to reach wide public circles.

It is extremely important to take into account how World War II contributed to the establishment of Soviet rule in Poland. The Polish example cannot be applied across the board to other East European societies, but many similarities can be found. Diplomatically speaking, a secret protocol signed by Molotov and British foreign secretary Anthony Eden in the autumn of 1944 directly conceded Soviet domination of Romania and Bulgaria in exchange for preponderant British influence in Greece. The agreement also provided for an equal role for the Soviets and British in Hungary and Yugoslavia. Although the agreement did not come about in precisely these terms, it illustrated both the Soviets' desire to establish a major zone of influence in Eastern Europe and the West's willingness to acquiesce to it under certain conditions. In practice, Czechoslovakia, Hungary, Romania, and Bulgaria faced the same artificially strong position enjoyed by their national communist parties, all of which were subordinate to Moscow and largely empowered by Soviet support. Communist-dominated military and police forces were established quickly after the arrival of Soviet troops.

Hundreds of thousands of people whose social roles and positions threatened future communist domination were eliminated—if they had not already been removed by the Germans—with the widespread assistance of the Red Army and the Soviet secret police. Noncommunist politicians in every country were assaulted by a familiar pattern of mysterious deaths, kidnappings, and arrests on specious charges of treason or other crimes against the state. By 1948 all centers of noncommunist political activity and independent civil society in Eastern Europe had been obliterated. The Polish case suggests that a wider range of factors should be examined in the context of East European Bolshevization. Especially interesting is how Nazi occupation paved the way for socialist policies to appear less alien than they have often been portrayed. The role and complicity of the Western Allies must not be ignored, either. These issues change the thrust of the question from Soviet intentions in Eastern Europe, which were fairly clear by 1942, to the nature of the process, which is a much more fruitful exercise in historical thinking.

–ANTON FEDYASHIN,
GEORGETOWN UNIVERSITY

References

Zbigniew K. Brzezinski, *The Soviet Bloc, Unity and Conflict* (Cambridge, Mass.: Harvard University Press, 1960).

Colin Elman and Miriam Fendius Elman, eds., *Bridges and Boundaries: Historians, Political Scientists, and the Study of International Relations* (Cambridge, Mass.: MIT Press, 2001).

Andrei Gromyko, *Memoirs,* translated by Harold Shukman (New York: Doubleday, 1989).

Melvyn P. Leffler, "Adherence to Agreements: Yalta and the Experiences of the Early Cold War," *International Security,* 11 (Summer 1986): 88–123.

Leffler, *A Preponderance of Power: National Security, the Truman Administration, and the Cold War* (Stanford, Cal.: Stanford University Press, 1992).

Norman Naimark and Leonid Gibianskii, eds., *The Establishment of Communist Regimes in Eastern Europe, 1944–1949* (Boulder, Colo.: Westview Press, 1997).

R. Craig Nation, *Black Earth, Red Star: A History of Soviet Security Policy, 1917–1991* (Ithaca, N.Y.: Cornell University Press, 1992).

Scott D. Parrish and Mikhail M. Narinsky, "New Evidence on the Soviet Rejection of the Marshall Plan, 1947: Two Reports," Working Paper 9 (Washington, D.C.: Cold War International History Project, Woodrow Wilson International Center For Scholars, 1994).

Vladimir O. Pechatnov, "The Big Three after World War II: New Documents on Soviet Thinking about Post War Relations with the United States and Great Britain," Working Paper 13 (Washington, D.C.: Cold War International History Project, Woodrow Wilson International Center For Scholars, 1995).

Antony Polonsky and Boleslaw Drukier, eds., *The Beginnings of Communist Rule in Poland* (London & Boston: Routledge & Kegan Paul, 1980).

Gale Stokes, ed., *From Stalinism to Pluralism, A Documentary History of Eastern Europe since 1945* (New York: Oxford University Press, 1991).

William Taubman, *Stalin's American Policy: From Entente to Détente to Cold War* (New York: Norton, 1982).

Athan G. Theoharis, *The Yalta Myths: An Issue in U.S. Politics, 1945–1955* (Columbia: University of Missouri Press, 1970).

United States Department of State, *Foreign Relations of the United States, Diplomatic Papers: The Conferences at Cairo and Tehran, 1943* (Washington, D.C.: Government Printing Office, 1961).

United States Department of State, *Foreign Relations of the United States, Diplomatic Papers: The Conferences of Malta and Yalta, 1945* (Washington, D.C.: Government Printing Office, 1955).

Natalia I. Yegorova, "The 'Iran Crisis' of 1945–1946: A View from the Russian Archives," Working Paper 15 (Washington, D.C.: Cold War International History Project, Woodrow Wilson International Center For Scholars, 1996).

SUEZ CRISIS

Was superpower pressure the determining factor in Gamal Abdel Nasser's ultimately successful nationalization of the Suez Canal Company?

Viewpoint: Yes. The Soviet threat of intervention and the lack of American support forced Britain, France, and Israel to withdraw from Egypt.

Viewpoint: No. The foreign occupation of the Suez Canal collapsed because of poor planning and inadequate diplomacy on the part of Britain and France.

The fate of European colonies was one of the most difficult themes in international relations after World War II (1939–1945). While colonial powers often withdrew from their possessions willingly, their many attempts to remain in control often led to disaster or potential disaster. The Suez Crisis (1956) was one such potential disaster. In July of that year Egyptian leader Gamal Abdel Nasser nationalized the Suez Canal Company, the governing authority of the strategic canal, which was controlled predominantly by Britain and France. After prolonged attempts to reach a peaceful solution, those two nations, in collusion with Israel, launched an attack on Egypt in late October. After only a few days the allies had occupied the canal and its surrounding areas. Despite this apparent success, the victorious powers almost immediately found themselves under international pressure to withdraw. The United Nations (UN) condemned their "unauthorized" use of military power, and its Security Council passed a resolution calling for their withdrawal from Egypt in favor of replacement by UN authorities. The United States, Britain's and France's staunchest ally, voted in favor of the resolution, as did the Soviet Union, which also intimated through other channels that it would retaliate with nuclear weapons if the allies failed to withdraw. Their forces left within a few weeks.

What were the reasons for that defeat? One argument assigns most of the responsibility to international pressure: when confronted with the lack of American support and the threat of Soviet missiles, the allies felt that capitulation was the only safe and realistic option. A counterargument suggests instead that poor diplomatic planning contained the seeds of defeat. The secrecy of the military operation, which was maintained even within the British and French governments, made unified support for the operation a near impossibility. It also offended the American government, which had consistently offered its support for a military solution as a last resort. When the operation failed, it was the fault of its executors.

Viewpoint:
Yes. The Soviet threat of intervention and the lack of American support forced Britain, France, and Israel to withdraw from Egypt.

There is no better illustration of the transfer of power from Europe to the United States in the Middle East during the twentieth century than the Suez Crisis (1956). The Eisenhower administration used America's economic and commercial power to force London, Paris, and Jerusalem to withdraw their forces from Egypt; to recognize Egypt's confiscation of Britain's and France's most valuable overseas asset, the Suez Canal; and to force Britain to accept humiliation and defeat in a fashion "that Germany in two world wars had not been able to do." For the first time in a century Britain had failed to defend its vital interests because of the actions of another nation. The fact that the United States, Britain's closest ally, had sided against it made the situation even more difficult to accept. As British prime minister Harold Macmillan wrote American secretary of state John Foster Dulles, "the British action [at Suez] was the last gasp of declining power. . . . Perhaps in two hundred years the United States [will] know how we felt."

Traditionally, historians describe the Suez Crisis as a watershed moment in twentieth-century history. The United States replaced France and Great Britain as the principal defender of Western interests in the Middle East and, along with the Union of Soviet Socialist Republics (U.S.S.R.), adopted a new position of regional prominence. Historians have stressed that the crisis must be understood within the context of a host of other factors: Cold War rivalries, France's war in Algeria, Egyptian leader Gamal Abdel Nasser's drive for independence, the Arab-Israeli conflict, decolonization, Great Britain's postwar decline, and a decade-long discourse in which Washington, fearful of communist subversion and Arab nationalism, worked to convince London and Paris to withdraw from their colonial possessions in the Middle East. The fact that World War I (1914–1918), Middle Eastern oil, and weak Soviet diplomacy created conditions that allowed Great Britain and France to dominate Middle Eastern affairs longer than they would have been able to do otherwise is often overlooked. Events during World War I and the interwar period set the stage for the two superpowers to play the decisive role in the Suez Crisis.

The 1910s and 1920s transformed the roles of Britain, France, the United States, and the U.S.S.R. in the Middle East. The Russian Revolution (1917) and the Central Powers' defeat in World War I crippled Britain's and France's principal Great Power rivals in Middle East politics—Germany, the Ottoman Empire (later the Turkish Republic), and Russia (later the U.S.S.R.)—and forced them to withdraw from active regional diplomacy. The Soviet Union, for instance, had initially terrorized British and French officials, who feared an alliance of Asian nationalists and Russian commissars and the impact of fierce Soviet anticolonial propaganda. The alliance never materialized, however, and Soviet diplomacy, intrigue, and influence in the region were negligible throughout the interwar period. Few prewar Arab nationalists or Islamic parties were interested in communism or seeking Moscow's assistance.

Without clear competitors, London and Paris formalized their wartime gains. They added to their empires in North Africa, Egypt, Iran, and the Persian Gulf region by dividing control over the new "mandate" states of Iraq, Syria, Lebanon, Palestine, and Transjordan (Jordan). Britain also encouraged European and American Jews to settle in Palestine. Jewish immigration was important to London because it was seen as the factor legitimizing Britain's presence in Palestine (through the Balfour Declaration of 1917), but it also laid the foundation for decades of violence. The potential cost of containing this violence was an important issue for both Britain and France because they had already strained their resources fighting in World War I and Turkey's war of independence (1919–1923) as well as suppressing revolts in Syria, Egypt, and Iraq. Early in the century both countries were forced to use U.S. capital, petroleum, and munitions to meet their needs.

That process, however, carried a high price internationally. U.S. conceptions of global security, international political and economic norms, and postwar settlements were inconsistent with those of Britain and France. On the one hand, London stressed the need for imperial preference and, along with France, wished to incorporate Middle Eastern territories into the imperial fold quickly without preconditions. On the other hand, Washington emphasized the rights of U.S. corporations in the Middle East and other overseas territories, self-determination for all peoples, and the promotion of a stable international order—particularly in underdeveloped regions—through cooperation among the Great Powers. Together, these principles constricted Britain's and France's freedom of action, limited the duration of their control over the new territories, and suggested the possibility of the breakup of all empires.

In the 1920s Washington employed these principles to press for U.S. access to the Iraqi oil

TAKING ISSUE WITH NASSER

On 27 July 1956 British prime minister Anthony Eden sent the following telegram to U.S. president Dwight D. Eisenhower concerning the seizure of the Suez Canal by Egyptian president Gamal Abdel Nasser:

This morning I have reviewed the whole position with my Cabinet colleagues and Chiefs of Staff. We are all agreed that we cannot afford to allow Nasser to seize control of the canal in this way, in defiance of international agreements. If we take a firm stand over this now we shall have the support of all the maritime powers. If we do not, our influence and yours throughout the Middle East will, we are all convinced, be finally destroyed.

The immediate threat is to the oil supplies to Western Europe, a great part of which flows through the canal. . . . If the canal were closed we should have to ask you to help us by reducing the amount which you draw from the pipeline terminals in the eastern Mediterranean and possibly by sending us supplementary supplies for a time from your side of the world.

It is, however, the outlook for the longer term which is more threatening. The canal is an international asset and facility, which is vital to the free world. The maritime powers cannot afford to allow Egypt to expropriate it and to exploit it by using the revenues for her own internal purposes irrespective of the interests of the canal and of the canal users. . . .

We should not allow ourselves to become involved in legal quibbles about the rights of the Egyptian Government to nationalize what is technically an Egyptian company, or in financial arguments about their capacity to pay the compensation which they have offered. I feel sure that we should take issue with Nasser on the broad international grounds.

As we see it we are unlikely to attain our objectives by economic pressures alone. I gather that Egypt is not due to receive any further aid from you. No large payments from her sterling balances here are due before January. We ought in the first instance to bring the maximum political pressure to bear on Egypt. For this, apart from our own action, we should invoke the support of all the interested powers. My colleagues and I are convinced that we must be ready, in the last resort, to use force to bring Nasser to his senses. For our part we are prepared to do so. I have this morning instructed our Chiefs of Staff to prepare a military plan accordingly.

However, the first step must be for you and us and France to exchange views, align our policies and concert together how we can best bring the maximum pressure to bear on the Egyptian Government.

Source: *Anthony Eden,* Full Circle *(Boston: Houghton Mifflin, 1960), pp. 476–477.*

---

fields under British control. Fortunately for London, Washington "refused to privilege foreign policy over domestic priorities" and preferred in the long run to allow Britain to protect American citizens and investments in the Middle East, which was far from the United States and without clear strategic U.S. interests. Both governments reached a compromise: U.S. companies gained access to Iraqi oil fields in exchange for British access to American oil fields and U.S. investments in London in sterling-denominated assets. This deal was important for London financiers, who were quickly losing their position as the center of global finance to New York. Still, it was clear that U.S. values could undermine European positions in the Middle East and that the loss of U.S. friendship could prove disastrous to Paris and London.

At the same time, one should not overemphasize U.S. leverage over European empires or the influence of American ideas and institutions. Few Americans were trained in Middle Eastern studies or languages or had links to the region before the 1950s. Middle Easterners had been familiar with ideas central to U.S. values for a century before the proclamation of Woodrow Wilson's Fourteen Points in 1918. Britain and France were rightly confident that they would be less dependent on the United States given that fighter aircraft, armored cars, machine guns, alliances with local leaders, and chemical weapons permitted control of ever larger territories at minimal cost and with a handful of regiments.

The confidence of Britain and France in their position in the Middle East was confirmed in the decade immediately after the war. Although they lost their mandates, both Britain and France retained close links to the local elite, maintained military bases in the region, and controlled many economic facilities, such as the Suez

SUEZ CRISIS

Canal and the oil refinery at Abadan, Iran. Withdrawal from Palestine (1948) freed London from the responsibility for resolving the many problems following the founding of Israel, many of which were caused by the Balfour Declaration. Britain and France were permanent members of the United Nations (UN) Security Council, the key to Great Power status. As the dispute between the United States and the U.S.S.R. intensified, Washington provided financial assistance to Britain and France to recover from World War II (1939–1945) and to regain control over their overseas empires, now seen as buffers against global Communism. This partnership was especially clear in the Middle East: British bases protected Middle East petroleum supplies, Washington aided the French in Algeria, and the United States and Britain overthrew Iranian prime minister Mohammad Mosaddeq (1953) after he nationalized Iran's oil production.

Changes in U.S. policy, however, were a double-edged sword. Faced with the Soviet threat, Washington prioritized foreign policy and abandoned the practice of paying Britain to protect U.S. interests in the Middle East, which bordered the U.S.S.R. American interests in the Middle East grew in the mid 1940s as new discoveries of oil made it clear that the region would soon win the balance of world oil production away from North America. This change partly explains Washington's conditions for assisting London in overthrowing Iran's government: majority interest in Iranian oil production, which was previously a British monopoly. U.S. interests became more complicated by Washington's recognition of Israel, an action generated by domestic constituents but opposed by regional oil producers. To address this problem, the U.S. government asked American oil companies to serve as surrogate representatives for U.S. interests and to allow Washington to support multiple, contradictory positions simultaneously. Ultimately, this process framed U.S. policy during the Suez Crisis, which attempted to check Soviet regional influence, support the existence of Israel, and guarantee access to Middle East oil.

Soviet policy underwent profound changes in the 1950s. The new Soviet leader, Nikita Khrushchev, abandoned the cautious foreign policies of his predecessor, Josef Stalin, in the Third World and aggressively courted the newly independent nations, even those that were not led by Communist parties. He hoped that the U.S.S.R.'s anti-imperialism, industrialization, and expertise in weapons and technology would appeal to nations eager to escape laissez-faire economics (often a precondition of Western aid) and all forms of Western "neocolonialism" in favor of independent foreign policies and planned economic growth. Starting with the Soviet-Indian trade treaty (1953), Moscow extended loans, trade credits, military advisers, and technological expertise to nations throughout Asia and Africa. Khrushchev ultimately aimed to counter Western influence in the Third World, break the U.S. cordon around the U.S.S.R., and demonstrate the "superiority" of the Soviet system.

Egypt was a key component of Khrushchev's strategy. Although Nasser opposed Communism, he refused to join the Baghdad Pact (1955), a British-led alliance to contain the U.S.S.R., and convinced other Arab states to do likewise. In his eyes the treaty was colonialism, no different than earlier stages of European occupation, such as the mandate system, the French occupation of Algeria, and Israel's domination of Palestine. After seizing power in a 1952 coup, Nasser worked to modernize Egypt's economy, end foreign control of domestic economic institutions, unify the Arabs, and defeat Israel, which had humiliated Egypt in 1948 and regularly raided Egyptian-controlled Gaza in response to Palestinian guerilla attacks. He was also determined to play the superpowers against each other and their allies. In 1955, for instance, Nasser obtained Soviet weapons through Czechoslovakia after his attempts to purchase Western weapons failed.

Nasser followed up the so-called Czech arms deal with a far bolder ploy: nationalization of the Suez Canal and construction of the Aswan Dam. The dam would have political benefits (increased prestige) and economic benefits (more water and electricity for Egypt). However, the costs of construction were beyond Egyptian means and necessitated seeking foreign assistance. When the United States withdrew a World Bank loan to pay for the dam, Nasser nationalized the Suez Canal on 26 July 1956. Many Arabs saw Nasser as a hero, and nationalization became a symbol of their liberation from oppression by outside interests. By contrast, Britain and France saw it as theft and compared Nasser to World War II German leader Adolf Hitler. Washington also saw Nasser's nationalization as counterproductive, but U.S. president Dwight D. Eisenhower opposed any military intervention because he feared jeopardizing his reelection campaign and his case against Moscow's repression of a liberal reform movement in Hungary. Moscow welcomed the nationalization and the problems it created for Washington.

Britain and France were determined to destroy Nasser. British prime minister Anthony Eden believed that the crisis over the nationalization of Iranian oil demonstrated that the only way to deal with Third World intransigence was through force and that the United States would eventually back its allies. The French were furious at the nationalization of their company and Nasser's spurring on the Algerians to resist France's presence in their country. Paris also hoped that Nasser's defeat would be seen by Algeria's rebels "as a demonstration of France's indomitable will to remain in Algeria." By October 1956 both nations were determined to overthrow Nasser and found an ally in Israel, which saw the invasion as an opportunity to rid itself of a key enemy. None of the states informed the United States of their plans before they launched a carefully orchestrated invasion of the Suez Canal zone later that month. This gamble was risky for London for two reasons: first, once the invasion began, Britain would no longer be able to import oil from the Near East and would have to rely on American supplies; second, given Britain's shaky finances, the invasion would certainly spark a run on the pound. If Washington did not support the invasion, the results would be disastrous for London.

It became obvious that Eden's assumptions about the United States were fatally wrong and that London's gamble failed miserably. Eisenhower reacted with fury to the invasion; he refused to aid London until British forces had withdrawn, telling an aide that Britain and France "should be left to work out their own oil problems—to boil in their own oil, so to speak." Though the invasion was successful militarily and Paris had made careful financial preparations to avoid blackmail, French forces withdrew along with the Israelis when Britain bowed to U.S. pressure. The Soviets co-authored with the United States a UN Security Council resolution condemning the invasion and made threats to use nuclear force against Britain and France if they did not withdraw. For his part, Nasser appeared to have brilliantly played the two superpowers off against each other and against the three intervening powers so that he alone emerged as the victim and the undisputed victor, the vanquisher of Great Britain from the Middle East and the new leader of the Arab world.

In reality, Nasser succeeded because of his political skills and his luck that superpower interests coincided with Egypt's. This reality was borne out a decade later in June 1967, when Nasser faced another Israeli war. At that time Nasser sought to retain his leadership of the Arab world by deploying troops to the Sinai and blockading the Strait of Tiran, which Jerusalem had made clear was a casus belli. Nasser's deployment was reckless since most of his army was in Yemen, but he gambled that superpower intervention would allow him to escape again. His gamble failed. The superpowers remained neutral, and in just six days the Israelis inflicted a defeat on Nasser as humiliating as the one Washington's actions had inflicted on its allies in 1956.

It is important to remember the consistency in U.S. thinking leading to Suez. Eisenhower weighed his options in the Middle East in much the same way that his predecessors had done during the 1920s. Eisenhower concluded that, given the sentiment in the Arab world, the costs of supporting Britain and France were higher than withdrawing support, no matter what Europe's feelings were. Eisenhower's decision revealed that American priorities could hinder Europe's position in the Middle East as much as assist it. The decision also revealed the degree of London's postwar dependence on Washington and how much Britain's Middle East empire depended on U.S. goodwill and Soviet weakness. When both of these factors changed, Britain's power in the Middle East crumbled. France fared little better, and its power collapsed by 1960. By that time the age of European politics in the Middle East was over, and the time of superpower politics in the region was well under way.

—SEAN FOLEY,
GEORGETOWN UNIVERSITY

Viewpoint:
No. The foreign occupation of the Suez Canal collapsed because of poor planning and inadequate diplomacy on the part of Britain and France.

Historians of the Cold War often treat the Suez Crisis (1956) as one of many "standoffs" in which the United States and the Soviet Union faced a threat to their uneasy peace. Superpower cooperation in defusing the crisis has been looked upon as an important case in which mutual interests and the use of their overweening power determined the outcome of an international problem. For a variety of reasons, however, the historian should note that Britain's and France's approach to Egypt contained many embarrassing flaws that doomed their expedition regardless of what the superpowers did.

By the time Egyptian leader Gamal Abdel Nasser nationalized the Suez Canal Company in July 1956, Britain and France were already on their way down as powers. Britain had been dramatically weakened by the two world wars, in addition to general trends of long-term decline, and had already divested itself of its major colonial possession, India. France had been absolutely defeated by Germany in World War II (1939–1945), subjected to a long and humiliating occupation, and liberated by foreign troops. Both nations had begun to bear massive expenses associated with expanded welfare states, and neither could claim its former military power and international prominence.

These factors strongly influenced London and Paris's reaction to Nasser's seizure of the canal. They knew that their straitened circumstances would never allow them to intervene directly, and both feared potentially hostile international opinion. Instead, they decided to use international law for their ends. After talks with the new nation of Israel, which coveted access to the Red Sea through Egyptian territory, they persuaded Prime Minister David Ben-Gurion to launch an attack. As the Israeli troops moved in, Britain and France planned to use their United Nations (UN) Security Council seats to call for a cease-fire, demand the withdrawal of Israeli and Egyptian forces from the Canal Zone, and propose that they police it themselves under a UN mandate. After Israel attacked on 29 October 1956, that is exactly what happened. Before securing UN approval, however, Britain and France dispatched airborne troops to occupy the canal. This bold move cost them any potential sanction under international law. After Soviet threats of military action, including a possible nuclear response, and the U.S. failure to support its allies diplomatically, the Security Council approved a resolution calling for Britain and France to withdraw in favor of a UN peacekeeping force. Within days of its appearance in Egypt the Anglo-French troop presence was doomed. They left in December, having done little more than make Nasser a hero to the Third World.

Obviously, this outcome suffered from poor diplomacy. Perhaps the most significant problem was that the British and French fundamentally failed to secure the support of their major ally, the United States. This development was curious, indeed, since President Dwight D. Eisenhower had previously assured them that if peaceful solutions failed, he would back military action. The type of military action that his allies pursued, however, was presented as a fait accompli. At no point did either government, or Israel, which the United States also supported, tell Washington what was about to happen or look to Washington as a bastion of support. Indeed, the British government did not even tell its ambassador to the United States, Sir Roger Makins, about its plans and summoned him home just before the attack occurred so that its actions could be obscured at the crucial time. Such tactics by their very nature excluded the possibility of U.S. support and the diplomatic or military benefits that it might have carried. Eisenhower may have had the more subtle intention of maneuvering the British and French into a position where their influence in the Middle East would be edged out in favor of American influence, but part of his failure to support his allies in the Security Council vote, and indeed even to vote with the Soviet Union against them, came from his sense that they were using his earlier abstract guarantee of support for a military solution more to exclude American influence than to benefit from multilateral backing.

Another crucial flaw in the diplomatic conduct of the Suez Crisis was that the collusion between Britain, France, and Israel was a secret so deep that even members of their governments were unaware of what was happening. British prime minister Anthony Eden failed to tell even members of his own cabinet about their plans, to say nothing of his party's rank-and-file members of Parliament or the opposition leaders. This decision proved damning, for as soon as the Anglo-French attack became known, both the opposition Labour Party and some of the Conservative Party's backbenchers subjected the government to scathing criticism. Eden's secrecy prevented him from forging a united approach to Egypt even in his own country. He was forced to resign in January 1957. In France, Premier Guy Mollet suffered less criticism, but his government nevertheless fell in May of that year.

From a strategic standpoint Britain's and France's association with Israel was also damning. Israel's emergence as an independent nation in 1948 had enraged the Arab world enough to cause them to go to war immediately thereafter. Colluding with Israel to attack an Arab state just eight years later could not have been worse for Britain's and France's already tense relations with the Middle East. In addition to making the two great powers seem to be great friends of Zionism, their reliance on Israeli military action, however marginal it was in the tactical execution of the British and French attack, made them look incredibly weak—as if they could not fight effectively in the Third World without the help of a small developing nation that had only just emerged from colonial rule. This "lesson" was well learned throughout the Arab world, which subsequently became more confident in its attitudes and bolder in its actions. The Algerian National Liberation Front, which was fighting for independence from France, was already directly supported by Nasser and, after seeing the apparent French weakness at Suez, escalated its resistance into a full-scale military confrontation in Algiers in 1957—only the beginning of France's painful withdrawal from North Africa. A nationalist coup in Iraq toppled that country's

Soviet cartoon celebrating Gamal Abdel Nasser's seizure of the Suez Canal in July 1956. The banner reads "Shares of the Suez Canal Co. Ltd."

(from Marcus Cunliffe, The Times History of Our Times, 1971).

pro-British monarchy in a bloody coup a year later.

Britain and France further revealed weakness in their response to Soviet threats. The Soviets delivered diplomatic notes on 5 November 1956 and threatened military action unless the occupying powers withdrew from the canal. Since the Soviets had no conventional forces anywhere close to Egypt, the threat implied nuclear war. The Soviet threat, however, was pure bluff. Even though Soviet tanks were moving into Hungary at the same time, it was highly unlikely that the Soviets would have launched a nuclear war to settle the Suez Crisis. Soviet leader Nikita Khrushchev's bluster was an empty threat, for his strategic nuclear forces were far weaker than

he said they were and far weaker than the Western response he would undoubtedly have faced. When Khrushchev was removed from power in October 1964, his critics in the Soviet leadership sharply criticized him for having brought the U.S.S.R. "within a hair's breadth of a big war" over Suez and accused him of "political adventurism," "blackmail," and an "irresponsible juggling with the fate of the country" in his policy toward the crisis. As the British and French should have known at the time, these critics were right. Despite the Security Council vote favoring UN peacekeepers over continued Anglo-French occupation, the United States was prepared to defend its allies. Following the delivery of the threatening Soviet notes Eisenhower ordered the U.S.

Sixth Fleet, already in position to help evacuate Americans in the Eastern Mediterranean, to high alert in anticipation of a general war. Reflecting on the Soviet ultimatum to American allies, the president remarked, "if those fellows start something, we may have to hit 'em—and, if necessary, with everything in the bucket." Britain and France were safe from nuclear attack. Their poor planning, weak diplomatic arrangements, and resulting confusion led them to back down.

The resolution of the Suez Crisis was a classic case of poor diplomacy. In their careless bumbling the British and French allied themselves with a state they did not need in a way that exacerbated their situation and made them appear feeble before the entire world, particularly their restless colonial populations. They then failed to gain the support of their greatest ally, support that was nevertheless at the ready when it was needed. Their failure to establish domestic support both frustrated the military operation and resulted in their leaders' fall from power only a few months later. At the climax of the crisis they fell for what was almost certainly a Soviet bluff, one that Eisenhower may have been prepared to call. Finally, their ultimate withdrawal lionized Nasser and energized opposition throughout the Arab world. Britain and France's freedom of action as great powers ended with a series of whimpers rather than bangs.

–PAUL DU QUENOY,
GEORGETOWN UNIVERSITY

References

William H. Becker and Samuel F. Wells Jr., eds., *Economics and World Power: An Assessment of American Diplomacy since 1789* (New York: Columbia University Press, 1984).

William L. Cleveland, *A History of the Modern Middle East* (Boulder, Colo.: Westview Press, 1994).

John DeNovo, "On the Sidelines: The United States and the Middle East between the Wars, 1919–1939," in *The Great Powers in the Middle East*, edited by Uriel Dann (New York: Holmes & Meier, 1988): 225–237.

Diane B. Kunz, *The Economic Diplomacy of the Suez Crisis* (Chapel Hill: University of North Carolina Press, 1991).

Melvyn Leffler, "1921–1932: Expansion Impulses and Domestic Constraints," in *Economics and World Power: An Assessment of American Diplomacy since 1789*, edited by Becker and Wells (New York: Columbia University Press, 1984).

William Stivers, "International Politics and Iraqi Oil, 1918–1928: A Study in Anglo-American Diplomacy," *Business History Review*, 15 (Winter 1981): 517–540.

Irwin M. Wall, "The U.S., Algeria, and the Fourth French Republic," *Diplomatic History*, 18 (Spring 1994): 489–511.

Has terrorism been an important factor in twentieth-century European history?

Viewpoint: Yes. Terrorism has afflicted most major European countries and has had a serious impact on national and international politics.

Viewpoint: No. Terrorist groups in twentieth-century Europe have been generally small, short-lived organizations that have employed ineffective tactics.

The attacks on the United States on 11 September 2001 placed terrorism at the center of the international agenda. Although this example of sudden violence occurred outside Europe, much global attention is now devoted to America's "war on terrorism." For Europeans this trope is familiar. From anarchists to the Irish Republican Army (IRA) and from communist radicals to the Palestine Liberation Organization (PLO), terrorism was a present factor in European life over much of the twentieth century.

The essays in this chapter debate the overall relevance of terrorist violence in the shaping of modern Europe. One argument draws upon the range of terrorist activity to suggest that it was of major significance. It affected most European countries, led governments to act in certain ways in certain circumstances, and brought attention to political issues through much publicized acts of violence and intimidation. Causes as seemingly unrelated as socialist revolution, Basque independence, and Arab nationalism all employed remarkably similar techniques of violence to achieve their aims, and they attracted major international attention in the process.

The counterargument suggests that terrorism has been confined in its reach. Practiced by marginal malcontents representing peripheral concerns to modern Europe, terrorism—as horrible as each instance of it may have been—involved relatively few people (perpetrators as well as victims) and in many notable ways did not have a major impact on daily life or national policies. As the beginning of the twenty-first century has shown that terrorism will almost certainly remain a concern of the whole world, its past relevance and effectiveness warrants serious consideration.

Viewpoint:
Yes. Terrorism has afflicted most major European countries and has had a serious impact on national and international politics.

Terrorism has been a cultural constant of the twentieth century. From the anarchist assassination of

U.S. president William McKinley in September 1901 to the horror of the World Trade Center attack one hundred years later every decade has had its own distinctive brand of terrorism. At the same time, almost every terrorist movement has been unsuccessful in achieving its proclaimed goals but often catastrophically successful in the effect of their tactical aims.

Irish Republican Army gunmen patrolling Grafton Street, Dublin, July 1922

(Hulton Picture Archive)

Terrorism can be defined as an ideologically motivated act of violence, generally committed by a relatively small group, designed to cause political change. European terrorism has often contained a shock element designed to increase its news value. In this definition the far more destructive state-sponsored terrorism is set aside. Thus, the unspeakable horrors perpetrated by the Gestapo (Nazi secret police) and the countless millions murdered by Soviet leader Josef Stalin will not be discussed in this essay.

The two terrorist operations most successful in attaining their stated goals occurred early in the twentieth century: the anarchists and the Irish Republican Army (IRA). Anarchism was much more a coffeehouse ideology than an organized movement. Its general aim was to create a classless society free of economic, aristocratic, and judicial restraints. Flourishing from the 1870s to 1914 in the United States and Europe, it had a distinctly Balkan flavor. Although generally depicted as a black-caped, bomb-throwing cabal, its violent actions were almost always the work of a lone individual who believed the way to their dream state was to destroy the holders of power. Over the span of their existence they

assassinated several national leaders, including a president of France, a king of Italy, and an empress of Austria. With the murder in June 1914 of Archduke Franz Ferdinand, heir apparent to the dual crown of Austria-Hungary, the anarchists succeeded beyond their wildest dreams. They plunged the whole of Europe into war and in the process brought down the four major monarchies and aristocratic societies—Germany, Austria-Hungary, Russia, and the Ottoman Empire—at the cost of more than ten million lives.

The second terrorist group of the twentieth century was more successful in its immediate and strategic goals, and the conflict that it began probably should be classified as the century's first war of national liberation. The IRA came into being after the collapse of the Easter Rebellion (1916). Eamon de Valera headed its political wing, Sinn Féin, while Michael Collins led the "action" wing. The IRA over the course of the next ten years launched a wave of political violence, especially urban guerrilla warfare against British rule. By 1922 the IRA's terrorist tactics compelled the British to consent to negotiations for Ireland's de facto independence as a free state and future as a de jure independent nation. Nevertheless, the continuing British presence in Northern Ireland has prompted an enduring campaign of terrorist attacks and other forms of violence. IRA attacks have included street violence and many bombings that have targeted, maimed, and killed several members of the British government, including Queen Elizabeth II's cousin Lord Mountbatten in 1979. Yet, Ireland has not been the only locus of terrorist activity. Basque separatists have carried out many attacks on judges and other officials in Spain, while activist Corsican terrorists have waged a sporadic terrorist campaign against personnel of the French government.

Terrorism after World War II (1939–1945) added several variations. The peace movement of the 1960s spawned ultraviolent Marxist-Leninist gangs, which specialized in car bombings, airline hijackings, and assassinations. Two of the most prominent and violent were the Baader-Meinhof Gang of West Germany and the Red Brigades of Italy. Although the West German group was responsible for many deaths, the Red Brigades organization was by far the more vicious. Its handiwork included the kidnapping and murder of former Italian prime minister Aldo Moro (1978), the kidnapping of American general James Dozier (1981), and the killing of Leamon Hunt, the U.S. chief of the Sinai Multinational Force and Observer Group (1984).

A new element in terrorism arose in the 1970s—the professional, mercenary terrorist. The most notorious and deadly was a South American from a wealthy family, Ilich Ramirez Sanchez, who went by the nom de guerre *Carlos the Jackal*. He worked for the Palestinians, Libyans, Red Brigades, and anyone else who was sufficiently radical and could meet his price. He was finally captured by Sudanese authorities in 1994 and turned over to the French government. He is spending a life sentence in closely guarded solitary confinement.

The Palestinians provided the most psychologically shocking attacks of the era, mostly in connection with their desire to end Israeli occupation of their traditional homeland. In 1972 a group calling itself Black September invaded the quarters of the Israeli athletes during the Munich Olympic games. Two athletes were killed in their room while nine others were taken hostage. In the following botched rescue attempt, all the hostages, five terrorists, and one German policeman were killed. It took Israeli intelligence agents ten years, but they ultimately found and executed most of the Black September members involved in the Munich Massacre.

Other Arab terrorist organizations operated through the 1980s. On 27 December 1985 a group of Palestinians led by Abu Nidal simulta-neously attacked the Rome and Vienna airports. They killed twenty travelers and wounded many more. That same year another group led by Abu Abbas highjacked the Italian ocean liner *Achille Lauro* and murdered an American passenger.

Europe has learned to accommodate acts of terrorism, a factor that has remained present in European life and important in the continent's political development. By causing the deaths of many national government officials, terrorism has changed history in many ways. Terrorist activities in Ireland, Spain, and France have highlighted nationalist tensions, while political terrorism marked enduring radicalism. Although the al-Qaida terrorist attacks of 11 September 2001 targeted the United States, they also claimed hundreds of European lives and led directly to much of Europe's (especially Britain's) alignment with the U.S. "war on terrorism." Terrorism is one of the most current issues affecting international politics today.

–JOHN WHEATLEY,
BROOKLYN CENTER, MINNESOTA

Viewpoint:
No. Terrorist groups in twentieth-century Europe have been generally small, short-lived organizations that have employed ineffective tactics.

The twentieth century was dominated by a series of organized, violent conflicts that engulfed the world. World War I (1914–1918), unique in its brutality and massive scale, was only to be surpassed by World War II (1939–1945). As World War II came to a close, so commenced the Cold War, launching the globe into a bipolar existence in which smaller, scattered wars flared up across continents. At the close of the century the collapse of the Berlin Wall signaled the termination of the Cold War period, and the post–Cold War era witnessed new regional powers struggling for a new balance yet vying for supremacy. More than any other factor, these tumultuous events molded European political development in the last century.

World War I and World War II along with the Cold War motivated European states to strive for unification and peaceful coexistence, propelling them to create the European Union (EU). The driving force behind the political movement that would obsess Europe for the latter half of the twentieth century was Europe's total collapse caused by the political devastation and economic disintegration that resulted from

EUROPEAN CONVENTION ON THE SUPPRESSION OF TERRORISM

Strasbourg, 27.I.1977

The member States of the Council of Europe, signatory hereto,

Considering that the aim of the Council of Europe is to achieve a greater unity between its members;

Aware of the growing concern caused by the increase in acts of terrorism;

Wishing to take effective measures to ensure that the perpetrators of such acts do not escape prosecution and punishment;

Convinced that extradition is a particularly effective measure for achieving this result,

Have agreed as follows;

Article 1

For the purposes of extradition between Contracting States, none of the following offences shall be regarded as a political offence or as an offence connected with a political offence or as an offence inspired by political motives:

a.) an offence within the scope of the Convention for the Suppression of Unlawful Seizure of Aircraft, signed at The Hague on 16 December 1970;

b.) an offence within the scope of the Convention for the Suppression of Unlawful Acts against the Safety of Civil Aviation, signed at Montreal on 23 September 1971;

c.) a serious offence involving an attack against the life, physical integrity or liberty of internationally protected persons, including diplomatic agents;

d.) an offence involving kidnapping, the taking of a hostage or serious unlawful detention;

e.) an offence involving the use of a bomb, grenade, rocket, automatic firearm or letter or parcel bomb if this use endangers persons;

f.) an attempt to commit any of the foregoing offences or participation as an accomplice of a person who commits or attempts to commit such an offence.

Article 2

For the purpose of extradition between Contracting States, a Contracting State may decide not to regard as a political offence or as an offence connected with a political offence or as an offence inspired by political motives a serious offence involving an act of violence, other than one covered by Article 1, against the life, physical integrity or liberty of a person.

The same shall apply to a serious offence involving an act against property, other than one covered by Article 1, if the act created a collective danger for persons.

The same shall apply to an attempt to commit any of the foregoing offences or participation as an accomplice of a person who commits or attempts to commit such an offence.

Article 3

The provisions of all extradition treaties and arrangements applicable between Contracting States, including the European Convention on Extradition, are modified as between Contracting States to the extent that they are incompatible with this Convention.

Article 4

For the purpose of this Convention and to the extent that any offence mentioned in Article 1 or 2 is not listed as an extraditable offence in any extradition convention or treaty existing between Contracting States, it shall be deemed to be included as such therein.

Article 5

Nothing in this Convention shall be interpreted as imposing an obligation to extradite if the requested State has substantial grounds for believing that the request for extradition for an offence mentioned in Article 1 or 2 has been made for the purpose of prosecuting or punishing a person on account of his race, religion, nationality or political opinion, or that that person's position may be prejudiced for any of these reasons.

Article 6

Each Contracting State shall take such measures as may be necessary to establish its jurisdiction over an offence mentioned in Article 1 in the case where the suspected offender is present in its territory and it does not extradite him after receiving a request for extradition from a Contracting State whose jurisdiction is based on a rule of jurisdiction existing equally in the law of the requested State. This Convention does not exclude any criminal jurisdiction exercised in accordance with national law.

Article 7

A Contracting State in whose territory a person suspected to have committed an offence mentioned in Article 1 is found and which has received a request for extradition under the conditions mentioned in Article 6, paragraph 1, shall, if it does not extradite that person, submit the case, without exception whatsoever and without undue delay, to its competent authorities for the purpose of prosecution. Those authorities shall take their decision in the same manner as in the case of any offence of a serious nature under the law of that State.

Article 8

Contracting States shall afford one another the widest measure of mutual assistance in criminal matters in connection with proceedings brought in respect of the offences mentioned in Article 1 or 2. The law of the requested State concerning mutual assistance in criminal matters shall apply in all cases. Nevertheless this assistance may not be refused on the sole ground that it concerns a political offence or an offence connected with a political offence or an offence inspired by political motives.

Nothing in this Convention shall be interpreted as imposing an obligation to afford mutual assistance if the requested State has substantial grounds for believing that the request for mutual assistance in respect of an offence mentioned in Article 1 or 2 has been made for the purpose of prosecuting or punishing a person on account of his race, religion, nationality or political opinion or that that person's position may be prejudiced for any of these reasons.

The provisions of all treaties and arrangements concerning mutual assistance in criminal matters applicable between Contracting States, including the European Convention on Mutual Assistance in Criminal Matters, are modified as between Contracting States to the extent that they are incompatible with this Convention.

Article 9

The European Committee on Crime Problems of the Council of Europe shall be kept informed regarding the application of this Convention.

It shall do whatever is needful to facilitate a friendly settlement of any difficulty which may arise out of its execution.

Article 10

Any dispute between Contracting States concerning the interpretation or application of this Convention, which has not been settled in the framework of Article 9, paragraph 2, shall, at the request of any Party to the dispute, be referred to arbitration. Each Party shall nominate an arbitrator and the two arbitrators shall nominate a referee. If any Party has not nominated its arbitrator within the three months following the request for arbitration, he shall be nominated at the request of the other Party by the President of the European Court of Human Rights. If the latter should be a national of one of the Parties to the dispute, this duty shall be carried out by the Vice-President of the Court or if the Vice-President is a national of one of the Parties to the dispute, by the most senior judge of the Court not being a national of one of the Parties to the dispute. The same procedure shall be observed if the arbitrators cannot agree on the choice of referee.

The arbitration tribunal shall lay down its own procedure. Its decisions shall be taken by majority vote. Its award shall be final.

Article 11

This Convention shall be open to signature by the member States of the Council of Europe. It shall be subject to ratification, acceptance or approval. Instruments of ratification, acceptance or approval shall be deposited with the Secretary General of the Council of Europe.

The Convention shall enter into force three months after the date of the deposit of the third instrument of ratification, acceptance or approval.

In respect of a signatory State ratifying, accepting or approving subsequently, the Convention shall come into force three months after the date of the deposit of its instrument of ratification, acceptance or approval.

Article 12

Any State may, at the time of signature or when depositing its instrument of ratification, acceptance or approval, specify the territory or territories to which this Convention shall apply.

Any State may, when depositing its instrument of ratification, acceptance or approval or at any later date, by declaration addressed to the Secretary General of the Council of Europe, extend this Convention to any other territory or territories specified in the declaration and for whose international relations it is responsible or on whose behalf it is authorised to give undertakings.

Any declaration made in pursuance of the preceding paragraph may, in respect of any territory mentioned in such declaration, be withdrawn by means of a notification addressed to the Secretary General of the Council of Europe. Such withdrawal shall take effect immediately or at such later date as may be specified in the notification.

Article 13

Any State may, at the time of signature or when depositing its instrument of ratification, acceptance or approval, declare that it reserves the right to refuse extradition in respect of any offence mentioned in Article 1 which it considers to be a political offence, an offence connected with a political offence or an offence inspired by political motives, provided that it undertakes to take into due consideration, when evaluating the character of the offence, any particularly serious aspects of the offence, including:

a.) that it created a collective danger to the life, physical integrity or liberty of persons; or

b.) that it affected persons foreign to the motives behind it; or

c.) that cruel or vicious means have been used in the commission of the offence.

Any State may wholly or partly withdraw a reservation it has made in accordance with the foregoing paragraph by means of a declaration addressed to the Secretary General of the Council of Europe which shall become effective as from the date of its receipt.

A State which has made a reservation in accordance with paragraph 1 of this article may not claim the application of Article 1 by any other State; it may, however, if its reservation is partial or conditional, claim the application of that article in so far as it has itself accepted it.

Article 14

Any Contracting State may denounce this Convention by means of a written notification addressed to the Secretary General of the Council of Europe. Any such denunciation shall take effect immediately or at such later date as may be specified in the notification.

Article 15

This Convention ceases to have effect in respect of any Contracting State which withdraws from or ceases to be a member of the Council of Europe.

Article 16

The Secretary General of the Council of Europe shall notify the member States of the Council of:

a.) any signature;

b.) any deposit of an instrument of ratification, acceptance or approval;

c.) any date of entry into force of this Convention in accordance with Article 11 thereof;

d.) any declaration or notification received in pursuance of the provisions of Article 12;

e.) any reservation made in pursuance of the provisions of Article 13, paragraph 1;

f.) the withdrawal of any reservation effected in pursuance of the provisions of Article 13, paragraph 2;

g.) any notification received in pursuance of Article 14 and the date on which denunciation takes effect;

h.) any cessation of the effects of the Convention pursuant to Article 15.

In witness whereof, the undersigned, being duly authorised thereto, have signed this Convention.

Done at Strasbourg, this 27th day of January 1977, in English and in French, both texts being equally authoritative, in a single copy which shall remain deposited in the archives of the Council of Europe. The Secretary General of the Council of Europe shall transmit certified copies to each of the signatory States.

Source: Council of Europe, European Treaties, ETS No. 90, "European Convention on The Suppression of Terrorism" <http://ue.eu.int/ejn/data/vol_b/ 4b_convention_protocole_accords/terrorisme/ 090texten.html>.

TERRORISM

the two world wars. The conviction most widely held was that integrated economies and political union would render impossible the repetition of such catastrophic military conflicts. The Cold War only reinforced the need for European integration as the weakness of a divided Europe became apparent in contrast to the military, political, and economic prowess of the two superpowers, the United States of America and the Soviet Union.

"Urban revolutions" and terrorist movements, which were ubiquitous in twentieth-century Europe, could neither compare to key catalysts such as World War I, World War II, or the Cold War in the European political equation, nor shape effectively the political future of Europe. That these wars were compelling forces driving European political development, however, also does not explain fully the malfunction and shortcomings of these terrorist movements. The abysmal failure of terrorism on the twentieth-century European political scene is a multifaceted phenomenon.

Terrorism has been defined as the "systematic inducement of fear and anxiety to control and direct a civilian population" in order to bring about political change. Although terrorism is frequently dramatic, rarely is it with political consequence.

Terrorism is certainly not a novelty of the twentieth century. The first written evidence of terrorism appeared in the 1798 supplement of the *Dictionnaire de la Académie Française* as *"système régime de la terreur."* Examples of terrorist organizations prior to World War I include the People's Will organization in Russia, the Irish Volunteers (forerunner of the Irish Republican Army, IRA) in the United Kingdom, the anarchists of the 1890s, and the Internal Macedonian Revolutionary Organization (IMRO) in the Kingdoms of Yugoslavia and Greece, among others. Minor fringe elements such as the Marxist-inspired Baader-Meinhof Gang in Germany or the Red Brigades in Italy, or national separatists such as the Basque *Euskadi Ta Askatasuna* (ETA) in Spain, the IRA, and the Corsican Liberation Front in France preoccupied Europe in the 1960s and 1970s. A marked increase in Palestinian-oriented acts of terror occurred after the defeat of the Arab states in their June 1967 war with Israel. Factions from the Middle East dominated the global terrorist scene. By the 1980s indigenous terrorist movements in Europe had petered out. The terrorists or "urban guerrillas" faded into history texts as footnotes, their efforts unsuccessful, causing temporary, sensational damage and limited political effect.

There is a variety of myths surrounding terrorism. Many people mistakenly believe that terrorism is a recent concept, but it is neither a new

nor an unprecedented occurrence in history. Nor were the movements predating the twentieth century lacking in sophistication or organization. For example, the Russian People's Will was ideologically and politically advanced and evolved, creating exemplary terrorist literature and propaganda that has yet to be surpassed and is reportedly still in use and circulation among modern-day terrorist organizations.

Another myth is that terrorism is equivalent to the desire for national liberation. However, most examples of terrorism occur not in closed societies but in democratic ones where participation in government is possible.

A third misconception is that terrorism evidences a political left-wing orientation. Actually, terrorist movements throughout the years have represented different shades of the political spectrum, ranging from ultra-right-wing and fascist to extreme Marxist.

Another fallacy is that the grievances of terrorists are legitimate. However, upon closer examination one sees that terrorism rarely occurs under the most oppressive of regimes.

Most people believe that terrorism is highly effective. Yet, no known case of a small terrorist group seizing and maintaining power has ever been recorded. Though terrorist acts may influence change, they rarely bring about lasting results. For such an outcome either a political mass movement is required to support the aims of the terrorists or the terrorist acts must occur within the framework of an already existing wider strategy.

Terrorists are frequently thought of as idealists. Given that terrorist acts have inhuman consequences and a vicious, cruel effect on the population in question, it would be difficult to define the intentions as idealistic. Terrorist acts challenge generally accepted universal values and principles.

Terrorism fails because of a variety of interrelated factors relating to either governmental impatience or the lack of popular support. Terrorist organizations may include only a select, minute portion of a population, thus suffering from a sort of exclusive, elitist affectation that alienates potential sympathizers. The organizations may be fraught with ideological division or fail to present a reasonable political platform with which mainstream individuals can identify. If a state's political system offers legal, nonviolent mechanisms or processes for its citizens to effect political change, then terrorism is not only morally and legally unappealing but also unnecessarily risky. Generally, governments are unwilling to tolerate or negotiate with terrorists, especially once terrorists pose not merely a nuisance but escalate to the status of a severe threat to the state. A state is likely to

TERRORISM

run damage control until the situation gets out of hand, and then usually the terrorists only succeed in provoking a government crackdown. Given that most of the targets of terrorist actions are expendable in the eyes of a state—such as statesmen, government buildings, and so on—governments are generally faced with more pressing and potentially dangerous political issues, such as the perceived Soviet threat of expansion during the latter half of the twentieth century.

These points can be illustrated by a case-by-case examination. Terrorist movements often represent a minor fraction of the population. They are small in number and short-lived. The Basque separatists, the ETA, do not dominate the industrial Basque cities, nor do they command their allegiance. The Basque movement will not accept Castilian-speaking immigrants. The Baader-Meinhof Gang consisted of between just five to fifty members. Their success was in publicity alone as Germany remains economically capitalist and politically democratic, not Marxist.

Regarding ideological division, Basque and Corsican terrorist organizations could not agree whether their goal should be autonomy or independence. Corsican terrorists were occasionally active since 1964 with a few shootings and bombings in Corsica and mainland France, mostly of public buildings and vacation homes, resulting in little loss of life. Corsica is still an integral part of France, just as the Basque region is of Spain. The governments provided both regions with a wide array of rights, such as language instruction or legislative bodies. The extremist nature of the radical Marxist platforms of the Baader-Meinhof Gang or Red Brigades did not appeal to the population at large in Germany or Italy, even though both countries possessed strong socialist elements. The IRA splintered into the Provisional Irish Republican Army (the "Provos" or PRIRA) and the "Real" IRA (or "dissident" IRA or RIRA); the former is actively participating in the peace process, whereas the latter attempts to disrupt the peace process, stating that its objective is the complete British withdrawal from Northern Ireland and unification of Northern Ireland with the Republic of Ireland.

The actual acts and tactics of terrorists can also be ineffectual. For example, the IMRO, led by Damian Gruev in the early 1900s, attempted to create a "Macedonian" state from territories in Greece, Serbia, and Bulgaria. However, it failed to achieve its objective and managed to lose more members of its terrorist organization than inflict damage.

A global consensus that collaboration with terrorists is unacceptable also renders terrorists impotent in the long run. Governments often overreact to terrorism, thereby establishing the contrary result of the terrorists' objective. In Spain, Francisco Franco's approach in the late 1960s and 1970s against ETA included such tactics as torture, arrests en masse, search, and seizure. In Northern Ireland the British police bombarded Catholic neighborhoods with tear gas in response to Catholic violence against Protestant mobs. Europeans states have devised more-effective responses, including concessions, thereby neutralizing terrorism. The present democratic regime in Spain granted autonomy to the Basque region and official status to the Basque language. The British government has attempted to maintain a "lower profile" and recently dissolved the Northern Irish Assembly in Belfast, in which the Protestant majority always outvoted the Catholic minority. In France, a Corsican assembly was created in 1982.

Many point to the assassination of Archduke Franz Ferdinand in June 1914 as a terrorist triumph. Although the assassination is still regarded as the historical event triggering World War I, military preparations and tensions among the key states already existed and a variety of foreign powers was involved. The assassination was more part of a historical process than a successful act of terrorism.

After forty-five years of peace European militarism and hypernationalism waned. Democratic principles became entrenched as a political way of life. Highly stratified European societies were leveling, and the bases of support for revolutionary elites were vanishing. Europe was steadily on the move towards unification and integration.

All of these factors took the proverbial wind out of the sails of terrorists in Europe. One terrorist organization after another capitulated, admitting defeat, and declared its purposelessness. In April 1998 the German Red Army Faction, which emerged from the Baader-Meinhof Gang, stated, "We are stuck in a dead end." In April 1984 the Italian Red Brigades stated that their struggle was pointless because "the international conditions that made this struggle possible no longer exist."

If the goal of terrorism is to influence the political behavior and attitudes of a target group wider than the immediate victims then terrorism failed in Europe. As each generation witnessed and struggled through the newly dawning conflict, whether it was the disillusioned "lost generation" heralding World War I as "the war to end all wars" or "Cold Warriors," a political movement of European unification grew and gained momentum regardless of terrorism. Democratic political principles and capitalist market economies stand as the pillars of the EU, the crowning achievement of the European twentieth century. Terrorism has fallen by the wayside in European politics.

—JELENA BUDJEVAC,
WASHINGTON, D.C.

References

Yonah Alexander and Kenneth A. Myers, eds., *Terrorism in Europe* (London: Croom Helm, 1982; New York: St. Martin's Press, 1982).

Alexander and Dennis A. Pluchinsky, eds., *European Terrorism Today & Tomorrow* (Washington, D.C.: Brassey's, 1992).

Luigi Bonanate, "Some Unanticipated Consequences of Terrorism," *Journal of Peace Research*, 16 (1979): 197–211.

Martha Crenshaw, "The Causes of Terrorism," *Comparative Politics*, 13 (July 1981): 379–399.

William A. Douglass and Joseba Zulaika, "On the Interpretation of Terrorist Violence: ETA and the Basque Political Process," *Comparative Studies in Society and History*, 32 (April 1990): 238–257.

Lawrence C. Hamilton and James D. Hamilton, "Dynamics of Terrorism," *International Studies Quarterly*, 27 (March 1983): 39–54.

Walter Laqueur, *A History of Terrorism* (New Brunswick, N.J.: Transaction Publishers, 2001).

Edward Mickolus, "Comment—Terrorists, Governments, and Numbers," *Journal of Conflict Resolution*, 31 (March 1987): 54–62.

Stephen Van Evera, "Primed for Peace: Europe after the Cold War," *International Security*, 15 (Winter 1990–1991): 7–57.

Raphael Zariski, "Ethnic Extremism Among Ethnoterritorial Minorities in Western Europe: Dimensions, Causes and Institutional Responses," *Comparative Politics*, 21 (April 1989): 53–272.

TOTAL WAR

Was total war a twentieth-century concept?

Viewpoint: Yes. Mass mobilization of peoples and resources for conflict did not occur until the twentieth century.

Viewpoint: No. Total war had precedents in earlier centuries; twentieth-century technology simply made military domination over civil authority easier to implement.

One characteristic of twentieth-century Europe has been its affliction by what many historians and other observers have come to call "total war"—conflict in which all aspects of a society are in some way employed in and affected by the fighting. Bombing civilians, marshalling all economic activity through the offices of the state, mobilizing entire populations for war-related labor, and other such measures redefined earlier forms of warfare, which had "rules" against harming civilians and confined destruction to the battlefield.

Was total war conceived in the twentieth century? As one argument maintains, its technological, ideological, and organizational bases came into being with the Industrial Revolution and the rise of the bureaucratic state. On one hand, while these innovations began in the nineteenth century, only in the twentieth century were they perfected to the point that total war was possible. On the other hand, one can look throughout history to find precursors to total war. Although twentieth-century technology vastly expanded the scope of war—controlling economic factors, targeting and mobilizing populations, and putting all of a society's efforts into fighting enemies—nothing in total war was new.

Viewpoint:
Yes. Mass mobilization of peoples and resources for conflict did not occur until the twentieth century.

The advent of "total war" in the twentieth century included mass mobilization of populations and marshaling of national resources to achieve victory. Casualties of this type of conflict surpassed the combined casualties from all wars prior to the twentieth century. Indeed, the term *total war* was coined to describe this unique phenomenon.

Before the twentieth century, destructive wars certainly occurred across the globe. Battles and sieges caused much loss of life, not only among combatants but also among noncombatants. Rome left Carthage desolated at the end of the Punic Wars (264–146 BCE). Genghis Khan's Mongol army captured the cities of Bukhara, Samarkand, and Harat and massacred their inhabitants (1219–1223). Prussia suffered the loss of one-third of its population during the Thirty Years' War (1618–1648). Union general William Tecumseh Sherman wreaked enough damage to "make Georgia howl" in his march to the sea and through the Carolinas during the American Civil War (1861–1865).

The administrative, technological, and ideological aspects of twentieth-century total wars also had their antecedents in earlier centuries. The rise of the modern nation-state with the ability to maintain large standing armies dated back to the seventeenth century. Louis XIV of France fielded an army in excess of three hundred thousand men during the War of the League of Augsburg (1689–1697). Mechanical weapons and industrial production of those weapons appeared in the nineteenth century. Various revolutionary ideologies raised popular support during the eighteenth and nineteenth centuries. Inspired in part by nationalism, hundreds of thousands of Frenchmen rallied to their flag in the revolutionary *levée en masse* (1793). In his seminal study *On War* (1832), military theorist Carl von Clausewitz outlined the concept of "absolute war," a conflict fought without restraints, in theory if not in practice. Administration, technology, and ideology did not, however, coalesce in a single conflict until the twentieth century. While perhaps "absolute" in some sense, previous wars were not "total."

Not even Clausewitz could have envisioned the totality of twentieth-century warfare, especially relative to the unlimited goals for which these conflicts were fought. At least one author, however, prophesied the coming totality of war. In *The Future of War in its Technical, Economic and Political Relations* (1899), Ivan S. Bloch described the "total war" of the future. It would include the mass mobilization of a nation's resources for war, the development of increasingly effective weapons, and unimaginable numbers of casualties, all on a scale heretofore unseen in human history. Particularly accurate was Bloch's prediction that such a conflict would sap the material and moral energies of all participating nations and lead to the collapse of organized society. Bloch also argued that technological advances would make future conflicts impossible to fight according to the past's rules and conventions. He was inaccurate only in part of this last prediction in the world wars. It is worth noting, however, that Bloch's observation that new technology could make traditional war making obsolete had much relevance to the Cold War, when weapons of mass destruction (WMD) loomed ominously as options.

The major strands of administration, technology, and ideology coalesced in World War I (1914–1918). In the weeks after the assassination of Archduke Franz Ferdinand in June 1914 the governments of Germany, France, Britain, and Russia activated their mobilizations and war plans. Some 65 million men from all nations took up arms during World War I. Although many had anticipated a short conflict, this war dragged on for four years of attrition and stalemate. Logistical requirements put the capabilities of national governments to the test. Keeping millions of men fed and armed on the battlefield, as well as keeping tens of millions of civilians patriotic and loyal on the home front, proved to be great challenges. In 1917 Russia buckled under the pressure of maintaining the total war effort and fell into revolution. Other nations sharply increased their industrial and agricultural production to meet the insatiable demands on resources. Governments exercised dictatorial control of industry and agriculture to ensure that the war effort remained efficient. Ultimately, France, Britain, Germany, and the late-arriving United States kept pace with wartime requirements with relative success. No conflict before World War I, the so-called Great War, had been so highly organized.

Technological innovations found their way onto battlefields, into the air, and on the oceans. The machine gun changed battlefield tactics by giving overwhelming superiority in firepower to defensive forces. German submarines preyed on warships and commercial vessels regardless of combatant or neutral status. Airplanes did not yet achieve a high level of development, but their use set the stage for the all-out strategic and terror bombing of the future. Furthermore, the Germans utilized scientific advances in chemistry to develop poison gas for use on the battlefield.

When World War I started, nationalism trumped all other worldviews and ideologies. Socialists, conservatives, liberals, feminists, and others joined in huge patriotic celebrations as a lust for war and a love of nation spread across Europe. Civilians and soldiers alike felt they had a vested interest in their national war effort, that they served a cause greater than themselves. Conscription was not immediately necessary because millions of men rushed to volunteer to fight. After protracted bloodbaths at the Somme and Verdun in 1916 many surviving soldiers lost much of their patriotic zeal. Civilians also began to question their great nationalist cause as their loved ones were killed or maimed. Consequently, to help ensure support for the war, national governments initiated massive propaganda campaigns. The German media portrayed the British as effeminate fops, whereas British propaganda made the Germans out to be evil and rapacious Huns. Both sides dehumanized their opponents.

The scale of popular support and mass mobilization during World War I had not been seen in history, nor had people witnessed the sizes of armed forces and the staggering number of casualties. When this deadly conflict finally ended, without a clear-cut resolution, the world attempted to return to the prewar social and

TOTAL WAR

political "normalcy." Hopefully, the combatants thought, World War I would be the "war to end all wars." Bitterness and disillusionment, however, gripped many Europeans. In two decades, another total war would be fought.

World War II (1939–1945) yielded a still more catastrophic level of total war. Administrative, technological, and ideological elements fueled the combatant nations. By 1944 some forty million men and women were under arms. Conservative estimates of deaths in World War II, both civilian and combatant, stand at sixty million.

World War II posed serious administrative challenges. Large armies required careful planning and elaborate logistical support to maintain combat readiness, let alone to fight battles. Lines of transportation and communication stretched across the vast Pacific, Atlantic, and Indian Oceans; across the plains of Eastern Europe; and over the mountains of Asia. In the U.S. armed forces fewer than 15 percent of soldiers, sailors, and marines ever saw combat. Others worked in logistical support roles that supplied, fed, armed, clothed, medicated, transported, and evacuated the combat troops. For combat on desolate islands in the Pacific the U.S. Navy utilized floating supply depots that furnished every soldier and marine with 1,300 pounds of equipment. On the home front governments once again marshaled all material and personnel for the war effort, which entailed not only managing the production of equipment through dictatorial government policies but also preserving domestic support through use of biased propaganda.

During World War II decades-old technologies achieved more effective application to warmaking, and new technologies also came into being. The use of airplanes in war reached its fullest potential. All sides employed "strategic bombing" of both military and civilian targets. Allied aircraft leveled most major cities of Germany and Japan. Incendiary bombs ignited massive firestorms, such as those in Dresden (February 1945) and Tokyo (March 1945), each of which claimed more than 100,000 lives. In total war, whole civilian populations mobilized by working in factories or reducing their consumption of food. This participation meant that the limits on civilian immunity were lifted. The use of American B-29 bombers to drop atomic bombs on Hiroshima (6 August 1945) and Nagasaki (9 August 1945) stands as an example of airpower contributing to the totality of war.

The atomic bombs grew out of the so-called Manhattan Project, part of an effort by the U.S. military to apply science to war in revolutionary and destructive ways. Thousands of scientists and engineers worked for years on the $2 billion exercise in research and development. The effort came to fruition with the killing of more than one hundred thousand Japanese civilians. Nazi Germany and militarist Japan also used technological innovations with devastating effects. The Germans developed rocket-propelled weapons that would evolve into Intercontinental Ballistic Missiles (ICBMs) just two decades later. The Japanese explored the possibilities of biological warfare in the super-secret Unit 731; Japanese scientists used Chinese prisoners as human experiments to explore the effects and means of transmission of diseases.

Perhaps most frightening of all the elements of total war in World War II was ideology. In addition to nationalism, other worldviews such as liberalism, Nazism, and communism provided incredibly high motivation for people. Liberalism drove the United States and Britain to fight against the militarist and totalitarian regimes of the Axis powers. Nazism and communism were locked in mortal combat as Germany and the Soviet Union fought massive battles in Eastern Europe. Indeed, ideological factors reached diabolical levels in the Holocaust, the calculated and systematic extermination of millions of Jews and others considered by the Germans to be "lesser" races. Driven by intense racial hatred, Nazis employed efficient management principles to maximize the number of deaths. Trains carried Jews to camps where they were methodically worked to death or immediately killed in gas chambers. Japan's treatment of Chinese in the "Rape of Nanking" (1937–1938) and elsewhere in East Asia rivaled the Nazi program in its racism and scope. World War II was not merely a total war because of mobilization of people and resources; it could also be considered a total war for those examples of wholesale extermination of populations.

Two images were burned into public memory at the conclusion of World War II: the mushroom cloud of an atomic explosion and the emaciated bodies of victims of the Holocaust. Both images bear witness to the totality of war in the twentieth century. The threshold of total war had been crossed. Following World War II, governments have been reluctant to employ increasingly effective weapons of mass destruction. Despite much rhetoric and posturing in the Cuban Missile Crisis (1962), for example, the use of nuclear weapons was not repeated. The Cold War, however, did generate much death in many conflicts. The Vietnam War (ended 1975) may have been comparatively limited in scope, but it cost millions of civilian and military lives. Moreover, Vietnam and other Cold War conflicts have also included the administrative, technological, and ideological elements of total war to one degree or another.

–DAVID J. ULBRICH,
TEMPLE UNIVERSITY

TOTAL WAR

Viewpoint:
No. Total war had precedents in earlier centuries; twentieth-century technology simply made military domination over civil authority easier to implement.

"Total war," like many twentieth-century concepts, has its historical roots in the past. Many scholars have defined total war in the context of World War I (1914–1918) and World War II (1939–1945), conflicts in which most, if not all, belligerents fully mobilized their human and material resources for a struggle of global domination. The absolute disregard for human life in the trenches at the Western Front, in the Nazi death camps, and in Hiroshima are the most concrete examples of the damage total war was meant to inflict. Nazi and Stalinist totalitarian ideals of stripping basic human rights to the point where the state alone had the power to determine what people could think or even who could exist are also key to this definition. Nevertheless, important precedents for this modern form of warfare, especially in terms of popular mobilization, nationalist ideals, military domination over civil authority, and the concepts of attrition and "unconditional surrender" are to be found from the seventeenth to late nineteenth centuries.

Seventeenth-century wars of religion involved far more than just princes and small numbers of armed followers. Indeed, many newly recruited adventurers, mercenaries, and fugitives throughout Europe devastated town and countryside alike. During the Thirty Years' War (1618–1648) continuous raids, campaigns, famines, and epidemics caused the death of up to one-third of the population in the Holy Roman Empire. Similarly, France also lost a significant proportion of its population during the Wars of Religion in the late sixteenth century. The majority of the French middle class was Huguenot and was either killed, forcibly converted, or exiled. The result of these bloody conflicts was that European states could now mobilize the masses around a distinctive national religious spirit. Those subjects who held a different faith were viewed as potential traitors.

The trend toward popular participation in military conflicts reached a turning point during the Napoleonic Era. The onset of the French Revolution in 1789 triggered a new ideological division in Europe. The Jacobin call for a republic based on popular representation and universal human rights challenged the continued existence of European monarchical and ecclesiastic orders by appealing to merchants, artisans, wealthy elite, and urban populations, all groups critical to maintaining the political and social order. The expansion of European literacy through newly established schools and a growing print culture amplified the demand for revolution among these groups. As a result, those who took up the cause of the French Republic certainly felt they had a personal stake in the matter.

However, those threatened by the Revolution were even more motivated to mobilize human and material resources to revitalize the ancien régime. It is no coincidence that British and German nationalism began to flourish in reaction to Napoleon's France. The European aristocracy largely supported such countermovements to popularize their own cause and ensure their own survival. Thus, both revolution and counterrevolution planted the idea of the nation-state among populations at large.

The most important military development of the Napoleonic era was conscription. The French Revolutionary government used the *levée en masse* (1793) to great effect. The French government ignored the European tradition of raising a small professional army and instead insisted that all men of fighting age join the army. As a result the French Army dwarfed its opponents. The Austrians, Prussians, Russians, and British tried to combine their armies to counter the French, but they had difficulty integrating troops with different loyalties, languages, and command structures. The result was a series of resounding defeats inflicted by Napoleon during the first decade of the nineteenth century. These governments were soon forced to employ mass conscription to counter Napoleon's armies.

The social effect of this measure was profound. Whereas men before the draft felt more ties to their region than to the nation, new draftees were galvanized into a new corporate fighting force where a feeling of national patriotism and loyalty was the order of the day. Veterans from this conflict usually did not abandon these feelings after they had left the battlefield. European governments were aware of this fact and played on these feelings whenever they wanted to drum up support for a new conflict. However, battlefield veterans also often made political demands on the government, a trend that sometimes threatened the preexisting political order.

The American Civil War (1861–1865) and Franco-Prussian War (1870–1871) introduced key new concepts to the development of total war. Perhaps the most obvious was the war of attrition utilized by Union generals against the Confederates. President Abraham Lincoln and the Union military high command decided in the late stages of the conflict that the only way to win the war was to have no mercy on the South, as General William Tecumseh Sherman's burn-

DRESDEN

Lothar Metzger, who was almost ten at the time of the attack on Dresden, describes the firebombing of the German city by Allied bombers on 13–14 February 1945:

About 9:30 PM the alarm was given. We children knew that sound and got up and dressed quickly, to hurry downstairs into our cellar which we used as an air raid shelter. My older sister and I carried my baby twin sisters, my mother carried a little suitcase and the bottles with milk for our babies. On the radio we heard with great horror the news: "Attention, a great air raid will come over our town!" This news I will never forget.

Some minutes later we heard a horrible noise—the bombers. There were nonstop explosions. Our cellar was filled with fire and smoke and was damaged, the lights went out and wounded people shouted dreadfully. In great fear we struggled to leave this cellar. My mother and my older sister carried the big basket in which the twins were lain. With one hand I grasped my younger sister and with the other I grasped the coat of my mother.

We did not recognize our street any more. Fire, only fire wherever we looked. Our 4th floor did not exist anymore. The broken remains of our house were burning. On the streets there were burning vehicles and carts with refugees, people, horses, all of them screaming and shouting in fear of death. I saw hurt women, children, old people searching a way through ruins and flames.

We fled into another cellar overcrowded with injured and distraught men women and children shouting, crying and praying. No light except some electric torches. And then suddenly the second raid began. This shelter was hit too, and so we fled through cellar after cellar. Many, so many, desperate people came in from the streets. It is not possible to describe! Explosion after explosion. It was beyond belief, worse than the blackest nightmare. So many people were horribly burnt and injured. It became more and more difficult to breathe. It was dark and all of us tried to leave this cellar with inconceivable panic. Dead and dying people were trampled upon, luggage was left or snatched up out of our hands by rescuers. The basket with our twins covered with wet cloths was snatched up out of my mother's hands and we were pushed upstairs by the people behind us. We saw the burning street, the falling ruins and the terrible firestorm. My mother covered us with wet blankets and coats she found in a water tub.

We saw terrible things: cremated adults shrunk to the size of small children, pieces of arms and legs, dead people, whole families burnt to death, burning people ran to and fro, burnt coaches filled with civilian refugees, dead rescuers and soldiers, many were calling and looking for their children and families, and fire everywhere, everywhere fire, and all the time the hot wind of the firestorm threw people back into the burning houses they were trying to escape from.

I cannot forget these terrible details. I can never forget them.

Now my mother possessed only a little bag with our identity papers. The basket with the twins had disappeared and then suddenly my older sister vanished too. Although my mother looked for her immediately it was in vain. The last hours of this night we found shelter in the cellar of a hospital nearby surrounded by crying and dying people. In the next morning we looked for our sister and the twins but without success. The house where we lived was only a burning ruin. The house where our twins were left we could not go in. Soldiers said everyone was burnt to death and we never saw my two baby sisters again.

Totally exhausted, with burnt hair and badly burnt and wounded by the fire we walked to the Loschwitz bridge where we found good people who allowed us to wash, to eat and to sleep. But only a short time because suddenly the second air raid began (February 14th) and this house too was bombed and my mother's last identity papers burnt. Completely exhausted we hurried over the bridge (river Elbe) with many other homeless survivors and found another family ready to help us, because somehow their home survived this horror.

In all this tragedy I had completely forgotten my l0th birthday. But the next day my mother surprised me with a piece of sausage she begged from the "Red Cross." This was my birthday present.

In the next days and weeks we looked for my older Sister but in vain. We wrote our present address on the last walls of our damaged house. In the middle of March we were evacuated to a little village near Oschatz and on March 3lst, we got a letter from my sister. She was alive! In that disastrous night she lost us and with other lost children she was taken to a nearby village. Later she found our address on the wall of our house and at the beginning of April my mother brought her to our new home.

You can be sure that the horrible experiences of this night in Dresden led to confused dreams, sleepless nights and disturbed our souls, me and the rest of my family. Years later I intensively thought the matter over, the causes, the political contexts of this night. This became very important for my whole life and my further decisions.

Source: *Lothar Metzger, "The Fire-bombing of Dresden: An Eye-witness Account," (May 1999), Timewitnesses: Memories of the Last Century <http://timewitnesses.org/english/~lothar.html>.*

ing of Atlanta, General Philip Sheridan's destruction of the Shenandoah Valley, and General Ulysses S. Grant's bloody campaign against General Robert E. Lee's army in the Wilderness campaign all demonstrated. Union policy makers decided to kill, capture, or immobilize as many Confederate soldiers as possible and also to try to break the South's moral and material resources needed to wage the conflict. The North accomplished this task largely by freeing approximately 3.5 million slaves and burning or capturing key Southern cities.

Both the Americans and the Prussians adopted a policy of accepting only total submission as a means to end each conflict. General Grant's practice of accepting only "unconditional surrender" in the early stages of the Civil War soon was adopted by President Lincoln and the Northern public. The Prussian leadership similarly imposed harsh terms on the French after their decisive victory over Napoleon III at Sedan (1870), annexing the territory of Alsace-Lorraine, exacting an enormous indemnity, and declaring the unification of Germany at the peace table in Paris. The victors no longer sought to reestablish a balance of power; nations were meant to dominate or destroy their enemy.

Both of the losing sides in these conflicts also took actions that approximated total war. For all of their talk about states' rights, the Confederacy actually enacted conscription earlier than the U.S. government. Likewise, the French drafted an army that was larger than the Prussians'. Although the Franco-Prussian War was too short to affect France's long-term economic development, the Confederacy made strides in developing its industries to meet its military needs. The South's ability to industrialize a cotton-dependent agrarian economy points to a familiar pattern that was to be repeated during the twentieth century. "Backward nations" would often use wars as a means to mobilize themselves to modernity. Total war became a program for socio-economic development.

Finally, the assertion of Prussian military control over civilian authority set a disturbing trend for later governments. Not only was Germany established as a nation in the wake of a military conquest, but the nature of the unification itself demanded further military glory to sustain it. Otto von Bismarck may have been chancellor of Germany, but the nature of his post was such that he, like the system he had created, was dependent on the will of a kaiser who took his place in the military circles that surrounded him. Even Bismarck could not prevent Kaiser Wilhelm II from embarking on a program of military and colonial expansion that inevitably collided with the interests of Great Britain, the leading maritime and colonial power. To Wilhelm II—like Colmar von der Goltz, a former Prussian general and interwar rightist intellectual who advocated a military regime continually resorting to total war—Germany was required to conquer all of its rivals in order to take its true place in the pantheon of nations. In this context the verses of Germany's national anthem "Deutschland, Deutschland über Alles" seemed to be totally appropriate.

Bismarck's unification of Germany—like many developments during the American Civil War, Napoleon's campaigns, and the European wars of religion—was an important milestone in the development of total war. Popular mobilization by means of religious or national identity during the Thirty Years' War and the French Revolution does not mean that one can classify either conflict as a total war. Later Western European and American governments (such as Germany and the United States) improved on the methods by harnessing their war efforts to their growing industrial power. As the Prussian leadership demonstrated in the late nineteenth century, war became an invaluable tool in achieving national greatness. Victorious wars of conquest meant that the kaiser did not have to surrender any rights and privileges. While none of these developments can be classified as a total war, they provided the blueprints for it. The great powers of Europe would not forget these lessons when war broke out in August 1914.

–YORK NORMAN,
GEORGETOWN UNIVERSITY

References

Ivan S. Bloch, *The Future of War in its Technical, Economic and Political Relations,* translated by R. C. Long (Boston: Ginn, 1899).

John Buckley, *Air Power in the Age of Total War* (Bloomington: Indiana University Press, 1999).

Carl von Clausewitz, *On War,* edited and translated by Michael Howard and Peter Paret (Princeton: Princeton University Press, 1976).

Edward Mead Earle, *Makers of Modern Strategy: Military Thought from Machiavelli to Hitler* (Princeton: Princeton University Press, 1943).

Stig Förster & Jörg Nagler, eds., *On the Road to Total War: The American Civil War and the German Wars of Unification, 1861–1871* (Washington, D.C.: German Historical Institute, 1997; Cambridge & New York: Cambridge University Press, 1997).

TOTAL WAR

J. F. C. Fuller, *The Conduct of War, 1789–1961: A Study of the French, Industrial, and Russian Revolutions on War and Its Conduct* (New Brunswick, N.J.: Rutgers University Press, 1961).

Michael Howard, *War in European History* (London & New York: Oxford University Press, 1976).

Arthur Marwick, *Britain in the Century of Total War: War, Peace and Social Change, 1900–1967* (London: Bodley Head, 1968).

Marwick, *War and Social Change in the Twentieth Century: A Comparative Study of Britain, France, Germany, Russia, and the United States* (London: Macmillan, 1974; New York: St. Martin's Press, 1974).

Richard A. Preston, Alex Roland, and Sydney F. Wise, *Men in Arms: A History of Warfare and its Interrelationships with Western Society*, fifth edition (Fort Worth, Tex.: Holt, Rinehart & Winston, 1991).

Hew Strachan, "Essay and Reflection: On Total War and Modern War," *International History Review*, 22 (2000): 341–370.

Charles Townshend, ed., *The Oxford Illustrated History of Modern War* (Oxford & New York: Oxford University Press, 1997).

Gordon Wright, *The Ordeal of Total War, 1939–1945* (New York: Harper & Row, 1968).

Yasushi Yamanouchi, J. Victor Koschmann, and Ryuichi Narita, eds., *Total War and "Modernization"* (Ithaca, N.Y.: Cornell University Press, 1998).

TOTAL WAR

TOTALITARIANISM

Can Josef Stalin's Soviet Union and Adolf Hitler's Germany accurately be described as totalitarian?

Viewpoint: Yes. Rulers such as Josef Stalin and Adolf Hitler created regimes that successfully controlled every aspect of government and society.

Viewpoint: No. Totalitarianism is a facile label that political theorists have applied to states, societies, and leaders that were far more complex and faced far more limitations than have conventionally been recognized.

Many thinkers have used the term *totalitarianism* to describe dictatorships in the twentieth century that appeared to control all aspects of social, economic, and political life. In their efforts to maintain "total" control of their people, leaders such as Josef Stalin of the Soviet Union and Adolf Hitler of Germany suggested the emergence of a new and sinister form of government. First pioneered by German political philosopher Hannah Arendt in *The Origins of Totalitarianism* (1951), this new concept drew direct comparisons between communism and fascism and impugned them as political philosophies that demanded nothing less than the slavery of humanity.

Are the conclusions of the totalitarian school valid? As one argument suggests, the huge volume of literature on Nazi Germany and emerging studies of the Soviet Union confirm that both states indeed aspired to the complete control of their populations and relied on an array of horrors to help them do it. Contrary to these studies, however, many historians argue that regardless of their intentions, totalitarian governments rarely succeeded in establishing total control of their societies. Corruption, disorganization, resistance, and other nuances, they suggest, denied them the ability to achieve anything more than superficial conformity. Looking at these states and societies simply as totalitarian might blind observers to their true complexities.

Viewpoint:
Yes. Rulers such as Josef Stalin and Adolf Hitler created regimes that successfully controlled every aspect of government and society.

In the broadest sense, *totalitarianism* is characterized by strong cen-tral rule that not only strives to control the major political institutions in a country but also seeks to subordinate all aspects of every individual's life to the authority of the government. Thus, in a veritable totalitarian state, nobody is left outside the state; people's political, socio-economic, and cultural activities are essentially controlled by the state; there are no organizations independent of the state; and any

Children's demonstration on a collective farm outside of Moscow in the 1930s. The banners bear slogans promising better productivity and protection of revolutionary goals.

(from Lewis Siegelbaum and Andrei Sokolov, Stalinism as a Way of Life, *2000).*

kind of opposition to the state is illegitimate and practically nonexistent.

Not all twentieth-century dictatorships fit this description. Some dictatorial regimes never aspired to be totalitarian, confining their authority to maintaining control over traditional political institutions; others, such as Benito Mussolini's Italy, aspired to, but never fully achieved, total control over all aspects of the individual's life. Of all twentieth-century dictatorships only Nazi Germany, the U.S.S.R., and its satellite communist regimes, as well as China, essentially possessed the major characteristics of a totalitarian state.

In these states an old order was swept away. Their social fabrics were weakened, and people became more amenable to absorption into a single, unified movement, which was led by a political party whose structure and elaborate ideology essentially coalesced with the political structure of the state. Usually the party ideology set a generic and unrealistic goal, such as world domination by the Aryan "master race" in Nazi Germany or an idealized communist society in the U.S.S.R. In both the U.S.S.R. and Nazi Germany the ruling party—the all-soviet Communist Party and the National Socialist German Workers' Party, respectively—were proclaimed the only legal parties, and it became a criminal offense to organize any new party. Traditional social institutions and organizations were replaced by ones related to and controlled by the state.

Such organizations incorporated people of different ages, sexes, and occupations and strived to organize and control people's lives not only with respect to their professional activities but also to their leisure time and family lives. Dissent and unwillingness to participate were proscribed, and specific social groups were designated as scapegoats to be blamed for real or anticipated troubles. Members of these groups were severely repressed and frequently killed—good examples in this regard were the genocide of Jews in Nazi Germany and the repressions against the kulaks (wealthy peasants) in Stalin's U.S.S.R. in the late 1920s and 1930s. A major building block in the party-state's coercive apparatus was a highly developed and centralized secret police whose major objective was to identify and persecute internal and external enemies of the state and thus instill fear and a sense of subordination in members of the totalitarian society. The army, economy, and media were also put under the ideological and political control of the state and had to comply with its goals and plans.

It is not difficult to identify the high degree of structural and functional similarity between the Nazi Party and the Communist Party (as well as the communist parties in other regimes). Although these left-wing (communist) and right-wing (Nazi, Fascist) totalitarian regimes had quite different ideologies, they were both highly centralized along vertical lines. The *Führerprinzip* (leader principle) and the similar principle of "democratic centralism" in the U.S.S.R. postulated that both the Nazi and Communist parties, and for that matter any organization in these totalitarian regimes, had a hierarchy of leaders who could demand absolute obedience from his subordinates and in turn owed similar obedience to his superiors. At the top of the state and party hierarchy stood the Leader or the General Secretary of the Party (in the Nazi and Soviet cases, respectively). He was perceived as the bearer of the collective will of the people. This cult of personality reached extremes in both Nazi Germany and the U.S.S.R. and assigned him a quasi-godly status. The average citizen was to serve his people, his leader, and his party.

Not less important to the centrality of the party-state in both the U.S.S.R. and Nazi Germany were the many party-controlled organizations. Special attention was paid to the ideological education and indoctrination of young people. Youth organizations such as the Hitler Youth and the Komsomol (Communist Youth) had a presence in schools, universities, recreational camps, and various other circles of interest. Among the objectives of these organizations was not only to indoctrinate young people but also to make sure that most of their time in school and outside was dedicated to activities incorporated into the framework of these party-controlled youth organizations. They were also intended to prevent young people from active membership in alternative organizations, such as religious groups, or any other associations that could claim any degree of independence from the party and the state.

Party-dominated organizations exercised considerable control over the activities of adult society as well. In 1933 Hitler's regime established the German Labor Front, a Nazi-dominated organization to which every worker had to belong, while the same held true for the all-Soviet Trade Unions in the U.S.S.R. Alternative labor organizations were banned, and collective bargaining and strikes were outlawed in both countries. Party-dominated trade unions—as well as other organizations of broader appeal such as Strength Through Joy, a subsidiary of the German Labor Front, and the Fatherland Front in the U.S.S.R.—provided a great variety of recreational facilities and a varied program of sports, education, and vacation trips. Journalists as well as artists and professionals were organized in associations controlled by the party and the state, and the right to practice their crafts was invariably linked to active membership in these organizations. Ideological education became an important part of army training in both Nazi Germany and the U.S.S.R., and in the latter political

officers were installed as deputy commanders in every army unit shortly after the 1917 Revolution. In Germany the paramilitary SA and SS formations were integral parts of the Nazi Party structure and police apparatus.

However, one should not confuse acceptance with enthusiasm. People's participation in state- and party-controlled activities and organizations was often achieved under strong political (and in some cases economic) pressure as well as under the sense of virtually constant fear of reprisals and repression. Importantly enough, one of the most effective controls over the individual citizen was making his job dependent on loyal cooperation. On the whole, the fear of jeopardizing one's livelihood and the need to support a family proved effective checks against any thought of active opposition or of openly criticizing the regime and its leaders.

In cases in which these checks were not sufficient, totalitarian states used a secret police to eliminate any vestiges of political opposition. This activity also contributed to the creation of a general atmosphere of fear and paranoia on the part of ordinary people. The powerful Gestapo in Nazi Germany and the various secret police organizations in the U.S.S.R., together with state-controlled special courts, stood ready to deal with any elements considered disloyal. The existence of these agencies served as a further deterrent against oppositional action, to say nothing of their free license to use arbitrary arrest, torture, concentration camps, and other instruments of intimidation to carry out their work. A network of informers and neighborhood groups watched the charges of the various national movements and associations and helped to make control over them truly total.

In this context it is not difficult to understand the absence of significant political opposition in totalitarian regimes. Opposition, if it developed at all, did so within the party establishment itself. Stalin's infamous purges in the Communist Party, state administration, and military in the 1930s were not aimed at wiping out real significant opposition to his rule but rather at strengthening further the atmosphere of fear and paranoia among the populace at all levels, and thus solidifying his position as leader of the regime. Similarly, in Germany, Hitler dealt with a few minor challenges from some party functionaries whose plans never assumed any concrete form. The Catholic and Protestant churches—the most powerful potential enemy of totalitarian regimes—were essentially subdued to the general interests and plans of the Nazi regime in Germany. Organized religion in the U.S.S.R. was heavily repressed by the institutions of the Soviet state. The Russian Orthodox Church was partially legitimized during World War II (1939–1945), but only as a means of mobilizing the remaining faithful in the interests of the state. Both regimes were able to mobilize public opinion or at least prevent any significant opposition against the persecution of whole social groups designated as scapegoats and enemies of the regime.

It is important to note one important difference between right-wing totalitarian regimes such as Nazi Germany and left-wing totalitarian regimes such as the U.S.S.R. While both types of regimes established firm control over the economy and tried to centralize economic development through central planning—the U.S.S.R. introduced its first five-year plan in 1928 while Nazi Germany started its four-year plan in 1936—communist regimes managed to achieve a practically unlimited control over economic development by eliminating private property, nationalizing private businesses, and collectivizing agriculture. The lack of a viable economic base inherently weakened any potential opposition.

Although it is certainly not applicable to all twentieth-century dictatorships, the term *totalitarian* is relevant to several regimes that managed to establish total or nearly total control over virtually all political, economic, social, and cultural life. While the term does not explain many important aspects of totalitarian regimes, such as their origins and ideological diversity, it appears a viable term with respect to the basic structure and mode of functioning of highly centralized repressive regimes such as Nazi Germany and Stalin's U.S.S.R. These regimes successfully controlled virtually every aspect of government and society.

—YORK NORMAN,
GEORGETOWN UNIVERSITY

Viewpoint:
No. Totalitarianism is a facile label that political theorists have applied to states, societies, and leaders that were far more complex and faced far more limitations than have conventionally been recognized.

Contrary to its conventional illustration as a concept born out of the political exigencies of the Cold War, the term *totalitarianism* has had a long and often contradictory history of its own before its systematization in the post-1945 period. Although the word was first used in the

political discourse in Italy only a few months after Benito Mussolini's rise to power in the 1920s, its meaning shifted throughout the interwar period. Used and often abused by both left and right—by Marxist theorists, democratic critics, and fascist sponsors—the "totalitarian" analysis was constructed on a rather nebulous basis, often as a vehement disapprobation but sometimes also as a positive force of dynamism. Antifascist analysts cast the term in a wholly negative light, in the sense that it militated against the trend of political pluralism, social individualism, and personal freedom that had made substantial inroads in Europe in the nineteenth and early twentieth centuries. By contrast, a steadily increasing number of fascist sympathizers in the 1920s and 1930s—including Mussolini—used the concept as a wholly positive force of, and prerequisite for, domestic unity and political progress.

In the postwar era the term *totalitarianism* became the conceptual basis upon which one of the most influential political theories of the twentieth century was erected. With the works of Hannah Arendt, Carl J. Friedrich, Zbigniew K. Brzezinski, Karl Dietrich Bracher, and Juan J. Linz—and this group is not an exhaustive accounting of the "totalitarianist" scholarly pantheon—the term was elevated to the status of an "ideal type" of political analysis, projecting the notion that a new, modern form of regime made its appearance in the first half of the century that had no precedent in the past. This line of analysis, based on a fundamental distinction between democratic-competitive and monocratic systems of rule, identified totalitarianism as a category of the latter variety, alongside the more traditional norm of authoritarian dictatorship. Unlike authoritarianism, however, totalitarian systems have been characterized by a fierce attack on any notion of pluralism and a desire to impose "total"—that is, limitless and holistic—control over societal functions. Although individual analysts have accentuated somewhat different aspects of this novel category of political rule, consensus on the main features of the totalitarian regime has crystallized around five main features: an elaborate ideology of legitimation; concentration of power in the hands of an omnipotent leader; a single mass party; full control of communications and flow of information; and monopoly of coercion, coupled with extensive use of terrorist methods. Such a broad delineation of the ideal type of totalitarianism empowered Western political scientists in the 1950s and 1960s to project their analysis on an intriguing comparative field, encompassing both fascist and communist regimes. In particular, given the well-documented limitations of the totalitarian practices of the Italian fascist regime, the bulk of the totalitarianist analysis has traditionally focused on the two arguably most successful systems of Nazi Germany and the Stalinist U.S.S.R.

This broadening of analytical focus raised the first eyebrows with regard to the political agenda implicit in the totalitarianist model of interpretation. Critics in both the West and the East pointed to the fact that, if indeed ideology has been accepted as a major definitional aspect of the theory, then there is little in common between the Nazi racial utopia and the massive project of social engineering in the Soviet Union beyond the extensive use of terror. As Soviet philosopher Alexander Zinoviev stressed, arguing from a Marxist point of view, socialism was neither an historical deviation (as National Socialism was) nor a system of unsolicited and objectless terror, but a social utopia of mass integration. Even if the two regimes in question used similar techniques for their consolidation and for eradicating internal opposition (and this similarity might warrant the application of the term to both initially), the subsequent development of the Soviet system took place in a decidedly "post-totalitarian" direction. In contrast, National Socialism—and fascism, in general—sanctioned the use of violence and terror as a primary ideological target, often divorced from any practical objective. Such fundamental differences, coupled with the widely accepted contrariety in the ideological visions by each regime, appeared to suggest that such a comparison was gravely incongruous and misguiding.

The implication of this objection to the widening of the totalitarianist analysis goes far beyond an academic dispute over methodology. At the heart of this critique lies a serious inference about the political motives behind the use of such a parallelism between Nazi Germany and the Soviet Union. At the height of the Cold War, when Adolf Hitler and his regime were still largely analyzed as a "demonic" historical aberration and were overwhelmingly associated with the most horrendous mass crimes in history, comparing the arch-ideological enemy of the West to National Socialism constituted a powerful emotive weapon for unconditionally denouncing communism. In other words, the main criticism was that totalitarianism served a political rather than an analytical function: while it offered limited (and questionable) insight into the practices of the two regimes, it was a convincing instrument of intensifying the Western "war on communism," both domestically and internationally, by appropriating the legitimacy of history and academic research.

Such an allegation might indeed be unfair to an extent, given the academic sophistication of some analytical models of totalitarianism. After all, none of the main exponents of the theory has ever seriously denied the fundamental differ-

---

YOUNG PIONEERS

Soviet state control of its citizens included indoctrination through the participation of children in the Young Pioneers. The pledge and rules of the organization were:

I, a young pioneer of the Soviet Union, in the presence of my comrades solemnly promise to love my Soviet Motherland passionately, and to live, learn and struggle as the great Lenin bade us and as the Communist Party teaches us.

A Pioneer loves his motherland and the Communist Party of the Soviet Union.

A Pioneer prepares himself to enter the Komsomol organization.

A Pioneer honors the memory of those who gave their lives in the struggle for freedom and for the prosperity of the Soviet Motherland.

A Pioneer is friendly to the children of all countries.

A Pioneer learns well.

A Pioneer is polite and well disciplined.

A Pioneer loves labor and is careful of public property.

A Pioneer is a good comrade: he cares for the young and helps the old.

A Pioneer is brave and unafraid of difficulties.

A Pioneer is honorable and values the honor of his detachment.

A Pioneer hardens himself, does physical exercises every day, and loves nature.

Source: *"The All-Union Lenin Pioneer Organisation,"* from Nigel Grant, Soviet Education *(Middlesex, U.K: Pelican, 1968); Perspectives on World History and Current Events: Documents and Excerpts <http://www.geocities.com/pwhce/doc1rus.html>.*

---

ences in worldview between National Socialist Germany and Stalinist Soviet Union. However, the counterargument offered, namely that the theory focuses on the actual exercise of power and promotion of mass control, has been far from immune to further criticism for its character. Talking of the importance of an elaborate holistic ideology, on the one hand, but showing no interest in the actual content of each ideological system, on the other, can hardly lead to valid comparative conclusions about the motives behind the way that power was consolidated and exercised in either of the two regimes in question here. In this respect the totalitarianist analysis is open to accusations of consciously excluding troublesome differences in order to sustain a cult of similitude between National Socialist Ger-

TOTALITARIANISM

many and Stalinist (or even post-Stalinist) U.S.S.R.

Leaving aside the questionable comparison between fascism and communism, the study of totalitarianism can tell little about fascism per se in its various interwar permutations. The general consensus among the most celebrated exponents of the theory is that fascist Italy should be excluded from a serious discussion of totalitarianism, on the basis of Mussolini's ostensible failure to promote an effective political and social totality. Here, references to Nazi ruthlessness in stamping out opposition, in surveillance techniques, and in the sheer terror unleashed through the regime's secret police and racialist policies make the Italian regime appear as a benign and rather unsuccessful totalitarian experiment. As much as Mussolini paid extensive lip service to the "ferocious total will" of his novel creed, the argument goes, it was the usual case of wishful thinking versus reality—propaganda as opposed to actual result. This conclusion may be true, at least to some extent. Yet, excluding Italy (and, of course, other interwar regimes with fascist tendencies that failed even more comprehensively in their totalitarian ventures) from comparative scrutiny does not advance the understanding of what fascism actually stood for in opposition to Soviet communism. For those who argue that National Socialism is fundamentally different from fascism—and should, therefore, be analyzed in isolation from other interwar ultranationalist regimes in Europe—this suggestion is rather welcome. For the champions of a generic fascist model of analysis such distinctions succumb to an idolatry of individual differences while losing sight of key similarities between National Socialism and other manifestations of fascism in interwar Europe.

The clash between the interpretations of totalitarianism and generic fascism brings us to a further question that concerns the difference between intentions and results. Theories of totalitarianism eliminate all fascist regimes, apart from that of Hitler, on the grounds that regardless of their ideological aims, their actions did not amount to a totalitarian exercise of power. Intentions are important, however; and it is exactly at this point that the scrutiny of the content of ideology (a concern that totalitarianist interpretations have largely disregarded) becomes instrumental. In recent decades the idea that the Nazi regime was a monolithic mechanism with a single will and direction has been successfully challenged, giving way to an interpretation that stressed its polycratic and often chaotic character. Although palpably more ferocious in its surveillance practices than any other similar institu-

tions in interwar Europe, the myth of the "omnipotent, omniscient, omnipresent" Gestapo (*Geheime Staatspolizei,* Secret State Police) has been substantially modified to highlight the system's gaps and inefficiencies. The failure of the Nazi Party to command the loyalties of the German population, to become the "total" repository of the national community's allegiance, and to overcome its widespread unpopularity have questioned the applicability of the totalitarianist theory to even such a fundamental aspect of its five-point checklist.

If even the Nazi regime fell short of its ideological intention to impose a truly total system of sociopolitical domination, then one is faced with two different conclusions: either the totalitarianism of specifically Hitler's regime was a mere illusion, in which case the whole theory rests on a false hypothesis; or the model depends more on intentions than actions, thereby making the exclusion of the Italian and other interwar regimes practically indefensible. The former conclusion renders the theory of totalitarianism so restricted that it becomes inapplicable, while the latter expands it to such an extent that the original premises of analysis become irrelevant. In either case, the model of totalitarianism appears awkwardly static in its formulaic list of basic features and bewilderingly ahistorical in its disregard for the vastly different ideological concerns of each system.

In recent years a revival of totalitarianist interpretations, ironically spearheaded by prominent scholars of Italian Fascism, seems to suggest that, rather than focusing on the actual exercise of power, the quest for totality was in fact an ideological pursuit of fascism per se. This new breed of totalitarianist theories appears more concerned with the intellectual components of fascism than with its alleged similarities to the Stalinist regime. For once, the collapse of the Soviet empire in Eastern Europe has at least removed the political necessity for a comparison between fascism and communism. The shift of attention from practice to ideology and from the static model of traditional totalitarianism to more dynamic theories of gradual implementation of a cult of totality has already contributed to the partial reinstatement of the concept. However, the totalitarianist theory of the 1950s and 1960s has essentially failed in its basic premise: that the duet of National Socialism and Stalinism could become the exclusive objects of a fruitful comparative analysis on the basis of the ideal type of totalitarian dictatorship. Perhaps the most eloquent proof of totalitarianism's failure lies in the fact that, in spite of some dissonant voices, National Socialism continues to be regarded as a more legitimate item of comparative analysis alongside Fascist Italy than Stalinist Russia.

–ARISTOTLE A. KALLIS,
UNIVERSITY OF BRISTOL

References

Hannah Arendt, *The Origins of Totalitarianism* (New York: Harcourt, Brace, 1951).

Carl J. Friedrich and Zbigniew K. Brzezinski, *Totalitarian Dictatorship and Autocracy* (Cambridge, Mass.: Harvard University Press, 1954).

Friedrich, ed., *Totalitarianism* (Cambridge, Mass.: Harvard University Press, 1954).

Irving Howe, ed., *1984 Revisited: Totalitarianism in Our Century* (New York: Harper & Row, 1983).

Stephen J. Lee, *The European Dictatorships, 1918–1945* (London & New York: Methuen, 1987).

Juan J. Linz, *Totalitarian and Authoritarian Regimes* (Boulder, Colo.: Lynne Rienner, 2000).

Luisa Passerini, ed., *Memory and Totalitarianism* (Oxford & New York: Oxford University Press, 1992).

Leonard Shapiro, *Totalitarianism* (London: Pall Mall Press, 1972; New York: Praeger, 1972).

Simon Torney, *Making Sense of Tyranny: Interpretations of Totalitarianism* (Manchester & New York: Manchester University Press, 1995).

Aryeh L. Unger, *The Totalitarian Party: Party and People in Nazi Germany and Soviet Russia* (London & New York: Cambridge University Press, 1974).

UNITED STATES AS A EUROPEAN POWER

Has the United States been "the greatest European power" since World War II?

Viewpoint: Yes. American involvement in World War II thrust the United States into a long-term and continuing role as the arbiter of European affairs.

Viewpoint: No. Although the United States had a pronounced role in European affairs immediately after World War II, its influence and presence on the Continent has steadily declined since the late 1940s.

Some historians have characterized post–World War II (1939–1945) United States as "the greatest European power." As much of a geographic misstatement as this assertion may be, the United States enjoyed the strongest military, diplomatic, and economic presence in Europe for decades after 1945, and some observers argue that this situation remains true today.

No one can dispute that America was predominant in Europe immediately after the war. U.S. forces had helped liberate much of the Continent from Nazi Germany. Tens of thousands of U.S. troops remained to occupy Germany, Italy, and Austria and to garrison bases and other installations in preparation for any potential war with the Soviet Union. U.S. diplomatic clout determined much of the Continent's development in the years after the war, playing an especially important role in the formation of the North Atlantic Treaty Organization (NATO) in 1949 and in decisions affecting European integration, West German rearmament, and the deployment of nuclear weapons. Economic assistance, which included the comprehensive Marshall Plan (1947) as well as a variety of other aid and development programs, stimulated the recovery of European industry, trade, and agriculture.

Yet, there is substantial debate about how long this situation persisted. One argument maintains that the U.S. presence, though diminished, remains strong, influential, and essential for European security after 2000. The sheer size and power of the U.S. military and its presence in Europe ensure a pronounced role even more than fifty years after World War II. America's overwhelming contribution to NATO forces, its perpetual control of the alliance's command structure, and its instrumental role in the crises in the former Yugoslavia in the 1990s continue to demonstrate and guarantee its clout.

A counterargument suggests that American influence has declined in a major way. Despite a continuing U.S. military presence, Europe has made substantial strides in the management of its own affairs. Economically, the combined wealth of the European Union (EU) is almost as great as that of the United States, while its population, and arguably its potential, is substantially larger. Diplomatically, individual European nations and, increasingly, the EU as an organization, show greater and greater resistance to U.S. world leadership. By the turn of the twenty-first century, this standing was not only true with regard to European affairs but also to matters concerning world trade, the environment, human rights, the authority of the United Nations (UN), and policy toward combating international terrorism. This situation suggests that U.S. influence in Europe has been experiencing an inevitable decline and may face complete evaporation in the future.

Viewpoint:
Yes. American involvement in World War II thrust the United States into a long-term and continuing role as the arbiter of European affairs.

From the moment in spring of 1945, when American and Soviet troops met in Germany, it is impossible to speak of "Europe" as a single geopolitical entity. The Soviet-controlled, eastern part had a different social and political history from the western part, dominated by the United States. The once-mighty European powers, which in 1914 ruled most of the world, had exhausted themselves in two world wars and lapsed into the shadows of the two new global giants. When the Soviet Union dissolved in 1991, the United States was left as the undisputed global superpower.

World War II (1939–1945) was not the first American intervention in European conflicts. In 1917 U.S. troops landed in France to help the beleaguered Entente gain the upper hand in what was then known as the Great War (World War I, 1914–1918). When the hostilities ended, the Americans withdrew. In 1945 they stayed, establishing military bases in occupied Germany and elsewhere, and facing off with their former Soviet allies in a new political confrontation dubbed the Cold War. This confrontation and its chief protagonists defined the military, economic, and political role of Europe in the postwar world.

The three main powers of Western Europe were all badly hurt by the war. Britain suffered heavy losses, both militarily and economically. France had been occupied for four years and was merely a shadow of its former self. Germany's infrastructure was nearly obliterated, and the country was divided between British, French, and U.S. troops on one side and the Soviets on the other.

In late 1946, however, the U.S. and British occupation zones were combined ("Bizonia"), prompting speculation about the reunification of Germany. The Soviets reacted by blockading Western-occupied parts of Berlin, deep inside their occupation zone, in June 1948. Instead of retreating, the United States and Britain organized an airlift that supplied Berlin for almost a year. Meanwhile, the French occupation zone joined its Anglo-American counterpart, and on 23 May 1949, they established the Federal Republic of Germany. A day later the Soviets ended the blockade of Berlin, as it had become pointless. Soon thereafter, the German Democratic Republic was established from Soviet-occupied German territories, cementing a division of Germany for the next forty years. The confrontation over Berlin and the partition of Germany were clear signs that the United States intended not to retreat from Europe but to remain a force in Continental affairs. For the next five decades, the United States was the dominant force in Western European affairs. This dominance continues even today, though somewhat subdued and tempered by the economic power of the European Union (EU).

American military dominance in Europe has been virtually unchallenged. In April 1949 the North Atlantic Treaty Organization (NATO) was formed, making the United States an inseparable component of European collective security. The position of Supreme Allied Commander, Europe (SACEUR) was created in 1950. All thirteen generals who have held that post have been Americans.

In 1966, Charles de Gaulle's government decided that France would stop its participation in the NATO command structure. Showing that France was not the linchpin of European security de Gaulle may have believed it to be, NATO simply relocated its headquarters to Belgium and continued operations.

Since the end of World War II, the United States has maintained many military bases in Europe. Nearly sixty years after the end of the war, twenty U.S. military bases are still located in Germany alone. Naples, Italy, hosts the headquarters for NATO's Southern Command, which includes a powerful U.S. naval force; the Aviano Air Base north of Venice has served as a launching pad for operations in the Balkans in the 1990s. In 1992 there were still more than 70,000 U.S. troops in Europe.

From an economic perspective, the situation has been slightly different. All of Europe suffered great losses of capital assets and infrastructure during the war. In 1947 the United States launched the Marshall Plan, a massive program of economic aid, aimed at rebuilding and revitalizing European nations. By the end of 1951, when the plan ended, the total aid to Western Europe amounted to more than $13 billion.

Stimulated by this capital infusion, Western Europe quickly recovered from the ravages of war. France, Italy, Belgium, Luxembourg, and

the Netherlands, along with the recently established Federal Republic of Germany, signed the Treaty of Paris (1951), establishing the European Coal and Steel Community (ECSC). The ECSC gradually expanded in both membership and scope, becoming the European Economic Community (EEC) in 1957. In December 1991 EEC members signed a treaty in Maastricht, the Netherlands, establishing the European Union (EU). In 2001 the estimated Gross Domestic Product (GDP) of the EU was $8 trillion, while that of the United States was $10 trillion. In 2001 the EU introduced a new currency, the euro, which has kept rough parity with the American dollar.

Even as the EU has come to rival the United States in the global markets, it has continued to defer to the U.S. politically. Western Europe's subordination to the United States has been keenly felt in the realm of foreign affairs. Even after fifty years of economic integration, there is still nothing even remotely resembling a joint European foreign or defense policy. Britain has crafted a particularly close relationship with Washington since 1945, which has often put it at odds with its European partners. Whether governed by Margaret Thatcher and the Conservatives or Tony Blair and the Labor Party, London

has provided nearly unconditional support to U.S. diplomatic and military initiatives. France has exhibited more independence, relying on a partnership with Germany, but its defiance has remained largely rhetorical and symbolic—such as the 1966 withdrawal from NATO's joint command structures. Germany—reunified in 1990 after the Soviet bloc collapse—has not defied the United States in any major way despite some provocative rhetoric during its 2002 parliamentary elections. Furthermore, because of constitutional constraints, the German military was unable to engage abroad before the late 1990s.

The extent to which the United States was a dominant force in European affairs was perhaps most readily apparent in the degree to which it took over the role European powers played in global affairs. The former European powers could no longer hold on to their colonial possessions. The United States encouraged the dissolution of colonial empires in Africa and Asia, replacing European power and influence with its own.

One example of this global shift in power is the Eisenhower administration's refusal to support French forces trying to repress an independence movement in Vietnam. In 1954 the

French were defeated at Dien Bien Phu and were forced to recognize the independence of Vietnam later that year. Vietnam was partitioned into the heavily communist North and a more pro-Western South. The United States, which did not sign the Geneva accords, almost immediately became involved in supporting the South Vietnamese regime against rebels who sought unification with the North. The war escalated in the mid 1960s and ended with a U.S. withdrawal in 1973 and a communist victory in 1975. Indeed, there is an argument to be made that America's Vietnam trauma was a direct consequence of its dominance in Europe.

In 1948 the United Kingdom retreated from its Palestinian mandate in the Middle East. The State of Israel was proclaimed almost immediately, leading to incessant warfare with the neighboring Arab states, which refused to recognize its legitimacy. Replacing Britain and France as the most influential powers in the region, the United States became more involved. In 1956 American diplomatic pressure forced Britain and France to end their campaign to reverse Egypt's nationalization of the Suez Canal. Washington gave direct military aid to Israel during its 1973 war with Egypt and Syria, stationed troops in Lebanon in the early 1980s, and mounted a large-scale campaign to liberate Kuwait from an Iraqi invasion in 1991. Iran (Persia) became hostile to the United States after the Islamic Revolution (1979), in part because the United States had helped engineer its monarch's seizure of full power in 1953 and supported the Shah thereafter.

Despite some early hopes, the collapse of communism and the end of the Cold War have not resulted in a dramatic diminution of U.S. involvement in Europe. Faced with a crisis in the former Yugoslavia, which exploded in violent civil wars just as the EU was committing itself to further political integration, Luxembourg foreign minister Jacques Poos enthusiastically chimed, "The hour of Europe has come!" Over the next four years, however, Europe was incapable of stopping the carnage in Yugoslavia. The United States, facing the prospect of insignificance in post–Cold War Europe, covertly and overtly interfered in the Yugoslav conflicts. Finally, an American-led military intervention stopped the war and forced a peace onto the warring factions in late 1995. Richard Holbrooke, the diplomat who spearheaded U.S. efforts in the Balkans, described it as "re-establishing [U.S.] leadership" in Europe. Far from lapsing into obscurity as its Soviet counterpart, the Warsaw Pact, did at the end of the Cold War, the American-led NATO asserted new roles for itself during the Balkans intervention and the follow-on peacekeeping mission in Bosnia. A strong difference of opinion between Europe and the United States regarding the Bosnian crisis was completely muted by the spring of 1999, when NATO again intervened at America's behest. By the end of 2002, NATO's projected expansion encompassed seven former Warsaw Pact members and even three former republics of the Soviet Union. The conclusion of the Cold War did not end the fifty-year American dominance of European affairs; it only made it stronger. After the tumultuous events of the 1990s, Europe has decided to accept U.S. leadership, even as its original purpose had been consigned to the dustbin of history.

–NEBOJSA MALIC,
WASHINGTON, D.C.

Viewpoint:
No. Although the United States had a pronounced role in European affairs immediately after World War II, its influence and presence on the Continent has steadily declined since the late 1940s.

American patriots might well believe that the United States was the greatest European power after World War II (1939–1945). After all, the economic, political, and military power of the United States seemed, at first blush, to be overwhelming. The United States also was more active than usual in European affairs. Through the occupation of Germany (1945), implementation of the Marshall Plan (1947), and establishment of the North Atlantic Treaty Organization (NATO, 1949) America's relationship with Europe has certainly been much more intense than it was in the years before the war.

A careful look at the record, however, indicates otherwise. American commitment to Europe has always been tenuous, and Washington has always had its eye on the exit door, despite the wishes of more internationally minded Americans. In the relationship between Europe and the United States, the big story has not been about the United States as the greatest European power; it has been about a newly emerging Europe that is its own master.

If the 1940s meant the high-water mark of American involvement in European affairs, then this commitment was shaky indeed. Perhaps the greatest U.S. commitment to Europe was the Marshall Plan, but this program, aimed at the expansion of free trade across Western Europe and sold to America as a bulwark against the spread of communism, was Washington's last significant contribution to Europe's well-being.

EUROPEAN COAL AND STEEL COMMUNITY

The articles of the document establishing the European Coal and Steel Community in 1952 are:

Article 1

By this Treaty, the HIGH CONTRACTING PARTIES establish among themselves a EUROPEAN COAL AND STEEL COMMUNITY, founded upon a common market, common objectives and common institutions.

Article 2

The European Coal and Steel Community shall have as its task to contribute, in harmony with the general economy of the Member States and through the establishment of a common market as provided in Article 4, to economic expansion, growth of employment and a rising standard of living in the Member States.

The Community shall progressively bring about conditions which will of themselves ensure the most rational distribution of production at the highest possible level of productivity, while safeguarding continuity of employment and taking care not to provoke fundamental and persistent disturbances in the economies of Member States.

Article 3

The institutions of the Community shall, within the limits of their respective powers, in the common interest:

ensure an orderly supply to the common market, taking into account the needs of third countries;

ensure that all comparably placed consumers in the common market have equal access to the sources of production;

ensure the establishment of the lowest prices under such conditions that these prices do not result in higher prices charged by the same undertakings in other transactions or in a higher general price level at another time, while allowing necessary amortization and normal return on invested capital;

ensure the maintenance of conditions which will encourage undertakings to expand and improve their production potential and to promote a policy of using natural resources rationally and avoiding their unconsidered exhaustion;

promote improved working conditions and an improved standard of living for the workers in each of the industries for which it is responsible, so as to make possible their harmonization while the improvement is being maintained;

promote the growth of international trade and ensure that equitable limits are observed in export pricing;

promote the orderly expansion and modernization of production, and the improvement of quality, with no protection against competing industries that is not justified by improper action on their part or in their favour.

Article 4

The following are recognized as incompatible with the common market for coal and steel and shall accordingly be abolished and prohibited within the Community, as provided in this Treaty:

import and export duties, or charges having equivalent effect, and quantitative restrictions on the movement of products;

measures or practices which discriminate between producers, between purchasers or between consumers, especially in prices and delivery terms or transport rates and conditions, and measures or practices which interfere with the purchaser's free choice of supplier;

subsidies or aids granted by States, or special charges imposed by States, in any form whatsoever;

restrictive practices which tend towards the sharing or exploiting of markets.

Article 5

The Community shall carry out its task in accordance with this Treaty, with a limited measure of intervention.

To this end the Community shall:

provide guidance and assistance for the parties concerned, by obtaining information, organizing consultations and laying down general objectives;

place financial resources at the disposal of undertakings for their investment and bear part of the cost of readaptation;

ensure the establishment, maintenance and observance of normal competitive conditions and exert direct influence upon production or upon the market only when circumstances so require;

publish the reasons for its actions and take the necessary measures to ensure the observance of the rules laid down in this Treaty.

The institutions of the Community shall carry out these activities with a minimum of administrative machinery and in close cooperation with the parties concerned.

Article 6

The Community shall have legal personality.

In international relations, the Community shall enjoy the legal capacity it requires to perform its functions and attain its objectives.

In each of the Member States, the Community shall enjoy the most extensive legal capacity accorded to legal persons constituted in that State; it may, in particular, acquire or dispose of movable and immovable property and may be a party to legal proceedings.

The Community shall be represented by its institutions, each within the limits of its powers.

Source: "Treaty Establishing the European Coal and Steel Community," Europa <http://europa.eu.int/abc/obj/treaties/en/entr30a.htm#Article_1>.

The only other significant American contribution to Europe has been defense, but this effort was always less extensive than was commonly believed. Between 1946 and 1949, when the NATO treaty was signed, America's military presence in Europe was evaporating. This tendency was slowed, but not reversed, by the events of 1948, in particular the Police Coup communist takeover of Czechoslovakia and the Soviet blockade of Berlin. The result of President Harry S Truman's reconsideration of American policy toward Europe was the establishment of NATO, but initially the treaty was more of a gesture than an actual functioning alliance. Already in April 1949 the limits of America's willingness and ability to contribute to European security were made clear. Immediately after the signing ceremony, Truman and Secretary of State George C. Marshall brought their European counterparts behind closed doors and confessed that, should there in fact be any need to activate NATO defenses, there was nothing that the United States could do to help its newly anointed European allies. This revelation was rather typical of the American stance toward Europe: there was a lot of rhetoric and some strong-arming to get Europe to come along, but when the real work was to be done, Washington always was behind on its commitments.

If the United States was to make up for its inability to defend Europe in April 1949, any such effort was sorely curbed by the outbreak of the Korean War (1950–1953) fourteen months later. Korea in fact proved to be the stimulus that was needed to promote European self-sufficiency in defense, politics, and economic growth. Korea meant that Germany was going to be rearmed and that European arms industries would be restored to supply the land armies of NATO. When the Korean War ended, Washington's policy kept this emphasis on European self-sufficiency. President Dwight D. Eisenhower's "New Look" provided American nuclear and air power, but the hard fighting was to be done by European troops. Eisenhower explicitly proclaimed that his ambition was to make Europe "a third great power bloc," a belief that he had already made clear as NATO commander in Europe in the 1940s. Europe would continue to be the backbone of NATO's defense, so much so that the largest army in NATO has perennially been Germany's.

One cause of this spotty involvement in Europe derived from American society's residual isolationism. The location of the United Nations (UN) in New York City is a reflection of this fact: it was reasoned by many that situating the organization in the United States would make world affairs that much harder for America to ignore. Amazingly, even at a time when U.S.

linkage to the outside world has been so dramatically demonstrated in the terrorist attacks of September 2001, there are still American calls to expel the UN from the United States. Most American support for internationalism has tended to be centered around the traditional East Coast elite, but the problem is that for the last fifty years, that population has become less and less influential.

Even this high-water mark was not as promising as it might seem. John F. Kennedy, the last U.S. president to enjoy strong popularity in Europe, nevertheless left much to be desired in terms of commitment to Europe. French president Charles de Gaulle's contempt for Kennedy is well known. Mostly, Kennedy's stance toward Europe fit the American pattern: great rhetorical shows, such as the 1962 European tour and the Berlin Wall standoff: beyond that, the Kennedy administration would brook no criticism from the Europeans and behaved in a high-handed fashion toward its NATO allies. One should not think that Europe was singled out in this way: Latin America and Asia received much the same treatment. This same administration also waded into the Vietnam War (ended 1975), which arguably did more to distance Europe and America than any other event of its time. It should not have come as a surprise to Washington when de Gaulle and German chancellor Willy Brandt tried to develop a more "Eurocentric" stance on world affairs: Europe had become tired of being bossed around without any commensurate U.S. contributions. American reluctance to meet the outside world on its own terms has constantly undermined any dedicated effort to remain engaged in European affairs, and has not gone unnoticed in Europe.

Of course, Europeans would have preferred to take care of their own affairs, and Washington's irregular involvement in them only made the point obvious on both sides of the Atlantic. Washington actively encouraged European efforts to improve integration and independence. In the end, what emerged was a single great European alliance in place of American power. The Marshall Plan was explicitly aimed at creating a larger pan-European economy, not especially subtly modeled after the American experience. Yet, whatever integration the Americans might have envisioned for Europe, the end result was homegrown. France's Schumann Plan resulted in the European Coal and Steel Community (1951), and in that same year tentative steps toward European integration were taken with the European Defense Community. The Treaty of Rome (1957) laid out the European Economic Community (EEC), and by the 1969 Summit the EEC proclaimed its intention to create a unified foreign policy. The Luxembourg

Report (1970) created the machinery for political cooperation in the EEC, and developments accelerated in the 1980s, culminating in the Maastricht Treaty (1992) creating a European Union (EU). The expansion of integrated Europe—beginning with Britain's, Ireland's, and Denmark's entry in 1973—spread the movement more widely, while the accession of formerly neutral nations (Austria, Sweden, Finland) in 1995 and the expected accession of eight former Eastern bloc nations, Cyprus, and Malta in 2004 have only further enhanced the EU's position.

Still, the EU's dominance has not been in the form of high-profile political pronunciations or statements, but rather in the day-to-day affairs of Europeans. Regulation and negotiation with outside powers has grown out of trade considerations. As envisioned by the founders of the EEC, economic cooperation has opened the door for political cooperation. Already in 1968, before the first expansion, the EEC had created common agricultural and trade policies. Nations from around the world sent embassies to Brussels to negotiate with Europe as a whole, and the political unity of Europe was made manifest by the Single Europe Act (1986) and the Maastricht Treaty. There is now a common EU foreign policy, and the disintegration of Yugoslavia in the 1990s was in large measure settled by the EU. Although American intervention may well have played its role, Washington's part has only been as partners with the Europeans.

While military and political developments were dominated by Europe, economic developments were not far behind. Europe has always been more populous than the United States, and since the 1950s, once its economy recovered from the devastation of the war, Europe's economy has been larger than America's. Most Americans are oblivious to the fact that the Europeans own large chunks of the American economy and infrastructure. During the 1980s, America was worried about the Japanese buying up the country, when in fact the largest foreign owner of

American property was Great Britain, followed by the Netherlands. British, Dutch, German, and French investors today own far more of the United States than the Japanese. Even tiny Denmark owns one of America's largest shippers, Mærsk Sealand.

Although many Americans might not know it, Europe is doing rather well, and outstrips the United States in many important measures. European integration arose against the backdrop of a sporadic American commitment to Europe. The greatest European power has absolutely not been the United States. It has been Europe.

–PHIL GILTNER,
ALBANY ACADEMY

References

Phillip Corwin, *Dubious Mandate: A Memoir of the UN in Bosnia, Summer 1995* (Durham, N.C.: Duke University Press, 1999).

Douglas Eden, ed., *Europe and the Atlantic Relationship: Issues of Identity, Security, and Power* (New York: St. Martin's Press, 2000).

David Hine and Hussein Kassim, eds., *Beyond the Market: The EU and National Social Policy* (London & New York: Routledge, 1998).

Richard Holbrooke, *To End a War* (New York: Random House, 1998).

Jolyon Howorth and John T. S. Keeler, eds., *Defending Europe: The EU, NATO and the Quest for European Autonomy* (New York: Palgrave Macmillan, 2003).

Robert Kagan, *Of Paradise and Power: America and Europe in the New World Order* (New York: Knopf, 2003).

David Owen, *Balkan Odyssey* (New York: Harcourt Brace, 1995).

UNITED STATES AS A
EUROPEAN POWER

UNITED STATES AND WESTERN EUROPE

Did the United States require the invitation of European leaders to assume a major role in Western Europe after World War II?

Viewpoint: Yes. Western European governments invited the relatively reluctant United States to safeguard Europe from communism.

Viewpoint: No. The United States needed no invitation to extend its influence in Europe and never would have abandoned its interests there.

After World War II (1939–1945) the United States stood at the height of international power. It established a long-term military presence and played a major economic role all over the world. In Western Europe the United States quickly established military bases, where tens of thousands of troops and vast quantities of supplies remained at the ready for a new conflict. It also took the lead in financing European recovery through hefty investment and generous loans and credit.

In a recent work, Norwegian historian Geir Lundestad argues that this large U.S. military and economic presence was the result of an invitation. He contends that European politicians actively invited the American presence to ensure their security and persuaded an otherwise reluctant U.S. leadership to accept that responsibility. The predominant U.S. role in European affairs after 1945, then, was an "empire by invitation."

Yet, this scenario was not necessarily the case. Regardless of whether Europeans delivered an invitation for American power to protect them, a wider perspective suggests that the United States would never have abandoned its growing hegemony. America's new world role did not allow it to ignore the health, stability, and security of its West European allies. Facing a totalitarian Soviet Union, after defeating Nazi Germany and authoritarian Japan, American idealists would not permit a renewed threat to European democracy. American business could not permit the collapse of its biggest prewar trading partners and most lucrative markets. America's projection of power into Western Europe was, in this view, a foregone conclusion.

Viewpoint:
Yes. Western European governments invited the relatively reluctant United States to safeguard Europe from communism.

Over the course of the Cold War, and particularly in the wake of American involvement in Vietnam (ending 1975), some observers came to see the rivalry between the United States and the Soviet Union as a conflict involving competing powers of roughly equivalent status. Those who saw this equivalence perceived both nations as imperialist powers dominating submissive allies. They saw the Americans and Soviets supporting governments for strategic

273

advantage without regard for the ideological considerations that supposedly underlay the rivalry between the capitalist, democratic United States and the communist Union of Soviet Socialist Republics (U.S.S.R.). They also saw the two superpowers looking primarily to promote their own power and strength against those of their chief competitors.

This development marked a sharp departure from prior understandings of the Cold War. Initially, American involvement in Europe had been explained as a reaction to Soviet efforts to expand the communist empire across Europe. In his seminal article "Empire by Invitation? The United States and Western Europe, 1945–1952," (1986), Norwegian scholar Geir Lundestad pointed out that while early Cold War scholarship had focused much attention on the expansion of Soviet control over Eastern Europe, the nation whose power and influence expanded most dramatically in the years following World War II (1939–1945) was not the Soviet Union but the United States. In explaining American success in expanding its "empire," Lundestad noted that the U.S. position in international affairs, and in Europe, had grown with the acquiescence and encouragement of the West Europeans, who became part of the American sphere of influence.

Lundestad's scholarship suggested themes that were later developed by John Lewis Gaddis in *We Now Know: Rethinking Cold War History* (1997). As Gaddis has explained it, "Western Europeans invited the United States to construct a sphere of influence and to include them within it." It would be erroneous, however, to suggest that the United States was dragged into an expanded role in world affairs against its will. At the same time, any contemplation of European affairs during the Cold War years must recognize that the greater American role was encouraged and promoted by the very Europeans who were part of the U.S.-led group of nations. While the Soviet Union had forced its will on the subjugated peoples of Eastern Europe, the Americans had not dictated to conquered peoples, but rather played the leading role in a coalition of democratic nations whose populations endorsed and supported their inclusion within this international grouping.

The performance in "liberated" areas of Europe by the Red Army in World War II, particularly in Poland, gave impetus to concerns among political leaders of the Western European democracies about their future security on a continent in which the Soviets were an unrivaled military power. The only power positioned to provide a convincing counterbalance to the Soviets was the United States, although the Americans had a history of preferring to remain nonaligned in Euro-

pean affairs during peacetime. Not only could the Americans balance Soviet power, but a permanent U.S. role in Europe would also guard against potential trouble with a resurgent Germany. After requesting U.S. economic aid to facilitate recovery and reconstruction, the European democracies encouraged American military involvement in Europe culminating in the formation of the North Atlantic Treaty Organization (NATO) in 1949. The NATO alliance, as one witticism has it, was desired by the Western European democracies "to keep the Americans in, the Russians out, and the Germans down." The accomplishment of this aim by the Western Europeans was a triumph of their diplomacy in engaging the United States first economically and then militarily.

The Americans became more involved economically in response to European needs. The British wanted the Americans to play a larger role in funding occupation costs in Germany after the British and Americans merged their zones of occupation. In addition, the British, French, and Italians all sought economic assistance from the United States during the years between the end of World War II and the establishment of the Marshall Plan (1947). The United States attached conditions to its economic assistance, certainly, and it is not clear that the European nations were satisfied with the quantities of aid they received from the Americans. Still, the United States provided money and was given the opportunity to impose conditions because of the desires of the Western Europeans.

European initiative was also important in the Marshall Plan, or European Recovery Program. U.S. secretary of state George C. Marshall, in his 1947 commencement address at Harvard University, announced that the Americans would be receptive to a European request for assistance and made clear that the program would be dependent upon European initiative. It had to be organized and requested by the Europeans. Not only did the European nations do so, but the British and French took the lead in responding to the request in a way that ensured Soviet rejection of the plan. At the Paris conference in the summer of 1947, the British, French, and Soviets met to discuss the European response to Marshall's offer. At various times it has been suggested that the Soviets only attended the conference to disrupt the proceedings, but Soviet foreign minister Vycheslav Molotov arrived with a large delegation of economic experts. The presence of these experts demonstrated that the Soviets took the plan seriously. Soviet leader Josef Stalin and other communist thinkers in Moscow expected capitalism to face a crisis without wartime demand, and they believed the Marshall Plan could have been

AMERICAN STRATEGY

Below is an excerpt from the influential article written by senior State Department official George F. Kennan:

It is clear that the United States cannot expect in the foreseeable future to enjoy political intimacy with the Soviet regime. It must continue to regard the Soviet Union as a rival, not a partner, in the political arena. It must continue to expect that Soviet policies will reflect no abstract love of peace and stability, no real faith in the possibility of a permanent happy coexistence of the Socialist and capitalist worlds, but rather a cautious, persistent pressure toward the disruption and weakening of all rival influence and rival power.

Balanced against this are the facts that Russia, as opposed to the western world in general, is still by far the weaker party, that Soviet policy is highly flexible, and that Soviet society may well contain deficiencies which will eventually weaken its own total potential. This would of itself warrant the United States entering with reasonable confidence upon a policy of firm containment, designed to confront the Russians with unalterable counterforce at every point where they show signs of encroaching upon the interests of a peaceful and stable world.

But in actuality the possibilities for American policy are by no means limited to holding the line and hoping for the best. It is entirely possible for the United States to influence by its actions the internal developments, both within Russia and throughout the international Communist movement, by which Russian policy is largely determined. This is not only a question of the modest measure of informational activity which this government can conduct in the Soviet Union and elsewhere, although that, too, is important. It is rather a question of the degree to which the United States can create among the peoples of the world generally the impression of a country which knows what it wants, which is coping successfully with the problem of its internal life and with the responsibilities of a World Power, and which has a spiritual vitality capable of holding its own among the major ideological currents of the time. To the extent that such an impression can be created and maintained, the aims of Russian Communism must appear sterile and quixotic, the hopes and enthusiasm of Moscow's supporters must wane, and added strain must be imposed on the Kremlin's foreign policies. For the palsied decrepitude of the capitalist world is the keystone of Communist philosophy. Even the failure of the United States to experience the early economic depression which the ravens of the Red Square have been predicting with such complacent confidence since hostilities ceased would have deep and important repercussions throughout the Communist world.

By the same token, exhibitions of indecision, disunity and internal disintegration within this country have an exhilarating effect on the whole Communist movement. At each evidence of these tendencies, a thrill of hope and excitement goes through the Communist world; a new jauntiness can be noted in the Moscow tread; new groups of foreign supporters climb on to what they can only view as the band wagon of international politics; and Russian pressure increases all along the line in international affairs.

It would be an exaggeration to say that American behavior unassisted and alone could exercise a power of life and death over the Communist movement and bring about the early fall of Soviet power in Russia. But the United States has it in its power to increase enormously the strains under which Soviet policy must operate, to force upon the Kremlin a far greater degree of moderation and circumspection than it has had to observe in recent years, and in this way to promote tendencies which must eventually find their outlet in either the breakup or the gradual mellowing of Soviet power. For no mystical, Messianic movement—and particularly not that of the Kremlin—can face frustration indefinitely without eventually adjusting itself in one way or another to the logic of that state of affairs.

Thus the decision will really fall in large measure in this country itself. The issue of Soviet-American relations is in essence a test of the overall worth of the United States as a nation among nations. To avoid destruction the United States need only measure up to its own best traditions and prove itself worthy of preservation as a great nation.

Surely, there was never a fairer test of national quality than this. In the light of these circumstances, the thoughtful observer of Russian-American relations will find no cause for complaint in the Kremlin's challenge to American society. He will rather experience a certain gratitude to a Providence which, by providing the American people with this implacable challenge, has made their entire security as a nation dependent on their pulling themselves together and accepting the responsibilities of moral and political leadership that history plainly intended them to bear.

Source: George F. Kennan, "The Sources of Soviet Conduct," as X, *Foreign Affairs,* 25 (July 1947): 566–582.

an effort by the Truman administration to obtain political advantage from the provision of credits that for reasons of economic self-interest the United States had to extend to Europe.

Since they saw this plan as an opportunity to obtain reconstruction assistance cheaply, the Soviets took Marshall's offer seriously. Actual Soviet participation might have made the European Recovery Program politically impossible for the U.S. Congress to pass. Even continued Soviet participation in deliberations could have posed unsolvable problems for the Americans and Western Europeans. While the Soviets wanted each nation to submit a list of its requirements individually, with priority on American aid going to those nations that had suffered the most and done the most during the war, the British preferred a response more in line with Marshall's suggestions. British foreign minister Ernest Bevin insisted that the Europeans reply with a multilateral, integrated response; French foreign minister Georges Bidault supported Bevin. Isolated, Molotov and the Soviets stormed out of the conference. The Western Europeans could now respond in the fashion that Marshall had indicated would draw a favorable response. It is true that the Truman administration was pleased by this outcome, and that the British and French had done what the Americans clearly signaled was essential to make the program work. This acquiescence was clear evidence that the Western Europeans were willing to make concessions to ensure that the United States played the larger role in Europe that Western European democracies desired.

Just as greater U.S. economic involvement in Europe resulted from Western European initiative, so too did the Western European democracies play a crucial role in bringing about permanent American military involvement with the continent. While the Western Europeans were struggling to recover economically, even with American assistance, they were concerned about maintaining the security that would be a necessary prerequisite for enduring economic prosperity. In particular, they were worried about the potential threat emanating from Moscow. The Soviets loomed as an ominous presence ever since the success of the Red Army in "liberating" Eastern Europe. The British and French, who had entered the war in defense of Poland, saw the appalling treatment of the victims of wartime Nazi—and Soviet—aggression. The Western Europeans could not have been pleased by the way the Soviets passed off the undemocratic aggregation of communist loyalists in the Lublin Committee as the government of Poland, nor could they have been happy about the Soviet refusal to provide more meaningful opportunities for the exiled prewar government to partici-

pate. Soviet delays and unwillingness to permit genuine democratic elections may have fallen within a plausible interpretation of the Yalta (1945) agreements, but they suggested the Soviets were aggressive, expansionist, and not really committed to the principles of the Atlantic Charter (1941).

While Soviet treatment of Poland caused concern in the West, a more dramatic example of Soviet brutality was evident in Germany. There the Soviets initially had hoped that indigenous communists would be able to capitalize on their war-won prestige and emerge as the democratically elected leaders of a unified Germany. This idea was not as far-fetched as it may at first appear. German communists had earned considerable goodwill as the most determined resisters of the Nazis, and the Red Army had won prestige for communism with its destruction of the German war machine. Yet, the brutishness of the Soviets in occupied Germany, including the rape of as many as 2 million women, left the Germans with little more enthusiasm for Soviet-supported communism than their former Polish opponents had.

The Soviet penchant for brutality, combined with the strength of the Red Army and Soviet willingness to use its power, caused growing concern among Europeans about their security. These worries became more pronounced after a coup in Czechoslovakia in February 1948 replaced a coalition government with a communist regime, convincing many in the West that Stalin had aggressive designs on Western Europe. Also in 1948 the Soviets aroused concern in the West with their pressure on Finland, and subsequent rumors of Soviet pressure on Norway. On May 5 General Lucius Clay, head of American forces in Germany, warned that tension over Berlin threatened to explode into war. Stalin further added to these fears with his blockade of ground routes to Berlin beginning in June 1948.

Facing this Soviet threat, the Western democracies showed that they had learned hard lessons in watching German leader Adolf Hitler's success in picking off nations one at a time while other democracies refused to get involved in hopes that they might be spared the Nazi onslaught. The case of Belgium in particular had been instructive: with a much sturdier army than many now recognize, the Belgians in coordination with the British and French could have made a stout defense against the Germans that would have greatly complicated Hitler's efforts to conquer France. Belgium's unwillingness to coordinate defenses with the British and French lest they give Hitler a pretext to attack left them easy prey. Recognizing the importance of coordinated efforts, the Belgians, Dutch, and Luxembourgers began working with the British and French to arrange common defense in the years following World War II.

Belgian and Dutch leaders, like Britain's Bevin, however, believed American participation in any Western defense arrangement was essential for its credibility. In February 1948 Bevin complained to the U.S. State Department that moves toward a Western European defensive grouping were being undermined by Washington's unwillingness to support such efforts publicly. In March the Americans announced their willingness "to proceed at once in the joint discussions on the establishment of an Atlantic security system." Later in March, Britain, France, Belgium, the Netherlands, and Luxembourg signed the Brussels Pact and established the Western Union. In April the United States adopted policies to support efforts to coordinate defenses in the North Atlantic. There was still some question about the form this coordination would take; the U.S. government preferred to avoid formal ties between the United States and the Western European democracies. Through 1948 and into 1949, several nations—including Britain, Canada, France, and Belgium—emphasized the need for U.S. commitment to a security grouping.

There were Americans who believed that the United States needed to commit formally to an alliance with the Western democracies, and to do so on an equal basis with the other participants. They were able to win the argument within the U.S. government because of the Western European demands for this American involvement. The Western Europeans got what they wanted when the United States entered the alliance, but they also desired more tangible expressions of American commitment. The United States appointed General Dwight D. Eisenhower as the Supreme Commander of the North Atlantic Treaty Organization (NATO), and agreed to station U.S. forces in Europe permanently. These gestures reassured Western Europeans of American commitment to the success of the new alliance.

In explaining the greater American involvement in European affairs after World War II, one must avoid the temptation to make the United States appear too much the passive agent. The United States had a vital interest in the reconstruction of strong, stable democracies in Western Europe. With the weakening of traditional European powers such as Britain, France, Germany, and even the smaller nations such as Belgium and the Netherlands, and with the disarming of Germany at the close of the war, the United States was likely to play a greater role in European affairs simply to prevent the power vacuum from being filled by the Soviets. Many

important American political and diplomatic leaders were interested in seeing the United States play such an expanded role.

Despite the apparent death of isolationism following the attack on Pearl Harbor (7 December 1941), there remained strong strains in American political thinking that would lead the United States toward a stronger role than the nation ultimately played. It was necessary for the Western Europeans to advocate a stronger role for the Americans. Just as some Americans realized that it was in their interest to play a larger role in Europe, there were Europeans who understood that their affairs would be safer, more secure, and more prosperous if the United States were involved. They had seen what Soviet "liberation" had done to Eastern Europe, and they wanted to avoid such tender mercies, but they needed American strength actively involved in the continent. This commonality of interests, especially the willingness of Europeans to promote it, moved Western Europe to encourage American establishment of a sphere of influence including Western Europe.

—JOHN A. SOARES JR.,
CINCINNATI, OHIO

Viewpoint:
No. The United States needed no invitation to extend its influence in Europe and never would have abandoned its interests there.

The United States needed no invitation to establish a major military and economic presence in Europe after World War II (1939–1945). Although many Western European statesmen, sensing their countries' weakness after the bloodiest and most destructive conflict in history, urged Washington to assist their recovery and defense, the U.S. government needed little persuasion.

Defending Europe from a resurgent Germany or an expansionist Soviet Union was no small element in American strategic thinking in the postwar era. Washington's main motivation for favoring the Entente and then entering World War I (1914–1918) on its side in 1917 was to prevent a prospective German victory and continental hegemony. Likewise, although the United States did not enter World War II until Nazi Germany declared war on it in December 1941, it nevertheless showed its strong favoritism and support for Britain and France at earlier stages, embraced policies that suggested a "drift" toward conflict, and ultimately provided the tools and leadership to offer effective resistance.

There was no reason why Washington should have abandoned its determination to prevent any single power from dominating Europe after 1945. As it became more and more apparent that rosy wartime relations among the victorious Allied powers would not endure, many American statesmen justifiably asked themselves whether they had marshaled U.S. power to crush the Nazi threat merely to hand a European hegemony to the Soviet Union. In the event, their reasons for opposing the possible extension of Moscow's influence westward were the same. A single power controlling all or most of Europe's resources would become not just a challenge to American world power but ultimately a threat to the security of the United States and to the survival of its free institutions. A hostile or potentially hostile hegemonic power in Europe could also close its markets to American commerce. Since the United States conducted nearly half of its foreign trade with Europe before 1939, this possibility was never a bright prospect. On a philosophical level, few Americans relished the idea of Europe—where most Americans had deep roots (more recent than today) as well as strong cultural ties—falling under dictatorship. Indeed, one condition of American participation in ending World War I had been President Woodrow Wilson's insistence on the democratization of the Allies' authoritarian opponents and the right of democratic self-determination for the continent's national groups. As imperfect as these policies were in conception and execution, they nevertheless betrayed the growing role of a democratic idealism in American foreign policy. In the early months of World War II, elite as well as popular opinion in the United States greatly favored the French Republic and America's democratic progenitors in Britain. The collapse of French resistance in June 1940 stimulated an outpouring of sympathy, while Britain's heroic resistance elicited more goodwill, increasingly larger packages of material assistance, and, by 1941, what amounted to an undeclared naval war between the United States and Germany.

There was plainly no reason why favorable attitudes toward helping democracies resist dictatorship should have paled after 1945. Few in the American establishment believed that the wartime cooperation with the Soviet Union would endure once Germany had been defeated, and most realized that Moscow's partnership with the West was little more than a marriage of convenience. Indeed, even that temporary alignment had depended on glossy depictions of the Soviet Union as one of the "democracies," a land with a government not all that different from those of the West. Most American leaders and experts on the Soviet Union, however, well knew that it was a dictatorship at least as tyrannical and blood-stained as Nazi Germany, and many speculated that it would use its position as a victor to push its own agenda in the postwar world. The dwindling number who disagreed were isolated and sidelined. Even before the end of World War II, U.S. officials had serious evidence that the Soviets were systematically breaking wartime agreements. It was also apparent that they were using their victor status and military power to place communists in crucial positions in the national governments of Eastern Europe, to sideline non- and anticommunist centers of power throughout the region, and to promote the success of communist parties in Western Europe. Soviet demands for occupation rights in Japan, base rights in Turkey and former Italian colonies, the right to annex territory in northern Iran, the right to join in the occupation of western Germany's industrial Ruhr region, and other demands that exceeded wartime agreements suggested that even if the Soviet Union, as some scholars now argue, was not prepared to go to war with the West, it was nevertheless interested in expanding its influence in the world as far as possible.

Resisting Russian expansion into central Europe and the Middle East was an old theme for the powers of Europe, but in the aftermath of World War II it became clear that they could no longer bear that burden on their own. Britain had played the leading role in checking Russian expansion into the region for more than a century by 1945, but its renewed activity there after the war was more than its weakened economic and military power could sustain. By early 1947, its government called on the United States to foot the bill for military aid to the restored Greek government in its civil war with communist guerillas and to support Turkey in its attempts to resist Soviet pressure to yield base and transit rights. U.S. president Harry S Truman agreed, and in March 1947 he issued a more general statement, the "Truman Doctrine," which committed the United States to resisting communist expansion anywhere. Senior State Department official George F. Kennan's anonymous article, "The Sources of Soviet Conduct," published in the influential journal *Foreign Affairs* in July 1947, but conceived of and reflected in American strategy in the months before, recommended that the United States actively pursue the "containment" of Soviet expansion. This strategy remained the cornerstone of American foreign policy until the 1970s.

Although these developments have been interpreted as the result of an "invitation," there are two reasons not to agree with this assessment. First, Britain's acknowledgment that it

U.S. president Harry S Truman signing the North Atlantic Treaty Organization (NATO) charter in August 1949

(Hulton/Archive by Getty Images)

could not back up the Greeks and the Turks was a candid admission of its weakness—a weakness so great that London could not even maintain the joint role that a true invitation might have implied. Calling on Washington to take over Britain's traditional role of checking Russia in the Eastern Mediterranean was more of a plea or a warning. Had Truman not stepped in, financial constraints would have forced the British to pull out anyway—just as they were pulling out of other costly commitments elsewhere at that time (they left India the same year and Palestine in 1948)—and the balance of power in the region might have changed. Truman was not responding to a simple invitation; his concern was to prevent a direct military threat to strategic lines of communication upon which his country and its closest ally depended for their economic and military strength.

Second, the Truman Doctrine went far beyond addressing Britain's strategic dilemma in the Eastern Mediterranean. Both taken and meant literally, Truman made a unilateral commitment of American power to any place where the Soviet Union or its allies were on the move. For the moment, that seemed to be Greece and Turkey, but later in the year it applied to China, where the anticommunist Nationalist forces began to receive American aid to fight the communists. In the following year it applied to Berlin, where the Soviets blockaded the Western powers' occupation zones of the city in an attempt to force them out. In 1950 it became relevant to South Korea when the communist North invaded with Soviet and later Chinese support. In the early 1950s it served as the basis for supporting French forces in Indochina against communist insurgents and, after the French were defeated, for full-scale American military involvement in the war between North and South Vietnam. It also underlay the rationale for the North Atlantic Treaty Organization (NATO), a multilateral defensive alliance formed with most nations of Western Europe and Canada in April 1949 (and later including Greece and Turkey), as well as the South East Asia Treaty Organization (SEATO), a similar alliance including the United States and its allies in East and South Asia, created in September 1954. The Doctrine's global relevance thus reflected the strategy advanced in existing American strategic thinking after World War II, and encapsulated in Kennan's article, rather than specifically British or general European concerns. Even if the British had explicitly invited the United States to support their efforts in Greece and Turkey, Truman and his advisers were already thinking bigger on their own.

American financial assistance to Western Europe has also been described as the result of an invitation. Yet, this policy, too, is best understood as a wise investment that needed little recommendation by Europeans. Because so much of America's prewar foreign trade had been conducted with Western Europe, it was unsurprising that Washington should have desired the restoration and support of stable and friendly governments there. Regardless of European entreaties for American financial aid, no responsible U.S. politician could have ignored the consequences of letting Western Europe struggle and starve. In the desperate postwar economic situation, communism threatened to gain ground. The French Communist Party won 26.6 percent of the vote in October 1945 elections to fill the assembly charged with drafting a new constitution, while Italian communists did even better in early postwar parliamentary elections. No American elite committed to resisting communist expansion could sit idly by while France and Italy, to say nothing of the other countries of Western Europe, turned Red. Reducing political extremism to impotence was a major goal of the immediate postwar American loans to Western Europe and of the more comprehensive Marshall Plan, a U.S.-directed program of aid to European economies announced by Secretary of State George C. Marshall in June 1947. Although there was some domestic resistance to financing Europe's recovery at a time when America itself was suffering a postwar recession and some potentially serious labor unrest, the desperate situation in Europe and its potential long-term consequences swayed the critics. It is exaggerated to credit American aid with all of Europe's postwar economic success, but it is entirely accurate to acknowledge that it primed the pump at just the right moment and helped moderate European governments marginalize political extremism at an auspicious time. Communism rapidly diminished in the region, while Western European nations recovered their economic health, reoriented their markets toward American imports, and began to redevelop their export industries to stimulate domestic growth. At every step of this vast business deal, Americans plunged in without the need to be invited.

American power after 1945 was not "empire by invitation." It was empire by power. A nation that had just destroyed two strong rivals, had a tradition of resisting any state that sought a European hegemony, was dedicated to ideals of democracy and capitalism, and was strenuously opposed to communism needed no additional motivation to adopt and defend the greatest role any nation has ever played. An economy that produced no less than half of the world's industrial output in 1950—this after several years of European recovery—did not have to be convinced that the stability of its principal markets and trading partners was vital to its continued success. Invitations were superfluous; America had arrived.

–PAUL DU QUENOY,
GEORGETOWN UNIVERSITY

References

John Lewis Gaddis, *We Now Know: Rethinking Cold War History* (Oxford: Clarendon Press, 1997; New York: Oxford University Press, 1997).

George F. Kennan, "The Sources of Soviet Conduct," as X, *Foreign Affairs,* 25 (July 1947): 566–582.

Melvyn P. Leffler, *A Preponderance of Power: National Security, the Truman Administration, and the Cold War* (Stanford, Cal.: Stanford University Press, 1992).

Geir Lundestad, "Empire by Invitation? The United States and Western Europe, 1945–1952," *Journal of Peace Research,* 23 (1986): 263–276.

Charles S. Maier, ed., *The Cold War in Europe: Era of a Divided Continent,* third edition (Princeton: Markus Weiner, 1996).

UNITED STATES AND
WESTERN EUROPE

VELVET REVOLUTIONS

Were the "Velvet Revolutions" of 1989 in Eastern Europe the result of Soviet weakness?

Viewpoint: Yes. The democratic revolutions in Eastern Europe during 1989 were peaceful because the Soviet Union lacked the strength and political will to preserve its position in the region.

Viewpoint: No. The peaceful demise of communist regimes in Eastern Europe occurred because Soviet leader Mikhail Gorbachev favored an end to the Cold War and a strategic partnership with the United States.

Over the course of 1989 Soviet hegemony in Eastern Europe, the product of victory in World War II (1939–1945) that had stood firm for more than four decades, was dissolved. Few observers in any country believed that the Soviet bloc could crumble with such speed, if at all. Within only a few months every communist government in the region fell from power and pro-Western, anticommunist political forces took control. To even greater astonishment, almost all of these transitions occurred peacefully, leading the surprised world to call them "velvet revolutions."

Why would the Soviet Union abandon such a substantial and advantageous position that it and the Russian Empire had coveted for centuries? The "triumphalist" argument, favored by the Western right, maintains that the Soviets realized their major weakness in economic power and military might. Moscow determined that no matter what it did, it would lag further behind its Western opponents. Essentially outspent, the Soviets were forced to retreat from Eastern Europe rather than face violent confrontations that they were likely to lose.

The alternate argument offers a fundamentally different explanation. Focusing on Soviet leader Mikhail Gorbachev, it suggests that he sought a fundamental transformation of the geopolitical structure of the Cold War. Realizing that the continuation of an uneasy truce with the West would be unproductive for both sides, Gorbachev pursued a peaceful program of foreign relations. To that end, he sought to end the division of Europe and to move U.S.-Soviet relations from antagonism to strategic partnership. An integral part of this strategy included the withdrawal of coercive Soviet power from Eastern Europe. Hoping to retain influence or at least "friendly" governments in the region, Gorbachev wanted to ensure Soviet security without preserving a pillar of contentious relations with the West. The "velvet revolutions" were necessary for his success.

**Viewpoint:
Yes. The democratic
revolutions in Eastern Europe
during 1989 were peaceful because
the Soviet Union lacked the strength
and political will to preserve its
position in the region.**

A storm of victorious democratic revolutions swept throughout Eastern Europe in 1989. These revolutions, with the exception of the Romanian uprising of December, involved no bloodshed and were named the "velvet revolutions" after the peaceful downfall of the communist regime in Czechoslovakia. To much surprise, the region where major Soviet foreign interventions had taken place and about 565,000 Soviet troops were stationed witnessed the unprecedented retreat of Moscow from its Eastern European empire. The majority of Western historians have come to the conclusion that the surprising success of the velvet revolutions seems to lie in the loss of political legitimacy of ruling communist parties, the progressive decay of the Soviet superpower that made it difficult to dominate Eastern Europe, and Soviet leader Mikhail Gorbachev's "hands-off" policy as the revolutions proceeded. Many scholars have credited Gorbachev for the dramatic transition in Eastern Europe and rightly point out that it could not have happened without Soviet *perestroika* (a program of economic and political restructuring).

At the same time, while addressing the so-called Gorbachev factor, it is important to look not just at Gorbachev's actions but why he took them. It was the rapid decline of Soviet power that influenced Moscow's calculations and/or miscalculations in the region, rather than Soviet goodwill, which contributed to the tremendous success of the velvet revolutions. Since almost all of these communist regimes were established by the Soviets, directly or indirectly, and none of them enjoyed real popular legitimacy, Soviet weakness was a key to their collapse. Moreover, as British historian Richard Vinen has noted, "the fall of communism should not be seen as a single dramatic event, but rather as the combination of changes that had been going on for years." Soviet weakness complemented a combination of socio-economic, political, military-strategic, ideological, and cultural trends and developments, all of which became increasingly interrelated and interdependent by the end of the 1980s.

Since the 1970s the communist countries of Eastern Europe moved into a protracted crisis as a result of the obsolescence of their industrial base and infrastructure, overcentralization, inflexibility, inefficiency, and corruption of their state-run economic system. This host of deficiencies led to several emergencies, misguided investments, and increasing consumer shortages. The disarray had particular and far-reaching consequences for Moscow's Eastern European satellites, especially for economic ties among the communist members of the Council for Mutual Economic Assistance (CMEA), the main pillar of Soviet economic dominance. The Soviet Union conducted more than half of its trade with CMEA countries, which benefited because of artificially low prices for energy resources, which were their principal imports from the Soviet Union. The Union of Soviet Socialist Republics (U.S.S.R.) in its turn, in fact, subsidized its Eastern European allies, paying relatively high prices for the machinery and consumer goods that Moscow imported from Eastern Europe. The Kremlin deliberately maintained such an expensive system of economic relationships for largely political reasons—to keep the region closely tied to the Soviet Union. As the economic situation in the U.S.S.R. deteriorated, Moscow became unable to provide its allies with raw materials and energy at previous levels and was forced to calculate the growing economic burden of maintaining its empire in Eastern Europe. The CMEA trade arrangements became too costly to sustain. This difficulty led, also, to mounting economic problems in the region, which already had all the indicators of systemic deterioration, similar to the Soviet crisis, and, consequently, to increasing popular frustration and dissatisfaction with the existing social and political system. Even some elements within the local ruling elite were looking beyond the Iron Curtain to gain much-needed foreign credits and investments.

The progressing decline of the U.S.S.R.'s military power—caused by technological backwardness, economic crisis, and many ills of the Soviet system—was of particular importance for prerevolutionary developments in Eastern Europe, as most of the communist regimes there were established and/or supported by Russian bayonets. Since the mid 1970s the Soviet Union had been slipping behind the West in terms of military power, particularly in technology and weaponry. The Russian defeat in the Afghan War (1979–1989) demonstrated the mounting shortcomings and inefficiencies of the Soviet military machine. It also damaged Moscow's prestige among the Eastern Europeans and proved the limits of military power in maintaining imperial control. Additionally, Soviet military weakness compromised the U.S.S.R.'s security guarantees to its satellites.

Worker preparing a statue of Klement Gottwald, president of Czechoslovakia from 1948 to 1953, for removal, January 1990. The graffito reads "Murderer of the Nation"

(Czech News Agency).

At the same time, these developments contributed to the decline of the Warsaw Pact, a main tool of Moscow's political and military control over Eastern Europe since its creation in 1955. As the Eastern European militaries were organized on the Soviet model—and the U.S.S.R. was also the main source of weaponry, munitions, supplies, and training for the Pact's armies—dependence on the Soviets unavoidably led to growing military obsolescence. Conversely, the military weakness and uncertain loyalty of the satellites made Eastern Europe a dubious asset in the strategic sense. Moreover, the real strategic importance of this buffer zone for the U.S.S.R. had been reduced in the age of nuclear weapons and intercontinental ballistic missiles (ICBMs), particularly when the Reagan administration surprised the Soviets with the "Star Wars" challenge—the development of an antiballistic missile defense system—announced in March 1983.

The growing international isolation of the Soviet Union, which resulted from its antagonism with almost all the industrial powers (the United States, Western Europe, and Japan) and China, contributed to disagreements between Moscow and its satellites. For example, in 1983–1984, defiant Hungary, Romania, East Germany, and Bulgaria objected to the Soviet hard line toward West Germany after the deployment of U.S. intermediate range nuclear missiles there.

Soviet decline had also demonstrated by the end of the twentieth century that the dogmas of Marxism-Leninism, the ideological and cultural foundation of communist society and the unifying bond of the Soviet Empire, simply did not work. This realization had devastating consequences for the Soviet imperial domain. As Zbigniew K. Brzezinski put it in his *The Grand Failure: The Birth and Death of Communism in the Twentieth Century* (1989), the ideological crisis of communism intensified nationalist aspirations in Eastern Europe and resentment toward the Soviet model of development. An increasing number of Eastern Europeans viewed Russian hegemony as a source of growing social, economic, and cultural retardation. Accordingly, they considered the elimination of Soviet domination and removal from power of its local leaders as necessary preconditions to social, political, economic, and cultural rebirth.

Communist ideology contributed enormously to the intellectual decline of the Soviet and Eastern European ruling elite, limiting significantly their understanding of the situation, while developing further their inflexibility and inability to pursue high-risk strategies in unfavorable domestic and international conditions—despite the presence of brilliant people

in party apparatus, governmental agencies, intelligence services, press, think tanks, and academia. This factor was of particular importance in weakening the U.S.S.R. *Perestroika* affected Eastern Europe in several interrelated ways. Since 1985 many half-measured attempts by the Kremlin to revitalize the socialist system, while not addressing the core of its crisis, interplayed with incompetence and corruption of the political establishment to make the bad economic situation much worse. These measures in fact disrupted and distorted the communist economy—and accelerated the collapse of the Soviet social and economic infrastructure—while the atmosphere of *glasnost* (openness) had demonstrated to the Eastern Europeans the real extent of physical, social, environmental, and moral degradation of Soviet society. Conversely, Moscow's initiatives to reform the Soviet bloc economies on the *perestroika* model turned out to be deeply destabilizing for the CMEA and its member states. Facing the cumulative consequences of the disintegration of the Soviet economy, some representatives of Moscow's political and academic elite discussed new priorities for Eastern European policy, suggesting the deconstruction of the empire. At the same time, *perestroika* and *glasnost* had a kind of revolutionizing effect on Eastern Europe, as they legitimized the idea of political and economic reforms throughout the Soviet bloc and prepared the ground for major changes.

After 1985 there were also major transformations in the foreign policy of the U.S.S.R., including the retreat from the confrontation with the West, stimulated by Soviet domestic and international weakness. While discussing the impact of those weaknesses on Eastern Europe, many historians point out that Gorbachev did not have a grand design for the region. Rather, his policy emerged gradually as a result of incremental changes and adjustments forced by the Soviet decline.

Contrary to the Kremlin's expectations, the effect of these changes eroded Soviet influence in the region. Initially, in 1985–1987, Moscow emphasized the close political, economic, and military integration of the bloc, almost completely ignoring the growing problems and contradictions. After 1987 the Soviet leadership encouraged the Eastern European old guard to adopt reforms and tried to create more-balanced relations with its satellites, based on partnership and tolerance of diversity. Rather than strengthening cohesion and Soviet influence within the bloc, however, Kremlin initiatives accentuated the divisions among communist states, splitting the Warsaw Pact into three camps: the reformist camp (the U.S.S.R., Poland, and Hungary), the so-called rejectionist or conservative camp (East Germany, Czechoslovakia, and Romania), and the middle camp (Bulgaria).

Additionally, the bureaucratic inefficiency of the decision-making process in Soviet East European policy—as well as the rivalry between the Foreign Ministry on the one side and the Communist Party apparatus, the *Komitet Gosudarstvennoy Bezopasnosti* (Committee for State Security, KGB), and the Ministry of Defense on the other—intensified significantly during the *perestroika* years and distracted the Kremlin's attention from the warning signals about the gathering storm in Eastern Europe. That is why, pushing for reforms and changes in Eastern Europe, the Soviet leadership over-optimistically perceived itself as a catalyst and chief guarantor of the democratic evolution inside the Iron Curtain and never anticipated the speed and character of the coming changes. Nor did it expect that the promotion of the principle of the freedom of choice would give way to the revolutionary surge and removal of communist regimes in Eastern Europe.

The Soviet reaction to the revolutions of 1989 was spontaneous and rather chaotic. Although there were some indications of KGB attempts to manipulate events in Czechoslovakia and Romania, these actions were too ill coordinated and limited to ensure Soviet control over the events. An increasingly divided U.S.S.R., already paralyzed by deepening domestic crisis, would not and could not intervene to uphold the disintegrating communist regimes in Eastern Europe. Additionally, the possibility of Soviet military intervention in 1989 was completely ruled out because of the "Afghan syndrome" within Soviet society and Gorbachev's unwillingness to risk his new détente with the West. Reversing the previous Soviet policy of armed intervention to prevent unwanted changes within the Warsaw Pact countries (the Brezhnev Doctrine), Gorbachev adopted a "Sinatra Doctrine" of letting the East Europeans "do it their way," allowing political upheavals in the satellite countries to run their course. While formulating the new Soviet doctrine of noninterference, Gorbachev referred to the smooth and peaceful democratic transitions in Poland and Hungary, hoping that the willingness of the Soviet Union to accept political pluralism within the bloc would support the pro-Moscow reformers and/or allow the U.S.S.R. to preserve its influence in the new Eastern Europe. The Kremlin's withdrawal of the threat of military intervention made it clear to hard liners in the German Democratic Republic, Czechoslovakia, and Bulgaria that they could no longer count on Soviet support. This move left them with no choice but to surrender power, as they did in October–November 1989. The victorious democratization of Eastern Europe made the neo-Stalinist regime in Romania hopelessly isolated and irrelevant. In December 1989 it was violently overthrown.

The Sinatra Doctrine also reflected Moscow's desire to prevent the West from exploiting the revolutionary developments in Eastern Europe, while gaining time to preserve and consolidate Soviet influence. During the Malta summit between Gorbachev and U.S. president George H. W. Bush in December 1989, the Soviets attempted to seek an understanding with the United States about the U.S.S.R.'s limits of involvement in the turbulent region. For the weakening U.S.S.R. this strategy was too late to be effective. The Soviet proposition reflected also Moscow's inability to face new and unfavorable realities and acknowledged for the first time since World War II that the fate of Eastern Europe was dependent on local political forces, which were becoming increasingly anticommunist and anti-Soviet. It should also be noted that even in January 1989 the Soviets were still guided by wishful thinking about U.S.S.R.-led reforms. The Soviets failed to respond positively to a similar Western initiative about superpower consultations and understanding on Eastern Europe (the "Yalta concept," as some historians called it), delivered to Gorbachev by former U.S. secretary of state Henry Kissinger. This failure illustrated, to the weakness of the Soviet position, that Gorbachev had not engineered the tumbling of the Eastern European communist dominoes nor had he foreseen the pace and sequence of events.

Many Soviet mistakes, misperceptions, and miscalculations immediately before and during the velvet revolutions were connected with the fundamental weakness of the U.S.S.R.'s posture in Eastern Europe. As many historians agree, for more than forty years Moscow attempted to impose an alien political, economic, social, and cultural system on unwilling people from the Baltic to the Balkans. Having misunderstood the historical nature of Soviet domination in Eastern Europe and forced by Soviet weakness to undertake political changes, Gorbachev advocated reforms and more openness within the Soviet bloc in the unrealistic hope that its members would voluntarily remain together under Soviet influence. In fact, this policy unleashed forces that took on a dynamic of their own and resulted in the collapse of communism in Eastern Europe.

–PETER RAINOW,
SAN MATEO, CALIFORNIA

VELVET REVOLUTIONS

WE ARE FACED WITH IMMENSE WORK

On 7 December 1988 Soviet leader Mikhail Gorbachev addressed the United Nations about conditions in the Soviet Union and Eastern Europe:

Freedom of choice is a universal principle to which there should be no exceptions. We have not come to the conclusion of the immutability of this principle simply through good motives. We have been led to it through impartial analysis of the objective processes of our time. The increasing varieties of social development in different countries are becoming an ever more perceptible feature of these processes. This relates to both the capitalist and socialist systems. The variety of sociopolitical structures which has grown over the last decades from national liberation movements also demonstrates this. This objective fact presupposes respect for other people's vie[w]s and stands, tolerance, a preparedness to see phenomena that are different as not necessarily bad or hostile, and an ability to learn to live side by side while remaining different and not agreeing with one another on every issue.

The de-ideologization of interstate relations has become a demand of the new stage. We are not giving up our convictions, philosophy, or traditions. Neither are we calling on anyone else to give up theirs. Yet we are not going to shut ourselves up within the range of our values. That would lead to spiritual impoverishment, for it would mean renouncing so powerful a source of development as sharing all the original things created independently by each nation. In the course of such sharing, each should prove the advantages of his own system, his own way of life and values, but not through words or propaganda alone, but through real deeds as well. That is, indeed, an honest struggle of ideology, but it must not be carried over into mutual relations between states. Otherwise we simply will not be able to solve a single world problem; arrange broad, mutually advantageous and equitable cooperation between peoples; manage rationally the achievements of the scientific and technical revolution; transform world economic relations; protect the environment; overcome underdevelopment; or put an end to hunger, disease, illiteracy, and other mass ills. Finally, in that case, we will not manage to eliminate the nuclear threat and militarism.

Such are our reflections on the natural order of things in the world on the threshold of the 21st century. We are, of course, far from claiming to have infallible truth, but having subjected the previous realities—realities that have arisen again—to strict analysis, we have come to the conclusion that it is by precisely such approaches that we must search jointly for a way to achieve the supremacy of the common human idea over the countless multiplicity of centrifugal forces, to preserve the vitality of a civilization that is possibl[y] th[e] only one in the universe. . . .

Our country is undergoing a truly revolutionary upsurge. The process of restructuring is gaining pace; we started by elaborating the theoretical concepts of restructuring; we had to assess the nature and scope of the problems, to interpret the lessons of the past, and to express this in the form of political conclusions and programs. This was done. The theoretical work, the re-interpretation of what had happened, the final elaboration, enrichment, and correction of political stances have not ended. They continue. However, it was fundamentally important to start from an overall concept, which is already now being confirmed by the experience of past years, which has turned out to be generally correct and to which there is no alternative.

In order to involve society in implementing the plans for restructuring it had to be made more truly democratic. Under the badge of democratization, restructuring has now encompassed politics, the economy, spiritual life, and ideology. We have unfolded a radical economic reform, we have accumulated experience, and from the new year we are transferring the entire national economy to new forms and work methods. Moreover, this means a profound reorganization of production relations and the realization of the immense potential of socialist property.

In moving toward such bold revolutionary transformations, we understood that there would be errors, that there would be resistance, that the novelty would bring new problems. We foresaw the possibility of breaking in individual sections. However, the profound democratic reform of the entire system of power and government is the guarantee that the overall process of restructuring will move steadily forward and gather strength.

We completed the first stage of the process of political reform with the recent decisions by the U.S.S.R. Supreme Soviet on amendments to the Constitution and the adoption of the Law on Elections. Without stopping, we embarked upon the second stage of this. At which the most important task will be working on the interaction between the central government and the republics, settling relations between nationalities on the principles of Leninist internationalism bequeathed to us by the great revolution and, at the same time, reorganizing the power of the Soviets locally. We are faced with immense work. At the same time we must resolve major problems.

We are more than fully confident. We have both the theory, the policy and the vanguard force of restructuring a party which is also restructuring itself in accordance with the new tasks and the radical changes throughout society. And the most important thing: all peoples and all generations of citizens in our great country are in favor of restructuring.

We have gone substantially and deeply into the business of constructing a socialist state based on the rule of law. A whole series of new laws has been prepared or is at a completion stage. Many of them come into force as early as 1989, and we trust that they will correspond to the highest standards from the point of view of ensuring the rights of the individual. Soviet democracy is to acquire a firm, normative base. This means such acts as the Law on Freedom of Conscience, on *glasnost,* on public associations and organizations, and on much else. There are now no people in places of imprisonment in the country who have been sentenced for their political or religious convictions. It is proposed to include in the drafts of the new laws additional guarantees ruling out any form of persecution on these bases. Of course, this does not apply to those who have committed real criminal or state offenses: espionage, sabotage, terrorism, and so on, whatever political or philosophical views they may hold.

The draft amendments to the criminal code are ready and waiting their turn. In particular, those articles relating to the use of the supreme measure of punishment are being reviewed. The problem of exit and entry is also being resolved in a humane spirit, including the case of leaving the country in order to be reunited with relatives. As you know, one of the reasons for refusal of visas is citizens' possession of secrets. Strictly substantiated terms for the length of time for possessing secrets are being introduced in advance. On starting work at a relevant institution or enterprise, everyone will be made aware of this regulation. Disputes that arise can be appealed under the law. Thus the problem of the so-called "refuseniks" is being removed.

We intend to expand the Soviet Union's participation in the monitoring mechanism on human rights in the United Nations and within the framework of the pan-European process. We consider that the jurisdiction of the International Court in The Hague with respect to interpreting and applying agreements in the field of human rights should be obligatory for all states.

Within the Helsinki process, we are also examining an end to jamming of all the foreign radio broadcasts to the Soviet Union. On the whole, our credo is as follows: Political problems should be solved only by political means, and human problems only in a humane way. . . .

Today I can inform you of the following: The Soviet Union has made a decision on reducing its armed forces. In the next two years, their numerical strength will be reduced by 500,000 persons, and the volume of conventional arms will also be cut considerably. These reductions will be made on a unilateral basis, unconnected with negotiations on the mandate for the Vienna meeting. By agreement with our allies in the Warsaw Pact, we have made the decision to withdraw six tank divisions from the GDR, Czechoslovakia, and Hungary, and to disband them by 1991. Assault landing formations and units, and a number of others, including assault river-crossing forces, with their armaments and combat equipment, will also be withdrawn from the groups of Soviet forces situated in those countries. The Soviet forces situated in those countries will be cut by 50,000 persons, and their arms by 5,000 tanks. All remaining Soviet divisions on the territory of our allies will be reorganized. They will be given a different structure from today's which will become unambiguously defensive, after the removal of a large number of their tanks. . . .

By this act, just as by all our actions aimed at the demilitarization of international relations, we would also like to draw the attention of the world community to another topical problem, the problem of changing over from an economy of armament to an economy of disarmament. Is the conversion of military production realistic? I have already had occasion to speak about this. We believe that it is, indeed, realistic. For its part, the Soviet Union is ready to do the following. Within the framework of the economic reform we are ready to draw up and submit our internal plan for conversion, to prepare in the course of 1989, as an experiment, the plans for the conversion of two or three defense enterprises, to publish our experience of job relocation of specialists from the military industry, and also of using its equipment, buildings, and works in civilian industry[.] It is desirable that all states, primarily the major military powers, submit their national plans on this issue to the United Nations.

Source: *"Gorbachev's Speech to the U.N.," Cold War: Historical Documents, CNN Interactive <http://www.cnn.com/SPECIALS/cold.war/episodes/23/documents/gorbachev/>.*

VELVET REVOLUTIONS

Viewpoint:
No. The peaceful demise of communist regimes in Eastern Europe occurred because Soviet leader Mikhail Gorbachev favored an end to the Cold War and a strategic partnership with the United States.

The "velvet revolutions" of 1989 were not the result of Soviet weakness. Although the Soviet Union was politically and economically weakened, its military was still quite strong. Yet, these simplistic assessments of strength and weakness do not explain Soviet policy in Eastern Europe. The peaceful transformation of Eastern Europe occurred because General Secretary Mikhail Gorbachev wanted a peaceful conclusion to the Cold War and the beginning of an honest strategic partnership with the Americans.

Certainly, in the 1980s the Soviet Union was weaker than it had been in political and economic terms. Gorbachev's selection as leader in March 1985 signified the recognition by members of the Politburo of the serious problems plaguing their country. Gorbachev, in an effort to modernize the economy, introduced sweeping reforms in all aspects of Soviet life; he believed that real economic reform could only be achieved through simultaneous economic and political changes. He undertook a parallel transformation of foreign policy to allow a reordering of domestic economic priorities.

Although Soviet weakness was not responsible for the velvet revolutions, it played a role in fomenting change in Eastern Europe. Gorbachev hoped that the Eastern European countries would follow his lead in reforming their economic and political systems. He frequently cajoled more traditionally minded leaders to adopt programs of reform similar to his own. His efforts in that respect met with limited success. Yet, his reforms often had unintended effects. Gorbachev did not foresee the delegitimizing effect that *glasnost* (openness) would have on the regimes of Eastern Europe, which led to growing protests against communist rule. Eastern Europeans began to question the Soviet role in their region and the role of communist parties in their countries. By 1989 this discontent led to demonstrations that culminated in revolution.

The Soviet Union, however, did not suffer major problems in its military sector. Gorbachev had withdrawn Soviet troops from Afghanistan by February 1989, thus freeing up

greater military resources. If Gorbachev had wanted to intervene in Eastern Europe, he could have done so. It is unclear, though, what effect such an action would have had. Unlike earlier invasions, in Hungary (1956) and Czechoslovakia (1968), Soviet intervention would likely not have enjoyed widespread Warsaw Pact support. If such a maneuver had reasserted temporary control, maintaining it would likely have been difficult and would have deprived the Soviet Union of important, scarce resources at a time when it was struggling to reform its own economy and political system. Gorbachev's decision not to intervene, however, was not determined by an analysis of military and political resources.

The most important factor that shaped Gorbachev's attitude was a new conception of the place of Eastern Europe in the Soviet empire, a rethinking that began in the late Brezhnev period. Soviet leader Leonid Brezhnev loosened the political relationship between the Soviet Union and Eastern Europe and attempted to change the economic relationship as well. This policy shift was a result of the high costs of continuing Soviet domination. Scholar F. Stephen Larrabee refers to this process as a movement from "cohesion to corrosion." Gorbachev increasingly questioned the need for the maintenance of the Eastern European bloc; he did not see the region as being as economically or strategically vital to the Soviet Union as it once was. This reassessment was especially true in light of the strain that holding on to Eastern Europe placed on the Soviet economy.

From a strategic point of view, Eastern Europe was no longer an essential buffer zone. This shift was caused in large part by the decline of Cold War tensions, characterized by Gorbachev's positive relations with U.S. president Ronald Reagan, British prime minister Margaret Thatcher, and West German chancellor Helmut Kohl. Similarly, Gorbachev's efforts to separate foreign policy from ideology rendered the preservation of the bloc less necessary. Gorbachev's ideological innovations, such as his rejection of the notion of inevitable conflict between the communist and capitalist systems, were essential to the peaceful end of the Cold War.

Even if it was not articulated until somewhat later, Gorbachev's "new political thinking" signified an end to the Brezhnev Doctrine, whereby the Soviet Union had claimed the right to intervene in a socialist state's development if it threatened common interests, as defined by Moscow. Gorbachev's repudiation of this doctrine effectively freed the East European countries to abandon communism. This shift and the Soviet withdrawal from Afghanistan were the results of a reassessment of the security interests of the Soviet Union and of the importance of ideology in determining military action. Gorbachev asserted that the Soviet Union would no longer use force as a means of supporting unpopular communist governments, as it had earlier in Hungary and Czechoslovakia. In light of the new Soviet approach to relations with the West, Gorbachev was able to announce in a United Nations (UN) speech in December 1988 that the Eastern European nations need not fear Soviet intervention and that he recognized their "freedom to choose" their respective political and economic systems. This new policy emboldened the Soviet and Eastern European peoples to express and mobilize their opposition. An examination of the dramatic upheavals of 1989 should not deny the significant role played by the people of Eastern Europe.

Gorbachev's strategic shift can be seen most clearly in the Soviet decision not to intervene in Poland in 1989. In partially free elections there, Solidarity, a dissident rival of the Polish Communist Party, garnered a majority of legislative seats. Gorbachev advised the head of the Polish Communist Party that the Soviets would accept a coalition government, confirming his rhetoric regarding the Eastern Europeans' "right to choose." By fall 1989 there was a noncommunist government in place. In allowing this first domino to fall, Gorbachev permitted the overwhelmingly peaceful collapse of communism in Eastern Europe and the Soviet Union. The developments in Poland were mirrored by similarly dramatic changes in Hungary, the German Democratic Republic, Czechoslovakia, and Romania. The change of power in Romania, however, was less peaceful than the revolutions elsewhere in Eastern Europe.

Some historians emphasize the extent to which Western liberal thought influenced Gorbachev's thinking in examining his decision to allow the dismantling of the Berlin Wall and his unwillingness to intervene in the velvet revolutions. Indeed, political scientist Robert D. English has described a process by which the Soviet elite, including Gorbachev and his supporters, reevaluated questions of national identity, ideology, and foreign policy caused by a long-term Westernization process. Exposure to contemporary Western political and social ideas as well as European leftist thought shaped the attitudes of Gorbachev and other Soviet elite toward the Soviet sphere of influence. In this new ideological context, Gor-

bachev would not compel the East Europeans to follow his course.

As Eastern Europe became less strategically and economically important to Gorbachev and the Soviet Union, the United States and Western Europe became more so. Gorbachev was especially focused on concluding conventional- and strategic-arms reduction agreements with the West. Gorbachev had been making considerable progress with Reagan, beginning with their 1985 summit in Geneva. Similarly, he hoped to gain financial and technical assistance from Western countries such as the United States and the Federal Republic of Germany. Soviet support for "new political thinking" in Eastern Europe considerably influenced a relaxation of tensions with the West and paved the way to Western economic assistance. Gorbachev regarded these objectives as essential to the survival and recovery of the Soviet Union. His interest in developing myriad positive relations with the West guided his actions concerning Eastern Europe; Gorbachev did not want to jeopardize his new relationship with the West. Gorbachev's avoidance of bloodshed in Eastern Europe and within the Soviet Union was in part a result of these outside factors. To provoke international outrage through large-scale violence such as that used by the Chinese government in the Tiananmen Square massacre (June 1989) would not have served Gorbachev's goal of modernization for the Soviet Union. Thus, Gorbachev's two aims were in conflict: the need to strengthen the Soviet Union to ensure its continued existence and the desire to prevent a fracturing or dissolution of the Soviet empire.

Gorbachev was unwilling to resort to large-scale bloodshed to maintain the informal Soviet empire in Eastern Europe. He acted in compliance with his declaration in 1988 that the Eastern European countries had the "freedom to choose." The Soviet Union did not intervene when the Berlin Wall fell in East Germany in November 1989, nor when peaceful political events in Eastern Europe resulted in a rejection of communism. Gorbachev demonstrated his recognition of the futility of Soviet military intervention: "What were we supposed to do? Should we have used axes and tanks and tried to teach them another lesson in how to live?" These words, however, do not indicate Soviet weakness, rather a more sophisticated worldview that no longer saw the continued membership of Eastern Europe in the Soviet empire as a means to a strategic and peaceful relationship with the West.

–SARAH SNYDER,
GEORGETOWN UNIVERSITY

VELVET REVOLUTIONS

References

Archie Brown, *The Gorbachev Factor* (Oxford & New York: Oxford University Press, 1996).

Zbigniew K. Brzezinski, *The Grand Failure: The Birth and Death of Communism in the Twentieth Century* (New York: Scribners, 1989).

John B. Dunlop, *The Rise of Russia and the Fall of the Soviet Empire* (Princeton: Princeton University Press, 1993).

Robert D. English, *Russia and the Idea of the West: Gorbachev, Intellectuals, and the End of the Cold War* (New York: Columbia University Press, 2000).

Raymond L. Garthoff, *The Great Transition: American-Soviet Relations and the End of the Cold War* (Washington, D.C.: Brookings Institution, 1994).

F. Stephen Larrabee, "Soviet Policy toward Eastern Europe: Interests, Instruments, and Trends," in *Soviet Foreign Policy in a Changing World*, edited by Robbin F. Laird and Erik P. Hoffmann (Berlin & New York: De Gruyter, 1986; New York: Aldine, 1986), pp. 531–548.

Janice Gross Stein, "Political Learning by Doing: Gorbachev as Uncommitted Thinker and Motivated Learner," *International Organization* (Spring 1994): 155–183.

Angela E. Stent, *Russia and Germany Reborn: Unification, the Soviet Collapse, and the New Europe* (Princeton: Princeton University Press, 1999).

Richard Vinen, *A History in Fragments: Europe in the Twentieth Century* (Cambridge, Mass.: Da Capo Press, 2001).

VERSAILLES TREATY

Did the Versailles Treaty (1919) precipitate the rise of Nazism?

Viewpoint: Yes. The harsh terms of the World War I peace treaty created an environment of mistrust, unrest, and economic hardship that provided fertile ground for German political extremism.

Viewpoint: No. The Versailles Treaty was a feasible peace settlement that had little to do with the rise of Nazism in Germany.

The conclusion of peace with Germany after World War I (1914–1918) came at French king Louis XIV's splendorous Versailles palace in 1919. The treaty, which the Germans were not allowed to negotiate, required Berlin to accept all responsibility for the war, pay large but undefined reparations to the victorious Allies, accept serious long-term limitations on the size and power of its armed forces, yield its colonial possessions, and cede important parts of its European territory.

Because Adolf Hitler came to power in Germany less than fourteen years after the Treaty of Versailles was signed, many historians have focused on its punitive terms to explain the rise of Nazism. National guilt, economic debility, military disarmament, and territorial truncation all seemed to play into the hands of an extremist movement that promised recovery and a redress of Germany's grievances. When the Germans supported Hitler, the argument follows, they were rejecting the consequences of the peace treaty.

A revisionist argument has reexamined this idea, however. Emphasizing the broader context of European diplomacy, it maintains that the Treaty of Versailles was far from exceptional and no more punitive than other peace settlements in modern European history. Many treaties before Versailles had also included territorial transfers, financial indemnities, and disarmament provisions without leading to a rise in political extremism in the defeated country. From that perspective the rise of Nazism after World War I was much more an exception than a rule, one that should provoke deeper reassessments of German history and politics.

Viewpoint:
Yes. The harsh terms of the World War I peace treaty created an environment of mistrust, unrest, and economic hardship that provided fertile ground for German political extremism.

The Treaty of Versailles (1919) was a critical factor in the rise of Nazism in Germany. The three major victorious powers of World War I (1914–1918)—Great Britain, France, and the United States imposed terms on the newly established Weimar Republic that succeeded in undermining the young democracy's legitimacy, paving the way for new extremist movements to carry out radical revisionist plans.

German acceptance of the "war guilt clause," Article 231 of the Versailles Treaty, was perhaps the most onerous part of the entire document. The article proclaimed that Germany alone was responsible for the war by carrying out an attack against France and Belgium and extending the war from Russia to Western Europe. These actions, in addition to certain war-crimes charges that were leveled at the Kaiser and other officials, made the Germans liable for impressive legal, monetary, and territorial penalties.

The first of these penalties was Germany's exclusion from major international agreements. Germany was not allowed to send representatives to the Versailles conference. Britain, France, the United States, Italy, and Japan sent two commissioners each to dictate terms of the treaty, while most decisions were made in consultation by the British, French, and American leaders. Moreover, the failure of the newly formed League of Nations to admit Germany as a member revealed contempt for Germany as a pariah of the civilized world. These actions discredited Germany's new republic and put the government on par with the Bolsheviks in terms of their international esteem. The German Republic soon took steps to work with Russia to destabilize the international order. Domestically, Nazis and other German extreme nationalists often worked hand in hand with German communists to destabilize the democracy that they saw as being tainted by the harsh peace imposed by the Western powers. The communists and Nazis soon became so powerful that nontotalitarian parties could not form a coalition on their own. By 1932 the surging popularity of the Nazis and, to a lesser extent, the communists threatened the Weimar Republic's democracy. Authoritarianism now had a growing popular mandate.

Allied demands for reparations had terrible economic and political consequences for both Germany and the world. The German republican government understood that it could only pay its debt of approximately $33 billion by inflating its own currency. By 1923 this inflation had a disastrous effect on the German economy by diluting savings and other liquid assets. The bankruptcy that this runaway inflation caused made the German middle and working class much more embittered, unstable, and willing to listen to extremists for solutions. Because democracy appeared to be turning into such a disastrous experience, what could they lose by trying out an alternative solution? Indeed, for German patriots leery of the Soviet-controlled German Communist Party, Adolf Hitler was seen as the country's last hope.

The German inflation crisis had a profound international impact. The collapse of German markets caused other European countries to restrict their trade. The resulting inactivity of international markets caused bankruptcies and depression throughout the continent. Economic hardship caused many Westerners to question the democracies that were at least partially responsible for the crisis. The rise of far-right parties during the interwar years was not limited to just Italy, Germany, and other Eastern European states but instead found audiences throughout the continent.

The Versailles Treaty also called for significant losses of German territory that embittered all future German governments, yet were lenient enough to permit Germany's eventual recovery. While France had sought to redeem the territory of Alsace-Lorraine since its loss in the Franco-Prussian War (1870–1871), French premier Georges Clemenceau's demands at the peace conference surpassed the prior expectations of the Allies and the Germans themselves. In compensation for the loss of the coal mining regions of eastern France, the French claimed the industrial Saar region, a rich, ethnically German region adjacent to Alsace-Lorraine. More significantly, the French also wanted to either annex the Rhineland territory or possibly detach it from Germany as an independent state.

Objections to these claims by U.S. president Woodrow Wilson and British prime minister David Lloyd George resulted in the worst possible solution. The Americans and British only agreed to an Allied occupation of the Saar and the Rhineland for a period of fifteen years, protesting that the seizure of both regions would have violated the Wilsonian principle of self-determination. The treaty also stipulated that the Saar would be allowed to hold a referendum whether it would join Germany or France at the end of its occupation. The Rhineland would be allowed to rejoin Germany, but it would remain permanently demilitarized in order to prevent future German aggression. In reality, these terms ensured that Germany would eventually reclaim the territories but still reminded the German people of their status as a losing power subject to military occupation. Hitler capitalized on these actions by whipping up hatred against those foreign and domestic powers responsible for the occupation of these regions. He later recognized French and British threats as bluffs and occupied the areas with armed forces in full violation of the treaty. Hitler even used Wilson's ploy of a popular plebiscite to justify these actions. As the Western powers' later acquiescence in Munich (1938) to similar actions in Czechoslovakia proved, the English

AWAY WITH VERSAILLES!

During a speech in 1941, German leader Adolf Hitler touched on his long-held views on the Treaty of Versailles (1919):

My programme was to do away with Versailles. People all over the world should not pretend to be simpletons and act as if I had only discovered this programme in 1933, or 1935 or 1937. These gentlemen should only have read what I wrote about myself a thousand times instead of listening to stupid emigre trash. No human being can have stated and written down as often as I what he wanted, and I wrote it again and again: "Away with Versailles!"

And this was not a whim of ours, but the reason was that Versailles was the greatest injustice and the most abject ill-treatment of a great people ever known in history. Without the abolition of this instrument of force—meant to destroy the German people—it would have been impossible to keep this people alive. I came forward as a soldier with this programme, and spoke about it for the first time in 1919. And I have kept to this programme as to a solemn obligation during all the years of the struggle for power. . . . I said to myself: "Thank God, for having brought me to a point where I can put my programme into action."

But again I did not want to do this with violence. I talked as much as any human being can. My speeches in the Reichstag, which cannot be falsified by democratic statesmen, are evidence for history. What offers did I make them! How I begged them to be reasonable! I begged them to see reason and not to interfere with the existence of a great nation. I proved to them that they themselves would derive no benefit from it. I told them it was senseless, and that they would only do themselves harm. What have I not done in all these years to pave the way to an understanding? It would never have been possible to begin this armament race unless others had wanted it. I made proposals to them. However, every proposal, coming as it did from me, was sufficient to cause excitement among a certain Jewish-international-capitalist clique, just as it used to happen formerly in Germany when every reasonable proposal was rejected only because it was made by National Socialists.

My Reichstag speech on 17th May 1933, or for that matter, my later speeches, my innumerable announcements at public meetings, all the memoranda which I wrote in these days—they were all governed by the one idea: whatever happened it must be possible to find a method for a peaceful revision of this Versailles Treaty. That this Treaty was an infamous document, all its authors finally admitted. In fact, the possibility of a revision was to be left open. Only they made the League of Nations the agent for this purpose, and this institution was quite unsuited for its task. The League of Nations was established on the one hand to prevent a revision of the Treaty, and, on the other hand, was to have jurisdiction for such a revision.

At first we were not members of the League, and later German participation amounted in the last analysis to nothing but the payments of yearly installments. That was the only positive thing as far as Germany could see. Of course, Germany was then a Democracy and the Democrats of Berlin begged, on their knees. They went to Geneva before the International Tribunal. They begged: "Give us a revision." Everything was in vain.

I, as a National Socialist, recognized after a few months that this Tribunal would not help us. Accordingly, I did what I could, but I say our adversaries always confused us with the people with whom they had dealt since November 1918. The German nation had nothing in common with those men. That was not Germany. They were miserable individuals kept by England and France, who had doped them. That was not the German nation, and to connect the nation with such people we regard as a defamation.

If the others believed they could apply the same methods to us they applied to the November men, they were greatly mistaken. In that event both sides were at cross purposes. They could not expect us to go to Geneva and continue begging, to receive kicks, and to beg again. If they expected that, they mistook the former German soldier for the traitor of 1918. Of course, those November men could not do anything but give in, for they were in fetters; they were caught in the fetters of that other world. We, however, have no reason to give in to that other world, or do the English perhaps believe that we have an inferiority complex when we compare ourselves with them.

Source: *"Text of Speech by Chancellor Adolf Hitler, at Berlin Sports Palace, January 30, 1941" <http://astro.ocis.temple.edu/~rimmermatext_of_speech_by_chancellor_ado.htm>.*

VERSAILLES TREATY

and French governments accepted that the "principle of national self-determination" trumped the necessity to prevent Germany from reattaining Great Power status.

The German loss of territories to the newly formed Polish Republic had similar consequences. Outside the industrial region of East Upper Silesia, Germany had also lost the so-called Polish corridor that formerly connected the German heartland to East Prussia. The Allies intended to grant this territory and the ethnically German "free city" of Danzig (Gdansk) to the Polish Republic in order to guarantee it access to the sea. The overall effect was to inspire German nationalists to seek revenge.

Likewise, the Allies failed to establish Poland as a state that could contain its German rival. Since the Treaty of Versailles redrew Polish borders by giving tracts of ethnically mixed territory from the former German, Habsburg, and Russian Empires, the government in Warsaw had difficulties in restraining the aspirations of its Ukrainian, German, and Jewish minorities for greater representation. The desire of the German and Soviet governments to reclaim lands populated by these groups created inherent instabilities that prevented democratic development. Poland, which itself had claims to land in Czechoslovakia, was all too willing to cut deals with enemy powers such as Germany to obtain these lands. The morally suspect actions of the Polish government provided Hitler with an important pretext for carrying out his own plans to oppress minorities and make additional territorial demands.

In sum, the Versailles Treaty set the stage for the rise of Hitler and the Nazi movement. The victorious powers of World War I had failed to diminish Germany's power. Although some German territories and wealth were taken away, the effects were only temporary. Within a generation, Hitler was able to play on feelings of economic insecurity and wounded national pride to build a new German state that was more authoritarian and militaristic then ever before. Germany's continued isolation only fed these feelings and helped Hitler to develop a new ideological hatred of foreigners that eventually translated into a program of genocide against the Jews, who, he said, shared blame with the Western powers for Germany's woes. The Nazi government's campaign of conquest and annexations in Eastern Europe soon led to dreams of global domination and a new world war. Never before had a treaty failed so completely to carry out its purpose of world peace.

–YORK NORMAN,
GEORGETOWN UNIVERSITY

Viewpoint:
No. The Versailles Treaty was a feasible peace settlement that had little to do with the rise of Nazism in Germany.

The rise of Adolf Hitler and Nazism is the bleakest aspect of German history. Historians, scholars, and propagandists have explained this occurrence in many ways; one of the most seductive, and flawed, is the argument that the severe terms of the Treaty of Versailles (1919) created a political atmosphere particularly conducive to and ultimately responsible for Hitler's rise to power. The problem with this monocausal explanation is not only that it exculpates the Germans from responsibility but also that it fails to consider the broader historical context in which the treaty existed. Appealing as it might be to impugn the treaty, this charge is too simplistic and thus is misleading. Instead, Versailles should be viewed as a feasible agreement that was entirely consistent with previous treaties in European history.

A common failing of most considerations of the Treaty of Versailles is that it is routinely studied without reference to the other treaties that comprised the Peace of Paris. Although each of these five treaties contained provisions specific to the individual countries involved, Versailles, the first to be written, provided a template for the others. Since Versailles established the rubric for the other treaties, and because all of the former Central Powers experienced a rise in political extremism after the war, some scholars have concluded that the Versailles model produced a political atmosphere especially amenable to the emergence of political extremism. This argument fails to consider the enormous political discontent that existed in nearly every one of these countries before the imposition of the Peace of Paris; in Germany, this discontent became revolutionary even before the conclusion of World War I (1914–1918). The roots of the German extreme right, including Nazism, can be found in the cultural, intellectual, and political history of Imperial Germany. Further, political extremism in Bulgaria, while frequently guised as nationalistic outrage for the loss of territory following the war, grew from cleavages that originated in the nineteenth century, not the Treaty of Neuilly (27 November 1919). Moreover, before the Hungarians signed the Treaty of Trianon (4 June 1920), they experienced 133 days of Communist rule, which was ended by the seizure of power by a right-wing authoritarian regime. The ancillary

treaties of the Paris Peace Settlement may have contributed to this extremism, but it is inappropriate to consider them as the genesis of political extremism in these countries.

The central tenet of most arguments that the Treaty of Versailles led to an atmosphere amenable to the rise of Nazism is that the treaty was too harsh. Professor Gerhard Weinberg has deflected this contention by arguing that the treaty left Germany principally intact and that the peripheral territorial losses Germany suffered hardly constituted a threat to its continued existence. Weinberg further maintains that, excepting Russia, the treaty left Germany as Europe's largest country in both geography and population. Moreover, the war strengthened Germany's geopolitical position because Germany suffered considerably less physical destruction than its principle European opponents. The Treaty of Versailles was harsh, yet the Germans should have anticipated such a peace and were fortunate not to have been subjected to one even more severe.

Although the Germans might have expected a harsher treaty, they also might have predicted stricter enforcement. Treaty conditions that called for the extradition and trial of German officers, bureaucrats, and even Kaiser Wilhelm II produced only forty-five trials and twelve convictions, all of minor officials and officers. Additionally, while the treaty strictly limited the size and power of the German military forces, this provision too proved to be permeable. The Germans consistently evaded the limits on the number of troops by creating

quasi-official paramilitary organizations often headed by military officers officially removed from active duty, establishing secret arms caches spread across Germany, and training pilots and tank crews secretly in the Soviet Union. Further, the dissolution of the Prussian General Staff, as required by Versailles, produced little more than a change in nomenclature as its functions were simply assumed by a "troop office." Arguments claiming that these breaches of the treaty were permitted only because the Allies lacked knowledge of them are incomplete and probably misguided. Thus, while the terms of the treaty were harsh, the Allies, almost from the first days of its implementation, indicated a willingness to tolerate quiet violations of the treaty.

While the German government believed it surrendered under U.S. president Woodrow Wilson's relatively conciliatory Fourteen Points, it should have anticipated a harsh peace. Conflict had long punctuated Franco-German relations. The Treaty of Frankfurt (1871), which ended Prussia's successful war against France, was harsh and encompassed many provisions that anticipated the Treaty of Versailles. It included unprecedented reparations payments, limited military occupation, and the annexation of Alsace-Lorraine, a wealthy and strategically important industrial region that had belonged to France for more than two centuries. The Treaty of Brest-Litovsk (1918), dictated to Russia by Germany only months before the conclusion of World War I, was one of the

Column of French troops marching into the Rhineland city of Mainz, January 1923

(from Stefan Lorant, Sieg Heil! Hail to Victory: An Illustrated History of Germany from Bismarck to Hitler, *1979)*

harshest treaties in modern European history. It deprived Russia of a swath of territory stretching from Finland to Georgia that contained 60 million people and much of Russia's wealth in industry and natural resources. Russia was also obliged to turn over vast quantities of raw materials. Neither of these treaties, however, produced a significant political movement, apart from the desire of French politicians to regain Alsace-Lorraine in the future. Radical political events that followed the signing of these treaties resulted from domestic conditions that existed before their implementation. No argument has suggested that either of these severe treaties was responsible for the development of political radicalism; why is such an argument reserved for the Treaty of Versailles, especially when it was the Germans who had themselves imposed harsh terms when they had been the victors?

One of the most vitriolic critics of the treaty was noted economist John Maynard Keynes, who expressed both his misunderstanding and enmity for the treaty in *The Economic Consequences of the Peace* (1919). Although he wrote the text to oppose the treaty in general, it is frequently considered in connection with the treaty's reparation clauses. While the specific reparations terms were unknown when Keynes published his text, it was properly assumed they would be huge. Many people have seized on the enormity of the final reparations as one of the reasons for the German economic collapse and subsequent rise of Nazism. This contention absolves the German government of responsibility for its poor financial policies and fails to consider the historical trend toward increasingly arduous reparations. The Treaty of Frankfurt had required the French to pay 4 billion francs, an enormous sum, in reparations. Moreover, not only did the latter treaty impose unprecedented reparations on the French, but it also permitted German troops to occupy French territory until the sum was paid in totality. This occupation makes the French occupation of the Ruhr, following German delays in payments, considerably less offensive. The Treaty of Versailles's tremendous reparations were not without precedent.

The decision by the Weimar government to pay the reparations by printing huge amounts of currency was not imposed by the authors of the Treaty of Versailles. This policy, which, it was hoped, would decrease the amount that Germany had to pay in relative terms, resulted in hyperinflation in the early 1920s and imposed financial ruin on the Germans. The subsequent economic crisis may have been the central factor in Hitler's rise to power, but the German government made a conscious decision to create massive inflation. By 1924, only three years after the reparations committee had fixed Germany's debt at $33 billion, the American-sponsored Dawes Plan reduced the overall amount to just $9 billion and provided a package of loans to help finance the payments. Five years later another debt restructuring, organized by American financier Owen Young, further reduced Germany's reparations and extended its payments over a fifty-nine-year period ending in 1988.

Even the tremendous strain that the German government placed on its people with its decision to inflate the currency did not necessitate the rise of Nazism. William Sheridan Allen's *The Nazi Seizure of Power: The Experience of a Single German Town, 1930–1935* (1965) has demonstrated the difficulty that the Nazis faced in coming to power. The most important issue in their rise was the economy, yet even with this powerful tool, the Nazis still had to work every German town, almost daily, to "seize" power. The stabilization of the German economy after 1923 marginalized Nazism and other political extremes. In the 1928 parliamentary elections they received only 2.8 percent of the vote. Their reemergence in the few years that followed came in the wake of the world economic crisis set off in 1929, a depression that hurt Germany especially badly. The poor economic conditions that fueled Nazism's march to power came from declining international trade, ill-conceived government austerity measures, and disappearing foreign investment, not from reparations payments. Indeed, even the drastically reduced payments mandated by the Young Plan only lasted until 1931, when U.S. president Herbert Hoover proposed a moratorium on reparations in light of the economic crisis.

The Nazis' electoral success in the elections of September 1930, July 1932, and November 1932, and Hitler's appointment as chancellor in January 1933 resulted from a variety of factors within German domestic political life. Responsibility for such a complex movement should not be attributed to one cause and certainly not blamed solely on the Treaty of Versailles. The authors of Versailles intended to punish the Central Powers for World War I, but only in Germany did a party as radical as the Nazis establish themselves in the government. The terms of the treaty, moreover, were not dramatically out of step with earlier international peace treaties, particularly those that Germany itself had imposed on France in 1871 and Russia in 1918. Several of Versailles' provisions, including the disarmament clauses and reparations payments, were significantly ameliorated over time. Responsibility for the economic crisis that propelled Hitler to power must instead lie with a German government that failed to deal effectively with its own problems.

–NILES ILLICH,
TEXAS A&M UNIVERSITY

References

Derek H. Aldcroft, *From Versailles to Wall Street, 1919–1929* (London: Lane, 1977; Berkeley: University of California Press, 1977).

William Sheridan Allen, *The Nazi Seizure of Power: The Experience of a Single German Town, 1922–1945,* revised edition (Chicago: Quadrangle Books, 1965).

Gerald J. De Groot, *The First World War* (Houndmills, U.K. & New York: Palgrave, 2001).

John Maynard Keynes, *The Economic Consequences of the Peace* (London: Macmillan, 1919).

Michael J. Lyons, *World War I: A Short History* (Englewood Cliffs, N.J.: Prentice Hall, 1994).

Charles L. Mee Jr., *The End of Order, Versailles, 1919* (New York: Dutton, 1980).

Gerhard Weinberg, *Germany, Hitler, and World War II* (Cambridge: Cambridge University Press, 1995).

VERSAILLES TREATY

VICHY FRANCE

Was Vichy France truly a puppet state of Nazi Germany?

Viewpoint: Yes. Vichy France was a collaborationist regime that fully supported the German war effort, willingly participated in the Holocaust, and forfeited the national sovereignty and honor of France.

Viewpoint: No. Vichy France was at the most an accommodationist regime that favored limited cooperation with Germany to minimize the impact of the defeat and to promote the long-term recovery of national sovereignty.

France's sudden and complete collapse in the summer of 1940 ushered in one of the most controversial and confusing periods in its history. On 10 July an impromptu gathering of the defeated Third Republic's parliament met and voted overwhelmingly to grant extraordinary powers to the aged Marshal Henri-Philippe Pétain, a hero of World War I (1914–1918) and a major political figure of the interwar era. Pétain's regime, based in the provincial spa town of Vichy, was authoritarian in form and represented many long-standing features of France's reactionary and conservative traditions. France's liberation in 1944 displaced the Vichy government in favor of General Charles de Gaulle's Provisional Government, which eventually restored a democratic order.

Historians of modern France have devoted a great deal of energy to studying what Vichy truly meant and what motivations drove its policies. After an initial period of national "purification," in which many Vichy acolytes were tried and punished for their actions during the war, the French nation tried hard to bury its Vichy past. By the late 1960s, however, a rising generation of students began to raise new doubts and put forward new accusations about France's domestic government during World War II (1939–1945). Partly encouraged by Marcel Ophüls' scathing documentary movie *Le chagrin et la pitié* (*The Sorrow and the Pity,* 1971), the older generation of Frenchmen was forced to confront difficult questions about what it had done in its wartime youth.

One of the major questions that historians have sought to answer is whether Vichy France was a collaborationist regime. American historian Robert O. Paxton, in *Vichy France: Old Guard and New Order, 1940–1944* (1972), argued that Vichy sought in almost every way to collaborate with the Germans. Pétain's government, he charged, went out of its way to please Nazi Germany by seeking a formal alliance, by participating in the Holocaust, by turning over forced laborers to Germany, and by trying its best to fulfill other German demands. Some subsequent studies confirmed Paxton's controversial allegations. Yet, in recent years, a growing revisionist historiography has detected much greater ambiguity in the Vichy years. New students of Vichy have argued that what occurred was little more than an accommodation, with many elements of French government and society doing the minimum necessary to survive Germany's oppressive occupation, and using their position in some ways to thwart the occupier's maximum goals through sloppy conformity.

Viewpoint:
Yes. Vichy France was a collaborationist regime that fully supported the German war effort, willingly participated in the Holocaust, and forfeited the national sovereignty and honor of France.

There are rarely easy answers in any debate over history, and those who condemn Vichy France should carefully consider every aspect of French life during the 1940–1944 occupation by German forces. France's military had fallen to the German onslaught, leaving the country at the mercy of German leader Adolf Hitler. Under the provisions of an armistice, Germany occupied the north and west of France, while a portion of the southeast remained nominally independent. Occupation was harsh. French citizens at all levels had to make the best of their new circumstances. Ordinary people had few role models had they chosen to resist. Indeed, the French leadership in 1940 had options it could have employed after its military defeat. Although the Germans had overrun France, it would have been possible for the French leadership to take the navy, flee to Africa, and continue to resist the German war effort. Instead, few at the upper levels condemned the armistice. The highest official to criticize it was Charles de Gaulle, who at the time was a minor general in the army. With such a leadership, what could ordinary people have done?

Although it is difficult to condemn the actions of the French people forced to live under German occupation, their experiences and those of their leadership deserve serious scrutiny. Ever since scholar Robert O. Paxton attacked the conventional wisdom of de Gaulle's acting as the sword of France while Henri-Philippe Pétain was its shield, this explanation of Vichy France has been subject to doubts. Paxton's *Vichy France: Old Guard and New Order, 1940–1944* (1972) raised troubling questions about French resistance. Paxton portrays most of the French as latecomers in the struggle against Hitler. After the war one heard many stories about the high level of participation in the Resistance. There is some truth here, depending on when one joined the struggle and how one participated. If reading anti-German literature and giving German soldiers wrong directions constituted resisting, then the ranks of the movement were high. If resistance meant joining genuine guerrilla movements and doing something against the occupying forces, the ranks of the movement drop considerably. Whereas France remained a

dangerous place as long as there were German troops on its soil, it was a far greater risk to join the movement before the Allied invasion of 6 June 1944. It was even riskier to support de Gaulle before 1943. In the early years of the war no one could be certain that Germany would lose. This possibility increased in the middle of 1943, after Nazi defeats at Stalingrad and Kursk, and was a foregone conclusion after the invasion of Normandy in 1944. Before 1943, when it seemed that German forces could remain in France for many years, only the brave or foolish resisted their occupiers. Paxton argues that few French citizens were willing to take this risk.

Using a wider variety of material, Philippe Burrin, in *France under the Germans: Collaboration and Compromise* (1996), has corroborated Paxton's indictment of the French leadership. Not only did the Vichy regime try to accommodate the Nazi occupation, but its head of state, Pétain, and its prime minister, Pierre Laval, believed they could convince Hitler to give France an important role in the new Nazi European order. Besides describing the frequent attempts by the Vichy leadership to appear as allies of Hitler, Burrin charts the government's fall from respect in 1940. He details the gradual loss of the little power initially allotted to the regime. Even when faced with the reality of German troops in "unoccupied" France, which the Germans designated as a zone of operations, Pétain and Laval held on to every bit of power granted them. Burrin also describes the progressive relinquishment of Vichy's role as protector of the French people, since by late 1942 Jews, communists, and anyone else considered threatening to the Germans had been sacrificed. If Pétain was the shield of France, this shield did not always extend to the Jews or communists. French prisoners of war did not always fare well, either, nor did those compelled to work in the German war industry. Any illusions the Vichy leadership had essentially disappeared in late 1942 with the German occupation of the entire country. The regime lost all its leverage, including its navy, and was no longer anything besides a shield for the German occupiers and for the French leaders themselves.

Initially, the Germans did not request the Vichy government to institute an anti-Semitic program against the approximately 300,000 Jews living in France in 1940. Nevertheless, harsh repressive measures were enacted, first against immigrant Jews, who were unwelcome in France, then against France's own Jewish citizens. Initially, French Jews were forced out of elected office, public positions, teaching, and the media. The government also barred Jews from moving to the unoccupied zone of France. Those who already lived there could remain. Gradually

**French police officers
swearing allegiance to the
Vichy government,
August 1942**

(Documentation Francaise)

more positions were closed to Jews, quotas were placed on the number of Jews allowed to enter universities and secondary schools, and a system was instigated in 1941 to confiscate Jewish property in the unoccupied zone. Beginning in May 1942 in the occupied zone, Jews were required to wear a yellow star; this measure, however, was never extended to those living in the unoccupied zone. The situation worsened once the Germans, with cooperation of the French government and police, began rounding up and deporting Jews. At first the victims were foreign Jews; regular deportation of them to Auschwitz commenced in May 1942. By June 1942 the Germans were demanding that France deport its own Jewish citizens. Laval resisted this measure somewhat; he preferred to deport foreign Jews. Nonetheless, more than 70,000 Jews were deported from France. One-third of them were French citizens. French forces assisted the Germans in locating and interning foreign Jews. Only 2,500 of the Jews who were deported survived.

During the war Germany was in constant need of laborers. The exploitation of Polish and Russian workers did not sufficiently fill Germany's economic needs; therefore, French citizens were pressed into service. Initially, these laborers consisted of the French POWs who

were still imprisoned in Germany; many of them worked in factories and farms that supported the German war effort. However, this measure was insufficient. The *relève* plan of 1942, in which Germany promised to exchange one POW for every three skilled workers sent to Germany, did not provide enough labor for the German economy, requiring the Germans to employ harsher means. Between August 1942 and February 1943 the Vichy regime began systematically to conscript French citizens for work in Germany. Maurice Larkin, in *France since the Popular Front: Government and People, 1936–1996* (1988), estimates that at least 650,000 Frenchmen were drafted to work in Germany. He indicates that their productivity was almost as high as their German counterparts and much higher than fellow Dutch or Danish conscripted labor. Although the evidence indicates that Vichy's forced-labor plans were the greatest cause of dissent among the people, they nevertheless helped the German war effort.

Pétain and Laval also hoped for a formal alliance with Hitler and tried to maintain a working relationship with him during the war years. Laval offered Germany unofficial help in the continued fight against Britain, including supplying two hundred "volunteer" pilots. Vichy forces in Dakar repulsed a combined Anglo-Gaullist invasion in late 1940. Anglo-Gaullist forces were compelled to occupy French Syria in summer 1941 after the Germans had installed air bases there. French troops initially fired on the Anglo-American invaders of North Africa (1942) before switching sides. There was also concern about the French navy. As part of the armistice of 1940, it was to be kept out of the war. This agreement did not prevent the British from attacking the fleet in 1940 or the French naval crews from scuttling the fleet to keep it out of German hands in 1942.

The French were relatively lucky during World War II. They did not experience the same fate as Poland or the Soviet Union. Occupation in France was bad, but it was far worse in the eastern conquests of Nazi Germany. However, there is no evidence that the decision to collaborate made life in France any better. Had the Poles tried to accommodate their German conquerors, they still would have suffered terribly under Nazi occupation. Greater resistance from France would have meant more violence and more suffering for the people, although it would have also slowed the German war effort and made it more difficult for them to find productive labor. In addition, Vichy's treatment of its Jews was a terrible crime. It may have tried to save French Jews, but it accomplished what little it could by sacrificing foreign Jews residing in the country. The efforts of average French citizens to survive after 1940 must be taken into context, but this reality does not absolve the Vichy leadership from the role it played in helping the German war effort and in the roundup and deportation of French Jews.

–DAVID MARSHALL,
UNIVERSITY OF CALIFORNIA, RIVERSIDE

Viewpoint:
No. Vichy France was at the most an accommodationist regime that favored limited cooperation with Germany to minimize the impact of the defeat and to promote the long-term recovery of national sovereignty.

Since Robert O. Paxton published his groundbreaking work, *Vichy France: Old Guard and New Order, 1940–1944* (1972), the dominant view of the regime that governed France between its defeat by Nazi Germany in 1940 and its liberation by the Allied powers in 1944 has been that the Vichy state was in every way a collaborationist regime. Some more-recent research, however,

has suggested that Vichy France's attitudes toward Germany were more defined by their ambiguity. While many French individuals and institutions had no choice but to accept their fate as a defeated nation, new evidence suggests that they were largely unwilling to collaborate wholeheartedly with the Germans.

The murkiness of Vichy France's willingness to collaborate with Germany began with its new government. While it is true that Henri-Philippe Pétain and his associates, especially Prime Minister Pierre Laval, sought a diplomatic accommodation with Germany, there were many compelling reasons to do so, few of which implied any degree of sycophancy. The end of combat did not translate into an end to the conflict. The armistice signed on 22 June suspended the fighting, but France still remained technically at war. According to terms of the armistice, about 60 percent of the country was to remain under German occupation, and France was to be saddled with its cost. Two million French prisoners of war were to remain in Germany as virtual hostages until the official end of hostilities.

The Vichy government's primary diplomatic concern was to end this precarious situation, a feat that could only have been accomplished by means of a permanent peace settlement. The moral cloud that has covered these leaders should be seen in that context. As far as the French leadership knew, Germany stood poised to win the war in short order. Britain appeared to be on the verge of collapse, and, eighteen months before Pearl Harbor (7 December 1941), there was no hint of American intervention. Germany and the Union of Soviet Socialist Republics (U.S.S.R.) were allies in June 1940 and remained so until Adolf Hitler invaded the Soviet Union a year later. Germany's campaign against the Soviet Union appeared triumphant until late 1942. The wisest course under these circumstances was to use whatever trump cards France had at its disposal—its fleet, its empire, and the cost to the Germans of occupying all of metropolitan France—to maintain a diminished position in what seemed to be an unavoidably German Europe and to wait for better times.

Were they kidding themselves? Vichy leaders had enough reasonable evidence to believe that accommodation was a viable policy. Britain's perceived lack of long-term commitment reinforced a long-held suspicion that Britain had betrayed its French ally. Its attack on the French fleet at Mers-el-Kébir in North Africa and its occupation of jealously guarded French colonial possessions made the alternative difficult to contemplate. Another major source of encouragement was that the Germans themselves were divided on how to proceed in the future. The bureaucracy of the occupying power was diffuse, split between the military administration, the

German Foreign Ministry, the SS, the German Ministries of Production and Labor, an Italian occupation zone in the southeast, and the separate authorities in Alsace-Lorraine and the region north of the Somme. The divided functions made it difficult to devise a cohesive policy, and a significant body of German opinion, including the diplomatic representatives in Paris and Production Minister Albert Speer, impressed the possibilities of collaboration upon a reasonably credulous Vichy government. Such accommodation was also successful in defending the French colonial empire's integrity against Italian and Spanish encroachments. Italian dictator Benito Mussolini wanted Tunisia, Corsica, Nice, and Savoy, while Spanish leader Francisco Franco wanted to expand his country's presence in Morocco at France's expense, but neither leader accomplished his goals.

Once it became apparent that Germany could be defeated, however, Vichy's position changed. Its failure to resist British and American occupation of French North Africa in November 1942 indicated that its inclination toward doing the Germans' bidding was not all that strong, especially after Germany abrogated a term of the armistice and marched into the unoccupied zone of France in retaliation. That same month the encirclement of the German armies at Stalingrad indicated that the tide of the war was turning. The period that followed saw the waning of Vichy's willingness to favor the Axis side, concede base rights to Germany in North Africa, or work for a lasting peace settlement. Indeed, Vichy's response to the German invasion of the unoccupied zone was to scuttle its fleet in port. Its new policy, accelerated by the German surrender at Stalingrad in February 1943 and the collapse of Mussolini's regime after an Allied invasion of Italy later that year, indicated that Vichy was playing a waiting game. By late 1943 organs of the Vichy military and civil administration were covertly preparing to join in armed resistance against the Germans. Pétain declined to execute his governing functions in early 1944, and his government's removal to Germany later in the year was more of an abduction than anything else.

High politics had particularly close parallels in the day-to-day experiences of average people. Like their leaders, ordinary Frenchmen began to think of the future in a Europe united under German leadership, but only when it was widely believed that Germany would win the war. Businessmen dealt with the Germans to survive economic hardship, avoid German confiscation of their industrial capital, and, in certain industries (banking, insurance, publishing), to prevent takeovers by German firms. Were those goals truly dishon-

orable in the circumstances, particularly if they intentionally robbed the Germans of the ability to take over the French economy and monopolize its resources for their war efforts? Had the French offered more resistance and not tried to get on with their daily lives, France could well have ended up like any other occupied country, where all resources were ruthlessly plundered by the Germans.

Yet, just as their leaders came to realize that accommodation was no longer really worth it after November 1942, so did the overwhelming majority of the French people distance themselves from it. For the millions who were simply doing their best to survive, French historian Philippe Burrin has recently argued, "it would not be fair systematically to ascribe either a positive or a negative connotation to the phenomenon of accommodation. . . . to be a hero is honourable; not to be one is not necessarily dishonourable." The general portrait emerging in the new historiography is of a people who were just trying to get through the ordeal and survive as best they could. In some cases this effort meant civil obedience and common courtesy toward the invader. At other times it called for avoidance or cool silence. The tiny minority of Frenchmen who actively resisted, however, did not have a monopoly on virtue, nor were their less-heroic compatriots the "nation of collaborators" that was later castigated.

Perhaps one of the most contentious subjects that historians of Vichy France have studied is its treatment of France's Jewish population. One of the most damning features of Vichy and its functionaries, they argue, was that they willingly participated in the Holocaust by turning over Jews to be murdered by the Nazis. Obviously, even the sacrifice of one human life should bring moral condemnation on the regime, but there are nevertheless ambiguities that must be considered. First, the terms of the armistice deprived the French government of its jurisdiction over much of its Jewish population. About half of its 300,000 Jews were noncitizens, many of whom had recently arrived from Germany and other lands that had been incorporated into the Greater Reich. Since Article XIX of the armistice required French authorities to surrender Reich citizens to the occupiers on their request, tens of thousands of Jewish refugees were thus abandoned to their fate, along with others who were wanted for political reasons. This acquiescence was of course horrible, but since representatives of the Third Republic signed the armistice nearly three weeks before Pétain was granted powers, his regime's culpability in the fate of individuals in this category should be considered carefully.

It is damning that other Jews were deported and killed, but no matter how histori-

ARMISTICE AGREEMENT
BETWEEN THE GERMAN HIGH COMMAND OF THE ARMED FORCES AND FRENCH PLENIPOTENTIARIES, COMPIÈGNE, JUNE 22, 1940

Between the chief of the High Command of the armed forces, Col. Gen. [Wilhelm] Keitel, commissioned by the Fuehrer of the German Reich and Supreme Commander in Chief of the German Armed Forces, and the fully authorized plenipotentiaries of the French Government, General [Charles L. C.] Huntziger, chairman of the delegation; Ambassador [Léon] Noel, Rear Admiral [Maurice R.] LeLuc, Army Corps General [Georges] Parisot and Air Force General [Jean-Marie Joseph] Bergeret, the following armistice treaty was agreed upon:

ARTICLE I.

The French Government directs a cessation of fighting against the German Reich in France as well as in French possessions, colonies, protectorate territories, mandates as well as on the seas.

It [the French Government] directs the immediate laying down of arms of French units already encircled by German troops.

ARTICLE II.

To safeguard the interests of the German Reich, French State territory north and west of the line drawn on the attached map will be occupied by German troops.

As far as the parts to be occupied still are not in control of German troops, this occupation will be carried out immediately after the conclusion of this treaty.

ARTICLE III.

In the occupied parts of France the German Reich exercises all rights of an occupying power[.] The French Government obligates itself to support with every means the regulations resulting from the exercise of these rights and to carry them out with the aid of French administration.

All French authorities and officials of the occupied territory, therefore, are to be promptly informed by the French Government to comply with the regulations of the German military commanders and to cooperate with them in a correct manner.

It is the intention of the German Government to limit the occupation of the west coast after ending hostilities with England to the extent absolutely necessary.

The French Government is permitted to select the seat of its government in unoccupied territory, or, if it wishes, to move to Paris. In this case, the German Government guarantees the French Government and its central authorities every necessary alleviation so that they will be in a position to conduct the administration of unoccupied territory from Paris.

ARTICLE IV.

French armed forces on land, on the sea, and in the air are to be demobilized and disarmed in a period still to be set. Excepted are only those units which are necessary for maintenance of domestic order. Germany and Italy will fix their strength. The French armed forces in the territory to be occupied by Germany are to be hastily withdrawn into territory not to be occupied and be discharged. These troops, before marching out, shall lay down their weapons and equipment at the places where they are stationed at the time this treaty becomes effective. They are responsible for orderly delivery to German troops.

ARTICLE V.

As a guarantee for the observance of the armistice, the surrender, undamaged, of all those guns, tanks, tank defense weapons, war planes, anti-aircraft artillery, infantry weapons, means of conveyance, and munitions can be demanded from the units of the French armed forces which are standing in battle against Germany and which at the time this agreement goes into force are in territory not to be occupied by Germany.

The German armistice commission will decide the extent of delivery.

ARTICLE VI.

Weapons, munitions, and war apparatus of every kind remaining in the unoccupied portion of France are to be stored and/or secured under German and/or Italian control—so far as not released for the arming allowed to French units.

The German High Command reserves the right to direct all those measures which are necessary to exclude unauthorized use of this material. Building of new war apparatus in unoccupied territory is to be stopped immediately.

ARTICLE VII.

In occupied territory, all the land and coastal fortifications, with weapons, munitions, and apparatus and plants of every kind are to be surrendered undamaged. Plans of these fortifications, as well as plans of those already conquered by German troops, are to be handed over.

Exact plans regarding prepared blastings, land mines, obstructions, time fuses, barriers for fighting, etc., shall be given to the German High Command. These hindrances are to be removed by French forces upon German demand.

ARTICLE VIII.

The French war fleet is to collect in ports to be designated more particularly, and under German and/or Italian control to demobilize and lay up—with the exception of those units released to the French Government for protection of French interests in its colonial empire.

The peacetime stations of ships should control the designation of ports.

The German Government solemnly declares to the French Government that it does not intend to use the French War Fleet which is in harbors under German control for its purposes in war, with the exception of units necessary for the purposes of guarding the coast and sweeping mines.

It further solemnly and expressly declares that it does not intend to bring up any demands respecting the French War Fleet at the conclusion of a peace.

All warships outside France are to be recalled to France with the exception of that portion of the French War Fleet which shall be designated to represent French interests in the colonial empire.

ARTICLE IX.

The French High Command must give the German High Command the exact location of all mines which France has set out, as well as information on the other harbor and coastal obstructions and defense facilities. Insofar as the German High Command may require, French forces must clear away the mines.

ARTICLE X.

The French Government is obligated to forbid any portion of its remaining armed forces to undertake hostilities against Germany in any manner.

[The] French Government also will prevent members of its armed forces from leaving the country and prevent armaments of any sort, including ships, planes, etc., being taken to England or any other place abroad. The French Government will forbid French citizens to fight against Germany in the service of States with which the German Reich is still at war. French citizens who violate this provision are to be treated by German troops as insurgents.

ARTICLE XI.

French commercial vessels of all sorts, including coastal and harbor vessels which are now in French hands, may not leave port until further notice. Resumption of commercial voyages will require approval of the German and Italian Governments.

French commercial vessels will be recalled by the French Government or, if return is impossible, the French Government will instruct them to enter neutral harbors.

All confiscated German commercial vessels are, on demand, to be returned [to Germany] undamaged.

ARTICLE XII.

Flight by any airplane over French territory shall be prohibited. Every plane making a flight without German approval will be regarded as an enemy by the German Air Force and treated accordingly.

In unoccupied territory, air fields and ground facilities of the air force shall be under German and Italian control.

Demand may be made that such air fields be rendered unusable. The French Government is required to take charge of all foreign airplanes in the unoccupied region to prevent flights. They are to be turned over to the German armed forces.

ARTICLE XIII.

The French Government obligates itself to turn over to German troops in the occupied region all facilities and properties of the French armed forces in undamaged condition.

It [the French Government] also will see to it that harbors, industrial facilities, and docks are preserved in their present condition and damaged in no way.

The same stipulations apply to transportation routes and equipment, especially railways, roads, and canals, and to the whole communications network and equipment, waterways and coastal transportation services.

Additionally, the French Government is required on demand of the German High Command to perform all necessary restoration labor on these facilities.

The French Government will see to it that in the occupied region necessary technical personnel and rolling stock of the railways and other transportation equipment, to a degree normal in peacetime, be retained in service.

ARTICLE XIV.

There is an immediate prohibition of transmission for all wireless stations on French soil. Resumption of wireless connections from the unoccupied portion of France requires a special regulation.

ARTICLE XV.

The French Government obligates itself to convey transit freight between the German Reich and Italy through unoccupied territory to the extent demanded by the German Government.

ARTICLE XVI.

The French Government, in agreement with the responsible German officials, will carry out the return of population into occupied territory.

ARTICLE XVII.

The French Government obligates itself to prevent every transference of economic valuables and provisions from the territory to be occupied by German troops into unoccupied territory or abroad.

These valuables and provisions in occupied territory are to be disposed of only in agreement with the German Government. In that connection, the German Government will consider the necessities of life of the population in unoccupied territory.

ans choose to present the information, a higher percentage of Jews survived in France than in Germany and in any other country occupied by Germany, with the sole exception of Denmark. The 24 percent of the total number of Jews in France that were deported was 24 percent too many, but neighboring Belgium lost 75 percent of its Jews, while the death toll among Dutch Jews reached to well over 90 percent. Neither country had an existing government in place to thwart German intentions. This caveat cannot excuse the deaths of the Jews in France or absolve Vichy officials of their due moral complicity, but the fact that an accommodationist regime and society existed nevertheless moderated what the Germans could do. The unoccupied zone effectively sheltered Jews from detention while it lasted. Many officials in the Vichy police and civil administration refused to cooperate, used their positions to warn Jews of their fate so they could avoid capture, or did a deliberately sloppy job of executing German directives. To cite one example, a roundup of Parisian Jews in July 1942 failed to detain more than half of its 25,000 intended victims, partly because French officials and others who were "in the know" warned or hid their Jewish neighbors ahead of time or did not execute their tasks. Cases of kindness, risk taking, and sheltering by sympathetic individuals, religious institutions, and organizations in civil society were numerous and aided many people who would otherwise have been deported and killed. Historian Susan Zuccotti, a leading expert on the issue, has suggested that the general attitude of passivity toward the Germans also saved many people. In practice the Germans had to rely largely on themselves to implement their policies in occupied France. Although some Frenchmen cooperated with them, many had nothing to do with the Vichy government, nor did they represent anything more than a fanatical element in French society that had unfortunately existed long before the war. Many aspects of Vichy's complicity were harrowing, particularly Laval's attempt to sacrifice the foreign Jews in France in exchange for German promises not to deport native-born French Jews, but its presence and the actions and inactions of its citizens and officials played a role in frustrating the Germans' attempt to carry out the Holocaust as thoroughly in France as they did almost everywhere else.

Vichy France remains a subject of enormous complexity. Yet, it has become difficult to condemn it unreservedly as a collaborationist regime. A public-opinion poll conducted in the early 1980s found that 66 percent of Frenchmen did not condemn Pétain for his actions in 1940–1944. He existed in what postmodernists call a "situational truth." His country was defeated

ARTICLE XVIII.
The French Government will bear the costs of maintenance of German occupation troops on French soil.

ARTICLE XIX.
All German war and civil prisoners in French custody, including those under arrest and convicted who were seized and sentenced because of acts in favor of the German Reich, shall be surrendered immediately to German troops.
The French Government is obliged to surrender upon demand all Germans named by the German Government in France as well as in French possessions, colonies, protectorate territories, and mandates.
The French Government binds itself to prevent removal of German war and civil prisoners from France into French possessions or into foreign countries. Regarding prisoners already taken outside of France, as well as sick and wounded German prisoners who cannot be transported, exact lists with the places of residence are to be produced. The German High Command assumes care of sick and wounded German war prisoners.

ARTICLE XX.
French troops in German prison camps will remain prisoners of war until conclusion of a peace.

ARTICLE XXI.
The French Government assumes responsibility for the security of all objects and valuables whose undamaged surrender or holding in readiness for German disposal is demanded in this agreement or whose removal outside the country is forbidden. The French Government is bound to compensate for all destruction, damage or removal contrary to agreement.

ARTICLE XXII.
The Armistice Commission, acting in accordance with the direction of the German High Command, will regulate and supervise the carrying out of the armistice agreement. It is the task of the Armistice Commission further to insure the necessary conformity of this agreement with the Italian-French armistice.
The French Government will send a delegation to the seat of the German Armistice Commission to represent the French wishes and to receive regulations from the German Armistice Commission for executing [the agreement].

ARTICLE XXIII.
This armistice agreement becomes effective as soon as the French Government also has reached an agreement with the Italian Government regarding cessation of hostilities.
Hostilities will be stopped six hours after the moment at which the Italian Government has notified the German Government of conclusion of its agreement. The German Government will notify the French Government of this time by wireless.

ARTICLE XXIV.
This agreement is valid until conclusion of a peace treaty. The German Government may terminate this agreement at any time with immediate effect if the French Government fails to fulfill the obligations it assumes under the agreement.
This armistice agreement, signed in the Forest of Compiègne, June 22, 1940, at 6:50 p.m., German summer time.

Source: United States, Department of State, Documents on German Foreign Policy 1918–1945, Series D, IX, Publication No. 6312 (Washington, D.C.: U.S. Government Printing Office, 1956), pp. 671–676; The Avalon Project at Yale Law School <http://www.yale.edu/lawweb/avalon/wwii/frgearm.htm>.

VICHY FRANCE

and occupied. Its only ally, which did not act in the most trustworthy manner after the armistice, looked as if it would also be defeated, and its strongest future liberator would not even enter the war for a year and a half after the defeat. Conversely, when it seemed that Germany would be defeated, Vichy failed to rally to its defense. It offered nonresistance to the Allies in North Africa in November 1942, scuttled its fleet when the Germans marched into the unoccupied zone, became notably less cooperative thereafter, and ceased to play any effective role under the Germans in the months before the June 1944 landings in Normandy. To condemn French society for its conduct is to condemn a nation of hapless people who were only trying to survive the war as best they could without allowing the Germans to destroy their lives and livelihoods any more than they already had.

–PAUL DU QUENOY,
GEORGETOWN UNIVERSITY

References

Philippe Burrin, *France under the Germans: Collaboration and Compromise,* translated by Janet Lloyd (New York: New Press, 1996).

John Hellman, *The Knight-Monks of Vichy France: Uriage, 1940–1945* (Montreal & Buffalo: McGill-Queen's University Press, 1993).

Julian Jackson, *France: The Dark Years, 1940–1944* (Oxford & New York: Oxford University Press, 2001).

Maurice Larkin, *France since the Popular Front: Government and People, 1936–1996* (Oxford: Clarendon Press / New York: Oxford University Press, 1988).

Robert O. Paxton, *Vichy France: Old Guard and New Order, 1940–1944* (New York: Knopf, 1972).

Susan Zuccotti, *The Holocaust, the French, and the Jews* (New York: Basic Books, 1993).

VICHY FRANCE

WORLD WAR I PEACE SETTLEMENT

Could World War I have been settled by a negotiated peace?

Viewpoint: Yes. Most participants in the conflict were willing to negotiate at various stages of the war, but diplomatic blunders and the interference of other powers prevented them from doing so.

Viewpoint: No. Until late in the war the major powers believed that they and their allies would emerge victorious.

More soldiers fell in World War I (1914–1918) than in all other European conflicts in the previous eight centuries combined. As the war consumed the Continent's youth and embroiled most of its nations in a heretofore unknown carnage, the thought of peace more than once crossed the minds of tired European leaders and their weary societies.

How realistic was the notion that World War I could have been settled through negotiation? As one contributor maintains, a negotiated peace was a wholly desirable and realizable goal. Nations strained to the breaking point naturally looked to diplomacy as a means of escaping conflict. Several efforts to make a diplomatic breakthrough were advanced by the major combatants, and only a series of high-level errors and blunders prevented them from leading to peace.

Yet, how realistic could this scenario be in an era of total war and in a conflict that most powers believed they would win? With economies oriented toward total victory, dehumanizing propaganda demonizing enemies, and overarching strategic goals requiring nothing short of the complete defeat of opponents, bringing a negotiated peace was as hopeless as breaking the stalemate on the Western Front.

Viewpoint:
Yes. Most participants in the conflict were willing to negotiate at various stages of the war, but diplomatic blunders and the interference of other powers prevented them from doing so.

By 1916 World War I (1914–1918)—contrary to all original expectations that it would be a short, mobile, and decisive conflict—had evolved into a total war of attrition.

All the combatants realized that victory was far off. While in 1914 and 1915 there were only a few efforts by the Allied or Central Powers to seek a peaceful solution to the conflict, the strategic stalemate on the major fronts and the growing cost of the war intensified the attempts of belligerents and neutral powers to seek a way out in the form of negotiated peace.

The first peace overture of 1916 was made by the United States, which was neutral at the time. In January and February U.S. president Woodrow Wilson sent his trusted and influential adviser Colonel

Edward M. House to Europe to study the possibility of American mediation between the conflicting sides. The House mission resulted in an agreement with Great Britain that called for the United States to sponsor a peace conference to reach a compromise solution. If Germany rejected the peace initiative, the United States could enter the war on the Allied side. At the same time, Britain, still hoping for military victory for the Allies, reserved the right to initiate American mediation and was reluctant to do so. This reluctance, as well as the approaching U.S. presidential election of 1916, in which neutrality was a major issue, forced Wilson to suspend his peace offer.

On 12 December 1916 German chancellor Theobald von Bethmann-Hollweg proposed peace negotiations between the Central Powers and the Entente. In the aftermath of German successes on the Eastern Front and under pressure from an optimistic German military, Bethmann-Hollweg insisted on the preservation of territorial gains, including the German occupation of Belgium and northern France—conditions unacceptable for the Allies. Following Wilson's renewed invitation of 18 December 1916, made after his narrow reelection in November, to seek a compromise between the belligerents, Germany modified its position and agreed to evacuate the occupied territories in Western Europe. Yet, the Central Powers firmly insisted on holding territorial gains in Eastern Europe and demanded additional colonies.

The Entente, which perceived the German proposal as an attempt to capitalize on military successes, responded on 30 December 1916 by demanding the withdrawal of German troops from all occupied territories and the liberation of minorities in Austria-Hungary and the Ottoman Empire. Western skepticism about German peace proposals had some grounds. Since fall 1916 Berlin had tried to approach Russia in order to conclude a separate peace in the east, which would allow Germany to concentrate all its efforts to achieve military victory in Western Europe. This overture received some support from reactionary Russian politicians and even from some figures in the Tsar's inner circle who desired to withdraw from the alliance with the Western democracies and restore the Holy Alliance of monarchies.

In a 22 January 1917 address to the U.S. Senate, Wilson appealed to the combatants to agree to "peace without victory." Exhausted by war, Britain and Austria-Hungary were ready to accept U.S. mediation, but the German declaration of unrestricted submarine warfare in order to achieve total victory killed this peace initiative. Attacks on American merchant shipping made U.S. neutrality impossible. In less than two weeks Washington severed diplomatic relations with Germany and, after several attacks at sea, declared war in April.

Yet, despite these events, in the spring of 1917 Emperor Karl of Austria-Hungary, a country that was desperately struggling for survival, approached Britain and France with peace proposals via his brother-in-law, Prince Sixtus of Bourbon-Parma, an officer of the Belgian army. The Austrians suggested some concessions in Italy and were prepared to support the reversion of Alsace-Lorraine, French territory lost to Germany in 1871, and Belgium's restored independence.

The question of whether Karl was prepared to make a separate peace with the Allies in the case of Germany's refusal or was merely trying to find a compromise basis for a general peace remains a matter of much controversy. As for Germany, when it learned about the Austrian move, it delivered its own proposals aimed to extend the Central Powers' influence in Poland, strengthen German domination in the Baltic provinces, and secure Austrian hegemony in the Balkans. Moreover, Berlin made no concessions on Alsace-Lorraine or Belgium. The Entente was inclined to make a separate peace with Austria-Hungary, but the German intervention and the fact that other allies—Italy, Romania, and Serbia—found the Austrian proposals unacceptable put an end to the initiative.

In July 1917 the German Reichstag passed a peace resolution that called on the government to renounce territorial demands in order to stimulate the search for a peace solution. The resolution was met with strong resistance from Kaiser Wilhelm II and the German military, but it nevertheless proved that a broad segment of German public opinion favored a peace settlement without any gains or losses for any combatant power.

On 1 August 1917 Pope Benedict XV sent a note to the belligerents, proposing a compromise peace without annexations and reparations. Particularly, the Pope proposed Germany's withdrawal from Belgium and France; the Allies' withdrawal from German colonies; the withdrawal of Germany and its allies from Serbia, Montenegro, and Romania; and the creation of an independent Poland. This proposal led to separate bilateral negotiations between the Holy See and the Entente and the Central Powers. In these negotiations the Central Powers demonstrated their reluctance to withdraw unconditionally from all territories they had occupied, particularly Belgium. The Allies, for their part, were not prepared to give up their long-term goals, such as regaining Alsace-Lorraine and seizing the ethnic Italian Trentino. There were also some German attempts to nego-

tiate with Britain through Spain, but growing disagreements within the German ruling elite prevented this move. While the politicians were ready to surrender Belgium and other occupied countries for peace, German generals insisted on retaining some territories for strategic and economic reasons. The generals won. When the Germans stated in October 1917 that they would never surrender, all hopes for a negotiated peace vanished.

The collapse of the Eastern Front in 1917 nevertheless allowed the Central Powers to realize their long-term goal—elimination of the two-front war. For sure, the Bolshevik government, which came to power in Russia in November 1917, proposed a general, just, and democratic peace without annexations and reparations. In fact, and in contrast to the other Allied governments, they were more interested in peace at any cost in order to secure and consolidate power at home. This motive, as well as an almost complete collapse of the Russian army, opened the way for the conclusion of the Treaty of Brest-Litovsk, a peace settlement signed by Soviet Russia and the Central Powers on 3 March 1918. With Russia out of the war, the

Central Powers could devote greater attention to the other fronts, particularly to the crucial Western Front.

The developments of 1916–1918 demonstrated that most participants in the conflict were willing to negotiate at various stages but were prevented from doing so by bad luck and the interference of other powers. Several peace proposals failed because the protagonists assumed that the war would end with a decisive outcome and were determined to achieve it. There was also a basic asymmetry in the strategic positions of the belligerents. While by 1916 Germany succeeded in dominating Central Europe as a zone of political, military, and economic hegemony, the Allies desperately tried to withstand it and reverse the Teutonic onslaught. Hence there was different and, moreover, mutually exclusive understanding of compromise by the warring sides. The Central Powers persistently tried at least to preserve the status quo that their armies had achieved by 1916. For the Allies, the ideal compromise solution was the prewar status quo. This principal contradiction could be resolved only by military victory. Neither side was ever ready to negotiate in real terms

Column of German troops evacuating a Belgian town in 1918

(from Stefan Lorant, Sieg Heil! Hail to Victory: An Illustrated History of Germany from Bismarck to Hitler, *1979)*

WORLD WAR I PEACE SETTLEMENT

SEEKING PEACE

Speaking before the Senate in January 1917, U.S. president Woodrow Wilson called for the warring sides in Europe to accept "peace without victory." A portion of his speech appears here:

The present war must first be ended; but we owe it to candour and to a just regard for the opinion of mankind to say that, so far as our participation in guarantees of future peace is concerned, it makes a great deal of difference in what way and upon what terms it is ended. The treaties and agreements which bring it to an end must embody terms which will create a peace that is worth guaranteeing and preserving, a peace that will win the approval of mankind, not merely a peace that will serve the several interests and immediate aims of the nations engaged. We shall have no voice in determining what those terms shall be, but we shall, I feel sure, have a voice in determining whether they shall be made lasting or not by the guarantees of a universal covenant; and our judgment upon what is fundamental and essential as a condition precedent to permanency should be spoken now, not afterwards when it may be too late.

No covenant of cooperative peace that does not include the peoples of the New World can suffice to keep the future safe against war; and yet there is only one sort of peace that the peoples of America could join in guaranteeing. The elements of that peace must be elements that engage the confidence and satisfy the principles of the American governments, elements consistent with their political faith and with the practical convictions which the peoples of America have once for all embraced and undertaken to defend. . . .

The terms of the immediate peace agreed upon will determine whether it is a peace for which such a guarantee can be secured. The question upon which the whole future peace and policy of the world depends is this: Is the present war a struggle for a just and secure peace, or only for a new balance of power? If it be only a struggle for a new balance of power, who will guarantee, who can guarantee, the stable equilibrium of the new arrangement? Only a tranquil Europe can be a stable Europe. There must be, not a balance of power, but a community of power; not organized rivalries, but an organized common peace. . . . it must be a peace without victory. . . . Victory would mean peace forced upon the loser, a victor's terms imposed upon the vanquished. It would be accepted in humiliation, under duress, at an intolerable sacrifice, and would leave a sting, a resentment, a bitter memory upon which terms of peace would rest, not permanently, but only as upon quicksand. Only a peace between equals can last, only a peace the very principle of which is equality and a common participation in a common benefit. The right state of mind, the right feeling between nations, is as necessary for a lasting peace as is the just settlement of vexed questions of territory or of racial and national allegiance.

The equality of nations upon which peace must be founded if it is to last must be an equality of rights; the guarantees exchanged must neither recognize nor imply a difference between big nations and small, between those that are powerful and those that are weak. Right must be based upon the common strength, not upon the individual strength, of the nations upon whose concert peace will depend. Equality of territory or of resources there of course cannot be; nor any other sort of equality not gained in the ordinary peaceful and legitimate development of the peoples themselves. But no one asks or expects anything more than an equality of rights. Mankind is looking now for freedom of life, not for equipoises of power.

And there is a deeper thing involved than even equality of right among organized nations. No peace can last, or ought to last, which does not recognize and accept the principle that governments derive all their just powers from the consent of the governed, and that no right anywhere exists to hand peoples about from sovereignty to sovereignty as if they were property. . . .

And in holding out the expectation that the people and Government of the United States will join the other civilized nations of the world in guaranteeing the permanence of peace upon such terms as I have named I speak with the greater boldness and confidence because it is clear to every man who can think that there is in this promise no breach in either our traditions or our policy as a nation, but a fulfilment, rather, of all that we have professed or striven for. . . .

I am proposing, as it were, that the nations should with one accord adopt the doctrine of President Monroe as the doctrine of the world: that no nation should seek to extend its polity over any other nation or people, but that every people should be left free to determine its own polity, its own way of development, unhindered, unthreatened, unafraid, the little along with the great and powerful.

I am proposing that all nations henceforth avoid entangling alliances which would draw them into competitions of power, catch them in a net of intrigue and selfish rivalry, and disturb their own affairs with influences intruded from without. There is no entangling alliance in a concert of power. When all unite to act in the same sense and with the same purpose, all act in the common interest and are free to live their own lives under a common protection.

I am proposing government by the consent of the governed; that freedom of the seas which in international conference after conference representatives of the United States have urged with the eloquence of those who are the convinced disciples of liberty; and that moderation of armaments which makes of armies and navies a power for order merely, not an instrument of aggression or selfish violence.

These are American principles, American policies. We could stand for no others. And they are also the principles and policies of forward-looking men and women everywhere, of every modern nation, of every enlightened community. They are the principles of mankind and must prevail.

Source: *"22 January, 1917: Address of the President of the United States to the Senate," The World War I Document Archive <http://www.lib.byu.edu/~rdh/wwi/1917/senate.html>.*

when the other side was, and, conversely, when one coalition faltered and proposed talks, the other became hopeful. In these circumstances the belligerents either failed to specify their war aims or insisted on territorial changes and political conditions that their enemies could never have accepted, including Germany's reluctance to restore Belgium's independence or Britain and France's demand for the liberation of the subject nationalities of Austria-Hungary.

Domestic political factors were also important. The rivalry between military and political leadership in Berlin significantly limited Germany's ability to deliver compromise peace proposals. The questionable loyalty of Austria-Hungary's subject nationalities, particularly the Slavs, its growing trends of disintegration, and Russia's rising political instability made these countries extremely vulnerable and weak parts of their respective coalitions. This fact precluded any significant support from more-powerful allies for possible peace moves by Vienna and Petrograd and undermined chances for a general peace settlement. Despite peace initiatives that were sincere and both taken and meant seriously, the war continued until the defeat of Germany and the armistice of 11 November 1918.

—PETER RAINOW,
SAN MATEO, CALIFORNIA

Viewpoint:
No. Until late in the war the major powers believed that they and their allies would emerge victorious.

Although diplomatic channels were used by all of the major combatants during World War I (1914–1918), the conflict could not have been settled by a negotiated peace. Some of the belligerents were alarmed by the devastation and sheer carnage of years of trench warfare, yet no combatant made any significant diplomatic efforts to end the conflict until 1916, when the bloodbaths at Verdun (1916) and the Somme (1916) on the Western Front left all the major belligerents exhausted by the stalemate. All diplomatic efforts that compromised the war aims of the various parties ended in failure. While domestic support for the war faltered throughout Europe by 1917, no government except for the Russian Bolsheviks was willing to make serious sacrifices. Moreover, Germany's imperial and military elite's aggressive foreign policy guaranteed that no peace negotiations short of their opponents' surrender would ever succeed.

Some may argue that opportunities for a negotiated peace existed from 1916 until the final stages of the war. For instance, the British sought to entice Bulgaria and the Ottoman Empire to make a separate peace with the Entente, thereby allowing the Allies to make significant strategic gains in the Balkans, the eastern Mediterranean, and the Middle East. Peace with Bulgaria would have injured the Habsburgs by allowing the Allied Expeditionary Force (AEF) in Greece to liberate occupied Serbia. Neutrality or alliance with the Ottoman Empire would have deprived the Central Powers of a major ally, supported British efforts in the Balkans and Middle East, and opened up lines of communication with Russia by means of the Black Sea and Persian Gulf.

Both of these efforts were doomed to failure. Earlier promises to Serbia and Greece prevented an agreement with the Bulgarians. The Bulgarians would only talk if they were given Macedonia and part of the Aegean Coast. This precondition was anathema to the Entente's Balkan partners, which were themselves at loggerheads over that region's future. The Ottomans may have been open to negotiations despite their leader Enver Pasha's pro-German orientation. Given the Empire's loss of Arab lands to the British, it was in the Turks' interest to end the war with at least part of its empire intact. Nevertheless, British concerns over defeating an "inferior" civilization and giving freedom to its many "peoples" (under British protection, of course) prevented any deal from being made. To the British, Enver's actions against the Armenians earlier in the war only confirmed the notion that the Turks were simply barbarians, while a 1916 agreement between Britain and France partitioned most of the Ottoman Empire's non-Turkish realms between them in the event of victory.

British ideological considerations also forestalled efforts for a separate peace with the Habsburg Empire, which, if successful, would have left the Germans hopelessly vulnerable to the Entente. In January 1917 the newly crowned

Karl I wished to extricate himself from the conflict that his predecessor, Emperor Franz Josef, had started. Acting independently from his generals, Karl hoped to save the monarchy by gaining peace. Even though some key British diplomats saw this interest as a golden opportunity to win the war, the British Foreign Office rebuffed what they believed to be a vague offer. Instead, the British and French called for the breakup of the Habsburg Empire and for the first time endorsed the efforts of Austria-Hungary's minority nationalities to seek independence. Thus, the Western Allies saw the Habsburgs, like the Ottomans, as historical anachronisms. A determined policy would ensure their defeat and extinction in ways that would benefit British and French interests after the war.

Although the enormous loss of life and deteriorating social conditions caused dissent among the major combatants, revolution alone could stop a government from continuing the war. For instance, the mutiny of more than half of the French army in the spring of 1917 was quickly suppressed. Many French patriots of all political persuasions saw cries for peace as treasonous, and censorship prevented further protests of the war effort. In Germany, deteriorating social conditions prompted a faction of the Social Democratic Party, the "Independent" Social Democratic Party (USPD), to break off in support of peace negotiations in April 1917. Although this action led to several illegal strikes, the USPD could not successfully challenge Germany's leadership either on the street or in Parliament. Revolution in Germany did not come about as a result of these disputes, but in reaction to Germany's defeat on the battlefield.

The Bolsheviks were the only government willing to negotiate with an enemy power. These efforts eventually culminated in the signing of the Treaty of Brest-Litovsk (March 1918), which gave nominal independence to vast tracts of territory including Ukraine, Poland, and Finland, as well as huge reparations to the Central Powers. Yet, this treaty was made out of necessity. After the decisive loss during the Brusilov Offensive (1916), the Russian army deteriorated to the point of ineffectiveness. Political dissent, social unrest, and a desire by the common Russian foot soldier to claim his land in the countryside completely demolished whatever order was left. Russian commissar of foreign affairs Lev Trotsky's policy of "neither war, nor peace" ignored these realities and only led to further German conquests. Continued war threatened not only Russia's survival but the survival of the Revolution as well. For Soviet leader Vladimir Lenin and the Bolsheviks, there was no choice but to make peace at any cost.

Finally, Germany's wartime leadership was hell-bent on total victory. From the outset of the war, Kaiser Wilhelm II and his generals used diplomatic negotiations as an extension of Germany's military efforts. The Germans showed their facetious attitudes toward negotiated peace in early 1917, when Wilhelm II worked together with the good offices of then-neutral U.S. president Woodrow Wilson to seek an end to the conflict. Rather than taking advantage of the attention that the British government gave to the peace proposal, the Germans chose to offer no specific terms and actually persuaded the Austrians, who were indeed interested in a separate peace, to follow suit. The Kaiser simply stated his willingness to end the conflict. As Wilhelm II later admitted, the statement was a ruse to break Germany's international isolation. The policy also sabotaged Vienna's separate efforts.

Perhaps the greatest example of German diplomatic intolerance was the Treaty of Brest-Litovsk. The Germans imposed a punitive peace on the Bolsheviks. While the annexation of Polish lands and the Baltic region, the establishment of a pro-German Ukrainian puppet state, and enormous reparations satisfied the German desire for territorial and monetary compensation for "total victory," these terms only harmed German war efforts. The Germans were forced to maintain a large occupational army, the critical force they needed to defeat the French in the remaining months before the American Expeditionary Force (AEF) could decisively alter the balance of power on the Western Front. As a result, the Great German offensive on the Western Front in the summer of 1918 soon stalled.

The fact that the Germans failed to capitalize on opportunities for negotiated peace was no accident. The vain Kaiser had no patience for the diplomatic and domestic intricacies that German chancellor Otto von Bismarck had dealt with in the wake of the Franco-Prussian War (1870–1871). Rather than maintaining his traditional alliance with Russia and acknowledging Britain as the premier naval and colonial power, Wilhelm II embarked on a naval development program and a quest for colonies that left Germany completely isolated. The Kaiser's failure to include wide sections of the population in the empire's political life frustrated the aspirations of an emerging working class and bourgeoisie and put political pressure on Prussia's military elite for a more popular government. Wilhelm II and the elite could only stymie these demands by waging a new war for even greater glory. Hopes for a total victory over France in the Great War papered over the gaps in Germany's political fabric in the name of national unity. As the German leadership was well aware, any thoughts of compromise, especially peace without victory, threatened the prestige, and perhaps the existence, of the monarchy itself. Wilhelm II's abdication in November 1918 and the collapse of the Hohenzollern dynasty after the declaration of an armistice proved these fears to be real.

Most powers were determined to fight World War I to its finish and punish the enemy powers to the greatest extent possible. Ideological, international, and domestic considerations ensured that a negotiated peace could not be made with the lesser powers—such as the Ottomans, Habsburgs, or even Bulgarians—not to mention a peace between the major combatants on the Western Front. Total war had come of age.

–YORK NORMAN,
GEORGETOWN UNIVERSITY

References

Fritz Fischer, *Germany's Aims in the First World War* (London: Chatto & Windus, 1967; New York: Norton, 1967).

Michael J. Lyons, *World War I: A Short History* (Englewood Cliffs, N.J.: Prentice Hall, 1994).

V. H. Rothwell, *British War Aims and Peace Diplomacy, 1914–1918* (Oxford: Clarendon Press, 1971).

A. J. P. Taylor, *The Struggle for Mastery in Europe, 1848–1918* (Oxford: Clarendon Press, 1954).

Z. A. B. Zeman, *The Break-up of the Habsburg Empire, 1914–1918: A Study in National and Social Revolution* (London & New York: Oxford University Press, 1961).

WORLD WAR II ALLIANCES

Was the World War II alliance of the United States, Great Britain, and the Soviet Union ironclad?

Viewpoint: Yes. The Allied powers presented a united front in the pursuit of victory.

Viewpoint: No. The Allies were consumed by mutual suspicions, strategic disagreements, and serious controversies over the postwar peace settlement.

Combining their efforts to defeat Nazi Germany in World War II (1939–1945), American president Franklin D. Roosevelt, British prime minister Winston Churchill, and Soviet dictator Josef Stalin became known as the "Big Three," fast and firm allies who shared not only the same military goal but also common values and a shared vision of the postwar international order. How truly fast and firm, however, was this alliance?

The classical view, reflected in wartime propaganda, is that the bonds among the Big Three were indeed unshakable. Threatening both Britain and the Union of Soviet Socialist Republics (U.S.S.R.) with total defeat, Adolf Hitler's Germany was simply too dangerous to either nation for it to resist alignment with the other, regardless of any differences they may have had. The threat of an Eastern Hemisphere controlled by Germany and America's Pacific enemy, Japan, left Washington with no choice but to support its traditional ally, Britain, and the Soviet Union, which it had long regarded with mistrust and suspicion. Strategic necessity and national survival made unity inevitable and total.

Yet, as some scholars argue, there were always fractures within the "Grand Alliance," disagreements that threatened to become insurmountable and that emerged in earnest almost as soon as Germany's defeat was assured. Diverse interests, ideologies, and security requirements ensured that no degree of commitment could have placed the solidity of the wartime alliance beyond doubt. At least a few policy makers in all three countries wondered whether wartime solidarity was worth the price of the war. No matter how cooperative the national leaders may have appeared, their visions of the postwar world diverged to the point of incompatibility, influencing not only the diplomacy of the alliance but even the conduct of its military operations. If the partnership was one of necessity, the argument follows, it was in many ways reluctant, conditional, and, ultimately, fragile.

Viewpoint:
Yes. The Allied powers presented a united front in the pursuit of victory.

The involvement of the Union of Soviet Socialist Republics (U.S.S.R.) and the United States in the war against the Axis Powers in 1941 not only transformed the European and Pacific wars into World War II (1939–1945) but also resulted in the emergence of one of the greatest coalitions ever known. At the center of the anti-Axis coalition was the Grand Alliance, or the Big Three—the United States, United Kingdom, and U.S.S.R. From the beginning of the war in Europe the United States strongly supported Britain, providing it with war matériel (Lend-Lease aid program) and political backing. When in June 1941 the Germans invaded the Soviet Union, British prime minister Winston Churchill—a longtime foe of communism—had no hesitation in proclaiming his firm support for the Soviets. All previous hostility toward the U.S.S.R. was overshadowed by the resolve to work together in the common interest—defeat of the Axis. The essence of the emerging Allied strategy was simple: the West should deliver to the Soviet Union as much matériel and arms as it could and invade Europe as soon as possible. It meant that the Red Army should hold the bulk of German forces at bay until the Allies were ready to open a second front in Western Europe.

As far as supplies for the U.S.S.R. were concerned, Britain had promised to render all possible aid to the Russians, but obviously only the United States could meet the enormous needs of its struggling ally. U.S. president Franklin D. Roosevelt, despite the fact that the United States until December 1941 kept formal neutrality, immediately moved to extend Lend-Lease aid to the U.S.S.R. after the German invasion. This aspect of cooperation proved successful. In total, the United States supplied the U.S.S.R. with more than $11 billion in vitally needed goods, including trucks, tanks, planes, rolling stock, machine tools, textiles, boots, oil, food, and raw materials. While Lend-Lease supplies were a relatively modest part of the Red Army's arsenal, in some Soviet military operations, particularly the large-scale spring offensive of 1944, they played an indispensable role.

There were also many examples of effective military coordination within the Grand Alliance. After 1941 the British and Soviets acted in concert in Iran, when they occupied the country to avert an imminent pro-German coup. As a result, Iran was secured for the coalition and became a major artery of supplies for the Soviet war effort. As for the Anglo-American invasion of Europe, the Soviets continuously called for a second front during

all interallied conferences in 1941–1943. In May 1942 Soviet foreign minister Vyacheslav Molotov visited London and Washington to explain his country's military situation and to request the opening of a second front by the Western Allies in order to relieve pressure on the Red Army. At the Moscow Conference (August 1942) Soviet leader Josef Stalin, Churchill, and Roosevelt's envoy W. Averell Harriman discussed the issue of a second front in Europe. The Soviets were informed about the planned operation (code-named "Torch") the Allied landing in North Africa (November 1942).

At the Moscow Conference of Foreign Ministers (October–November 1943) the Grand Alliance formulated its main strategic aim for the end of the war—the doctrine of unconditional surrender that Roosevelt and Churchill had articulated in Casablanca (January 1943). At the Teheran Conference (November–December 1943) Churchill, Roosevelt, and Stalin made concerted military and political plans for the Anglo-American invasion of France (operation "Overlord") and a coordinated Russian offensive on the Eastern Front. Stalin also promised that the Soviet Union would enter the war against Japan three months after the defeat of Germany. The coordination of the common struggle against Japan was a matter of discussion during the last Big Three summit at Potsdam (July–August 1945), and indeed, the Soviets attacked Japanese forces in Manchuria and Korea on 8 August, exactly three months after Germany's surrender on 8 May.

The political aspects of coalition warfare were of much importance as well. At an interallied conference in London (September 1941) the Soviets pledged their adherence to the principles of the Atlantic Charter, adopted by Churchill and Roosevelt in August 1941, which called for Allied unity in the struggle against Germany and supported every nation's freedom to choose its government. On 1 January 1942 in Washington the Big Three and twenty-three other nations at war with the Axis powers concluded a pact not to make separate armistices with the enemy. The Washington Pact became the nucleus of the United Nations (UN). The official name of the anti-Axis coalition expressed the hopes that wartime alliance would be transformed into postwar international organization to preserve peace, security, and cooperation.

At the 1943 Moscow meeting the Big Three furthermore agreed on provisional formulas for joint military/political decision making in liberated countries, the restoration of democracy in Austria and Italy, and the punishment of German war criminals. They also agreed to establish the European Advisory Commission in London to discuss the future of Germany. Political cooperation within the alliance reached a new level at the Moscow summit between Stalin and Churchill in

COLLABORATION

On 19 June 1942 Soviet foreign minister Vyacheslav Molotov reported to the Supreme Soviet about his treaty negotiations with the British:

The second part of the treaty is comparatively new. The significance of this part of the treaty consists, first, in the fact that it lays down for the first time basic principles for friendly collaboration between the USSR and Great Britain after the war. It also provides for collaboration by both countries with the other United Nations in the peace settlement and in the postwar period. This collaboration is conceived along the lines of the basic principles of the well known Atlantic Charter, to which the USSR in good time adhered.

There can be no doubt that an agreement of this kind will be of great significance in the entire future development of Europe. Both countries agreed to work together after the re-establishment of peace "for the organization of security and economic prosperity in Europe." The treaty states that both countries "will take into account the interests of the United Nations in realizing this objective and will act in accord with the two principles of not seeking territorial aggrandizement for themselves and of non-interference in the internal affairs of other states."

These principles of the treaty fully accord with the well known pronouncement made by the head of the Government of the USSR, Comrade Stalin, on November 6 last year, when he said: "We have not and cannot have any such war aims as the seizure of foreign territories and the subjugation of foreign peoples, whether it be peoples and territories of Europe or peoples and territories of Asia, including Iran."

Stressing their lack of any desire for territorial aggrandizement for themselves and their policy of non-interference in the internal affairs of other states, the Soviet Union and Great Britain proclaim the friendly principles of their policy toward all freedom-loving nations and at the same time point to the fundamental difference between their policy and the aggressive policy of Hitlerite Germany, which is fighting for seizure of the territory of other nations and for their enslavement. . . .

The clear and categorical nature of this mutual undertaking is of high importance to the countries which are striving to ensure a stable peace after the victorious termination of this war. Further, everyone realizes the importance of the fact that both Governments have agreed that all the above-mentioned obligations relating to the post-war period shall remain in force for a prolonged period, 20 years being the term envisaged, with the possibility of its prolongation.

It is also asked whether, in addition to the published treaty, any secret agreements were concluded between the USSR and Great Britain. I must declare, with a full sense of responsibility, that these assumptions are absolutely unfounded and that no secret Anglo-Soviet agreements exist, as likewise there exist no secret Soviet-American agreements.

After all that has been said, one cannot help associating oneself with the words uttered by Mr. Eden in his speech on the signing of the treaty, when he said: "Never before in the history of our two countries has our association been so close or our mutual pledge for the future so complete. This is surely a happy augury." . . .

. . . Serious attention was naturally paid in our negotiations both in London and in Washington to problems of a second front in Europe. The results of these negotiations are dealt with in similar words both in Anglo-Soviet and Soviet-American communiqués. Both communiqués declare that in the negotiations "complete understanding was reached with regard to the urgent tasks of creating a second front in Europe in 1942."

This statement is of great importance to the peoples of the Soviet Union, since the creation of a second front in Europe will make insuperable difficulties for Hitler's armies on our front. Let us hope that our common enemy will soon experience to his cost the results of the ever growing military collaboration of the three great powers.

Furthermore, questions were discussed of further improving and increasing munitions deliveries to the Soviet Union from the United States and Great Britain. Here too positive results may be recorded. In the second half of the current year deliveries of munitions and supplies to the USSR by the Allies will be increased and accelerated. This is confirmed above all by the increasing dimensions of deliveries from the United States.

As we know, last November the United States of America decided to accord the Soviet Union a loan of $1,000,000,000 to pay for munitions deliveries to the Soviet Union. As for the new program of deliveries, the United States fixes its total value at $3,000,000,000. Thus we have a further substantial increase in the military-economic assistance rendered to the Soviet Union by the United States of America, as well as the consent of Great Britain to further improve munitions deliveries.

In this connection we must recognize the supreme importance of the "agreement between the Governments of the Union of Soviet Socialist Republics and the United States of America on principles applying to mutual aid in the prosecution of the war against aggression" signed in Washington June 11, which follows the lines of a similar agreement between the United States and Great Britain. This agreement is of a preliminary nature and lays down only principles of future agreement between the two governments in question.

The significance of this Soviet-American agreement lies in that it not only proceeds from recognition of the fact of the fighting collaboration established between the Soviet Union and the United States of America in the present war against Hitlerite Germany, but also provides for coordinated action between the two countries in the post-war period. The agreement implies an understanding between the USSR and the United States as regards the improvement of international relationships after the war in the interests of the stability of the peace. Consequently, the Washington agreement is of great significance to the United States and the Soviet Union as well as to other nations.

Source: *"Molotov's Report on Ratification of the Anglo-Soviet Treaty to the Supreme Soviet of the Union of Soviet Socialist Republics: Moscow, June 19, 1942," Information Bulletin, Embassy of the U.S.S.R., Washington, D.C., 19 June 1942.*

October 1944, when both leaders agreed on the division of Eastern Europe into zones of influence. The British accepted Soviet dominance in Romania and Bulgaria, while Stalin agreed to British influence in Greece and Yugoslavia, with leverage in Hungary split between the two powers.

At the Yalta Conference in February 1945 the Big Three reached agreement on immediate postwar issues: German reparations, four-power occupation of the defeated country, and the trial of major war criminals. While issues of the postwar status of Eastern Europe, particularly the Polish Question, were frequent matters of disagreement between the U.S.S.R. and the West, the need for military and political cooperation prompted the Allies to compromise. In 1943–1945 the United States and Britain recognized the Soviet annexation of Poland's former eastern territories and accepted the idea that Poland should be compensated for its territorial losses with German territory. The Soviets on their part agreed to coalition governments for Poland and other Eastern European countries. Discussions on a new international organization culminated in the signing of the Charter of the United Nations at the San Francisco Conference in April 1945. Final arrangements for the postwar settlement, including the peace treaty with former enemies, were discussed at the Potsdam Conference.

It should be noted that contacts among the Big Three contributed to the practice of international relations. The United States and Britain coordinated strategic and political decisions to an extent and by means unprecedented in earlier wars. While the Western Allies institutionalized their cooperation in an integrated military command and close collaboration on atomic weaponry, contacts with the Soviets relied mainly on personal connections between the Allied heads of governments. The Big Three held in their hands the power to make major decisions in war and diplomacy—therefore, the development of personal relations and trust between Roosevelt and Churchill on the one hand, and these two leaders and Stalin on the other, was of cardinal importance. Additionally, the war occurred at a time when communications had developed sufficiently to alter the nature of diplomacy and decision making. Air travel facilitated personal contacts between political leaders on short notice. Interallied relations also initiated the birth of direct "summit" diplomacy at the expense of traditional diplomatic channels and institutions.

The Allied powers were firmly united in their pursuit of ultimate victory. Ideological differences between the West and the Soviets were overlaid by the pronouncement of the Grand Alliance's anti-fascist and democratic principles. This overarching concern allowed the United States, Britain, and the Soviet Union to develop the strategic, politi-cal, and military cooperation that was closer and more effective than the enemy's and that was one of the reasons for the Axis's total defeat in a global war. As Churchill said after his first encounter with Stalin in 1942, "we were good and faithful comrades in this war."

—PETER RAINOW,
SAN MATEO, CALIFORNIA

Viewpoint:
No. The Allies were consumed by mutual suspicions, strategic disagreements, and serious controversies over the postwar peace settlement.

During World War II (1939–1945) Soviet leader Josef Stalin told his Yugoslav communist comrades, "This war is not as in the past; whoever occupies a territory also imposes on it his own social system as far as his army can reach. Everyone imposes his own system as far as his army can reach. It cannot be otherwise." Consistent with this thinking, when Stalin signed the Atlantic Charter (1941), with its pledges of democracy and multilateral international trade, he added the reservation that "practical application of these principles will necessarily adapt itself to the circumstances, needs, and historic peculiarities of particular countries." With Stalin's views so sharply divergent from those of his Western allies, there was little chance the wartime cooperation of the Grand Alliance (the United States, Great Britain, and the Union of Soviet Socialist Republics) would continue into the postwar period. Despite efforts, especially by U.S. president Franklin D. Roosevelt, to smooth over differences among the Allies, there were simply too many sources of disagreement. The Grand Alliance was never based on a shared vision of the postwar world. Rather, nations with different worldviews were thrust together by the threat of Nazi ascendancy in Europe. With the defeat of German leader Adolf Hitler and the destruction of Nazi Germany, there was no longer sufficient glue to hold the alliance together.

While Cold War hostilities, pitting the United States and Britain against the Soviet Union after World War II, were not unanticipated, it bears mentioning that during the war many in the United States expected greater difficulty in postwar relations with the British. While the Soviets maintained their empire of contiguous peoples whose ethnic or linguistic distinctions were often lost on Americans, the British had an extensive overseas empire that seemed to

Josef Stalin, Franklin D.
Roosevelt, and Winston
Churchill (l-r)
at the Teheran
Conference in 1943

*(Imperial War Museum,
London)*

clash with the promises of self-determination and multilateral trade of the Atlantic Charter. Many Americans expected that the British would strive to maintain their imperial system against U.S. efforts to encourage self-government, in places such as India, and to reduce trade barriers generally.

Not only were there disagreements between the United States and Britain on the specifics of the postwar world but they also clashed about wartime strategy. The Americans were far more eager than the British to launch a cross-channel invasion of France that American military planners thought was essential to ending the war. British determination to fight in the Mediterranean seemed to be a distraction from the true focus of Allied efforts to defeat the Nazis. The Americans ultimately vetoed post-Normandy (1944) efforts by Churchill to land forces in the Balkans to try to strengthen Britain's traditional position in the eastern Mediterranean and to halt Soviet progression through Eastern Europe that was causing worry among diplomats representing the United States and the United Kingdom.

While disagreements between the Americans and the British showed the difficulties of maintaining the Grand Alliance even among nations of similar language, law, and customs, the U.S.-U.K. disputes paled in comparison to philosophical differences between the United Kingdom and the United States on the one hand and the Soviet Union on the other. The postwar division of Europe, and the acceptance of that division, suggests that the two sides might have found ways to maintain their wartime relationship, but ideological hostility and mutual suspicions dating back to the establishment of the Bolshevik regime in 1917 were too much to overcome. In addition, the Soviets were gravely weakened by their wartime exertion; historian Thomas G. Paterson has noted that the Soviets, as winners, had suffered greater damage than the losers of earlier wars. This weakness brought on by wartime devastation encouraged Stalin's suspicions and further precluded the possibility that the two sides would build a trusting relationship.

Despite their ideological differences and a mutual enmity that lasted until 1989–1991, the

Western Allies and the Soviets eventually reached a modus vivendi in a divided Europe in which each side implicitly recognized the other's interests. This arrangement suggests the possibility that such a division could have occurred without the hostility that marked postwar Europe. In this regard the role of the Nordic countries appears instructive. Without warfare, and with less tension than was present elsewhere in Europe, the Nordic countries divided their loyalties in the Cold War while retaining cordial relations among themselves. The five Nordic Council nations—Iceland, Norway, Denmark, Sweden, and Finland—took different approaches to the Cold War while continuing their cooperation. Finland developed close ties with the Soviets while remaining technically neutral. Sweden was officially neutral while quietly developing closer ties with Western Europe. Norway, Denmark, and Iceland joined the United States and United Kingdom in the North Atlantic Treaty Organization (NATO). The Soviets eventually recognized the importance of Norway, Denmark, and Iceland to American lines of communication, while the Western allies eventually conceded the importance of Finland to Soviet defenses, and each side recognized that Sweden was not worth a general European war. Yet, even in this part of Europe, tensions and hostility were problematic. Some NATO members wanted to include Finland for fear that abandonment of the Finns would lead to their absorption by the Soviets. The Soviets permitted the Finns to keep their independence for a variety of reasons that were not replicated elsewhere in Europe; there was little chance that the Soviets would have permitted other Eastern European nations to enjoy the Finnish combination of internal independence and Soviet-oriented defense policies. Before accepting Norwegian involvement with the Western European democracies, the Soviets made overtures to the Oslo government suggesting that they sought bases on the North Sea that would have threatened the Western democracies' lines of communication.

The Nordic countries are also instructive to considerations of postwar possibilities for the Grand Alliance because of Soviet actions in, and Western response to, the Winter War in Finland (1939–1940). After the German attack on the Soviet Union most of Stalin's activities prior to June 1941, including the invasion of Finland, were explained away in the West as part of his efforts to prepare to defend against the coming Nazi onslaught. The reality, however, is that Stalin sought to take advantage of the disarray in Eastern Europe and his treaty with Hitler to expand Soviet territory and influence. The Soviets had participated in the partitioning of Poland with the Nazis in 1939. Moreover, the Soviets had much more expansive designs on Finland before the realities of the Winter War forced a

revision of Soviet intentions. Before launching their invasion of Finland, the Soviets unleashed a campaign of invective against the Finns, classifying their Nordic neighbors as "pigs, reptiles, bandits and warmongers." Presaging what they would do when "liberating" Poland toward the end of World War II, the Soviets established a People's Democratic Government of Finland in the first border town they seized; this entity was designed to become the government in Helsinki after the Finns were defeated. Following Hitler's example from his attack on Poland, the Soviets fabricated a border incident to charge that the Finns had attacked them first. Like the Nazis in Poland, the Soviets followed up their introduction of military forces by bombing cities, a policy designed to terrorize the civilian population.

Stalin in this case, however, benefited from his own military ineptitude: when the Red Army encountered considerable difficulty in subduing the Finns, he negotiated a peace in which he accepted much more limited territorial gains than he initially had expected. This reversal made it possible for his apologists in the West later to characterize the Soviet effort against the Finns as a merely defensive attempt to prepare for coming Nazi aggression. The apologists did not need to deal with the efforts to establish a Communist dictatorship in Finland, as they had to explain away Soviet complicity in the division of Poland, or the similarity between Stalin and Hitler in their tactics for instigating aggressive wars with smaller neighbors. Stalin's aggressive designs on Poland, Finland, and the Baltic republics closely resembled the aggressive expansionism of Hitler, Italian leader Benito Mussolini, and the Japanese. Despite this similarity in aims and methods between the Soviets and the Axis powers, Roosevelt's understanding of the potential utility of the Red Army against Nazi Germany prevented him from taking steps in response to Soviet conduct that would have undermined possibilities for cooperation between the Western democracies and the Soviets.

Roosevelt's commitment to make common cause with the Soviets, shared with Churchill despite his history of antipathy to communism, made obvious sense from a strategic standpoint. This combination would permit the Western democracies to defeat Hitler more assuredly and at much lower cost. However, the willingness of Roosevelt and Churchill to pursue distasteful short-term policies overlooking Soviet aggression in the interest of larger strategic goals should not be confused with a genuine similarity of interests between the Western democracies and Soviet totalitarianism.

Despite the stark differences in worldview among the members of the Grand Alliance, wartime propaganda in the West, particularly in the

United States, suggested that the war was having a purifying effect on the Soviet Union. Americans could read or see the 1943 movie version of Joseph E. Davies' pro-Stalin memoir *Mission to Moscow* (1941), which was denigrated as "Submission to Moscow" because of its fawning over the dictator. Or they could see Frank Capra's movie *The Battle of Russia* (1943) and hear its paeans to religious freedom in the U.S.S.R. and descriptions of Soviet peoples fighting for "freedom." Those individuals exposed to such distorted views of life under Stalin could be forgiven for thinking that there was significant common ground among the Allies. However, despite Roosevelt's efforts to reassure Stalin that he envisioned the Soviets playing an important role, on par with that of the United States and United Kingdom, in the postwar world, the Soviet dictator remained committed to unilateral efforts to impose his will as far as his armies reached. The disparity in thinking between Roosevelt and Stalin was made clear in Poland. Roosevelt in the Yalta agreements appeared willing to give Stalin considerable latitude in the construction of a government as long as the dictator provided some appearance of following the forms of democracy envisioned in the Declaration on Liberated Europe (February 1945). When Stalin established a brutal pro-Soviet dictatorship there, the disparity between the two sides and their aims became unmistakably clear.

Disagreements among the Grand Alliance in the later years of World War II were nothing new. In fact, the legacy of suspicions between the Western Allies and the U.S.S.R. dated back so far, and involved so much history, that it would have been an almost Herculean task for the leaders to overlook it. American refusal to recognize the Communist government until 1933, the intervention of Western forces in the Russian Civil War (1918–1920), Western resistance to Soviet proposals calling for collective security measures against Hitler in the 1930s, America's refusal to deliver a warship Roosevelt promised to Stalin, repeated delays in the promised Second Front in France, and failure to share with Stalin details about the atomic weapons project (that he knew about through espionage), all conspired to convince the Soviets of inherent Western hostility. At the same time, Soviet refusal to pay debts the Americans expected as part of the agreement conferring diplomatic recognition on Moscow, the Soviet agreement with Hitler that made World War II possible, the brutality of the Soviet invasion of democratic Finland, unsuccessful Soviet efforts to establish a Communist Finnish government, and Soviet espionage to penetrate wartime allies on a scale usu-ally reserved for enemies, all suggested the Soviets would be at best reluctant collaborators in a peaceful, democratic postwar world.

The fact that the United States and the United Kingdom on the one hand, and the Soviet Union on the other, had such different views of what constituted peace and democracy meant that there was little chance that their wartime cooperation would continue into the postwar period. Hitler had required them to overcome their suspicions and hostility to ensure his defeat, but even while cooperating they could not completely set aside their suspicions. Without the war, the legacy of suspicion and the different ideologies made continued cooperation a task of insurmountable difficulty. The Grand Alliance could not be sustained in peacetime.

–JOHN A. SOARES JR.,
CINCINNATI, OHIO

References

Robert Beitzell, *The Uneasy Alliance: America, Britain, and Russia, 1941–1943* (New York: Knopf, 1972).

George N. Crocker, *Roosevelt's Road to Russia* (Chicago: Regnery, 1959).

Herbert Feis, *Churchill, Roosevelt, Stalin: The War They Waged and the Peace They Sought* (Princeton: Princeton University Press, 1957).

John Lewis Gaddis, *We Now Know: Rethinking Cold War History* (Oxford: Clarendon Press, 1997; New York: Oxford University Press, 1997).

Steven Merritt Miner, *Between Churchill and Stalin: The Soviet Union, Great Britain, and the Origins of the Grand Alliance* (Chapel Hill: University of North Carolina Press, 1988).

Robert Nisbet, *Roosevelt and Stalin: The Failed Courtship* (Washington, D.C.: Regnery Gateway, 1988).

Thomas G. Paterson, *On Every Front: The Making and Unmaking of the Cold War,* revised edition (New York: Norton, 1992).

Amos Perlmutter, *FDR & Stalin: A Not So Grand Alliance, 1943–1945* (Columbia: University of Missouri Press, 1993).

R. C. Raack, *Stalin's Drive to the West, 1938–1945: The Origin of the Cold War* (Stanford, Cal.: Stanford University Press, 1995).

REFERENCES

1. GENERAL

Aldcroft, Derek H. *From Versailles to Wall Street, 1919–1929*. London: John Lane, 1977; Berkeley: University of California Press, 1977.

Aron, Raymond. *In Defense of Decadent Europe*. Translated by Stephen Cox. South Bend, Ind.: Regnery/Gateway, 1977.

Barraclough, Geoffrey. *An Introduction to Contemporary History*. London: Watts, 1964.

Black, C. E. and E. C. Helmreich. *Twentieth Century Europe: A History*. New York: Knopf, 1950.

Ferro, Marc. *Colonization: A Global History*. Translated by K. D. Prithipaul. Quebec: World Heritage Press, 1997.

Holborn, Hajo. *The Political Collapse of Europe*. New York: Knopf, 1951.

Kennedy, Paul M. *The Rise and Fall of the Great Powers: Economic Change and Military Conflict from 1500 to 2000*. New York: Random House, 1987.

Palmer, R. R. and Joel Colton. *History of the Modern World*. Sixth edition. New York: Knopf, 1984.

Sontag, Raymond J. *A Broken World, 1919–1939*. New York: Harper & Row, 1971.

Spellman, W. M. *Monarchies 1000–2000*. London: Reaktion, 2001.

Taylor, A. J. P. *The Struggle for Mastery in Europe, 1848–1918*. Oxford: Clarendon Press, 1954.

Toynbee, Arnold. *The World and the West*. New York: Oxford University Press, 1953.

Vinen, Richard. *A History in Fragments: Europe in the Twentieth Century*. Cambridge, Mass.: Da Capo Press, 2001.

2. BIOGRAPHY

Ascher, Abraham. *P. A. Stolypin: The Search for Stability in Late Imperial Russia*. Stanford, Cal.: Stanford University Press, 2001.

Bullock, Alan. *Hitler: A Study in Tyranny*. New York: Harper, 1952.

Carrère d'Encausse, Hélène. *Nicholas II: The Interrupted Transition*. Translated by George Holoch. New York: Holmes & Meier, 2000.

Fest, Joachim C. *Hitler*. Translated by Richard and Clara Winston. New York: Harcourt Brace Jovanovich, 1974.

Kaplan, Alice. *The Collaborator: The Trial & Execution of Robert Brasillach*. Chicago: University of Chicago Press, 2000.

Payne, Robert. *The Life and Death of Adolf Hitler*. New York: Praeger, 1973.

Réau, Elisabeth du. *Edouard Daladier, 1884–1970*. Paris: Fayard, 1993.

3. CENTRAL & EASTERN EUROPE

Berend, Ivan T. *Decades of Crisis: Central and Eastern Europe before World War II*. Berkeley: University of California Press, 1998.

Crampton, R. J. *Eastern Europe in the Twentieth Century—and After*. Second edition. London & New York: Routledge, 1997.

Denitch, Bogdan. *Ethnic Nationalism: The Tragic Death of Yugoslavia*. Revised edition. Minneapolis: University of Minnesota Press, 1996.

Glenny, Misha. *The Balkans: Nationalism, War, and the Great Powers, 1804–1999*. New York: Viking, 2000.

Haviv, Ron. *Blood and Honey: A Balkan War Journal*. New York: TV Books, 2000.

Jászi, Oszkár. *The Dissolution of the Habsburg Monarchy*. Chicago: University of Chicago Press, 1929.

Jelavich, Barbara. *History of the Balkans*. Cambridge & New York: Cambridge University Press, 1983.

Johnson, Lonnie. *Central Europe: Enemies, Neighbors, Friends*. New York: Oxford University Press, 1996.

Naimark, Norman and Leonid Gibianskii, eds. *The Establishment of Communist Regimes in Eastern Europe, 1944–1949*. Boulder, Colo.: Westview Press, 1997.

Okey, Robin. *Eastern Europe 1740–1985: Feudalism to Communism*. Minneapolis: University of Minnesota Press, 1986.

Polonsky, Antony and Boleslaw Drukier, eds. *The Beginnings of Communist Rule in Poland*. London & Boston: Routledge & Kegan Paul, 1980.

Ramet, Sabrina. *Balkan Babel: The Disintegration of Yugoslavia from the Death of Tito to the Fall of Milosevic*. Fourth edition, enlarged. Boulder, Colo.: Westview Press, 2002.

Rothschild, Joseph. *East Central Europe between the Two World Wars*. Seattle: University of Washington Press, 1974.

Rothschild. *Return to Diversity: A Political History of East Central Europe since World War II*. New York: Oxford University Press, 1989.

Seton-Watson, Hugh. *Eastern Europe between the Wars, 1918–1941*. Third edition. New York: Harper & Row, 1967.

Zeman, Z. A. B. *The Break-up of the Habsburg Empire, 1914–1918: A Study in National and Social Revolution*. London & New York: Oxford University Press, 1961.

4. COLD WAR

Brzezinski, Zbigniew K. *The Grand Failure: The Birth and Death of Communism in the Twentieth Century.* New York: Scribners, 1989.

Chand, Attar. *Nuclear Disarmament and Foreign Policy.* New Delhi: Akashdeep, 1992.

English, Robert D. *Russia and the Idea of the West: Gorbachev, Intellectuals, and the End of the Cold War.* New York: Columbia University Press, 2000.

Fedorowich, Kent and Martin Thomas, eds. *Diplomacy and Colonial Retreat.* London & Portland, Ore.: Frank Cass, 2001.

Gaddis, John Lewis. *The United States and the End of the Cold War: Implications, Reconsiderations, Provocations.* New York: Oxford University Press, 1992.

Gaddis. *We Now Know: Rethinking Cold War History.* Oxford: Clarendon Press, 1997; New York: Oxford University Press, 1997.

Garthoff, Raymond L. *The Great Transition: American-Soviet Relations and the End of the Cold War.* Washington, D.C.: Brookings Institution, 1994.

Jakobson, Max. *Finland: Myth and Reality.* Helsinki: Otava Publishing Company, 1987.

Leffler, Melvyn P. *A Preponderance of Power: National Security, the Truman Administration, and the Cold War.* Stanford, Cal.: Stanford University Press, 1992.

Mark, Eduard. "Revolution by Degrees: Stalin's National-Front Strategy for Europe, 1941–1947." Working Paper 31, Washington, D.C.: Cold War International History Project, Woodrow Wilson International Center for Scholars, 2001.

Oberdorfer, Don. *The Turn: From the Cold War to a New Era: The United States and the Soviet Union, 1983–1990.* New York: Poseidon Press, 1991.

Parrish, Scott D. and Mikhail M. Narinsky. "New Evidence on the Soviet Rejection of the Marshall Plan, 1947: Two Reports." Working Paper 9. Washington, D.C.: Cold War International History Project, Woodrow Wilson International Center For Scholars, 1994.

Paterson, Thomas G. *On Every Front: The Making and Unmaking of the Cold War.* Revised edition. New York: Norton, 1992.

Pechatnov, Vladimir O. "The Big Three after World War II: New Documents on Soviet Thinking about Post War Relations with the United States and Great Britain." Working Paper 13. Washington, D.C.: Cold War International History Project, Woodrow Wilson International Center For Scholars, 1995.

Polvinen, Tuomo. *Between East and West: Finland in International Politics, 1944–1947.* Edited and translated by D. G. Kirby and Peter Herring. Minneapolis: University of Minnesota Press, 1986.

Raack, R. C. *Stalin's Drive to the West, 1938–1945: The Origin of the Cold War.* Stanford, Cal.: Stanford University Press, 1995.

Ruddy, T. Michael, ed. *Charting an Independent Course: Finland's Place in the Cold War and in U.S. Foreign Policy.* Claremont, Cal.: Regina Books, 1998.

Schweizer, Peter. *Victory: The Reagan Administration's Secret Strategy that Hastened the Collapse of the Soviet Union.* New York: Atlantic Monthly Press, 1994.

Stent, Angela E. *Russia and Germany Reborn: Unification, the Soviet Collapse, and the New Europe.* Princeton: Princeton University Press, 1999.

Taubman, William. *Stalin's American Policy: From Entente to Détente to Cold War.* New York: Norton, 1982.

Yegorova, Natalia I. "The 'Iran Crisis' of 1945–1946: A View from the Russian Archives." Working Paper 15. Washington, D.C.: Cold War International History Project, Woodrow Wilson International Center For Scholars, 1996.

5. FRANCE

Agulhon, Maurice. *The French Republic, 1879–1992.* Translated by Antonia Nevill. Oxford & Cambridge, Mass.: Blackwell, 1995.

Ardagh, John. *France in the New Century: Portrait of a Changing Society.* Revised edition. London & New York: Penguin, 2000.

Bernard, Philippe and Henri Dubief. *The Decline of the Third Republic, 1914–1938.* Translated by Anthony Forster. Cambridge & New York: Cambridge University Press, 1985; Paris: Maison des sciences de l'homme, 1985.

Berstein, Serge. *La France des années 30.* Paris: Colin, 1988.

Blatt, Joel, ed. *The French Defeat of 1940: Reassessments.* Providence, R.I.: Berghahn Books, 1998.

Bloch, Marc. *Strange Defeat: A Statement of Evidence Written in 1940.* Translated by Gerard Hopkins. London & New York: Oxford University Press, 1949.

Burrin, Philippe. *France under the Germans: Collaboration and Compromise.* Translated by Janet Lloyd. New York: New Press, 1996.

Crémieux-Brilhac, Jean-Louis. *Les Français de l'an 40.* 2 volumes. Paris: Gallimard, 1990.

Duroselle, Jean-Baptiste. *La Décadence: Politique étrangère de la France, 1932–1939.* Paris: Imprimerie Nationale, 1979.

Fenby, Jonathan. *France on the Brink.* New York: Arcade, 1999.

Hellman, John. *The Knight-Monks of Vichy France: Uriage, 1940–1945.* Montreal & Buffalo: McGill-Queen's University Press, 1993.

Irvine, William D. *French Conservatism in Crisis: The Republican Federation of France in the 1930s.* Baton Rouge: Louisiana State University Press, 1979.

Kedward, Roderick and Roger Austin, eds. *Vichy France and the Resistance: Culture & Ideology.* London: Croom Helm, 1985; Totowa, N.J.: Barnes & Noble, 1985.

Knapp, Andrew and Vincent Wright. *Government and Politics of France.* Fourth edition. London & New York: Routledge, 2001.

Kolodziej, Edward E. *French International Policy under de Gaulle and Pompidou: The Politics of Grandeur.* Ithaca, N.Y.: Cornell University Press, 1974.

Lacaze, Yvon. *La France et Munich: étude d'un processus décisionnel en matière de relations internationales.* Berne & New York: Peter Lang, 1992.

Larkin, Maurice. *France since the Popular Front: Government and People, 1936–1996.* Second edition. Oxford & New York: Clarendon Press, 1997.

May, Ernest R. *Strange Victory: Hitler's Conquest of France.* New York: Hill & Wang, 2000.

McMillan, James F. *Twentieth-Century France: Politics and Society 1898–1991.* London & New York: Arnold, 1992.

Newhouse, John. *De Gaulle and the Anglo-Saxons.* London: Deutsch, 1970; New York: Viking, 1970.

Paxton, Robert O. *Vichy France: Old Guard and New Order, 1940–1944.* New York: Knopf, 1972.

Prost, Antoine. *In the Wake of War: Les anciens combattants and French Society.* Translated by Helen McPhail. Providence, R.I.: Berg, 1992.

Rioux, Jean-Pierre. *The Fourth Republic, 1944–1958.* Translated by Godfrey Rogers. Cambridge & New York: Cambridge University Press, 1987.

Rousso, Henry. *The Vichy Syndrome: History and Memory in France since 1944.* Translated by Arthur Goldhammer. Cambridge, Mass.: Harvard University Press, 1991.

Soucy, Robert. *French Fascism: The First Wave, 1924–1933.* New Haven: Yale University Press, 1986.

Soucy. *French Fascism: The Second Wave, 1933–1939.* New Haven: Yale University Press, 1995.

Sternhell, Zeev. *Neither Right nor Left: Fascist Ideology in France.* Translated by David Maisel. Berkeley: University of California Press, 1986.

Stevens, Anne. *The Government and Politics of France.* New York: St. Martin's Press, 1992; London: Macmillan, 1992.

Weber, Eugen. *Action Française.* Stanford, Cal.: Stanford University Press, 1962.

Weber. *The Hollow Years: France in the 1930s.* New York: Norton, 1994.

Wright, Gordon. *France in Modern Times: From the Enlightenment to the Present.* Fifth edition. New York: Norton, 1995.

Young, Robert J. *In Command of France: French Foreign Policy and Military Planning, 1933–1940.* Cambridge, Mass.: Harvard University Press, 1978.

Zuccotti, Susan. *The Holocaust, the French, and the Jews.* New York: Basic Books, 1993.

6. GERMANY

Allen, William Sheridan. *The Nazi Seizure of Power: The Experience of a Single German Town, 1922–1945.* Revised edition. New York: Watts, 1984.

Berghahn, V. R. *Germany and the Approach of War in 1914.* London: Macmillan, 1973; New York: St. Martin's Press, 1973.

Bracher, Karl Dietrich. *The German Dictatorship: The Origins, Structures, and Effects of National Socialism.* Translated by Jean Steinberg. New York: Praeger, 1970.

Craig, Gordon A. *Germany, 1866–1945.* Oxford: Clarendon Press, 1978; New York: Oxford University Press, 1978.

Gay, Peter. *Weimar Culture: The Outsider as Insider.* New York: Harper & Row, 1968.

Koch, H. W., ed. *Aspects of the Third Reich.* London: Macmillan, 1985; New York: St. Martin's Press, 1985.

Morris, Warren B. Jr. *The Weimar Republic and Nazi Germany.* Chicago: Nelson-Hall, 1982.

Panayi, Panikos, ed. *Weimar and Nazi Germany: Continuities and Discontinuities.* Harlow, U.K. & New York: Longman, 2001.

Shirer, William L. *The Rise and Fall of the Third Reich: A History of Nazi Germany.* New York: Simon & Schuster, 1960.

7. GREAT BRITAIN

Balfour-Paul, Glen. *The End of Empire in the Middle East: Britain's Relinquishment of Power in Her Last Three Arab Dependencies.* Cambridge & New York: Cambridge University Press, 1991.

Boyce, D. George. *Decolonization and the British Empire.* New York: St. Martin's Press, 1999.

Darwin, John. *Britain and Decolonisation: The Retreat from Empire in the Post-War World.* New York: St. Martin's Press, 1988.

Gilbert, Bentley B. *Britain, 1914–1945: The Aftermath of Power.* Wheeling, Ill.: Harlan Davidson, 1995.

Harris, Kenneth. *The Queen: Royalty and Reality.* New York: St. Martin's Press, 1995.

Hazlehurst, Cameron. *Politicians at War, July 1914 to May 1915: A Prologue to the Triumph of Lloyd George.* London: Cape, 1971.

James, Lawrence. *Imperial Rearguard: Wars of Empire, 1919–85.* London & Washington, D.C.: Brassey's Defense Publishers, 1988; Elmsford, N.Y.: Pergamon Press, 1988.

James. *The Rise and Fall of the British Empire.* London: Little, Brown, 1994.

Johnson, Paul. *The Offshore Islanders.* London: Weidenfeld & Nicolson, 1972.

Marwick, Arthur. *Britain in the Century of Total War: War, Peace and Social Change, 1900–1967.* London: Bodley Head, 1968.

Schmidt, Gustav. *The Politics and Economics of Appeasement: British Foreign Policy in the 1930s.* New York: St. Martin's Press, 1986.

Taylor, Anthony. *"Down with the Crown": British Anti-monarchism and Debates about Royalty since 1790.* London: Reaktion, 1999.

Wilson, Keith M. *The Policy of the Entente: Essays on the Determinants of British Foreign Policy, 1904–1914.* Cambridge & New York: Cambridge University Press, 1985.

8. INTERNATIONAL RELATIONS & DIPLOMACY

Burns, Richard Dean, ed. *Encyclopedia of Arms Control and Disarmament.* 3 volumes. New York: Scribners, 1993.

Carley, Michael Jabara. *1939: The Alliance That Never Was and the Coming of World War II.* Chicago: Dee, 1999.

Eden, Douglas, ed. *Europe and the Atlantic Relationship: Issues of Identity, Security, and Power.* New York: St. Martin's Press, 2000.

Elman, Colin and Miriam Fendius Elman, eds. *Bridges and Boundaries: Historians, Political Scientists, and the Study of International Relations.* Cambridge, Mass.: MIT Press, 2001.

Hanhimäki, Jussi M. *Containing Coexistence: America, Russia, and the "Finnish Solution."* Kent, Ohio: Kent State University Press, 1997.

Haslam, Jonathan. *The Soviet Union and the Struggle for Collective Security in Europe, 1933–1939.* New York: St. Martin's Press, 1984.

Hine, David and Hussein Kassim, eds. *Beyond the Market: The EU and National Social Policy.* London & New York: Routledge, 1998.

Howorth, Jolyon and John T. S. Keeler, eds. *Defending Europe: The EU, NATO and the Quest for European Autonomy.* New York: Palgrave Macmillan, 2003.

Kagan, Robert. *Of Paradise and Power: America and Europe in the New World Order.* New York: Knopf, 2003.

Kitching, Carolyn J. *Britain and the Geneva Disarmament Conference: A Study in International History.* New York: Palgrave Macmillan, 2003.

Lamb, Richard. *Drift to War, 1922–1939.* London: W. H. Allen, 1989.

Langhorne, Richard. *The Collapse of the Concert of Europe: International Politics, 1890–1914.* New York: St. Martin's Press, 1981.

MacMillan, Margaret. *Peacemakers: The Paris Conference of 1919 and Its Attempt to End War.* London: Murray, 2001.

Roberts, Geoffrey. *The Soviet Union and the Origins of the Second World War: Russo-German Relations and the*

REFERENCES

Road to War, 1933–1941. New York: St. Martin's Press, 1995.

Sur, Serge, ed. *Disarmament and Limitation of Armaments: Unilateral Measures and Policies.* New York: United Nations, 1992.

Tanner, Fred, ed. *From Versailles to Baghdad: Post-war Armament Control of Defeated States.* New York: United Nations, 1992.

Taylor, Telford. *Munich: The Price of Peace.* Garden City, N.Y.: Doubleday, 1979.

Tilford, Roger, ed. *The Ostpolitik and Political Change in Germany.* Farnborough, U.K.: Saxon House, 1975; Lexington, Mass.: Lexington Books, 1975.

Towle, Philip. *Enforced Disarmament: From the Napoleonic Campaigns to the Gulf War.* Oxford: Clarendon Press, 1997; New York: Oxford University Press, 1997.

Windsor, Philip. *Germany and the Management of Détente.* London: Chatto & Windus, 1971; New York: Praeger, 1971.

Yoder, Amos. *World Politics and Causes of War since 1914.* Lanham, Md.: University Press of America, 1986.

9. MEMOIRS, AUTOBIOGRAPHIES, & PRIMARY DOCUMENTS

Brandt, Willy. *My Life in Politics.* London & New York: Hamilton, 1992.

Corwin, Phillip. *Dubious Mandate: A Memoir of the UN in Bosnia, Summer 1995.* Durham, N.C.: Duke University Press, 1999.

Daniels, Robert V., ed. and trans. *A Documentary History of Communism in Russia: From Lenin to Gorbachev.* Third edition. Revised and updated. Hanover, N.H.: University Press of New England, 1993.

Gromyko, Andrei. *Memoirs.* Translated by Harold Shukman. New York: Doubleday, 1989.

Holbrooke, Richard. *To End a War.* New York: Random House, 1998.

Meese, Edwin III. *With Reagan: The Inside Story.* Washington, D.C.: Regnery Gateway, 1992.

Owen, David. *Balkan Odyssey.* New York: Harcourt Brace, 1995.

Stokes, Gale, ed. *From Stalinism to Pluralism, A Documentary History of Eastern Europe since 1945.* New York: Oxford University Press, 1991.

Trotsky, Leon. *The Essential Trotsky.* New York: Barnes & Noble, 1963.

United States Department of State. *Foreign Relations of the United States, Diplomatic Papers: The Conferences at Cairo and Tehran, 1943.* Washington, D.C.: Government Printing Office, 1961.

United States Department of State. *Foreign Relations of the United States, Diplomatic Papers: The Conferences of Malta and Yalta, 1945.* Washington, D.C.: Government Printing Office, 1955.

10. MIDDLE EAST & EUROPE

Cleveland, William L. *A History of the Modern Middle East.* Boulder, Colo.: Westview Press, 1994.

Dann, Uriel. *The Great Powers in the Middle East.* New York: Holmes & Meier, 1988.

Kunz, Diane B. *The Economic Diplomacy of the Suez Crisis.* Chapel Hill: University of North Carolina Press, 1991.

Owen, Roger. *The Middle East in the World Economy, 1800–1914.* London & New York: Methuen, 1981.

11. RUSSIA & THE SOVIET UNION

Bradley, John F. N. *Allied Intervention in Russia.* London: Weidenfeld & Nicolson, 1968.

Brooks, Jeffrey. *When Russia Learned to Read: Literacy and Popular Literature, 1861–1917.* Princeton: Princeton University Press, 1985.

Brown, Archie. *The Gorbachev Factor.* Oxford & New York: Oxford University Press, 1996.

Brzezinski, Zbigniew K. *The Soviet Bloc: Unity and Conflict.* Cambridge, Mass.: Harvard University Press, 1960.

Cohen, Stephen F. *Rethinking the Soviet Experience: Politics and History since 1917.* New York: Oxford University Press, 1985.

Conroy, Mary Schaeffer, ed. *Emerging Democracy in Late Imperial Russia: Case Studies on Local Self-Government (the Zemstvos), State Duma Elections, the Tsarist Government, and the State Council before and during World War I.* Niwot: University of Colorado Press, 1998.

Cracraft, James, ed. *Major Problems in the History of Imperial Russia.* Lexington, Mass.: Heath, 1994.

Dunlop, John B. *The Rise of Russia and the Fall of the Soviet Empire.* Princeton: Princeton University Press, 1993.

Figes, Orlando. *A People's Tragedy: The Russian Revolution, 1891–1924.* New York: Viking, 1997.

Gregory, Paul. *Before Command: An Economic History of Russia from the Emancipation to the First Five Year Plan.* Princeton: Princeton University Press, 1994.

Haigh, R. H., D. S. Morris, and A. R. Peters. *Soviet Foreign Policy, the League of Nations, and Europe, 1917–1939.* Aldershot, U.K.: Gower, 1986; Totowa, N.J.: Barnes & Noble, 1986.

Hamm, Michael F. *Kiev: A Portrait, 1800–1917.* Princeton: Princeton University Press, 1993.

Hosking, Geoffrey. *The First Socialist Society: A History of the Soviet Union From Within.* Second edition. Enlarged. Cambridge, Mass.: Harvard University Press, 1993.

Kennan, George F. *Soviet-American Relations, 1917–1920.* 2 volumes. Princeton: Princeton University Press, 1958.

Kotkin, Stephen. *Armageddon Averted: The Soviet Collapse, 1970–2000.* Oxford: Oxford University Press, 2001.

Kotz, David M. and Fred Weir. *Revolution from Above: The Demise of the Soviet System.* London & New York: Routledge, 1997.

Laird, Robbin F. and Erik P. Hoffmann, eds. *Soviet Foreign Policy in a Changing World.* Berlin & New York: de Gruyter, 1986; New York: Aldine, 1986.

Lieven, Dominic. *Empire: The Russian Empire and Its Rivals.* London: Murray, 2000.

Lieven. *Nicholas II: Twilight of the Empire.* New York: St. Martin's Press, 1994.

Lindenmeyr, Adèle. *Poverty Is Not a Vice: Charity, Society, and the State in Imperial Russia.* Princeton: Princeton University Press, 1996.

McDaniel, Tim. *Autocracy, Capitalism, and the Revolution in Russia.* Berkeley: University of California Press, 1988.

Menning, Bruce W. *Bayonets Before Bullets: The Imperial Russian Army, 1861–1914.* Bloomington: Indiana University Press, 1992.

Morley, William J. *The Japanese Thrust into Siberia, 1918.* New York: Columbia University Press, 1957.

Nation, R. Craig. *Black Earth, Red Star: A Hisory of Soviet Security Policy, 1917–1991.* Ithaca, N.Y.: Cornell University Press, 1992.

Odom, William E. *The Collapse of the Soviet Military.* New Haven: Yale University Press, 1998.

Petro, Nicolai N. *The Rebirth of Russian Democracy: An Interpretation of Political Culture.* Cambridge, Mass.: Harvard University Press, 1995.

Pipes, Richard. *The Russian Revolution.* New York: Knopf, 1990.

Rabinowitch, Alexander. *The Bolsheviks Come to Power: The Revolution of 1917 in Petrograd.* New York: Norton, 1976.

Riasanovsky, Nicholas V. *A History of Russia.* Sixth edition. New York: Oxford University Press, 2000.

Riha, Thomas, ed. *Readings in Russian Civilization.* 2 volumes. Second edition. Revised. Chicago & London: University of Chicago Press, 1969.

Silverlight, John. *The Victors' Dilemma: Allied Intervention in the Russian Civil War.* New York: Weybright & Talley, 1971.

Somin, Ilya. *Stillborn Crusade: The Tragic Failure of Western Intervention in the Russian Civil War, 1918–1920.* New Brunswick, N.J.: Transaction, 1996.

Suny, Ronald Grigor. *The Soviet Experiment: Russia, the USSR, and the Successor States.* New York: Oxford University Press, 1998.

Ullman, Richard H. *Anglo-Soviet Relations, 1917–1921.* 2 volumes. Princeton: Princeton University Press, 1961, 1968.

Unterberger, Betty Miller. *America's Siberian Expedition, 1918–1920: A Study of National Policy.* Durham, N.C.: Duke University Press, 1956.

Von Laue, Theodore H. *Why Lenin? Why Stalin? Why Gorbachev? The Rise and Fall of the Soviet System.* New York: HarperCollins, 1993.

Winters, Paul A., ed. *The Collapse of the Soviet Union.* San Diego, Cal.: Greenhaven Press, 1999.

Wolfe, Bertram D. *Three Who Made a Revolution: A Biographical History.* New York: Dial, 1948. Fourth edition, revised, 1964.

12. TERRORISM

Alexander, Yonah and Kenneth A. Myers, eds. *Terrorism in Europe.* London: Croom Helm, 1982; New York: St. Martin's Press, 1982.

Alexander and Dennis A. Pluchinsky, eds. *European Terrorism Today & Tomorrow.* Washington, D.C.: Brassey's Defense Publishers, 1992.

Laqueur, Walter. *A History of Terrorism.* New Brunswick, N.J.: Transaction, 2001.

13. TOTALITARIANISM

Arendt, Hannah. *The Origins of Totalitarianism.* New York: Harcourt, Brace, 1951.

Friedrich, Carl J., ed. *Totalitarianism.* Cambridge, Mass.: Harvard University Press, 1954.

Friedrich and Zbigniew K. Brzezinski. *Totalitarian Dictatorship and Autocracy.* Cambridge, Mass.: Harvard University Press, 1954.

Howe, Irving, ed. *1984 Revisited: Totalitarianism in Our Century.* New York: Harper & Row, 1983.

Lee, Stephen J. *The European Dictatorships, 1918–1945.* London & New York: Methuen, 1987.

Linz, Juan J. *Totalitarian and Authoritarian Regimes.* Boulder, Colo.: Lynne Rienner, 2000.

Passerini, Luisa, ed. *Memory and Totalitarianism.* Oxford & New York: Oxford University Press, 1992.

Shapiro, Leonard. *Totalitarianism.* London: Pall Mall Press, 1972; New York: Praeger, 1972.

Torney, Simon. *Making Sense of Tyranny: Interpretations of Totalitarianism.* Manchester & New York: Manchester University Press, 1995.

Tucker, Robert C. *The Marxian Revolutionary Idea.* New York: Norton, 1969.

Unger, Aryeh L. *The Totalitarian Party: Party and People in Nazi Germany and Soviet Russia.* London & New York: Cambridge University Press, 1974.

14. WAR

Bloch, Ivan S. *The Future of War in Its Technical, Economic and Political Relations.* Translated by R. C. Long. Boston: Ginn, 1899.

Buckley, John. *Air Power in the Age of Total War.* Bloomington: Indiana University Press, 1999.

Clausewitz, Carl von. *On War.* Edited and translated by Michael Howard and Peter Paret. Princeton: Princeton University Press, 1976.

Earle, Edward Mead. *Makers of Modern Strategy: Military Thought from Machiavelli to Hitler.* Princeton: Princeton University Press, 1943.

Förster, Stig and Jörg Nagler, eds. *On the Road to Total War: The American Civil War and the German Wars of Unification, 1861–1871.* Washington, D.C.: German Historical Institute, 1997; Cambridge & New York: Cambridge University Press, 1997.

Fuller, J. F. C. *The Conduct of War, 1789–1961: A Study of the French, Industrial, and Russian Revolutions on War and Its Conduct.* New Brunswick, N.J.: Rutgers University Press, 1961.

Howard, Michael. *War in European History.* London & New York: Oxford University Press, 1976.

Marwick, Arthur. *War and Social Change in the Twentieth Century: A Comparative Study of Britain, France, Germany, Russia, and the United States.* London: Macmillan, 1974; New York: St. Martin's Press, 1974.

Preston, Richard A., Alex Roland, and Sydney F. Wise. *Men in Arms: A History of Warfare and Its Interrelationships with Western Society.* Fifth edition. Fort Worth, Tex.: Holt, 1991.

Townshend, Charles, ed. *The Oxford Illustrated History of Modern War.* Oxford & New York: Oxford University Press, 1997.

Wright, Gordon. *The Ordeal of Total War, 1939–1945.* New York: Harper & Row, 1968.

Yamanouchi, Yasushi, J. Victor Koschmann, and Ryuichi Narita, eds. *Total War and "Modernization."* Ithaca, N.Y.: Cornell University Press, 1998.

15. WORLD WAR I

Bourne, J. M. *Britain and the Great War 1914–1918.* London & New York: Arnold, 1989.

Charmley, John. *Splendid Isolation?: Britain, the Balance of Power, and the Origins of the First World War.* London: Hodder & Stoughton, 1999.

De Groot, Gerald J. *The First World War.* Houndmills, U.K. & New York: Palgrave, 2001.

Farrar, L. L., Jr. *The Short War Illusion: German Policy, Strategy & Domestic Affairs, August–December 1914.* Santa Barbara, Cal.: ABC-Clio, 1973.

Ferguson, Niall. *The Pity of War.* New York: Basic Books, 1999.

Fischer, Fritz. *Germany's Aims in the First World War.* London: Chatto & Windus, 1967; New York: Norton, 1967.

Kennedy, Paul, ed. *The War Plans of the Great Powers, 1880–1914.* London & Boston: Allen & Unwin, 1979.

Keynes, John Maynard. *The Economic Consequences of the Peace.* London: Macmillan, 1919.

Lafore, Laurence. *The Long Fuse: An Interpretation of the Origins of World War I.* Philadelphia: Lippincott, 1965.

Lyons, Michael J. *World War I: A Short History.* Englewood Cliffs, N.J.: Prentice Hall, 1994.

Mee, Charles L., Jr. *The End of Order, Versailles, 1919.* New York: Dutton, 1980.

Remak, Joachim. *The Origins of World War I, 1871–1914.* New York: Holt, Rinehart & Winston, 1967.

Rothwell, V. H. *British War Aims and Peace Diplomacy, 1914–1918.* Oxford: Clarendon Press, 1971.

Steiner, Zara S. *Britain and the Origins of the First World War.* London: Macmillan, 1977.

Stone, Norman. *The Eastern Front: 1914–1917.* London: Hodder & Stoughton, 1975; New York: Scribners, 1975.

Terraine, John. *White Heat: The New Warfare 1914–18.* London: Sidgwick & Jackson, 1982.

Turner, John. *British Politics and the Great War: Coalition and Conflict, 1915–1918.* New Haven: Yale University Press, 1992.

16. WORLD WAR II

Beitzell, Robert. *The Uneasy Alliance: America, Britain, and Russia, 1941–1943.* New York: Knopf, 1972.

Churchill, Winston. *The Second World War.* 6 volumes. Boston: Houghton Mifflin, 1948–1953.

Clark, Alan. *Barbarossa: The Russian-German Conflict, 1941–1945.* New York: Morrow, 1965.

Crocker, George N. *Roosevelt's Road to Russia.* Chicago: Regnery, 1959.

Feis, Herbert. *Churchill, Roosevelt, Stalin: The War They Waged and the Peace They Sought.* Princeton: Princeton University Press, 1957.

Fugate, Bryan I. *Operation Barbarossa: Strategy and Tactics on the Eastern Front, 1941.* Novato, Cal.: Presidio Press, 1984.

Herring, George C. *Aid to Russia, 1941–1946: Strategy, Diplomacy, and the Origins of the Cold War.* New York: Columbia University Press, 1973.

Keegan, John. *Barbarossa: Invasion of Russia, 1941.* New York: Ballantine, 1971.

Kershaw, Robert J. *War without Garlands: Operation Barbarossa, 1941/1942.* Shepperton: Ian Allan, 2000.

Miner, Steven Merritt. *Between Churchill and Stalin: The Soviet Union, Great Britain, and the Origins of the Grand Alliance.* Chapel Hill: University of North Carolina Press, 1988.

Murray, Williamson. *The Change in the European Balance of Power, 1938–1939: The Path to Ruin.* Princeton: Princeton University Press, 1984.

Nisbet, Robert. *Roosevelt and Stalin: The Failed Courtship.* Washington, D.C.: Regnery Gateway, 1988.

Overy, Richard. *Why the Allies Won.* London: Random House, 1995.

Parrish, Michael, ed. *Battle for Moscow: The 1942 Soviet General Staff Study.* Washington, D.C.: Pergamon-Brassey's Defense Publishers, 1989.

Perlmutter, Amos. *FDR & Stalin: A Not So Grand Alliance, 1943–1945.* Columbia: University of Missouri Press, 1993.

Taylor, A. J. P. *The Second World War.* London: Athlone Press, 1974.

Trotter, William R. *A Frozen Hell: The Russo-Finnish Winter War of 1939–1940.* Chapel Hill, N.C.: Algonquin Books of Chapel Hill, 1991.

Tuyll, Hubert P. van. *Feeding the Bear: American Aid to the Soviet Union, 1941–1945.* Westport, Conn.: Greenwood Press, 1989.

United States, President. *Report to Congress on Lend-Lease Operations.* 43 volumes. Washington, D.C.: Government Printing Office, 1941–1960.

Wegner, Bernd, ed. *From Peace to War: Germany, Soviet Russia and the World, 1939–1941.* Providence, R.I.: Berghahn Books, 1997.

Werth, Alexander. *Russia at War, 1941–1945.* New York: Dutton, 1964.

Whaley, Barton. *Codeword BARBAROSSA.* Cambridge, Mass.: MIT Press, 1973.

Wieczynski, Joseph L., ed. *Operation Barbarossa: The German Attack on the Soviet Union, June 22, 1941.* Salt Lake City: Schlacks, 1993.

REFERENCES

CONTRIBUTORS

BLAIR, Catherine: Doctoral student at Georgetown University; earned a B.A. in history and Russian from the University of North Carolina at Chapel Hill and an M.A. in history from Georgetown University; she is researching pretenders to the throne in seventeenth- and eighteenth-century Russia.

BUDJEVAC, Jelena: Studied history and international relations at George Washington University and Univerzita Karlova (The Charles University in Prague); she currently works in communications and is a freelance writer in Washington, D.C.

CRANE, Richard F.: Associate professor of history at Greensboro College in North Carolina; completed a Ph.D. at the University of Connecticut in 1994; author of *A French Conscience in Prague: Louis Eugene Faucher and the Abandonment of Czechoslovakia* (1996); author of an article on French Catholicism and the 1940 Nazi victory in *Catholic Historical Review* (forthcoming).

FEDYASHIN, Anton A.: Ph.D. student at Georgetown University; he is researching Russian liberal thought during the Witte reforms; earned a B.A. from St. John's College in Annapolis and a M.A. from the Davis Center for Russian studies at Harvard University; he is a citizen of Russia.

FOLEY, Kerry: Earned an M.A. in Russian and Eastern European studies, with a certificate in refugees and humanitarian emergencies, from Georgetown University in 2002; worked for the Damascus office of the United Nations High Commissioner for Refugees (October 2002–December 2003); consulted for the Damascus office of the International Organization for Migration.

FOLEY, Sean: Ph.D. candidate in modern Middle East history at Georgetown University; Fulbright scholar in Damascus, Syria, and Istanbul, Turkey (January 2002–December 2003); author of various publications on Middle Eastern history and politics as well as U.S. diplomatic history.

FRANK, Matthew: Visiting lecturer with the Civic Education Project at the history faculty of Omsk State University in western Siberia; doctoral candidate at St. Antony's College, Oxford University; his thesis on Britain and the transfer of Germans from East Central Europe (1939–1947) will be submitted in 2004.

GILTNER, Philip: Earned a doctorate in modern European history from the University of Toronto; currently teaches at the Albany Academy; taught at the United States Military Academy at West Point, Pace University, and Mercy College; author of *"In the Friendliest Manner": German-Danish Economic Cooperation during the Nazi Occupation of 1940–1945* (1998); he lives in Kinderhook, New York.

HELM, Lawrence A.: Strategic policy consultant for NASA; earned an M.A. in history from George Washington University; oversaw IT Research initiatives at NASA Headquarters for ten years and was involved in the earliest Internet deployments for the agency.

ILLICH, Niles: Graduate student in the Department of History at Texas A&M University, College Station.

KALLIS, Aristotle: Lecturer in modern European history in the Department of Historical Studies at the University of Bristol; he is the author of *Fascist Ideology: Territory and Expansion in Italy and Germany, 1922–1945* (2000) and the editor of *The Fascism Reader* (2003).

KING, Joe: A graduate of Georgetown University's School of Foreign Service; he is currently chairman of Tours.com.

MALIC, Nebojsa: Holds a B.A. in history from Graceland University in Iowa; currently resides in Washington, D.C.; writes a weekly commentary on Balkans issues for Antiwar.com.

MARSHALL, David E.: Earned a Ph.D in modern European history from the University of California, Riverside; holds an M.A. in history from the University of California, Riverside and an M.A. in German literature from San Francisco State University.

NORMAN, York: Ph.D. candidate in history at Georgetown University; holds an M.A. in Eastern European history from Indiana University and an M.A. in Ottoman history from Bilkent University, Turkey; his fields of study are Ottoman history and early modern Europe.

PARKS, Mary: Independent scholar, Austin, Texas.

PORTER, Thomas Earl: Associate professor of modern European and Russian history at North Carolina A&T State University in Greensboro, N.C.; received a doctorate in history from the University of Washington in 1990; published several articles on the zemstvo, the development of civil society, and the government and politics of late Imperial Russia.

QUENOY, Paul du: Doctoral candidate in Russian history at Georgetown University; author of several articles on Russia, Ukraine, and the Soviet Union; co-editor of *History in Dispute, Volume 6: The Cold War, Second Series* (2000).

RAINOW, Peter: Author and co-author of six books and more than sixty chapters on international history published in the United States, the United Kingdom, Italy, Russia, and Ukraine; visiting scholar at Stanford University (1996–1997); participated in the Consensus Project on the future of international relations at the John M. Olin Institute of Strategic Studies, Harvard University (1991–1992).

SANKEY, Margaret: Assistant professor of history at Minnesota State University, Moorhead; specializes in British and military history; author of *Jacobite Prisoners of the 1715: Preventing and Punishing Insurrection in Early Hanoverian Britain* (forthcoming); she has published several journal articles on Jacobitism.

SCHNEIDER, Brandon C.: Graduate student in Russian history at Georgetown University; his dissertation will focus on railroad planning and transportation issues in the Russian Empire; received a B.A. from Youngstown State University and an M.A. in Russian history from Georgetown University.

SHOWALTER, Dennis: Professor of history at Colorado College; president of the Society for Military History; visiting professor at the U.S. Military Academy and U.S. Air Force Academy; author and editor of many books; joint editor of *War in History*.

SNYDER, Sarah: Graduate student in history at Georgetown University; earned a B.A. in history from Brown University and an M.A. in history from University College of London; her dissertation examines the influence of the Helsinki process on American foreign policy, Soviet-American relations, and the end of the Cold War.

SOARES, John: Received a Ph.D. in history from George Washington University; he has taught courses on U.S. history and international relations at Montgomery College, George Washington University, and the University of Cincinnati; he is currently working on a book about the Cold War and international ice hockey.

TSYGANKOV, Andrei P.: Teaches international relations and political science at San Francisco State University; holds a Candidate of Sciences degree from Moscow State University and a Ph.D. from the University of Southern California; author of *Pathways after Empire: National Identity and Foreign Economic Policy in the Post-Soviet World* (2001) and *Whose World Order?* (forthcoming); his current research explores Russian international relations theory and foreign policy; he is a native of Russia.

ULBRICH, David J.: Doctoral candidate in history at Temple University; awarded the 2003–2004 Lemuel C. Shepherd Dissertation Fellowship by the U.S. Marine Corps Heritage Foundation, which supports his research for "Managing Marine Mobilization: Thomas Holcomb and the U.S. Marine Corps, 1936–1943."

VARHO, Scott: Summa cum laude graduate of Amherst College in European Studies; earned an M.A. with honors from the Politics and European Studies Department at Palacky University in Olomouc, Czech Republic; has done extensive research in European development; his undergraduate thesis was on the formation of Czechoslovakia during World War I; he focused on European integration issues throughout his graduate studies; co-author and presenter of a document outlining the state of Czech legislation in the areas of company law, audit, accounting, and intellectual property to the Senate of the Czech Republic Committee on European Integration (2002), which was unanimously adopted as the Committee's official position regarding these legislative areas.

VOURKOUTIOTIS, Vasilis: Lecturer in modern European history at the University of Ottawa, Canada; received a Ph.D. from McGill University, Montreal; author of *Prisoners of War and the German High Command: The British and American Experience* (2003); author of articles and reviews in academic journals in Canada, the United States, and Europe.

WHEATLEY, John: Independent scholar, Brooklyn Center, Minnesota.

INDEX

183, 185, 189, 243, 264–266, 268, 271; XIV
14; XV 37; XVI 186
impact on Nazi collaboration IV 131
policy of Nazi Party XI 103
Soviet Union XV 253
Anti-Submarine Detection Investigation Committee
VIII 196
Anti-Tactical Ballistic Missiles (ATBM) I 195
Anti-Tank Guided Missiles (ATGMs) VI 172
antiwar movement II 159, 161
demonstrations II 3
impact on American politics II 3
Apache helicopter VI 173
apartheid II 20, 100; VI 6; VII 5, 7; XI 167; XIV 221
Apollo 8 (1968) II 257–258
Apollo 11 (1969) II 258
Apollo 12 (1969) II 259
Apollo Theatre III 188
Appalachian Mountains XII 199, 230
settlers banned from crossing XII 53
appeasement I 300; IV 16–21; XI 14
Appolinaire, Guillame VIII 191
April Laws XI 94
April Theses IX 199
Aquinas, Thomas X 179; XI 19, 23; XII 258–259; XIII
17
Arab-American Corporation (ARAMCO) II 145
Arab Bank for Economic Development in Africa
(ABEDA) XV 142
Arab Cooperation Council (ACC) XV 147
Arab Federation XV 120
Arab Fund for Technical Assistance (AFTA) XV 142
Arab Higher Committee for Palestine VII 137
Arab Human Development Report (AHDR) XIV 56,
59, 83, 92
Arab-Israeli conflict XIV 61, 89; XV 51–57, 68, 102,
142, 144
Arab-Israeli peace process XIV 31, 36
Arab-Israeli War (1947–1949) XIV 159, 179, 220; XV
21, 30, 33, 35, 37, 45–46, 65–66, 144, 191,
213, 244, 253
Arab-Israeli War (Six-Day War, 1967) II 142, 148, 150;
VI 31; XIV 144, 151–152, 160, 193, 220,
268, 270; XV 20–25, 37, 40–41, 45–46, 70,
73, 93, 102, 130, 134–140, 144, 149, 191,
198–199, 211–214, 219, 223, 225, 237, 242,
247, 253, 255, 261, 267; XVI 239
Arab-Israeli War (Yom Kippur War, 1973) I 156–157,
159, 162, 222, 308–317; VI 41, 43, 107, 161,
163, 166, 171, 204, 268; VII 135–136, 140;
XIV 89, 145, 195, 221, 245; XIV 217; XV 20,
40, 46, 49, 54, 56, 106, 139, 175, 213, 218–
220, 225–226, 237–241, 252–254, 257, 261,
268
aftermath I 312
Gaza Strip I 314
Golan Heights I 314
Sinai Peninsula I 314
West Bank of the Jordan River I 314
Arab League (League of Arab States) VI 135, 161;
XIV 55, 110, 148, 150, 180, 205, 247–248,
289; XV 45, 49, 57, 89, 91, 104, 127, 133,
141–147, 193, 198–199, 204, 214, 239, 261,
275–276
Arab Maghreb Union (UMA) XIV 69–76, 114; XV 147
Arab Monetary Fund XIV 247
Arab News Network (ANN) XIV 29
Arab nationalism VI 161, 163; XV 30, 64–65, 101,
165–170, 206, 249, 274–276; XVI 236, 243
Arab Nationalist Movement (ANM) XV 49
Arab oil embargo (1973) VI 107; XIV 212, 217
Arab Radio and Television (ART) XIV 29
Arab Revolt (1916) VIII 37–42, 214
Arab Revolt (1936–1939) XV 89, 146
Arab socialism XIV 47
Arab States Broadcasting Union XIV 34
Arab Steadfastness Front XIV 198
Arab Women's Organization (AWO) XIV 289

Arabia VIII 37, 41, 212; IX 96; XIV 159, 188, 201, 206,
244
Arabian Peninsula VIII 38; XIV 133, 176–177, 201; XV
146
Arabic (British ship), sinking of VIII 288; IX 21
Arabic (language) X 4, 6; XIV 180, 201–203, 205, 209
Arafat, Yasser I 159; XIV 19, 22, 24–27, 61, 63, 95–96,
99, 100–101, 103, 106–107, 166, 179, 197,
225; XV 41, 44, 76, 89–91, 93, 127, 135, 149,
153, 182–184, 186–187, 191, 193, 195, 198–
200, 255, 266
Aragon X 2, 4, 30, 35, 41, 159
Jews in X 15
Aramco XV 177, 179
Aravalli Mountains VII 125
Arbenz Guzmán, Jacobo I 24, 49, 66, 93, 123–126,
129–131, 211
Guatemala I 70
overthrow of government in Guatemala III 53
Arcadia Conference (1941–1942) IV 209, 212; V 38
Arctic Sea IX 194
Ardennes Forest XVI 115
Arendt, Hannah I 135; III 103; V 166; XVI 259, 262
Arévalo, Juan José I 24, 123, 126
Argentina I 24, 54, 94; VI 194, 266; XIV 71; XV 33;
XVI 81, 98, 110–111
Adolf Eichmann in XI 37, 40
attacks against Jews in XIV 125–126
Communist guerrilla movements I 125
human rights record I 143
immigrants XI 59
military coups I 26
nuclear nonproliferation I 224
nuclear weapons development I 219, 223
reduction of U.S. military aid I 141
slavery in XIII 272
War of the Triple Alliance I 125
war with Great Britain VI 8, 13
Argoud, Antoine XV 12, 15
Argov, Shlomo XV 127, 132
Arianism X 17
Arias, Oscar VI 191
Arias peace process VI 194
Arif, Abdul Salaam XV 122–124
Aristotle X 69; XII 110, 119, 122; XIII 17, 166
Arizona VII 211–212, 214–216
water policy in VII 108–115, 152–153
Arizona v. *California* (2000) VII 168, 290–303
Ark of the Covenant XIV 159, 163
Arkansas
African Americas in IX 4
slavery in XIII 282
Arkansas River VII 10–16
Arkhipov, Ivan VI 44
Arlington Dam (United States) VII 54
Armenia VIII 41, 208, 212, 214, 216; X 93, 185, 187–
188, 201; XI 79, 169; XVI 18
mandate in VIII 12
massacres in VIII 216; XI 172
occupies Caucasia VIII 217
Soviet Republic VIII 214
war against populace VIII 213
Arminianism XII 150
arms race I 180–187, 262; II 49, 56, 65
Armstrong, John XII 224–225, 227, 229
Armstrong, Louis "Satchmo" II 218; III 79; IX 4
Armstrong, Neil II 257, 259
Army of Northern Virginia VIII 49
Army of the Republic of Vietnam (ARVN) VI 98–99
Army War College, Carlisle Barracks, Pennsylvania VIII
16
Arndt, Ernst Moritz XI 247
Arnold, Benedict XII 9–16, 39, 44–45, 80, 161, 306
Arnold, Henry Harley "Hap" V 5, 51, 88, 91, 98–99
Ar-Rashid, Harun X 287
Arrow Cross XI 177
Arrowrock Dam (United States) VII 26
Art, avant-garde IX 87

British North America Act (Constitution Act, 1867) VII 117

British Petroleum XIV 211–212; XV 108, 156, 172–173, 176, 178–179

British Royal Flying Corps IX 217, 220

British South Sea Company XIII 272

British-United States Agreement (BRUSA) VI 11

British West Indies XII 290, 295, 310–316
    slavery in XII 311

Brittain, Vera VIII 266

Broadcasting Board of Governors XIV 233, 235

Brodie, Bernard I 165; II 65

Brodsky, Joseph XIV 233

Brooke, Alan Francis V 43, 76

Brooke, Rupert VIII 188; IX 149

Brookings Institution XV 220

Brooks, John XII 222–224

Brooks, William K. VII 40, 43, 46–47

Broom and Whisk Makers Union II 191

Brotherhood of Sleeping Car Porters II 189, 217–218

Brower, David Ross VII 110, 112

Brown, Harold VI 42–43

Brown, John XII 11; XIII 4

Brown v. *Board of Education of Topeka, Kansas* (1954) II 20, 23–24, 26, 45, 80, 90–91, 136–143, 270, 280, 286, 293, 295; III 27, 185

Brown Synod (1933) XI 27

Brown University XIII 31, 198

Bruchmuller, Georg IX 127–129

Brüning, Heinrich XVI 148, 151

Brusilov, Aleksey VIII 266; IX 60–66, 193, 242; XVI 204

Brusilov Offensive (1916) IX 72, 137, 155, 193, 243, 252; XVI 312

Brussels Treaty (1954) I 208; VI 101

Bryan, Samuel XII 76

Bryan, William Jennings III 32, 34, 36–37; VIII 204; IX 19, 21, 246
    Scopes Trial III 33

Brzezinski, Zbigniew I 135, 143, 146; VI 42, 166, 256, 263; XIV 8; XV 220; XVI 122, 262

Buchanan, James XIII 195, 278

Buchenwald (concentration camp) V 57; XI 45, 236, 245
    German people's reaction V 215

Buck v. *Bell* (1927) III 18, 21

Buckingham Palace XVI 178

Buddhist monks, immolation of VI 23

Bukovina IX 136; XVI 34, 99

Bulganin, Nikolai A. VI 135; XVI 84

Bulgaria I 107, 294; II 39, 153; VI 251–252, 261, 274, 276, 280; VIII 11, 14, 44, 46, 95, 212, 216–217, 230; IX 120, 171, 203–206, 270, 272; XI 214, 220; XIV 176, 178; XV 120; XVI 32, 36, 76, 104, 122, 124, 185, 192, 233, 249, 284–285, 317
    ally of Germany VIII 278
    Fatherland Front XVI 124
    monarchy XVI 180
    U.S. push for greater freedoms I 110
    U.S. recognizes communist government I 303
    World War I XVI 312

Bulgars X 29

Bull, William XII 215

Bull Moose Party III 243

Bullitt, William XVI 2

Bund Deutscher Mädel (German Girls' Organization) IV 191

Bund Naturschutz in Bayern (BUND) VII 206, 210

Bundestag (Federal Diet) VI 102

Bundy, McGeorge I 29, 294; II 6
    flexible response I 120
    use of nuclear weapons policy I 171

Bureau of Indian Affairs (BIA) III 141, 143; VII 55–56, 59, 166–167, 169, 172

Burger, Justice Warren E. II 182, 221, 284; XII 283

Burgess, Guy I 243, 245; VI 11

Burgh, James XII 278

Burgoyne, John XII 10, 15, 39, 45–47, 80, 95–96, 100, 103, 155, 158, 162, 181, 267–274, 305

Burke, Edmund XII 29–30, 139, 143, 166

Burke, Thomas XII 185

Burma VIII 35; XII 33; XIV 177; XV 14
    fall of V 197
    opium trade I 15

Burns, William XIV 100, 107

Burundi II 101, 155

Bush, George H. W. VI 28, 51, 58, 61, 191, 195, 205, 226, 229, 242, 257; X 56; XIV 97, 100, 198, 247; XV 102, 182, 258, 260; XVI 60, 285
    Africa policy VI 7
    civil war in Somalia II 155
    foreign policy "balance of power" II 155
    international political experience II 152
    Iraq XV 73–79
    Madrid Conference XV 184
    New World Order II 152–158; XV 81
    nuclear nonproliferation policy I 224
    Panama intervention II 155
    Persian Gulf crisis II 153
    Persian Gulf War XV 80–87
    relationship with former Yugoslavia II 155
    role of United States II 155
    U.S. spying on Soviet Union I 191
    unilateral U.S. foreign policy II 156

Bush (George H. W.) administration II 100; VI 120; XIV 199
    arms-control agreements VI 20
    defense spending VI 224
    envisionment of New World Order II 155
    Iraq XV 73–79, 81, 84, 86
    nuclear-nonproliferation policy I 217
    policy on Afgahnistan I 14–16

Bush, George W. VII 224; XIV 13–15, 33, 37–38, 41, 43, 88, 112, 168, 193, 228–229, 239, 247, 267; XV 78
    governor of Texas XIV 103
    Iraq XV 80, 87
    Middle East XIV 95–108
    on terrorism XIV 126

Bush (George W.) administration XIV 109, 193, 231, 247, 238, 239; XVI 95
    Bush Doctrine XIV 14, 17, 43, 237, 239–240
    conservative ideology XIV 16
    Middle East XIV 95–108
    response to World Trade Center attack XIV 228
    terrorism XIV 10, 13, 17
    view on Hizbollah XIV 126

Bushido code III 13

Butler, Justice Pierce III 25

Butler, Pierce XII 296

Butler, Smedley, IX 96

Butterfield, Herbert X 278, 304

Buxton, Thomas Fowell XIII 131, 159

Byrd II, William XIII 150–151, 207

Byrnes, James F. I 28, 31, 263, 304; II 206; V 51, 53; XI 256

Byzantine Empire X 33, 73, 88, 92, 107–108, 110, 112, 118–119, 121, 128, 138, 150–151, 156, 172–174, 188, 205, 208–209, 215, 238–239, 249–250, 262, 269, 280, 282, 284, 287; XIII 167; XIV 261
    Crusades X 15, 24–31
    relations with the West X 24–31

C

Cable News Network (CNN) XIV 29, 34, 61, 66

Cabora Bassa Dam (Mozambique) VII 237, 239, 240

Cadwalader, John XII 98

Caesar, Julius XII 302

cahiers des doleances (notebooks of grievances) XII 129, 133

Cairncross, John VI 11
    Soviet nuclear spying I 243–245

Cairnes, John E. XIII 174, 240, 242

Index

INDEX

INDEX

E

Index

Gregorian reform X 36, 94, 115, 217
Gregory I X 229
Gregory VII X 81, 85, 98–99, 104–105, 115–122, 130,
164, 205, 208, 213, 219–220, 224, 227–228,
267, 279, 284–285, 289; XI 80
Gregory VIII X 130, 254, 256, 260, 294, 297
Gregory IX X 92–96, 180, 206, 226, 266
Gregory X X 67, 70, 210
Gregory of Tours X 104, 229
Grenada I 56–57; II 44, 58; VI 83, 165, 194, 221–222,
234, 237, 261, 270; XII 311, 313
maroons in XII 314
Grenville, George XII 53, 139, 141, 149, 190, 231, 236
Grey, Edward IX 102; XVI 24
Griswold v. *Connecticut* (1965) II 281–283, 286
Groener, Wilhelm VIII 96, 143, 246; XVI 173
Gromyko, Andrey VI 75, 116; XV 258; XVI 227
Gropius, Walter IX 86
Group for Environmental Monitoring (GEM) VII 238
Group of Seven XIV 109
Group of 77 (G-77) VI 271
Groupe Islamique Armee (Armed Islamic Group,
GIA) XV 2, 5
Groves, Leslie I 28, 235, 247
Guadeloupe IX 111
Guantanamo Bay VI 64
Guatemala I 54–56, 70, 89, 94, 122–133; II 40, 103;
VI 21, 131, 194, 266
Agrarian Reform Law (1952) I 123, 126
CIA involvement I 211; XV 157
CIA trained anti-Castro Cubans in VI 141
coup of 1954 I 123
human rights violations in VI 241
Marxist guerrillas in VI 193
military coup of 1963 I 24
1954 coup I 128
United Fruit Company I 70
U.S. intervention (1954) I 15, 123–133
Guchkov, Aleksandr XVI 50–51, 53
Guderian, Heinz W. IV 282; V 123–127
Guevara, Ernesto "Che" I 93; II 160, 215; VI 70; XV
49
death I 126
role in communist revolution in Bolivia I 126
Guibert of Nogent X 72, 97–98, 100, 103, 128, 164,
212–213, 234, 281
Guigo de Castro X 162–163
Guiscard, Robert X 73, 121–122, 220, 228, 269, 284–
285
gulag archipelago VI 250
Gulf Cooperation Council (GCC) XIV 114, 180, 247;
XV 141, 147
Gulf of Aqaba XV 20–21, 135, 137, 170, 247, 250
Gulf of Sidra VI 165, 234; XIV 198
Gulf of Tonkin incident (1964) I 291; VI 144
Gulf of Tonkin Resolution (1964) I 91; II 7; VI 139,
284, 287; XII 31
Gulf Oil Company XIV 211–212; XV 172–173, 177,
178
gunboat diplomacy VI 166
Gurion, David Ben I 216
Guy of Lusignan X 52, 251, 256, 259
Guyana. *See* British Guiana
Gypsies, murder of VIII 94–95; XI 66, 71, 73, 147, 149,
153, 171, 186, 190, 242–243, 247, 257

H

Haas, Richard XIV 97, 100
Habash, George XV 41, 90, 199
Habeas Corpus VI 9
Haber, Fritz VIII 241–242
Habib, Philip Charles VI 229; XV 132, 153
Habitat Patch Connectivity Project VII 232
Habsburg Empire VI 217; VIII 43, 257, 281; IX 133–
138, 206, 225, 266–267; XII 189; XVI 76,
99, 100, 312
collapse of XVI 29–37

ethnic groups in XVI 30
Habsburgs XVI 104, 195, 211–213, 216, 294
Hachani, Abdelkader XV 4–5, 8
Hadid, Muhammad XV 122–123, 124
Hadrian XI 19
Hafiz El Assad II 146
Hafsids X 66, 146
Hague, The XVI 92
Hague Conference (1911–1912) III 137; VIII 240
Hague Conventions (1907) V 222, 264; VIII 244; XI
258; XV 79
Haig, Alexander M. I 56; II 179; VI 44, 225, 229, 231;
XIV 198
Haig, Douglas VIII 52, 56, 77, 79, 103–104, 106, 108,
114, 218–221, 223, 26, 271–273; IX 34–39,
107–108, 110, 120, 123, 211
Hainburg Dam Project (Austria) VII 105
Haiti I 51, 125; II 100; III 50; VI 58, 194, 213, 217,
283; IX 96; XII 169; XIII 156, 209–216
Haitian Revolution XIII 209–216
Haldane Reforms (1906) IX 51
Haldeman, Harry R. VI 24
Halder, Franz V 126–127, 227
Ha-Levi, Yehuda ben Shemuel X 273, 275
Hallstein Doctrine VI 208, 210
Halsey Jr., William F. IV 173
Hamad XIV 61–63
Haman Act VII 47
Hamas XIV 24, 41, 93, 103, 105, 107, 127, 148, 184,
230; XV 90, 182, 186, 194, 201, 264
Hamilton, Alexander XII 34, 58, 65, 68, 70, 73, 97,
114, 119–122, 127, 162, 222–224, 228–229,
258, 279, 289–291, 296; XIII 281; XVI 66
Hamilton, Ian VIII 118–119, 122
Hammarskjold, Dag XV 247
Hammond, James Henry XIII 27, 48, 81, 83, 87, 218–
219, 240, 264–265
Hampton, Wade XIII 155, 233, 235
Hancock, John XII 110, 291; XIII 48
Handel, George XVI 23
Hankey, Maurice VIII 79
Hannibal VIII 179, 249
Hanoi I 41–47
Hanoverians XII 136
Haram al-Sharif 19, 22–23, 159–160, 165–167
Hardin, Garrett VII 47, 70, 72–73
Harding, Warren G. III 25, 69, 175–178; IX 92; XI 56
Harding administration IX 171
Harkin, Thomas R. VI 194
Harlan, John Marshall II 23, 282–283; XIII 57
Harlem Renaissance III 78–84, 118–120, 184; IX 1, 4
Harper, William XIII 70, 73–74, 165, 217, 267
Harper's Ferry (1859) XIII 4
Harriman, W. Averell I 306; II 264; V 312; XV 160;
XVI 227, 315
Harrington, James XII 119, 122–123, 209
Harris, Sir Arthur "Bomber" V 87, 91
Harrison, Earl G. XI 122–124
Harrison Act (1914) III 133, 137
narcotics legislation III 137
Hart, Sir Basil Henry Liddell V 23, 102
Harvard University VI 90, 129, 199, 203, 258; XIII
198; XIV 14
Hashemite Arabs VIII 40–41; XIV 245
Hashemite Kingdom XIV 160, 166; XV 32, 34, 41–42,
44–45, 116, 121, 142, 146, 273, 275
Hassan II XIV 74, 209, 278, 282–283; XV 44
Hat Act (1732) XII 198, 202, 243
Hatch Act (1939) III 11
Hauptmann, Bruno III 110–116
Hausner, Gideon XI 38–41
Hawaii IX 96
Hawatmah, Nayef XV 41, 90, 199
Hayden, Carl Trumbull VII 109, 112, 154–155
Hayes, James Allison VII 274
Hays, Mary Ludwig (Molly Pitcher) XII 263
Hazen, Moses XII 12
Heady, Earl O. VII 187

Index

INDEX

Index

INDEX

INDEX

N

"positive neutrality" II 148

Nation of Islam II 93–95

National Aeronautics and Space Administration (NASA) II 246, 258, 260; XI 152
    creation of II 242
    funding of II 261

National Association for the Advancement of Colored People (NAACP) II 19–20, 23, 25, 27, 44–45, 90, 94, 138, 140–141; III 80, 93, 118, 121, 182, 184–186, 217, 270–274; IX 2, 4; XIII 256, 277
    opposition to Model Cities housing projects II 277
    Scottsboro case III 185

National Association of Black Journalists II 96

National Association of Broadcasters II 123

National Association of Colored Women III 167

National Audubon Society VII 215

National Black Political Convention (1972) II 95, 198

National Committee of Negro Churchmen II 95

National Committee to Re-Open the Rosenberg Case II 228

National Conference of Christians and Jews XI 159

National Council of Negro Churchmen (NCNC) II 94

National Council of Mayors VII 258

National Council of Slovenes, Croats, and Serbs XVI 36, 100

National Defense and Interstate Highway Act (1956) II 107

National Defense Highway Act (1956) II 249

National Education Association II 190–191

National Environmental Policy Act (NEPA) II 183; VII 31, 176, 266, 269,

National Farmers Process Tax Recovery Association III 159

National Front for the Liberation of Angola (*Frente Nacional de Libertação de Angola* or FNLA) VI 1, 6, 87, 165

National Guard Act (1903) VIII 301

National Guidance Committee (NGC) XIV 25

National Industrial Recovery Act (NIRA, 1933) III 27–28, 62, 65, 149,154
    Supreme Court ruling III 25

National Intelligence Estimates (NIEs) VI 256–258, 260

National Iranian Oil Company (NIOC) XV 175

National Labor Relations Act (Wagner Act, 1935) III 149, 193

National Labor Relations Board (NLRB) II 188; III 30, 62, 149, 190–191, 193, 195

National Liberation Front (NLF) I 296; II 119, 263–264, 266

National liberation movements VI 183–187

National Negro Congress (NNC) III 184

National Negro Convention XIII 234

National Organization of Women (NOW) II 78

National Organization for Women v. *Joseph Scheidler* (1994) II 223

National Parks Association VII 30

National Pollutant Discharge Elimination System VII 264

National Prohibition Act (1919) III 200

National Reclamation Act (1902) III 243

National Recovery Administration (NRA, 1933) III 30, 154

National Security Act (1947) I 5, 7, 64, 69; VI 61

National Security Agency (NSA) I 74; II 230; VI 157

National Security Council (NSC) I 54, 64, 83, 121; VI 41, 90, 96, 196, 231; XIV 107, 235; XV 31, 158
    Action No. 1845-c XV 166
    Alpha Plan XV 170
    Directive 5820/1 (1958) XV 165–170
    Memorandum 68 (NSC-68) I 83–84, 89, 149, 182, 211, 274; XIV 107–108
    Policy paper 5428 (1954) XV 166

National Security Decision Directives (NSDD) VI 13, 32, 82, 166

National Security Strategy (NSS) XIV 107

National Socialist German Workers' Party (Nazi Party, Nazis) I 35; IV 267; VI 49, 176, 254, 274, 277; VIII 92, 94, 167; XI 4–5, 21–23, 28–29, 32–33, 35, 55, 59, 67, 70, 72, 74–75, 77, 80–81, 83, 87–88, 90, 93–95, 98, 102–103, 105–107, 111, 113, 121, 128, 138–140, 142, 169, 171, 183–184, 186, 189, 202–203, 207–208, 211, 217, 223, 238–239, 245, 253, 255–257, 264, 266, 268, 270–271; XII 259; XVI 9, 13, 76, 130, 140–142, 148–149, 151, 176, 186, 216, 229, 260–261, 264, 298
    criminality of XI 166–173
    euthanasia XI 83, 270
    medical experiments of XI 146–154
    Night of the Long Knives (1934) XI 243
    public health XI 47
    racial ideology XI 118
    resistance to XI 268
    war crime trials 252–264

National Socialist Party of Austria XI 36

National Union for the Total Independence of Angola (*União Nacional para a Independência Total de Angola* or UNITA) VI 1–2, 6, 87, 165

National Urban League II 94; III 80, 184; IX 2, 4

National Water Act of 1974 (Poland) 18

Native Americans VIII 23, 27; X 10, 179; XII 18, 34, 37, 53, 73, 95, 199, 217, 263, 279, 282, 285; XIII 161; XV 39
    advocate breaching dams VII 221
    American Revolution XII 44, 49, 173–180, 268
    assimilation of VII 55, 168
    blamed for reducing salmon catch VII 199
    Canary Islands, brought to XIII 168
    control of resources on reservations VII 166–173
    Creek confederacy XII 295
    dam income VII 59
    dam monitoring by Columbia River tribes VII 223
    displacement of VII 27
    environmental damage to land VII 111
    extermination of XI 71, 169
    First Salmon ceremony VII 56
    fishing VII 57, 197, 220
    fishing rights of VII 198, 202
    Great Rendezvous at Celilio Falls VII 56
    impact of dams on VII 29, 51–61, 108, 110
    impact of diseases upon XIII 162
    ingenuity of VII 11
    intermarriage with non-Indians VII 169
    loss of rights VII 151
    on Columbia River VII 202
    opposition by non-Indians living on the reservations VII 172
    protest movements VII 199
    relocation of burial grounds VII 60
    relations with maroons XIII 110
    relationship with U.S. government III 139–146
    reservations of VII 28
    sacred sites endangered by dams VII 25
    symbolism of U.S. flag XIII 270
    threat to western expansion XII 18
    treaties VII 56, 222
    used as slaves XIII 162

Native Americans, tribes
    Aymara Indians (Peru) XII 74
    Aztec XIII 162
    Cherokee XII 264
    Chippewa XII 175–176, 178
    Cocopah VII 151
    Delaware XII 175
    Flathead VII 167, 169–170
    Hopi VII 169
    Hualapai VII 110, 114
    Inca XIII 162
    Iroquois XII 41, 173–180
    Kootenai VII 167, 171–172
    Miami XII 175–176
    Mohawk XII 173–175, 177, 179

P

Pacific Gas and Electric Corporation (PG&E) VII 177–178

Pacific Northwest VII 55; XII 171
dams in VII 51
industrialization in VII 51–53
railroads in VII 52
water policy in VII 110

Pacific Northwest Development Association VII 53

Pacific Ocean VII 220; XVI 65, 91, 254
dumping ground for thermal waste VII 178
during World War I VIII 31, 33, 72, 133, 137
islands XII 171

Pacific Salmon Crisis VII 219

Pacific Southwest Water Plan VII 109

Pacific Western (oil company) XV 180

Pahlavi, Mohammad Reza Shah I 11, 70, 141–146; II 97; VI 166, 266; XIV 37, 174; XV 73, 100, 106–115, 156–164, 228–236

Pahlavi, Reza Shah XV 102, 106, 108, 156–157, 163

Paine, Thomas XII 54, 110, 113, 121, 143, 153, 261; XIV 77; XVI 181–182

Pakistan I 89, 158; II 85, 172; VI 53, 83, 88, 149, 201, 214–215, 219, 238; XIV 2–7, 11–12, 16, 79, 81, 88, 141, 144, 147–148, 177, 180, 186, 190, 228–230, 260; XV 26, 29, 59, 117, 271–272; XVI 45, 71
anti-Taliban assistance to United States XIV 13
assists Taliban XIV 11
Baghdad Pact I 161
Inter-Services Intelligence Division (ISID) XIV 4, 6
nuclear alliance with Libya I 223
nuclear weapons I 15, 217, 219, 221, 223, XIV 3, 6, 40; XVI 98, 109
refugee population in XIV 7
religious indoctrination in XIV 92
terrorism XIV 14

Paleologue, Georges IX 198

Palestine I 160, 164, 317; II 144; VI 164, 188; VII 81–82, 138, 139; VIII 37, 39–40, 82, 103, 163, 166, 208, 212–213, 216, 221; IX 67, 72, 93, 96, 206; X 10,15, 47, 62, 89, 113, 159, 170, 183, 191–192, 281, 306; XI 60, 62, 64, 93, 120, 123–124, 127, 177; XIV 32–33, 55, 63, 79, 87, 95–108, 112, 116, 148, 152–153, 155, 157, 159, 163, 166, 176, 180, 186, 191, 197, 199, 246, 258; XV 24, 33–37, 39, 41–42, 46, 52–54, 79, 83, 134, 137, 139, 142, 144, 146, 222, 226, 240, 248, 253, 260, 263, 274; XVI 13, 81, 88, 236, 238
British withdrawal from VI 83
Central Council (CC) XV 195
corruption in XIV 49
Declaration of Principles (1993) XV 189, 198
diaspora X 63, 306
disenfranchisement in VII 135
intifada XIV 7, 19–27; XV 89–96
Jewish homeland in VIII 37, 168
Jewish immigration XVI 236
mandate VIII 166; XVI 269
Occupied Territories XIV 20, 22, 25–27
Oslo accords XV 182–192
partition of XIV 160
refugees XIV 179, 220–226; XV 21, 183, 191, 214
Rejection Front XV 198
sugar cane in XIII 167
Unified National Leadership (UNL) XIV 26
water VII 140; XIV 269
women XIV 121, 123
Zionist refuge XI 11, 57

Palestine Communist Party (PCP) XV 95

Palestine Legislative Council (PLC) XV 194

Palestine Liberation Front XV 90

Palestine Liberation Organization (PLO) I 156; VI 54, 163, 201; XIV 23–26, 61, 107, 125–126, 131, 184, 197, 225; XV 20, 22, 40–42, 44–46, 48, 54, 57, 76, 83, 89–91, 93–95, 127, 129, 131–132, 144, 148–150, 153, 187, 193–201, 216, 220, 222, 255, 266; XVI 243
Constitution XV 195
Oslo accords XV 182–192

Palestine National Council XIV 25; XV 193–195, 198–199

Palestine National Front (PNF) XIV 25

Palestine People's Conference (PPC) XV 198

Palestinian Authority (PA) VII 136; XIV 19, 24, 25, 27, 87–88, 95–96, 101, 103, 114, 152, 167, 225, 239; XV 183–186, 194–195, 201
Preventive Security Service XIV 102

Palestinian Islamic Jihad XIV 41

Palestinian Legislative Council XIV 102

Palestinian Liberation Front XIV 199; XV 77

Palestinian National Congress XV 22

Palmares XIII 104–105, 107, 212

Palmer, A. Mitchell III 221–223, 226

Palmer, Joel VII 56

Palmer raids III 221, 223, 234

Pan-African Congress (1919) III 122; VII 239

Panama Canal I 53; II 257; III 243, 247; VI 40, 190; XVI 65, 69

Panama Canal Treaty I 52

Panama Canal Zone XV 247

Panama Refining Company v. *Ryan* (1935) III 28

Pan-Arabism XIV 190, 193–194, 205; XV 12, 20, 42, 102, 146

Pan-Asianism IX 164

Panda (Moscow TV show) VII 23–24

Panic of 1819 XIII 176

Panic of 1837 XIII 176

Pan-Slavism VIII 207, 228; IX 99

Papacy X 26, 122, 204, 206, 208, 216, 220, 238, 285

Papen, Franz von XVI 148–149, 154

Paracelsus XIII 183

Paraguay XIV 71

Paris, Matthew X 34, 145, 235

Paris Agreement (1945) XI 214

Paris Bourse (French Stock Exchange) XV 246

Paris Commune (1871) VIII 147

Paris Peace Accords (1973) I 142; VI 222

Paris Peace Conference (1919) VIII 12, 150, 217; IX 93, 107, 165, 171–174, 250; XVI 7, 91, 93, 107

Paris Summit (1960) I 276

Parker, Billy VII 56

Parker, Dorothy III 177

Parker River Wildlife Refuge VII 277–278

Parks, Rosa II 140

Partiya Karkeren Kurdistan (Kurdistan Workers Party or PKK) XIV 265

Partnership for Peace (PfP) XIV 264

Party Kings X 244, 246

Party of Democratic Socialism (PDS) XVI 77

Pasha, Enver XVI 312

Pasic, Nicola IX 267; XVI 100, 103, 194

Pastors' Emergency League XI 29, 31, 32

Pathet Lao VI 141–142

Patriot Party (1994) II 195, 198

Patriotic Union of Kurdistan (PUK) XIV 169, 173

Patton, George S. V 2, 43, 44, 125, 127–129, 136; VIII 19, 219
Battle of the Bulge IV 195
Italian campaign IV 144
military background IV 193
Operation Torch IV 193
reputation IV 192–199

Paul, Marcel VII 97

Pawnbroker, The (1964) XI 159

Peabody Coal Company VII 111

Peace and Freedom Party II 197

Peace Corps I 24; II 116; VI 140

Peace of God (989) X 36, 85, 165, 217

Peace of Paris (1763) XII 139

Peace of Westphalia. *See* Treaties

Peace Water Pipeline Project VII 79, 83

INDEX

INDEX

INDEX

Stone, Justice Harlan III 25
Stone, Livingston VII 197
Stono Rebellion (1739) XIII 124, 235
stormtroopers IX 126, 129–130
Stowe, Harriet Beecher XIII 4, 89
Strait of Tiran XV 20–21, 24, 135, 137, 225, 245, 247, 250, 254; XVI 239
Straits of Gibraltar XVI 65
Straits of Malacca XVI 65
Strategic Air Command (SAC) I 188; VI 263
Strategic Arms Limitation Treaty (SALT I) I 190, 199; II 171; VI 30, 35, 41, 43; XV 257; XVI 95
Strategic Arms Limitation Treaty (SALT II) I 10, 12, 143, 146, 191; VI 2, 35, 166
    Soviet criticism of VI 43
Strategic Arms Reduction Treaty (START) I 199, 224; VI 44; XVI 95; XVI 98
Strategic bombing
    postwar I 4, 6, 8
    postwar role I 5
Strategic bombing in World War II I 3–4
Strategic Defense Initiative (SDI) I 186, 195–196, 199; II 58; VI 3, 22, 36, 109, 223, 226, 229, 234, 239; XVI 40, 45, 95
Strauss, Richard IX 84
Stravinsky, Igor IX 84
Streicher, Julius V 224; XI 185, 254, 258
Stresemann, Gustav XVI 209, 211–212
Strong, Ted VII 61
Stuart, John XII 53, 143, 192
Student League for Industrial Democracy (SLID) II 160
Student Nonviolent Coordinating Committee (SNCC) II 22, 28, 91, 93, 161; VI 25
Student, Kurt V 14
Students for a Democratic Society (SDS) II 7, 160, 162
Submarines V 255–261; VIII 11, 287–294; IX 183
    antisubmarine warfare (ASW) V 256
    antiwarship (AWS) operations V 259
    Dolphin-class (nuclear) XIV 148
    Great Britain V 260
    I-class V 258
    Italy V 261
    Japanese Navy V 258, 261
    Kriegsmarine (German Navy) V 261
    RO-class V 258
    Soviet Union V 261
    United States V 261
    unrestricted warfare VIII 22, 204, 287–294, 296
Suburbia II 249–255, 293–294
    suburban developments II 160
Sudan VII 3; XIV 52, 55–56, 79, 81, 87, 134, 136, 141, 176–177, 180, 183, 186, 190, 197, 231; XV 23, 239, 271, 276
    female circumcision XIV 288
    genocide in XIV 140
    National Islamic Front (NIF) XIV 140
    water XIV 270
    women XIV 121
Sudeten German Party XI 207
Sudetenland IX 272; XI 14, 60, 207; XVI 101–102, 104
    Munich Agreement (1938) I 300
Sudetenland crisis (September 1938) IV 125, 248; XI 15
Suez Canal VI 10, 80, 270; VII 2, 147; VIII 38, 213; XIV 175; XV 19, 23, 33, 56, 65–66, 68, 70, 137, 166, 170, 223, 225, 237–238, 240–241, 244, 246, 254; XVI 23, 64–65, 68, 81, 88, 136
    nationalization of (1956) XV 166
Suez Canal Company XV 66, 70, 168, 245–246, 250; XVI 80, 84, 235, 239
Suez Crisis (1956) I 192, 289; II 52, 148; VI 8, 11, 80–81, 106, 130, 133, 135, 160, 188, 209, 270; XIV 144; XV 168; XVI 84–85, 88, 95, 111, 136, 235–242, 269
    U.S. position I 185; VI 270

Suez War (1956) XV 19–21, 24, 32, 58, 62, 70, 116, 169, 213, 225, 244–251, 253, 270, 272, 275
Suffolk Resolves XII 54
Sufism XIV 206, 208
Sugar Act (1764) XII 2, 55, 149, 200, 207, 231, 233, 236, 240, 313–314
Sukarno I 110, 273, 277, 283; VI 81, 268
Sukhomlinov, Vladimir IX 158–159, 192–193, 238; XVI 201
Sullivan, John XII 179, 302
Sulz Valley VII 207
Summerall, Charles VIII 27–28
Summi Pontificatus (1939) XI 192
Sunnis XV 126, 146
Supreme Muslim Council XV 195
Surinam XIII 104, 133, 190, 212
    maroons in XIII 105, 108, 110
    slave revolts XIII 154
Susquehanna River XII 186
Sussex (British ship), sinking of IX 21, 247
Sutherland, Justice George III 25
Suzuki, Kantaro III 15
Swampland Grants (1849 and 1850) VII 272
Swann v. Charlotte-Mecklenburg Board of Education (1968) II 293, 296
Swaziland VII 236
Sweatt v. Painter, 1950 II 141
Sweden XI 174–176, 178; XV 215; XVI 45, 212–214, 272, 319
    monarchy XVI 178, 180–181
    offers Poland environmental help VII 20
    opposition to African dams in VII 240
    saves Dutch and Norwegian Jews XI 174
    slave trade XIII 270
Swift, Jonathan XII 124
Swiss National Bank XI 178
Switzerland VII 229; VIII 110, 235; IX 196, 200; XI 61–62, 131, 174–176, 178; XVI 45, 58, 213
    Jewish policy of XI 177
    Nazi gold XI 178–180
    treatment of Jewish passports XI 2
Syankusule, David VII 242, 246
Sykes-Picot Agreement (1916) VIII 41
Symington, Stuart I 6, 119, 188–189, 217–218
Symington Amendment (1976) I 218
Syngman Rhee VI 147, 150–151
Syria I 159, 308–309; VI 54, 163, 201, 215, 261, 268; VII 135, 138, 148–149; VIII 39, 41, 104, 213, 216; IX 92, 96; X 46–49, 108–110, 185–187; XIV 29, 41, 52, 55–56, 60–61, 63–64, 79, 87, 97, 110, 112, 114, 125–126, 146, 148–149, 177, 179–181, 190, 193, 195, 198, 201, 220, 225, 230, 242, 252, 255, 265; XV 20–21, 23, 25, 32, 34, 37, 41, 44–45, 48, 53, 57, 59, 61–62, 70, 75, 79, 81, 83, 91, 116, 127, 129, 131, 133–137, 141–142, 144–150, 152–153, 155, 166, 168, 183, 193, 199–200, 206, 213–214, 216, 219–220, 222, 225–226, 238, 240, 245, 254, 255, 257; XVI 98, 236, 269
    Alawi sect XIV 67
    alleviating poverty XIV 65
    Arab Socialist Party (ASP) XV 271
    Arab Socialist Resurrection Party (ASRP) XV 271
    attacks Israel I 316; VI 161, 163; XIV 145
    Baath Party XIV 82, 253; XV 135, 270–271, 273, 275–276
    CIA plot XV 157
    closes al-Jazeera office XIV 65
    Communist Party XV 271
    conflict with Jordan I 157
    cotton and textile exports XIV 45
    dams in VII 76–84
    de-liberalization XIV 64
    deportations to VIII 166
    economy XIV 51, 54
    fundamentalist movements I 163
    immigration and population problems VII 82
    Israel, negotiations with XV 33, 260–269

INDEX

INDEX

Soviet intervention in I 73, 258; XV 253
U.S. aid to resist Soviet influence I 176
War of Independence (1919–1923) XVI 236
water VII 76–84; XIV 268–271
women XIV 121
Young Turk revolution VIII 45; XV 274
Turkish-Iraqi Mixed Economic Commission VII 79
Turkish Petroleum Company (TPC) XV 176
Turkish-Pakistani Treaty (April 1954) XV 31
Turkish Straits XVI 66, 194
Turkmenistan XIV 2, 180, 228, 231
Turner, Frederick Jackson
frontier thesis II 245
Turner, Nat XIII 54, 91, 124, 156–158, 235–236
Tuskegee Institute III 268–272
Twenty-One Demands (1915) IX 164, 166, 168
Tyre X 47–49, 53, 75, 128, 148, 150, 152, 154, 170, 192,
247–249, 251, 254, 256, 261

U

U-2 spy plane incident (1960) I 65–66, 70, 189–190,
192, 194; II 38, 54, 229, 260; VI 64
U-2 spy plane reconnaissance VI 70–71
U.S.-Middle East Partnership Initiative (1997) XIV 114
U.S. Steel Corporation VII 269; VIII 296; XI 60
U Thant VI 75; XV 23, 135, 137, 217, 225
U-boats. See *Unterseeboote*
Udall, Morris King VII 109, 114
Udall, Stewart Lee VII 109, 112, 259, 267
Uganda XIV 197–198
genocide in XI 71
Uighurs XIV 12
Ukraine VI 133, 136, 215, 218, 251; VII 248, 252; VIII
94, 96–99, 280; XI 115, 175; XVI 6, 18, 29–
30, 32–34, 88, 98, 163, 189, 294, 312–313
Chernobyl accident in VII 18, 22
Cossacks VIII 99
forest clear-cutting in VII 254
German atrocities in XI 268
mass executions in VI 251
nuclear-deterence theory I 231
pogroms VIII 168–169
Rada (parliament) XVI 18
Russian conquest of XVI 70
surrender of nuclear weapons to Russian
Federation I 220
Ukrainian Insurgent Army (UPA) IV 130
Ukrainian Military Congress XVI 18
Ulbricht, Walter I 35, 38
Berlin I 120
Ulster Volunteers VIII 155, 161
Ultra IV 260–264; V 79, 85
Battle of the Atlantic, 1941–1945 IV 263
Battle of Britain, 1940 IV 264
Battle of the Bulge, 1944 IV 264
contribution to Allied invasion plans IV 262
North Africa campaign IV 264
role in D-Day planning IV 261
Umkhonto we Sizwe (MK) VII 239
Uncle Tom's Cabin (1852) XIII 4
Unconditional surrender policy V 46, 53, 270–275
German reaction V 272
Japanese reaction V 273
Uniates XVI 30
Union Army XIII 54
black soldiers in XIII 53, 55
Union of Arab Community Based Association XIV 116
Union of Soviet Socialist Republics (U.S.S.R.). *See*
Soviet Union
Union Pacific Railroad VII 60
United Arab Emirates (UAE) XIV 11, 50, 55, 148, 177,
179, 212, 215, 217, 247
economy XIV 51
water XIV 269
United Arab Republic (UAR) I 282; II 147–148
Soviet ties II 148
United Auto Workers (UAW) II 189; III 191, 194

United Fruit Company I 70, 123, 125–126, 129–130
United Kingdom XVI 186, 248
Lend Lease aid XVI 162, 167
United Mine Workers II 190–191
United Mine Workers Strike (1902) III 244
United Nations I 29–30, 50, 53, 98, 194, 217, 219–220,
278, 284, 288–289, 305; II 20, 40, 46, 51,
53, 61, 71, 87, 100, 115; VI 31, 135–136, 147,
151, 158, 234, 261; VII 2, 65, 79, 81, 240,
245; VIII 11; IX 171; XI 37, 121, 124; XIV
12, 14, 17, 55, 85, 96, 103, 106, 144, 146,
149, 159–160, 173, 180, 192, 195, 199, 219,
225, 228, 231, 237, 247, 265, 277, 282, 287;
XV 15, 21, 24, 34, 74, 80–81, 84, 91, 97, 100,
102, 120, 141, 153, 198, 203, 205, 219, 237,
253; XVI 57, 76, 87–88, 98, 157, 230, 267,
271, 289, 315, 317
adopts TVA model VII 1
agencies working in Latin America I 22
Atomic Energy Commission I 27, 29
censure of Soviet Union for invasion of
Afghanistan I 12
Charter XV 245
China seat VI 44, 148
Convention on the Law of the Sea (1982) XV 247
Council for Namibia VII 241
creation of II 100, 208
Decade for the Rights of Indigenous Peoples XIV
207
Declaration of Human Rights XV 79
Declaration on the Granting of Independence of
Colonial Countries and Peoples (1960) XIV
277
Economic Commission for Latin America
(ECLA) I 20
Economic Commission for the Middle East XIV
177
Fourth Committee on Decolonization XIV 277
General Assembly XIV 277; XV 34, 200, 254
human rights I 146
Hungarian uprising (1956) VI 270
Interim Force in Lebanon (UNIFIL) XV 153
International Law Commission XIV 274
intervention in the Congo II 115
Korea VI 146
Mission for the Referendum in Western Sahara
(MINURSO) XIV 278
nuclear weapons I 28
Observation Group in Lebanon (UNOGIL) XV 61
Palestinian refugees XIV 179
Panel on Water VII 286
Partition of Palestine XIV 163; XV 190
Persian Gulf War XV 73–79
Relief and Works Agency for Palestine Refugees in
the Near East XIV 179; XV 204
Resolution 181 XIV 152, 165; XV 181 37, 38
Resolution 194 XIV 221, 225
Resolution 338 VI 163
Resolution 339 VI 163
Resolution 340 VI 163
response to invasion of South Korea II 37
Security Council II 100; VI 11, 13, 163, 284; XIV
179, 228, 239, 278, 280, 284 ; XV 23, 81, 148,
150, 245, 247, 250, 258; XVI 84, 238, 240–241
Security Council Resolution 242 XIV 162; XV 40,
42, 46, 89, 134–135, 184, 198–199, 211–218,
220, 226, 257, 261, 263
Security Council Resolution 339 XV 220
Security Council Resolution 497 XV 263
Security Council Resolution 678 XV 81, 258
Security Council Resolution 687 XIV 75, 237
Security Council Resolution 1397 XIV 100, 105
Security Council Resolution 1441 XIV 239, 240
sets tone on water policy VII 286
Slavic Bloc XVI 123
Special Commission (UNSCOM) XV 75
Special Committee on Palestine (UNSCOP) XI 126
status of Taiwan I 269

INDEX

INDEX

Webster, Daniel XIII 4
Webster v. *Reproductive Health Services* (1989) II 222
Wedemeyer, Albert Coady V 42–43, 126, 149, 280
Wehrmacht (German Army) IV 19, 24, 85–86, 88, 108,
   125, 130, 141, 167, 230, 277; V 37, 96, 104,
   106, 118, 125–126, 132, 135, 153, 179, 211,
   219, 226, 229, 232, 244, 272, 275, 282–283;
   VIII 92; XI 33, 83, 117–118, 169, 267; XVI
   118, 185, 188–189
  Case Yellow IV 282
  early victories V 213
  Hitler's ideology V 137–144
  Manstein Plan IV 107
  mechanized warfare IV 282
  myth IV 286
  opinion of guerrilla warfare IV 93, 101
  panzer divisions IV 284
  reputation IV 281, 287
  role in war atrocities IV 85–94
  Tank Forces development IV 106
  utilization of tanks IV 283
  weapons development IV 105
Weimar Republic IV 270; V 115, 210–211; VI 176;
   VIII 144, 284–285; IX 260; XVI 176, 209,
   212
Weinberger, Caspar W. VI 2, 21, 221–222, 229, 231;
   XVI 44
Weizmann, Chaim XI 62, 121
Weld, Theodore Dwight XIII 31, 142
Welles, Orson III 237
Wells, H. G. IX 220
Wells, Ida B. XIII 57
Wells, Sumner V 58; XI 60
Weltpolitik VIII 31, 44, 249, 266
Wemyss, James XII 41, 186
Wends X 179, 225
Wesley, John XII 151
West Africa IX 113, 115–116, 118; XII 165
  culture XIII 206
  interdiction of slave trade from XII 167
  religion in XIII 187
  slave trade XIII 36–38, 40
  slaves from XIII 168
West Bank XIV 20, 22, 25–26, 100, 105–106, 112, 160,
   162, 220–221, 223, 226, 230; XV 20–21, 23,
   25, 34, 37, 41–42, 45, 48– 49, 52–53, 57, 61,
   78–79, 89–95, 131–132, 134, 136–137, 139,
   182–183, 185–186, 190–191, 194–195, 198–
   200, 213–215, 219, 222, 226–227, 242, 261,
   263
  settlements in XIV 151–158
West Berlin I 194, 288, 293; VI 147–149
  Soviet blockade (1948) I 238
West Caprivi Game Reserve VII 35
West Germany I 113, 154; VI 101, 103, 121, 168–169,
   201, 204, 206–212; XI 181, 214–215; XI 35,
   256, 260; XV 14; XVI 77, 156, 267–268;
   XVI 155–156, 284
  aid received from U.S. I 158
  antinuclear protests VI 16
  emigration VI 118
  entry into NATO I 206
  joins NATO I 108
  military I 255
  Minister of Federal Transportation VII 207
  nuclear proliferation I 223
  nuclear weapons development I 222
  opposition to African dams in VII 240
  postwar economy I 174
  relations with Poland VI 211
  relations with the Soviet Union VI 211
  Social Democrats I 36
  terrorism XVI 245, 248
West India Company XIII 270
West Indies XII 22, 37, 79, 167; XIII 7, 18, 136, 181,
   235, 243, 270
  British troops in XII 186
  death rates of imported slaves XIII 134

Loyalist refugees flee to XII 189
slave trade XIII 273
slavery in XIII 65, 80
threatened by French XII 182
trade with New England XIII 195
West Point XII 9–10, 13
West Virginia XV 267
Western Desert Project (Egypt) VII 2
Western Ghats VII 125
Western Kansas Groundwater Management District No.
   1 VII 185
Western Sahara XIV 70–75, 209, 276–285
  Green March (1975) XIV 284
  refugees XIV 284
Westminster Abbey XII 159
Westmoreland, William C. I 291; II 5
  Vietnam War policy I 299
wetlands VII 271–279
  private property VII 272
  scientific understanding VII 273
Wheeler, Burton K. II 209; III 26
Whigs XII 110, 128, 254; XIII 21, 281–283
Whiskey Rebellion (1794) XII 125, 219, 277, 283
White, Thomas W. XI 57, 62
White, Walter II 44; III 218
  march on Washington III 219
white flight II 250, 292–293
  Boston II 298
White League XIII 55
White Panther Party II 95
White Paper (1922) XV 34
White Paper (1939) XV 34
White Pines Act (1729) XII 243
White Sea XVI 184
white supremacy XIII 224
Whitefield, George XII 148, 150–152
Whitehouse, Joseph VII 171
Whitney, Eli XIII 7, 43
Whittier, John Greenleaf VII 275
Wickes, Lambert XII 79, 106
Wiener Landesgericht prison XI 149
Wiesel, Elie XI 50, 52, 142, 164, 218, 223, 228, 230–
   231
Wilberforce, William XIII 31, 157, 159
Wild and Scenic Rivers Act (1968) VII 31
Wilde, Oscar IX 87, 146, 148
Wilderness Act (1964) VII 31
Wilderness Society VII 30, 112, 258
Wilhelm II 24, 29–31, 35, 72, 97, 152, 184, 209, 213,
   226, 229, 252, 257, 282; IX 32, 42, 44, 75,
   98–101, 103, 139–140, 142, 146, 160, 222,
   226, 257; X 57, 305 ; XI 169; XVI 35, 183,
   192, 194, 257, 295, 308, 313
Wilkes, John XII 30, 167–168
Wilkins, Roy XIII 256
Wilkomirski, Binjamin XI 52, 53
William, Frederick IX 100
William II XII 243
William of Malmesbury X 215–216
William of Newburgh X 16, 33, 277
William of Tyre X 197, 201, 211, 214–215, 218–219, 305
William of Upper Burgundy X 119, 285
William the Conqueror XVI 181
Williams, Robin XI 160
Wilson, Edward O. VII 234–235
Wilson, Harold XV 135
Wilson, Henry Hughes VIII 77, 108, 237
Wilson, James XII 65, 74, 139, 281
Wilson, Woodrow I 88, 151, 285; II 8, 46, 145, 156,
   199; III 25, 55, 98–99, 175, 208, 211, 223,
   244; VI 57, 77, 188; VIII 11–12, 16–18, 22,
   96, 204, 228, 261, 277–278, 281–282, 295,
   298–299; IX 7, 19, 21, 24, 26, 31, 57, 105,
   168, 173, 225, 245–247, 250, 270; XIV 43;
   XVI 2, 4, 7, 34, 36, 76, 87, 100–102, 111, 292,
   307–308, 310, 313
  flu epidemic III 100
  foreign policy III 46

INDEX

272-273, 276, 282; IX 12-13, 15-16, 27, 29-
31, 33-34, 38, 40, 48-49, 53, 61, 65-67, 71-
73, 104-110, 114, 118, 120, 122, 124, 128,
131, 190, 193, 203, 225, 231-232, 234-235,
253-254; XVI 5-6, 34, 37, 201, 309, 312-
313
women in VIII 296, 298
World War II (1939-1945) I 61, 91; III 11, 50, 250-
257; VI 8, 27, 31, 36, 49, 77, 79, 126, 146,
179, 267; VII 27, 29, 53, 69, 90, 93, 109,
152, 168, 174, 188, 199, 202, 204, 236-237,
257, 263-264, 273, 278, 287; IX 22, 27; X
14, 272, 300, 305; XI , 9-10, 14, 18, 36-37,
45, 56, 70, 81, 103, 106, 114, 117-118, 121,
126, 139-140, 148, 168, 171, 174, 181, 187,
191-192, 211, 214, 227, 243, 249, 252-253,
255-257, 260; XII 30, 33, 64, 171; XIII 198;
XIV 2, 17, 37, 40, 71, 171, 174, 176, 181, 188,
192, 211, 230, 238, 245, 261; XV 12, 18, 29-
30, 34-35, 65, 70, 87, 106, 108, 116, 126,
141, 146, 156, 163, 172-173, 176-177, 202,
229, 252-253, 274; XVI 11, 36, 39, 41, 44,
61, 63, 65, 69, 76, 80-81, 84-85, 91, 94, 99,
100, 104-105, 111, 113, 118, 121-122, 125,
134, 137, 140, 158, 163, 171, 181, 208, 211,
213, 216, 218, 221, 226, 228-229, 233, 238,
240, 245, 254, 255, 262, 266, 267, 269, 281,
285, 298, 301
African American contributions IV 221; IX 115
Allied bombing XI 13
Allies V 27-33; VI 169
Anglo-American alliance IV 208; XVI 314-320
antisubmarine defense IX 79
Axis powers V 62-67
Balkans V 68-78
Catholic Church VIII 209
display of Confederate flag during XIII 277
Eastern Front IV 53-60; XI 169, 177; XVI 315
casualties IV 55
Soviet advantages IV 55
effect on Great Depression III 63
homefront segregation IV 218
impact on Civil Rights movement IV 220
impact on colonial powers VI 183
Japanese internment III 102-109
Kyushu invasion III 13
labor impressment IX 114
movies about XI 155
Okinawa III 15
Operation Olympic III 14
Operation Overlord II 39
Pacific theater III 13, 214; VI 254
Pearl Harbor III 214-215
relationship of Great Britain and U.S. II 31
resistance movements V 243-247
role of tanks IV 238-251
Soviet casualties II 38
strategy: IV 104-128; Allied V 19-26; Anglo-
American disputes V 34-40; Anglo-Americn
relations V 41-47; atomic bomb V 48-55;
Axis V 62-67; Balkans 68-78; bomber
offensive V 86-100; Eastern Front IV 53-
60; Italian campaign IV 143-150; Operation
Barbarossa V 226-234; Operation Dragoon
V 235-242; unconditional surrender V 270-
277; Yalta conference V 309-316
submarines V 255-261
Teheran Conference (1943) II 32
threat of Japanese invasion III 108
Tokyo trials (1945-1948) V 263-269
unconditional surrender policy V 270-276
U.S. combat effectiveness V 278-286
U.S. Marine Corps V 295-301
War Plan Orange III 108
women's roles V 302-308; VIII 130
Yalta Conference (1945) II 39
World's Fair, Chicago (1933) III 2

World's Fair, New York (1939) II 122
World's Fair, St. Louis (1904) III 242
World Water Commission VII 280, 281
World Water Forum (2000) VII 286
World Wildlife Fund (WWF) VII 107
World Zionist Organization XI 60, 124
Wyandot XII 175-176
Wye River Agreement (1998) 185, 264

X

Xangô XIII 192
Xhosa VII 67, 242

Y

Yad Vashem XI 161, 164, 202-203, 206
Yakama Reservation VII 60
Yakovlev, Aleksandr N. I 104, 152
Yale College XII 10
Yale University XIII 198
Yalta Conference (1945) I 73, 110, 252, 254, 256-257,
259, 273, 285, 288, 300-307; II 39, 205,
211; V 32, 75, 88, 252, 309-315; VI 126,
153, 158, 267; XI 261; XVI 74, 122, 127,
226-227, 230, 317
"betraying" east European countries I 59
criticism of I 302, 306
"Declaration of Liberated Europe" I 300
Far East I 303-304
German war reparations I 300
Poland V 310-311
Stalin's promise of elections I 151
United Nations V 310, 314
Yamagata Aritomo IX 164, 167
Yamamoto, Isoroku IV 2, 6
Yamani, Ahmed Zaki XIV 214, 218
Yamashita, Tomoyuki
trial of V 265
Yarmuk River VII 78, 81
Yasui, Minoru V 188-189
Yasui v. U.S. (1943) V 188
Yates v. United States (1957) I 81; II 281
Yatskov, Anatoli II 230
Year of Eating Bones VII 242
Yellow Sea VII 148
Yeltsin, Boris VI 113-114; XVI 77
Yemen VIII 39, 41, 212; XIV 52, 55, 68, 79, 146, 177,
179, 181, 248, 291; XV 57, 62, 81, 141, 144,
146, 166, 204
Arab Republic XV 276
assasination of Ahmad I 282
civil war (1962) II 150
Cole attack (2000) XIV 16
pan-Arab campaign I 281
People's Democratic Republic XV 276
revolution I 158
terrorism XIV 14
UAR XV 270, 271, 273, 276
water XIV 269
women XIV 291
Yom Kippur War. See Arab-Israeli War, 1973
Yosemite National Park VII 112
Young Lords II 94, 197
Young Plan (1929) IV 270; IX 92, 171; XVI 148, 296
Young Turks VIII 37, 45, 211; XI 172
Yugoslav Communist Party XVI 100
Yugoslav National Committee XVI 36
Yugoslav National Council (YNC) IX 267
Yugoslavia I 36, 108, 273, 277, 294; II 154, 156; VI
134, 136, 175, 181, 217, 219, 226-227, 243-
244, 265, 271, 273-275, 277; VII 248-249,
252-254; IX 93, 203, 208, 266-272; XI 10,
174; XV 68, 120, 167; XVI 36, 41, 76, 98-
100, 102-104, 115, 123-124, 213, 233, 248,
269, 272, 317
collapse of XVI 57-63
collectivization VI 274

ISBN 1-55862-479-1

90000